Camilla Hélena von Heijne

The Messenger of the Lord in Early Jewish Interpretations of Genesis

Beihefte zur Zeitschrift für die alttestamentliche Wissenschaft

Herausgegeben von
John Barton · Reinhard G. Kratz
Choon-Leong Seow · Markus Witte

Band 412

De Gruyter

Camilla Hélena von Heijne

The Messenger of the Lord
in Early Jewish Interpretations of Genesis

De Gruyter

ISBN 978-3-11-022684-3
e-ISBN 978-3-11-022685-0
ISSN 0934-2575

Library of Congress Cataloging-in-Publication Data

A CIP catalogue record for this book is available from the Library of Congress.

Bibliographic information published by the Deutsche Nationalbibliothek

The Deutsche Nationalbibliothek lists this publication in the Deutsche
Nationalbibliografie; detailed bibliographic data are available in the Internet
at http://dnb.d-nb.de.

© 2010 Walter de Gruyter GmbH & Co. KG, Berlin/New York

Printing: Hubert & Co. GmbH & Co. KG, Göttingen
∞ Printed on acid-free paper
Printed in Germany
www.degruyter.com

To My Beloved Mother
and in Loving Memory
of My Father

The Patriarch Jacob's struggle with the angel at the ford of Jabbok (1855),
portrayed by the French artist Gustave Doré (1832–1883)

Preface

As far back as I can remember I have been fascinated by the intriguing stories of the Bible. This naturally made me interested in how these texts have been interpreted, understood and applied throughout history. Since the Bible originated on Israelite/Jewish soil, the Jewish religion and culture attracted my attention in a special way. All these factors resulted in my decision to begin theological studies at Uppsala University.

At the end of my undergraduate education I had the privilege to receive a scholarship from the Church of Sweden Mission in order to study at the Swedish Theological Institute in Jerusalem. I am very grateful for this grant and also wish to express my sincere appreciation to my teachers and co-students who made my spring term in Jerusalem an unforgettable experience. The semester in Jerusalem gave me a glimpse of the treasure that lies hidden in Jewish biblical exegesis. The study of Midrash was like the opening of a different world and gave me many new insights. I discovered that the Scripture has indeed 70 faces, as in the famous Rabbinic saying.

Thus, my semester at the Swedish Theological Institute had a decisive impact on my life and contributed to my decision to pursue postgraduate studies in Old Testament Exegesis. The first step on this journey was to produce a Master thesis in this field and I chose to write about the binding of Isaac in early Jewish interpretation, the Aqedah (Gen 22:1-19). It was later published in a shortened version in *Svensk Exegetisk Årsbok*, vol. 62, 1997. In this context, I wish to thank Professor Dr. Stig Norin for accepting me as a doctoral student in Old Testament Exegesis.

Since my first extended stay in Israel had been such a great experience, I wished to return. Grants from *Thanks to Scandinavia, Friends of the Hebrew University in Sweden*, and *Sven Linder's scholarship* made my dream come true, and I spent my first academic year as a postgraduate student at the Hebrew University of Jerusalem. During my year in Israel, I studied ancient and modern Hebrew, biblical studies, Midrash, Second Temple literature, and the historical geography of Jerusalem. It was an invaluable period of my life, and I wish to express my sincere gratitude to all of my teachers at the Hebrew University.

When the time came for me to select a topic for my doctoral dissertation, I wished to deepen my studies in Jewish exegesis and decided to
write about the angel/messenger of the Lord in early Jewish interpretations of Genesis. An additional reason for my choice was that the ambiguity of these biblical texts intrigued me, i.e., the ambivalence between
God and His angel/messenger. I have always been interested in how
the relationship between God/the divine sphere and humankind is
portrayed and perceived in different religions and their sacred scriptures.

In my book, I have included the illustration of Jacob's struggle at
the ford of Jabbok, portrayed by Gustave Doré. Since Genesis 32 is one
of the main narratives discussed in my dissertation, I find this illustration by Gustave Doré apt, but this is not the only reason. As the patriarch Jacob/Israel represents the Jewish people, his combat with God/the
angel at Jabbok may be interpreted symbolically as depicting the early
Jewish sages' grappling with 'the angel of the Lord-texts'. Additionally,
the process of writing and finally completing this dissertation has been
a long journey and in many ways a struggle.

Since no scholarly author is an island, there are many persons who
have contributed in different ways to my project, and I wish to thank
all of them.

First and foremost, I would like to express my deep gratitude and
appreciation to my supervisor, Associate Professor Dr. Tord Fornberg,
without whose support and commitment this book would never have
been completed. He has helped me immensely by his reading of and
constructive comments on my manuscript. His enthusiasm, encouragement, and patience during this long journey have been most important, and I thank him from the depth of my heart for never having
doubted my potential and ability to reach my goal and complete the
project I had begun.

When I presented my licentiate thesis at the Higher Seminar of Old
Testament Exegesis in June 2006, Professor Dr. Staffan Olofsson was the
opponent. I wish to thank him sincerely for his constructive sugges-
tions and comments, which have been very valuable in completing this
dissertation. Moreover, I wish to thank all the participants of the
Higher Seminar and especially Professor Dr. Stig Norin. Professor
emeritus Dr. Lars Hartman has been a frequent participant at my presentations in the Higher Seminar, and his constructive comments have
proved very useful. In this context, I also wish to thank all the participants of the joint Uppsala–Åbo–Helsingfors Seminars. The present
study would not have been possible without the people who taught me
Hebrew, Aramaic and Greek, thus I am indebted to all my teachers of

these languages. I would also like to thank my students in the course entitled *The Hebrew Bible from a Jewish Perspective – Introduction to Jewish Exegesis* for stimulating discussions.

Associate Professor Dr. LarsOlov Eriksson was referee at the colloquium where I presented a preliminary draft of my dissertation and I wish to express my gratitude for his helpful remarks. Over the years there have been many scholars, both in Sweden and abroad, who have contributed to my work with this book in various ways, and I am grateful to them all. Among those, I especially wish to mention Professor Dr. Reinhard Kratz (University of Göttingen) who recommended my monograph for publication in the BZAW series. Thus, the present book is a slightly revised version of my dissertation publicly examined at Uppsala University the 15th of December 2008 for the degree of Doctor of Theology.

I also wish to express my appreciation to many friends outside the academic world who have been a great help over the years by their support and encouragement as well as to Monique Federsel and Gullvi Nilsson for proofing my manuscript.

Naturally, financial support in a dissertation project is of decisive importance, and in this context I wish to mention the following foundations: *Olaus Petri Stiftelsen, Lars Hiertas Minne, Bertil och Kaj Malers Minne*, and *Fredrika Bremer Förbundet*, as well as a scholarship from the Church of Sweden for higher theological studies, in addition to several scholarships granted by the Swedish House of Nobility and Uppsala University during my years of study, for example, *Banérs, Bielkes*, and *Jubelfest.*

Last, but not least, from the depth of my heart, I wish to express my profoundest gratitude and appreciation to my beloved parents, Ulla and Richard von Heijne. They have always believed in my potential and their constant support and encouragement have been of the utmost importance. For this I remain forever grateful. I dedicate this book to my parents with deep love.

Uppsala, March 2010

Camilla von Heijne

Notes on Abbreviations and Pictures, etc.

The abbreviations used are from the list in *Anchor Bible Dictionary* (*ABD*) vol. 1, 1992, with the exception of the abbreviation of *Dictionary of Deities and Demons in the Bible* (*DDD*) which is not included in the above mentioned list.

Unless otherwise stated, whenever a Bible text is quoted in English translation the New Revised Standard Version (NRSV) is used.

In the end of Excursus 2, there are three pictures showing:

1 Doura Europos synagogue, painting on the upper panel of Torah shrine (third century C.E.).

2 Beth Alpha synagogue, floor mosaic (ca. 525 C.E.).

3 Sepphoris synagogue, floor mosaic (fifth/sixth century C.E.).

Contents

1. Defining the Issue

1.1 Aim and Scope of the Study

In the Bible[1] we encounter the enigmatic figure 'the messenger/angel of the Lord/YHWH/God/Elohim' several times. The relationship between God and this angel is far from clear and the identity of YHWH and His angel is merged in many texts, e.g., Gen 16:7-14; 21:17-20; 22:1-19; 31:10-13; 48:15-16; Exod 3:1-6; Josh 5:13-15; 6:2, and Judges chapters 6 and 13. In these pericopes, 'the angel of YHWH'[2] seems to be completely interchangeable with YHWH Himself. According to Exod 23:20-21, the angel possesses the name of God, it is 'in him', and it appears to be implied that this 'divine name angel' has the power to forgive sins, an ability that elsewhere in the Bible is reserved for God. This angel is always anonymous and speaks with divine authority in the first person singular as if he is God Himself, thus there is no clear distinction between the sender and the messenger. [3] Unlike other biblical angels, the 'angel of the Lord' accepts being worshipped by men and seems to be acknowledged as divine; e.g., Gen 16:13; 48:15-16; Josh 5:13-15, and Judg 13:17-23.[4]

The aim of the present study is to explore the ambiguous relationship between God and His angel in early Jewish biblical interpretation

---

1   In my analysis of the biblical texts, I follow the Jewish division of the Hebrew Bible: Torah, (the Pentateuch) Neviim (the former Prophets: Josh – 2 Kings, the latter Prophets: Isaiah – Malaki), and Ketuvim (the Writings: Psalms – 2 Chronicles, including Daniel), cf., Luke 24:44. I use the Hebrew Masoretic text (MT) of Biblia Hebraica Stuttgartensia, 1990, and the New Revised Standard Version (NRSV), 1989, if not otherwise stated. Since the thesis concerns Jewish reception history, the term 'Bible' generally refers to the Jewish Canon, i.e., the Hebrew Bible, if not otherwise stated.

2   For the sake of simplicity, I will generally use the terms 'the angel of the Lord' or מלאך YHWH/יהוה.

3   See also Meier 1995a, 87-88.

4   Even if the figure 'the angel of the Lord' is not mentioned in Josh 5:13-15, it seems apparent that the "man" who Joshua encounters is a divine emissary of a similar kind, i.e., an implicit reference to 'the angel of the Lord'. See section 1.3.1, and chapter 3 below. Cf., Rev 22:8-9.

and theology, focusing on sources from roughly 200 B.C.E. to 650 C.E.
How did the early Jewish interpreters treat this perplexing phenomenon? Who is 'the angel of the Lord'? How is he related to God and to
other heavenly emissaries? How is the angel of the Lord depicted in the
various sources? Was the angel understood as a manifesta-
tion/revelation of God Himself, or as an independent angelic being, a
messenger distinct from God? A third alternative between these two
extremes may be that 'the angel of the Lord' was regarded as a hypostasis of God, a personification/an extension of the divine will, possessing a certain degree of independent personhood but not completely
separate from God.

A related question is in which ways the view of God was influenced by the angelology[5] of early Judaism and/or vice versa as well as
how the relationship between man and the divine realm is constituted.
The present thesis is not primarily a study of the designation 'the angel
of the Lord' *per se*[6] but the heart of the problem is the *ambivalence* between God and this angel that appears in many biblical texts. How did
the early Jewish interpreters handle this issue?

In order to define the identity of 'the angel of the Lord' in early
Jewish exegesis, we need to examine how he is portrayed in his relationship on the one hand to God, and on the other to so-called ordinary
angels. The interpretations of the identity of 'the angel of the Lord'
cannot be studied in isolation but must be seen in a wider religious
context as part of the development of the angelology and the concepts
of God in the various forms of early Judaism.

At first, my ambition was to study the early Jewish interpretations
of this phenomenon in the Bible as a whole. However, because of the
vastness of the area, I had to restrict my focus to the relevant texts in
Genesis and how they have been interpreted in early Jewish literature.
Thus, the purpose is not to explore the perception(s) of the ambiguous
relationship between the 'angel of the Lord' and God in early Judaism
in general but to investigate the early Jewish treatment of this issue in a
specific sample of biblical texts. How is 'the angel of the Lord' identified by the early Jewish interpreters in these texts? Are there any main
patterns of interpretation? Is there a uniform answer, or is the appearance of 'the angel of the Lord' in the various biblical texts perceived

---

5   I use the term 'angelology' with some reservation, since we cannot talk about any
     uniform systematic doctrine of angels in the various forms of early Judaism. See,
     e.g., Olyan 1993, 1, and Hurtado 1998, 24-25.
6   There are also texts in which he appears to be distinct from God, e.g., 2 Sam 24:15-16,
     and 2 Kgs 19:35.

differently, and, if so, why? Are there any discernable differences in the interpretations that may depend on the character of the divergent biblical texts as such? Do the discussed Jewish sources differ from each other in their treatment of the issue? Is it possible to discern any chronological development in the interpretations of the texts during the chosen time-span? However, in addition to the fact that around 800 years separate the dating of the earliest and the latest source, it must also be taken into consideration that the material represents different strands of Judaism, from pre-Christian Apocalyptic Judaism (e.g., *Jubilees*, Qumran), the writings of Josephus, and the Hellenistic, Alexandrian branch represented by, for example, Philo and the Wisdom of Solomon, to later Rabbinic Judaism, i.e., the Talmud and the Rabbinic Midrashim.

1.2 Earlier Research – Some Remarks

The identification of the angel of the Lord in the Bible has been the subject of much scholarly discussion. In March 1979, Fritz Guggisberg presented a doctoral dissertation on the subject, entitled *Die Gestalt des Mal'ak Jahwe im Alten Testament*.[7] The main focus of my study, however, is the early history of Jewish interpretation of 'the angel of the Lord-texts' in Genesis, as opposed to the biblical texts themselves. To the best of my knowledge, such an investigation has not yet been conducted. The role of angels in general in early Jewish exegesis is discussed by, for example, Saul Olyan in his monograph *A Thousand Thousands Served Him. Exegesis and the Naming of Angels in Ancient Judaism* (1993).[8]

A systematic analysis of the concept 'the angel of the Lord' in early Jewish biblical interpretation has yet to be made. Jarl E. Fossum has carried out a thorough investigation of the Jewish and Samaritan concepts of intermediation and the origin of Gnosticism.[9] The monograph by Alan F. Segal[10] deals with the early Rabbinic polemic against what was labeled the heresy of 'two powers in heaven', i.e., the belief in an

---

7   See also Röttger 1978, and Stier 1934.
8   Concerning angelology in general, much has of course been written. See e.g., Shinan's article about the angelology of the Palestinian Targums to the Pentateuch in *Sefarad*, 1983, 181-197. See also Reiterer et al. (ed.) 2007. The monographs by, among others, Mach 1992, Rofé 1979, Schäfer 1975, Rowland, 1982, Sullivan, 2004, and Tuschling 2007 are also worth mentioning.
9   Fossum 1985. See also Barker 1992.
10   *Two Powers in Heaven. Early Rabbinic Reports about Christianity and Gnosticism*, 1977.

intermediary divine agent at God's side,[11] and the possible roots and proponents of the heresy. Segal's study has shown that the cryptic portrayal of God in some texts in the Bible, including the ambivalence between God and His angel in, for example, Exodus 23, was considered problematic by the early Rabbis, since these texts were used by heretics as support for their standpoint. One Rabbinic response was to list those passages as dangerous.[12] Thus, the issue discussed by Segal has many aspects in common with my own work but we differ in our approach. Segal's investigation may be described as a thematic study of a phenomenon in early Judaism, while I analyze the early Jewish interpretations of a specific sample of biblical texts.

Charles Gieschen and Larry Hurtado,[13] among others,[14] have written about the Jewish religious background in relation to the development of early Christology, and the present author feels indebted to them. However, they are New Testament scholars and thus approach the issue from a different perspective. My purpose, however, is to make a systematic analysis of the various early Jewish interpretations of the Genesis pericopes in question.

1.3 Material and Approach

1.3.1 Biblical Texts

The study concerns the interpretations of the biblical texts in the form in which they existed during the period of Jewish history mentioned above. The pericopes encountered by the early Jewish interpreters were probably very similar to those found in the Masoretic text (MT),[15] although important issues of textual criticism and linguistic problems will be discussed. Differences between the MT and other ancient ver-

---

11   That is, a belief in two complementary heavenly powers, God and His vice-regent who had assisted God in creating the world. Thus, the heresy did not necessarily include dualism, something which was also considered heretical by the Rabbis. See Segal 1977, 3-73, and 121-155. See also Fossum 1985, 307-338.

12   Segal 1977, 33-83, and 121-155. The problematic passages include, e.g., texts where verbs are used in the plural in references to the God of Israel, e.g., Gen 1:26-27, and Gen 35:7 (sic!). See also *b. Sanhedrin* 38b.

13   See Gieschen 1998, and Hurtado 1998.

14   See for example Barker 1992, Stuckenbruck 1995, Hannah 1999, and Newman et al. (ed.) 1999.

15   Tov 2003, 243.

sions are crucial but issues of tradition history such as source-criticism are beyond the scope of this thesis.

The Jewish interpreters did not regard Genesis as an isolated book but read it in the light of the rest of the Bible, which they understood as a unity, in which everything belongs together.[16] Genesis will therefore not be treated in isolation. The Bible itself contains examples of texts which allude to each other: Hos 12:4-6 (in NRSV vv. 3-5) refers to Jacob's struggle in Genesis 32 and Isa 63:9-10 alludes to Exod 23:20-23, and 33:14. The account of the visit of 'the angel of the Lord' in Judges 13 may be influenced by Genesis 18 and 32, and/or vice versa.[17] As the reader of this thesis will discover, 'the angel of the Lord-texts' are closely interrelated in early Jewish interpretation. Therefore, in the analysis of the interpretations of Gen 16:7-14 the reader will find references to other biblical texts, e.g., Genesis 18; Judges 13, and so on.

The 'angel of the Lord-texts' in Genesis may be divided into two categories. Firstly, those that *explicitly* mention 'the angel of the Lord'. These pericopes, with one exception, display the above mentioned merged identity between the angel and God. The texts in question are: Gen 16:7-14; 21:17-20; 22:1-19;[18] 24:7, 40; 31:10-13, and 48:15-16. In Genesis, chapter 24 contains the only reference to an angel in the singular where the distinction between God and His angel seems clear. The text is nevertheless included in my study because of its exceptional character. As it constitutes an exception to the rule, the question arises as to whether it is treated differently to the other pericopes by the interpreters.

Gen 16:7-14 and 21:17-20 will be studied together, as they are parallel texts. Since the angel of God who appears to Jacob in Gen 31:10-13 identifies himself as the God of Bethel who spoke to him in Gen 28:10-22, this pericope will also be taken into consideration. The same applies to Gen 35:1-15, a text also connected to Jacob's dream at Bethel in Genesis 28. In Gen 35:1, God says to Jacob: "Arise, go up to Bethel, and settle there. Make an altar there to *the God* who appeared to you, when you fled from your brother Esau". God is thus talking about 'the God of

---

16 Holtz 1984b, 11-29, and 1984a, 179-186, Syrén 2000, 247-248.

17 Syrén 2000, 248-259. See also Kugel 1990, 1, and Olyan 1993, 11, 19-20.

18 In my study, I generally refer to both the narrative in Genesis 22 and its interpretations as 'the Aqedah', i.e., 'the binding of Isaac', which has become the standard designation of the pericope in Jewish tradition; for this inclusive usage see, e.g., Kalimi, 2002, 1-58. However, I am well aware that there are scholars who have criticized this loose use of the term, e.g., Davies and Chilton (1978, 514-546). In their opinion, the designation 'Aqedah' should only be used to denote the Rabbinic, post-Mishnaic expiatory interpretation of the (near) sacrifice of Isaac.

Bethel' in the *third* person. Is this therefore a reference to 'the angel of God'?, compare Genesis 31.

A few texts in Genesis mention angels in the plural. These angels, who seem to be distinct from God, appear in the contexts of 'the angel of the Lord-texts'. Thus, in Gen 28:12, Jacob dreams of angels ascending and descending on a heavenly stairway/ladder and sees God standing above it, v. 13, [19] and before Jacob reaches the ford of Jabbok, he meets angels of God; Gen 32:1-2.

Secondly, there are texts which I term *implicit* references to 'the angel of the Lord'. Despite the fact that the designation 'the angel of the Lord' is not mentioned, these pericopes describe divine revelations of a similar character and exhibit the same ambiguity between God and the divine emissary(-ies). Thus, these texts also belong to 'the angel of the Lord traditions'.[20]

In Genesis there are two such pericopes, Genesis 18, the account of the visit of the three "men" to Abraham and Sarah, and the struggle of Jacob with an unknown "man" at the ford of Jabbok in Genesis 32. Contextually, Genesis 18 and 19 belong together. Two of Abraham's guests are depicted in Gen 19:1, 15 as angels/messengers but the leader of the company seems somehow to be an appearance of God in person; Gen 18:9-15. The "man" who confronts Jacob at Jabbok is anonymous, similar to the 'angel of the Lord'. The "man" refuses to reveal his name, Gen 32:29,[21] cf., Judg 13:17-18, and has the power to bless and rename Jacob, one of the patriarchs. Moreover, the meaning of his new name 'Israel' is said to be that Jacob had indeed striven with God Himself.[22] In the same way as Hagar, Jacob appears to identify the divine emissary as God in person; Gen 32:30[23], cf., Gen 16:13.[24] The patriarch's encounter with the "man" is connected to Hos 12:3-5 (MT vv. 4-6):

> [Hos 12:3] In the womb he [Jacob] tried to supplant his brother, and in his manhood he strove with God. [4] He strove with the angel and prevailed, he wept and sought his favor; he met him at Bethel, and there he spoke with him [5] The LORD the God of hosts, the LORD is his name!

The prophet Hosea alludes to the tradition of Jacob's wrestling bout and designates his combatant as a מלאך, an angel/messenger. However,

---

19   An alternative interpretation of Gen 28:13 is that God is said to be standing in front of or beside Jacob.
20   See also Gieschen 1998, 57-69.
21   Verse 30 in the MT.
22   See also Köckert 2007, 52, and Eynikel 2007, 113-114.
23   Verse 31 in the MT.
24   See also Judg 6:22-23, and 13:21-23.

he does not mention Jabbok as the site of the confrontation but refers to Bethel as the location of the divine encounter, the מלאָך/'angel' is said to be the one who spoke to Jacob at Bethel, i.e., God Himself. Thus, the "angel" is equated with God, cf., Gen 48:15-16, where the designations 'God' and 'angel' also are used synonymously and in parallel. Different strands of the Jacob-tradition appear to have been fused in this statement. The passage is also related to Gen 28:10-22; 31:10-13, and 35:1-15 by the reference to Bethel.

In the present thesis I have chosen to focus primarily on the first category of texts, i.e., the so-called explicit references to 'the angel of the Lord' but Genesis 32 is an exception to this rule. It is included as a main text in my study for two reasons. Firstly, it constitutes an inseparable part of the Jacob-saga as a whole, as all the Jacob-pericopes are closely interrelated. Secondly, although strictly speaking the designation 'the angel of the Lord' does not occur in Genesis 32, the prophet Hosea explicitly identifies Jacob's opponent as an angel, who in turn appears to be equated with God.[25] However, the narrative of the visitation of the three "men" in Genesis 18 and its interpretations will not be focused upon in the study, although references to the pericope are unavoidable, since all 'the angel of the Lord-texts' in Genesis are interconnected.

Some persons in Genesis, e.g., Melchizedek,[26] Enoch, and Jacob/Israel[27] have been endowed with a kind of angelic character in early Jewish legends, and it could be assumed that, for example, the Enoch/Metatron-traditions of early Judaism would be included in my study. However, although the disappearance of Enoch in Gen 5:24 is indeed mysterious and served as the starting point for many of the Enoch/Metatron-speculations[28], there is no ambivalence between God and Enoch in the biblical text as such, and the same applies to Melchizedek. However, because of the connection with Genesis 32, the tradition of Jacob's angelic identity/counterpart will be taken into consideration.

---

25 As will be shown below, there are scholars who even consider the word מלאָך in Hosea 12 as a glossa, and in reference to Genesis 32, they interpret this passage in Hosea to mean that Jacob had struggled with God.

26 In 11QMech (11Q13), Melchizedek is identified as the leader of the heavenly armies. See also *2 Enoch* 69-73, and Wassén 2007, 503-505.

27 See, e.g., the *Prayer of Joseph,* and chapter 4.2 below.

28 See, e.g., *1 Enoch* 70-71; *2 Enoch* 22. In *3 Enoch*, these Enoch-speculations reach their climax and Enoch is explicitly identified as the angel Metatron. See also Segal 1977, 60-73, Fossum 1985, 307-314, and Gieschen 1998, 146, 156-158.

1.3.2 Post-Biblical Sources

As previously mentioned, I focus on Jewish sources dating from roughly 200 B.C.E. to 650 C.E.[29] The reasons for this choice of time-span are
firstly that we may assume that the books of the present Jewish biblical
canon were in the main complete by the start of that period. The Pentateuch was most certainly already "canonized," and even books such as
Chronicles, Ezra-Nehemiah, Psalms and Daniel were considered by
many as 'Holy Scripture'.[30] Secondly, the completion of the Babylonian
Talmud and the emergence of Islam in the 7th century C.E. mark the
end of a period in Jewish history.[31]

However, the dating of ancient sources is a complicated matter and
I will also discuss a few sources edited after the 7th century C.E., since
they contain material from earlier times. Thus *Targum Pseudo-Jonathan*,
which is difficult to date, will be included.[32] The date of the original
composition of the Pseudepigraphical work *The Ladder of Jacob* is unknown. The book may be based on a Jewish source dating from around
the first century C.E.[33] The Midrash *Pirqê de Rabbi Eliezer* is another exception to my general chronological limitation, since it shares many
traditions with, for example, *Genesis Rabbah*, the Pseudepigrapha of the
Old Testament (OT), and *Targum Pseudo-Jonathan*.[34]

The sources to be studied thus include the Targums to Genesis,[35]
since they are not merely Aramaic translations of the Bible but often
contain a great deal of elaboration on the biblical texts. The *Samaritan
Targum* is not strictly Jewish and will therefore be omitted. The schism
between Jews and Samaritans is very old and goes back to at least Per-

---

29   When quoting biblical references and other primary sources, I will sometimes place
      chosen words in italics in order to emphasize them. However, if not otherwise
      stated, in quotations from the Targums the words in italics are not my own but the
      system used by the English translators. In this manner the targumic deviations are
      highlighted in accordance with their policy. See, for example *The Aramaic Bible*, vol.
      6, the Editors' Foreword, 1988, viii. Regarding *Genesis Rabbah*, the translators have
      chosen to render the commented verse in question in capital letters, while italics are
      used for the supporting biblical references.
30   Here I take the same position as Kugel, (1998, 29-30).
31   See e.g., Illman/Harviainen 1993, 14, 94, and Jaffee 1997, 20. See also chapter 2 below.
32   It is generally acknowledged that this Targum contains early material. See chapters
      2.2.3, and 4.5.1 below.
33   E.g., Lunt introduction in *OTP*, vol. 2, 1985, 404, and Kugel 1995, 209-210.
34   Friedlander 1916, introduction to *Pirqê de Rabbi Eliezer*, xix-lv, Bowker 1969, 85, Maher
      1992, introduction to Targum *Pseudo-Jonathan*, 5-12, and Strack/Stemberger 1991, 357.
35   The Targums in question are *Onqelos*, *Neofiti 1*, *Pseudo-Jonathan*, the *Genizah Frag-
      ments*, and the *Fragment-Targums*.

sian times.[36] I will also examine the writings of Josephus and Philo. Apocryphical books and Pseudepigraphs, such as the book of Tobit, Wisdom of Solomon, *Jubilees*, *Prayer of Joseph*, *Testament of Jacob*, and early Rabbinic Midrashim, e.g., *Genesis Rabbah*, will also be considered.[37] As for the Qumran literature, although there are many angels mentioned in these sources, the material contains little of relevance for our subject. However, in 4Q225, the so-called '*Pseudo-Jubilees*', there is a rendering of the Aqedah of interest for our task, and in 4Q158 a fragmentarily preserved paraphrase on Genesis 32. The New Testament (NT) will also be treated against the background of early Jewish interpretation of the Hebrew Bible.[38]

Roughly speaking, I will use three kinds of interpretative material in my study. Firstly, there are sources that explicitly "translate", comment on, or rewrite the biblical narratives, e.g., the Targums, the works of Philo, *Genesis Rabbah*, *Jubilees*, and the *Judean Antiquities* by Josephus. Secondly, we have sources that share the same motif(s), theme(s) and/or literary structure as our texts, connected to the role of 'the angel of the Lord'. By the use of a biblical theme or motif familiar to the reader, the

---

36 The reason for omitting the *Samaritan Targum* is that the split between Jews and Samaritans is so ancient. Samaritan history goes back to the destruction of the northern kingdom of Israel and its capital Samaria in 721/722 B.C.E. The Assyrians then deported some of the population and in their place brought in alien people. In the eyes of the people of Judah, the inhabitants of the north were becoming pagan (cf., 2 Kgs 17:24-41). During the time of Ezra the returning Jews thus considered the Samaritans a mixed people. The Samaritans, however, claimed to be the descendants of the northern Israelites. In contrast to the Jews, the Samaritans claimed that the proper place to worship God was at Mt. Gerizim and not Jerusalem. This conflict eventually resulted in a final break between Jews and Samaritans when the Hasmonean king John Hyrcanus destroyed the Temple on Mt. Gerizim in 128 B.C.E. However, the "divorce" between the two peoples and their religious traditions is in practice much older, well before the period covered in this study. The Samaritans only consider the Torah or Pentateuch as Holy Scripture, a fact which indicates that this part of the Hebrew Bible was "canonized" at the time of the schism between Jews and Samaritans. Since the parting of Jews and Samaritans goes so far back in time, the *Samaritan Targum* represents an own, perhaps Israelite but not Jewish, tradition of interpretation. The conflict between Jews and Samaritans is attested in the book of ben Sirach (50:25), and the NT, e.g., John 4:5-22. See also Jaffee 1997, 135-138. The *Samaritan Targum* is generally discussed separately by scholars.

37 *Pseudo-Philo* or *Liber Antiquitatum Biblicarum* (*L.A.B.*) has only a short summary of Genesis 12-50 in chapter 8, where nothing of relevance to the present study is mentioned, although there are some scattered references to our texts in other chapters.

38 Because the focus of this dissertation is early Jewish reception history, the definition 'post-biblical sources' refers to sources outside the Jewish Canon, i.e., the Hebrew Bible. In contrast to the *Samaritan Targum*, the NT originated in a Jewish context, long after the split between Jews and Samaritans, see, e.g., John 4:19-22.

author invites the audience to understand his/her story in the light of an already well-known biblical text. Robert Alter terms this literary method a use of type-scenes. For example, a common function of 'the angel of the Lord' is to announce the birth of a child, e.g., Gen 16:7-14, and Judges 13.[39] This motif and the literary structure of these texts recur in the NT, Luke 1:8-20, 26-38.[40] As will be shown in the following, despite the fact that the book of Tobit is not an explicit commentary on a specific biblical text, the plot seems to have been modeled on Genesis 24, where an angel is also said to accompany the traveler, although this angel does not play such an active part in the narrative as Raphael, whose role in Tobit is reminiscent of other biblical 'angel of the Lord-texts'.

A third interpretative method comprises explicit allusions or references to biblical events, circumstances or persons. Wisdom of Solomon chapter 10 and John 1:51 may be seen as expressions of this kind of biblical interpretation.[41]

In two excurses, I will also take a look at the portrayal of the 'angel of the Lord-motif' in early Jewish liturgical poems and art.

1.3.3 Outline of the Thesis

As mentioned above, the interpretations of the identity of 'the angel of the Lord' must be seen in the context of the development of the angelology and concepts of God in the various forms of early Judaism. Thus, as background information, I will briefly discuss the development of angelology in section 1.4, and in chapter 2 I will present a survey of early Jewish exegesis. The main focus of this chapter is the emerging Rabbinic Judaism and its literature, i.e., the Talmud, Targums, and Rabbinic Midrashim. However, I define midrash as an interpretative method in a broader sense, encompassing such non-Rabbinical works as *Jubilees* and other Pseudepigrapha. The analysis of Philo's and Josephus' interpretations of the texts includes a general introduction concerning their characteristics as exegetes.

---

39 See also Genesis 18, and 1 Samuel 1.
40 See Alter 1981, 47-62, esp. p. 51. As other examples of biblical type-scenes, Alter mentions the encounter with the future betrothed at a well and the testament of the dying hero (e.g., Genesis 49 and Deuteronomy 32-33), etc. The betrothal type-scene also includes the traveling of the hero to a foreign land, see e.g., Genesis 24; 29:1-20; Exod 2:15-22, and the book of Tobit. See also Teugels 2004, 45-57.
41 See also Dimant 1988, 383, 391- 400, and chapters 2 and 4.1 below.

Although the subject of my thesis is to examine the early Jewish interpretations of the Genesis texts in question, an analysis of the biblical texts as such is necessary as a basis for the investigation. Therefore, chapter 3 contains a detailed examination of the relevant Genesis-texts with text-critical analysis. Important differences between the Septuagint (LXX) and the MT are thus discussed in this chapter. For the sake of clarity, I have included a survey of all the 'angel of the Lord-texts' in the Bible but the main focus is on Genesis. As mentioned above, the early Jewish interpreters did not treat Genesis as an isolated book and all 'the angel of the Lord-texts' are interconnected, thus this chapter is intended as a general overview. It also serves as an introductory chapter to the problem/phenomenon of the merged identity of God and His angel in the Bible itself. At the end of chapter 3, we look briefly at how this problem has been dealt with in modern historical-critical exegesis.

The main part of my thesis is chapter 4, in which I analyze the interpretations given in the various Jewish sources of the appearance of 'the angel of the Lord' in the chosen Genesis texts. My ambition has been to investigate the material chronologically, thus starting the analysis with the earliest works, the book of Tobit and Wisdom of Solomon. However, other considerations such as genre, the kind of interpretative method(s) employed in the sources and the interrelationships between them have also been decisive in the ordering of the material. For example, all the Rabbinic material is discussed in chapter 4.5, and the Gospel of Luke is treated in the same chapter as the book of Tobit (4.1), despite the fact that there is a considerable time-span between them. Moreover, because many scholars have seen a connection between John 1:51 and the interpretation of Genesis 28 in, for example, the Targums and the Rabbinic Midrashim, the discussion of the Gospel of John has been placed after the chapter on these Rabbinic sources. In two excurses, I will briefly discuss the treatment of 'the angel of the Lord-motif' in early Jewish liturgical poems and art.

After the discussion of the interpretations of the texts in each section, a summary of the results is provided. Finally, in chapter 5 I summarize and discuss the conclusions of the investigation.

1.4 Angelology – Some Introductory Remarks

What is an angel? The most common word for angel in Hebrew is מַלְאָךְ, which originally means *messenger*. It is an instrumental noun derived from the ancient Semitic root לְאַךְ found, for example, in Ugaritic, where it means 'to send with a commission/message'. A מַלְאָךְ is thus 'one who

is sent'.[42] The noun is used in the Bible to refer to both human and supernatural messengers, and it is sometimes unclear which meaning is
intended.[43] The sender can likewise be either human or divine. The
same applies to the Greek word ἄγγελος, the most common translation
of מלאך in the LXX.[44] However, while ἄγγελος in the LXX can denote
both human and heavenly agents, the word πρέσβυς is often used for
human messengers.[45] The terms ἄγγελος and מלאך were not originally
used to denote Cherubs and Seraphs, due to the fact that they are not
messengers.[46] In contrast to Cherubs and Seraphs, the heavenly מלאכים
'angels' are depicted as similar to humans in appearance, and without
wings. Sometimes they are simply called 'men', e.g., Gen 19:5, 10; Ezek
40:3; Josh 5:13; Zech 1:8-12, and Dan 10:5, 15-18.[47] However, in the later
texts of the Hebrew Bible, the Apocryphal books, and the NT, מלאך and
ἄγγελος became generic terms for any of God's supernatural ser-

---

42   Meier 1995a, 81, Bamberger 1971, 957, and von Rad 1964, 76-77.
43   In, e.g., 1 Sam 19:20, Hag 1:13, the word is clearly used for humans, while other texts
      are more ambiguous, e.g., Judg 2:1; Isa 44:26; Mal 3:1. The reference is undisputedly
      to angels in, e.g., Gen 28:12. The divine messengers are often termed messen-
      gers/angels of God (or YHWH), although that is not always the case, e.g., Gen 48:16.
      See also Eynikel 2007, 110-112.
44   Bamberger 1971, 957, van Henten 1995a, 90, and Freedman-Willoughby 1997, 309.
45   White 1999, 300. Newsom (1992, 249) states: "Nevertheless, there are indications that
      already in the LXX angelos was beginning to take on the quasi-technical meaning of
      heavenly being ..."
46   E.g., Gen 3:24; 1 Sam 4:4; Ps 18:11; Isaiah 6, and Ezekiel 1 and 10. The 'living crea-
      tures' of Ezekiel 1 are in 10:15, 20-22 identified as Cherubs. See Meier 1995a, 83-84
      and Newsom 1992, 251. There are also other designations for 'angelic beings' in the
      Bible; 'sons of God' (Satan is mentioned among them), e.g., Job 1:6; 'sons of
      gods'/'divine beings' e.g., Ps. 29:1; 89:7 (NRSV 89:6); 'gods', e.g., Ps 82:1; 'holy ones',
      e.g., Ps 89:6, 8 (NRSV 89:5, 7); 'spirits', e.g., 1 Kgs 22:21; Ps 104:4, 'ministers' is used
      parallel to מלאכים /messengers in Ps 103:20-21. In the LXX, the designation 'sons of
      God' is often translated by the term ἄγγελοι; Newsom 1992, 248-249. See also
      Köckert 2007, 53. Because of the "scandal" that angels could be spoken of in the Bible
      as mingling in the flesh with human women, the angelic interpretation of the 'sons
      of God' in Gen 6:1-4 has been rejected in some ancient Jewish sources. That angels
      might be capable of sexual relations was considered repulsive (cf., Matt 22:30). For
      example, in Targum Onqelos and Neofiti 1 to Genesis, the 'sons of God' are depicted
      as humans descended from important families. This text in Genesis, however, is the
      source of the oldest legend concerning the fallen angels (1 Enoch 6) and the interpre-
      tation also has modern supporters, see e.g., von Rad 1985, 114. It is noteworthy,
      however, that the pericope itself does not contain any clear denouncement of 'the
      sons of God' marrying the women. See also Marmorstein 1971, 966, Hogeterp 2007,
      379-381, and Wassén 2007, 500-501.
47   See also von Rad 1964, 80, and Köckert 2007, 51-52. Female 'angelic beings' are men-
      tioned only once in the Bible, in Zech 5:9-11.

vants.[48] During the Second Temple era, the supernatural status of the heavenly servants of God became more significant, while their role as messengers receded into the background. The angels are often named, and appear as independent individuals, sometimes even in opposition to God.[49]

The word מלאך eventually ceased to be used for human messengers and postbiblical Hebrew employs other terms.[50] In the Vulgate, the distinction between human and heavenly messengers is clear; *angelus* is used to designate the supernatural ones, while *nuntius* refers to human agents.[51] This differentiation can also be found in *Targum Jonathan* and the Syriac Peshitta.[52]

Angels appear as theologically important creatures and are mentioned more often in the later religious literature of Israel, from the third century B.C.E. and onward. Thus it seems that God's transcendence increased in this later stage, and the angels' roles as mediators were emphasized; God prefers to send subordinate emissaries to communicate with humankind.[53] This does not necessarily imply that angels in earlier times of Jewish history did not play a part in the popular

---

48 Meier 1995a, 84, 89. Newsom (1992, 251) writes: "Later tradition interpreted both seraphim and cherubim as classes of angels." According to Köckert (2007, 54) the ideas of a heavenly council and that of a messenger were fused. In the NT the Greek word ἄγγελος is used only three times for human messengers sent by other men; Luke 7:24; 9:52, and Jas 2:25. John the Baptist is referred to by Jesus in Matt 11:10 (Mark 1:2) as "the messenger of the covenant" (cf., Mal 3:1). Otherwise ἄγγελος is used exclusively to refer to angels in the supernatural sense of the word. Human messengers in the NT are generally referred to by other words, such as οἱ πεμφθέντες (Luke 7:10), etc. See Kittel 1964, 83.

49 Meier 1995a, 89-90, Newsom 1992, 251-253, and Eynikel 2007, 110-116. See also Gutmann/Editorial staff 1971, 961-966.

50 E.g., שליח. Bamberger 1971, 957. Divine messengers do not appear in all sections of the Hebrew Bible. For example, they are not mentioned in the P and D sections of the Pentateuch, at least not in the MT, see also Meier 1995a, 84. However, even if the word מלאך does not appear in the MT of Deuteronomy, Deut 33:2 says that God came with "myriads of holy ones [i.e., angels?]…" cf., the LXX rendering of the same verse and Ps 89:6, 8. In addition to the reference in Deut 33:2, angels are mentioned the LXX version of Deut 32:8. According to this verse, God set the bounds of the nations according to the number of His angels. All nations thus have their own appointed guardian angel. In MT the bounds are set according to the number of the Israelites. In both the LXX and the MT it is stated that the people of Israel are the Lord's own portion; v. 9. See also Hannah, 2007, 422-423.

51 Meier 1995a, 82, and Köckert 2007, 51. See also Eynikel 2007, 110-112.

52 אזגדא is normally used for human messengers in *Targum Jonathan*, while מלאכא designates heavenly agents, see also Kasher 2007, 555-556. However, there are a few exceptions to this rule, see Smelik 1995, 349-50.

53 Meier 1995a, 84, van Henten 1995a, 90-94. Gutmann/Editorial staff 1971, 961-962.

mythology among the people but it was not until the Hellenistic period that the conditions for a more developed angelology were present.[54] During the Second Temple period, the dominant view was that it was only the great prophets of long ago who had been given the privilege of direct contact with God, while in later generations God used angels as intermediaries.[55] However, the view that the development of the belief in angels is due to a growing sense of distance between humankind and a transcendent God has been contested. For example, Olyan argues that the explanation is mainly to be found in the biblical exegesis of that time.[56]

Based primarily on Acts 23:8; "The Sadducees say that there is no resurrection, or angel, or spirit; but the Pharisees acknowledge all three," it is commonly assumed that the Sadducees denied the very existence of angels. This may be an exaggeration, based on their rejection of apocalyptic teachings. It is true that the Sadducees did not acknowledge the authority of the oral traditions of the Pharisees but angels are mentioned in the Hebrew Bible, even in the Torah itself, and it is unlikely that the Sadducees consistently rationalized the biblical appearances of angels into human messengers, although they certainly rejected as superstition the exuberant angelology and demonology which was popular among apocalyptic circles, for example, the Essenes.[57] The difference between the Sadducees and Pharisees may be that they represented different kinds of angelology; while the latter regarded angels as independent, distinct personalities with wills of their own, the Sadducees maintained an older view and perceived them as mere impersonal extensions of the Deity.[58] The implied meaning of Acts 23:8 may thus be that the Sadducees refused to accept the later angelology embraced by the Pharisees and other Jewish groups.[59]

---

54 Gutmann/Editorial staff 1971, 961.
55 Gutmann/Editorial staff 1971, 961.
56 Olyan 1993, 8-13. For more information on Olyan's reasoning, see chapter 2.2.2. See also Hurtado 1998, 24-27, and Wassén 2007, 519-520.
57 Moore 1927 vol. 1, 68, Schiffman 1991, 110, and Gutmann/Editorial staff 1971, 962.
58 See Finkelstein 1929, 235-240. According to *j. Rosh ha-Shana* 1.2, the names of the angels were brought back by Israel from Babylonia.
59 Another interpretation is advocated by Tuschling (2007, 28-33) among others, who suggests that the words 'spirit' and 'angel' should be understood as synonymous. The doctrine that is denied is the continued existence of the deceased in any form; they will not be resurrected nor will they continue their existence after death in the form of angels/spirits.

2. Early Jewish Exegesis – A Survey

2.1 General Background

2.1.1 The Written and the Oral Torah

Knowledge of the Hebrew Bible alone is not sufficient for a proper understanding of Judaism. A person gains approximately the same amount of knowledge of Judaism as of Christianity by confining his/her study to these Holy Scriptures.[1] In addition to the Bible, Judaism has an oral tradition, the oral Torah. In the same way as Christianity, Judaism has a dual Canon. According to tradition, both the written Torah (the Bible) and the oral Torah were revealed by God at Sinai. [2]

The Torah is the heart of Rabbinic Judaism[3] and is often compared to a marriage contract, Israel being the wife of God.[4] One of the few dogmas of Rabbinic Judaism is the divine and Mosaic origin of the Torah.[5] The term 'Torah' is a somewhat complicated concept. The translation 'law' is too narrow, as the term rather implies 'instruction', 'teaching' or 'guidance in life'. In its most limited sense 'the (written) Torah' indicates the Pentateuch, the most holy part of the Bible in Judaism. In relation to the Pentateuch, the rest of the biblical books are considered "commentaries" on the Mosaic revelation, although the concept can also signify the Bible as a whole.

---

1   As Holtz (1984b, 181) states: "Without knowing the rabbis' interpretation of the Bible, one does not understand either Jewish thought or Jewish practice." See also Adania 2002, 20-21.

2   Trebolle Barrera 1998, 21-22, and Signer 1994, 66-67.

3   The main focus is on so-called 'Rabbinic Judaism', but the term 'midrash' is used in a broad sense, thus encompassing a wide spectrum of early Jewish biblical interpretation in various sources, e.g., *Jubilees,* and not only as a designation of the Rabbinic Midrashim. Philo and Josephus as interpreters of the Bible will be discussed in their respective chapters.

4   Holtz 1984b, 183-184.

5   Adania 2004, 14.

According to traditional Orthodox Judaism, the Bible is eternally relevant and infallible, inspired by a perfect author, God himself. [6] He has entrusted his word to Israel, and all possible Jewish interpretations are inherent in the biblical texts. The Bible is full of hidden implications.[7]

The Jewish religion is often described as primarily orthopraxy, a way of life, rather than as orthodoxy.[8] The emphasis is not on theological doctrines to the same degree as in Christianity. But the eternal interpretability of the Bible can be designated as a dogma of Rabbinic Judaism. A famous passage in Mishnah states: "Turn it over and over because everything is in it."[9] Every detail in the Biblical texts is important and they do not contain any unnecessary repetitions.

In contrast to the written Torah, the "closed" biblical canon, the oral Torah constitutes an open, unfinished and living process of interpretation. Examples of institutions deriving from the oral Torah are the festivals of Purim and Hanukkah, both established in "post-Mosaic times."[10] According to the Rabbis, in its widest definition the Torah encompasses the whole Jewish religious tradition[11] and includes all possible Jewish interpretations of the Bible. Even the Talmud has never been completed. In sum, Torah designates divine revelation.[12]

Since the Hebrew Bible was translated into Greek, the Rabbis designated the oral Torah as the 'secret of Israel', a sign of the divine election of the Jewish people.[13] A passage in *Pesikta Rabbati* illustrates this:

> [Piska 5.1] ... Moses asked that the Mishnah also be in written form, like the Torah. But the Holy One, blessed be He, foresaw that the nations would translate the Torah, and reading it, say, in Greek, would declare: "We are Israel; we are the children of the Lord." And Israel would declare: "We are the children of the Lord" The scales would appear to be balanced between both claims, but then the Holy One, blessed be He, would say to the nations: "What are you claiming, that you are my children? I have no way of knowing other than my child who possesses My

---

6   Since the more liberal forms of Judaism, the Conservative and Reform movements, are relatively recent phenomena, they will not be considered in my survey.

7   Holtz 1984a, 12-17, 185.

8   Illman/Harviainen 1993, 92-93.

9   The reference is to *m. Abot* 5.22 (Eng. trans. Neusner 1988, 689). See also Holtz 1984b, 185.

10   Maccoby 1988, 6. As I understand Maccoby, the point is that neither Purim nor Hanukkah is mentioned in the Pentateuch. Purim, however, is mentioned in the Hebrew Bible, while Hanukkah is not.

11   Jaffee 1997, 78-80.

12   Steinsaltz 1976, 47 and 272-275. Adania 2002, 19, Holtz 1984a, 11-29, and 181-185.

13   Bowker 1969, 12-13. See also Levine 1988, 143.

secret lore." The nations will ask: "And what is Thy secret lore?" God will reply: "It is the Mishnah."[14]

This teaching was partly connected to the popularity of the LXX among the early Christians.[15] The LXX therefore gradually gained a bad reputation in Judaism, and new Jewish-Greek translations were made, such as the one by Aqvila.

A main characteristic of the oral Torah is that of *discussion*; there may be more than one interpretation of the same biblical text.[16] In contrast to the written Torah (and the nucleus mentioned below), another characteristic of the oral Torah is its fallibility. The oral traditions are not regarded as inspired by the Holy Spirit in the same way as the Bible. The oral Torah is considered a process, as opposed to a fixed revelation.[17] God has entrusted His word to Israel. Rabbinic disputes are solved in a democratic way; the majority is right.

According to the Rabbinic interpretation of Deut 30:12-14, the written Torah is indeed from heaven, but its practical application, the oral Torah, is earthly and as such subject to human imperfection.[18] Thus, the status of the NT in Christianity and the oral Torah in Rabbinic Judaism is not comparable. Both constitute interpretations of the Hebrew Bible but, according to Christian belief, the NT is part of the Bible itself, and most Christians consider it to be of greater importance than the OT. The "canonical" works of the oral Torah, the Mishnah and the Babylonian Talmud, are not regarded as divinely inspired in the same way as the Bible. As a Christian counterpart, Hyam Maccoby mentions the status of the works of Thomas Aquinas in the Catholic Church.[19] It is clear, however, that the Mishnah has a high authority of its own and its laws can be taught independently of the Bible.[20]

In Christianity, Christ is the centre of the divine revelation, while in Judaism the Torah occupies this position. Jews and Christians thus study the Hebrew Bible/OT from different paradigms of interpretation. For Judaism the Torah is the centre, while Christians tend to read the

---

14　*Pesikta Rabbati*, vol. 1 (ed. and trans. Braude) 1968, 93.

15　Bowker 1969, 49. See also Trebolle Barrera 1998, 106-107.

16　Maccoby 1988, 1-3, and 8.

17　Maccoby 1988, 2-5.

18　Maccoby 1988, 5. Maccoby refers here to the famous story of the dispute between Rabbi Joshua and Rabbi Eliezer in the Babylonian Talmud (*b. Baba Mezia* 59b). See also Steinsaltz 1976, 217-218.

19　Maccoby 1988, 6-7, and 25-29.

20　Bowker 1969, 46-47.

Scriptures from a Christological perspective.[21] Jews and Christians have different "eyeglasses," the oral tradition of the Rabbis and the NT respectively. [22]

2.1.2 The Origin and Growth of the Oral Torah

As the main corpus of the oral Torah was transmitted by word of mouth for a long time it is very difficult to date these traditions. However, it is logical to assume that some kind of oral applications must have accompanied the written Torah from the very beginning.[23] The oldest parts of the Hebrew Bible may predate 1000 B.C.E., and it can be assumed that the interpretation of the Bible goes back as far as the oldest texts within it. Evidence of this process can be found within the Bible itself.[24]

According to Rabbinic tradition, the oral Torah was transmitted in an unbroken chain from Moses and his successor Joshua via the religious leaders in each generation down to the Pharisees and the earliest

---

21 Cf., Luke 24:44-47. See also Trebolle Barrera 1998, 20-23. It is important to bear in mind that in Galatians Paul is writing to gentile Christians. Cf., Acts 15:12-29 and 21:17-26. Rom 10:4 is translated in the NRSV as: "For Christ is the *end* of the law…" The Greek word τέλος can, however, also mean *goal.*

22 See also Fornberg 1988, 43. Note what Jesus says in Matt 5:17-18: "Do not think that I have come to abolish the law or the prophets; I have come not to abolish but to fulfill. For truly I tell you, until heaven and earth pass away, not one letter, not one stroke of a letter, will pass from the law until all is accomplished."

23 Cf., Deut 17:8-11. Steinsaltz 1976, 10-17. See also Adania 2002, 20. Both Steinsaltz and Adania mention the prescription in Deut 24:1 that a man who wishes to divorce his wife should write her a 'bill of divorce'. The text does not, however, specify any details. Another example they mention is the commandment in Deut 12:21: "… then you may slaughter from your flock which the Lord has given you, *just as I have commanded you* …" (My italics). The wording "just as I have commanded you" presupposes a certain procedure already known from an oral tradition. Geza Vermes also mentions the divorce law in Deut 24:1-4 as an example of the early need for biblical exposition. He writes that: "Would it be too extravagant to suggest that the permissive interpretation of the divorce law […] may belong to the pre-Ezra period?" (p. 209) His conclusion is that this tradition may very well be pre-exilic: Vermes 1970, 199- 231, esp. pp. 205-209.

24 Kugel 1998, 1-2. See also Trebolle Barrera 1998, 20-22, 47, 104-107, and 430-435. Vermes (1970, 209) concludes that: "First, biblical law was part of the real life of the community before, as well as after, the Exile. As such it was bound to be accompanied by a legal commentary… This commentary was not affected by the canonization of the Torah, and the earliest exegetical traditions doubtless derive from and may sometimes even be identical with, the immediate pre-canonical understanding of the Bible."

Rabbis. In this 'chain of transmission' a group called 'the men of the Great Assembly' is mentioned, an institution probably founded during the Persian period:[25]

> Moses received the [oral] Torah at Sinai and handed it on to Joshua; Joshua to the elders, and elders to the prophets. And prophets handed it on to the men of the great assembly. They said three things: Be prudent in judgement. Raise up many disciples. Make a fence for the [written] Torah.[26]

This passage from *Mishnah Abot* actually mentions *two kinds of Torah*. According to the Rabbis, it is the oral Torah, i.e., the orally transmitted tradition that constitutes the "fence" around the written Torah, the Bible. The oral Torah contains the authentic interpretation and application of the biblical revelation.[27] It is probable that the origin of the Torah-oriented branch of Judaism, which later became known as Rabbinic Judaism, is to be traced to the Persian period.[28] According to Jewish tradition, the priest and scribe Ezra, the religious leader during the return from Babylon, played a prominent role in this development.[29]

However, it is a misunderstanding to assume that the early Rabbis really claimed that *all* of the oral Torah had been given once and for all on Sinai. The relationship between the written word of God and the oral traditions is complex. The Rabbis thought that the *nucleus* of the Oral Torah was given to Moses by God. These traditions are called *halakhot le-Moshe mi-Sinai* (laws of Moses from Sinai) and are considered equal in authority to the written Torah. The rest of the oral traditions are thus regarded as being of lesser authority, although the total development of the oral Torah throughout the centuries may have been in the mind of Moses *in potentia*.[30]

After the Babylonian exile, the Jews who returned home found themselves in a totally new situation. They had to rebuild the Temple,

---

25 Goldenberg 1984, 130, and Kugel 1986, 64-67.

26 *The Mishnah. A New Translation. m. Abot* 1.1 (ed. and trans. Neusner 1988, 672). To this day, a chapter of this tractate is read by pious Jews every Shabbat, beginning with the first Shabbat after Passover. It is therefore included in the Jewish prayer book.

27 Jaffee 1997, 83. This does *not* imply that there is only *one* correct interpretation of the biblical texts. As we will see, the Rabbis promote multiple interpretations of the Bible.

28 Kugel 1986, 64-67. According to Holtz (1984a, 12), the Rabbinic dogma that the oral Torah was given at Sinai need not be taken literally. The message is that all Jewish Bible study is Torah and has the validity of divine revelation. All Jewish interpretations are already "hidden" in the biblical texts.

29 Steinsaltz 1976, 10-17. Runesson 2003, 63-84.

30 Maccoby 1988, 4-6. See also Kugel 1986, 65-69.

and the world around them had altered considerably, both culturally and politically. All this gave rise to new biblical applications and interpretations.[31]

Maccoby compares the destruction of the First Temple and the Babylonian exile with the situation after the fall of the Second Temple in 70 C.E. Each of these national disasters led to a consolidation of the Jewish religion, and if the first resulted in the "canonization" of the Hebrew Bible, the Rabbinic literature (e.g., the Talmud) was the product of the second.[32]

Moreover, at the beginning of our era, the biblical canon was not yet completely fixed. Many books claiming divine inspiration were still being written, for example at Qumran. Thus the initial Rabbinic reluctance to write down the oral traditions was grounded in an attempt to protect the status of the biblical books. When the biblical canon was firmly established, it became easier to allow the publication of other religious works.[33]

The origin of the Mishnah is debated among scholars, and some claim that it is not a commentary on the Bible but an independent collection of rules.[34] Gary Porton uses this as an argument to prove that the Pharisaic Judaism of the Second Temple era was not exclusively centered on the Bible.[35] On the other hand, it has been pointed out that although the Mishnah rarely quotes the Bible, its laws derive from the written Torah.[36] Both positions have supporters.[37] Daniel Patte concludes that there are two sources for the oral Torah: cultural customs and traditions and biblical interpretation. Revelation has two loci; the Bible and the cultural changes of history.[38]

---

31 Kugel 1998, 2-14, and Steinsaltz 1976, 14-17.
32 See Nehemiah 8-10, and Maccoby 1988, 16-17. The renewal of the covenant after the return from exile is described in Neh 9:38-10:39. Of course Maccoby here refers to the Rabbinic literature in its written and "canonized" form. The five books of Moses were probably "canonized" during the time of Ezra and Nehemiah. Vermes (1970, 199) states that the biblical canon was established at about the end of the third century B.C.E. Only the book of Daniel was later added, see also Jaffee 1997, 54-73.
33 Maccoby 1988, 6-7.
34 Porton 1979, 113-116.
35 Porton 1979, 116.
36 Bowker 1969, 46-47.
37 Strack/Stemberger 1991, 142-143.
38 Patte 1975, 90-100.

2.1.3 The Rabbis and the Oral Torah

The oral traditions are mentioned by Josephus.[39] In the NT they are termed 'the traditions of the elders' and associated with the scribes and the Pharisees, see, for example, Matt 15:1-2 and Mark 7:1-4. The oral Torah was rejected by the Sadducees.[40] The early Rabbis considered themselves heirs to the Pharisaic movement.[41]

The origin of the Pharisees remains disputed. Did they represent the mainstream interpretation of Judaism from the beginning, as the Rabbis claim, or were they originally only one group among several?[42] The title 'Rabbi' makes its appearance in the first century C.E., but the function of the Rabbinic sage is certainly much older.[43]

According to John Bowker, it is a mistake to assume that Rabbinic Judaism rapidly excluded all other forms after the fall of the Second Temple; it was a process that took time. The Hellenistic branch of Judaism was powerful and also influenced the Rabbis.[44] The belief in the immortality of the human soul is a concept that entered Rabbinic Judaism through Greek influence.[45] Martin Jaffee even claims that the most profound change in early Judaism did not occur until the middle of the 7th century C.E., after the Islamic conquest. Before the coming of Islam, Judaism was not a uniform movement.[46]

The traditional view of Rabbinic Judaism is that the Holy Spirit had been withdrawn from Israel after the death of the last biblical prophets and that *direct* divine inspiration therefore ceased.[47] The scribes and the

---

39 *Ant.* 13.297. Josephus will be discussed in his own right in chapter 4.4.
40 Steinsaltz 1976, 21, and Bowker 1969, 42.
41 Bowker 1969, 42, Goldenberg 1984, 130, see also Jaffee 1997, 78-85. In the light of the polemic against the Jewish religious leaders, e.g., the Pharisees, in the NT, Jesus' statement in Matt 23: 1-3 is remarkable, since his words may be read as an assent to their authority and the oral Torah; it is not the teaching of the scribes and the Pharisees that is wrong, the problem is that they do not live as they teach.
42 Kugel 1986, 67. See also Maccoby 1988, 11-16.
43 Kugel 1986, 64.
44 Bowker 1969, 36-38.
45 Holtz 1984b, 182-183.
46 Jaffee 1997, 18-20. See also Levine 1988, 148.
47 Bowker 1969, 44. According to Levine 1988, 3, there is a significant difference in Rabbinic tradition between inspiration and canonicity. He writes: "...whereas an inspired book was a work deemed to have been composed under divine inspiration, a canonical book was one considered authoritative for determining religious practice and doctrine. The biblical canon of the Rabbis consisted of texts they considered both inspired and canonical." The book of ben Sirah is considered inspired but was not

Rabbis gradually took the place of the prophets as the spiritual leaders of Israel.[48] By studying the written word of God in the light of contemporary circumstances, they explored the will of God for His people, i.e., the 'oral Torah'. God did not, however, leave Israel, and the Rabbinic sources often speak of the *bath qol*/ 'daughter of His voice' and the Shekinah/ 'the divine presence'.[49]

According to Bowker, the term *bath qol* represents the Rabbinic belief that God remains in communication with humanity but not in the same immediate sense as prophecy. It signifies divine inspiration and is in many ways an equivalent to 'the Holy Spirit'. However, the sectarians' (e.g., early Christians and the Qumran community) use of the latter concept "… explains why the Pharisees/Rabbis increasingly restricted the functions of *ruah haQodesh* and why they tended to substitute other terminology."[50]

2.1.4 The Evolvement of the Synagogue

It has been pointed out that it is wrong to depict the Torah as the sole centre of the Jewish people after the Babylonian exile. It is true that the Scriptures were important, but as long as the Temple stood the cult and the priesthood were equally important, perhaps even more so. The Temple cult and the Torah constituted two ways to God.[51] The High priest Shimon the Righteous (about 200 B.C.E.) is said to have been one of the last of the members of 'the Great Assembly.' In *m. Abot* 1.2 we have a saying attributed to him:

> He [Shimon] would say: "On three things does the world stand:
> 1. On the Torah,
> 2. and on the Temple service
> 3. and on deeds of loving kindness." [52]

---

officially canonized. Jaffee (1997, 88) writes that ben Sirah has a quasi-scriptural status and is often cited by the Rabbis. See also Kugel 1998, 32-33.

48   Kugel 1998, 9-14, and Patte 1975, 118-119. As long as the Temple stood, the priests retained their position as spiritual leaders alongside the Rabbinic sages. Besides their cultic function, many priests were also teachers of the Bible.

49   Bowker 1969, 44.

50   Bowker 1969, 44-45.

51   Porton 1979, 112-114.

52   Eng. trans. Neusner 1988, 673.

There was most certainly a difference between Jews living in the Diaspora and those in the land of Israel concerning the importance of the Temple in Jewish religious life.[53]

Porton claims that it is doubtful that the Torah was read in the synagogues before 70 C.E.[54] The origin and function of the first synagogues are disputed. Most scholars, however, agree that the reading of the Torah in the synagogue was a well established custom before the fall of the Second Temple.[55] From passages in the NT, it is quite clear that the synagogue institution had this function during that period. Synagogues are mentioned many times in the NT, both in the gospels and in Acts.[56] At Masada, for example, the remains of a synagogue that was in use *before* the fall of the fortification in 73 C.E. have been found.[57] Josephus and Philo also refer to the existence of synagogues.[58] The Theodotus inscription, dating from before 70 of our era can also be mentioned.[59] The earliest proofs of synagogues are Egyptian inscriptions and papyri from the third century B.C.E.[60]

Until the 1970s, the general view among scholars was that the synagogue institution originated during the Babylonian exile.[61] Today, the trend is to date the origin of the institution to the Hellenistic era, but the traditional view has not been totally abandoned.[62] The reason for modern doubts about Babylonian origin is lack of evidence, even if the theory seems historically plausible.[63] Anders Runesson dates the beginnings of the synagogue to the Persian period but admits that a major

---

53 In stating that the Bible and the Temple cult were equally important, Porton refers to the religious life of "Palestinian Jews," 1979, 114. Since 'Palestine' was a name given to the land by the Romans in 135 C.E., I will here generally use the Jewish terms for the region, i.e., 'the land of Israel or Judea, Samaria, and Galilee'. Cf., Matt 2:20. See also Illman/Harviainen 1993, 75-76.

54 Porton 1979, 115-118.

55 See, for example, Perrot 1988, 137, and 149, Tov 2003, 237-255, Runesson 2003, 63-84, Falk 2003, 404, and Schürer (revised English edition by Vermes, Millar, Black) 1979, vol. 2, 424-427. The part concerning the school and the synagogue has been revised by Cave. See also L. I. Levine 2003, 1-21.

56 E.g., Luke 4:16-22; Matt 13:54; Mark 1:21; John 6:59; Acts 15:21, and 18:4.

57 See also Tov 2003, 237-255.

58 Philo, *Flaccus* 47, and *On the Embassy to Gaius* 132-135; Josephus, *The Wars of the Jews* 7.3.3, L. I. Levine 2003, 6, and 18. Philo will be discussed in his own right in chapter 4.3.

59 Perrot 1988, 137.

60 Claussen 2003, 147-148.

61 Cf., Moore 1927, vol. 1, 281-307. See also Runesson 2003, 63.

62 See Runesson 2003, 63-64.

63 Runesson 2003, 63. See also Claussen 2003, 147.

development of the institution probably took place during the Hellenistic era.[64] The synagogue was still an evolving institution during the first centuries C.E.[65]

In addition to the books of Ezra and Nehemiah, two other biblical texts may be mentioned in connection with the debate on the origin of the synagogue institution. The first is Psalm 74, which probably dates from exilic times:[66]

> [Ps 74:7] They set your sanctuary on fire; they desecrated the dwelling place of your name, bringing it to the ground. [8] They said to themselves, "We will utterly subdue them"; they burned *all the meeting places of God* [כל מועדי אל] in the land.

The old King James Version translates כל מועדי אל as "all the *synagogues* of God." This interpretation is also found in the ancient Greek Aquila and Symmachus translations. The New International Version is more imprecise and says "every place where God was worshipped." The Swedish translation from 1917 says "alla Guds församlingshus" [all God's houses of assembly], and the version from 2000 has "alla gudshus" [all houses of God] (my translations).[67] It is noteworthy that כל מועדי אל refers to something in the *plural*, which cannot be the Temple, since it is mentioned in v. 7: "your sanctuary/ the dwelling place of your name." Is this perhaps an early reference to synagogues? In his dissertation Runesson refers to J. Morgenstern, who dates the origin of the synagogue institution as far back as the Josianic reform and uses Ps 74:8 in support of pre-exilic "synagogues."[68] In the revised English version of Emil Schürer's handbook it is stated that מועדי אל refers to synagogues.[69] The arguments for a Josianic origin are unconvincing, although the Psalm may indicate the existence of some kind of "synagogues" in exilic times.

However, one quite weighty counter argument is that the LXX does not understand the expression as 'synagogues' but translates מועדי אל in Ps 74:8 as τὰς ἑορτὰς Κυρίου/"the feasts of the Lord." This rendering of the verse is also found in the Targum to Psalms, Peshitta,

---

64 Runesson 2003, 63-84. See also Runesson 2001.
65 L. I. Levine 2003, 2.
66 Tate 1990, 246-247.
67 The Swedish Bible translation from 2000 has a note to Ps 74: 8: "The meaning of the original text is uncertain and also depends on the age of the Psalm (local cult centers in ancient times, the precursors of the synagogues in later times). In general the expression signifies a place where God reveals himself" (my translation).
68 Runesson 2001, 105.
69 Schürer (revised English edition by Vermes, Millar, Black) 1979, vol. 2, 425-426. The part concerning the school and the synagogue was revised by Cave.

and the Vulgate. The problem with this interpretation, however, is that the מועדי אל in v. 8 are objects of *burning* while the LXX instead says ... καταπαύσωμεν/"let us *abolish* ..."[70] Marvin Tate states that this rendering seems to involve too much change to be likely, and I tend to agree with him.[71] He writes that the מועדי אל in v. 8 probably refers to the precursors/prototypes of the synagogues.[72] The second text is Ezek 11:16:

> Therefore say, 'Thus says the Lord GOD: "Although I have cast them far off among the Gentiles, and although I have scattered them among the countries, yet I shall be *a little sanctuary* [מקדש מעט] for them in the countries where they have gone.'"[73]

The LXX translates מקדש מעט as ἁγίασμα μικρόν. According to both the Babylonian Talmud and the Targum to this verse, this is an exilic reference to the synagogue institution.[74] This may of course be a later retrojection but the text is used as an argument by scholars who support the exilic origin of the synagogue institution.[75]

As mentioned above, most scholars consider that the reading of the Torah in the synagogues was a well established custom during the Second Temple era but their liturgical function during that time is a more controversial matter. According to Bowker, the origin of the synagogue was closely associated with the reading and study of the Torah. As long as the Temple stood, the synagogue in Judea was not a 'house of prayer'. It developed this function only after the ending of the Temple cult. In the Diaspora, 'houses of prayer' may have existed but, according to Bowker, they were originally distinct from synagogues.[76] He derives the origin of the synagogues in the land of Israel to the so-called *ma'amadoth*.[77] Bowker writes:

> The *ma'amadoth* were divisions of people throughout Judea, which were intended to correspond to the twenty-four courses of the priests in the Temple. In this way all the people were involved in the duties and sacrifices of the Temple, even though they could not be present in Jerusalem. Each

---

70 Anderson 1972, vol. 2, 541.
71 Tate 1990, 243.
72 Tate 1990, 249-250.
73 NKJV.
74 *Targum Jonathan* Ezek 11:16, and *b. Megillah* 29a.
75 E.g., Runesson 2001, 112-123. See also Zimmerli 1979, vol. 1, 261-262. However, the meaning of the Hebrew word מעט is here ambiguous, as it may also be translated temporally, i.e., 'for a little while', e.g., see NRSV: "... yet I [the Lord] have been a sanctuary to them [the Israelites] for a little while ..."
76 Bowker 1969, 9-12.
77 Literally 'places of standing'.

ma'amad assembled, when its turn came, to read passages of Scripture corresponding to the sacrifices taking place in Jerusalem. It was from these
'assemblies' that 'synagogues' in Palestine seem to have developed.[78]

Other scholars hold the opinion that from the beginning prayer was a
central factor in the synagogues.[79] In ancient sources, the synagogue is
sometimes designated as προσευχή 'house of prayer'.[80] Maybe there
was a difference in function between synagogues in the Diaspora and
the land of Israel, and perhaps also between synagogues in the Galilee
and Judea as long as the Temple stood.[81]

To conclude, it must be stated that the importance of the synagogue
and the Torah after the fall of the Second Temple is undisputed. It was
then that the Pharisaic/Rabbinic branch of Judaism gradually became
normative. It was able to survive since it was not dependent on the
Temple cult. The Torah became the 'portable sanctuary' and "homel-
and" of the Jews.[82] The crises of 70 and 135 C.E. eventually resulted in
the writing down of the core documents of the oral Torah, Mishnah,
and its commentary Gemara, that is, the Talmud.[83]

2.2 An Introduction to the World of Midrash

2.2.1 Definitions of Midrash

The noun מדרש/'midrash' derives from the root דרש. In biblical Hebrew
דרש as a verb means 'to search/seek', 'investigate', 'inquire about',
'examine', 'turn to question', 'care about,' 'study', 'expound', etc.[84] The
verb is found in, for example, Ezra 7:10: "For Ezra had set his heart *to
study* [לדרוש] the law of the LORD, and to do it, and to teach the statues
and ordinances in Israel."[85] In late biblical Hebrew the verb had ac-

---

78   Bowker 1969, 9.
79   E.g., Patte 1975, 31-35.
80   See, for example, L. I. Levine 2003, 1-21, and Claussen 2003, 147. As an example we
      may mention the inscription from Schedia south of Alexandria from the time of Pto-
      lemy III (Euergetes, reigned 246-221 B.C.E.).
81   See, for example, L. I. Levine 2003, 1-21, and Falk 2003, 404-428.
82   Bowker 1969, 42, Holtz 1984a, 17.
83   The very meaning of the word *Talmud* is *study*, that is, *study of the Torah*.
84   In the Bible, the most usual object of דרש is God, and can in these cases also have the
      meaning 'worship', Ezra 4:2; 6:21.
85   The NKJV says here: "For Ezra had prepared his heart *to seek* the Law of the LORD,
      and to do it, and to teach statues and ordinances in Israel." See also Ps 119:94, 155,
      and 1 Chr 28:8. Cf., Lev 10:16; Deut 13:15 (v. 14 in NRSV), and Isa 55:6.

quired the sense of '*inquiring in order to do*'[86] and in Rabbinic literature is mainly associated with biblical interpretation.[87] The noun 'midrash' is found only twice in the Bible; 2 Chr 13:22 and 24:27. In both cases the word seems to denote some kind of book or study, but we cannot be certain:[88] "The rest of the acts of Abijah, his behavior and his deeds, are written in the *story* [במדרש] of the prophet Iddo" (2 Chr 13:22). In the LXX the word βιβλίον is used in this context.[89]

As previously mentioned, in Rabbinic literature midrash primarily denotes biblical study and interpretation. The noun is used to signify both the *process* whereby the Bible is expounded and *the result* of that exegesis.[90] There have been several attempts to define midrash, but no general consensus on the matter has been achieved. Most scholars do, however, recognize that midrash in its widest sense refers both to an *exegetical method*, the *result of interpreting* (the exegetical exposition of a certain biblical unit or verse), and the *midrashic compilations*, e.g., *Genesis Rabbah*. The term can thus in its widest sense be applied to any Jewish biblical interpretation and not only the Rabbinic Midrashim.[91] Accordingly, even a book like *Jubilees* can be said to be a midrashic work.[92]

The midrashic *method* is considered very ancient; indeed 1-2 Chronicles have been designated a kind of midrash, mainly of 1-2 Samuel and the books of Kings.[93] Some scholars have also claimed that Deuteronomy and the book of Ezekiel contain midrashic elements.[94] We can also mention some of the titles of the biblical Psalms; for example, the introduc-

---

86   Porton 1979, 106.
87   Porton 1992a, 818, and Jastrow 1971, 325. Jastrow lists three categories of meanings of the verb in Rabbinic Hebrew: 1) to examine, question 2) to expound, interpret 3) to teach, lecture/preach.
88   Porton 1992a, 818.
89   In 2 Chr 24:27 the LXX has the word γραφή. See also Sir 51:23 where a 'house of learning'/בת מדרש is referred to.
90   Porton 1992a, 818.
91   The masculine plural form 'Midrashim' is a rather late creation and alludes only to the midrashic compilations. The plural used in early Rabbinic literature is the feminine 'Midrashot'. Trebolle Barrera, 1998, 476-477, and Maccoby 1988, 23.
92   This is the general view among scholars: e.g., Porton 1979, 108-109, Zetterholm 2001, 4, Bowker 1969, 46, and Neusner 1987, 7-12. Maccoby, however, prefers to use midrash in a more restricted sense and only applies it to denote *the Rabbinic* interpretations found in the Midrashim. However, he considers the term '(h)aggadah' to have a wider range and admits that haggadah may also be found in non-Rabbinic works (1988, 22-25). See also Trebolle Barrera 1998, 437, and Herr 1971, 1508-1509.
93   E.g., Porton 1992a, 819, cf., 2 Samuel 7, and 1 Chronicles 22.
94   Vermes 1970, 199.

tion to Psalm 51:[95] "To the leader. *A Psalm of David, when the prophet Na-than came to him, after he had gone in to Batsheba.*"[96] The Gemara is some-times said to be a kind of midrash on the Mishnah, but the prime object of interpretation is the Bible.[97] The word midrash has thus come to signi-fy ancient Jewish (and to a certain degree ancient Christian) biblical interpretation.[98] Midrash has been defined as

> ... a type of literature, oral or written, which stands in direct relationship to a fixed, canonical text, considered the authoritative and revealed word of God by the midrashist and his audience, and in which this canonical text is explicitly cited or clearly alluded to.[99]

This definition has not, however, been generally accepted.[100] Inner-biblical exegesis does not quite fit this definition of midrash, as the Bible does not comment upon itself in the same way as later midrashic works.[101] Rabbinic midrash may, however, be seen as a development of a process of interpretation dating back to biblical times.[102] In my view, Porton's definition is somewhat too narrow if we want to include, for example, the Targums as midrash. Porton nevertheless counts them as examples of midrashic activity.[103] The Targums are certainly witnesses of the midrashic *method*, which will be discussed in more detail further on in this chapter.

Attempts to describe midrash as a literary genre have been objected to as too narrow a classification; it is rather a certain *attitude towards*

---

95   Jaffee 1997, 71-73. Even the contents of some Psalms are midrashic, e.g., Psalm 78.

96   Cf., 2 Samuel 12.

97   Holtz 1984b, 178.

98   See Kugel 1990, 1-2, and Signer (1994, 68) who writes: "There are some remarkable parallels between the Midrashim and patristic literature, both Greek and Syriac, in hermeneutical methods. Origen and Jerome both reveal an awareness of Midrashic literature." The NT is considered by many scholars as a source of early midrashic in-terpretations, e.g., Neusner 1987, xi, 7-8, and 37-40, see below. Cf., also Horbury 1988, 770-776. As a complement to midrash, Jewish sages have always used the liter-al interpretation of Scripture: No matter how mystical and deep the meaning we can discover in the biblical texts, it cannot annul the obvious, plain sense of the peri-copes. The literal approach (peshat) became increasingly popular during the Middle Ages as a result of Islamic influence and as a polemical weapon directed against Christian allegorization of Scripture. Trebolle Barrera 1998, 475-476, Levine, 1988, 37, and Greenstein 1984, 213-223.

99   Porton 1992b, 62.

100 Zetterholm 2001, 6.

101 Porton himself admits that the notion of post-biblical midrash being different from biblical midrash merits investigation. Porton 1992b, 69.

102 Zetterholm 2001, 8. See also Kugel 1998, 29-30.

103 Porton 1992b, 70.

Scripture, a way of thinking.[104] James Kugel summarized four basic assumptions underlying all ancient biblical interpretation:[105]

1. The Bible is a *fundamentally cryptic document*. Behind the apparent meaning of the texts, there are hidden esoteric messages. For example, when it is said in Exod 15:25 that Moses cast a *tree or stick* in the waters of Marah, the word tree actually means *divine teachings*! One may compare with Matt 2:15: "… and remained there until the death of Herod. *This was to fulfill what had been spoken by the Lord through the prophet, 'Out of Egypt I have called my son.'*" Here Matthew interprets the prophecy of Hosea as referring to Jesus, but the *apparent meaning* in Hos 11:1 is that the prophet is referring to *Israel* as the son of God. This text in Hosea cannot be regarded as a "messianic prophecy" in "the plain sense", as for example Isaiah chapters 9 and 11. The prophet Hosea is not talking about the coming of the Messiah, but making a statement about Israel's exodus from Egypt.

2. The Bible is a *book of instruction that is relevant* for the time of the interpreter and his audience. In the Qumran society, for example, many of the biblical prophecies were understood as referring to the political situation of their own day. As another example, Kugel refers to what Paul says in 1 Cor 10:11: "These things happened to them [the Israelites during their 40 years of wandering in the desert] to serve as an example, and they were written to instruct us, on whom the ends of the ages have come." In Rabbinic Judaism, midrash is used to bridge the gap between the biblical world and the time of the Rabbis. Midrash is thus an *actualization* of Scripture, where the biblical message and commandments are adapted to new circumstances. Midrash is a profoundly religious activity, close to what we may call homiletics.

3. The Bible is *perfect and perfectly harmonious* and contains no mistakes. Contradictions or inconsistencies are viewed as illusions. The biblical revelation is seen as a harmonious whole, and one biblical text can thus illuminate another. Scripture is to be interpreted by Scripture. Every detail in the Bible is important; everything is in there for a reason.[106]

4. The Bible is divinely sanctioned or inspired.

---

104 Patte 1975, 117, and Zetterholm 2001, 5-7.
105 Kugel 1998, 14-19.
106 Cf., above, section 2.1.1.

As mentioned above, the verb דרשׁ means 'to search/seek', 'to inquire', 'investigate', etc. The midrashic method of interpretation is thus concerned with putting questions to the biblical texts. Theological problems and contradictions have to be explained and gaps in the texts filled in. For example; what happened to Isaac after he was nearly sacrificed by his father? Gen 22:19 merely states that *Abraham* returned to his servants and they went together to Beer-sheva. But where was Isaac? Why did God command Abraham to sacrifice him in the first place? Who is God talking to in Gen 1:26? Midrash hates anonymity; what was the name of Cain's wife? What did Cain say to Abel in Gen 4:8, and why did he kill his brother? What happened to Enoch after "God took him"? (Gen 5:24).

Midrash answers questions and adds "missing" details to the sparse biblical narratives. The idea is to read "between the lines" of the Bible, an activity sometimes described as *'creative historiography'*.[107] Kugel terms this 'narrative expansion'.[108] According to the midrashic view, the biblical texts have manifold meanings, and the Rabbis promote multiple interpretations of Scripture.[109]

Another characteristic of midrash is *'creative philology'*. Hebrew is considered the holy language and every detail, indeed every single letter, is significant.[110] For example, the creation story in Genesis begins with a ב, a closed letter, indicating that it is not intended for us humans to speculate about what was before the creation of the world, etc.[111] Wordplays are usual in midrash.[112] In summary, the Bible is an inexhaustible source of divine teaching and possible meanings "hidden" in the texts. Jacob Neusner distinguishes between three kinds of midrashic methods of interpretation:

1. Midrash as a *parable or allegory*, e.g., the bride in Song of Songs is understood by Jews as referring to Israel and by Christians as referring to the Church. Behind the 'plain meaning' of the biblical texts there lie deeper meanings. According to Neusner, this is the common approach in the Rabbinic Midrashim.[113]

---

107 Holtz 1984b, 189.
108 Kugel 1990, 3-4.
109 Porton 1992, 820. The multiple meanings of the Hebrew words naturally play an important role.
110 Holtz 1984b, 189.
111 Porton 1979, 132. E.g., *Gen. Rab.* 1.10. See *Midrash Rabbah* (ed. Freedman/Simon, translation Freedman) vol. 1, 1939, 9.
112 Holtz 1984b, 189, and Adania 2004, 16.
113 Neusner 1987, 8, 44. See also, for example, 1 Cor 10:1-13.

2. Midrash *as prophecy*, reading in the Bible the prediction of contemporary events, e.g., the common use of Scripture at Qumran (see above) and the many statements in the NT that Jesus fulfilled messianic prophecies.[114]

3. Midrash *as paraphrase*, for example the 'adding of missing details' in the Bible as mentioned above, or simply a rewriting of the biblical narrative in one's own words. Neusner places the Targums in this group of midrashic works.[115]

To the modern mind, the midrashic interpretations may sometimes appear far-fetched and imaginative. For this reason, Albert van der Heide claims that midrash cannot be called exegesis at all. He would rather designate it 'a kind of theology'.[116] There is indeed a great difference between midrash and what we today define as *historical-critical* exegesis. It is also true that the Midrashim bear witness to Rabbinic theology. But it is nevertheless appropriate to classify midrash as a method of interpretation, albeit not in the "modern" sense of the word. Patte makes a distinction between *exegesis* and *hermeneutics* and writes that, in early Judaism, the only conscious use of Scripture was hermeneutical.[117]

There is a debate among scholars as to whether midrash should be viewed primarily as biblical exegesis or as a vehicle for the expression of Rabbinic theology, with biblical verse merely serving as a pretext.[118] Karin Zetterholm discussed this issue in her dissertation and concluded that midrash is actually both,[119] a view shared by the present author. Kugel admits that although many midrashic interpretations may be ideologically motivated, they are nevertheless *always anchored in the biblical texts*. Midrash is presented as exegesis. The Rabbis had a genuine desire to explain and understand the Bible.[120] Their worldview naturally affected their understanding but the texts also had an influence on them. Even so-called scholarly exegesis is not objective; we all have ideologically colored "eyeglasses." There is interaction, dialogue, and mutual influence between the text and its reader. Biblical interpretation *per se* may have a role in the formation of ideological and theo-

---

114 Neusner 1987, 1-2. E.g., Matt 2:1-6. Neusner actually talks about "... the *Christian Judaism* of the Gospel of Matthew ..." (my italics).
115 Neusner 1987, 7.
116 van der Heide 1999, 7-18.
117 Patte 1975, 2-8.
118 Zetterholm 2001, 14.
119 Zetterholm 2001, 11-22.
120 Kugel 1998, 20-21, and 1990, 6-7, 251.

logical positions.[121] Alexander Samely states that it is impossible to establish the amount of Rabbinic theology that has an exegetical origin. Biblical interpretation, however, certainly played an important role. [122] Theology and exegesis are intertwined in the history of the Jewish religion. Kugel concludes that:

> ... it is usually difficult to decide whether a given interpreter set out to patrol all of Scripture in search of a place to "plant" an expression of his own ideology, or whether, on the contrary, faced with a particular exegetical stimulus in the biblical text–an unusual word, an apparent incongruity, or the like–the interpreter came up with an explanation that, in one way or another, also reflected his own ideology or issues of his day.[123]

2.2.2 Some Examples of Midrashic Influence on Angelology

Saul Olyan emphasizes the increasing importance of exegesis in early Judaism for the development of angelology and argues that much of the angelology in the Second Temple period and after originated as a result of it.[124] He also mentions other influences and admits the likelihood of an interaction between several factors but considers biblical interpretation as the most crucial.[125] In his own words:

> I argue that this tendency *to fill in the gaps*, to increase knowledge, to derive information from the biblical text, so well described by a number of scholars with respect to *midrash*, is precisely what was at work from the beginning in the gradual articulation of the angelic host [...] Through *careful study* of the text, ancient and medieval exegetes *discovered new information about angels*: their names, the designation of their orders, their functions, their appearance, even their personalities.[126] (my italics)

Olyan demonstrates that the angelic brigades as well as the personal names of many angels in early Jewish angelology are derived exegetically.[127] Only Michael and Gabriel are explicitly mentioned in the Hebrew Bible but Jewish sources also refer to other angels, including

---

121 Kugel 1998, 20-21, Boyarin 1990, 12-21, and 57-79.
122 Samely 1992, 81-85.
123 Kugel 1998, 22.
124 Olyan 1993, 9-13, 118.
125 E.g., the desire to avoid anthropomorphic depictions of God. Olyan, however, rejects the idea that the angels' primary function was to bridge the gap between an inaccessible God and humanity. Olyan 1993, 6-9, 118.
126 Olyan 1993, 10.
127 Olyan 1993, chapter 2, pp. 31-69, and chapters 3-4, pp. 70-115.

Mastema, Penuel, Doqiel, Lahtiel, Mahphekiel, and Haphekiel/Haphkiel.[128] In addition to the Cherubs and Seraphs, interpreters have also "discovered" the angelic hosts *Hayyoth, Ophannim, Galgallim, Maasim, Hashmallim,* and *Tarshishim* in the theophany described in Ezekiel 1 and 10.[129] The angelic class *Shinaim* is derived from the obscure text in Ps 68:18 (v. 17 in NRSV):[130] "With mighty chariotry, twice ten thousand, thousands upon *thousands* [(?) שנאן], the LORD came from Sinai into the holy place." The meaning of the word *Shinan,* a *hapax legomenon,* is unclear. This is a typical example of a common pattern in midrashic exegeses; angelic names and brigades often have their origin in *linguistic problems and rare words* in the Hebrew texts.[131] The fallen angel Azazel, mentioned in *1 Enoch* and the *Apocalypse of Abraham,* is derived from the strange word found only in Lev 16:8, 10 and 26.[132]

Theological problems often constitute the starting point for many midrashic interpretations. Why did God command Abraham to sacrifice his son? According to *Jub.* 17.16, it was the demonic angel *prince Maste-*

---

128 Olyan 1993, 25-27, 66-67, and 105-109. Another prominent angel is of course Raphael, a main character in the book of Tobit. In Jewish tradition, Raphael is counted among the archangels together with Gabriel and Michael. With regard to Raphael, Mastema, and Penuel, see also below. According to Olyan, the angelic name Doqiel is derived from an interpretation of Isa 40:22, where the noun *doq* appears. It is a *hapax legomenon,* and the context in Isa 40:22 is a theophany. Olyan 1993, 78-79. The angel Doqiel is mentioned in the *T. Ab.* 13.10 (rec. A). The angel Lahtiel is probably derived from the word *'lahat'* flame, in Gen 3:24. This angel is mentioned in the Hekalot literature, Olyan 1993, 71-73. The angels Mahpekiel and Haphekiel/Haphkiel are mentioned in a Jewish Aramaic inscription on a Babylonian magic bowl. Haphekiel/Haphkiel appears in a magic book from the Cairo Genizah, see Olyan 1993, 83-84. Their function is said *to turn around* [הפך] the heavens and the earth, the stars and constellations. The origin of their names is probably connected with an interpretation of God's *overthrow* of Sodom and Gomorrah in Genesis 19, where two unnamed angels are mentioned. Cf., Gen 19:25: "... and he *overthrew/wayyahpok* [ויהפך] those cities ..." and Gen 19:29b: "... God remembered Abraham, and sent Lot out from the midst of the *overthrow*"/*hahapheka* [ההפכה] ... See, for example, Isa 13:19, Deut 29:22 and Olyan, 1993, 83-85, see also Milik's/Black's comments in *The Books of Enoch. Aramaic Fragments from Qumran Cave 4,* 1976, 128.

129 Olyan 1993, 32-50. These angelic hosts are mentioned in the Hekalot literature. See also, for example, *Pesikta Rabbati* 20.4 and 7.2, *1 En.* 61.10; 71.7, and *3 En.* 6.2; 7.1. Concerning the *Maasim,* cf., Ps 103:22 and the Qumran Angelic Liturgy.

130 Olyan 1993, 50. See also *3 En.* 7.1. Also Ps 68:12-13 has given rise to angelic interpretations; who are the messengers in v. 12, and who are the kings of the armies that flee in v. 13? Many manuscripts have מלאכי/'angels/messengers' instead of מלכי/'kings' in v. 13, see also Olyan 1993, 21-22.

131 Olyan 1993, 30, 68-69, 87, 116-117.

132 Olyan 1993, 109-111. Cf., *1 En.* 8.1; 9.6; 10.4-6, 8; 13.1-2, etc. See also *Apoc. Ab.*13.6-14; 14.6-14, etc.

ma who challenged God and provoked Him to test Abraham by commanding the latter to sacrifice Isaac (cf., Job 1:6-12).[133] According to Olyan, the name Mastema is derived from the noun מַשְׂטֵמָה which only occurs in Hos 9:7 and 8.[134] To support his view, Olyan points out that the root of מַשְׂטֵמָה [שׂטם: 'bear a grudge against', 'harbor animosity toward'] is very similar to the root of *satan* [שׂטן: 'to accuse', 'act as adversary'] both in form and meaning.[135]

Another angel mentioned in *Jubilees* is the *angel of the Presence*, probably first derived from Isa 63:9: "In all their affliction He [God] was afflicted, And the *Angel of His Presence* saved them …"[136] This angel is the narrator in *Jubilees*, but the book also mentions other angels of the Presence. These angels are of a very high rank in ancient Jewish literature, often equated with the archangels.[137] According to Jan Willem van Henten:

> … the group of four archangels[138] probably developed from the four living creatures from Ezek 1. They are standing on the four sides of the divine throne (cf. the 'Angels of Presence,' e.g. 1QH 6:12-13; 1QSb 4:25-26; 4Q400 col. 1 lines 4 and 8) and say praises before the Lord of Glory (*1 Enoch* 40), pray on behalf of the righteous on earth (*1 Enoch* 40:6; Tob 12:15) and act as intercessors for the souls of the righteous ones who have died (*1 Enoch* 9; *T. Abr.* 14).[139]

Margaret Barker, however, claims that the concept of four archangels may have been derived from the four titles of the Messiah according to the MT of Isa 9:5:

> [Isa 9:6 in NRSV] For a child has been born for us, a son given to us; authority rests upon his shoulders; and he is named *Wonderful Counselor, Mighty God, Everlasting Father, Prince of Peace.* [my italics].

---

133 See also Olyan 1993, 25-26.

134 Verbal forms of this root occur in Gen 27:41; 49:23; 50:15, and Job 16:9; 30:21.

135 Olyan 1993, 66-67. Both in late biblical and Rabbinic Hebrew, final mem and nun are sometimes confused. In the Qumran War Scroll (e.g., 1QM 13.1), Belial is called *mal'ak mastema*. *Prince Mastema* is also mentioned in later Christian Coptic sources, see Müller 1959, 187, 190-193, 196. There is also a plurality of demonic angels termed *mastemot* in a Qumran sectarian apocalypse, 4Q390 1.11.

136 NKJV. See Olyan 1993, 108. See also for example *Jub.* 1.27-29.

137 *Jubilees* and other ancient Jewish sources also mention several 'angels of the Presence' in the plural. E.g., *Jub.* 2.2, 18; 15.27; 31.14; *T. Jud.* 25.2 and, *T. Levi* 3.5. According to *1 Enoch*, they are the angels Michael, Gabriel, Raphael, and Phanuel (sometimes Raphael and Gabriel are interchanged). See also Luke 1:19. Gutmann/Editorial Staff 1971, 963.

138 The archangels are sometimes said to be seven in number. Gutmann/Editorial Staff 1971, 962.

139 van Henten 1995b, 152.

In the LXX these four designations are combined into one, 'The Angel of Great Counsel.'[140] Barker writes:

> The Angel was fourfold. It has been suggested that the four titles of the Angel were individually represented by the four archangels and these eventually obscured the single identity of the original Angel [...] In Isaiah's prophecy Wonderful Counsellor was Michael, as can be seen from the themes of Job and Second Isaiah that Yahweh's incomparability lay in his wisdom (Job 38-9; Isa. 40, 43). Mighty God was Gabriel, Everlasting Father was Raphael and Prince of Peace was Phanuel, the Angel of the Presence and Light of God. The Great Angel was thus a figure of four aspects but these were known as late as the time of the translation of the LXX to have been four aspects of One.[141]

The angel Penuel/Phanuel mentioned above may have been derived from Exod 33:14-15 and Deut 4:37, where the divine presence (lit. 'face') receives special figurative treatment. The name could also have its origin in the exegesis of Gen 32:24-33; the wrestling of Jacob with an unknown man at *Peniel*. Jacob gives the place this name, because "... I have seen God *face to face* [פנים אל פנים] and my life is preserved." [142]

The idea that God should have tried to kill Moses as stated in Exod 4:24-25 seemed very strange to the ancient Jewish exegetes, thus in *Jubilees* and the Babylonian Talmud this deed is ascribed to *Mastema* and *Satan* respectively.[143] In *Targum Pseudo-Jonathan*, the attacker is first depicted as '*the angel of the Lord*', later called '*the destroying angel*'.[144]

A common targumic feature is to insert angels into biblical stories dealing with the connection between mankind and the divine realm where the Bible does not explicitly refer to angels. This is done for two main reasons; in order to solve a theological problem or to refrain from anthropomorphism.[145] A typical example is the translation of the

---

140 See also below, chapter 3.4.1.

141 Barker 1992, 36. The angel Phanuel, 'Presence of God', later becomes Uriel, 'Light of God'; see Barker 1992, the same page. See also Guiley 2004, 23, 310, where she writes that the archangels Michael, Gabriel, Raphael, and Uriel/Phanuel are aspects of the angel of the Lord.

142 Olyan 1993, 105-109.

143 Olyan 1993, 27-28. See *Jub.* 48.2-4, and *b. Nedarim* 32a.

144 Cf., Exod 12:23b; 2 Sam 24:16, and 1 Chr 21:15.

145 Shinan 1983, 182, and Maher 1992, 7. However, in this context it must also be pointed out that Rabbinic literature exhibits an ambivalent view on angels. On the one hand, angels may be introduced in order to avoid anthropomorphic depictions of God but, on the other, the Rabbis wished to play down the angels' roles in order to protect the monotheistic concept of God. A too high angelology could pose a threat to the uniqueness of God and invite heresies, such as the worship of angels

Hebrew אלהים as 'angels',[146] e.g., Gen 32:30b where Jacob exclaims; "…
For I have *seen God* face to face…" is rendered in *Targum Neofiti 1* as "I
have seen *angels from before the Lord* face to face…"[147] In *Targum Pseudo-Jonathan*, whenever God speaks in the plural form, the interpretation is
often that he is addressing the angels, e.g., God's words in Gen 1:26;
"… Let *us* make humankind in our image, according to our likeness …"
are thus understood as God speaking to angels.[148]

Besides the addition of angels where the biblical texts "require"
them, *Targum Pseudo-Jonathan* presents a special case among the Targums by inserting angels for no apparent reason, e.g., the reference to
Samael, the angel of death in Gen 3:6. This Targum also mentions angelic names that are not known from the Bible or the Rabbinic tradition,
e.g., Zagnugel in Exod 3:2, and often ascribes miraculous interventions
on behalf of humans to angels (e.g., Gen 27:25 and Exod 15:2). Although evil angels also occur in the other Targums, the dualism is more
accentuated in *Targum Pseudo-Jonathan*. It is generally acknowledged
that stronger folkloristic influences can be detected in *Targum Pseudo-Jonathan*, but the precise reasons for this difference between this and the
other Targums is still a subject of discussion.[149]

The above mentioned examples are but a few of the many difficult
texts where the ancient Jewish exegetes inserted or "discovered" angels. Olyan concludes that much of the angelology from the Second
Temple period and onwards has its origin in midrashic activity.[150]

2.2.3 The Midrashic Sources

So far we have mainly discussed midrash as an exegetical method. We
will now turn to the midrashic material.

Examples of midrashic interpretations are found in at least four
kinds of ancient Jewish sources (in addition to the Bible itself, both the
Old and the New Testament):

---

and the belief in two divine powers. See also chapter 1, *b. Sanhedrin* 38b, and Rebiger
2007, 630, 641.

146 Shinan 1983, 183, and Kasher 2007, 562-563. Other examples are the targumic renderings of Gen 3:5; 31:24; and 33:10.

147 Eng. trans. McNamara 1992, 159.

148 Shinan 1983, 184. Other examples are the renderings of Gen 3:22 and 11:7 in *Targum
Pseudo-Jonathan*.

149 Shinan 1983, 184-197, and Maher 1992, 6-8. See also Kasher 2007, 583-584.

150 Olyan 1993, 116-120.

1. Translations/paraphrases of the Bible, e.g., the LXX and the Tar-
    gums
2. The 'rewritten Bible', e.g., *Jubilees*
3. The Pesharim of Qumran
4. The Rabbinic Midrashim

(1) It is a well known fact that all translation involves interpretation
and thus even the LXX is to some extent a proof of early midrashic
activity. For example, in the above mentioned pericope, the LXX agrees
with *Targum Pseudo-Jonathan*; the attacker in Exod 4:24 is 'an angel of
the Lord', and not God Himself. Though containing interpretative elements, the LXX is relatively close to the original Hebrew text.

The Targums, on the other hand, can generally be said to incorpo-
rate larger amounts of midrashic material. However, there are differences between the various Targums concerning this matter, as well as
differences within the Targums themselves. Some pericopes (even
verses) contain more interpretative material than others. The two "canonized"/official Targums of Rabbinic Judaism, *Targum Onqelos* to the
Pentateuch and *Targum Jonathan* to the Prophets, are generally considered quite literal renderings of the Hebrew original.[151] The so-called
Palestinian Targums to the Pentateuch; *Neofiti 1, Targum Pseudo-
Jonathan*, the *Genizah Fragments*, and the *Fragment Targums* are usually
said to contain more interpretation.[152]

The Targums consist of a mixture of word-for-word translations of
the biblical texts and explanatory additions. They are full of 'narrative
expansions' interwoven with the translation. Philip Alexander has distinguished between two different kinds of exegesis in the Targums:

---

151 E.g., Maccoby 1988, 29-30.
152 Due to considerations of space, this is not the place to enter into the extensive dis-
     cussion concerning details of the different Targums, their place of origin, inter-
     relationships, editing, age, and so on. All Targums are generally considered to
     (mainly) encompass material originating during the time-frame of this thesis, rough-
     ly from the Second Temple era until soon after the appearance of Islam. Each of the
     extant Targums may contain material from different periods. *Targum Pseudo-
     Jonathan*, for example, refers both to "Yohanan the High Priest," Deut 33:11 (John
     Hyrcanus, 134-104 B.C.E.), and to a wife and daughter of Mohammad, Gen 21:21.
     Many scholars believe that all of the Targums originated in Palestine/Israel, e.g., Por-
     ton 1992b, 70. It is usually assumed that the original Hebrew text behind the Tar-
     gums was very close (if not identical) to the present MT, see, e.g., Tov 2003, 237-255.
     There is, however, no general consensus concerning this matter. Perhaps in this case
     there is a difference between the "official" Targums and the so-called Palestinian
     ones. Cf., Patte 1975, 52. For more information, see for example Bowker 1969, 3-28,
     Levine 1988, Alexander 1992, 320-330, and 1988, 217-250. See also chapter 4.5 below.

Firstly, additions are presented in such a way that they can be bracketed out and the base translation of the original text is easily discernible. Secondly, the translation and comment are inseparably fused together, and the original cannot be distinguished.[153]

Bowker classifies the Targums as a "genre" midway between the LXX and the works belonging to the 'rewritten Bible' type.[154] Samely does not wish to designate the Targums as biblical translations at all, in order not to obscure the formal differences between them and the LXX, Peshitta, and Vulgate.[155] Instead, he chooses to define the Targums as; "… an Aramaic *narrative paraphrase* of the biblical text in exegetical dependence on its wording"[156] (my italics). The purpose of the Targums is to express *the meaning* of the biblical texts, rather than to serve as literal translations.[157] We may mention the famous Talmudic dictum: "If one translates a verse literally, he is a liar; if he adds thereto, he is a blasphemer and a libeller."[158] Étan Levine provides us with an example of the application of this "rule:"

> Scriptural phrases such as "and they saw the God of Israel" (Ex 24:10) cannot be translated literally since God cannot be seen by man, yet to insert the word "angel" would be a blasphemy, since the angel would be *substi-*

---

153 Alexander 1988, 228-237.

154 Bowker 1969, 8-9. Neusner, however, points out that, linguistically, Aramaic is much closer to Hebrew than Greek, and the Targums do not need to alter the original word sequence. In this way, the Targums are closer to the original texts than the LXX. On the other hand, they contain more 'midrash as paraphrase', to use Neusner's (1987, 26-27) designation. Trebolle Barrera (1998, 325) writes: "The Targummim lie halfway on the path between a literary version and the long midrashic commentaries of the Rabbinic period." He also states that the LXX is one of the literary sources of *Targum Onqelos* and *Targum Jonathan*, 1998, 326.

155 Samely 1992, 159. Samely does not wish to designate the Aramaic translation of Job found in Qumran as a Targum in the usual sense of the word. He prefers to call it a translation, belonging to the same group as, for example, the LXX. We must also remember that the Targums were *never intended to replace* the reading of the Hebrew Bible in the synagogue service. The Targums were never used as substitutes for the Bible, but were *complementary translations/explicative paraphrases* of the original texts. Fraade 1992, 256-259 and 282-286, and Alexander 1988, 238-239. Hebrew (though not in its biblical form) continued to be a popular spoken language in the land of Israel, even after the fall of the Second Temple in 70 C.E. The final blow to Hebrew was probably the crushing of the bar Kochba revolt by the Romans in 135 C.E., Levine 1988, 8. Fraade (1992, 274) claims that Hebrew continued to be a popular spoken language in the land of Israel even after this catastrophe.

156 Samely 1992, 180.

157 Bowker 1969, 5, and Levine 1988, 9.

158 *b. Qiddushin* 49a. See also Levine 1982, 353.

tuting for God. Consequently, it is said, the correct rendering is "And they saw the glory (yeqara) of the God of Israel."[159]

It is generally assumed that a common characteristic of the Targums is the avoidance of anthropomorphisms.[160] In this context, scholars often refer to the targumic use of the concept 'Memra/Word' as a circumscribing of God. Other such concepts are 'Yeqara/Glory' (see above) and Shekinta/Presence. In contrast to the latter two, 'Memra' is only to be found in the Targums.[161] The employment of these concepts has been the subject of many scholarly discussions, and I will limit myself to a few comments upon the subject. The targumic avoidance of anthropomorphism is likewise a subject of debate, and some scholars have pointed out that the Targums are not consistent in this regard.[162]

The most characteristic designation for God in the Targums is 'the Memra of the Lord'. The Aramaic word *memra* is the definite form of *memar*, the Aramaic counterpart of the Late Hebrew *ma'amar*, from *amar*, 'to say'. The word also means 'to issue a command'.[163]

Most scholars agree that it is a misconception to interpret 'the Memra' as a kind of divine hypostasis. The concept is generally seen as a buffer word used by the Targums to prevent any direct contact between God and the world of humankind.[164] For example, whenever the Bible states that God will be with someone, the Targums in general employ 'the Memra'.[165]

However, the fact that apparently anthropomorphic statements have nevertheless sometimes been left unchanged in the Targums has led scholars to seek alternate explanations for the employment of the term. It has been proposed that the Memra also has a deep theological significance. 'The Memra' connotes the manifestation of God's creative power in the world, but it should not be understood as an intermediary "being" between mankind and God.[166]

The relationship between 'the Memra' and Philo's 'Logos' has naturally been the subject of many discussions. The general conclusion has been that the Targumists and Philo, despite the superficial terminological

---

159 Levine 1988, 59.
160 E.g., Le Déaut 1989, 586-587, Patte 1975, 66, and Trebolle Barrera 1998, 325.
161 Abelson 1912, 150.
162 Alexander 1988, 226, and Levine 1988, 45-61. Alexander and Levine both claim that the concern in the Targums is *reverence* for *God*, rather than avoidance of anthropomorphisms.
163 Moore 1922, 47, and Grossfeld 1988, 25.
164 See, for example Moore, 1922, 41-55, Grossfeld 1988, 25-27, and McNamara 1992, 38.
165 See, for example Hayward 1981, 148.
166 See, for example Abelson 1912, 150-167, and Hayward 1981, 147-149.

similarity, are basically speaking about two different things. However, some scholars have argued for a connection between 'the Memra' and 'the Logos' of John's Gospel.[167]

Robert Hayward sees 'the Memra' as originally substituting for the Tetragrammaton. Accordingly, the fact that 'the Memra' in, for example *Targum Neofiti 1*, is often connected to God's mercy has led him to suggest that this may explain the Rabbinic association of the divine attribute of Mercy with the divine name YHWH.[168]

The expression *yeqara* has the abstract meanings 'honor', 'glory', 'splendor', and 'majesty' and is the Aramaic equivalent of the Hebrew *kabod*. It is employed in the Targums in order to safeguard the transcendence of God. In *Targum Neofiti 1* it is most commonly used in combination with the term *shekinta*, the Aramaic counterpart of the Hebrew word *shekinah*, denoting the divine presence. The combined expression 'the Glory of the Shekinah of the Lord' is there very common. The concept 'Shekinah' derives from the verb *shaken*, 'to dwell, settle down, abide'. Although the noun *shekinah* does not occur in the Bible, the verb is often used to denote God's dwelling among His people (e.g., Exod 25:8; 29:46, Num 5:3, and Ezek 43:9).[169]

Most scholars believe that the Targums originated as oral Aramaic translations and interpretations of the readings of the Scriptures in the synagogues.[170] According to Jewish tradition, the 'targumic institution' dates back to the time of Ezra.[171] The Targums belong to the oral Torah. As such, the Targums are witnesses of Rabbinic traditions and theology, particularly *Targum Onqelos* and *Targum Jonathan*. The *meturgeman*/translator was bound by Jewish tradition.[172]

As stated above, Judaism of the Second Temple era was not a uniform religion, and several strands existed. The "victory" of Rabbinic Judaism was a long drawn-out process and some of the material in the Targums may be from an earlier period. Levine writes that during the Second Temple era; "…the basic criteria for orthodoxy were recognition of the God of Israel, belonging to the people of Israel, and following the

---

167 See, for example Abelson 1912, 158-167, and Grossfeld 1988, 25-29.
168 Hayward 1981, 147-149.
169 McNamara 1992, 36-37. See also Grossfeld 1988, 29-30, and Moore 1922, 55-59. In *Targum Onqelos, shekinta* is more often used on its own. For further information, see Grossfeld 1988, 29-30. The expression is of course also employed in *Targum Pseudo-Jonathan*.
170 E.g., Le Déaut 1989, 563-575, and Alexander 1988, 238-239.
171 Cf., Neh 8:8. The only occurrence of the verb לתרגם / 'to translate' in the Bible is in Ezra 4:7. See also Alexander 1988, 239-241, and Metzger 1962, 749.
172 Patte 1975, 65, and Alexander 1983, 23-26, and 1988, 238-239.

Law of Moses." This was a "creed" that all Jewish groups could accept, even Jewish Christians.[173]

Many scholars claim that the 'targumic institution' was never totally under Rabbinic control.[174] To some degree the Targums contain folkloristic traditions.[175] This is apparent in the so-called Palestinian Targums.[176] *Targum Pseudo-Jonathan* includes interpretations that were censured in Rabbinic literature, sometimes as early as the Mishnah.[177] Alexander Díez Macho claims that *Targum Neofiti 1* contains paraphrases from pre-Christian times, due to the fact that they favor Christian interpretations of Scripture[178] that were later censured by the Rabbis because of the polemical struggle between Judaism and Christianity regarding, e.g., the "correct" interpretation of the Hebrew Bible/OT.

The *Sitz im Leben* of the Targums was the synagogue service, private devotion, and the (religious) school.[179] The Targums are designated as a branch of study that falls between the Bible and the Mishna.[180] The liturgical use of the Targums gradually ceased with the coming of Islam and the emergence of Arabic as the vernacular in the Middle East.[181] The Yemenite Jewish liturgy is an exception, and *Targum Onqelos* is still used in the synagogue service.[182] The Targums *Jonathan* and *Onqelos* are to this day studied in Jewish religious schools and in private devotion.[183] The Targums are invaluable sources of knowledge about early Jewish interpretation and, as such, belong to the 'world of midrash'.

---

173 Levine 1988, VIII.
174 Levine 1988, VIII and 154-166. Flesher claims that the Palestinian Targums and the original form of *Targum Onqelos* originated in priestly circles, and that the priests, and not the Rabbis, were the main leaders of Jewish society even long after 70 C.E. Flesher 2003, 467-501. See also Cohen 1992, 157-173, L. I. Levine 1992, 201-222, and Shinan 1992, 241-251.
175 Shinan 1992, 241-251.
176 E.g., Alexander 1988, 249.
177 Alexander 1992, 322.
178 Díez Macho 1960, 225-233.
179 Alexander 1988, 238-241, 247-250, and Le Déaut 1989, 564-568.
180 Grossfeld 1971, 842, and Fraade 1992, 263, and Levine 1988, 10.
181 Alexander 1988, 250. Levine (1982, 365) writes that the *terminus ad quem* for the "official" Targums must be the Sassanid regime in Babylon; "… for there are no clear references to the fall of Babylon by the Arabian conquest, nor any references to the Arabs at all. Nor are there any Arabic linguistic criteria which would suggest dating the final redaction of the targum later than 640 C.E."
182 Alexander 1988, 250, and Grossfeld 1971, 844.
183 Alexander 1988, 250, and Grossfeld 1971, 844-845.

There are, however, marked differences between the Targums and other kinds of midrashic sources. The exegetical *method* in the Targums is that of midrash, but in *literal form* the Targums are "translations"/paraphrases and not Bible commentaries as the Rabbinic Midrashim. The Targums, for example, never refer to Rabbinic authorities by name, and seldom openly quote the Bible.[184] The Targums also distinguish themselves from the works of the 'rewritten Bible', though they may be closer to them in genre.

(2) Examples of sources belonging to *the second* category of midrashic sources, the so-called 'rewritten Bible', are *Jubilees*, *Genesis Apocryphon*, and *Liber Antiquitatum Biblicarum* [*L.A.B.*], sometimes called *Pseudo-Philo*.[185] The differences between these works and the Targums are that the latter are *bound by the wording* of the original Hebrew text. The 'rewritten Bible' sets out to *retell* the biblical narrative in *its own words*, and with its own literary devices. The 'rewritten Bible' could be said to be interested in *story*, while the Targum is interested in the biblical *text*.[186] Porton does not want to classify the *Judean Antiquities* by Josephus or Philo's *Life of Moses* as midrashic works because both of

---

184 Alexander 1983, 16-17.

185 This is not the place to present a detailed description of these works. In short, *Jubilees* is a rewriting of biblical history from Genesis 1– Exodus 14 and claims to be an account given by the angel of the Presence regarding the revelations given to Moses during the forty days that he spent on Sinai (Exod 24:18). Cf., the tradition that the Torah was transmitted to Moses through the mediation of angels: Deut 33:2-3 in the LXX, the Vulgate, Peshitta and the Targums and Acts 7 in the NT. See also chapter 4.2, Nickelsburg 1984, 97-104, Wintermute, introduction in *OTP* 1985, 35-50, and Jaffee 1997, 74-78. The *Genesis Apocryphon* scroll found in Qumran Cave 1 is a compilation of patriarchal narratives, covering the period from Lamech to Abraham. The scroll ends abruptly in the middle of an expanded version of Gen 15:1-4 (22:27-34). The "author" might have used *Jubilees* as one of his sources, but this work is an even freer paraphrase of Genesis. The scroll was composed in Aramaic around the turn of the era. Nickelburg 1984, 104 107. *Liber Antiquitatum Biblicarum* (*L.A.B.*) or *Pseudo-Philo* is an account of the history of Israel from Adam to the death of King Saul. See also chapter 4.2 and Bowker 1969, 30-31, Harrington, introduction in *OTP* 1985, 297-303, and Nickelsburg 1984, 107-110. Both *Pseudo-Philo* and *Jubilees* belong to the so-called Pseudepigrapha, while *Genesis Apocryphon* does not. These works are included in neither the LXX nor the Hebrew biblical canon and have been suppressed by Rabbinic Judaism. In the Ethiopian Orthodox Church, as well as among Ethiopian Jews, *Jubilees* is considered a part of the Bible.

186 Samely 1992, 160-162, and Bowker 1969, 8-9.

them seem to have been written for non-Jews.[187] They are, however, similar to the 'rewritten Bible' in literary form.[188]

Patte points out that the view on revelation expressed in *Jubilees* is very different to that of Rabbinic Judaism. Far from being a source of 'divine revelation', the cultural changes of history are more or less looked upon as evil. The Pharisees/Rabbis were open to Hellenistic influence, but in 'Apocalyptic Judaism', to which *Jubilees* bears witness, the Hellenistic culture is considered heathen and thus evil.[189] The prior Persian culture may, however, have had an *unconscious* influence upon the Apocalyptists; their dualistic worldview, angelology, etc.[190]

According to Rabbinic Judaism, the oral Torah is not a new revelation but an unfolding of the message already given in the written Torah. *Jubilees*, on the other hand, claims to contain additional revelations, 'heavenly secrets' not found in the Bible.[191] This is apparently in contradiction to the Rabbinic "doctrine" that no part of the Torah/divine revelation has been left behind in heaven, see, e.g., *Deut. Rab.* 8.6.[192] *Jubilees* thus represents a different form of Judaism, and in contrast to, for example, *Targum Onqelos*, it does not belong to the framework of the Rabbinic oral Torah. In Jaffee's words: "… tradition is Torah *only* if it is transmitted by a Rabbinic sage."[193]

(3) The *third* type of midrashic sources are the Pesharim of Qumran. These are a kind of 'Bible commentaries'. Like *Jubilees*, they are witnesses of the 'Apocalyptic Judaism' that flourished in the land of Israel during the Second Temple era. A chief characteristic of the Pesharim is the attempts to demonstrate that biblical prophecies were being fulfilled in the history and life of the Qumran community. Eschatology is a major theme. Neusner calls it 'midrash as prophecy'. In this respect the Pesharim differ from the Rabbinic Midrashim and there are also significant stylistic differences between them. For example, the Rabbinic Midrashim are collections of interpretations by different Rabbis, while the Pesharim are always anonymous and appear to be unitary biblical commentaries. Moreover, the Rabbinic Midrashim often quote single

---

187 Porton 1992b, 72.
188 With regard to Philo, some of his works must be considered more as proper 'Bible commentaries', for example, his treatise *Questions and Answers on Genesis*.
189 Patte 1975, 145-157.
190 Patte 1975, 155.
191 Patte 1975, 151-157. Cf., *Jub.* 32.21-22.
192 See *Midrash Rabbah*, Deuteronomy (ed. Freedman and Simon, translation Rabbinowitz), 1939, 153.
193 Jaffee 1997, 82-83. See also pp. 74-78 and 88.

words and phrases and present multiple interpretations, whereas the Pesharim comment on entire pericopes of Scripture. [194]

(4) The *fourth group* of midrashic sources, the Rabbinic Midrashim, can also be designated as 'Bible commentaries', though of a different character than the Pesharim. There are different kinds of Rabbinic Midrashim. Scholars sometimes talk about *halakhic* Midrashim versus *haggadic* Midrashim.[195]

A definition of Rabbinic terminology is here appropriate. Halakah derives from the root הלך '*to walk*' and signifies legal material. Halakhic Midrash thus answers the questions '*how?*', '*when?*', and '*where?*' Halakah consists of *concrete rules* about *how* the biblical commandments should be put into *practice* in different situations; how a person can *walk* in 'the path of the Torah'.

Haggadah, on the other hand, derives from the root נגד '*to tell/to explain*' and haggadic midrash answers the question '*why?*' Haggadah explains the *meaning* of the commandments and describes Rabbinic theology. One important purpose of haggadah is *to inspire* the Jews to live according to halakha. Haggadah is a wide ranging term referring to homilies, legends, parables as well as theological and ethical statements. One may compare haggadah with the parables of Jesus. In summary, haggadah encompasses all *non-legal* Jewish interpretations of Scripture. Halakha has a more binding character than haggadah. [196] This latter term is often called *aggadah*, in order to distinguish it from the Passover Haggadah, the earliest known Rabbinic Midrash on Deut 26:5-8.[197]

The Mishnah mainly contains halakha. According to Neusner, the Rabbinic Midrashim and the increasing Rabbinic interest in aggadic exegesis was partly due to the challenge of Christianity. With the advent of Christianity, it became more important to discuss theological issues.[198] About a quarter of the material in the Babylonian Talmud is

---

194 Porton 1992a, 819, and 1979, 125-128.
195 *Mekhilta de Rabbi Ishmael* and *Sifra* on Leviticus (both edited during the third century C.E.) are often classified as halakhic Midrashim, while for example *Genesis Rabbah* is a haggadic Midrash, Strack/Stemberger 1991, 261-308. However, they use these designations with some reservation, because there is no such thing as "pure" halakhic or haggadic Midrashim.
196 Bowker 1969, 40-48, Holtz 1984b, 178-179, and Maccoby 1988, 17-22.
197 Herr 1971, 1509.
198 Neusner 1987, 44-51. According to Neusner, it was the establishment of Christianity as the state religion in the Roman Empire that made it impossible for the Rabbis to ignore the Christian challenge.

aggadic.[199] The oral Torah thus consists of both aspects of Jewish interpretation. It is therefore very misleading to talk about 'the oral law'.[200]

There is very little in Jewish literature that can be described as "pure" halakha or aggadah.[201] For this reason, Porton avoids classifying the different Rabbinic Midrashim as halakhic or aggadic. He also points out that the word 'aggadah' originally meant *exegesis,* and the term 'midrash aggadah' is thus a tautology. Porton distinguishes between two kinds of Rabbinic Midrashim, the *expositional* and the *homiletical.* The expositional Midrash is a running commentary on a biblical text. *Genesis Rabbah* belongs to this group.[202]

Barry Holtz prefers to classify the above mentioned Midrash as *exegetical,* since it constitutes a detailed verse by verse commentary on Genesis. On the other hand, he designates *Pirqê de Rabbi Eliezer* as a *narrative* Midrash, similar in style to the 'rewritten Bible'.[203] *Pirqê de Rabbi Eliezer* has many similarities with *Targum Pseudo-Jonathan.*[204] The two scholars are, however, in agreement concerning the homiletical Midrashim group, which strictly speaking does not contain 'Bible commentaries' but collections of 'homilies' on the main themes of the Torah readings in the synagogue, and often only comments on a few verses of a biblical passage. As an example we can mention *Pesiqta de Rab Kahana,* which seems to be organized around verses read on special festivals and holy days.[205] The early Midrashim all appear to have originated in the land of Israel.[206]

---

199 Steinsaltz 1976, 251.
200 Maccoby 1988, 20.
201 Holtz 1984b, 179.
202 Porton 1992a, 820, and 1979, 128.
203 Holtz 1984b, 187-188. See also Bowker 1969, 69-92. *Pirqê de Rabbi Eliezer* was probably written in the land of Israel during the eighth or ninth century C.E. Strack and Stemberger do not want to classify it as a Midrash in the real sense but rather as belonging to the 'rewritten Bible' category. It appears to be the work of a single author. Strack/Stemberger 1991, 356-357.
204 Bowker 1969, 85.
205 Porton 1992a, 820, and Holtz 1984b, 186, see also Bowker 1969, 72-77. Strack/Stemberger (1991, 321) date *Pesiqta de Rab Kahana* to the fifth century C.E. It is disputed whether these Midrashim contain sermons actually held in the Synagogues, see Strack/Stemberger 1991, 261-262.
206 Herr 1971, 1510. The earliest Midrashim were all edited sometime during the timeframe of this thesis, e.g., *Genesis Rabbah* is usually said to have been edited during the 4th to 5th centuries C.E. Scholars sometimes talk about Tannaitic and Amoraitic Midrashim. *Genesis Rabbah* is often classified as an Amoraitic Midrash. Porton, however, believes that this designation is inappropriate, since these sources are difficult to date and Tannaitic sages are also cited in the so-called 'Amoraitic Midrashim' (1992b, 78 and 1992, 820). The Tannaim (from Aramaic *tanna* 'to repeat/learn') were

In discussing the different genres employed in the early Jewish interpretation of the Bible, Devorah Dimant concluded that we can roughly distinguish between two kinds of use of Scripture; the expositional and the compositional mode. In the expositional function, the biblical element is explicitly presented and commented on as sacred text. Dimant places the Rabbinic Midrashim and the Pesharim of Qumran in this group.[207]

The compositional use of Scripture, on the other hand, can be found in, for example, the works belonging to the 'rewritten Bible' genre. In these works, the biblical elements are integrated into the structure and presented without any formal marker. The compositional use of Scripture may also be expressed by mere allusions to the Bible; hints at terms or motifs taken from biblical accounts well-known to the reader. As an example, Dimant mentions the book of Tobit, where Tobit's character seems to have been modeled on Job's personality in the Bible.[208] Dimant's description of this last mentioned compositional function of biblical elements in early Jewish interpretation thus has a clear similarity to what Robert Alter defines as use of biblical literary themes, or type-scenes to use his own expression.[209]

There are scholars who want to limit the term 'midrash' to signify *only the Rabbinic Midrashim*. Maccoby, for example, prefers to use midrash in this restricted way. However, he endows the term '(h)aggadah' with a wider scope and admits that it may also be found in non-Rabbinic works. He claims that this is the original Jewish usage of the terminology and that this distinction may help us to avoid an overlap between midrash and (h)aggadah.[210] Julio Trebolle Barrera writes:

> Properly speaking, midrash assumes the existence of a biblical text which is already established and "canonized". Given the various forms of interpretation of biblical texts (midrash, pesher, prophecy applied to the present, rewriting of narratives of biblical laws, etc.), it would be better if the term "midrash" were reserved for Rabbinic midrash and did not include the different forms of biblical interpretation under the name "midrash", which otherwise becomes to generic and is no longer precise. [211]

---

the earliest group of Rabbinic sages, from the time of Jesus until the early third century C.E. They were followed by the Amoraim (*amar*, to say, /to comment, the commentators of Tannaitic teaching (200-500 C.E.). Mishnah is a Tannaitic work, while Gemara is the product of the Amoraim. See Strack/Stemberger 1991, 7-8, 300-307.

207 Dimant 1991, 74-75.
208 Dimant 1991, 73-80.
209 Alter 1981, 47-62. See also Teugels 2004, 51-52.
210 Maccoby 1988, 22-25. See also Teugels 2004, 135-169.
211 Trebolle Barrera 1998, 437.

Their wish to restrict the range of midrash is worth considering. It is important to distinguish between midrash as an exegetical *method* and a literary *genre*. With regard to genre, we should perhaps restrict ourselves to discussing the Rabbinic Midrashim, whereas we might find the midrashic exegetical method at work in other Jewish sources.

3. The Ambiguous Identity of the Angel

3.1 Introduction

As mentioned in previous chapters, the mysterious being called 'the angel of the Lord' who appears for example in Genesis, constitutes a perplexing phenomenon in the angelology of the Hebrew Bible. This angel/messenger differentiates himself from other heavenly emissaries[1] and it is often difficult to distinguish him from God. One proposed explanation of the merged identity of God and this angel is that messengers in the ancient Near East did not need to distinguish between themselves and the ones who sent them. In my opinion this is not a valid theory. According to Samuel A. Meier, the puzzling narratives about 'the angel of the Lord' are the *only* texts in biblical and ancient Near Eastern literature where no distinction is made between sender and messenger. Although the messengers sometimes speak in the first person as if they were the senders of the message, they normally report who sent them.[2]

This מלאך 'angel' is thus unique among messengers in the Ancient Near Eastern literature, which raises the question as to whether he is a messenger at all or YHWH Himself appearing to people in the form of an "angel."[3] There are many narratives in the Bible where God communicates in a direct way with human beings, without any reference to the מלאך YHWH e.g., Genesis 12 and 15. There are also texts where the

---

1   See, for example, von Rad 1964, 77-80.
2   Meier 1995a, 87-88. Meier writes on p. 88:

> It must be underscored that the angel of YHWH in these perplexing biblical narratives does not behave like any other messenger known in the divine or human realm. Although the term 'messenger' is present, the narrative itself omits the indispensable features of messenger activity and presents instead the activities which one associates with Yahweh and other gods of the ancient Near East.

3   Meier 1995a, 88. Freedman-Willoughby (1997, 321): "From these passages it is evident that the *mal'ak* YHWH is closely associated with Yahweh in name, authority, and message, and that he represents Yahweh in the human realm, whereas Yahweh's own immediacy is actualized in realms outside human perception."

מלאך YHWH seems to be distinguished from God, e.g., 2 Sam 24:15-16 and 2 Kgs 19:35 with parallel texts in Chronicles and Isaiah.[4]

As previously mentioned, midrashic exegesis takes its starting point in theological and linguistic problematic issues in the Bible. Thus, the purpose of this chapter is to illuminate the problem of the merged identity of God and His angel in the biblical texts as such. Which questions related to the aim of this study are raised when reading these texts? Since the early Jewish interpreters did not regard Genesis as an isolated book, I will present a survey of all 'angel of the Lord-texts' in the Bible.[5] However, it is the early Jewish interpretation of the Genesis pericopes that is the subject of this dissertation. Thus these texts will be studied in greater detail.

As already stated, I distinguish between explicit references to the angel of the Lord, i.e., texts in which the angel is mentioned, e.g., Genesis 16, and texts describing divine encounters of a similar kind, e.g., Jacob's struggle with his mysterious combatant in Genesis 32. Another example is the visitation of the three "men" to Abraham and Sarah in Genesis 18. However, as stated in chapter 1, only Genesis 32 will be analyzed closely, while Genesis 18 (and 19) will be treated in less detail. Despite my decision to focus on explicit references, Genesis 32 is included as a main text for two reasons. Firstly, it forms an important part of the 'Jacob saga' as a whole and, secondly, the prophet Hosea explicitly identifies[6] Jacob's contender as an 'angel' מלאך.[7] Thus there are connections between Hosea 12 and Genesis 32 as well as between the appearance of the angel in Genesis 31 and the theophanies in Genesis 28 and 35. Each main section will be followed by a short summary of the results. However, because of the brevity of section 3.5, the discussion of the Writings will form an exception to this rule.

---

4   The parallel texts are to be found in 1 Chr 21:14-30; 2 Chr 32:20-22, and Isa 37:36. Note that it is YHWH who tells David to number the Israelites in 2 Sam 24:1, while according to 1 Chr 21:1 it is Satan. This incident, referred to in 2 Samuel 24 and 1 Chronicles 21, is the *only* biblical case where it is stated that the angel of the Lord turned against Israel. This gives rise to the possible understanding of 'the destroying angel' in 1 Chr 21:14-15 as a demonic figure, in spite of the fact that it is stated that YHWH sent him, cf., 1 Sam 16:14.

5   These texts are also discussed in Guggisberg 1979.

6   The originality of this identification, however, is intensely debated among scholars, see below.

7   Hos 12:4-6 (vv. 3-5 in NRSV) will also be discussed in greater detail because of the pericope's connection to Gen 32:22-32; 28:10-22, and 35:1-15.

3.2 Genesis

3.2.1 Hagar and the Angel

Genesis 16

We first encounter the angel of the Lord in Gen 16:7-14.[8] This pericope has much in common with Gen 21:17-20, and they are often designated as parallel texts. The two pericopes describe a meeting between Hagar and the angel/messenger of the Lord/God. In both cases, the angel comes to the rescue of Hagar and her (in Genesis 16 still unborn) son.

According to both texts, the angel of the Lord/God delivers a message of crucial importance and speaks with divine authority. In the two stories, the divine angel/messenger speaks in the first person as if he is God Himself (Gen 16:10 and 21:18, cf., Gen 12:1-3 and 17:3-8), although he also refers to God in the third person (Gen 16:11 and 21:17). The angel never explicitly identifies himself. The texts are ambiguous. *Who* is the angel of the Lord/God? His identity is veiled in obscurity.

When she has fled from Sarai, Hagar meets the angel in the desert:

[Gen 16:7] The angel of the LORD found her [Hagar] by a spring of water in the wilderness, the spring on the way to Shur. [8] And he said, "Hagar, slave-girl of Sarai, where have you come from and where are you going?" She said, I am running away from my mistress Sarai [9]. The angel of the LORD said to her, "Return to your mistress, and submit to her." [10] The Angel of the LORD also said to her, "I will so greatly multiply your offspring, that they cannot be counted for multitude." [11] And the angel of the LORD said to her: "Now, you have conceived, and shall bear a son; you shall call him Ishmael, for the LORD has given heed to your affliction. [12] He shall be a wild ass of a man, with his hand against everyone, and everyone's hand against him; and he shall live at odds with all his kin." [13] So she named the LORD who spoke to her, "*You are El-roi*" [ותקרא שם יהוה הדבר אליה אתה אל ראי] for she said, "*Have I really seen God and remained alive after seeing him?*" [הגם הלם ראיתי אחרי ראי]9 [14] Therefore the well was called Beer-lahai-roi; [באר לחי ראי] it lies between Kadesh and Bered.

The angel finds the pregnant, runaway Hagar by a spring of water in the wilderness (v. 7) and asks her: "Hagar, slave-girl of Sarai, where have you come from and where are you going?" (v. 8a). Initially, the meeting between Hagar and the angel seems very ordinary; it is a meeting en route and not described as a divine revelation, vision or epipha-

---

8   See also Guggisberg, 1979, 32-34.
9   In the NKJV Gen 16:13b reads: ... "You-Are-*the-God-Who-Sees*"; for she said, "have I *also seen Him who sees me?*"

ny. It is a meeting between two persons in the desert.[10] The curious thing is that the angel is obviously familiar with Hagar, since he addresses her by name and refers to her position in Abraham's household. The question in v. 8a is thus most probably rhetorical, as the angel already knows the answer; it is a kind of greeting. The angel of the Lord does not introduce himself to Hagar; in the words of Claus Westermann; "… he is unknown, he comes from and returns to the unknown."[11]

Hagar replies that she has fled from her mistress, but the angel encourages her to return to Sarai and submit herself (vv. 8b-9). The angel of the Lord also promises Hagar abundant offspring (v.10), tells her to give her yet unborn son the name Ishmael [ישמעאל]; "… for the LORD has given heed [שמע lit. 'heard'] to your affliction" (v.11). The interpretation of the name constitutes a unique phrase in the Hebrew Bible, being an amalgam of two distinct idioms. Generally, God *sees* [ראה] affliction, e.g., Gen 29:32; Exod 4:31, and He *hears* [שמע] the outcry of the oppressed, as in Exod 3:7 and Deut 26:7.[12] The angel predicts Ishmael's life and destiny, v.12.

It is probably the content of the message that makes Hagar realize that she has met a divine emissary.[13] She seems to identify the angel/messenger of the Lord with God Himself, since she exclaims (v. 13b): "… 'You are El-roi/ *You-Are-the-God-Who-Sees*';[14] [אתה אל ראי...]"[15]

---

10   In this respect, there is an apparent difference between Gen 16:7 and Gen 21:17, see below. Like Manoah and his wife, Hagar does not at first realize that she is meeting a heavenly emissary. In Judg 13:2-22, the angel of the Lord appears to the couple as a man, in "human form." Although it is not explicitly stated in the text, it is highly probable that the angel of the Lord likewise appeared to Hagar in human form, since she does not at first recognize him as a heavenly messenger. See Isaacs 1998, 6, and Westermann 1985, 243. As we have seen in chapter 1.4, the heavenly messengers/ מלאכים, in contrast to Cherubs and Seraphs, are generally depicted in the Bible as similar to humans in appearance and are sometimes simply called 'men.' See, for example, Gen 19:5, 10.

11   Westermann 1985, 243. According to Westermann, the מלאך YHWH is a messenger of God who in human form meets a person on earth. The initial greeting of the מלאך is a key to our understanding of the 'phenomenon.'

12   See also Sarna 1989, 121.

13   See also Köckert 2007, 53.

14   NKJV.

15   The epithet אל ראי is open to multiple interpretations depending on the vocalization of the second word. Possible translations are: 'God of seeing', that is, the all-seeing God, 'God of vision', 'God of my seeing', that is, whom I have seen, and 'God who sees me'. According to Sarna (1989, 121), it is likely that the various meanings were intended to be apprehended simultaneously. In his words: "When God 'sees' it is, of course, that He shows His concern and extends His protection; when Hagar 'sees,' she experiences God's self-manifestation."

... 'Have I really seen God and remained alive after seeing him'" [הגם הלם ראיתי
אחרי ראי]? In v. 14 we read: "Therefore the well was called Beer-lahai-roi
[באר לחי ראי]; it lies between Kadesh and Bered."[16] As in Judg 13:19-23,
for instance, the messenger is not recognized as a divine emissary until
his departure.[17]

The Hebrew text of v. 13 is obscure and difficult to translate.[18]
Many scholars today have adopted John Wellhausen's emendation,[19]
according to which the last part of v. 13 should be rendered as follows:
הגם אלהים ראיתי ואחי meaning: "Have I really seen God and remained
alive/and I (still) live! As shown in the quotation above, this rendering
is chosen in the NRSV.[20] This is in accordance with the name of the well
in v. 14, which could be translated as "the well of the living one who
sees me/the well of one who sees and lives." Hagar is amazed that she
has seen God, and yet survived (cf., Gen 32:30; Exod 33:20; Judg 6:22-
24, and 13:22).[21] According to this rendering, the name of the well is
thus to be understood in the light of the concept that normally one who
really sees God must die. Hagar, however, appears to be an exception
to that rule.

According to Westermann, Wellhausen's emendation is worthy of
consideration, because it makes such good sense in the context of the
pericope. However, he also maintains that another "solution" to the
problematic verse could merely be the changing of הלם to אלהים. In the
latter case, the verse should be translated: "I have seen God after he
saw me."[22] Westermann interprets vv. 13-14 as Hagar says that God
saw her in her misery and came to her aid, hence God is her savior, cf.,
Ps 113:6.[23]

---

16 See also Westermann 1985, 247.
17 Cf., Westermann 1985, 242-243.
18 A quite strange but literal translation can be: "...Have I here seen behind (the back
    of/after) Him who sees me" (?) According to Westermann, v.13 could also be trans-
    lated as follows: "...you are the God of my seeing [...] God I have seen after he saw
    me". Westermann (1987, 126) interprets this verse to mean that Hagar exclaims that
    she met God after He saw her in her misery. God saw Hagar's distress in this situa-
    tion. The text does not necessarily imply a vision. According to Wevers (1993, 226),
    the LXX rendering of Gen 21:13b, which he translates as "...For even in person have
    I seen the one who appeared to me", may possibly reflect Exod 33:23 where it is
    stated that Moses is allowed to see God's back. See also below.
19 E.g., Speiser 1964, 118-119.
20 The latest Swedish Bible translation, Bibel 2000, also follows Wellhausen's emenda-
    tion.
21 See also Gieschen 1998, 57-58.
22 Westermann 1985, 248.
23 Westermann 1985, 247.

In the LXX, vv. 13-14 are rendered as follows:

[13] καὶ ἐκάλεσεν Ἁγὰρ τὸ ὄνομα κυρίου τοῦ λαλοῦντος πρὸς αὐτήν, Σὺ ὁ θεὸς ὁ ἐπιδών με, ὅτι εἶπεν Καὶ γὰρ ἐνώπιον εἶδον ὀφθέντα μοι/And Hagar called the name of the Lord who spoke to her, "You are the God who sees me/looks upon me;" for she said, "For I have openly [or: in person, see below] seen him that appeared to me." [14] ἕνεκεν τούτου ἐκάλεσεν τὸ φρέαρ, Φρέαρ οὗ ἐνώπιον εἶδον.../ ...The well of him whom I have openly seen ...

John W. Wevers points out that the LXX obviously interprets the epithet אל ראי in v. 13 as Hagar proclaims the messenger as "the God who looks upon me", thus reading ראי as a participle with a first person pronominal suffix; God is the One who pays attention to and provides for her.[24] Wevers further remarks that since the ἄγγελος in v. 7 is unarticulated, it should be rendered 'a messenger'.[25] However, in v. 13 this messenger is apparently identified as the Lord/God Himself, thus the ambiguous relationship between God and His angel/messenger is preserved in the LXX.[26] Wevers takes the word ἐνώπιον adverbially to mean 'in person, face to face', and he translates v. 13b accordingly; "... for even in person have I seen the one appearing to me."[27] The Hebrew name of the well in v. 14 is not translated in the LXX but rendered in accordance with the reading in v. 13: "...Φρέαρ οὗ ἐνώπιον εἶδον .../"the well of him I have openly seen/ the well of the one whom I saw in person"[28] The same Hebrew designation of the well recurs in Gen 24:62 and 25:11 but there the LXX renders it as τὸ φρέαρ τῆς ὁράσεως/"the well of the vision", thus alluding to the appearance of the "angel" to Hagar.[29]

The noun ὅρασις occurs in the LXX Pentateuch eight times, only two of which describe ordinary human vision; Gen 2:9 and Lev 13:12. In all other cases, like the one in Gen 24:62, the word designates visions of a supernatural kind.[30] According to Robert Hayward, the choice of ὅρασις in the LXX rendering of Mizpah, the name of the place where

---

24   Wevers 1993, 225. See also the Vulgate Gen 16:13.

25   Wevers 1993, 222.

26   Wevers 1993, 222, 225-226.

27   Wevers 1993, 225-226.

28   The second alternative is Wevers' (1993, 226) translation. Wevers (same page) concludes that: "Presumably, Hagar has seen the Lord, though only in his form as ὁ ἄγγελος κυρίου, since according to Exod 33:20 'no man can see my (i.e. God's) face and live'."

29   See also Wevers 1993, 373.

30   See also, e.g., Num 24:4, 16, where the word designates an original Hebrew מחזה 'vision' of God.

Jacob and Laban made a covenant (Gen 31:49), may signify that the translator(s) understood the pact between Jacob and Laban as having included a revelation of God.[31]

It is possible to understand the text to mean that God spoke to Hagar through an angel. In her exclamation, she recognizes God as the source of the message and her deliverance. God saw Hagar in her distress and sent an angel. This interpretation, however, is doubtful because of the text's ambiguity. Why does the heavenly messenger first talk to Hagar as God Himself in the first person and then switch to the third person? (Gen 16:10-11).

The angel speaks and blesses in the first person as if he were God: "I will so greatly multiply your offspring …"[32] He never says that God sent him or that his message comes from God. It is only in v. 11 that the angel talks about YHWH as someone distinct from himself. The angel talks with divine authority. He does not identify himself, but Hagar has the impression that she has met God.[33]

The angel of the Lord always has a special reason for his appearance, such as the delivery of a crucial message, of great importance in the (salvation-) history of Israel. The announcement of the birth of a child or of salvation (cf., Judg 13:2-5; Gen 18:9-15; 21:17-20; 22:11-18) is very common. In this case, both of these elements are combined.[34]

---

31 Hayward 2005, 46-49.

32 Cf., how God speaks with Abram in Gen 12:1-3 and 17:3-8.

33 See also Eynikel 2007, 113-114. Newsom (1992, 250) writes: "The apparent interchangeability of the *mal'ak yhwh* and Yahweh cannot be resolved by assuming a clumsy merging of two traditional stories. The same ambiguity occurs in many narratives (e.g. Gen 21:15-21; 22:11-12; 31:11-13; Exod 3:2-6; Judg 6:11-24)". Let me here quote a peculiar interpretation of Gen 16:7-14; 22:1-19, and Judges 13. Freedman-Willoughby (1997, 319) writes: "Hagar's comment that she has seen an Elohim may indicate that she herself is clear about having seen 'a divine being' rather than God himself [...] Since in Gen 22:1-19 one cannot determine the E source with any certainty, Elohim may very well be a generic term for 'a divine being.' Be that as it may, the author did not distinguish between God who tested and the angel who spoke the command." Likewise, Freedman-Willoughby claims that it could be that Manoah and his wife in Judges 13 had not seen God Himself, because they did not die, but "only" a divine being: "Jgs. 13 shows with marvelous clarity the overlapping terminology, and further examples can be found in Gen. 32:22-32(21-31); 2 S. 24:17; Hos. 12:5(4); Zech. 1:9-6:5." This interpretation, however, seems to be quite unusual.

34 See also Westermann 1985, 242.

Genesis 21

The time has now come for a comparison between Gen 16:7-14 and 21:17-20.[35] In the context of the latter pericope, we are told that Hagar has been driven away by Abraham due to Sarah's fear that Ishmael might inherit from her husband and diminish/annul the inheritance of Isaac. Abraham felt compelled to expel her because of this conflict but does so very unwillingly and only after God has told him to heed his wife Sarah:

> [21:11] The matter was very distressing to Abraham on account of his son. [12] But God said to Abraham, "Do not be distressed because of the boy and because of your slave woman; whatever Sarah says to you, do as she tells you, for it is through Isaac that your offspring shall be named for you. [13] As for the son of the slave woman, I will make a nation of him also, because he is your offspring."[36]

In contrast to the narrative in Genesis 16, Ishmael is now born and Hagar has not run away but been cast out of her master's household. Hagar and her son are lost in the wilderness of Beersheba:

> [21:15] When the water in the skin was gone, she cast the child under one of the bushes. [16] Then she went and sat down opposite him a good way off [...] for she said, "Do not let me look on the death of the child." And as she sat opposite him, she lifted up her voice and wept.[37]

In this critical, desperate situation, the angel of God once more appears as her comforter and rescuer. It is worth noting that it is the *angel/messenger who speaks* to Hagar but it is *God who hears* the boy's cries and shows her the well:[38]

> [21:17] And *God* [Elohim] heard the voice of the boy; and *the angel of God* called to Hagar *from heaven*, and said to her, "What troubles you, Hagar? Do not be afraid, *for God* has heard the voice of the boy where he is. [18] Come, lift up the boy and hold him fast with your hand, for *I will* make a great nation of him." [19] Then *God opened* her eyes and she saw a well of water. She went, and filled the skin with water, and gave the boy a drink. [20] God was with the boy, and he grew up; he lived in the wilderness, and became an expert with the bow.

In contrast to the narrative in Genesis 16, the angel of God does not encourage Hagar to return to Abraham and Sarah but promises that God will take care of her and her son. As in Gen 16:10, the angel says

---

35 See also Guggisberg 1979, 45-47.
36 Note that God speaks directly to Abraham, no angel being mentioned.
37 According to the LXX Gen 21:16b, it was the boy, not Hagar, who wept.
38 According to Westermann (1985, 339), we cannot ignore the differences between Genesis 16 and 21. Despite the similarities, they are two different narratives.

that he will give her abundant offspring, Gen 21:18. In both pericopes the angel blesses Hagar with divine authority in first person singular: "... *I will so greatly multiply* your offspring ... (Gen 16:10), "... *I will make* a great nation of him ..." (Gen 21:18). This is precisely what God Himself tells Abraham in Gen 21:13. But the angel also refers to God in the third person, Gen 16:11 and 21:17. Both narratives mention a well/a spring of water, perhaps the same one.

There are many parallels between the two pericopes, e.g., the angel of the Lord/God plays a similar role, that of savior. One major difference in the portrayal of the divine messenger, however, is that the angel of God calls to Hagar *from heaven* according to Gen 21:17, whereas in Gen 16:7 the angel meets her *on earth*: "The angel of the Lord found her by a spring of water in the wilderness ..." Westermann writes about Gen 21:17: "The messenger of God who is encountered on earth (cf. Gen 16:7b) has become an 'angel', a heavenly being who calls from heaven."[39]

Another obvious difference is of course the designation of the Deity in the texts, YHWH versus Elohim. The designation 'the angel of YHWH/the Lord' is the most common in the Bible (58 times), while 'the angel of Elohim/God' only occurs 11 times.[40]

Concluding Remarks

The narratives about Hagar's encounter with the divine messenger tell us something important about God's character. God sees Hagar's distress and delivers her and her son, even though she is only a bondwoman; God shows her mercy. God is impartial and He does not abandon the outcast. God's grace and blessing is not restricted to Isaac's line.[41] It is noteworthy that Hagar, Ishmael's mother, is the only biblical woman who gives God a "name," an epithet:"You-Are-the-God-who-Sees ..." (Gen 16:13).[42]

It is possible to understand the texts as if God spoke to Hagar through an angel, although this interpretation is hardly tenable because of the ambiguity of the narratives. As mentioned in chapter 2.2.1, midrashic exegesis takes its point of departure in questions put to the biblical texts. One purpose of midrash is to solve theological problems

---

39 Westermann 1985, 342. See also Köckert 2007, 69-70.
40 Westermann 1985, 242.
41 See also Westermann 1985, 343-344.
42 NKJV.

in the Bible. Our two present pericopes are no "simple" texts. The ambiguous identity of the angel of the Lord/God is one of the apparent exegetical problems in the texts. Who is it that speaks to Hagar in these narratives?

A connected issue is how we should interpret the obscure verses Gen 16:13-14. Is Hagar really proclaiming that she has seen God and gives Him a name in v. 13? If she saw God, why did she survive since, according to Jewish theology, no one can see God and live? Does she actually identify the angel of the Lord as God Himself? What is the role of the angel of the Lord/God in the interpretations of these two texts? How is he related to God and to Hagar? Do the interpreters have any comments as to why the angel of God calls to Hagar from heaven in Gen 21:17, whereas he seems to meet her on earth in Gen 16:7? How are the two texts related to each other?

3.2.2 The Three Heavenly Visitors and the Doom of Sodom and Gomorrah

In Genesis 18-19:29 we can discern three main sections, the visitation of the three "men" to Abraham and Sarah, Gen 18:1-15 (16),[43] Abraham's negotiation with YHWH, Gen 18:17-33, and the doom of Sodom and Gomorrah, Gen 19:1-29.[44] In the Bible these sections form a single, integrated narrative. However, the original unity of Gen 18-19:29 is debated among scholars, but that is a subject for another thesis.[45] The focus here is the interpretation of the texts in their present form. Gen 18:1-15 reads:

> [Gen 18:1] The LORD appeared to Abraham by the oaks of Mamre, as he sat at the entrance of his tent in the heat of the day. [2] He looked up and saw three men standing near him. When he saw them, he ran from the tent entrance to meet them, and bowed down to the ground.[46] [3] He said, "My lord [אדני], if I find favor with you [בעיניך lit. "in your (2nd pers. sing.) eyes"],

---

43　Some scholars wish to include v. 16 in this passage. However, the scene itself covers Gen 18:1-15, while v. 16 serves as a bridge to the subsequent sections, see further Hamori 2004, 13-14, and Westermann 1985, 282.

44　See also Hamori 2004, 13-33. Some scholars have suggested a pre-Israelitic origin of the Genesis narrative in a myth of a visitation of three gods, see the discussion in Westermann 1985, 275-276, and Hamori 2004, 48-73.

45　See also Hamori 2004, 13-33, Westermann 1985, 274-275, and van Seters 1975, 215-216.

46　Abraham's reverent greeting indicates that he acknowledges his visitors as being of higher rank than himself. See also Westermann 1985, 278, and Letellier 1995, 82.

do not pass by your servant. [4] Let a little water be brought, and wash your feet, and rest yourselves under the tree. [5] Let me bring a little bread, that you may refresh yourselves [...]" So *they* said, "Do as you have said." [8] ... and he [Abraham] stood by them under the tree while they ate. [9] *They* said to him, "Where is your wife Sarah?" And he said, "There, in the tent."[10] Then *one* said [ויאמר], "*I* will surely return to you in due season, and your wife Sarah shall have a son." And Sarah was listening at the tent entrance behind him. [13] *The LORD* [יהוה] said to Abraham, "Why did Sarah laugh, and say, "Shall I indeed bear a child, now that I am old?" Is anything too wonderful for the LORD? At the set time *I* will return to you, in due season, and Sarah shall have a son. [15] But Sarah denied, saying, I did not laugh, for she was afraid. He said, "O yes, you did laugh."

We are told by the narrator in v. 1 that the Lord appeared to Abraham by the terebinth trees of Mamre, and this divine revelation is connected to the visit of three 'men' [אנשים] to the patriarch. In the context, one of the men seems to be identified with YHWH (vv. 13-33), though it is unlikely that Abraham recognizes him at first.[47] This "man" talks with divine authority in the first person singular as if he is God Himself and promises Abraham and Sarah a son (vv. 10-15). In the same manner as the angel of the Lord, he comes in order to deliver a message of crucial importance.[48] The sudden shift from the third person plural (vv. 5, 9) to the first person singular in v. 10 is somewhat confusing. Likewise, it is also peculiar that Abraham greets his three visitors in v. 3 in the singular form, as "... my lord [LORD/Adonai][49] if I find favor with you [lit. "in your eyes/sight", בעיניך (2nd pers. sing.)][50] do not pass on by your servant." In vv. 4-5 on the other hand, he addresses the men in the plural and invites them to a meal.[51] The greeting, "my lord" אדני(v. 3) is vocalized by the Masoretes as if signifying YHWH, i.e., 'Adonai/LORD',[52] although that was hardly the narrator's original intention, but probably an interpretation based on the "heading" in v. 1: "The LORD appeared to Abraham ..."[53] Abraham's greeting in the singular is presumably to be understood as indicating that he recogniz-

---

47 See also Letellier 1995, 80-103.

48 See also Westermann 1985, 275, and Barr 1960, 33.

49 "... my lord" is the translation chosen in the NRSV, but אדני is in the MT vocalized as Adonai/LORD.

50 In Samaritanus the word is inflected in the plural and thus refers to all three of the men; "your eyes..."

51 Hamori (2004, 33-36) argues that the shift from singular to plural may be understood in the light of the conversation recorded in 2 Kgs 18:17-18.

52 See also the MT Gen 19:17-19, where the same problem recurs, cf., the rendering in the LXX.

53 See, e.g., Westermann 1985, 278, and Letellier 1995, 82-83.

es one of the men as their leader.[54] It is probably not until v. 10, when the man confirms the divine promise of a son, that he realizes who is speaking to him.[55] The content of the message reveals the "men's" heavenly origin, cf., Genesis 16.[56] In the following verses (vv. 13-14), the leader is explicitly identified as YHWH and shows Himself to be omniscient.

In v. 16 we read that the men left Abraham's tent and he accompanied them on their way. In v. 22 a distinction is again made between the visitors: "So the men turned from there, and went toward Sodom, while Abraham remained standing before the Lord."[57] By now, we know for certain that Abraham is aware of who he is talking to and he pleads with God to spare the people of Sodom (vv. 23-33). The two other men are identified in chapter 19 vv. 1, 15 as messengers/angels/מלאכים, but in some verses they are still called 'men'; (vv. 5, 8, 10, 12, 16).[58] In contrast to the leader of the company in chapter 18, these two men appear to be "mere" angels, sent by God to do his bidding, see Gen 19:13.[59] However, in Gen 19:17 and 21 we again find examples of a mysterious shift from the plural to the singular form in the Hebrew text.[60]

According to Ester Hamori, the narratives in Genesis 18 and 32 distinguish themselves by being so-called ''îš theophanies' to use her term, i.e., theophanies in which God appears in concrete human form. She states that normally, the distinction between God and man is clear in the Bible, but these two texts are exceptions. In Genesis 18 and 32, God is not described metaphorically as a man, as is the case in Exod 15:3 and Isa 42:13. In the theophanies of the Genesis texts, God appears in the

---

54 See also Hamori 2004, 34-36, and Letellier 1995, 82-83.
55 Hamori (2004, 131-132) points out that both Genesis 18 and 32 deal with the confirmation of a divine promise to one of Israel's forefathers. Moreover, in both narratives God appears in concrete human form, the so-called ''îš theophany' to use Hamori's designation, a fact that she takes as an illustration of the special relationship between God and the patriarchs. Regarding the ''îš theophany', see further below. See also Letellier 1995, 88-89.
56 See also Hamori 2004, 44-47.
57 According to a text critical note to v. 22, the original wording of the verse was: "and the *Lord* remained standing before Abraham".
58 Samaritanus has מלאכים in Gen 19:12.
59 In this verse the two angels refer to God in the third person.
60 The seemingly pleonastic repetition of "from YHWH" in Gen 19:24 gave rise to the interpretation that the second reference to YHWH in fact refers to the angel Gabriel. This interpretation could be taken as support for the 'two-powers-heresy' and the passage was included among the "dangerous texts" by the Rabbis, see, e.g., *b. Sanhedrin* 38b. See also Segal 1977, 121-134.

tangible, physical body of a man. Both pericopes describe a concrete meeting with God in human form, not a vision or dream. [61]

The term 'the angel of the Lord' is not mentioned in Genesis 18, although the narrative is in many ways reminiscent of 'the angel of the Lord-texts', which also describe the appearance of a divine messenger in the form of a man.[62] In both Genesis 18 and Judges 13, the reason for the heavenly visitations is the annunciation of the birth of a son to a barren woman.[63] In both cases, the divine emissaries are invited to share a meal with their hosts.[64] Hamori admits that the man/angel of the Lord in, for example, Judges 13 appears in concrete human form, but she remarks that the narrative lacks the realistic anthropomorphism which characterizes Genesis 18 and 32.[65] In contrast to the three "men," the divine messenger in Judges 13 refuses to eat the food offered to him. She further points out that, although the two angels in Genesis 19 are clearly depicted as having a physical human form, since the men of Sodom even wish to have sex with them,[66] they behave in an utterly superhuman way when they blind the inhabitants of that city.[67]

Robert I. Letellier, however, sees no major difference in the degree of anthropomorphism between Genesis 18 and the explicit narratives of the appearance of the מלאך יהוה /'the angel of the Lord' in the OT. In both Genesis 18 and the 'angel of the Lord-texts' the central issue is the appearance of the Lord in human shape, but this should not be confused with mere anthropomorphism. Although YHWH is depicted as eating in Genesis 18, his external appearance is not described.[68] Letellier writes:

> The element of ambiguity is not that YHWH appears to men, but that he [in Genesis 18] is accompanied by *mal'akim* who later move to Sodom and continue the effect of the theophany there, carrying God's presence into the city and eventually seeming to merge into the person of YHWH himself when they speak to Lot in the singular and with the voice of omnipotence (19, 21). The voice and presence of the *mal'ak* varies in a number of stories, seeming to appear and speak for YHWH so closely that it is difficult to un-

---

61 Hamori 2004, 1-8.

62 See also Barr 1960, 32-38, esp. pp. 33-34, and Gieschen 1998, 51-69.

63 This type-scene recurs in the NT, see the annunciations to Zechariah, the father of John the Baptist and Mary, the mother of Jesus in Luke's Gospel. See also Brown (reprinted ed.) 1999, 155-158, 268-269, and Letellier 1995, 103-107.

64 Cf., Heb 13:2.

65 For a discussion of Genesis 32, see below.

66 Gen 19:4-5.

67 Hamori 2004, 43-44, and 141-147.

68 Letellier 1995, 90-91.

derstand him merely as a substitute for God. This is particularly the case in Gen 16,7-14 […]. The *mal'ak* passages, far from establishing a remoteness or transcendence of YHWH, perhaps in an attempt at combating primitive anthropomorphism, sustain an ambiguity of identity and increase mystery. The *mal'ak* does not dilute the theophany, but must be understood as accompanying the self-revelation of God in human form …[69]

Concluding Remarks

I agree with Letellier that the main mystery of the narrative in Genesis 18-19 lies in the ambiguous relationship between the three divine visitors. The story may be interpreted as an appearance of YHWH and two angels, or that YHWH was somehow present in all three of them, although the statements in Gen 18:22 and 19:1 indicate that God was accompanied by two angels.[70] In this way, Genesis 18-19 present the same problem as most of the 'angel of the Lord-texts'. However, it is true that the human appearance of Abraham's visitors is made remarkably concrete by their eating of his food, a behavior which has no counterpart in any other biblical text.

3.2.3 The Aqedah and the Angel

Gen 22:1-19 is a very central pericope in Judaism and consequently the object of careful analysis and interpretation.[71] The angel of the Lord does not play such a significant role, the main characters being Abraham and Isaac. In Jewish tradition, the pericope is called '*the Aqedah*' or '*Aqedat Isaac*', that is, 'the binding of Isaac', a reference to the fact that he was bound on the altar, but not sacrificed. Isaac thus plays an im-

---

69   Letellier 1995, 90-91. See also p. 92.
70   See also Köckert 2007, 63-67, and Eynikel 2007, 114.
71   According to Jewish tradition the Aqedah was the tenth and final trial of Abraham, cf., *Targum Neofiti 1* Gen 22:1, *Pirqê de Rabbi Eliezer* 31, *Genesis Rabbah* 56.11. See also Neh 9:7-8; Sir 44:19-21. In early Jewish Interpretation the pericope is connected to two of the most important Jewish holidays; Pesach and Rosh haShana. In modern Jewish liturgy, this text is read in the Synagogue service on the second day of Rosh haShana. The blowing of the shofar ram's horn, cf., Lev 23:23-25 and Num 29:1) on Rosh haShana is connected to the ram that was sacrificed instead of Isaac. Cf., Lewis 1971, 1443-1447 and Jacobs 1971, 481-482.

portant role, even overshadowing Abraham in many early Jewish interpretations of the text.[72]

The primary focus of this study, however, is not Isaac but concepts
of God and angelology with specific reference to the angel of the Lord
in the early Jewish exegesis of the text.

The first and most obvious problem in Gen 22:1-19 is *why* a loving
God commands Abraham to sacrifice Isaac, the son of promise. In v. 1 it
is stated that "After *these things* God tested Abraham ..." The readers
are informed of something that Abraham did not know when he was
commanded to sacrifice his son, that the whole scenario is "only" a
trial. But why is it necessary for an all-knowing God to test a man? Did
God not know that Abraham feared him, even without testing him (v.
12)? What was the purpose of the trial? Moreover, what words or
events [דברים] are referred to in v. 1?

Another peculiarity in the pericope is the altering of the divine
"name." It is *God/Elohim* who commands Abraham to sacrifice Isaac (v.
1) but it is the angel of the *Lord/YHWH* who intervenes at the last moment and manages to stop Abraham from completing the sacrifice
(vv. 11-12). Both designations of God are used five times in the text.
Does this have any significance?[73]

What kind of place is the land of Moriah (v. 2)? The only additional
scriptural reference to Moriah is in 2 Chr 3:1, where it is said that king
Solomon built the Temple on Mount Moriah in Jerusalem (cf., 2 Sam
24:16-25 and 1 Chr 21:15-28). In the LXX the sacrificial place is called
'the high land', the Vulgate says 'the land of vision', and in Peshitta we
read 'the land of the Amorites'. It is worth noting that the name Moriah
has similarities to the Hebrew words for myrrh, fear/reverence and the
hiphil participle of the verb ראה 'see'.

---

72   There is an apparent parallel between God's initial calling of Abraham in Gen 12:1
     and His command to sacrifice Isaac in Gen 22:2 by the use of the Hebrew phrase לך לך
     / "Go forth...!", which does not occur again in the Bible, constitutes a kind of so-
     called inclusio connecting Abraham's calling to be a servant of God and the conclu-
     sion of his spiritual odyssey. In *Jub.* 17.15-18.19 Abraham is the main character (cf.,
     Heb 11:17-19; Jas 2:21-24) but at an early stage of Jewish theology the focus was
     transferred to Isaac, who was depicted as a prototype of the Jewish martyr, e.g., 4
     Macc. 13.12-15, 16.20-21 and *L.A.B.* 40.1-9. See also Josephus' rewriting of the peri-
     cope in his *Judean Antiquities*. This was also the main interpretation of the Aqedah
     during the crusades in the Middle Ages. In many Jewish interpretations, Isaac's wil-
     lingness to sacrifice himself is also viewed as a kind of atonement, e.g., *L.A.B.* 18.5;
     32.1-4. See also the interpretation of the Aqedah in, for example, the Palestinian Tar-
     gums, *Genesis Rabbah* and *Pirqê de Rabbi Eliezer*. Cf., von Heijne, 1997, 57-86, Kugel
     1998, 296-326 and van Bekkum 2002, 86-95.

73   See also Köckert 2007, 70-71.

There is an apparent connection between v. 2 and the problematic v. 14. The latter verse can be translated in several ways. The Hebrew wording is as follows:

ויקרא אברהם שם המקום ההוא יהוה יראה אשר יאמר היום בהר יהוה יראה

The verse can be translated: "Abraham called the name of the place the Lord sees/chooses, as it is said today, on the mountain of the Lord it is *seen/revealed*" (my translation).[74] In the Hebrew text it is unclear who or what is seen on the mountain. Who or what does the last part of v. 14 refers to; the ram, God, the angel of the Lord, or something/someone else? The translators of the LXX as well as the Swedish Bible 2000 interpret the end of the verse as referring to the Lord, LXX: Ἐν τῷ ὄρει κύριος ὤφθη /Bible 2000: "… på berget där Herren blir sedd" ["on the mountain where *the Lord is seen*," my translation]. This understanding of the verse is of interest for our subject, since it is the angel of the Lord who reveals himself and talks to Abraham in vv. 11-12 and 15-18. Are the angel of the Lord and the Lord Himself identical? The NRSV, on the other hand, translates the verb ראה as *'provide'*: "So Abraham called that place 'The LORD will *provide*'; as it is said to this day, "On the mount of the LORD *it shall be provided*."

The biblical pericope has six/seven actors: God (Elohim/YHWH), Abraham, his two servants,[75] Isaac, the angel of the Lord (YHWH), and the ram. The focus of the study is the role of the angel of the Lord in early Jewish interpretation. The main question is whether the angel is actually seen as a revelation of God Himself or "only" as His messenger? The biblical text is ambivalent on this point. Are God and the angel of the Lord identical, and does our narrative therefore only have six actors?

As mentioned above, the text contains both biblical "names" of God, YHWH and Elohim, and the angel is called 'the angel of YHWH'.

The angel is the deliverer of Isaac and therefore also of his descendants, the people of Israel. The angel appears for the first time in vv. 11-12 and saves Isaac at the last moment from being sacrificed by his father. The angel of the Lord speaks with divine authority in the first person singular, as if he is God himself, although he also refers to God in the third person:

---

74 There are some text critical remarks pertaining to this verse in BHS. The issue is the grammatical form in which we are to read the verb ראה 'to see' the first and second time it appears in the verse. It all depends on how we choose to vocalize the word. The MT first uses an active and then a passive form.

75 The two young men, the servants of Abraham, are identified as Ishmael and Eliezer in *Pirqê de Rabbi Eliezer* 31 and *Targum Pseudo-Jonathan* Gen 22:3.

[Gen 22:11] But the angel of the LORD called to him from heaven, and said, "Abraham, Abraham!" And he said, "Here I am." [12] He said, "Do not lay your hand on the boy or do anything to him; for now *I know* that you *fear God*, since you have not withheld your son, your only son *from me.*"

In v. 15 we read that the angel of the Lord calls to Abraham a *second time* from heaven. Why a *second* time? The angel says to Abraham:

[Gen 22:16] ... "By myself I have sworn, says the LORD [נאם יהוה]: Because you have done this, and have not withheld your son, your only son, [17] I will indeed bless you, and I will make your offspring as numerous as the stars of heaven and as the sand that is on the seashore. And your offspring shall possess the gate of their enemies, [18] and by your offspring shall all the nations of the earth gain blessing for themselves, because you have obeyed *my* voice."

In verse 16 the angel uses the so-called 'messenger-formula'/ נאם יהוה/ 'says the Lord'. Most scholars think that this does not solve the problem of the angel's identity. The angel never indicates that God sent him, as other messengers usually do. It is also noteworthy that the phrase נאם יהוה only occurs at this point in Genesis and that no other biblical מלאך uses it. [76]

The fact that *God swears by Himself* is something unique in the Aqedah and is only mentioned again in Exod 32:13, where the text alludes to this episode. [77] The angel of the Lord confirms and expands on the divine promises previously given to Abraham (Gen 12:1-3; 15:4-21; 17:1-8).

In Gen 22:19 we read that Abraham returned to his servants and they went together to Beersheba, but Isaac is not mentioned. Where is Isaac? He must still be alive, since we read that the angel of the Lord prevented Abraham from completing the sacrifice. As in Genesis 16 and 21, the angel intervenes as a savior. In the same way as he came to the rescue of Ishmael and his mother in the desert he saves Isaac's life at the last moment in Genesis 22.

Concluding Remarks

There are some similarities between Gen 16:7-14 (21:17-20) and 22:1-19. Both Abraham and Hagar meet the angel of the Lord who comes to rescue them and their sons and shows them a solution. Hagar catches

---

76 See above and, e.g., Meier 1995a, 87-88, 103.

77 This oath, however, is mentioned in, for example, Gen 26:2-5; Ps 105:9-11, and Sir 44:20-21. In the NT, the fact that God swore by Himself is referred to in Hebr 6:13-18.

sight of a well of water (Gen 21:19), while Abraham discovers a ram to sacrifice instead of his son (Gen 22:13). Hagar calls God 'the God who sees' (Gen 16:13). There is an apparent similarity between the name of the well in Gen 16:14: "… Beer-lahai-roi /באר לחי ראי/ the well of the Living One who sees me…" [78] and the naming of the sacrificial site in Gen 22:14: "On the mountain of the Lord it is seen/revealed/on the mountain the Lord is seen."[79] Both Hagar and Abraham are promised abundant offspring by the angel of the Lord, see Gen 16:10 and 22:17 respectively.

In both pericopes, God's and the angel's identities are fused together, the angel talks in the first person singular as if he is God Himself, but at the same time refers to God in the third person, Gen 16:10-11 and Gen 22:11. However, the angel in Genesis 22 distinguishes himself by using the 'messenger-formula' in v. 16, which is not used by any other biblical מלאך but, as mentioned, most scholars do not consider that the use of the phrase eliminates the problem of the angel's merging with God. Since he does not report who sent him, the angel does not behave like any other biblical messenger and thus differs from a prophet speaking on God's behalf. *Who* then, is the angel of the Lord, and why does he call to Abraham a *second* time from heaven? As we will see in the following, other angels are mentioned in many of the interpretations of Genesis 22. How is the angel of the Lord related on the one hand to these angels, and on the other to God Himself?

3.2.4 The Wooing of Rebekah – the Angel as a Protector and Guide

In Gen 24:1-4 we read that Abraham commands his servant to swear that he will go to his master's old homeland in order to search for a suitable wife for Isaac, a woman from among Abraham's relatives. When the servant says that she might not want to follow him back to Canaan (v. 5), Abraham answers him as follows:

> [Gen 24:6] … "See to it that you do not take my son back there [to Mesopotamia]. [7] The Lord, the God of heaven,[80] who took me from my father's house and from the land of my birth, and who spoke to me and swore to

---

78   My translation. In connection with the well, it is worth noting that in its rewriting of Gen 22:1-19, *Jubilees* refers to a well near the sacrificial site. Abraham bids his servants to stay there, while he and Isaac continue on (*Jub.* 18.4). In the LXX Beer Sheba (Gen 22:19) is translated as φρέαρ τοῦ ὅρκου/'the well of the oath'. Cf., *Jub.* 18.17-18.

79   My translations. See also Westermann 1985, 247

80   LXX adds "…and the God of the earth…" Concerning the title of YHWH as 'God of heaven', see also Niehr 1995, 702-705.

me, saying, 'To your offspring I will give this land,' *he will send his angel*[81] *before you, and you shall take a wife for my son from there.* [הוא ישלח מלאכו לפניך ולקחת אשה לבני משם] [8] But if the woman is not willing to follow you, then you will be free from this oath of mine; only you must not take my son back there."

The commission of the angel is to accompany Abraham's servant to Mesopotamia.[82] The angel will protect him during his journey and lead him to the proper woman. As we know, the journey is successful and the servant finds Rebekah, the grand-daughter of Abraham's brother. He meets her at a well outside the city of Nahor, when she comes to draw water. The servant considers their meeting as an answer to his prayer, i.e., as a divine intervention (vv. 12-27). His personal prayer plays an important role in the narrative; see vv. 26-27:

> [Gen 24:26] The man bowed his head and worshipped the LORD [27] and said, "Blessed be the LORD, the God of my master Abraham, who has not forsaken His steadfast love and his faithfulness toward my master. As for me, being on the way, the LORD has led me on the way to the house of my master's kin."

The servant is warmly welcomed by Rebekah's family and tells them about the reason for his journey, namely to find a wife for Isaac, vv. 29-41. In v. 40, the servant refers to Abraham's words in v. 7 concerning the angel. As a matter of fact, vv. 37-41 repeat vv. 2-9 and vv. 42-48 repeat vv. 11-27. Rebekah's father and brother both acknowledge the hand of God behind the events:

> [Gen 24:50] Then Laban and Bethuel answered, "The thing comes from the LORD; we cannot speak to you [the servant of Abraham] anything bad or good. [51] Look, Rebekah is before you, take her and go, and let her be the wife of your master's son, as the LORD has spoken." [52] When Abraham's servant heard their words, he bowed himself to the ground before the LORD.

Rebekah thus follows the servant back to Canaan and marries Isaac:

> [24:66] And the servant told Isaac all the things that he had done. [67] Then Isaac brought her into his mother Sarah's tent. He took Rebekah, and she became his wife; and he loved her. So Isaac was comforted after his mother's death.

According to Meier, a common function of a messenger in the Ancient Near East was to escort persons who were traveling under the protection of the sender. The same applies to the biblical messenger of God,

---

81 Westermann (1985, 378) has chosen the translation 'messenger' in Gen 24:7, while in his second commentary on Genesis (1987, 167) he uses the translation 'angel.'

82 See also Guggisberg 1979, 39-40.

who is often depicted as a protector of travelers in order to bring them safely to their destinations and help them accomplish their tasks. The present text is an obvious example, and Meier also refers to many others; Exod 14:19; 23:20-23; 32:34; 33:2; 1 Kgs 19:5-6, and Tob 5:21. Meier states that "... the later angelic protection of God's people in any context can be perceived as an extension of this original messenger task (Dan 3:28; 6:23[22]; Bar 6:6 [= Ep Jer 6])."[83]

In its present form, Genesis 24 is a tale of divine providence. God leads the servant to Abraham's relatives and a suitable wife for Isaac. The protection of the angel guarantees the success of the commission.[84]

According to Westermann, the theme of divine providence in Genesis 24 is the result of a reworking of an originally "pure" family narrative. The words of Abraham in v.7 "he [God] will send his angel before you..." are thus a later insertion. As support for his claim, Westermann writes that Abraham's assurance to his servant here is

> ... a traditional fixed expression for God's assistance and it occurs also in Ps. 91:11, which is an assurance of blessing to an individual at a relatively late period (cf. Ps 121); the reworking of Gen. 24 into its present form may be temporally close to it.[85]

Concluding Remarks

As stated above, the only reference to an angel in the singular in Genesis, where the distinction between God and His angel seems clear, is in Gen 24:7, 40. In the narrative of the wooing of Rebekah, the angel plays a very anonymous, "back stage" role; he does not speak (cf., Genesis 22) and is only referred to in the third person.

---

83   Meier 1995a, 85. See also Gutmann/Editorial Staff 1971, 964, Newsom 1992, 250, 252, and Ps 34:7 (v. 8 in the MT).

84   See also Köckert 2007, 71-72. At the same time, Genesis 24 is a family tale, whose primary goal is marriage. In this respect, the pericope has many similarities to Gen 29:1-14 and Exod 2:15b-22. All three narratives describe a meeting at a well between a stranger from afar and local people, a meeting that results in marriage. The common theme of all three narratives, the meeting with a future spouse at a well, may be defined as a so-called type-scene in the Hebrew Bible, see Alter 1981, 47-62. The element of 'divine guidance' is, however, absent in the two last mentioned pericopes. Nevertheless, the fact that God is not explicitly mentioned in Gen 29:1-14 and Exod 2:15b-22 does not exclude the implication of His action in the narratives, see, for example, Westermann 1985, 383.

85   Westermann 1985, 383-384. See also Eynikel 2007, 114, and Köckert 2007, 72.

Westermann's theory possibly explains why the angel in Genesis 24 seems to be clearly distinguished from God, in contrast to the other pericopes in Genesis where a divine messenger is mentioned in the singular form, e.g., Gen 16:7-14. Be that as it may, in its present form the narrative is a typical tale of divine providence and angelic protection.

3.2.5 Jacob and the Angel

Introduction

The explicit 'angel of the Lord-texts' in the Jacob cycle[86] are Gen 31:10-13, where the angel of God appears to Jacob and orders him to return to his homeland, as well as Jacob's equation of God with His angel in Gen 48:15-16. Both texts are in turn closely connected to Gen 28:10-22 and 35:1-15. All these pericopes have in common that they mention an encounter between God and Jacob at Bethel (except Gen 48:15-16, but Luz, i.e., Bethel is mentioned in that context, vv. 3-4).[87] Because of the close relationship of the texts, I have included them all in my analysis, even though the angel of God (in the singular form) is explicitly mentioned only in Gen 31:10-13 and 48:15-16.

The implicit 'angel of the Lord-text', the story of the struggle between Jacob and the unnamed man in Gen 32:24-32 (vv. 25-33 in the MT), is in many ways reminiscent of these texts, since it also describes an encounter between Jacob and the divine world, either God Himself or a divine being/an angel. It is apparent that the "man" who wrestles with Jacob is not an ordinary opponent.

There is also a connection between Gen 32:27-28[28-29] and 35:9-10, since both pericopes describe the bestowal of the name of Israel on Jacob and are in turn related to Hos 12:4-5 (vv. 5-6 in the MT). The latter text will be discussed in section 3.4.

---

86 See also Guggisberg 1979, 50-57.
87 According to Gen 28:19, it is Jacob who gives the city of Luz the name of Bethel, cf., Gen 35:6.

The Revelation at Bethel

Genesis 31

Let us begin by looking at Jacob's account of his encounter with God's angel during his service with Laban:

> [Gen 31:10] "… During the mating of the flock I once had a dream in which I looked up and saw that the male goats that leaped upon the flock were striped, speckled, and mottled. [11] Then *the angel of God* [מלאך האלהים] said to me in the dream, 'Jacob,' and I said, 'Here I am!' [12] And he said, 'Look up and see that all the goats that leap on the flock are striped, speckled, and mottled; for I have seen all that Laban is doing to you. [13] *I am the God of Bethel, where you anointed a pillar and made a vow to me.* Now leave this land at once and return to the land of your birth'"/ [אנכי האל בת אל אשר משחת שם מצבה אשר נדרת לי שם נדר עתה קום צא מן הארץ הזאת ושוב אל ארץ מולדתך]

Here Jacob addresses his two wives Rachel and Leah and tells them about a revelation in a dream. In the context of the pericope we read that Laban and his sons have become jealous of Jacob because of his increasing wealth, vv. 1-2. God then exhorts Jacob to return to his homeland, v. 3.[88] He decides to flee and therefore summons his wives to explain the situation, v. 4. Jacob tells them that Laban has behaved unjustly but that God has been with him, vv. 5-9. Jacob attributes the increase in his livestock to a divine revelation in a dream, vv. 10-12.

It is noteworthy that Jacob refers to '*the angel of God*' in v. 11. Diana Lipton points out that although angels appear elsewhere in Genesis, this is the only dream which is mediated by an angel, speaking in God's name, and she further remarks that in the middle of v. 12 the angel's voice has become indistinguishable from that of God. Despite this ambiguity, Lipton claims that the angel in Genesis 31 is to be understood as a distinct being, separate from God, a conclusion she bases on the similarities between the function of the angels in Gen 31:10-13 and Zech 5:5-6. Like Zechariah's angel, Jacob's angel appears as an *angelus interpres*, i.e., an interpreter of dreams and visions. Because Zechariah's angel is clearly depicted as an independent being, she claims that the same most probably applies to the angel who appeared to Jacob.[89] I admit that there

---

88 Cf., the "angel's" instruction in Gen 31:13. D. Lipton (1999, 30) remarks that the dream reported in Gen 31:10-13 is the only Genesis-dream not announced by the narrator, possibly because the dream and God's instruction in v. 3 were regarded as another version of one and the same event.

89 Lipton 1999, 30, 115-121. Lipton apparently does not take into consideration the question of the "angel's" own identification as 'the God of Bethel', see the discussion above.

is a genuine affinity *in function* between the two angels, but this fact alone does not *per se* place them in the same category.

In Gen 31:13, the angel of God identifies himself as *'the God of Bethel'*. The Hebrew wording in this verse is strange; אנכי האל בית אל can be translated as "I am the God Bethel." In the words of Nahum Sarna;

> ...the succeeding double use of "where," (Heb. *sham*), shows that "Bethel" here is a place name, not a divine name.[90] The title is intended not to limit the living God to a specific locale but to call to mind the original theophany [Gen 28:10-22], specifically the promise of constant protection and safe return. In like manner, the emphasis on the vow is a reminder to the patriarch that his self-imposed obligation assumed at Bethel has yet to be discharged ...[91]

The LXX is clearer than the MT in v. 13, where the angel of God says to Jacob:

> [Gen 31:13] ἐγώ εἰμι ὁ θεὸς ὁ ὀφθείς σοι ἐν τόπῳ θεοῦ / I am the God that appeared to you in the place of God.[92]

According to Hayward, the translators of the LXX modeled their account of the angel's appearance to Jacob on Moses' calling-experience at the burning bush.[93] They interpreted Jacob's life as prefiguring the destiny of his descendants, the people of Israel. Jacob's servitude in the house of Laban foreshadows the slavery of Israel in Egypt. God intervenes in both cases; in Gen 31:12, the angel says to Jacob "... for I have seen all that Laban is doing to you," compare with God's words to Moses in the LXX Exod 3:7 "... I have observed the misery of my people who are in Egypt ..." God/the angel of God exhorts Jacob to "leave this land at once"[94] and God tells Moses that He has come down in order to "bring them [the people of Israel] up out of that land

---

90 Bethel was the name of a pagan god once worshipped by some of the peoples in the Ancient Near East, cf., Jer 48:13. Likewise, the place known as Bethel was most certainly already a sacred Canaanite cultic site before and during the patriarchal period. See Sarna 1989, 398-400. For further discussion, see below.

91 Sarna 1989, 215.

92 The LXX also uses the definite form when referring to the angel in v. 11: ὁ ἄγγελος τοῦ θεοῦ ..., because the "angel" has already made himself known to Jacob in Genesis 28. This probably explains the definite form in verse 13, both in the Greek and the Hebrew texts: "... I am *the* God of Bethel/*the* God who appeared to you in the place of God..." God is reminding Jacob of their previous encounter at Bethel. The Swedish Bible translation (Bibel 2000) of Gen 31:13a reads: "Jag är den Gud som visade sig för dig i Bethel ... /I am the God who appeared to you in Bethel ..." [My translation]. According to Wevers (1993, 501-502), it is made totally clear in LXX vv. 12-13 that the "angel" is none other than God Himself.

93 Hayward 2005, 41-43.

94 Gen 31:13b.

[Egypt]."[95] The addition to the angel's speech in the LXX Gen 31:13; "…
and I will be with you,"[96] is regarded by Hayward as an allusion to
God's promise in Exod 3:12.[97]

The angel of God identifies himself in Gen 31:13 as the God ὁ
ὀφθείς σοι ἐν τόπῳ θεοῦ/ "who *appeared* to you in the place of God", a
clause that is reminiscent of Exod 3:2 where it is stated in the LXX:
Ὤφθη δὲ αὐτῷ ἄγγελος κυρίου …/… "And an angel of the Lord *appeared* to him [Moses]…" Jacob is thus compared to Moses; both had a
vision of God/His angel. In the two narratives, the identities of the angel and God are blurred; when we continue to read Exodus 3,[98] the
angel of the Lord seems to be none other than God Himself.[99] Hayward
further points out that the LXX designation of Bethel as 'the place of
God' may be intended to remind the reader of the place of God's *appearance* to Moses in the burning bush, which is explicitly described as
'holy ground', see Exod 3:5.[100]

Genesis 28

The angel/messenger of God hence claims to be none other than God
Himself who appeared to Jacob in Bethel. Gen 31:13 thus refers back to
another divine revelation in a dream, described in Gen 28:10-22:

> [10] Jacob left Beer-sheba and went toward Haran. [11] He came [ויפגה][101] to
> a certain place [במקום] and stayed there for the night, because the sun had
> set. Taking one of the stones [ויקח מאבני][102] of the place [המקום], he put it un-
> der his head and lay down in that place. [12] *And he dreamed that there was a
> ladder set up on the earth, the top of it reaching to heaven; and the angels of God
> were ascending and descending on it.* / ויהלום והנה סלם מצב ארצה וראשו מגיע השמימה]

---

95   Exod 3:8.

96   This concluding phrase has no counterpart in the MT. However, it is employed in
     God's previous exhortation to Jacob to return home, see Gen 31:3b.

97   See Hayward 2005, 38-44.

98   See, e.g., Exod 3:4b in the LXX and the MT. See also Hayward 2005, 42-43.

99   The similar ambivalence between God and His angel apparent in Exodus 3 and Gen
     31:11-13 is not discussed by Hayward, whose focus differs from that of the present
     investigation.

100 See Hayward 2005, 42-43. Cf., also Jacob's designation of Bethel according to Gen
     28:16-17. The Hebrew word מקום 'place' occurs no less than six times in the account
     of Jacob's dream at Bethel and is apparently a key-word in the story. It also has the
     connotation of 'holy place/site', see below.

101 Literally: "he *met* a certain place …" According to Westermann (1985, 452), the verb
     פגה 'meet' constitutes a link to Gen 32:1-2, where the same verb is employed. See also
     Philo's interpretation of the verb in his analysis of Genesis 28 in *On Dreams* 1.70-71
     and *Pirqê de Rabbi Eliezer*, see below.

102 Literally; "… from the *stones* [in plural!] of that place …" See the analysis of the
     Targums below.

[13] And *the LORD stood beside him*[103] and said [והנה מלאכי אלהים עלים וירדים בו], "I am the LORD, the God of Abraham [... [והנה יהוה נצב עליו ויאמר], אני יהוה אלהי אברהם] your father and the God of Isaac; the land on which you lie I will give to you and to your offspring; [14] and your offspring shall be like the dust of the earth, and you shall spread abroad to the west and to the east, and to the north and to the south; and all the families of the earth shall be blessed in you and in your offspring. [15] Know that I am with you [... והנה אנכי עמך] and will keep you wherever you go, and will bring you back to this land; for I will not leave you until I have done what I have promised you." [16] Then Jacob woke from his sleep and said, "Surely the LORD is in this place—and I did not know it!" [17] And he was afraid, and said, "How awesome is this place! This is none other than the house of God, and this is the gate of heaven." / וייקץ יעקב משנתו ויאמר אכן יש יהוה במקום הזה ואנכי לא [16] ידעתי [17] ויירא ויאמר מה נרא המקום הזה אין זה כי אם בית אלהים וזה שער השמים.

[18] So Jacob rose early in the morning, and he took the stone [האבן][104] that he had put under his head and set it up for a pillar [מצבה] and poured oil on the top of it. [19] *He called that place Bethel* [ויקרא את השם המקום ההו בית אל]; but the name of the city was Luz at the first. [20] Then Jacob made a vow, saying, " If God [אלהים] will be with me, and will keep me in this way that I go, and will give me bread to eat and clothing to wear, [21] so that I come again to my father's house in peace, then the LORD [יהוה] shall be my God [לי לאלהים], [22] and this stone, which I have set up for a pillar, shall be God's house [בית אלהים]; and of all that you give me I will surely give one tenth to you."[105]

This dream is the initial theophany in the life of Jacob and constitutes the first occasion when God appears and speaks to him. In a sense the vision can be designated as his calling as a servant of God.[106] Jacob is to be the one who will carry on the spiritual heritage of his fathers. The pericope belongs to the narratives of encounters with God and of sacred sites inserted in the Jacob-Esau story (see also Gen 32:1-2, 22-32; 35:1-15).[107]

God introduces Himself as "... the LORD, God of Abraham your father and the God of Isaac ..." This is clearly an allusion to the covenant made with Abraham and Isaac. God links Himself to Jacob's fathers and continues by repeating the promises of land, abundant offspring, and blessings previously given to the earlier patriarchs (vv. 13-14), see, for example, Gen 12:1-3; 13:14-17; 22:15-18; 17:6-8 (Abra-

---

103 Or: above him/it (the ladder).

104 Cf., Gen 28:11.

105 Cf., Gen 31:13.

106 Cf., the calling of the prophet Isaiah; Isaiah 6. See also Westermann 1985, 454-455, and Kugel 1995, 211.

107 Westermann 1985, 452.

ham), and 26:2-5, 23-25 (Isaac). One purpose of the vision is thus to confirm Jacob as the heir to the divine promises and the third patriarch.

In contrast to his predecessors, Jacob meets God in a dream. As mentioned before, early Jewish exegesis takes its point of departure in problems found in the texts. One intriguing question is why God chose to address Jacob in a *dream*.[108] Why could He not talk to him directly, as he did with Abraham and Isaac?[109] As shown above, according to Gen 31:10-13, the angel of God also appeared to Jacob in a dream.[110]

Another question is the meaning of the vision of the heavenly ladder or stairway[111] with angels going up and down on it. If the purpose of the dream was merely that God wanted to assure Jacob that "… the land on which you lie I will give to you and to your offspring" (v. 13),

---

108　Cf., Num 12:6b-8a:

[Num 12:6b] …When there are prophets among you, I the LORD make myself known to them in *visions*; I speak to them in *dreams*. [7] Not so with my servant Moses; he is entrusted with all my house. [8] With him I speak face to face–clearly, not in riddles; and he beholds the form of the LORD …

According to Guiley (2004, 105-109), the early Jews placed a high value on dreams as real experiences of the direct voice of God. Divinely inspired dreams are common in the Bible. Besides Jacob, his son Joseph and the prophet Daniel are well-known biblical characters who can be mentioned in this context. It is sometimes difficult to distinguish between dreams and visions in the Bible. Expressions such as "I continued looking, in the visions of my head as I lay in bed …" (Dan 4:13) may refer to dreams.

109　We may, however, interpret Gen 15:12-16 as God talking to Abraham in a dream, although this is unusual in the case of Abraham, cf., Gen 12:1-3; 13:14-17 etc.

110　According to Gen 31:24, God also appears to Laban in a dream when he pursues the fleeing Jacob and warns him: "Take heed that you say not a word to Jacob, either good or bad." According to Gen 46:2-4, God appeared to Israel (i.e., Jacob) in the visions of the night, presumably a dream, thus Jacob/Israel had a total of three divine dream revelations.

111　The Hebrew word סלם is a *hapax legomenon*. Its etymology and meaning is uncertain; it may derive from the root סלל 'to heap/pile up'. According to Koehler/Baumgartner (2001, 757-758), Sarna 1989, 198, Westermann (1985, 454), and, for example The New International Version, 'stairway' is probably the correct translation. In addition to the New Revised Standard Version cited above, the New King James Version also uses the translation 'ladder'. According to Sarna (1989, 198), the inspirational stimulus for the image of the 'ladder' is either the ladder of ascent to heaven known from Egyptian and Hittite sources or the Babylonian ziggurat/temple tower. The gods were considered to contact humanity from the top of the ziggurat, and the temple priests went up and down in the service of the deities. The angels may thus play a priestly role in Jacob's dream. See also Alter 1996, 49. Another interpretation is that Genesis 28 depicts Yahweh as a king and the angels as his emissaries who are sent out from His throne on various missions and afterwards return to report. See Lewis/Oliver 1996, 229.

there would have been no need for the heavenly ladder/stairway.[112] Among the patriarchs this revelation is unique to Jacob. Neither Abraham nor Isaac are ever said to have seen a heavenly ladder in their dreams. What was the vision of the angels climbing up and down on it intended to communicate?[113] Another question is what the ladder looked like. Its appearance is not described.

The ascending and descending angels underscores the connection between heaven and earth. The stairway is set/מצב at the place where Jacob is sleeping thereby marking the spot as holy.[114]

'The angels of God'/מלאכי אלהים in v. 12 are clearly *heavenly beings, sharply distinguished* from the מלאך יהוה/'the angel of the Lord' in the singular form. The angels of God in Gen 28:12 may be defined as similar to the sons of God mentioned in, for example, Job 1:6; 2:1.[115] Linguistically speaking, it is possible to interpret the last part of v. 12 as meaning that the angels are going up and down "on" for the sake of *Jacob*. The Hebrew word בו may refer to either Jacob or the ladder, but the most natural is of course the latter.[116]

According to Sarna, the angels play no role in the dream but their presence may

> ... reflect the notion of angelic beings who patrol the earth and report back to God. It is also possible that the notion of angelic activity may symbolize Jacob's personal hopes and fears, his prayers for protection, which rise to heaven and receive a response.[117]

Jacob's designation of the place of the revelation in v. 17 as the gate of heaven signifies that it is the place where the angels ascend to and descend from heaven.[118]

The expression מלאכי אלהים occurs only here and in chapter 32:1-2 in Genesis.[119] Both pericopes are connected to the life of Jacob. As men-

112 For reasons of simplicity, I will in general use the word 'ladder', because this is the translation in the NRSV.

113 See also Kugel 1995, 211.

114 See Köckert 2007, 57, and Westermann 1985, 454-455. According to Walters (1992, 602), the ladder is "... a symbol of the accessibility of God's help and presence, a theme distinctive to the Jacob stories."

115 See also Köckert 2007, 54, 57, Westermann 1985, 454-455, and Murphy 1989, 30.

116 See Kugel 1990, 114-120.

117 Sarna 1989, 198. Cf., for example Zech 1:7-11. It is noteworthy that the riders [angels?] who patrol the earth are clearly distinguished from the angel of the Lord, see vv. 10b-11: "... They are those whom the LORD has sent to patrol the earth. Then they spoke to the angel of the LORD who was standing among the myrtle trees, 'We have patrolled the earth, and lo, the whole earth remains at peace.' " Cf., Job 1, 2.

118 Sarna 1989, 199. According to Sarna, the idea of such places was widespread in the Ancient Middle East. See also Ps 78:23 and Westermann 1985, 457.

tioned above, these two texts and Genesis 19 are the only examples of
מלאכים/angels in the plural in Genesis. The appearance of the angels is
not described in Genesis 28.

The heavenly ladder and the angels certainly have a deep symbolic
significance. I question Sarna's statement that the angels play no role in
the dream. If so, why are they in it? Kugel remarks that it is peculiar
that the angels are said to be going *up and down*, in that order. In his
own words: "Angels are said to reside in heaven; they should therefore
more properly be said to *go down and up*."[120] It remains to be seen
whether the early Jewish interpreters bothered with this question.

The meaning of Gen 28:13a is debated. Does God stand upon/above
the ladder, or is He depicted as standing beside/in front of *Jacob*? The
Hebrew wording here is; "... והנה יהוה נצב עליו" and the question is what
or who the suffix attached to the preposition על alludes to, the ladder or
Jacob? Since the ladder is mentioned in v. 12, it seems likely that the
suffix refers to it, and this is also the translation we find in NKJV; "...
And behold, the Lord stood above *it* [the ladder] ..." This is also the
rendering in the LXX,[121] the Vulgate and Peshitta.[122]

Westermann however, claims that the reference is to Jacob and that
the verse should be translated accordingly; "And Yahweh stood before
him and said ..."[123] He bases his interpretation on the fact that Jacob is
addressed by God in the following, vv. 13b-15.[124] This appears to be a
weak argument, as God can talk to Jacob even if He is standing
above/on the ladder.

From the point of view of content, the question of where God is
standing may appear to be of little significance but if God is depicted as

---

119 The expression does not occur anywhere else in the Bible, with the exception of 2
    Chronicles 16, where the meaning is different, see Westermann 1985, 452.
120 Kugel 1995, 213. Linguistically speaking, there is nothing strange about the order of
    the verbs in Gen 28:12. In Hebrew as in English, things are generally said to 'go up
    and down', not 'down and up'. See also Kugel 1990, 114.
121 The wording of Gen 28:13 in the LXX is as follows: ... ὁ δὲ κύριος ἐπεστήρικτο ἐπ᾽
    αὐτῆς καὶ εἶπεν, Ἐγὼ κύριος ὁ Θεὸς Ἀβραὰμ τοῦ πατρός σου ... / "... the Lord
    stood upon it [the ladder] and said, 'I am the Lord, the God of Abraham your father
    ..." Since the word for 'ladder' in Greek, κλίμαξ, is feminine, the reference can here
    only be to the ladder, not to Jacob, who is obviously masculine.
122 See also Sarna 1989, 198 and 364. According to him, this is also the choice of Rashi,
    ibn Ezra, and Rambam, whereas Saadiah refers the preposition to Jacob. See also the
    New International Version which states in v. 13: "There above it [the ladder] stood
    the LORD ..."
123 Westermann 1985, 451 and 455, thus also the New Revised Standard Version and the
    latest Swedish Bible translation, Bibel 2000.
124 Westermann 1985, 455.

standing upon the ladder, it and God become more closely connected to each other.[125] Otherwise, it is possible to interpret God's speech to Jacob and the vision of the ladder as two separate revelations, thus in accordance with Westermann.[126] Sarna also translates v. 13a in this way: "And the LORD was standing beside him [Jacob] and He said …"[127]

Regardless of how we understand v.13, it is clear that the God who talks to Jacob is distinguished from the angels going up and down on the ladder. Nevertheless, the angel of God who appears to Jacob in Haran refers to himself as 'the God of Bethel,' Gen 31:13. This is accordingly no "ordinary angel," unlike the angels in Gen 28:12.

As we have seen, Jacob encounters God/the angel of God in a dream vision in both Gen 28:10-22 and 31:10-13. The two pericopes also have in common that Jacob finds himself in awkward situations. In Genesis 28, Jacob is on the run towards Haran in order to escape the revenge of his brother Esau. In Genesis 31, he has found himself forced to flee once more, this time because of the jealousy of Laban and his sons. In both situations, the divine revelation is intended as an encouragement. In Gen 28:15, God says to Jacob:

> "… Know that I am with you and will keep you wherever you go, and will bring you back to this land; for I will not leave you until I have done what I have promised you."

In contrast to the previous promises in vv. 13-14, this one concerns Jacob personally in his present predicament.[128] God speaks to Jacob during his flight and promises to protect him and bring him safely back home.

These two themes, the promise of divine protection during a journey[129] and the importance of marrying a relative, remind us of Genesis 24, the story of Abraham's servant's match-making trip to Haran. One difference between the two narratives is that in Genesis 28 it is God

---

125 If we understand the "ladder" in Jacob's dream as modeled on the Babylonian ziggurat/temple tower, it seems most probable that God is depicted as standing on/above the "ladder."

126 Westermann 1987, 200.

127 Sarna 1989, 198. Sarna also claims that the ladder did not function as a channel of communication between man and God, a statement that he leaves unexplained.

128 As mentioned above, Jacob is on the run. As a result of the conflict with his brother, Jacob is told by his mother to leave the land of his family and flee to Laban, his uncle in Haran; Gen 27:42-45; 28:1-2. Isaac exhorts his son to take as wife one of the daughters of Laban, that is, a relative.

129 See also Westermann 1985, 455-456, 460.

Himself who promises to look after Jacob, whereas Abraham in Genesis
24 refers to God's angel who will accompany his servant.[130]

The Hebrew word מקום 'place' in Genesis 28 is significant, because it
has a double connotation; the word can also mean 'a holy site.' However, when Jacob lodges there for the night, he treats the place as profane.
For him it is just a suitable spot to sleep.[131]

The last verses of our pericope, Gen 28:16-20, describe Jacob's response to the divine revelation. According to vv. 16-17, when Jacob
awakes from his sleep, he exclaims:

> [Gen 28:16] … "Surely the LORD is in this place–and I did not know it!"
> [17] And he was afraid, and said, "How awesome is this place! This is none
> other than the house of God, and this is the gate of heaven." / אכן יש יהוה [16]
> במקום הזה ואנכי לא ידעתי [17] ויירא ויאמר מה נרא המקום הזה אין זה כי אם בית אלהים וזה שער
> השמים.

Jacob's amazement reveals that he was initially ignorant of the sacredness of the place where he chose to spend the night. The heavenly vision was unexpected and the divine encounter surprised him.[132]

In addition to his astonishment, Jacob also reacted with awe and
fear: "And he was afraid, and said, 'How awesome is this place! This is
none other than the *house of God* …' " (v. 17). The Hebrew root ירא occurs twice in this verse. Kugel remarks that the fear of the patriarch
may have puzzled the early Jewish interpreters of the text. What could
possibly be so terrifying about a ladder with angels on it?[133] Jacob's fear
distinguishes him from his predecessors; neither Abraham nor Isaac are
said to have become afraid when God appeared to them. See, for example, Gen 12:7-9; 13:14-18 (Abraham), and 26:2-6 (Isaac).

However, Jacob's fear when encountering the transcendent and
numinous as described here is a universal human reaction to the expe-

---

130 See also Köckert 2007, 58, who interprets the angels on the ladder as symbolizing
     Jacob's divine protection, cf., God's promise in Gen 28:15.
131 Sarna, 1989, 197, 199, 400, and Westermann 1985, 454. The Swedish Bible translation
     from 1917 says in Gen 28:11: "Och han kom då till *den heliga platsen* …/And hence he
     came to *the holy place* …" (my translation). In Rabbinic terminology, the word מקום
     came to be employed as a divine epithet, meaning 'the Omnipresent'. According to
     Koehler/Baumgartner (2001, 627), it already had this meaning in Esth 4:14. See also
     Marmorstein 1927, 92-93, and Deut 12:5; 14:23; 16:2, 6, where the word is used to des-
     ignate God's chosen abode. The expression 'house of God' is a designation for the
     Temple in Jerusalem in, e.g., Ps 42:5; 1 Chr 6:33; 22:2, 11.
132 Jacob's surprise may also be interpreted in the light of his past behavior toward his
     brother. Because of feelings of guilt, he may be surprised that God still is concerned
     about him. See Sarna, 1989, 199.
133 Kugel 1995, 211.

rience of 'the holy'.[134] Because he treated the place irreverently, the discovery of its sanctity frightens Jacob, although it should be noted that the Hebrew word for 'holy', קדשׁ, does not occur in the pericope.[135]

The following morning Jacob begins to act upon his vision. He erects the stone he slept on as a pillar and pours oil on it, v. 18. This action presupposes the already existing rite of the anointing of the מצבה. The stone marks out the place of the revelation and functions as a 'witness' to Jacob's subsequent vow to God in vv. 20-21,[136] cf., Gen 31:45-54 and Josh 24:27. The מצבה is intended as a 'witness' to the divine presence at the site and is hence called בית אלהים /'house of God', v. 22.[137] In verse 19 Jacob calls the place Bethel, the name having the same meaning. See also Gen 31:13a, where the angel of God refers to this event and says: "I am the God of Bethel, where you anointed a pillar and made a vow to me."[138] The story has thus an etiological purpose; to derive the initial holiness of the site from Jacob's dream-vision.[139]

The Septuagint version of Genesis 28 does not mention the name Bethel at all. In v. 19 the expression is literally translated in accordance with its Hebrew meaning; 'house of God'; ... καὶ ἐκάλεσεν Ἰακὼβ τὸ ὄνομα τοῦ τόπου ἐκείνου Οἶκος θεοῦ .../ "... And Jacob called the name of that place *the house of God ...*"

Jacob's Struggle at the Ford of Jabbok

Yet another text, Gen 32:22-32,[140] tells about God (or a divine being/an angel?) appearing to Jacob and confronting him at the ford of Jabbok.

---

134 See also, e.g., Judg 13:20-22 and Luke 1:11-12. Hagar (Gen 16:7-14; 21:17-20), however, is not said to have shown any fear when she encountered the angel of the Lord.

135 See, for example, Westermann 1985, 460. According to him, God's presence in history and the importance of cultic worship are the two main messages of the text.

136 Westermann 1985, 457-458, Sarna 1989, 199-200.

137 Sarna 1989, 201. The מצבה may also be understood as a 'witness' to Jacob's dream vision, Westermann 1985, 457. In v. 22 the stone is hence given the same name as the place, cf., vv. 17, 19.

138 See also Hos 12:4b-5 (vv. 5b-6a in the MT): "He met him [Jacob] *at Bethel,* and there he spoke with him. The LORD the God of hosts, the LORD is his name!"

139 See Köckert 2007, 57, Westermann 1985, 452-454, and Sarna 1989, 199, and 398-400. Etiological narratives are frequent in Genesis. The naming of a place is often described as a response to a divine revelation. See Gen 16:14; 22:14; 32:1-2, 30, and 35:7, 15.

140 The numbering of the verses differs between the MT and NRSV; Gen 31:55 in the NRSV corresponds to Gen 32:1 in the MT. If not otherwise stated, the following discussion adheres to the NRSV.

Before we analyze the narrative, let us begin by taking a look at the context of this incident. In Gen 32:1-3 we read that when Jacob departs from Laban, he meets angels of God, מלאכי אלהים. When Jacob sees them he exclaims "… This is God's camp!" As a result of this experience, Jacob names the place 'Mahanaim'. Jacob's reaction tells us that the encounter was not with ordinary human messengers but with angels of God. As mentioned above, besides Gen 28:12 this is the only occurrence of the expression מלאכי אלהים in Genesis and it has the same meaning in both cases; it is divine beings/angels whom Jacob meets and not the specific 'angel of the Lord' who is always referred to in the singular. Westermann interprets the name Mahanaim as referring to God's power; Jacob is worried because of the impending confrontation with his brother and is met by God's host/army, most probably signifying divine protection.[141] In the same way as the departure of Jacob from the land of his birth was marked by the appearance of angels, so too is his return to his native land.[142]

When Jacob hears that Esau is coming toward him with 400 men, he is terrified and prays to God for help, vv. 9-12. His supplication recalls God's promises of land, protection, blessing, and prosperity in Gen 28:13-15 as well as God's/the angel of God's exhortation to return home, cf., Gen 32:9 and 31:3, 13.

There is also an obvious connection between Gen 32:27-30 and 35:9-15, the second narrative about Jacob becoming Israel. In spite of the fact that Hos 12:3-5 (MT vv. 4-6) will be treated later on, it must be stated here that the prophet makes an allusion to the tradition(s) of Jacob's encounter with God/the angel of God[143] as related in both of the above-mentioned pericopes.[144]

Let us now consider Jacob's nightly confrontation with the unknown man in Gen 32:22-32. A common scholarly view is that the story has a mythological origin; the folkloristic legend about a river-demon trying to prevent a traveler from crossing its domain. The narrative in Genesis 32 is supposed to be a reworking of this myth in order to make it compatible with Israel's monotheistic faith.[145]

According to Westermann, even in its present form the story is to be understood in this way. In his interpretation, the man/איש who wres-

---

141 Westermann 1985, 505. See also Sarna 1989, 223.
142 See also Köckert 2007, 58-59, Alter 1996, 177, and Sarna 1989, 223.
143 Cf., Hos 12:4 (v. 5 in the MT).
144 See also Vawter 1977, 349-350, and Hayward 2005, 18-24.
145 See Vawter 1977, 349, Hamori 2004, 86-95, Hayward 2005, 25, Westermann 1985, 515, and Sarna 1989, 403.

tles with Jacob is not God, but 'a divine being', 'a demon'.[146] Westermann takes the fact that the assailant shuns the daylight as proof of his
demonic identity; God does not fear the dawn.[147] Moreover, the God
whom Jacob had invoked in prayer could not possibly be the one who
attacked him. On the contrary, Jacob's victory over the demon is God's
answer to his prayer for divine intervention.[148]

Another interpretation of the text is to identify Jacob's contender as
an angel of God.[149] This view is represented by, for example, Sarna,
who points out that, because he blesses Jacob, the antagonist cannot be
a demon, a conclusion I find reasonable.[150] As Hamori remarks, it is
indeed very telling that Westermann finally puts the word 'blessing'
within quotation marks in his discussion of the narrative, because it
does not fit in with his demon interpretation.[151] In support of his identification of the contender, Sarna also refers to Hosea 12 and other biblical accounts where the designations איש 'man' and/or אלהים 'divine
beings' are used for angels; Genesis 18-19; Josh 5:13-15, and Judges
13.[152] The last argument is weak, since these biblical references are highly ambiguous, all of them belonging to 'the angel of the Lord-texts'.[153]

Sarna connects Jacob's wrestling bout with his return to the Promised Land and the subsequent confrontation with Esau, as the river

---

146 Westermann 1985, 515-518. Westermann and Vawter (1977, 349) interpret the word
     איש in Genesis 32 as meaning 'someone'. Vawter concludes that in v. 31 it becomes
     "... quite clear that a super-human, God-like character is the one with whom Jacob
     has contended at the Jabbok."
147 Westermann, 1985, 521. Westermann (1985, 516-517) also refers to Exod 4:24-26,
     where it is stated that YHWH attacked Moses at night. He claims that the reference
     to YHWH is secondary and that the attacker was originally a demon, see also the
     discussion of this text in chapter 2.
148 Westermann 1985, 521.
149 See also Hamori 2004, 95.
150 Sarna 1989, 403. See also Köckert (2007, 60-61) who remarks that demons do not
     usually give blessings. However, Köckert questions the identification of Jacob's op-
     ponent as an angel, since Jacob's new name as well as his reaction recorded in v. 30
     [31] "...For I have seen God face to face..." implies that he had struggled with none
     other than God Himself.
151 Hamori 2004, 94. A more likely variant of the 'demon-interpretation' is to read the
     story psychologically; Jacob wrestles with his "inner-demons" (as well as God) at
     night; i.e., his conscience and fears, when faced with the impending confrontation
     with Esau. See also Alter 1996, 181. Walters (1992, 605) interprets Jacob's wrestling
     bout at Jabbok as representing his struggle with both men (Esau, Laban, Isaac) and
     God throughout his life. At Jabbok, Jacob was forced to face his own character, his
     relations with other people as well as with God.
152 Sarna 1989, 227-228, 383-384, 404, and 414.
153 See also Köckert 2007, 61-62.

Jabbok constitutes a border of the future land of Israel.[154] The angel who tries to prevent Jacob from crossing the river is thus none other than Esau's celestial patron, cf., Dan 10:13, 20-21 and the LXX Deut 32:8. By renaming and blessing Jacob, his opponent acknowledges him as the rightful heir to the land. Jacob has thus nothing to fear when he finally meets his brother.[155]

As mentioned above, together with Genesis 18, Hamori regards the story of Jacob's physical combat with the unknown man as an '᾽îš theophany', the appearance of God in the concrete, physical form of a man, an interpretation that I find likely. The divine status of this man is indicated by several details in the text. He has the authority to bless Jacob as well to give him a new name, Israel:[156]

> [Gen 32:26] Then he [the man] said, "Let me go, for the day is breaking." But Jacob said, "I will not let you go, unless you bless me." [27] So he said to him, "What is your name?" And he said, "Jacob." [28] Then the man said, "You shall no longer be called Jacob. But Israel, for you have striven with God and with humans, and have prevailed."/ ויאמר לא יעקב יאמר עוד שמך כי אם ישראל כי שרית עם אלהים ועם אנשים ותוכל[157]

It is not only the authority to rename Jacob which demonstrates the divine nature of the man but also the significance of the new name itself. The explanation given in v. 28 indicates that Israel means 'he strives with God'.[158] Hamori refutes the argument that the word אלהים in this context may signify 'divine beings,' since it is used as an equivalent to אל, 'God/El', in v. 28 (v. 29 in the MT). However, Jacob's question in v. 29 may still express his doubts concerning the identity of his opponent, perhaps he still wonders what kind of אלהים/divine being he really is:[159]

> [Gen 32:29] Then Jacob asked him, "Please, tell me your name." But he said, "Why is it that you ask my name?" And there he blessed him. [30] So

---

154 Sarna 1989, 403. See also Num 21:24; Deut 2:37; 3:16; Josh 12:2, and Judg 11:13, 22.

155 Sarna 1989, 404. According to Sarna (1989, 227), the bestowal of the name Israel constitutes the blessing of Jacob, but there is no general consensus concerning this matter.

156 See also Hamori 2004, 82-83. Hamori compares this renaming of Jacob with Hos 1:6-2:1 (v. 3 in the MT). As will be shown below, Jacob/Israel has been bestowed with a kind of angelic character in some early Jewish sources, see also Gieschen 1998, 152-183.

157 Verse 29 in the MT.

158 However, in names formed by a verb (in this case שרה 'strive/struggle/contend') combined with the divine element אל/'god', God is usually the subject of the action, not its indirect object, hence 'God strives'. See also Sarna 1989, 26. The meaning of this name has been much debated, see below.

159 See also Hamori 2004, 85-86.

Jacob called the place Peniel, saying, "For I have seen God face to face, and yet my life is preserved."/ ויקרא יעקב שם המקום פניאל כי ראיתי אלהים פנים אל פנים ותנצל נפשי[160]

When Jacob/Israel asks for the man's name, he receives no reply (v. 29). Bruce Vawter compares the man's refusal to tell his name with God's cryptic answer to Moses in Exod 3:14: "I AM WHO I AM."[161] After the man has left, Jacob/Israel names the place Peniel, 'face of God', since he is shaken by the experience that he has met God in person and yet survived. This reminds us of Hagar's reaction after seeing the angel of the Lord, Gen 16:13, as well as of the name of the well, v. 14.[162]

According to Hamori, the man's counter question in Gen 32:29 "Why is it that you ask my name?" and his blessing of Jacob finally confirm his identity as God Himself. Furthermore, she claims that Jacob's naming of the place Peniel cannot be separated from his exclamation in v. 30 "For I have seen God [אלהים] *face to face;*" once more אלהים is used as an equivalent to אל/El.[163]

Jacob's reaction in v. 30 clearly indicates that the narrative in its present form describes a meeting with God.[164] The patriarch's wonder that he is still alive must be seen in the light of the Israelite conviction that no man can see God's face and live, compare Exod 33:20, where God says to Moses, "… you cannot see my face and live, for no one shall see me and live."[165] However, the case of Moses is highly ambiguous, because in Exod 33:11 it is stated that "… the Lord used to speak to Moses face to face, as one speaks to a friend," and in Deut 34:10 Moses is said to have been exceptional in this regard. Hamori claims that the stories of Jacob and Abraham in Genesis 18 and 32 similarly describe an intimate relationship with God. She further points out that in both narratives God confirms His promises to the patriarchs.[166]

Jacob's naming of the place and the word פנים 'face' in v. 30 (31) is a key-word.[167] It denotes personal presence, in this case divine presence.[168] To seek God's face is to seek His presence.[169]

---

160 Verse 31 in the MT.
161 Vawter 1977, 351.
162 Cf., Gideon's exclamation in Judg 6:22.
163 Hamori 2004, 77, 83-86. Cf., the discussion of the angelic name Phanuel, see chapter 2.
164 See also Köckert 2007, 61.
165 See also Murphy 1989, 34.
166 Hamori 2004, 130-132, 189-190.
167 See also Hamori 2004, 83-86.
168 Seow 1995, 609.
169 See, e.g., Ps 105:3.

The phrases פנים אל פנים and פנים בפנים[170] 'face to face' are only used in
the Bible to denote human-divine encounters.[171,] That the expression
signifies the Deity in person is shown in Exod 33:14-16:[172]

> [v. 14] He [God] said "My *presence* [פנים lit. 'face'] will go with you, and I
> will give you rest." [v. 15] And he [Moses] said to him, "If your *presence*
> [פנים] will not go, do not carry us up from here. [v. 16] For how shall it be
> known that I have found favor in your sight, I and your people, unless *you*
> go with us? In this way, we shall be distinct, I and your people ... [173]

In these verses, the presence [פנים] of God is said to go with the people
and God is depicted as personally accompanying them but, in Deut
4:37, YHWH is said to have led His people out of Egypt with (by means
of) His פנים:

> And because he loved your ancestors, he chose their descendants after
> them. He brought you out of Egypt with his own presence [בפניו], by his
> great power ...

According to Choon-Leong Seow, in this case the פנים *represents* the
divine presence and not literally God in person. He concludes: "The
Hebrew Bible uses the term pānîm to speak of the presence of God,
sometimes obliquely: the pānîm either *is*, or *represents*, the appearance
of the deity."[174] Thus if Seow is to be believed, the פנים 'presence' of God
in Deut 4:37 plays a role similar to 'the angel of the Lord' in many texts,
see, for example, Exod 23:20-24. However, in my opinion, the difference
between Exod 33:14-16 and Deut 4:37 is very subtle and many scholars
interpret the latter passage as also referring to God in person, as will be
shown in section 3.3.

The meaning of Jacob's new name 'Israel'/ישראל has been much discussed in scholarly circles. The explanation provided in v. 28 (29) indicates that it means 'he strives/contends with God', although most probably God is to be understood as the subject of the verb שרה
'strive/contend', hence 'God strives'.[175] However, additional etymolo-
gies of the name have also been suggested, for example a derivation of

---

170 See Deut 5:4.
171 Seow 1995, 609. See also Sarna 1989, 228.
172 See also Seow 1995, 611.
173 Cf., the LXX translation of the word in Exod 33:15: αὐτὸς σὺ 'you yourself'.
174 Seow 1995, 607-613, esp. p. 612. See also the discussion of Exodus, Judges, and Isaiah
     below (with regard to Isaiah 63, see also chapter 2).
175 This verb is most unusual and only found here and in Hos 12:4. Its meaning is con-
     tentious. Some scholars suggest that its proper meaning is 'have dominion, rule',
     thus the same as שׁרר/שׁור, see above and the note below. Hence Alter (1996, 182) un-
     derstands the name as meaning 'God will rule' or 'God will prevail.' See also Sarna
     1989, 405.

the verb שׁוּר, a by-form of שׂרר meaning 'rule, direct, act as a prince, have dominion', an interpretation based on Hos 12:5, compare Judg 9:22 and Hos 8:4.[176] As will be shown below, this understanding of the name Israel seems to be implied in, for example, the LXX and the Targums.[177] The Hebrew root ישׁר 'to be upright' has also been discussed by modern exegetes in this context. The narrative in Genesis 32 is then understood as a description of the patriarch's transformation from the deceitful Jacob into the upright Israel.[178] Philo related the name to 'seeing God', thus connecting it to either [179]ראה or שׁוּר meaning 'to see'.[180]

The LXX rendering of the event is slightly different to that of the MT:

> [Gen 32:24(25)] And Jacob was left alone; and a man wrestled with him [ἐπάλαιεν ἄνθρωπος μετ᾽ αὐτοῦ] till the morning. [28(29)] And he said to him, your name shall no longer be called Jacob, but Israel shall be your name, for you *have prevailed/ been strong/strengthened yourself with God*, [ἐνίσχυσας μετὰ θεοῦ] and with men [you are] *mighty/powerful* [καὶ μετὰ ἀνθρώπων δυνατός[181]]. [30(31)] And Jacob called the name of that place *the face/visible form/shape of God* [Εἶδος θεοῦ]; for [he said] I have seen God face to face [εἶδον γὰρ θεὸν πρόσωπον πρὸς πρόσωπον] and my life was preserved.

Interestingly enough, there are some late text witnesses of the LXX which have ἄγγελος/'angel' instead of ἄνθρωπος/'man' in v. 24 (25). This reading is probably an interpretation influenced by the reference to an angel in Hosea 12 but it is not attested in the oldest and most reliable manuscripts.[182] Hayward, with reference to M. Harl, points out

---

176 Several scholars thus derive the verbal form וישׁר in Hos 12:5 from the root mentioned above and propose that the correct translation is "he had dominion", although it is unclear who had dominion over whom, Jacob or the angel. See Hamori 2004, 79-80, and Sarna 1989, 405.

177 In the Targums, Jacob/Israel is entitled 'a prince of God', see below.

178 See Sarna 1989, 405, who points out that Israel/Jacob is used synonymously with Jeshurun in Deut 32:15; 33:15, 26, and Isa 44:2. Vawter (1977, 351) concludes that the purpose of the narrative is to demonstrate that Jacob was a man not only marked by struggling with men, i.e., Laban and Esau, but had also contended with God and prevailed, resulting in a transformation of his personality. However, as Alter (1996, 182) points out, it is noteworthy that the patriarch's new name (Israel) does not replace the old one (Jacob) completely (as is the case with Abram/Abraham) but instead becomes a synonym for it, see, e.g., Gen 49:2.

179 Thus, אישׁ ראה אל = Israel, 'a man seeing God'.

180 See Sarna 1989, 404-405, and Hayward 2005, 27-28. See also the discussion of Philo's interpretation of the pericope below.

181 Some MSS add here ἔση 'you shall be', see Wevers (ed.) 1974, text critical note to the LXX Gen 32:28.

182 See Wevers 1974, 314. See also Hayward 2005, 58.

that the most common meaning of the Greek preposition μετά is 'in company with/together with' rather than against, which indicates the possibility that the LXX translators wished to imply that the man wrestled with/alongside Jacob against some unmentioned foe,[183] an interpretation I find farfetched.

It is obvious, however, that the meaning of v. 28 (29) is ambiguous, in the words of Hayward, "... Has Jacob been strong with God in the sense of prevailing over him; or has he strengthened himself with the help of God, and, as a result, gained power over men?"[184]

The verb ἐνισχύειν used in this verse also occurs in, for example, Deut 32:43, where we find it in an exhortation to the angels of God to "be strong with/in God". According to Hayward, the use of the same verb in Gen 32:28 may imply that the name/title Israel has a kind of angelic status/dimension.[185]

The designation of the place as 'face/form of God'/Εἶδος θεοῦ in v. 30 (31) is obviously a literal translation of the Hebrew name Peniel, compare with the rendering of Bethel as 'house of God', see above. This translation forges an etymological link to the following verb εἶδον 'I have seen.'[186] The LXX version of our pericope echoes God's words to Moses in Exod 33:18-20, thus implying that the name Israel has to do with the exceptional ability to see God's face.[187]

The stories in Genesis 18 and 32 have similarities with the account in Judges 13, in which an angel is mentioned. As in Genesis 18 and 32, the divine messenger in Judges 13 appears in human form. In Judg 13:17, Manoah asks for the visitor's name but receives the answer "Why do you ask my name? It is too wonderful", a parallel to the man's response to Jacob's question in Gen 32:29.[188] This parallel is even more evident in a gloss in some LXX versions of the latter verse, where the man adds "and it [the name] is to be wondered at", a rendering which is most probably an attempt to identify Jacob's unknown contender in the light of Judges 13.[189] The words of Manoah to his wife in v. 22 echo

---

183 Hayward 2005, 59.
184 Hayward 2005, 62. See also Hamori 2004, 76-77.
185 See Hayward 2005, 64-66. Hayward (2005, 28) also notes that the form of the new name is reminiscent of the likewise theophoric names of the great angels; Michael, Gabriel, Raphael, and Uriel, a resemblance that also may indicate Israel's angelic status.
186 Hayward 2005, 67.
187 Hayward 2005, 67-70. He also refers to the LXX rendering of Exod 24:10, 17 with the word εἶδος, signifying the vision of God's glory. See also Hamori 2004, 130-132.
188 See Westermann 1985, 518.
189 See Hayward 2005, 66-67, and Wevers 1993, 544.

the reactions of Jacob/Israel and Hagar in Gen 32:30 and 16:13 respectively: "… We shall surely die, for we have seen God [אלהים]."[190]

Many scholars thus maintain that the account in Judges 13 is a key to understanding the complex texts in Genesis 16; 18 and 32, and vice versa. The connections between the pericopes indicate that the stories about the mysterious men in Genesis 18 and 32 should be interpreted in the light of 'the angel of the Lord traditions'.[191]

However, as mentioned previously, the only two narratives in the Bible that Hamori classifies as so-called ''îš theophanies' are Abraham's and Jacob's encounters with God in Genesis 18 and 32.[192] In her view, these two stories distinguish themselves from, for example, Judges 13, by what she defines as 'realistic anthropomorphism'; the man who confronts Jacob at the ford of Jabbok physically wrestles with him. The mysterious stranger is not supernaturally strong and it is stated "that he saw that he could not prevail against Jacob …" In the case of Genesis 18, the three men gladly eat the food that Abraham offers them.[193]

Although the 'angel of the Lord' in Judges 13 is designated איש 'a man',[194] described in both Judges 6[195] and 13 as having a physical human form and initially believed to be a fellow human by Gideon as well as by Manoah and his wife, he does not engage in such human behavior as eating or wrestling. In contrast to the men in Gen 18:5-8, the angel of the Lord does not eat the food offered by Gideon and Manoah, see Judg 6:19-21 and 13:15-20.[196]

Hamori also points out other differences between the pericopes, for example, the use of the term מלאך 'angel/messenger' in Judges 6 and

---

190 Gen 32:31 in the MT. See also Judg 6:22-23:

> [22] Then Gideon perceived that it was the angel of the LORD; and Gideon said, "Help me, Lord God! For I have seen the angel of the Lord face to face" [פנים אל פנים]. [23] But the LORD said to him, "Peace be to you; do not fear, you shall not die."

191 Gieschen 1998, 57-69. See also Syrén 2000, 247-251.

192 Hamori 2004, 1-8, 133-190.

193 See Gen 32:25; 18:5-8, and Hamori 2004, 1-8, 141-155.

194 See Judg 13:6, 8-11. Note, however, that the designation 'man'/'man of God' in the story clearly reflects Manoah's and his wife's misconception of the identity of the angel of the Lord. It is not the perspective of the narrator, see, e.g., Judg 13:3, 9, 13, 15-16. In the narrative, it is not until vv. 20-22 that Manoah and his wife realize his true identity.

195 In Judges 6 the angel of the Lord is never designated as 'a man'. However, in addition to Genesis 18 and 32, the divine emissary who meets Joshua (chapter 5) is also referred to as 'a man', see below.

196 Hamori 2004, 141-155. However, she admits that the narratives in Genesis 19; Judges 13, and Josh 5:13-15 are closely related to the ''îš theophany texts'.

13,[197] which in her view leaves us in no doubt concerning the "man's" identity; he is an angel, not God in person. Hamori consequently interprets Manoah's exclamation in v. 22 as a reference to the vision of a divine being, since in the previous verse Manoah had just realized that the heavenly visitor was the angel of the Lord.[198] Finally, she also remarks that, in both Judges 6 and 13, the angel of the Lord vanishes from sight in a highly superhuman manner, see Judg 6:21 and 13:20: "When the flame went up toward heaven from the altar, the angel of the LORD ascended in the flame of the altar while Manoah and his wife looked on …"[199]

I only partly agree with Hamori's reasoning. While it is true that the anthropomorphic character of the theophanies in Genesis 18 and 32 could be labeled as more concrete and realistic than the encounters with the angel of the Lord in Judges 6 and 13, who neither eats nor physically wrestles with anyone, there is an obvious ambivalence between God and His angel/messenger in the two latter pericopes. There are no clear distinctions between the "angel" and God.[200]

In my view, her argument in support of the understanding of אלהים as 'divine being' in Judg 13:22 but not in Gen 32:30 is inadequate. It is indeed remarkable that both Gideon and Manoah react in a similar way to Jacob and are amazed that they are still alive after seeing the angel of the Lord/God. Gideon even uses the same phrase as Jacob, פנים אל פנים, an expression that appears to be reserved for divine-human encounters.[201]

Jacob's Return to Bethel and the Blessing of His Grandsons

Jacob's pilgrimage to Bethel

As mentioned above, according to Gen 31:13, the angel of God orders Jacob to return to the land of his birth, which is the contextual background of chapter 35; Jacob and his family have reached Canaan after a

---

197 See, e.g., Judg 6:11-12, 20-21, and 13:9, 13, 21. It is also noteworthy that in Judges 6, the angel of the Lord/God is never designated 'man'/ איש.

198 Hamori 2004, 145-146.

199 The departures of the angel of the Lord in these stories thus differ from God's less spectacular departures in Genesis 32 and 18. See Hamori 2004, 143-150.

200 See, e.g., Judg 6:12, 14, 16, 20, and 13:20-23. Hamori's reasoning (2004, 153-155) appears slightly contradictory, as she seems to admit that there is indeed an ambiguous relationship between YHWH and His angel in the Bible and writes on p. 155: "This may be a particular manner of reference to a theophany, or may be the result of the angelic role in some texts having been blurred with Yahweh himself."

201 See above and Seow 1995, 609.

long journey (Gen 33:18). By now, Jacob has been confronted by the mysterious "man" who wrestled with him at the ford of Jabbok, Gen 32:22-32. He and his brother Esau have also been reconciled, chapter 33.

Now, when Jacob has come home to his land, God again reminds him to fulfill the vow that he made in Bethel, see Gen 28:20-22; 31:13. We read in Gen 35:1-3:

> [Gen 35:1] God [אלהים] said to Jacob, "Arise, go up *to Bethel* [בית אל] and settle there. *Make an altar there to the God* [לאל],[202] *who appeared to you when you fled from your brother Esau."* [2] So Jacob said to his household and to all who were with him, "Put away the foreign gods that are among you, and purify yourselves, and change your clothes; [3] Then come, let us go up to *Bethel, that I may make an altar there to the God* [לאל],[203] *who answered me in the day of my distress and has been with me wherever I have gone."*

The words in Gen 35:1b; "… the God, who appeared to you when you fled from your brother Esau," clearly allude to the divine revelation in Genesis 28. In this vision, God promised Jacob a safe return; "Know that I am with you and will keep you wherever you go, and will bring you back to this land …" (Gen 28:15). God exhorts Jacob to make an altar to God/El in Bethel, the place of the revelation, a symbolic act to prove Jacob's fulfillment of his vow. The wording of this verse is somewhat puzzling; why does God/Elohim refer to God/El in the *third* person, as to someone distinct from Himself?

Jacob apparently acknowledges that God has kept his promise, v. 3, and that the time has now come for the fulfillment of his own vow, namely that YHWH should be his God, cf., Gen 28:20-21. It seems as if Jacob considers the divine encounter in Genesis 28 as an answer to his prayers. Here, the use of the designation 'El' for God is not coinciden-tal, as it is a component of the name Bethel.[204]

In order to fulfill his vow, Jacob orders his household to purify themselves[205] and get rid of all their foreign gods as a sign of loyalty to YHWH. The journey to Bethel has the character of a pilgrimage to a holy site.[206] Jacob goes there to commemorate his first encounter with God.

In Gen 35:5 we read that God once more protected Jacob on his journey. The protection was greatly needed, because of the conflict with

---

202 In the MT, the definite form is used; literally: "to *the God* who appeared to you in Bethel," this God was already known to Jacob, hence the use of the definite article.
203 Also here the Hebrew uses the definite article.
204 Sarna 1989, 239.
205 Cf., Exod 19:10-11 and Josh 3:5. See also Sarna 1989, 240.
206 Westermann 1985, 550, Sarna 1989, 239

Shechem and his father on account of Dinah, Jacob's only daughter (Genesis 34). Jacob and his company eventually arrive in Bethel:

> [Gen 35:6] Jacob came to Luz (that is, Bethel), which is in the land of Canaan, he and all the people who were with him, [7] and there he built an altar and called the place [המקום] [207]*El-bethel*, [אל בת אל] because it was there that God had revealed himself to him [כי שם נגלו אליו האלהים] when he fled from his brother.

According to Gen 28:18, Jacob erected a מצבה but there is no reference to an altar in the text. Now, after he has returned safely home, Jacob builds an altar in thanksgiving and honor of the God who appeared to him and since then has protected him. The altar is built in memory and celebration of his first encounter with God.

As shown in the quotation, the Hebrew text of v. 7 is rather strange; why is the verb גלה 'to appear/reveal' rendered in the *plural* form? האלהים/'the God/the gods/divine beings'[208] is of course grammatically plural but in meaning usually singular, at least when the reference is to the God of Israel. Accordingly, the verb referring to God is usually in the singular form, with few exceptions, e.g., Gen 20:13. Most probably the verb in Gen 35:7 in the same way as in Gen 20:13, is singular in meaning.[209] Gen 35:7 was considered a dangerous passage by the early rabbis, since the grammatical plural of the verb referring to God invited heresies which questioned the unity of God and introduced the idea that God was assisted by a "second Deity" when creating the world.[210]

Sarna interprets v. 7 as a reference to *the angels*, who, according to Gen 28:12, went up and down on the ladder. According to Sarna, the word אלהים thus means *'divine beings'* in this context, an interpretation that I find doubtful.[211] Samaritanus, the LXX, Peshitta, and the Vulgate all render the verb in v. 7 in the singular form. In the LXX, Gen 35:7b is rendered as follows:

> … καὶ ἐκάλεσεν τὸ ὄνομα τοῦ τόπου, Βαιθήλ· ἐκεῖ γὰρ ἐπεφάνη αὐτῷ ὁ θεὸς …/… and he [Jacob] called the name of that place Bethel, because there (the) God had appeared to him …[212]

---

207 Here the Hebrew word most certainly also means 'holy site', see above and Sarna 1989, 240.

208 Again, the definite form is used, literally: "… because there *the God* appeared to him …"

209 See also Westermann 1985, 552. Cf., also Gen 1:26.

210 See *b. Sanhedrin* 38b and Segal 1977, 121-134, 33-73. Other scriptural verses used by the heretics in support of their theology were e.g., Gen 1:1-2, 26-27; 11:5-7; 19:24; Deut 4:7; 2 Sam 7:23-24, and Dan 7:9-14.

211 Sarna 1989, 241.

212 Note that LXX here uses the name Bethel, contrary to its rendering of Genesis 28 and 31.

Hayward points out that the verb used in this verse, ἐπιφαίνω, is very unusual in the LXX Pentateuch and is only employed in two additional texts, both of which describe an epiphany of God. In the first pericope, Num 6:25, the divine epiphany is connected to the priestly blessing of Israel and, in the second text, Deut 33:2, God is, according to the LXX, accompanied by angels, compare Genesis 28. Hayward thus concludes that, in the mind of the LXX translators, Jacob's dream in Bethel was an epiphany, and the appearance of God seems to be connected to blessing (cf., Gen 35:9-15) and the presence of angels.[213]

In Gen 35:9 it is said that God appears once more to Jacob and blesses him. In verse 10 God says to Jacob:

> [Gen 35:10] ... "Your name is Jacob; no longer shall you be called Jacob, but Israel shall be your name." So he was called Israel. [214]

This is an echo of Gen 32:28, as here God confirms Jacob's new name when he arrived in the Promised Land.[215] According to Sarna, it was not God in person who changed Jacob's name the first time (Gen 32:28) but an angel. The new name therefore needs to be confirmed and validated by God Himself.[216] Jacob is Israel, the ancestor of the people of Israel. Thus, the following verses (vv. 11-12) concern divine promises on a national level.[217]

God introduces Himself in Gen 35:11 as אל שדי/'El Shaddai'.[218] This divine epithet is translated in the NRSV as 'God Almighty'. The original meaning of the divine "name" may have been 'God of the Wilderness/Mountain' but its etymology and meaning are the subject of debate.[219] It is consistently used in the Bible as an epithet for YHWH, with the sole exception of Job 19:29.[220]

---

213 Hayward 2005, 81-90.

214 The name Israel may mean 'he who sees God,' or 'he who strives with God', although it is more likely that God is the subject of the verb, hence 'God strives' or 'God rules', see the discussion of the name above.

215 Jacob's struggle with the unknown man in Genesis 32 and his subsequent renaming takes place on the other side of the Jordan. See also Sarna 1989, 242.

216 Sarna 1989, 241-242. Cf., the interpretation of Gen 35:10 in Rabbinic midrash, see chapter 4.5 below.

217 Being the ancestor, Jacob/Israel is a common collective designation for the people. See, for example, Deut 32:9; Jer 10:25; 30:7; Isa 10:21-23; 29:22-23; 40:27; 41:8-14; 43:1-5, 22; 44:1-5, 21-23; 48:12; 49:5-6, et al. See also Walters 1992, 607-608.

218 Cf., Exod 6:3, where God says to Moses: "I appeared to Abraham, Isaac, and Jacob, as *God Almighty*, [אל שדי] but by my name 'the LORD [YHWH]' I did not make myself known to them."

219 Knauf 1995, 1416. See also Sarna 1989, 384-385. Based on his observation of the occurrence of the divine epithet in the Bible, Sarna concludes that El Shaddai is a very ancient designation of God in the Israelite religion. In the LXX, 'El Shaddai' in Gen

The use of this divine epithet in Gen 35:11 connects our pericope to Gen 28:3-4, where Isaac prayed that "May *God Almighty* [El Shaddai] bless you [Jacob] …" God now answers Isaac's prayer concerning his son, Gen 35:11-12. These verses are reminiscent of God's promises in Gen 17:1-8, in which God also designated Himself 'El Shaddai' and changed Abram's name to Abraham, a parallel to the renaming of Jacob to Israel in Gen 35:10. [221]

The blessing of Ephraim and Manasseh

The context of Gen 48:15-16 shows Jacob on his deathbed, his long-lost son Joseph visits him and asks Jacob to bless his two sons, Ephraim and Manasseh. When Joseph enters, Jacob gathers his remaining strength and says:

> [Gen 48:3] … "God Almighty [אל שדי] appeared to me at Luz [that is, Bethel] in the land of Canaan, and he blessed me, [4] and said to me, 'I am going to make you fruitful and increase your numbers; I will make of you a company of peoples, and will give this land to your offspring after you for a perpetual holding.'

Jacob refers to God as 'El Shaddai', compare Gen 35:11. Jacob is dying and, when looking back at his life, recalls his meeting(s) with God at Bethel and refers to the divine promises given to him as stated in Gen 35:11-12 (see also Gen 28:13-14). [222] Because Jacob is blessed by God, he has the ability to bestow the divine blessing on his grandsons. We thus read in Gen 48:15-16 that Jacob prays for Ephraim and Manasseh:

> [Gen 48:15] … "*The God* [האלהים] before whom my ancestors Abraham and Isaac walked, the God who has been my shepherd all my life to this day, [16] *the angel* [המלאך][223] who has redeemed me [הגאל אתי] from all harm, bless the boys …"[224]

35:11 is rendered simply as ὁ θεός σου/"your God." See also the LXX Gen 28:3, where Isaac refers to God as: "… my God …," and 48:3, where Jacob refers to God as "…my God…"

220 See Knauf 1995, 1416-1423, esp. p. 1417.

221 Jacob's response to the revelation is to set up a pillar מצבה, once again at the place where God spoke to him. It is unclear whether this is a rededication of the original pillar, or a new one. This time he not only pours oil on it but also a drink offering. Finally, we have a repetition of Jacob naming the place as Bethel, vv. 14-15.

222 Sarna 1989, 325.

223 Cf., Gen 31:11-13.

224 The LXX reads [Gen 48:15] … Ὁ θεός, ᾧ εὐηρέστησαν οἱ πατέρες μου ἐναντίον αὐτοῦ Ἀβραὰμ καὶ Ἰσαάκ, ὁ θεὸς ὁ τρέφων με ἐκ νεότητος ἕως τῆς ἡμέρας ταύτης, [16] ὁ ἄγγελος ὁ ῥυόμενός με ἐκ πάντων τῶν κακῶν εὐλογήσαι τὰ παιδία ταῦτα …

"The angel" is here equated with God. Moreover, "the angel" is designated as the one who has redeemed [הגאל] Jacob from all evil. The verb
גאל is often applied to YHWH in the Bible, e.g., Exod 6:6; 15:13; Ps 74:2;
Ps 103:1-4; 107:1-3, and Isa 44:22-24. The substantive גאל /'redeemer' is
an epithet metaphorically used for YHWH in the Bible. In Deutero-
Isaiah it is a common title for YHWH, used in parallel with such standard epithets as 'the Holy One of Israel' and 'YHWH Zebaot'. See for
example Isa 41:14; 43:1; 47:4, and 54:5.[225]

The parallelistic structure of verses 15-16 also strongly indicates
that 'the angel' is here an epithet for God.[226] "The angel" in v. 16 is none
other than God who has kept His promise and blessed and protected
Jacob all the days of his life, cf., Gen 28:13-15; 31:11-13. According to
Sarna, this is the most probable interpretation, and I tend to agree with
him.[227] He writes:

> ... No one in the Bible ever invokes an angel in prayer, nor in Jacob's sev-
> eral encounters with angels is there any mention of one who delivers him
> from harm. When the patriarch feels himself to be in mortal danger, he
> prays directly to God, as in [Gen] 32:10-13 and it is He who again and again
> is Jacob's guardian and protector (28:15,20; 31:3; 35:3). Admittedly, "Angel"
> as an epithet for God is extraordinary, but since angels are often simply ex-
> tensions of the divine personality, the distinction between God and angel
> in the biblical texts is frequently blurred (cf. Gen. 31:3,11,13; Exod. 3:2,4).
> Nevertheless, this verse may reflect some tradition associated with Bethel,
> not preserved in Genesis, concerning an angelic guardian of Jacob (cf.
> 31:13; 35:3). An echo of this may be found in Hosea 12:5.[228]

Sarna thus points out that the epithet 'angel' for God in v. 16 is something extraordinary and Samaritanus has here used the rendering
המלך/'the King'.

---

225 See also Ps 78:35; Prov 23:11; Jer 50:34. In Job 19:25 the term, however, may refer to
    another heavenly figure, a mediator between God and Job. This mediator is desig-
    nated by Elihu as a מלאך/messenger/angel, Job 33:23-24. For more information, see
    Mullen 1995, 706-708. He writes on p. 706: "On an individual level, Yahweh ransoms
    the pious and the needy, most specifically the widow and the orphan (Gen 48:16...)."
226 Cf., Hosea 12. See also Köckert 2007, 62-63.
227 In his translation of Gen 48:16 Sarna (1989, 328) has written "the Angel," with a
    capital A. He states that this is because he interprets the designation as an epithet for
    God Himself (cf., the NKJV Gen 48:16).
228 Sarna 1989, 328.

Concluding Remarks

An important difference between Genesis 28; 31 and 35 is that 'the angel of God' (in the singular form) is only mentioned in Genesis 31. In Gen 31:11 it is 'the angel of God' who addresses Jacob, whereas in the other pericopes it is 'God.' In Gen 31:13 'the angel' identifies himself as God: "*I am the God of Bethel*, where you anointed a pillar and made a vow to *me*", and in Gen 35:1b Jacob is commanded to return to Bethel and there make an altar to "… the God, who appeared to you when you fled from your brother Esau …", a clear reference to the dream in Genesis 28. For these reasons, it seems apparent that 'the angel of God' in Gen 31:11 is identical to God Himself. It appears to be the same person who talks to Jacob in all three narratives.[229]

As we have seen, the narratives in Genesis 28 and 31 have in common that God/the angel of God is said to have appeared to Jacob in a *dream*. The theophany of Genesis 35 thus differs from the others in that God speaks to Jacob when the latter is awake.

In Genesis 35 God's exhortation to Jacob to return to Bethel and fulfill his vow is in many ways a difficult text. It is indeed peculiar that God/Elohim refers to God/El in the third person, as to someone distinct from Himself. Likewise, the use of the plural form of the verb גלה 'to appear/reveal' in v. 7 is quite strange. In this way, the narrative of Jacob's return to Bethel contains an ambiguity similar to that of the explicit 'angel of the Lord-texts'.

Genesis 35 is the final chapter in 'the Jacob cycle', and although Jacob lives on and is mentioned in several later chapters, he is no longer the main character. Genesis 36 focuses on his brother Esau, while 'the Joseph cycle' begins in chapter 37. We have seen that Gen 35:1-15 refers back to Jacob's dream in Bethel. Thus, 'the Jacob story' in the Bible both begins and ends at the same place, in the LXX designated as 'the

---

229 Cf., also Hos 12:3-5 (vv. 4-6 in the MT):

[3] In the womb he [Jacob] tried to supplant his brother, and in his manhood he *strove with God.* [4] He *strove with the angel* and prevailed, he wept and sought his favor; he met him at *Bethel,* and there He spoke with him. [5] The *LORD the God of host, the LORD is his name!*

Because of the parallelistic structure of these verses, it seems evident that the "angel" (God, cf., v. 3.) mentioned by the prophet Hosea who struggled with Jacob at the ford of Jabbok is the same person who Jacob is said to have encountered in Bethel (Genesis 28 and 35).

place/house of God'.[230] Jacob and Bethel are very closely connected; his 'calling-experience' there (Gen 28:10-22) marked him for life.

The only one of the discussed Jacob narratives in which Bethel is not mentioned is the patriarch's nightly struggle with the unknown man, although the prophet Hosea appears to have located this event in that place. Possibly the prophet fused the different traditions of Jacob being named Israel, one of them connected to Bethel (Gen 35:9-10), see below for further details.

There have been various attempts to identify Jacob's opponent; he is either seen as a 'divine being', i.e., an angel or a demon, or assumed to be God in person. Hamori adopts the latter view and argues that the divine encounters of Genesis 18 and 32 are the only two so-called ''îš theophanies' in the Bible because of their concrete anthropomorphic character. Considering Jacob's reaction when he realizes who he has met; "for I have seen God face to face and my life is preserved" (Gen 32:30, cf., Gen 16:13 and Judg 6:22; 13:22), an understanding of the opponent as God Himself seems plausible.

Along with the identity of Jacob's contender, the meaning of the patriarch's new name has been much discussed. Proposed interpretations are, for example, 'God strives', 'he strives with God' or 'God will rule/prevail'.

Finally, in Genesis 48 the patriarch looks back on his life and tells Joseph about the God who appeared to him at Luz (i.e., Bethel). When he blesses his grandsons he equates this God with "the angel who has redeemed me from all harm..." Thus, Jacob seems to identify the "angel" as God.

3.2.6 Conclusions

To conclude, it may be stated that regarding the explicit references to the angel of the Lord in Genesis, we find a merged identity between God and the "angel" in the following texts: Gen 16:7-14 (the parallel text to Gen 21:17-20); 22:1-19; 31:10-13, and 48:15-16. The only reference to an angel in the singular in Genesis where the distinction between God and His angel seems clear is to be found in chapter 24, vv. 7 and 40. A few texts in Genesis mention מלאכים/angels in the plural, namely

---

230 Properly speaking, the Jacob story begins in Gen 25:19, but since Jacob has his first encounter with God in Genesis 28, this is the starting point of his life as God's servant. This divine revelation has been designated by scholars as the central event in the Jacob story, e.g., Westermann, 1985, 405-409. See also Walters 1992, 599-608.

Gen 19:1, 15; 28:12, and 32:1. These angels seem to be distinguished from God. It is remarkable that the angel of God/Elohim who appears to Jacob in Gen 31:10-13 identifies himself as the God of Bethel who addressed Jacob in Gen 28:13.

The narratives of Genesis 18-19 and 35 contain ambiguities similar to the explicit 'angel of the Lord-texts'. As for Genesis 32, it is clearly not an "ordinary", earthly man who struggles with Jacob, but some kind of supernatural opponent. Like 'the angel of the Lord', he acts with divine authority, blessing the patriarch and giving him a new name, cf., Gen 16:10-12; 17:5-8, and 35:9-10. There is an apparent resemblance between Hagar's and Jacob's reactions to the divine encounters, see Gen 16:13-14 and 32:29-30.

3.3 The Rest of the Pentateuch and the Books of the Former Prophets

3.3.1 Exodus

After Genesis, we first encounter the angel of the Lord/YHWH in Exodus 3, appearing to Moses in the burning bush, vv. 1b-6:

> [Exod 3:1b] ... he [Moses] led his flock beyond the wilderness, and came to Horeb, the mountain of God. [2] There *the angel of the LORD* appeared to him in a flame of fire out of a bush; he looked, and the bush was blazing, yet it was not consumed. [3] Then Moses said, " I must turn aside and look at this great sight ... [4] When *the LORD* [*YHWH*] saw that he had turned aside to see, *God* [*Elohim*] called to him out of the bush, "Moses, Moses!" And he said, "Here I am." [5] Then he said, "Come no closer! Remove the sandals from your feet, for the place on which you are standing is holy ground." [6] He said further, "I am the God of your father, the God of Abraham, the God of Isaac, and the God of Jacob." And Moses hid his face, for he was afraid to look at God.[231]

The angel is only mentioned in v. 2. From v. 4 onwards it is God Himself who talks to Moses, reveals His personal divine name, and calls him to deliver the people of Israel from slavery in Egypt. This is the

---

231 In the NT, this incident is referred to in Acts 7:30-35, where Stephen uses an indefinite form; "*an angel* appeared to him in the wilderness of Mount Sinai, in the flame of a burning bush..."

sole case where the angel of the Lord only appears at the very beginning of a narrative.[232]

The revelation of the divine name connects the above mentioned narrative to Exod 23:20-24:

> [20] *I am going to send an angel* in front of you, to guard you on the way and to bring you to the place that I have prepared. [21] Be attentive to him and listen to his voice; do not rebel against him, for *he* will not pardon your transgression; *for my name is in him.* [22] But if you listen attentively to *his voice* and do all that *I say*, then *I* will be an enemy to your enemies and a foe to your foes. [23] When *my angel* goes in front of you, and brings you to the Amorites, the Hittites, the Perizzites, the Canaanites, the Hivities, and the Jebusites, and *I* blot them out, [24] you shall not bow down to their gods…[233]

In this text, the angel is apparently distinct from God and yet not completely separate from Him. By possessing the divine name, he also shares the divine power and authority.[234] Compare this to the Deuteronomistic theology, in which the concept of 'the name of God' is used to

---

232 The terminological confusion in the pericope has been explained by Freedman-Willoughby (1997, 320) in three ways: "(1) Yahweh might have transmitted his message to Moses by his *mal'ak*, but the author used the terms Yahweh and Elohim since in his opinion the message came directly from God. The occurrence of *mal'ak* at the beginning of the narrative qualifies the subsequent use of Yahweh and Elohim. (2) The importance of the call of Moses, the initiation of God's personal name did not allow the narrative to be dominated by a *mal'ak*. The significance of the narrative itself required the direct intervention of God. (3) Yahweh himself spoke to Moses, but since Moses was not allowed to see him, the intercession of the *mal'ak* was necessary." According to Fabry (1997, 320), Exodus 3 is not considered a literary unit in recent academic exegesis. See also Guggisberg 1979, 40-41.

233 Cf., also the *Targum to Chronicles*, 1 Chr 17:21:

And who is like your people Israel, a people *unique and select* in the earth, *for* whom *an angel sent from before the Lord appeared* to deliver a people to be his own, to make a name *for himself and to do for them* great and *mighty* deeds by driving out *the* nations from before the people whom you had delivered from Egypt? [Eng. trans. McIvor 1994, 107. The words in italics are the Targumic derivatons from the MT].

234 See also Gieschen 1998, 57. In the NT, this parallels the hymn in praise of Jesus in Phil 2:9-11:

[9] Therefore God also highly exalted him and gave him the name that is above every name, [10] so that at the name of Jesus every knee should bend, in heaven, and on earth and under the earth, [11] and every tongue should confess that Jesus Christ is Lord, to the glory of God the Father.

describe the way in which YHWH is present in the Temple of Jerusalem.[235]

With reference to Hos 12:13,[236] some scholars have proposed that the מלאך in Exodus 23 should be identified as a human guide and leader, presumably Moses or Joshua. There are two major objections to this interpretation: firstly, the מלאך is not said to be speaking in God's name as a prophet, but it is stated in v. 21 that "… my [i.e., God's] name is *in* him…" Secondly, it seems to be implied in the same verse that the מלאך has the power to forgive Israel's sins, a capacity that elsewhere in the Bible is reserved for God.[237]

In Exod 14:19, the angel of God is connected to the pillar of cloud leading and protecting the Israelites during their exodus from Egypt:

> [Exod 14:19] *The angel of God* [Elohim], who was going before the Israelite army moved and went behind them; and *the pillar of cloud* moved from in front of them and took its place behind them.

In Exod 13:21-22 and 14:24, however, it is stated that it was *God* (YHWH) *who manifested Himself* in this pillar. In Exodus 33[238], the angel seems to be a being distinct from God. The Lord says to Moses in vv. 2-3:

> [Exod 33:2] *I will send an angel* before you,[239] and *I will drive out* the Canaanites, the Amorites, the Hittites, the Perizzites, the Hivites, and the Jebusites. [3] Go up to a land flowing with milk and honey; *but I will not go up among you, or I would consume you on the way* …

Later on in this chapter, it is stated that the Lord/YHWH spoke to Moses face to face, as a man speaks to his friend (v. 11) and that the presence of God was manifested in the pillar of cloud:

> [Exod 33:9] When Moses entered the tent, *the pillar of cloud* would descend and stand at the entrance of the tent, and *the LORD* [YHWH] would speak with Moses.

---

235 Newsom 1992, 250. See also Hannah 1999, 21, Fischer 2007, 84-91, and, e.g., Deut 12:5, 11; 14:23; 1 Kgs 8:16, 29; 9:3, and Jer 7:12.

236 See also Judg 2:1-5, discussed below.

237 See also Ausloos 2008, 8-10. According to Segal (1977, 68-70), this passage was considered problematic by the Rabbis in their attempts to combat the 'two-powers-heresy' because of the "angel's" remarkable ability. Cf., the debates in the NT between the Jewish leaders and Jesus, where one of the things that seemed to upset the Jewish authorities the most was that Jesus claimed to have the power to forgive sins, see, e.g., Mark 2:1-12. See also Gieschen 1998, 32-33, 71-78, and Guggisberg 1979, 60-61.

238 See also Guggisberg 1979, 62-64.

239 Here the NKJV follows the LXX; "And I will send my Angel before you…" The MT, however, lacks the first person singular suffix attached to the word מלאך 'angel' and refers thus simply to "…an angel…", cf., NRSV cited above. In this context the image of the מלאך seems to be used to denote the absence of God. See also Exod 32:34.

The conversation takes place after the incident with the golden calf, chapter 32. Moses pleads that he and the people may find grace before God and that YHWH Himself will go with them, vv. 12-13. God answers him and says

[Exod 33:14] He said, *"My presence* [פָּנַי] will go with you, and I will give you rest."

At the end of the conversation, when Moses asks to see the Glory of God, he receives the answer:

[Exod 33:19] ... "I will make all my goodness pass before you, and will proclaim before you the name, 'the LORD'; ...." [20] "But", he said, "you cannot see my face; for no one shall see me and live." [23] then I will take away my hand, and you shall see my back; but my face shall not be seen."[240]

This gives the impression that when it is said in vv. 9-11 that God talked to Moses 'face to face', it should not be understood literally; God had somehow "hidden" Himself in the pillar of cloud. This is essentially the so-called 'identity theory', which claims that the angel of the Lord and the pillar of cloud, etc, are revelations of God in different disguises in order to spare the life of those who see Him (see below).[241]

The astounding theophany described in Exod 24:9-11 is a remarkable exception from the above-mentioned pattern. No mediator is mentioned there:

[Exod 24:9] Then Moses and Aaron, Nadab, and Abihu, and seventy of the elders of Israel went up, [10] and *they saw the God of Israel.* Under his feet there was something like a pavement of sapphire stone, like the very hea-

---

240 According to Jewish tradition, the following theophany in Exod 34:5-7 is one of the most central episodes in the Bible as God reveals His very character to Moses:

[5] Now the LORD [YHWH] *descended in the cloud* and stood with him there, and proclaimed the name "The LORD" [YHWH]. [6] The LORD [YHWH] passed before him and proclaimed, "The LORD [YHWH], the LORD [YHWH] a God [El], merciful and gracious, slow to anger, and abounding in steadfast love and faithfulness, [7] keeping steadfast love for the thousandth generation, forgiving iniquity and transgression and sin, yet by no means clearing the guilty, but visiting the iniquity of the parents upon the children and the children's children to the third and the fourth generation."

God is thus depicted here both as the severe and righteous Judge and the forgiving and merciful Father. In Jewish tradition, the two main designations of God, Elohim (El) and YHWH are connected to the two chief attributes of the God of Israel. YHWH refers to the mercy of God, while Elohim stands for His justice. See G. Larsson 1993, 299-301, and Spiegel 1993, 121-122.

241 See Gieschen 1998, 55.

ven for clearness. [11] God did not lay his hand on the chief men of the people of Israel; *also they beheld God, and they ate and drank.*[242]

Along with some other scriptural passages, Exod 24:10 was considered a problematic and "dangerous" passage by the early Rabbis, since it contradicts the Rabbinic "dogma" that no man can see God and live. However, if it was an angel that Moses and the elders of Israel saw, it undermines the unity of God and may invite the heretic interpretation of two divine powers in heaven.[243]

There exists a widespread Jewish belief that the Torah was given to Israel through the mediation of angels. This tradition is also present in the NT, see Heb 2:2 and Gal 3:19 (angels in the plural). In Acts 7 Stephen first refers to *a specific angel* in the singular, definite form but later on he mentions *unspecified angels* in this context: [244]

> [38] "He [Moses] is the one who was in the congregation in the wilderness with *the angel* who spoke to him at *Mount Sinai,* and with our ancestors; and he received living oracles to give to us [...] [53] You are the ones that received *the law as ordained by angels,* and yet you have not kept it."[245]

In the LXX the one who intends to kill Moses over the issue of circumcision in Exod 4:24 is identified as an angel of the Lord, although in the MT it is YHWH Himself. The angel may have been substituted for YHWH by the LXX translators for theological reasons.[246] However, the angel of the Lord is generally described as a benefactor of Israel, who protects and guides the people (e.g., Exod 14:19; 23:20). When humans are compared with the angel of the Lord, it indicates a great appreciation of their personalities: good, discerning and wise (1 Sam 29:9; 2 Sam 14:17, 20). The angel is *the Redeemer* [הגאל], cf., Gen 48:16. The only con-

---

242 Cf., Ezek 1:26-28. However, the statement a few verses below, in Exod 24:17; "Now the appearance of the glory of the Lord was like a devouring fire on the top of the mountain in the sight of the people of Israel" (cf., the burning bush in Exod 3), can be taken as a qualification of the earlier assertion, i.e., it was "only" the Glory of the Lord that the elders of Israel beheld. This is one possible interpretation, but the passage could just as well be understood to imply a difference between the "common" people of Israel and the leaders; the elders saw God in person, but the people saw His Glory. See also Thompson, 2007, 221-222.

243 See also *b. Sanhedrin* 38b, where the 'divine name-angel' in Exod 23:21 is discussed. For further elaboration of this issue, see chapter 2 above and Segal 1977, 33-73.

244 See also Ps 68:18 (verse 17 in NRSV).

245 This tradition is also attested in the translations of Deut 33:2-3 in the LXX, Vulgate, Peshitta, and the Targums to the Pentateuch. See also the *Targum to Chronicles,* 1 Chr 29:11, Shinan 1983, 183-184, and Kittel 1964, 83. However, in the account of the divine revelation at Sinai in Exodus 19, neither the LXX nor MT refer to any angels, although *a cloud* on the mountain is mentioned.

246 See also chapter 2 above.

crete occasion when the angel is depicted as turning against Israel is in 2 Sam 24:15-16 (cf., 1 Chr 21:14-30).[247]

3.3.2 The Books of Joshua and Judges and Other Texts

There are other texts in which it is difficult to distinguish between this angel and God Himself, such as the story of Balaam (Num 22:22-35)[248] and several pericopes in the book of Judges (2:1-4; 5:23; 6:11-24, and 13). Both in Num 20:15-16 and Judg 2:1-4 we read that it was *the angel* who led Israel out of Egypt, although in Exod 15:1-19 and Deut 4:37 this deed is solely ascribed to YHWH.[249] In 2 Kings 1 the angel of the Lord appears and gives orders to Elijah (vv. 3, 15) on two occasions.[250] This is noteworthy, because otherwise God Himself speaks directly to this prophet.[251]

The Appearance of the Angel in Judges 2; 13 and 6

In Judges 2 there is an additional example of the tradition linking the מלאך with the deliverance from Egypt previously encountered in Exodus:

> [Judg 2:1] Now the angel of the LORD went up from Gilgal to Bochim, and said: "I brought you up from Egypt, and brought you into the land that I

---

247 See also Eynikel 2007, 112-113, von Rad 1964, 77, and Freedman-Willoughby 1997, 318.

248 Samaritanus mentions an angel/מלאך also in Num 22:20; 23:4, 5, and v. 16. The MT has Elohim in 22:20; 23:4 and YHWH in 23:5, 16.

249 However, as shown above, scholars differ about the interpretation of Deut 4:37. Cf., also Isa 63:9-10, see below. In Exod 12:22-28 it is not clear whether it was God Himself who killed the firstborn sons of the Egyptians, because in v. 23b it seems as if God used *the Destroyer* to do this. The same word 'the Destroyer'/המשחית is employed to denote the angel of the Lord who executed God's punishment for the sin of David in 2 Sam 24:16 and 1 Chr 21:15; 'the destroying angel:' [מלאך המשחית]. However, in 2 Kgs 19:35 and the parallel texts of Isa 37:36 and 2 Chr 32:20-22 concerning the killing of the Assyrians by the angel of the Lord, a word from a different root is used. See also what Paul writes in 1 Cor 10:10: "… and do not complain, as some of them [the Israelites] did, and were destroyed by *the destroyer* [ὁ ὀλεθρευτής]." The same word as in the LXX Exod 12:23b is here used by Paul. Curiously enough, the Modern Hebrew translation of the NT (the Bible Society in Israel, 1995) uses the concept המלאך המשחית in 1 Cor 10:10.

250 In 1 Kgs 19:5-8 there is also a reference to an angel who speaks to Elijah.

251 Meier 1995b, 104.

had promised to your ancestors. I said, 'I will never break my covenant
with you. [2] For your part, do not make a covenant with the inhabitants of
this land [...]' But you have not obeyed my command [...] [3] So now I say,
I will not drive them out before you; but they shall become adversaries to
you, and their gods shall be a snare to you." [4] When the angel of the
LORD spoke these words to all the Israelites, the people lifted up their
voices and wept. [5] So they named that place Bochim, and there they sacrificed to the LORD.

This passage is much discussed in scholarly circles, because the motif of
the מלאך יהוה 'the angel of the Lord' bringing the Israelites out of Egypt
and into the Promised Land contradicts Deuteronomistic theology,
which ascribes this deed to God in person, see Deut 4:37. Although
scholars differ on the exact meaning of the reference to God's presence
[פנים], there is no מלאך in this passage. In fact, Judg 2:1-5 constitutes an
exception by being the only text in the Deuteronomistic literature
where this motif is present.[252]

The מלאך in Judges 2 has been identified by some scholars as a human prophet, speaking on God's behalf.[253] This interpretation seems to
be implied in the LXX version of the passage, where the phrase 'so says
the Lord' is put into the mouth of the מלאך in v. 1.[254] Moreover, the מלאך
does not simply appear as does, for example, Hagar's angel or descend
from heaven but instead arrives from Gilgal. However, the connection
of the מלאך to the Exodus and the people's reaction in renaming the
place and sacrificing to the Lord speak in favor of the interpretation of
a divine messenger, compare Exod 23:20-23; 33:2; Gen 28:19-22; 32:30,
and Judg 6:24.[255]

In Judges 13, the birth of their son Samson is announced by a divine
emissary to Manoah and his wife:

[Judg 13:3] And *the angel* [מלאך] *of the Lord* [YHWH] appeared to the woman
and said to her, "Although you are barren, having borne no children, you
shall conceive and bear a son."[6] Then the woman came and told her
husband, "*A man* [איש] *of God* [Elohim] came to me, and his appearance was
like that of *an angel of God* [Elohim], most awe-inspiring; I did not ask him
where he came from, and he did not tell me his name..."

---

252 According to Judg 6:7-10, it was God himself who delivered the Israelites from
      slavery in Egypt and led them into the Promised Land. See also Guggisberg 1979, 64-
      65, and Ausloos 2008, 1-12.
253 See above and Newsom 1992, 249, Sullivan 2004, 57, and Ausloos 2008, 1-12.
254 In *Targum Jonathan*, the מלאך in Judges 2 is explicitly identified as a prophet, see
      Harrington and Saldarini (Eng. trans.) 1987, 61. See also Kasher 2007, 558-559, and
      Smelik 1995, 349-352.
255 See Ausloos 2008, 1-12, Fischer 2007, 89-91, and Sullivan 2004, 57.

[8] Then Manoah entreated the Lord [YHWH], and said, "O, LORD, I pray, let the man of God [Elohim] whom you sent come to us again..." [9] God [Elohim] listened to Manoah, and the angel of God [Elohim] came again to the woman as she sat in the field; but her husband Manoah was not with her. [10] So the woman ran quickly and told her husband, "The man who came to me the other day has appeared to me." [11] Manoah got up and followed his wife, and came to the man, and said to him, "Are you the man who spoke to this woman?" And he said, "I am." [12] Then Manoah said, "Now when your words come true, what is to be the boy's rule of life; what is he to do?" [13] The angel of the LORD [YHWH] said to Manoah, "Let the woman give heed to all that I said to her."

[15] Manoah said to the angel of the LORD [YHWH] "Allow us to detain you, and prepare a kid for you." [16] The *angel of the LORD* [YHWH] said to Manoah, "If you detain me, I will not eat your food, but if you want to prepare a burnt offering, then offer it *to the LORD* [YHWH]." (For Manoah did not know that he was *the angel of the LORD*) [YHWH.] [17] Then Manoah said to *the angel of the LORD* [YHWH], "What is your name, so that we may honor you when your words come true?" [18] But *the angel of the Lord* [YHWH] said to him, "Why do you ask my name? It is too wonderful."

[19] So Manoah took the kid with the grain offering, and offered it on the rock to the LORD, to him who works wonders. [And He did a wondrous thing while Manoah and his wife looked on ... NKJV] [20] When the flame went up toward heaven from the altar, *the angel of the LORD* [YHWH] ascended in the flame of the altar while Manoah and his wife looked on; and they fell on their faces to the ground. [21] *The angel of the LORD* [YHWH] did not appear again to Manoah and his wife. Then Manoah realized that it was *the angel of the LORD* [YHWH]. [22] And Manoah said to his wife, "We shall surely die, for we have seen *God* [Elohim]."

The same figure is here identified as *the angel of the Lord, God, the man, the man of God, and the angel of God.* In v. 6 the two last mentioned identities are combined. It seems that different strands of 'the angel of the Lord traditions' have been consciously united in this story, compare Genesis 18 and 32.[256] The similarities between Judg 13:19-22 and Judg 6:19, 21-23 are striking:[257]

[Judg 6:19] So Gideon went into his house and prepared a kid, and unleavened cakes from an ephah of flour [...] and brought them to him [the angel of the LORD], under the oak and presented them ... [21] Then the angel of the LORD reached out the tip of the staff that was in his hand, and touched the meat and the unleavened cakes; and fire sprang up from the

---

256 Gieschen 1998, 62.

257 See also the whole narrative of Gideon's encounter with the angel of the Lord in Judg 6:11-24. Although the angel of the Lord appears to Gideon, it is God who speaks to him, see e.g., Judg 6:14, 16, cf., Exodus 3. For Judges 6 and 13, see also Guggisberg 1979, 66-72, and Mach 1992, 39-45.

rock and consumed the meat and the unleavened cakes; and the angel of
the LORD vanished from his sight. [22] Then Gideon perceived that it was
the angel of the LORD; and Gideon said, "Help me, Lord God! For I have
seen the angel of the Lord face to face." [23] But the LORD said to him,
"Peace be to you; do not fear, you shall not die."

Both Manoah and Gideon prepare a kid for their guests, but these
refuse to eat and the food is consumed supernaturally by fire, whereupon the heavenly visitors vanish suddenly from sight. This highly superhuman disappearance makes Manoah and Gideon finally realize
that they have met a divine messenger and they consequently fear for
their lives.

As mentioned previously, the story in Genesis 18 has often been
compared to Judges 13, but a major difference between the two narratives is that Abraham's guests in fact eat the food offered to them. In
both Judges 6 and 13 the supernatural character of the visitors is be-
trayed by their behavior, while in Genesis 18, only the message itself
indicates their heavenly origin. Accordingly, of these accounts only
Genesis 18 is classified by Hamori as an ''îš theophany.'[258] See above for
further discussion of this issue.

Joshua's Encounter with the Commander of the Army of the Lord

In Josh 5:13-15 there is also a divine messenger, despite the fact that the
term 'the angel of the Lord' is not used:

> [13] Once when Joshua was by Jericho, he looked up and saw *a man* [איש]
> standing before him with a drawn sword in his hand. Joshua went to him
> and said to him, "Are you one of us, or one of our adversaries?" [14] He
> replied, "Neither, but as commander [שר] of the army of the LORD I have
> now come." And Joshua fell on his face to the earth and worshipped, and
> he said to him, "What do you command your servant, my lord?" [15] The
> Commander of the army of the LORD said to Joshua, "Remove the sandals
> from your feet, for the place where you stand is holy." And Joshua did so.

The messenger identifies himself as "commander of the army of the
Lord."[259] Joshua's reaction tells us that he recognizes the "man" as being of divine origin, either a revelation of God Himself or one of his
angels, and the passage may hence be defined as an implicit 'angel of

---

258 Hamori 2004, 145-147.
259 One of the divine titles of God in the Bible is the 'Lord of Hosts/YHWH Zebaot', e.g.,
Ps 89:9 (v. 8 in NRSV). The angels constitute the heavenly armies (צבאות) and council
of God. See also, e.g., 1 Sam 1:3; 2 Sam 5:10; 1 Kgs 22:19; 2 Kgs 6:17; Zech 1:12-13, and
Ps 48:9 (v. 8 in NRSV).

the Lord-text'.[260] The "man" seems to distinguish between himself and the Lord/YHWH in v. 14, but at the same time he accepts the worship of Joshua.[261]

The exhortation in Josh 5:15 recalls the command of God (the angel of the Lord?) in the burning bush to Moses in Exod 3:2-6. The appearance of the "man" as a warrior holding a sword parallels the description of the angel of the Lord confronting Balaam in Num 22:23.[262] The angel who leads the Israelites out of Egypt and into the Promised Land can also be mentioned.[263] Worth noting is that in the context of the above cited verses, it is the Lord Himself who continues to speak to Joshua in chapter 6:1-6.

According to Hamori, the encounter recorded in Josh 5:13-15 constitutes the closest angelic parallel to the '´îš theophany'. As in Genesis 18 and 32, the divine messenger is called איש 'a man' and, in contrast to the divine visitors of Manoah and Gideon, he does not engage in any supernatural act. However, Hamori claims that by presenting himself as 'commander of the army of the Lord' and by declaring the sanctity of the place of his appearance, "the man" immediately identifies himself as a divine being. Additionally, unlike the divine agents in Genesis 18 and 32, he does not participate in any specific human activity, such as wrestling or eating.[264]

3.3.3 Conclusions

In Exodus, the מלאך and God appear to be interchangeable. In Exod 14:19 the מלאך seems to be present in the pillar of cloud, but in other texts it is said that it was God who manifested Himself in this pillar. By

---

260 In *Targum Jonathan*, the "man" is identified as "an angel from before the Lord," see Josh 5:14, Harrington/Saldarini (Eng. trans.) 1987, 25.

261 This "man" has been identified as Michael, the guardian angel of Israel by some later interpreters, cf., Dan 10:21; 12:1. Maybe this is because the same title, namely שר/prince/commander, is used to designate both Michael and the "man" who meets Joshua. In the LXX this term is in these cases translated by the word ἄγγελος. See also *Joseph and Aseneth* 14, where the heavenly man says to Aseneth: "I am the chief of the house of the Lord and the commander of the whole host of the Most High..." See also Sullivan 2004, 55-56.

262 This reminds us of 'the destroying angel' who according to 1 Chr 21:16 was holding a drawn sword in his hand. See also 2 Sam 24:15-16; 2 Kgs 19:35; Isa 37:36. In Josh 23:3, 9-10 it is said that it was God who fought for Israel.

263 Cf., Exod 23:20-23; 33:2-3, and Judg 2:1-5 (see above).

264 Hamori 2004, 147-150. It is indeed remarkable that the "man" accepts the worship of Joshua, cf., Rev 19:9-10. See also Gieschen 1998, 33.

possessing the divine name and being capable of forgiving sins (Exod 23:21), the מלאך is depicted as sharing divine authority. The attempt to identify the מלאך in Exodus as a human leader, e.g., Moses, thus seems farfetched. However, unlike 'the angel of the Lord' in Genesis, the divine messenger in Exodus is sometimes spoken of by God in the third person (e.g., Exod 23:20-24; 33:2-3). Perhaps Exodus bears witness to a development in terms of the separation of God and His messenger, although the process is far from complete.[265] In Judges 6 and 13, the fusion of the מלאך and God is obvious.

On the other hand, the identification of the מלאך in Judges 2 as a divine messenger is more dubious. However, considering the people's reaction in Judg 2:5 I find it likely that this is also an example of the Exodus-tradition of 'the angel of the Lord' bringing the Israelites out of Egypt and into the Promised Land.

In the same way as the narratives in Genesis 18 and 32, the passage in Josh 5:13-15 may be classified as an implicit reference to 'the angel of the Lord'. As Jacob's contender at Jabbok he is called 'a man' but his title and acceptance of Joshua's worship reveal his divine identity.

3.4 The Books of the Latter Prophets

Apart from Ezekiel and Zechariah, angels are not often mentioned in the books of the Latter Prophets and the distinction between God and the angel/angels is clearer.[266] Exceptions are Hos 12:4-6 (vv. 3-5 in NRSV) where we find an allusion to the tradition of Jacob's struggle with the unknown, mysterious man (cf., Gen 32:24-32), Mal 3:1-2 where we encounter the מלאך of the covenant, and Isa 63:9-10, which mentions 'the angel of His Presence' [מלאך פניו]. Let us begin by looking at the latter pericope.

---

265 See also Hannah 1999, 21. According to Eynikel (2007, 113-121), 'the angel of the Lord-texts' in both Exodus (with the exception of Exodus 3) and Judges display an angelology characteristic of the pre-exilic period of Israelite history, i.e., a stage between the oldest conception of angels as "mere" extensions of God Himself (e.g., Genesis 16) and the later post-exilic view, displayed in, for example, the book of Daniel. I agree that the description of 'the divine name angel' (whom God refers to in the third person) in, e.g., Exodus 23, may represent this 'midway-stage' in the development of Israelite angelology. However, as stated above, in my view the fusion of God and the מלאך is obvious in Judges 6 and 13.

266 Strictly speaking, the concept 'the angel of the Lord' does not appear in Ezekiel, while in Zechariah we find it in 1:11; 3:1-6; 12:8. The angel of the Lord who appears in Isa 37:36 seems to be distinguished from God.

3.4.1 Isaiah

[Isa 63:9] In all their affliction He was afflicted, And *the Angel of His Presence* saved them; In His love and in His pity He redeemed them; And He bore them and carried them All the days of old. [10] But they rebelled and grieved *His Holy Spirit*; So He turned Himself against them as an enemy, And he fought against them.[267]

This is probably an example of inner biblical exegesis. Isaiah may be alluding to 'the divine name angel' in Exod 23:20-23 as well as to God's promise in Exod 33:14 that "My presence' (פָּנַי) will go with you", i.e., Israel. Charles Gieschen writes: "Thus, Isa 63.9 interpreted the Divine Name Angel who went *before* Israel to be God's Presence *with* Israel."[268] He also notes the words in Exod 23:22 that if Israel listened to this angel, YHWH would be "an enemy of their enemies." Because of the disobedience of the people, the opposite happened, Isa 63:10. In the LXX, however, Isa 63:9 is rendered: "... not an ambassador, nor a messenger – but [he] *himself* saved them."[269]

In the prophecy of Isaiah 9 it is the other way around. Here the LXX mentions a messenger/angel, while the MT does not:[270]

[6] For a child is born to us, and a son is given to us, and his name is called *the Messenger of great council* [Μεγάλης βουλῆς ἄγγελος] ...[271]

---

267 NKJV. Cf., Judg 2:1-5. See also Guggisberg 1979, 87-88.

268 Gieschen 1998, 117-118.

269 The LXX rendering appears thus to be influenced by Deuteronomistic theology, which leaves no place for the מַלְאָךְ but maintains that it was God in person who led the Israelites out of Egypt and into the Promised Land, see Ausloos 2008, 7-8. This interpretation of Isa 63:9a is chosen in the NRSV: "It was no messenger or angel, but his presence that saved them ..." In later Midrash, this interpretation prevailed, see the Passover Haggadah and Goldin 1968, 412-424. However, in the *Targum to Isaiah* 63:8b-9 we read:

[8b] ... and his Memra was their saviour. [9] Whensoever they transgressed before him, so as to bring affliction upon them, he did not afflict them, *but an angel sent from before him delivered them*; in his mercy and in his pity for them he rescued them, and bare them, and carried them all the days of old. [Eng. trans. Stenning 1949, 208, 210, my italics].

270 See also Mach 1992, 79-81.

271 The NRSV follows the MT:

[Isa 9:6/v. 5 MT] For a child has been born for us, a son given to us; authority rests upon his shoulders; and he is named Wonderful Counselor, Mighty God, Everlasting Father, Prince of Peace.

See also Guiley 2004, 23, 310, who claims that the four titles of the Messiah in the MT may have been given to the four archangels Michael, Gabriel, Raphael, and

As mentioned above, there is also a difference between the LXX and MT in Exod 4:24, since it is an angel of the Lord who tries to kill Moses in the LXX, while it is God in the MT.[272]

3.4.2 Hosea

In his call for repentance, the prophet Hosea alludes to Jacob's wrestling bout at the ford of Jabbok:

> [Hos 12:3/4] In the womb he [Jacob] tried to supplant his brother, and in his manhood he *strove with God* [שׂרה את אלהים] [4/5] He *strove* [וישׂר] *with the angel* [אֶל מלאך] and prevailed, he wept and sought his favor; he met him *at Bethel*, and there He spoke with him.[273] [5/6] The LORD the God of host, the LORD is his name! [274]

At first sight, the mysterious man who encounters Jacob according to Gen 32:24-32 seems to be identified by the prophet Hosea as an angel. However, in vv. 3-4 [4-5] אלהים 'God' and מלאך 'angel'/'messenger'[275] are used in parallel, as if the terms are synonymous, compare Gen 48:15-16 where angel and God are likewise equated with each other.[276]

Moreover, the מלאך/'angel' in v. 4 [5] is said to be the one who spoke with Jacob at Bethel (cf., the theophanies in Genesis 28 and 35), and in v. 5 [6] he is explicitly identified as "the LORD the God of hosts..."[277]

Uriel/Phanuel as the four aspects of the angel of great counsel/the angel of the Lord. See also Barker, 1992, 36 and 70-94. Cf., above, chapter 2.2.2.

272 Tuschling (2007, 83), claims that the expression chosen by the translator implies that the LXX supports an understanding of 'the angel of the Lord' as a hypostasis of God, not an "ordinary" angel.

273 MT has 'with us' (cf., NKJV cited below) but, e.g., the LXX has 'with him', see the text critical apparatus to the verse.

274 The translation in the NKJV is slightly different:

[Hos 12:3] He [Jacob] took his brother by the heel in the womb, and in his strength he struggled with God [4] Yes, he struggled with the Angel and prevailed; He wept, and sought favour from Him. He found him in Bethel, and there he spoke to us – [5] that is the Lord [YHWH] God of hosts, the Lord is his memorable name.

Note the connection to Bethel (cf., Gen 28:12-17; 31:11-13). The "man" in Gen 32:24-30 might be the "angel" that Jacob/Israel refers to in Gen 48:15-16.

275 If the word מלאך is original, Hosea is the only pre-exilic prophet who refers to an angel, since Jacob's opponent is clearly not a human messenger. See also Sullivan 2004, 47.

276 Cf., Judges 6 and 13 where the designations 'God' and 'angel/messenger of the Lord/God' are used alternately for the divine visitors. See also Andersen/Freedman 1980, 612-613.

277 However, v. 6 is considered by some scholars to be a gloss, see e.g., Whitt 1991, 25.

This passage of Hosea is thus ambiguous; the identities of God and His "angel" are fused together, there is no clear distinction between them, and they appear to be one and the same person. Accordingly, Dennis J. McCarthy[278] understands the word 'angel/messenger' in this context as equivalent to God,[279] while James L. Mays interprets Hosea's words as referring to traditions concerning Jacob's encounters with God, compare Genesis 32 and 28.[280]

The peculiar Hebrew wording, אֶל מַלְאָךְ, in MT v. 5 has been much discussed. Most English translations have chosen the emendation to read אֶל as אֶת 'with', but there are many scholars who opt to retain אֵל, read it as אֵל 'El/God' and delete מַלְאָךְ as a gloss, thus resolving the ambiguity of the text.[281] Given the parallelistic structure of vv. 4-5 (NRSV vv. 3-4), this solution seems possible.[282] If the unique phrase אֵל מַלְאָךְ (possibly meaning 'the divine messenger') is indeed original, this is its only occurrence in the entire Bible.[283]

However, despite the uniqueness of the phrase, Francis I. Andersen and David Noel Freedman maintain its originality and consider the equation of 'angel' and 'God' in Gen 48:16 as a close analogy to Hos 12:5 and later make quite a remarkable statement:

> The phrase 'ēl/mal'āk, "god, angel," is a unity, split up over two parallel lines. The base is "the Angel of God," representing the deity himself, though the phrase mal'āk 'ēl is unattested. It is probable that the mal'āk yhwh, who would never have been called that in patriarchal times, was mal'āk 'ēl in the preliterate traditions. And Hosea's material could go right back to such terminology.[284]

This is a truly interesting theory, but I find it quite hypothetical and am not entirely convinced by the line of argument. However, while Hos 12:3-5 [4-6] clearly alludes to the tradition of Jacob's wrestling bout,[285]

---

278 Roland E. Murphy has revised the *JBC* article by Dennis J. McCarthy.

279 McCarthy/Murphy1989, 227.

280 Mays 1969, 162-165. In this context, Mays (1969, 163) refers to the appearance of God in the form of an angel to the patriarchs in the E tradition; Gen 21:17; 31:11.

281 See e.g., Wolff 1974, 206, 212-213, Whitt 1991, 31-32. Both Wolff and Whitt point out that Hosea does not mention angels elsewhere and Whitt also remarks that Hos 12:4-5 is the only case in which מַלְאָךְ and אֱלֹהִים/אֵל are used in parallel in biblical poetry. See also Hamori 2004, 143-144. Hosea also uses אֵל to designate the deity in 12:1b and 11:9. See further Wolff 1974, 209-210, 212-213.

282 El and Elohim are a quite common word pair in the Bible, see e.g., Isa 46:9; Ps 7:12, and Job 5:8. See also Whitt 1991, 32.

283 See also Hamori 2004, 143-144, and Whitt 1991, 32.

284 Andersen/Freedman 1980, 613.

285 In the Bible the verb שׂרה 'to strive/struggle/contend' is only found in Hosea 12 and Genesis 32.

there are some differences between Hosea's version and that recorded in Genesis. There is a discussion among scholars concerning which version is the oldest one. It may very well be that Hosea 12 predates the narrative in Genesis 32 in its present form. According to William D. Whitt, both Hosea and the author of the Genesis story used a common source.[286] Kevin P. Sullivan concludes that, since Jacob's weeping in supplication has no counterpart in the Jabbok narrative in Genesis, it indicates either that Hosea might have known a different tradition or that the prophet altered the Genesis story.[287] In either case, Sullivan argues that:

> ... this lends credence to the possibility that the מלאך was indeed original [...] the Genesis passage was vague enough to allow room for interpretation and it seems that regardless of when it occurred, the author/redactor of Hosea 12 altered the Genesis tradition of Jacob wrestling with God to Jacob wrestling with an angel.

Be that as it may, scholars generally agree that Hosea refers to ancient Jacob traditions.[288] Another striking difference between the narrative and Hosea's statement is that the prophet does not mention the ford of Jabbok but refers to Jacob's encounters with God at Bethel, see Genesis 28 and 35. Thus, Hosea appears to have combined various Jacob traditions.[289] Another difference is of course the use of the word מלאך in designation of Jacob's contender, who is simply called 'a man' in Genesis 32 but, as mentioned above, this rendering has been questioned. Possibly, the word was added as a result of a later interpretation of Jacob's opponent as an angel.[290]

In the case of the Genesis-text, it is when the patriarch receives his new name that the "man" acknowledges that Jacob/Israel has prevailed. Hosea, on the other hand, does not mention the renaming of Jacob and does not explicitly state who was victorious in the combat.[291] As mentioned in the analysis of Genesis 32 above, many scholars derive the verb וישׂר in Hos 12:5 from the root שׂרר 'to rule', 'have dominion' and not from שׂרה 'to strive/struggle'. The subject of the verb however,

---

286 Whitt 1991, 41.
287 Sullivan 2004, 49.
288 See, e.g., Mays 1969, 162-165, Wolff 1974, 211-213, McCarthy/Murphy 1989, 227, and Hamori 2004, 79-82.
289 See also Wolff 1974, 213, and Hayward 2005, 21.
290 See also Wolff 1974, 212, Hamori 2004, 143-145, and Köckert 2007, 62. Köckert (same page) suggests that the equation of 'man' = 'angel' in Hosea 12 may be derived from Genesis 18-19. Cf., Sullivan 2004, 49.
291 See also Mays 1969, 163-164.

is debated.[292] As shown in the quotation above, Jacob is presented as victorious in the NRSV, where the translators have chosen to retain the word מלאך 'angel'.[293]

However, many scholars argue that it seems to be implied that God/the "angel" ruled and prevailed over Jacob. If Jacob were the victor, why would he weep[294] and seek the favor of his combatant?[295] The interpretation of God as victorious also makes sense in the context; in his call to the sinful people of Israel to repent, the prophet alludes to traditions concerning the patriarch Jacob's surrender to God. As the ancestor of the nation he represents and embodies his descendants.[296] In this light, the shift to the Hebrew imperfect tense ימצאנו 'he [God] finds us' and ידבר 'he speaks' is also explicable, as is the rendering עמנו 'with us' instead of 'with him' at the end of v. 5 in the MT. In the words of Mays:

> the verbs [...] shift from the narrative perfects and consecutives [...] to imperfects as if to bring the events of the line nearer to the audience. God still meets *them* at Bethel and speaks with *them* there![297]

Whitt argues that in this way Hosea bears witness to the original tradition: Jacob is defeated and begs for mercy, but in Genesis 32 the roles have been reversed, probably in order to present the patriarch in a better light.[298] Additionally, he claims that the author of the Genesis version has substituted איש for the already existing gloss מלאך.[299]

Both Whitt and H. L. Ginsberg interpret Hos 12:5 בית אל ימצאנו in the light of Gen 31:13 אנכי האל בית אל "I am the god Bethel" and identify Jacob's opponent as a god by the name of 'Beth-el'.[300] However, a great

---

292 See also Wolff 1974, 212-213, Sarna 1989, 404-405, and Hamori 2004, 79-82.
293 See also Whitt 1991, 32, who argues that the way one reads the subject depends on whether one retains the term מלאך or dismisses it as a gloss.
294 The weeping of Jacob is not mentioned in Genesis 32, though his request for a blessing in v. 26 may be interpreted as a prayer/supplication, hence 'to seek favor'.
295 However, as mentioned above, the Hosea text is unclear regarding who was victorious in the combat, Jacob or the "angel" and, linguistically speaking, the pericope can be interpreted to mean that it was the latter who wept and sought favor with Jacob. According to Köckert (2007, 62), this may be the reason for the transformation of Jacob's combat with God into a combat with an *angel* in Hosea 12, because such a statement can be made about an angel but certainly not about God.
296 See also Wolff 1974, 211-213, Mays 1969, 163-164, McCarthy/Murphy 1989, 227, and Hamori 2004, 80-82.
297 Mays 1969, 164. See also Wolff 1974, 213, and Walters 1992, 607-608.
298 Whitt 1991, 33-34.
299 Whitt 1991, 33.
300 Whitt 1991, 35-43, and Ginsberg 1961, 339-347. In addition to Genesis 31, Whitt also refers to Genesis 28.

difference between the two scholars is that Whitt maintains that the god Beth-el was merged with YHWH in later tradition,[301] while Ginsberg interprets Hosea's statement as a condemnation of the cult of the 'angel El-beth-el', to use his designation.[302] The identification of Jacob's contender as a god named Bethel appears to me as somewhat far-fetched, and I prefer to interpret 'Bethel' in Hos 12:5 as a reference to the place of the divine encounter.[303] In the LXX, Hos 12:3b-4[304] is rendered as follows:

[3b] ... καὶ ἐν κόποις αὐτοῦ ἐνίσχυσε πρὸς θεόν. [4] καὶ ἐνίσχυσε μετὰ ἀγγέλου καὶ ἠδυνάσθη·ἔκλαυσαν καὶ ἐδεήθησάν μου, ἐν τῷ οἴκῳ Ὢν εὑροσάν με, καὶ ἐκεῖ ἐλαλήθη πρὸς αὐτόν/αὐτούς.[305]/... and in his labors he [Jacob] had power with God. And he prevailed/was strong/strengthened himself with the angel and was strong, they wept, and entreated me, they found me in the house of On/the Being/the Existent/the Eternal, and there was spoken to him/them.

As shown in the quotation, the LXX states that Jacob "prevailed with the angel," thus maintaining the ambivalence between God and the angel, vv. 3-4. According to the LXX version, Jacob is the victor, but in v. 4b the subject changes to plural, "they wept, and entreated me ..." The explanation is certainly that the patriarch Jacob is seen as a representative of the collective, i.e., the people of Israel, cf., above.

Sullivan considers the LXX reading ... καὶ ἐνίσχυσε μετὰ ἀγγέλου... in Hos 12:4 as a support for the originality of 'the angel'/מלאך in this verse and if the word actually is a gloss, it must have been inserted at a fairly early stage.[306]

As we have seen in the discussion of the Jacob texts in Genesis, the Hebrew place-name Bethel is most commonly translated as τόπος/οἶκος θεοῦ, 'place/house of God' or transcribed as Βαιθήλ. The rendering in Hos 12:4 is thus a bit peculiar. One possible explanation could be that the phrase οἶκος Ὢν refers to a sanctuary at Bethel,[307] the house of God, i.e., the house of YHWH, whose name signifies 'the Being/the Existent/the Eternal', rendered in Greek as ὁ Ὤν, compare Exod 3:14:

Καὶ εἶπεν ὁ θεὸς πρὸς Μωυσῆν Ἐγώ εἰμι ὁ ὤν·καὶ εἶπεν, Οὕτως ἐρεῖς τοῖς υἱοῖς Ισραήλ Ὁ ὢν ἀπέσταλκέν με πρὸς ὑμᾶς./ And God spoke to

---

301 Whitt 1991, 35-43.
302 Ginsberg 1961, 339-347.
303 See also, e.g., Andersen/Freedman 1980, 614.
304 The numbering of the verses differs between the MT and the LXX.
305 Some mss have αὐτούς.
306 Sullivan 2004, 48.
307 See also Amos 7:13, and Mays 1969, 164.

Moses: I am the Being/the Existent/the Eternal and he said, thus shall you say to the sons of Israel, the Being/the Existent /the Eternal has sent me to you.[308]

3.4.3 Conclusions

As shown above, Isa 63:9-10; 9:6 and Hos 12:3-5 [4-6] are text critically, linguistically and theologically complicated passages. Both the passage in Hosea 12 and that in Isaiah 63 contain some kind of 'inner biblical exegesis'.

The phrase in Hosea 12:5 אֶל מלאך is much discussed because of its peculiarity, and there are basically two different "solutions"; the emendation to read אֶל as את 'with', or to retain אל and read it as אֵל 'El/God', while deleting מלאך as a gloss. In the latter case, the term is explained as an insertion in Hosea's text, based on a presumed later interpretation of Jacob's combatant as an angel, cf., the LXX version. The theory of Andersen and Freedman appears to be an exception to the rule and, although interesting, their explanation seems highly speculative. However, even if we keep מלאך, Jacob's contender was most certainly not seen as an "ordinary" angel by Hosea, as he is equated with God, cf., Gen 48:15-16. Those scholars who retain מלאך often refer to the presence of the "angel" in the LXX Hosea 12 and if the word is indeed a gloss, it must have been inserted at an early stage. Moreover, the LXX rendering of the Hebrew place name Bethel in Hos 12:4 is quite remarkable.

Speaking of the LXX, we have seen above that the versions of Isa 63:9 and 9:6 differ significantly from their counterparts in the MT, and the main issue in these pericopes is also the presence or absence of an angel/divine messenger.

The analysis makes it evident that all of these texts were perceived as difficult from early times, and the heart of the problem was (and remains to this day) the relationship between God and His מלאך/"angel".

3.5 The Writings

In the Writings, the book of Daniel often mentions angels and gives them names: Gabriel and Michael (e.g., Dan 9:21 and 10:13). Here we

---

308 Cf., also Rev 1:4, 8.

also encounter 'the son of God/the angel', Dan 3:25, 28, and 'one like the son of man'[309]/'one like a human being', Dan 7:13.[310] In Psalms, the angel of the Lord is mentioned in Ps 34:8[7] and 35:5-6, described as a guardian angel sent by God to protect and deliver the pious and to pursue their enemies. In Chronicles we have the parallel texts to 2 Sam 24:16 and Isa 37:36; 2 Kgs 19:35 (1 Chr 21:15 respectively 2 Chr 32:21). In Eccl 5:6[5] we read: "Do not let your mouth lead you into sin, and do not say before the messenger [מלאך][311] that it was a mistake ..." The curious thing is that the phrase "before the messenger" in the LXX is translated as πρὸ προσώπου τοῦ θεοῦ, "in the presence of God." This is a unique case. In the book of Job, Elihu refers to the מלאך as a mediator between God and humankind, Job 33:23

3.6 Attempts at Explanation in Modern Exegesis

3.6.1 Introductory Remarks

As stated above, the purpose of this investigation is to deal with the relevant texts in the book of Genesis and their interpretations in early Jewish sources. This restriction is due to considerations of space but for the sake of clarity it has also been necessary to survey the other texts concerning the problematic identification of the angel of the Lord. It is now time to take a closer look at the main solutions proposed for resolving this problem.

A feature common to most of the different explanations concerning the shift between YHWH and his angel in some texts is that the theophany must be mediated in some way.[312] This seems credible, but it does not answer the question why the angel appears in some but not all of the narratives. Carol A. Newsom writes:

---

309 NKJV.

310 Daniel 7 was considered a dangerous passage by the early Rabbis, as it can be interpreted as referring to two divine beings, 'the Ancient One' and 'one like the son of man', see further Segal 1977, 33-39. In Dan 4:10-20 we encounter the term 'îr/watcher, a designation for some kind of angelic beings found in post-exilic Jewish literature but canonically only in the book of Daniel, see also Noll 1997, 942.

311 The NJKV adds the designation "of God," while like the MT, the NRSV refers to an *unspecified* messenger/מלאך. From the context of Eccl 5:5 in the MT it is unclear whether a human (a prophet?) or a divine messenger is intended.

312 The interpolation theory can be seen as an exception in this case because, according to this view, it was originally God Himself who was the agent in these narratives.

But the explanation that seems most likely is that the interchange between Yahweh and *mal'ak yhwh* in various texts is the expression of a tension or paradox: Yahweh's authority and presence in these encounters is to be affirmed, but yet it is not possible for human beings to have an unmediated encounter with God.[313]

As I see it, she actually does not solve the problem of the identity of the angel of the Lord but instead states that the very point of these texts is that "the unresolved ambiguity in the narrative allows the reader to experience the paradox." She also maintains that it would be misleading to suggest that this perspective was a dogmatic belief in ancient Israelite religion. As mentioned, there are biblical texts in which God communicates with humans with no reference to the angel of the Lord (e.g., Genesis 15), while sometimes the distinction between God and the angel is clear (e.g., 1 Kgs 19:5-7).[314] There is a general consensus between scholars that there are different kinds of 'angel of the Lord texts'. The problematic pericopes are those where we find the above mentioned merging of the identity of the angel and God Himself.[315]

3.6.2 The Interpolation Theory

One quite frequent approach to this problem is the interpolation theory. According to this view, the word מלאך was inserted in certain contexts by the editors. The ambiguity between the angel of the Lord and God Himself is due to the fact that originally it was God alone who was the agent in these texts.[316] Gerhard von Rad supports this theory and writes:

> What distinguishes these passages from the others is that it is impossible in them to differentiate between the מ׳ [מלאך יהוה] and Yahweh Himself. The One who speaks or acts, i.e., Yahweh or the מ׳ is obviously one and the same person. Yet in the apparently haphazard alternation between the two there is a certain system. When the reference is to God apart from man, Yahweh is used; when God enters the appreciation of man, the מ׳ is introduced [...] Originally the stories probably referred quite naively to purely sensual theophanies.[317]

---

313 Newsom 1992, 250.

314 Newsom 1992, 250. I am not convinced that the angel in 1 Kings 19 is distinct from God. However, there is a clear distinction between the two in 2 Kgs 19:35.

315 E.g., von Rad 1964, 77, and Meier 1995b, 96-108. For this whole chapter, see also Guggisberg 1979, 133-155.

316 Cf., the discussion of the originality of the word מלאך in Hosea 12 above.

317 von Rad 1964, 77-78.

The editors are said to have inserted the concept of 'the angel of the Lord' for diverse theological reasons, for example to soften the anthropomorphic depictions of God in the stories.[318] This is the solution proposed by Meier. In addition, he claims that another reason for supporting this theory is that the term מלאך is not found in all text witnesses. One example is Exod 4:24, where the MT states that it was God who sought to kill Moses. As this idea was theologically difficult, the translators of the LXX inserted an angel.[319]

Meier also argues that the phrase מלאך יהוה should be understood as indefinite and thus translated 'an (unspecified) angel/messenger of the Lord'. He argues that since the Hebrew definite article cannot be employed in the construct when the nomen rectum is a proper name, a translation in definite form is equally possible and a matter of interpretation.[320] As support for a translation in indefinite form, Meier also refers to many cases in the LXX where the angel makes his first appearance.[321] Sure enough, both in Gen 16:7; 21:17, and 22:11, the LXX has an indefinite form: ἄγγελος κυρίου/θεοῦ: 'an angel of the Lord/God'. This is of interest, since the chosen translation of מלאך יהוה might indicate how the translator viewed this 'being'. That the LXX uses the definite form in, for example, Gen 16:8-10: ὁ ἄγγελος κυρίου/'the angel of the Lord', is probably because the angel has already been introduced in verse 7.[322] In accordance with his chosen translation of the concept, Meier also claims that the phrase מלאך YHWH is to be understood as a title designating several of God's supernatural envoys.[323] However, many scholars maintain that a translation in the definite form is proba-

---

318 von Rad 1964, 77-78. See also Meier 1995b, 106, Sarna 1989, 383, and Gieschen 1998, 54.

319 Meier 1995b, 96-108. Cf., also the scholarly discussion of the מלאך in Hosea 12 referred to above.

320 Meier mentions two different Bible translations in order to illustrate this; the Jewish Publication Society typically translates מלאך יהוה as an angel of the Lord, while the New Revised Standard Version translates the concept in the definite form.

321 Cf., for example 2 Chr 32:1, and 2 Kgs 19:35. Meier 1995b, 98-108.

322 Meier 1995b, 98-108. He writes on pp. 98-99:

Because Greek, like English, usually distinguishes definite from indefinite in genitive constructions (unlike Hebrew and Latin), early evidence from Greek is invaluable in discerning how the Bible's earliest accessible interpreters understood the phrase. The NT knows of no single "The angel of the Lord/God"....The Septuagint generally follows suit in translating mal'ak YHWH in the OT, although there are a few exceptional cases where the definite article appears when the figure first appears in a narrative (Num 22:23; Jud 5:23 [LXX cod. A]; 2 Sam 24:16; contrast the far more numerous cases where LXX presents the figure as indefinite: Gen 16:7; 22:11, 15; Exod 3:2 …)

323 Meier 1995b, 107.

bly correct and thus consider it a 'special title', reserved for a particular divine messenger.[324]

The interpolation theory has not been accepted by all scholars.[325] As we have seen, it cannot explain many of the texts where God speaks directly to humans without the mention of this 'mediating figure', including such bold anthropomorphic narratives as that of the visit of the three "men" to Abraham in Genesis 18.[326] James Barr opposes the interpolation theory:

> Firstly, the introduction of the *mal'ak* is too extremely spasmodic, and leaves too many fierce anthropomorphisms untouched, for its purpose to be understood in this way. The voice and presence of the *mal'ak* alternates in a number of stories so much with the voice and appearing of Yahweh that it is hardly possible to understand his place as a substitute for the latter. Secondly, far from the *mal'ak* representing a later and more sophisticated feature, it is found deeply embedded in stories of great antiquity; the best example is the J story of Gen xviii, where to be sure the term *mal'ak* does not appear until xix 1 and there in the plural, but where it is indisputable that we have the same general phenomenon as the *mal'ak* of other stories.[327]

Westermann writes that even if the interpolation theory may explain the role of the angel of the Lord in the later period of Israel's religious thinking, it cannot explain the fact that in the old narratives YHWH and his messenger are alternated in one and the same story.[328]

3.6.3 Theories that Focus on the Function of the Angel

Two main groups can be distinguished among the additional theories that attempt to explain the ambiguity between God and his angel, those that focus on the *function* of the angel/messenger in the narratives and those that concern the *essence* of this 'being'.[329]

The first category includes the messenger and representative theories. The former has been mentioned above and claims that the solution to the problem can be found in the union between the sender and the messenger. This theory can in turn be divided into two different ap-

---

324 See Gieschen 1998, 56, and Newsom 1992, 250.
325 Newsom, see above. See also Köckert 2007, 73-75, and Fabry 1997, 321-322.
326 The Jahvistic account in Genesis 2-3 is also worth mentioning for its anthropomorphic description of God.
327 Barr 1960, 33-34.
328 Westermann 1985, 243. See also Hamori 2004, 153-155.
329 Fabry 1997, 322.

proaches. The מלאך is either seen as an extension of God Himself and not a being distinct from God[330] or as a supernatural being sent by God as his messenger.[331] As we have seen, this explanation has been disputed by, among others, Meier, who claims that the messenger and sender could not be merged in the Ancient Near East.[332]

According to the closely related representation theory, the angel of the Lord is not identical with God but is His ambassador, speaking and acting with divine authority on His behalf. Gieschen argues that even if this theory can be used to explain texts where the angel of the Lord is depicted as distinct from God (e.g., 2 Sam 24:16; 2 Kgs 19:35) it cannot solve the problem of the merged identity in other narratives.[333] Westermann also focuses on the function of the angel/messenger of the Lord:

> ... But if one begins from the texts and the function which the *m.y.* [מלאך YHWH] plays therein, then it is obvious that a clear distinction must be made between *(a)* heavenly beings as, e.g., the seraphs in Is 6, and *(b)* any other type of theophany or divine manifestation. One must realize that the designation *m.y* has undergone profound changes from its earliest occurrence in the patriarchal stories down to the postexilic period. It is important that in the early narrative the *m.y.* is the one who meets. He is there only in the meeting. He is not a figure, nor a representative, nor some manifestation of God [...] he is only the one who meets [...] God is present not in the messenger, but in the message.[334]

---

330 This theory has been proposed by van der Woude (1963/64, 6-13). He prefers to translate the concept מלאך YHWH in indefinite form, because the angel is an extension of God Himself. In this way he agrees with Meier, although otherwise they have different opinions concerning this issue. See above. If we are to believe Finkelstein (1929, 235-240), the Sadducees advocated precisely this view on angels as mere extensions/emanations of the Deity and with no independent existence or personality of their own. As is well known, the Sadducees strongly objected to the Pharisaic view on angels as individual beings. See also chapter 1.4 above.

331 Meier 1995b, 105. See also Johnsson (1942, 5-41), who appears to advocate a kind of combination of the messenger and representative theories. In his discussion of the appearance of angels/'mysterious men' in Genesis, Köckert (2007, 51-78, see esp. pp. 53, 69-75) also emphasizes their function as divine messengers but does not make any clear distinction between the above mentioned messenger theory subgroups.

332 Meier 1995a, 87-88, and 1995b, 105.

333 Gieschen 1998, 55.

334 Westermann 1985, 243-244.

3.6.4 Theories that Focus on the Nature of the Angel

The second category of explanations focuses on the essence of the nature of the "angel" in question. Firstly, there is the identity theory where the angel of the Lord is a manifestation of God Himself. God reveals Himself in the form of an angel, a man, or a pillar of cloud, in order not to destroy those who see Him.[335] Secondly, the angel of the Lord is understood as a hypostasis of God.[336] Here we have subgroups of theories; the angel of the Lord is an aspect of God's personality or God's means of communication with the world, the so-called 'Logos-theory'[337] and, finally, according to some Christian interpreters; the angel of the Lord is the preincarnate Christ.[338]

3.7 Conclusions

I have presented a survey of the divergent explanations of the merged identity of God and His מלאך in some texts. However, there is no uniform 'angel of the Lord tradition' in the Bible. Sometimes the angel is presented as distinct from God, e.g., in 2 Kgs 19:35, and in Exodus God

---

335 Fabry 1997, 322, Gieschen 1998, 55, and Hannah 1999, 20. According to Meier (1995b, 105), a theory also exists in which "… the angel of the Lord is a means of crystalliz-ing into one figure the many revelatory forms of an early polytheism." A rather spe-cial variant of the 'communication theory' is represented by Ackerman (1921, 145-149), who equates the expressions 'the word of the Lord' with 'the angel of the Lord' and regards them as expressing the same thing, i.e., divine revelation (cf., Genesis 15 and 16). The distinction between the 'word of the Lord/God' and 'the angel of the Lord/God' is, according to Ackerman, that the phrases signify different modes of re-velation. On p. 147 he claims: "…the "word" of the Lord implies an idea whose source is peculiarly subjective [an inner reflection], and the "angel" of the Lord im-plies a suggestion that arrives objectively from without and is definitely connected with a specific thing" [i.e., a well or a burning bush]. Thus, Ackerman makes quite a physiological interpretation of the appearance of the 'angel of the Lord' in the Bible.
336 See also Tuschling 2007, 93-101.
337 Fabry 1997, 322, Gieschen 1998, 55-56.
338 Meier 1995b, 105. This interpretation was common among the Church fathers, e.g., Justin Martyr, and similar views can also be found among modern exegetes. Wes-termann (1987, 127) maintains: "Of all the modes of divine revelation in the Old Tes-tament, the revelation of God in a messenger comes closest to the New Testament self-revelation of God in the person of Jesus. The fact that Jesus, in human form, brings a message from God, that he speaks the words of God and performs the acts of God, has an Old Testament parallel in the 'messenger of Yahweh.' The creedal formula 'truly God and truly human' can be understood after this analogy from the Old Testament narratives of God's messenger."

sometimes refers to the מלאך in the third person (e.g., Exod 23:20-24; 33:1-2). However, by possessing the divine name, the מלאך of Exodus shares the divine nature and power and cannot be seen as completely separate from the Deity.[339] In the 'angel of the Lord narratives' of Genesis and Judges, with the possible exceptions of Genesis 24 and Judges 2, the oscillation between God and His מלאך is undeniable. These differences within the Bible may possibly mirror a historical development of the מלאך-concept.

Regarding the fusion of God and the מלאך, the various suggested "solutions" may be divided into three main categories; the interpolation theory, i.e., the idea of a later insertion of the מלאך into the text, and theories that focus on the function or nature of the מלאך. Sometimes it may be hard to distinguish between the various hypotheses. For example, the borderline between the interpretations of seeing the מלאך as an extension or a manifestation of YHWH is quite narrow.

---

339 The connection between the divine name and the angel recalls the so-called 'revelation hypothesis' proposed by H. Junker (1995, 76-77). He views the angel as the companion and bearer of the glory of YHWH, revealing the presence of YHWH when he appears, but YHWH Himself remains invisible to humans.

4. The Angel of the Lord – Early Jewish Interpretations of Genesis

This chapter will discuss the understanding of 'the angel of the Lord' in early Jewish exegesis. Who is this "angel"? Related issues are the descriptions of God, as well as the relationship of the texts to early Jewish angelology in general. Are there any other angels mentioned in the interpretations of the relevant pericopes? If so, how are they related to 'the angel of the Lord'? What is the relationship between God and His "angel"? How is God depicted and what significance does it have for our subject?

4.1 The Book of Tobit and Wisdom of Solomon and the Gospel of Luke

4.1.1 Introduction

Type-scenes and Allusions – Some Remarks

As mentioned in chapter 2.2.3, the Bible is used in two different ways in early Jewish interpretation, namely the expositional and compositional modes. In the former, the biblical text(s) is (are) explicitly presented and commented on. The Rabbinic Midrashim belongs to this category.[1]

The compositional mode, on the other hand, is characterized by an implicit use of the Bible; the biblical material is woven into the structure of the work and presented without any formal external marker. The compositional mode can take three different forms. In addition to the biblical expansion in the so-called 'rewritten Bible', it can be recognized by the presence of allusions to biblical motifs, themes, scenarios, and/or models. From the reader's perspective, the identification of such implicit biblical allusions requires a certain degree of familiarity with

---

1   See also Dimant 1991, 73-80.

the Bible.[2] This interpretative method is very similar to what Robert Alter defines as a use of biblical type-scenes.[3]

As will be shown in the following, although the book of Tobit is not an explicit commentary on any biblical text, it nevertheless contains allusions to biblical motifs or type-scenes.[4] The same applies to the annunciation in the Gospel of Luke, which echoes many other angelic annunciations in the Bible.[5] Both books display the same kind of interpretative method and there are also certain parallels between the resurrection narrative in the Gospel of Luke and Raphael's role in the book of Tobit, thus these books are treated together in this chapter.

A third expression of the compositional mode consists of explicit allusions or references to biblical events, circumstances or persons. Wisdom chapter 10 may be seen as an example of this kind of biblical interpretation.[6]

The Book of Tobit

It is difficult to date the book of Tobit. The setting of the plot is the end of the 8th century B.C.E. It is a story about an Israelite family who has been deported as captives of war to Assyria. The book, however, is from a much later period, and its story is generally considered fictional.[7]

Most scholars date the book of Tobit to somewhere between 250 and 175 B.C.E., after the completion of the prophetical writings of the Bible but before the Maccabean period.[8] The geographical origin of the

---

2   Dimant 1991, 73-80, and 1988, 400-419.

3   Alter 1981, 47-62. See also chapter 1.3.2 in this thesis.

4   See Spencer 1999, 157-160.

5   See the analysis below and Brown 1999, 156-158, 268-269.

6   See also Dimant 1988, 383, 391-400, where on p. 383 she defines this as a middle type between the compositional and expositional mode. The allusion to Jacob's ladder (Genesis 28) in John 1:51 also belongs to this category of biblical interpretation, see also chapter 4.6 below.

7   Moore 1996, 3-11. It is generally assumed that the author of Tobit used components from folktales when writing the book, e.g., 'the monster in the bridal chamber.' See, for example, Moore, 1996, 11-14, and Otzen 2002, 8-26, 57-59. In addition to these folktales, there are many echoes of the Hebrew Bible in Tobit, notably Genesis, the book of Job and Deuteronomy. As will be shown below, the author was most certainly inspired by Genesis 24. See also Spencer 1999, 156-162, Fitzmyer 2003, 34-41, and Moore 1996, 20-21.

8   The prophets are quoted and alluded to in the book of Tobit, e.g., Amos in Tob 2:6. See Moore 1996, 40-42, and Fitzmyer 2003, 50-52. See also Nowell 1996, 568, and Otzen 2002, 56. The book of Tobit may be based on early oral traditions, see Spencer 199, 152.

book is unknown. Palestine/the land of Israel, Egypt and Mesopotamia have all been proposed as the place where it was composed.[9]

The author of the book of Tobit remains anonymous; all we can say with certainty is that he was a pious and Torah-observing Jew.[10]

The book of Tobit was probably originally written in Aramaic (or perhaps Hebrew) but the oldest complete recensions available today, one short (GI) and one long (GII) version, are in Greek. The longer version of Tobit has a clear Semitic flavor and the Aramaic/Hebrew fragments of Tobit discovered at Qumran are in general similar to GII. [11] There is also an incomplete Greek recension that preserves only the text of Tob 6:9-12:22. This version appears to be mainly based on GII.[12]

The genre of the book may be defined as a short Jewish romance or legend, with a profoundly religious character. The book is characterized by a deuteronomistic perspective on history. The purpose of the author was both to edify and entertain. The power of prayer, belief in divine justice and providence are themes which penetrate the book; although the just may suffer, God always remembers His faithful and ultimately rewards them.[13]

The Wisdom of Solomon

This book goes by two names; in the Latin tradition (i.e., the Vulgate) it is called 'the Book of Wisdom' but in the LXX it is entitled 'the Wisdom of Solomon'.[14] The latter name was given to the book since its author purports to be King Solomon, even though he never explicitly calls him-

---

9   Moore 1996, 42-43, Fitzmyer 2003, 52-54, and Otzen 2002, 57-59.
10   The 'Book/Law of Moses' is referred to in Tob 6:13 and 7:13. See Moore 1996, 39, and Otzen 2002, 57-59.
11   In previous years, GI was generally regarded as the version closest to the original form of Tobit but today GII has assumed that position. Accordingly, most Bible translations today are mainly based on GII, e.g., the NRSV, the translation used in this thesis. This recension of Tobit is relatively intact only in the Codex Sinaiticus. Regarding details about the mss used in the NRSV for the translation of Tobit, see the preface "To the Reader."
12   See Moore 1996, 33-64, Fitzmyer 2003, 3-17, Di Lella 2000, 198-199, and Otzen 2002, 60-66. Concerning the status of the book of Tobit and the terms 'Apocrypha' and 'deuterocanonical', see Moore 1996, xiv, 48-53, and Fitzmyer 2003, 55-57.
13   Moore 1996, 17-24, Nowell 1996, 568-569. See also Otzen 2002, 27-56, Fitzmyer 2002, 29-41, and Spencer 1999, 160.
14   See Murphy 1996, 83, Wright 1989, 510, and Clarke 1973, 1. For reasons of simplification, I will henceforth refer to the book as 'Wisdom'.

self by that name.[15] An anonymous 'I' addresses us in the book but the author's implied identification with the King is clear.[16] The claim of Solomonic authorship is best explained as a literary device to increase the book's authority, King Solomon being the archetypal wise leader in Jewish tradition. In this way, the author connected his work to the two most important earlier books of the wisdom tradition, Proverbs and Ecclesiastes, biblical books likewise attributed to the legendary wise king.[17]

The true identity of the author is unknown but he was most probably a learned, Greek-speaking Jew living in Alexandria, a main centre of the Jewish Diaspora in his time.[18] Some scholars have questioned the unity of Wisdom, but the predominant view today is that the book is the work of a single author. Wisdom was most certainly originally written in Greek.[19]

The date of Wisdom is debated; its composition has been placed from approximately 200 B.C.E to 50 C.E. Most scholars tend to date Wisdom to the latter half of the first century B.C.E.[20] Thus it is probably later than Ben Sirah, the other apocryphal/deuterocanonical book belonging to the wisdom "genre."

David Winston argues for its composition to be early first century C.E., more specifically during the reign of Caligula, 37-41 C.E.[21] It is generally acknowledged that the author made use of the LXX, the composition of which thus constitutes a *terminus post quem*. The influence of Wisdom on the NT has often been assumed, although there are no clear quotations from Wisdom in the NT.[22]

---

15   Cf., Eccl 1:1.
16   See e.g., Wisdom 8-9.
17   See for example Wright, 1989, 510, and Murphy, 1996, 83-84.
18   Most scholars assume Alexandria to be the most likely place of the book's composition, e.g., Murphy 1996, 83, Wright 1996, 510, Winston 1992, 123, Grabbe 1997, 90-91, and Clarke 1973, 1-3. The alleged reasons for an Alexandrian context of the book are manifold, for example, the focus on Egypt in chapters 11-19 as well as the Jewish-Hellenistic thought milieu reflected in the text, which closely resembles other Jewish-Alexandrian works from the same period. However, although likely, the Alexandrian origin of the book is by no means certain, and other places of composition have also been suggested, e.g., Jerusalem and Syria, see Grabbe 1997, 123.
19   See Winston 1979, 12-14, and 1992, 121-122, Grabbe 1997, 24-25, and Wright 1996, 510-511. The homogeneity of the language and the structure of the book are two main issues often pointed out as support for its unity.
20   See for example Clarke 1973, 1-2, Murphy 1996, 83, and Wright 1996, 510.
21   Winston 1979, 20-25, Cf., Grabbe (1997, 87-90) who questions Winston's dating and puts the writing of Wisdom in the era of Augustus.
22   See, for example, Murphy 1996, 83, cf., Grabbe 1997, 28-29, 88.

According to Wis 1:1 and chapters 6-9, the intended readers of the book are the kings and rulers of the earth but in view of the content of Wisdom, its author certainly had a much wider audience in mind. The author's main purpose was probably to encourage and strengthen his fellow Jews and to warn against assimilation.[23]

There are similarities between Wisdom and Philo's writings, and Philo has even been suggested as its author. This theory may be hard to prove but it is obvious that Philo and the author of Wisdom worked and lived in a similar intellectual and religious environment. They were both most probably Jewish residents of Alexandria and may have been roughly contemporary with each other.[24] Winston has proposed that the author of Wisdom was influenced by Philo,[25] although the common assumption is that Wisdom pre-dates Philo's works.[26]

The Gospel of Luke

It is firmly based in ancient Christian tradition that Luke, the physician and companion of the apostle Paul, is the author of the third Gospel.[27]

This is not the proper place for a discussion of Luke's sources but it is generally assumed that he used Mark's Gospel as well as the so-called Q-source. When it comes to the birth-narratives, he seems to have had access to other traditions as well. Luke's home-church is often identified as the congregation of Antioch and this is possibly also where the Gospel was composed.[28]

The Gospel of Luke was presumably written after the fall of Jerusalem in 70 C.E. It is commonly dated somewhere between 80-85 C.E., thus later than Tobit and Wisdom.[29]

---

23 See Winston 1992, 126, Murphy 1996, 84, and Grabbe 1997, 91-94. Thus, the conventional view is that the book was primarily written for the Jews of Alexandria, even though an intended gentile readership cannot be excluded.
24 Wright 1996, 510, Winston 1979, 59-63, Davis 1984, 49-62, and Murphy 1990, 83.
25 Winston 1979, 59-63.
26 See, e.g., Wright 1996, 510, and Clarke 1973, 2.
27 See, e.g., the Muratorian Canon, the attribution at the end of the oldest extant copy of the Gospel (175-225 C.E.) and Irenaeus' prologue to the Gospel. See Karris 1989, 675, and Nolland 1989, xxxiv-xxxv.
28 Marshall 1978, 30-35. See also Karris 1989, 675-676.
29 Marshall 1978, 34-35, and Karris 1989, 675-676. See also Nolland 1989, xxxvii-xxxix. The Gospel of Luke thus probably pre-dates Josephus' works. According to himself, Luke wrote his Gospel before his composition of Acts, see Acts 1:1-5.

Luke was probably not of Jewish origin[30] and presumably wrote his Gospel primarily for Gentile-Christians and presumptive Gentile converts, maybe the so-called 'God-fearers' who already were familiar with the God of Israel and the Jewish faith.[31] Luke dedicated his Gospel to a man named Theophilus, who otherwise, unfortunately, remains totally unknown.[32]

4.1.2 The Book of Tobit and the Gospel of Luke – Type-scenes

The Angel of the Lord as Traveling Companion, Protector and Guide

The book of Tobit contains a tale that has a great deal in common with Genesis 24. The author was most certainly inspired by that text.[33] As in Genesis 24, we have both a family tale about the marriage of two relatives and a tale of divine guidance.[34]

In both Genesis 24 and the book of Tobit, an angel plays the role of protector and guide during a journey to a distant land, although Raphael plays a far more active part in the plot of the book of Tobit compared to the anonymous angel mentioned in Gen 24:7, 40. But in both cases, it is the presence and guidance of the angel that ensures the success of the mission, see the text analysis of Genesis 24 above.[35] As a literary character Tobit appears to a high degree to be modeled on the patriarch Abraham.[36]

The Israelite family at the centre of the story is living in exile in Assyria. As for Abraham in Genesis 24, it is important for Tobit that his son Tobias should marry a relative and not take as wife a woman belonging to the strangers amongst whom they live.[37] The story has a happy end, and Tobias marries his relative Sarah.[38]

---

30   Nolland 1989, xxxv.
31   See Nolland 1989, xxxii-xxxiii, and Karris 1989, 676. Marshall (1978, 35-36), however, suggests that Luke wrote primarily for the "simple folk" among the people of Israel.
32   See Luke 1:1-4. The name Theophilus, meaning 'friend of God' may possibly be a pseudonym for God-fearing readers in general. See also Nolland 1989, xxxiii.
33   See also Moore 1996, 8-9, 20, 188-191, 217.
34   See also Westermann 1985, 392, and Spencer 1999, 158-159.
35   See also Nickelsburg 1996, 341, van den Eynde 2005, 273-280, Otzen 2002, 21-23, and Mach 1992, 144-148.
36   See, for example, Nowell 2005, 3-11.
37   See Tob 4:12-13. See also Nowell 2005, 3-11, Nickelsburg 1996, 341, van den Eynde 2005, 273-280, Otzen 2002, 21-23.
38   See Tobit chapters 5-11.

A main difference between the two narratives, however, is that To-bit does not send away his son for the explicit purpose of finding a bride. As a result of poverty, Tobit sends his son Tobias to Media in order to fetch some money which he has deposited in the hands of a man called Gabael.[39] As in Genesis 24, an angel is sent to accompany the traveler. Tobias, however, is unaware of his heavenly protection. He thinks that his guide is an Israelite man, by the name of Azariah.[40] In reality, his companion is no less than the angel Raphael:[41]

> [Tob 5:4] So Tobias went out to look for a man to go with him to Media, someone who was acquainted with the way. He went out and found the angel Raphael standing in front of him; but he did not perceive that he was an angel of God. [5] Tobias said to him, 'Where do you come from, young man? "From your kindred, the Israelites;" he replied, "and I have come here to work." Then Tobias said to him, "Do you know the way to go to Media?" [6] "Yes," he replied. "I have been there many times; I am acquainted with it and know all the roads..."

As will be shown below,[42] in Jewish tradition Raphael is one of 'the angels of Presence'.[43]

As in Genesis 24, prayer plays a central role in the story.[44] The angel is sent as an answer to prayer.[45] Although at this stage of the story both Tobit and Tobias are unaware of it, Raphael's commission is more than just to act as Tobias' guide; he was sent by God in order to heal Tobit

---

39 See also Otzen 2002, 21-23.

40 See Tob 5:13. The name Azariah means 'YHWH has helped', which is exactly the function that the angel has in the story. See also Fitzmyer 2003, 184, 192-193.

41 The name Raphael means 'God has healed', yet another hint concerning his role in the narrative, see also Fitzmyer 2003, 160-161.

42 See chapter 4.2.

43 See also Ego 2007, 244-245, and Barker 2006, 118-128. Although never denoted as such in the book of Tobit, Raphael is later regarded as one of the archangels. See Mach 1995, 1299-1300, and Newsom 1992, 252. Raphael is frequently mentioned in the Pseudepigrapha and in Qumran sources, e.g. 1 En. 20.1-7, and 40.1-10. See also Gieschen 1998, 135-136, and Moore 1996, 160-161, and 271-272. See also Otzen 2002, 45-49, and Skemp 2005, 51-53.

44 See also Reiterer 2007, 271-273, and Ego 2007, 245-246. The title 'God of heaven' used in prayer by both Abraham (Gen 24:3,7) and Raguel, Sarah's father (Tob 7:12; 8:15), is an additional connection between the two narratives. See also Nowell, 2005, 4-6.

45 When Raphael reveals his true identity to Tobit and Tobias he says that it was he who transmitted Sarah's and Tobit's prayers to God; Tob 12:12 see below. He is a mediator between God and humanity, an angelic function typical of Second Temple apocalyptic writings, see, for example, 1 Enoch 9; 40; 99.3, 104.1, and Rev 8:3-4. See also Nickelsburg 1996, 344, Fitzmyer 2003, 294-295, Skemp 2005, 53 and Barker 2006, 120.

and to arrange the marriage between Tobias and Sarah, thus delivering her from the demon that afflicts her.[46]

The readers of the book of Tobit know more than the characters in the narrative. They are informed from the outset that Raphael is an angel and that a main issue in the plot is the quest for a bride; facts that recall other stories of journeys in order to acquire a bride from one's own people, such as Genesis 24 and 28-29. In many ways, Raphael's function as a match-maker seems to be modeled on the role of Abraham's servant in Genesis 24.[47] However, an obvious difference is of course that Raphael is an angel, thus reminding the readers of the servant's invisible companion.[48] When he sends his son away, Tobit says to him:

> ...May God in heaven bring you safely there [Media] and return you[49] in good health to me; and may his angel, my son, accompany you both [Tobias and Raphael/Azariah] for your safety. [Tob 5:17, cf., Gen 24:7][50]

When they leave, Tobias' mother starts to cry, and Tobit comforts his wife and says:

> Do not worry, our child will leave in good health and return to us in good health [...] Do not fear for them, my sister. For a good angel[51] will accompany him; his journey will be successful, and he will come back in good health. [Tob 5:21-22].[52]

Considering the fact that the readers are by now informed that Tobias is actually traveling together with the angel Raphael, the story is here

---

46   Tob 3:16-17. See also Nowell 2007, 230-231, Moore 1996, 29-30, and van den Eynde 2005, 274-279. As mentioned above, providence is a major theme both in Tobit and in Genesis 24. The marriages of both Isaac and Tobias are decided and arranged by God, see Gen 24:50, and Tob 7:11. See also Fitzmyer 2003, 218.

47   See Nickelsburg 1996, 341, and Otzen 2002, 21.

48   When discussing the similarities between the book of Tobit and Genesis 24, Otzen (2002, 21) holds that the weak point in the comparison of the two narratives is that the servant travels alone, a statement that I find highly peculiar in light of Abraham's words in Gen 24:7. Although the angelic companion remains invisible and silent in Genesis 24, it does not imply that he is not present.

49   In all the extant versions of Tobit, the Greek word for "you" is here in the plural form. Tobit is thus praying for divine protection for both his son and his (de facto) angelic companion, thus heightening the irony of the tale. See also Fitzmyer 2003, 196.

50   See also Tob 5:15-16.

51   It seems apparent that the author of Tobit also believed in "bad" angels. See also Moore 1996, 190.

52   In the LXX, the same Greek verb εὐοδόω, 'succeed' which is used in Tob 5:17 (and in 10:11, 14) is also used in Gen 24:40 (and in vv. 21, 42, 48, 56). See also Fitzmyer 2003, 199, and Otzen 2002, 21.

slightly ironic.[53] According to Carey Moore, Tobit's certainty of angelic protection:

> ... for the reader familiar with Gen 24:40, it foreshadows how Tobit's Sarah will be delivered, that is, in Gen 24:40 Eliezer tells Laban that in his search for a wife for Isaac an invisible angel would accompany him.[54]

The quest for a bride and angelic company on a journey are thus common motifs in the two stories, creating a type-scene. The readers and author of Tobit were certainly familiar with the narrative in Genesis 24, and the similarities are most certainly not coincidental.[55] In the words of Hedvig Larsson: "By using this kind of type-scene a narrator could alert his audience that they could expect the narrative to develop in a certain pattern."[56]

There are also parallels between the book of Tobit and Jacob's journey to Haran and subsequent marriage to his cousins Rachel and Leah in Genesis 28-29. Both Tobit and Isaac suffer from blindness[57] and both fathers admonish their sons to marry a woman of their own kin and, like Tobit, Isaac sends his son on a journey to a distant land.[58] The theme of divine/angelic protection of a traveler is also present in the Jacob-narrative, see for example, Gen 28:10-15; 31:3-22.

As will be shown in chapter 4.2, there is a clear similarity between Isaac's words to his wife when Jacob leaves home in *Jub.* 27.13-18 and Tob 5:21-22 quoted above. Most probably, the author of *Jubilees* made use of the book of Tobit.[59]

The angel Raphael hence accompanies Tobias to Media. During the journey, Raphael arranges a meeting between Tobias and his relative Sarah, who becomes his wife, chapters 6-8. Raphael also instructs Tobias how to repel the demon Asmodeus[60] and in this way saves Sarah

---

53 See also Nowell 2007, 233-237, and Fitzmyer 2003, 184-185, 196-199.

54 Moore 1996, 188. See also pages 190-191. The protecting role of the angels is a popular motif in pseudepigraphical works of the Second Temple period. E.g. *1 En.* 100.5; *T. Jud.* 3.10.

55 See van den Eynde 2005, 275-280 and Fitzmyer 2003, 161. As mentioned in the text analysis of Genesis 24, the motif of angels as protectors is frequently found in the Bible, e.g., Exod 14:19-20; 23:20-23, and Ps 91:11. See also Skemp 2005, 52.

56 H. Larsson 2006, 67.

57 Gen 27:1, cf., Tob 2:7-10.

58 Gen 28:1-5. See for example Nowell 2005, 5-11, and van den Eynde 2005, 275-278. There are striking similarities in wording between the LXX Gen 29:4-6 and Tob 7:3-5.

59 See also Moore 1996, 193-194, Otzen 2002, 23, and Spencer 1999, 160-161.

60 The demon Asmodeus is also mentioned in, for example, the Babylonian Talmud, e.g. *b. Gittin* 68a-b; *b. Pesahim* 110a. He likewise appears in *Testament of Solomon*, chapter 5, where Raphael is mentioned as the angel who thwarts him. Moore (1996, 147) writes: "... scholars are still debating whether the name is based upon the Heb.

once and for all from the demon who had killed all her former husbands, see chapters 3 and 8.[61] According to Moore, the book of Tobit

> ... represents a major step in the evolution of the biblical understanding of demons [...] and, especially, of angels [...]. Here are mentioned for the first time in Scripture two supernatural creatures who will figure quite prominently in subsequent Jewish and Christian traditions: the archangel Raphael and the demon Asmodeus.[62]

Tobias returns safely to his parents with the money and his wife, chapter 11. Raphael is also active in curing the blindness of Tobit, see 6:2-9; 10:14, and 11:7-8.[63]

The Doxology in Tobit 11

According to Charles Gieschen, Tob 11:14-15 deserves our special attention because of the veneration of the angels expressed in the doxology. In his discussion of the verses, he refers to Loren Stuckenbruck, who claims that the recension of the verses in the Codex Sinaiticus is earlier than the type which appears in other Greek manuscripts. In this version the doxology is in the third person and contains two blessings of angels:[64]

šmd, 'to destroy', [Cf., Exod 12:23] or represents the Persian *aeshma daēva* or *aesmadiv*, 'the demon of anger', who accompanied Ahriman (*Angra Mainyu*), the God of Evil." See also Hutter 1995, 197-200, and Fitzmyer 2003, 150-151.

61 See also the Pseudepigraphical book *Joseph and Aseneth*, wherein an angel plays an active role in the arrangement of the marriage of the two main characters, chapters 14-17.

62 Moore 1996, 28. See also Hutter 1995, 197-200. In *1 En.* 10.4 Raphael is ordered by God to handle another demon in a similar way: "... bind Azazel by his hands and feet and throw him into the darkness; and split open the desert that is in Dudadel and throw him there." The belief in demons and spiritual warfare that we encounter in the book of Tobit is reminiscent of the demonology and exorcism of the NT. See also Skemp 2005, 58-60, Fitzmyer 2003, 243, Otzen 2002, 47-49, and Nickelsburg 1996, 344. The predominant view among scholars is thus that the book of Tobit bears witness to a rather developed angelology, see, for example, Fitzmyer 2003, 160. Barker (2006, 118-128), however, appears to be of a different opinion. For a more detailed discussion of this issue, see below.

63 According to the book of Tobit, Raphael thus had three tasks to accomplish; the cure of Tobit's blindness, the arrangement of Sarah's and Tobias' marriage and the expulsion of the demon Asmodeus. This contradicts later Rabbinic tradition that one angel cannot perform more than one mission. See chapter 4.5 below and Barker 2006, 126.

64 In the text version generally used, the doxology is in the 2nd person and contains only one blessing of the angels. See Gieschen 1998, 136, and Stuckenbruck 1995, 164-167.

[Tob 11:14b] Blessed God and Blessed his great Name and Blessed all his holy angels; may his great Name be upon us, and *blessed all the angels unto all ages.* [15] For he has afflicted me. But now I see my son Tobias![65]

According to Gieschen, it is significant that God and the angels are praised side by side in the doxology, something that Stuckenbruck also acknowledges. However, Gieschen also points out that we here may have "… the possible identification of the Divine Name Angel who may be addressed in this prayer as 'His Name.'" This would mean that Tobit is not only praising all the angels but possibly one angel individually as the hypostatized name. This doxology indicates that individuals did not only worship together with angels but also venerated them along with God.[66]

To me, the assumed connection between the divine-name angel (Exod 23:20-21) and this doxology seems far-fetched but the veneration of the angels alongside God is nevertheless noteworthy, as it is somewhat unusual in Jewish sources. However, the blessing of the angels does not necessarily indicate that they are placed on the same level as God.

Angels in Human Disguise

A major issue in the plot of the story of Tobit is the fact that Raphael initially conceals his angelic identity and presents himself as an Israelite man.[67] Like the three "men" in Genesis 18-19, Raphael also appears in human disguise. This is a very common phenomenon in biblical angelophanies, see also, for example, Hagar's encounter with the angel of the Lord in Genesis 16[68] and the narratives in Genesis 32, Joshua 5, as well as Judges 6 and 13. The revelations of the heavenly messengers often seem to follow a similar pattern: They appear in human form, deliver a crucial message and are not recognized as divine emissaries

---

65   Eng. trans. Gieschen 1998, 136 [my italics]. In this case, the translators of the NRSV including Apocrypha (1989) do not follow the Codex Sinaiticus, and Tob 11:14b-15 is translated in the following way:

[14] "Blessed be God, and blessed be his great name, and blessed be all his holy angels. May his holy name be blessed throughout all the ages. [15] Though he afflicted me, he has had mercy upon me. Now I see my son Tobias!"

66   Gieschen 1998, 136.

67   See also Nowell 2007, 233-237.

68   Although it is not explicitly stated that the angel of the Lord appeared to Hagar in the form of a man, it seems to be implied in the story, see chapter 3.

until their departure. We may define this scenario as a type-scene common to many of these narratives. The divine emissaries are also very often offered hospitality in the form of food; Genesis 18-19; Judges 6 and 13. The allusion in Hebr 13:2 bears witness to this tradition:[69] "Do not neglect to show hospitality to strangers, for by doing that some have entertained angels without knowing it." In contrast to both Raphael and the angel of the Lord in Judges 6 and 13, however, Abraham's three visitors are said to have eaten the food offered to them.[70]

When Tobias and his father want to reward the man who accompanied him on the journey, Raphael, to their astonishment, reveals who he is:

> [Tob 12:6] Then Raphael called the two of them [Tobit and Tobias] privately and said to them, "Bless God and acknowledge him in the presence of all the living for the good things he has done for you... [11] "I will now declare the whole truth to you and conceal nothing from you... [12] So now when you [Tobit] and Sarah prayed, it was I who brought and read the record of your prayer before the glory of the Lord...[14] I was sent to you to test you [Tobit]. And at the same time God sent me to heal you and Sarah your daughter-in-law. [15] I am Raphael, one of the seven angels who stand ready and enter before the glory of the Lord."[71] [16] The two of them

---

69 See also Sullivan 2004, 37-83, 179-195, Kolenkow 1976, 153-162, and Fitzmyer 2003, 187-188. Moore (1996, 183-184) writes: "Starting with Genesis (18:1-8; 19:1-3) and continuing through the New Testament (cf., Heb 13:2), angels are virtually indistinguishable from human beings. In fact, they are often mistaken for mortals. The depiction of angels, complete with wings and haloes, so common in Christian paintings and sculpture, represents artistic conventions, not biblical descriptions."

70 During Second Temple times, the standard Jewish interpretation of Genesis 18-19 was that the three men did not actually eat at Mamre, it was only a vision. Cf., Josephus' interpretation of Genesis 18 in *Ant.* 1.196-198 and that of Philo in *On Abraham* 118 as well as the Palestinian Targums to Gen 18:8, e.g., *Tg. Neof.*: "Then he [Abraham] took curds and milk and the calf which he had prepared, and placed it before them [his three guests]; and he stood beside them under the tree and *they were giving the impression of eating and drinking*" (Eng. trans. McNamara 1992, 104). In the Talmud as well as in Cabbalistic lore, Raphael is said to be one of the three angels who visited Abraham. He is credited with the healing of Abraham from the pain from his circumcision. See Scholem 1971, 1549, and Guiley 2004, 311. See also the treatment of Genesis 18 in the *Testament of Abraham*. Considering the question whether or not angels eat, see Goodman 1986, 160-175. In Tob 6:6, there is a difference between the versions GII and GI. In the latter, it is explicitly said that not only Tobias but *both* he and Raphael ate the fish caught from the river Tigris, a statement that is corrected by Tob 12:19; Raphael did not really eat, it was a vision. See also Ego 2007, 249.

71 Note that Raphael designates himself as one of the seven highest angels, angels standing before God's throne. The later tradition of seven archangels is thus anticipated in the book of Tobit. Cf., Luke 1:19: "And the angel [Gabriel] answered him

were shaken; they fell face down, for they were afraid. [17] But he [Raphael] said to them, "Do not be afraid;[72] peace be with you. Bless God forevermore. As for me, when I was with you, I was not acting on my own will, but by the will of God. Bless him each and every day... [19] Although you were watching me, I really did not eat or drink anything–but what you saw was a vision. [20] So now get up from the ground, and acknowledge God. See, I am ascending to him who sent me. Write down all these things that have happened to you."[73] [21] Then they stood up, and could see him no more. [22] They kept blessing God and singing praises, and they acknowledged God for these marvelous deeds of his, when an angel of God had appeared to them.

Raphael and the angel of the Lord in Judges 6 and 13

The disclosure of the identity of the angel Raphael in Tobit 12 is similar in many ways to the narrative in Judges 13, another text where an angel of the Lord plays a central role. There are clear parallels between Tobit 12 and the revelation of the angel of the Lord to Manoah and his wife. Alexander Di Lella has pointed out no less than eight intertextual connections between the two stories and he concludes that the author of Tobit most assuredly modeled his narrative of Raphael's disclosure of his true identity on Judges 13.[74] One such connecting link is the fact that Raphael says that in reality he did not eat or drink anything, it was a vision; Tob 12:19. The angel of the Lord refuses to eat the food that Manoah offers him:

> [Judg 13:16] The angel of the LORD said to Manoah, "If you detain me, I will not eat your food; but if you want to prepare a burnt offering, then offer it to the LORD." (For Manoah did not know that he was the angel of the LORD.)[75]

[Zechariah] and said to him, 'I am Gabriel who stands in the presence of God...'" See also Rev 1:4; 3:1; 4:5; 8:2, and Zech 4:10; *T. Levi* 3.4-8, and *1 En.* 71.8-9.

72   A typical angelic exhortation, see also, for example, Gen 21:17; Dan 10:12, 19; Luke 1:13, 30; 2:10.

73   The commission to write down the past events/visions in a book is quite common in angel-ophanies, especially in apocalyptic writings, see Daniel 10-12, Rev 19:9; 22:9-10, and Nickelsburg 1984, 46.

74   Di Lella 2000, 205. According to Di Lella, some similarities between the two narratives are the healing of Manoah's wife from barrenness which corresponds to Raphael's healing of Tobit's blindness (cf., Gabriel's promise of a son to the elderly and barren couple Zechariah and Elizabeth in Luke 1 and the prediction of Isaac's birth to Abraham and Sarah in Genesis 18), the initial human disguise of the angelic visitor, the theme of prayer, the offering of food, and the ascension of the heavenly messenger. For details, see Di Lella 2000, 199-206.

75   It is also noteworthy, that similar to Jacob's contender in Gen 32:29, the angel of the Lord in Judg 13:17-18 refuses to reveal his name to Manoah and his wife.

Like Tobias and his father, Manoah and his wife did not at first realize that they were visited by a divine messenger. The wife designates him "a man of God" or simply "the man," Judg 13:6, 10. It is not until their departure that the heavenly visitors reveal who they really are. The reaction of Tobias and his father to this disclosure is similar to that of Manoah and his wife. Compare Tob 12:16-21 cited above with Judg 13:20-21:

> [20] When the flame [of the burnt offering] went up toward heaven from the altar, the angel of the LORD ascended in the flame of the altar while Manoah and his wife looked on; and they fell on their faces to the ground. [21] The angel of the LORD did not appear again to Manoah and his wife. Then Manoah realized that it was the angel of the LORD.

This scenario closely resembles the account in Judg 6:18-20 where we read that Gideon prepared a meal for the angel of the Lord but the food was consumed by fire and his heavenly visitor vanished.[76] In the same way as the angel of the Lord, Raphael also disappears very suddenly; "Then they [Tobit and Tobias] stood up, and could see him no more" [Tob 12:21].

However, an important difference between the book of Tobit and the narrative in Judges 13 is expressed by the words of Manoah to his wife in Judg 13:22: "*We shall surely die, for we have seen God.*" In contrast to the angel of the Lord in Judges 13, Raphael is very careful to distinguish between himself and God. He encourages Tobit and Tobias to praise and worship God, not himself. See, for example, Tob 12:18: "... *As for me, when I was with you, I was not acting on my own will, but by the will of God. Bless him each and every day ...*"[77]

The angel of the Lord in Judges 13, on the other hand, seems to accept worship. As in, for example, Genesis 16, the identity of the angel and God is merged in Judges 13, in clear contrast to Tobit 12. The difference between the two heavenly messengers is similar to the distinction between the angel of the Lord in Genesis 16 and the angel Gabriel who appears to Mary in Luke 1, and I will discuss these two texts below. But first, let us take a closer look at another narrative in the Gospel of Luke, the encounter with the risen Christ in chapter 24, which in many ways is reminiscent of Raphael's role in Tobit 5-12, as well as the appearances of the angel of the Lord in Judges 6 and 13.

---

76   See also Di Lella 2000, 202-205, and Goodman 1986, 166-169.
77   Cf., Rev 19:9-10; 22:8-9. See also Ego 2007, 251-252.

The risen Christ in Luke 24

In many ways Luke presents the resurrected Jesus in angelic terms. Like Tobias, the two men heading for Emmaus are accompanied on their journey by an incognito heavenly being, though the readers are informed of his true identity; Luke 24:15-16, cf., Tob 5:4. The disciples do not recognize the risen Christ until he breaks the bread and suddenly vanishes from their sight; Luke 24:30-32, cf., Tob 12:21-22. In the 'breaking of the bread' scholars have seen an allusion to the Eucharist, the Christian "sacrifice," and some of them interpret Luke 24:30-32 in the light of the angelophanies in Judges 6 and 13; when the angel of the Lord is offered food/a sacrifice, he ascends to heaven.[78]

However, Luke's resurrection narrative does not end there. According to Luke 24:36-50, the risen Christ appeared once more to his disciples, this time in Jerusalem. The disciples are frightened when they see him, and they think that he must be a ghost/spirit. Jesus' sudden appearance surely has angelic connotations.[79] In order to assure them of his corporality, Jesus eats in their presence, thus abolishing all their doubts.[80]

In this narrative, it seems evident that Luke wanted to counterfeit the assumption that the risen Christ is to be understood as an angel, since according to Jewish belief, angels do not eat, cf., Tob 12:19, and Judg 13:16.

We may conclude, however, that in his description of the risen Christ, Luke appears to have been inspired by Jewish traditions concerning encounters with heavenly beings, such as those contained in the book of Tobit and Judges 13.[81]

The Angelic Annunciation of the Birth of a Special Child

As shown in chapter 3 'the angel of the Lord' is generally described in the Bible as a benefactor,[82] and has always a special reason for his appearance. He delivers a crucial message, of great importance in the (salvation-) history of Israel. Very common is the announcement of the

---

78 See Fletcher-Louis 1997, 62-63, Sullivan 2004, 191-192, and Skemp 2005, 54-58. Cf., also Raphael's words in Tob 12:20 with Jesus' words in John 16:5: "But now I am going to him who sent me…"

79 Cf., Luke 24:36-37, and Tob 12:16-17.

80 Luke 24:41-43.

81 Fletcher-Louis 1997, 63-71, Skemp 2005, 53-58 and Goodman 1986,168.

82 As we have seen above, the angel is *the Redeemer* [הגאל], cf., Gen 48:16.

birth of a child, or the announcement of salvation, two elements that are often combined.[83] The angelic promise of a child follows a distinct pattern. The child is a special gift from God, and the woman in question is often described as barren. The birth of the child is a miracle. The parents of Ishmael, Isaac, Samson, John the Baptist[84] and Jesus all encounter divine emissaries.[85] This angelic annunciation is so frequent in the Bible that it may be defined as a so-called type-scene.[86]

Hagar and the angel and the annunciation of Mary
There are some striking parallels between the story of Hagar in Gen 16:7-14 and the annunciation in Luke 1:26-38.[87] Of course an obvious difference between Hagar and Mary (as well as Elizabeth and Manoah's wife) is that the former is already pregnant by natural means when she meets the angel but the angelophany in both annunciation-stories follows a similar pattern.

According to both Gen 16:8 and Luke 1:28, the angel first addresses Hagar and Mary with a greeting. In neither of the stories does he introduce himself to the woman. According to Westermann, in the original narrative, vv. 11-12 in Genesis 16 followed immediately on the greeting in v. 8.[88]

---

83   Cf., Judg 13:2-5; Gen 18:9-15; 16:7-14; 21:17-20; 22:11-18. See also Westermann 1985, 242. The only concrete occasion when the angel is depicted as turning against Israel is in 2 Sam 24:15-16, cf., 1 Chr 21:14-30, see also von Rad 1964, 77 and Freedman-Willoughby 1997, 318. See also above, sections 3.2.1 and 3.3.3.

84   There are evident structural similarities between the annunciations to Mary and Zechariah According to Luke 1:11-20, the angel Gabriel appeared to the father of John the Baptist. Gabriel foretells the *birth of a son* to him and his wife, despite their old age, and *predicts the name and the destiny/task* of their child. According to, for example, Brown (1999, 269), Luke was clearly influenced by the narrative of the divine promise of the birth of a son to another elderly and barren couple, Sarah and Abraham. See also Nolland 1989, 17-36.

85   See also the story about Hannah and her son in 1 Samuel 1-2. Although no angel is mentioned, it is apparent that the birth of Samuel is a special gift from God, an answer to Hannah's prayer. Jesus' case is of course unique, since the NT here speaks about a virgin birth. Joseph is his adoptive father. An angel of the Lord appears to Joseph in his dream; see Matt 1:20-21 and 2:13. See also Brown (reprinted ed.) 1999, 156-158, 231, note 1, and 268-269. For a discussion of Brown's book, see, for example, Conrad 1985, 656-663.

86   See chapter 1.3.2 above, Alter 1981, 47-62, and Coleridge 1993, 31-37.

87   See also Westermann 1985, 242-243, and 245-246.

88   Westermann 1985, 245. He writes on the same page: "The promise in vv. 11-12 has a defined structure, attested by a series of parallels, which points to a narrative form which has its base in the oral tradition stage."

There is, however, an important difference between the pericopes. In Luke 1:26, the narrator informs us that it was *the angel Gabriel* who was sent to Mary in Nazareth. The identity of the angel is thus clear.[89] Gabriel always refers to God in the third person; he is clearly separate from God. In contrast, the angel of the Lord in Genesis 16 appears very suddenly and unexpectedly, he comes from "nowhere" and speaks to Hagar. As Westermann says, "… he is unknown; he comes from and returns to the unknown."[90] The identity of the angel and God is here merged in a confusing way. These characteristics of the angel of the Lord are not present in the narrative of the annunciation in Luke 1. There are, however, obvious structural similarities between the two texts.[91] In both cases, the divine emissary delivers a message concerning the birth of a son. After his greeting, the angel tells the mother what name she shall give her son and predicts his destiny:[92]

---

89   Note that Gabriel in Luke 1:26-38 is never called 'the angel of the Lord'.
90   Westermann 1985, 243. See also chapter 3 above.
91   Westermann (1985, 245) writes:

This [the similarity of Gen. 16:8, 11-12 and Luke 1:28, 30b-32] is a rare and astounding example of the perseverance of a form over a period of more than a thousand years […]

A comparison with Lk. 1:11-17 shows that the form is open to variation […] The form has the following parts: (1) Introduction: a messenger of God is there (greeting); (2) announcement of pregnancy and a birth of a son is introduced by הנה; (3) specification of the name of the son with the reason explaining the name; (4) announcement of what will become of the child. The constant element, which is never missing, is the announcement of the birth of a son; and this is what the form as a whole is all about; all other parts are directed to or subordinated to this: originally it is probably the announcement of the birth of a son to a childless woman. It is as such the announcement of salvation or of the turning point in a crisis and so coincides with the narratives of a messenger of God; he comes to announce the change in the lot. But the examples show that the form can also be used in other situations, as in Gen. 16, where the announcement leads to another crisis.

92   Cf., the words of the angel of the Lord to Samson's mother in Judg 13:3-5, where the message of the angel of the Lord also follows a similar pattern. See also Klein 2007, 318-319.

Gen 16:8, 11-12 and Luke 1:28, 31-33

[Gen 16:8] And he [the angel of the Lord] said; "Hagar, slave-girl of Sarai, where have you come from and where are you going?"	[Luke 1:28] And he [the angel Gabriel] came to her [Mary] and said, "Greetings, favored one! The Lord is with you."
[11] …"Now you have conceived and shall bear a son;	[31] "… And now, you will conceive in your womb and bear a son,
you shall call him Ishmael,	and you will name him Jesus.
for the LORD has given heed to your affliction.	[32] He will be great, and will be called the Son of the Most High, and the Lord God will give to him the throne of his ancestor David.
[12] He shall be a wild ass of a man, with his hand against everyone, and everyone's hand against him; and he shall live at odds with all his kin."	[33] He will reign over the house of Jacob forever, and of his kingdom there will be no end."

The commissions of the angels are similar in these cases; the annunciation of the *birth of a son*, his *name*, and a *foretelling of his task/destiny*. The content of the tasks/destinies of Ishmael and Jesus is of course different but the literal structure of the messages to the two women follows the same pattern. Likewise, the function of the heavenly emissary is the same in both narratives. The pericopes share the same motif, the angelic announcement of the birth of a son.[93] According to John Collins, the archangel Gabriel in the Gospel of Luke "…is a messenger from God and takes over the role of the 'Angel of the LORD' of the Hebrew Bible, in announcing the birth of John the Baptist and Jesus."[94]

However, the ambivalence concerning the merged identity between God and the messenger that we find in Genesis 16 does not appear in Luke 1. Hagar's response to the words of the divine emissary is that she indeed has seen God, v. 13. Mary's reaction to the angel's message is to question how all this is about to happen, since she has no husband, v. 34. The angel who visits Mary is explicitly identified as Gabriel by the narrator, v. 26.

---

93 However, the annunciation of the birth of Jesus to Mary also strongly evokes the calling-narratives of the OT, e.g., Judg 6:11-24; Exodus 3, and Jer 1:4-10. See also Wyler 1996, 136-138, and Nolland 1989, 39-59.

94 Collins 1995, 641.

In fact, the merged identity between the angel of the Lord and God Himself is not found anywhere in the NT. In this respect, Samuel Meier is correct, when he writes that " … the NT knows of no single 'The angel of the Lord/God,' for the definite article never appears when a figure identified by this phrase makes its first appearance–it is always 'an angel of the Lord' (Matt 1:20; 2:13,19; 28:2; Luke 1:11; 2:9; John 5:4; Acts 5:19; 8:26; 10:3 ["of God"]; 12:7.23; Gal 4:14)."[95]

Concluding Remarks

Let us now turn to a comparison of the angelology presented in these various pericopes. The angel who guides Tobit is named[96] but the angel in Genesis 24 is anonymous. The angel Raphael plays a much more active part in the story than the angel in Genesis 24, who is mentioned only in vv. 7 and 40.

The reason for the more developed angelology of the book of Tobit compared to Genesis 24 is most probably that Tobit reflects a later stage in the development of the Israelite religion. As a named angel with a distinct personality, Raphael distinguishes himself from 'the angel of the Lord', the theophanic angel.[97] It is also worth noting that the OT texts that seem to distinguish between the angel of the Lord and God are generally to be found in later biblical texts, e.g., 1 Chr 21:14-15.[98]

However, in this respect there is an important difference between Genesis 16 and Judges 13 compared to Genesis 24. In the latter, we do not find the merged identity of the angel and God. As mentioned above in the text analysis, this is the only reference to an angel in the singular in Genesis, where the distinction between God and His angel seems clear. The angel in Genesis 24 may very well be an "ordinary" one. If Claus Westermann is correct in his assumption that the reference to the angel in Genesis 24 is a later insertion,[99] this could thus explain the distinction between the angel and God in this pericope.

The religion of the Hebrew Bible/OT must not be confused with the many forms of Jewish faith at the time of Jesus. There is a considerable timespan between the writing down of Genesis 16 and Luke 1. The merging of the identity of the divine messenger and God can be ex-

---

95   Meier 1995b, 98.
96   Cf., the angel Gabriel in Luke 1:26-27.
97   See, e.g., Fitzmyer 2003, 160, and Finkelstein 1929, 238.
98   Cf., above, chapter 1.4.
99   Westermann 1985, 383-384. See also the text analysis in chapter 3.2.4 above.

plained as characteristic of an earlier time. During the Second Temple period, the angelology of Israel became more developed; the angels received names and thus became individualized.[100] It may well be that the distance between God and humanity was regarded as greater at a later stage in Israel's history; God prefers to send angels to communicate with His people.

As shown in chapter 1.4, the Sadducees regarded the angels who appear in the Pentateuch as a kind of impersonal extension of God. The statement in Acts 23:8 should not be understood to mean that the Sadducees denied the existence of angels altogether but that they rejected the idea of angels as independent spiritual beings with a distinct personality and will of their own, an angelology which the Pharisees embraced.[101]

While most scholars regard the description of Raphael in the book of Tobit as an example of this kind of later angelology, Barker understands him "... as a manifestation of one aspect of the Lord,"[102] an interpretation that seems quite close to the Sadduceean view of angels.

According to Margaret Barker, the book of Tobit preserves memories of the religion of Israel during the First Temple period, before the reform of king Josiah and the victory of the Deuteronomistic "school;" the religion of Isaiah and Job.[103] In her view, the dualism present in the books of Tobit and Job is an expression of this older theology; the misfortunes of Sarah and Job are caused by an evil supernatural being, their sufferings are not a punishment for sin.[104] On the basis of the merged identity of the angel of the Lord and God in Genesis and, for example, Isa 9:6 (v. 5 in the MT), Barker argues that in the older Israelite religion, the divine presence had been manifold and that the angels had represented divergent divine characteristics before they came to be understood as distinct beings, separate from God. Accordingly, Raphael, for example, whose name means 'God heals' had formerly been the healing aspect of the Lord and, of the four 'throne names' in

---

100 E.g., Dan 9:21; 10:12-14, 12:1, and Tob 12:11-15. See also Brown 1999, 129 and 260.

101 See also Finkelstein 1929, 235-240.

102 Barker 2006, 118-128, esp. p. 124.

103 Barker 2006, 118-119, 128. As support for her theory, Barker points out that the Deuteronomistic theology does not seem to leave any room for angels. As support she refers to Isa 37:16 versus 2 Kgs 19:15, see Barker 2006, p. 119 and note 4. As is well known, there are no angels mentioned in the MT-version of Deuteronomy.

104 According to Barker (2006, 118-119), the books of Job and Tobit thus do not conform to the Deuteronomistic theory of divine reward-retribution. However, this seems to be rather a marginal standpoint. As stated above, many scholars see clear examples of a Deuteronomistic influence on the theology of the book of Tobit.

Isaiah 9, 'Prince of Peace' represents Raphael. Barker thus claims that during the Second Temple period the Lord was still remembered as "a cluster of angels," to use her expression.[105]

It seems reasonable that the revelations of 'the angel of the Lord' in, for example, Genesis 16 and Judges 13 are expressions of this early stage of the Israelite religion; 'the angel of the Lord' may be seen as a manifestation of God on earth. However, I agree with most scholars that the angel Raphael in the book of Tobit can hardly be put into the same category.

Like Gabriel in Luke 1, Raphael is clearly presented as an individual separate from God. The mere fact that they both have their own names indicates their independency as distinct personalities and distinguishes them from the angel of the Lord, who is always nameless and anonymous.[106]

It is also highly questionable that the presence of demonic characters (Satan and Asmodeus) in Job and Tobit respectively is an expression of Israel's pre-Josianic faith, since both are portrayed as angelic/spiritual beings acting independently and in opposition to God.[107]

4.1.3 The Wisdom of Solomon – Allusions

Wisdom and the Angel of the Lord – Some Introductory Remarks

In the Wisdom of Solomon there are some notable connections to 'the angel of the Lord' in Genesis and Exodus. There is much to say about the concept of wisdom but this is not the proper place for an elaboration of the 'wisdom-theology' of Israel in general. However, in order to demonstrate the parallels between the two concepts, I wish to briefly point out the Exodus connections, although the main focus is on the Genesis-texts.

---

105 Barker 2006, 123-126. Isa 9:5 [6] is rendered differently in the MT and the LXX, see also chapters 2.2.2 and 3.4.1 in this dissertation. As shown in chapter 2.2.2, in an earlier book Barker (1992, 36) instead attributes the title 'Prince of Peace' to the angel Phanuel, while Raphael is associated with the title 'Everlasting Father.'

106 Note that the angel of the Lord in Judg 13:18 refuses to reveal his name, as does Jacob's contender in Gen 32:30. Cf., Luke 1:19 where the angel identifies himself in front of Zechariah and proclaims: "I am Gabriel. I stand in the presence of God, and I have been sent to you…" See e.g., Tob 12:15, and Finkelstein 1929, 219-220.

107 According to, for example, Skemp (2005, 58-60), the book of Tobit and the NT in many ways share a similar demonology.

According to Lester Grabbe, Wisdom chapters 10-19 may be labeled a kind of Hellenistic Jewish Midrash on the biblical history in Genesis and Exodus.[108] This section is of interest for our quest, since it bears witness to the same ambiguity between God and 'Lady Wisdom' found between 'the angel of the Lord' and God in these biblical books. Regarding the Wisdom of Solomon Helmer Ringgren writes:

> The relation of Wisdom to God is here dealt with in greater detail than in the other [wisdom-] books, but at the same time it remains obscure in a peculiar way. This is most apparent in the last chapters of the book, 10-19. For in Chap. 10 Wisdom is the divine power, active in history. In the following chapters the grammatical subject changes imperceptibly and becomes God himself.[109]

Wisdom chapter 10 constitutes a hymn dedicated to the personified 'Lady Wisdom' and her works from the creation of humankind to the exodus of Israel from Egypt.[110] She is described as the one who led and protected the Israelites during their exodus from Egypt (Wis 10:17-19) and also to have guided them through the desert (chapter 11),[111] acts that the Hebrew Bible ascribes to either God Himself (Exod 13:21-22; 14:24, and 15:1-19; Deut 4:34-38; Ps 105:23-45) or the angel of God (Exod 14:19; 23:20-23; Num 20:15-16; Judg 2:1).[112] Thus, she plays the same role as the "angel" of the Exodus-tradition.[113] The same parallelism that exists between the angel and God Himself is applicable to the relationship between God and 'Lady Wisdom':

> [Wis 10:15] A holy people and blameless race wisdom delivered from a nation of oppressors. [16] She entered the soul of the servant of the Lord [Moses][114] and withstood dread kings with wonders and signs […] [17b] she guided them [the Israelites] along a marvelous way, and became a shelter to them by day, and a starry flame through the night. [18] She brought

---

108 Grabbe 1997, 18-25, 39-43.

109 Ringgren 1947, 115, see also pp. 116-119 and Winston 1979, 34.

110 See also Perdue 1994, 308-310. According to Winston (1992, 124), in contrast to the earlier wisdom books of Proverbs, Job and Ben Sira, 'Lady Wisdom' in the Wisdom of Solomon may be classified as a hypostasis. See also Grabbe 1997, 77-80, and Ringgren 1947, 115-119. However, according to Murphy (1992, 926), it is better to talk about 'Lady Wisdom' in this book also as a personification of God's wisdom, rather than as a hypostasis, which view is shared by Dunn (1989, 163-176).

111 See also Perdue 1994, 310-313.

112 The exact meaning of Deut 4:37 and Judg 2:1 is, however, debated, see chapter 3 above.

113 See also Gieschen 1998, 98-99, and Fossum 1995, 57-62.

114 Cf., Exodus 3 where 'the angel of the Lord' is said to have appeared to Moses in the burning bush, although the one who speaks to him is clearly God Himself, see chapter 3 above.

them through the Red Sea, and led them through deep waters, [19] but she drowned their enemies […] [20] Therefore the righteous plundered the ungodly, they sang hymns, O Lord, to your holy name, and praised with one accord your defending hand …

In Exod 14:19 the angel of God appears in the pillar of cloud, while we read in v. 24 that "the Lord in the pillar of fire looked down on the Egyptian army, and threw the Egyptian army into panic".[115] But according to the rendering of the exodus in Wis 10:15-20, it is 'Lady Wisdom' who becomes 'a starry flame' and the hand of God seems to be equated with her.[116]

The imagery of 'God's Hand' in Wis 10:20 recalls the song of Moses in Exod 15:1-18, which is explicitly alluded to in this verse. In the song of Moses as well as in Wisdom, 'the Hand' clearly represents God but in the later text it seems to be yet another epithet for 'Lady Wisdom'.[117] Compare also Wis 11:17 with Wis 9:1-2, where God's Word/'Logos', 'Lady Wisdom' and 'God's Hand' are equated with each other as instrumental in the creation of the world.[118] In Wis 18:15 the 'Logos of God' is said to be the one who killed the firstborn of the Egyptians. Thus the 'Logos' seems to be identified with 'the Destroyer'/המשחית mentioned in Exod 12:23b, and in Wis 18:16 the 'Logos' clearly represents 'the Destroying Angel'/מלאך המשחית in 2 Sam 24:16 and 1 Chr 21:15.[119] This is noteworthy, since scholars generally agree that 'Lady Wisdom' and 'Logos' are used synonymously in Wisdom. Here, the 'wisdom-tradition' is fused with the 'Logos-tradition' of Hellenistic Judaism.[120] Compare, for example, also Wis 18:15 and 9:10; both 'Lady Wisdom' and the 'Logos' are depicted as having their abode in heaven,

---

115 See also Isa 63:9 in the MT where 'the angel of His (God's) presence' is credited with having delivered Israel out of Egypt. However, in the LXX rendering of this verse, any angelic involvement is explicitly denied; the deed is ascribed to God Himself. See further chapter 3.4 above and Fossum 1995, 57-59.

116 Cf., also Sir 24:4 "I ['Lady Wisdom'] dwelt in the highest heavens, and my throne was in a pillar of cloud." See also Wis 18:3 and 19:7-8.

117 See also Gieschen 1998, 100-101, and Jude 5, where according to some mss Jesus is identified as the one who brought Israel out of Egypt. See also 1 Cor 10:4 and Matt 11:19; 23:34; cf., Luke 7:35; 11:49. For a discussion of this issue and connections to 'the angel of the Lord', see further Fossum 1995, 41-69. See also Col 2:1-3, 1 Cor 1:24, and Suggs 1970, 31-61.

118 For a quotation of these verses, see Excursus 2 below. See also Wis 8:4; 9:9; 2 En. 30.8-12, Winston 1979, 38-39, Fossum 1985, 288, and Gieschen 1998, 93, 100-101.

119 See also Wis 18:25, Fossum 1995, 51, 55-62; 1985, 228, and Gieschen 1998, 105-107. Cf., Rev 19:11-16.

120 See e.g., Winston 1979, 38-40, and 1992, 125. See also Grabbe 1997, 76-80.

on God's throne. How then, are we to define the nature of 'Lady Wisdom'? In an attempt to answer this question, Gerhard von Rad writes:

> ... None the less it is correct to say that wisdom is the form in which Jahweh's will and his accompanying of man (i.e. his salvation) approaches man [...] Still, the most important thing is that wisdom does not turn towards man in a shape of an "It", teaching, guidance, salvation or the like, but of a person, a summoning "I". So wisdom is truly the form in which Jahweh makes himself present and in which he wishes to be sought by man. "Whoso finds me, finds life" (Prov. VIII. 35). Only Jahweh can speak in this way. And yet, wisdom is not Jahweh himself: it is something separate from him ...[121]

This description of 'Lady Wisdom' is in many ways reminiscent of the function of the angel of the Lord as God's means of communicating with the world, compare the scholarly discussion regarding the relationship between God and the "angel" recorded in chapter 3.6.[122]

According to Winston, the Wisdom of Solomon represents a further step in the evolution of the concept of wisdom in Israelite religion compared to Proverbs, Job and Ben Sirah, since 'Lady Wisdom' is described as an eternal emanation of God,[123] which has no counterpart in these other books. However, Winston points out that the same idea appears in the writings of Philo, who in many ways appears to have a similar 'wisdom-theology'.[124] 'Lady Wisdom' is a mediator of divine revelation; e.g., Wisdom 8-9.[125] Moreover, she is depicted as a savior in Wisdom, a quality which in the Hebrew Bible is reserved for God and the 'angel of the Lord'.[126]

When comparing Wis 9:10 and 10:17, we see that she appears to be equated with God's Spirit, and in Wis 9:4 she is depicted as seated by God's throne.[127] She is clearly ascribed divine characteristics; see Wis 7:22-8:8.[128] In contrast to in Ben Sirah, 'Lady Wisdom' is never explicitly identified as the Torah in the Wisdom of Solomon but she is the personification of divine providence. She is credited with having guided the

---

121 von Rad 1962, 444.
122 See also Dunn's statement (1989, 176) concerning 'Lady Wisdom'.
123 Wis 7:25, cf., Heb 1:3. See also Winston 1979, 33-43, 59-63, 1992, 124-125, and Ringgren 1947, 116-119.
124 Winston 1979, 33-43, 59-63, and 1992, 124-125.
125 See also Winston 1979, 42-43.
126 E.g., Wis 9:18; 10:6-15. The depiction of 'Lady Wisdom' as a savior is thus unique to the Wisdom of Solomon. See further Grabbe 1997, 79-80.
127 See also *1 En.* 84.2-3, Gieschen 1998, 93-97, and Bauckham 1999, 43-71, esp. p. 56.
128 Cf., Col 1:15-16. See also Ringgren 1947, 115-119, Wright 1989, 512, Murphy 1995, 228-231, and Barker 1992, 62-67.

saints as well as the course of history.[129] In addition to her role in the account of the exodus from Egypt, she also appears to have overtaken the role of 'the angel of the Lord' in Wisdom's review of the life of the patriarchs.

The Aqedah

In Wis 10:5 it is stated that it was 'Lady Wisdom' who gave Abraham strength during the Aqedah:[130]

> [Wis 10:5] Wisdom also, when the nations in wicked agreement had been put to confusion, recognized the righteous man and preserved him blameless before God, and kept him strong in his compassion for his child.

In Genesis 22, it is 'the angel of the lord' who addresses Abraham and rescues Isaac but in Wis 10:5 it is instead 'Lady Wisdom' who is involved in the Aqedah.[131]

Jacob and the Angel

In Wis 10:10-12 we read about 'Lady Wisdom's' involvement in Jacob's life:

> [Wis 10:10] When a righteous man [Jacob] fled from his brother's wrath, she guided him on straight paths; she showed him the kingdom of God, and gave him knowledge of holy things; she prospered him in his labours, and increased the fruit of his toil. [11] When his oppressors were covetous, she stood by him and made him rich. [12] She protected him from his enemies, and kept him safe from those who lay in wait for him; in his arduous contest she gave him the victory, that he might learn that godliness is more powerful than anything else.

She is here credited as the one who protected and guided Jacob, a role that the Bible assigns to God/the angel of God.[132] When he runs away to escape the revenge of Esau, 'Lady Wisdom' is said to have guided him,

---

129 Winston 1992, 125. See also Suggs 1970, 40-43.

130 In the so-called Apocryphal or Deuterocanonical Scriptures of the OT there are a few allusions to Gen 22:1-19, namely in Judith 8:26-27, 1 Macc 2:52; Wis 10:5, and Sir 44:19-21. Of these, only the one in Wis 10:5 is of interest for our study.

131 See also the allusion to the destruction of Sodom and Gomorrah in Wis 10:6-8, where 'Lady Wisdom' is credited with having saved Lot, cf., Genesis 19. See also Winston 1979, 215-216, and Fossum 1995, 45-51.

132 See e.g., Gen 28:13-15; 31:3, 11-13, and 48:15-16. Cf., Raphael's function as a protector and guide in the book of Tobit.

shown him the kingdom of God and to have given him knowledge of holy things,[133] most certainly an allusion to Jacob's revelation at Bethel. Another possible translation of v. 10 is to read 'holy ones' instead of 'holy things'. If we choose this rendering, 'the holy ones' are probably the angels he saw in his dream.

In Gen 28:15a we read that in the dream God says to Jacob: "Know that I am with you and will keep you wherever you go ..." 'Lady Wisdom' is also said to have increased the fruit of Jacob's toil while he was in the service of Laban, something that Jacob himself tells his wives was an act of the angel of God (Gen 31:4-13). Gieschen states that in this speech Jacob refers to the God who exhorted him to leave Laban (Gen 31:3) as identical to this "angel."[134] Wis 10:12 seems to allude to Gen 31:24, where we read that when Laban pursued the fleeing Jacob, God appeared to the former in a dream and warned him not to harm Jacob. The last part of Wis 10:12 is probably an allusion to Jacob's contest with 'the unknown man' in Genesis 32.[135]

For these reasons it is apparent that the role of 'Lady Wisdom' in the passage quoted above is rooted in angelomorphic traditions. Thus, I fully agree with Gieschen when he writes: "One can see from the Genesis narrative that most of the events related in Wis. 10.10-12 involved

---

133 According to Winston (1979, 217), 'the holy things' may here consist in a vision of the future Temple and the Levite priesthood, an interpretation he bases on a presumptive influence of the *Testament of Levi*. Cf., the Targumic renderings of Genesis 28, see below. See also Wright 1989, 517.

134 Gieschen 1998, 102.

135 See also Winston 1979, 217-218. Since 'Lady Wisdom' in the passage quoted above is depicted as the protector of Jacob, it seems likely that she is not to be understood as Jacob's opponent in Wis 10:12 but rather as the one who strengthened him in the contest and ensured his victory, cf. Gen 32:28 [29] in the LXX. Thus Wis 10:12, in turn, reminds me of Hayward's interpretation of Luke 22:43-44 in the light of the LXX rendering of this verse (see further the discussion of LXX Genesis 32 in chapter 3.2.5. According to Hayward (2005, 321-327), the LXX version of Jacob's struggle may be understood as meaning that the angel fought alongside Jacob against some unnamed foe and he argues that Luke had Jacob's struggle in mind when he wrote his version of the night time anguish of Jesus at Gethsemane. In both cases, he argues, an angel was sent to strengthen Jacob and Jesus. Thus, according to Hayward's interpretation of Luke's passion narrative, the Evangelist modelled his version of Jesus' night at Gethsemane on Jacob's struggle at Jabbok; like Jacob, an angel comes to support Jesus against the foe, who in Luke 22:53 is explicitly defined as 'the power of darkness'. Cf., Westermann's identification of the man of Genesis 32 as representing the demonic powers (see chapter 3.2.5). However, he does not presuppose a third person at Jabbok. To me, Hayward's connection of the two narratives appears rather speculative, because it is hard to imagine a third, unmentioned person at the ford of Jabbok.

the actions of God as the Angel of the Lord."[136] In Wisdom, the hypostatized divine Wisdom has taken over the role of the angel of God as the one who guided and protected Jacob. In the same way as the "angel," the personified 'Lady Wisdom' appears to be equated with God Himself.[137]

Concluding Remarks

As we have seen, there are several examples where the actions of 'the angel of the Lord' in the Bible have been attributed to 'divine wisdom' in Wisdom. It seems therefore probable that the personification of wisdom in this book is dependent upon angelomorphic traditions, to use Gieschen's expression.

4.1.4 Summary and Conclusions

The book of Tobit is full of implicit allusions to Genesis 24. This early Jewish novel is not an explicit interpretation or rewriting of the pericope but the author was certainly inspired by the biblical narrative about the wooing of Rebekah. He seems to have modeled his own story on Genesis 24 as a kind of prototype. The two stories share at least two basic motifs; the importance of marrying a relative and angelic protection on a journey. Both Tobit and Genesis 24 are family narratives and at the same time tales of divine guidance and providence. In both stories, prayer plays a prominent role.

The words of Tobias' father to his wife in Tob 5:22, "*A good angel will accompany him, his journey will be successful, and he will come back*," remind the reader of the words of Abraham to his servant in Gen 24:7b; "*... he [God] will send His angel before you, and you shall take a wife for my son from there*." Angelic guidance and protection of a traveler is an important element of the plot in both narratives and may be labeled as a kind of common type-scene. Raphael guides Tobias to Sarah and her family, and God (by His angel) leads the servant of Abraham to the proper wife for Isaac. In both the book of Tobit and Genesis 24, the

---

136 Gieschen 1998, 102. Even though the angel in Gen 31:11 is called 'the angel of God', Gieschen (1998, 27) has chosen to consistently refer to this figure as 'the angel of the Lord'.

137 Gieschen 1998, 98-103.

marriages of the two relatives (Isaac and Rebekah respectively Tobias and Sarah) are seen as divine arrangements.

The doxology in Tob 11:14-15 is significant, because of the parallelism of the blessing of the angels alongside God (twice in codex Sinaiticus), something quite exceptional in Jewish angelology.

The disclosure of the true identity of Raphael also recalls another 'angel-narrative' in the Bible, Judges 13. There are clear parallels between Tobit 12 and the revelation of the angel of the Lord to Manoah and his wife. In both narratives, the heavenly emissaries are at first mistaken for humans. It is not until their departure that the heavenly guests reveal who they really are. Both Raphael in Tob 12:21 and the angel of the Lord in Judg 13:19-21 disappear very suddenly. We may define this scenario as another type-scene common to many of these narratives, cf., Gen 16:7-14 treated above.

There are, however, also differences between the depictions of the heavenly messengers in Tobit 12 and Judges 13. In contrast to Tobit 12, the identity of the angel and that of God are merged in Judges 13. Raphael, on the other hand, clearly distinguishes between himself and God, e.g., Tob 12:18. The difference between the two heavenly messengers is similar to the distinction between the angel of the Lord in Gen 16:7-14 and the angel Gabriel who appears to Mary and Zechariah in Luke 1. It is here worth mentioning, that both Raphael and Gabriel identify themselves as angels who stand in the presence of God, see Tob 12:15 and Luke 1:19.

As we have seen, the angels of Genesis 24 and in the book of Tobit are both depicted as distinct from God. They both play the role of guide and protector of a traveler. In both cases, the angels have a match-making commission. Accordingly, the story in Genesis 24 has more in common with the tale of Tobit than with Genesis 16 and Judges 13. But there are also differences. The angel who guides Tobit is known by the reader as Raphael, (cf., Luke 1:26-27) but the angel of Genesis 24 is anonymous. Raphael plays a far more active part in the course of events than the angel in Genesis 24, who is referred to only in verses 7 and 40.

My conclusion, based on these observations, is that the role of the angel in Genesis 24 may be interpreted as representing a stage in the evolution of the Jewish religion midway between such texts as Genesis 16 and Judges 13 and the more developed angelology found in the book of Tobit and Luke 1.

The Wisdom of Solomon, the second apocryphal/deuterocanoical book investigated above, is of a totally different genre and character than Tobit. It is not a novel but belongs to the 'wisdom-literature' of Israel and is a kind of 'exhortatory discourse' dedicated to the subject of wisdom. As we have seen, chapters 10-19 can be labeled a Hellenistic Jewish Midrash on the biblical history in Genesis and Exodus.

In this chapter, we have mainly focused on Wisdom 10, with its several allusions to 'the angel of the Lord-texts' in Genesis and Exodus where 'Lady Wisdom' has assumed the role of the "angel" in the Hebrew Bible. The role of 'Lady Wisdom' in this book may be defined as a manifestation/revelation of God in His dealings with humankind. She is depicted as a mediator of divine revelation and an executor of God's will and salvation. In this way, her role is reminiscent of that of 'the angel of the Lord' in the early stage of Israel's angelology, represented by such texts as Genesis 16; 22 and Judges 13, where the ambiguity of the "angel" and God is still evident.

Thus, a possible conclusion may be that, although the angelology developed in the direction of seeing angels as independent personalities, Judaism still had room for the idea of divine hypostases. It is therefore noteworthy that the 'Logos', an equivalent of 'Lady Wisdom' in Wis 18:16 plays the role of the angel of the Lord in 1 Chr 21:15, a text where the angel seems to be distinct from God.

4.2 The Pseudepigrapha and the Qumran Documents

4.2.1 Introduction

The main sources discussed in this chapter are the Pseudepigrapha *Jubilees, Liber Antiquitatum Biblicarum,* the *Ladder of Jacob,* the *Testament of Jacob,* the *Prayer of Joseph, Joseph and Aseneth, Demetrius the Chronographer,* and the Qumran document labeled 4Q225. All of these works contain interpretative material concerning some or all of the following explicit 'angel of the Lord-texts': Gen 21:17-21; Gen 22:1-19; 31:10-13; and 48:15-16. Gen 28:10-22 and 35:1-15 are closely connected to Gen 31:10-13 and are therefore included in the study. The story of Hagar and the angel has its only counterpart in the Pseudepigrapha by a rewriting of Genesis 21 in *Jubilees,* while the more complicated parallel-text, Gen 16:7-14, is omitted.

The implicit reference to 'the angel of the Lord' in Genesis 32, the tale of Jacob's struggle at the ford of Jabbok (Gen 32:22-30), is clearly the main exegetical background for the depiction of the patriarch as an angel in the *Prayer of Joseph.*[138] In 4Q158 there is a rewritten version of Genesis 32 and short allusions to the pericope are also extant in some of the other above mentioned sources. The *Prayer of Joseph* is also connected to some of the other biblical 'Jacob narratives'.[139]

Jubilees

Jubilees (*Jub.*) describes itself as a revelation given to Moses on Sinai by *the angel of the Presence.* According to the book's own account, this angel dictated the content of *Jubilees* 2-50 to Moses. The angel of the Presence is thus the alleged narrator of *Jubilees.*[140] Compare the tradition that the Torah was transmitted to Moses through the mediation of angels: Deut 33:2-3 in LXX, the Vulgate, Peshitta, and the Targums, see also Acts 7:38, 53; Gal 3:19, and Heb 2:2. *Jubilees* was most probably written in Hebrew in the land of Israel during the middle of the second century B.C.E. It seems to have been popular in the Qumran community.[141]

---

138 See the introduction by Smith in *OTP* vol. 2, 1985, 699-712.
139 Although *Jubilees* contains quite an extensive rewriting of the Jacob narrative in Genesis, Jacob's struggle at Jabbok has been excluded.
140 I use the English translation of *Jubilees* by Wintermute in *OTP* vol. 2, 1985, 52-142.
141 The only complete extant form of *Jubilees* is an Ethiopic translation. See the introduction by Wintermute in *OTP,* vol. 2, 1985, 35-50. Cf., chapter 2.2.3.

As mentioned previously, the concept 'the angel of the Presence' is probably derived from Isa 63:9 as recorded in the MT: "In all their affliction He [God] was afflicted, And *the Angel of His Presence* saved them ..."[142] The angel is first mentioned in *Jub.* 1.27, and in verse 29 we read: "And *the angel of the Presence,* who went before the camp of Israel, took the tablets of the division of the years... " The identity of this angel seems therefore to be based also on an interpretation of Exod 14:19; 23:20-23; 32:34, and Num 20:16.[143] According to *Jubilees*, it was the angel of the Presence who brought the Israelites out of the slavery in Egypt.

In addition to this heavenly mediator of the divine revelations, *Jubilees* mentions several angels of the Presence: *Jub.* 2.2, 18; 15.27, and 31.14. The narrator is one of them, often identified as Michael.[144] According to *Jubilees*, the angels of the Presence and the angels of sanctification are the two highest orders of angels: *Jub.* 2.18.[145] They were created on the first day of the Creation: *Jub.* 2.2. Besides Michael, angels like Gabriel, Raphael, Phanuel, Raguel, Sariel, and Uriel are often designated as angels of the Presence.[146] Compare the words of Gabriel to Zechariah when the latter doubted his message in Luke 1:19: Ἐγώ εἰμι Γαβριὴλ ὁ παρεστηκὼς ἐνώπιον τοῦ Θεοῦ .../ "I am Gabriel. I stand in the presence of God ..." Concerning Raphael, see also Tob 12:15.

The angelic narrator of *Jubilees* nevertheless distinguishes himself from all other angels mentioned in the book. In many passages of *Jubilees*, this specific angel of the Presence ascribes to himself words and deeds which are credited to God in the Bible, e.g., *Jub.* 6.19 and 12.22

---

142 Olyan 1993, 108-109. The quotation of Isa 63:9 is taken from the NKJV, which here is based on the MT. The NRSV, however, translates the verse according to the Septuagint's version: "... it was no messenger or angel, but his presence that saved them ..." See also chapters 2 and 3.

143 In Exod 23:20-23 the angel is linked to God's own name, cf., also Exod 13:21-22. See VanderKam 2000a, 385-388, and 2001, 86-89. See also Olyan 1993, 108-109, and van Ruiten 2007, 593-594.

144 Guiley 2004, 45.

145 Guiley 2004, 45. The angels of the Presence are often equated with the four or seven archangels. Angelic hierarchies built upon four archangels usually include Michael, Gabriel, Raphael and Uriel/Suriel. See Gutmann/Editorial Staff 1971, 962-963, Scholem 1971, 1549, and van Henten 1995b, 150-153.

146 Gutmann/Editorial staff 1971, 962-963. Guiley's list includes (besides Michael): Metatron, Suriel, Sandalphon, Astanphaeus, Sarakiel, Phanuel, Jehoel, Zagzagael, Uriel, Yefefiah, Sabaoth, and Akatriel. According to her, the angels of the Presence are also equated with the angels of Glory. Guiley 2004, 45. In addition to *Jubilees*, the angels of the Presence are mentioned in the *Testaments of the Twelve Patriarchs*, *1 Enoch* and in the *Life of Adam and Eve*. They appear also in the Qumran literature, see Seow 1995, 611-613, and Olyan 1993, 108.

(cf., Exod 24:8; 34.10, 27; Deut 4:23; 5:2; 9:9, and Gen 12:1).[147] There thus appears to be a merging of God's and this angel's identity in *Jubilees*, as is the case concerning God and the angel of the Lord in the Bible.[148]

4Q225

This Qumran manuscript has been classified as part of '*Pseudo-Jubilees*'. The account of the Aqedah in this document is similar to that in *Jubilees* but there are also differences. The manuscript probably bears witness to yet another version of Gen 22:1-19. It is unclear whether or not the document is an original version of *Jubilees*. The manuscript is written in Hebrew and can be dated sometime between the last years of the first century B.C.E. and the beginning of the first century C.E.[149]

4Q158

This Qumran document belongs to a group of five poorly preserved manuscripts which have been classified as reworkings of the Penta-teuch, all of which may be dated to the first century B.C.E. 4Q158 is included in my analysis because it contains a fragmentary paraphrase of Genesis 32.[150] The manuscript exhibits a noteworthy deviation from the MT that will be discussed below but, because of the briefness of the section dealing with this source, there will be no summary of the re-sults.[151]

Liber Antiquitatum Biblicarum

Liber Antiquitatum Biblicarum is also known as *Pseudo-Philo*, because for a long time it was wrongly ascribed to Philo of Alexandria. Today howev-

---

147 See also VanderKam 2000a, 390-392.
148 See also Ashton, (1994, 83) who likewise has noted that the voice of the angel of the Presence and the voice of God are merged in *Jubilees*.
149 Besides 4Q225, there are also fragments of the Aqedah account in 4Q226 and 4Q252. A document labeled 4Q227 is also called *Pseudo-Jubilees*, see Vermes 1997, 507-508, and García Martinez 2002, 44-45. Concerning the relationship between *Jubilees* and the so-called *Pseudo-Jubilees*, see VanderKam 1997, 241-261. I mainly use the tran-scription and English translation of the Hebrew text by García Martinez 2002, 46-47.
150 See Vermes, 1997, 442.
151 I use the English translation by Vermes 1997, 442.

er, it is generally acknowledged among scholars that he was not the author. The Pseudepigraphon is a free retelling of the biblical history from Adam to King David, and as such it belongs to the 'rewritten Bible' genre. Its author remains unknown. It is certain that the work was originally written in Hebrew and composed in the land of Israel. There are indications that support a dating of the original Hebrew version to the time before the fall of the Second Temple in 70 C.E. The author/compiler may thus have been contemporary with Jesus of Nazareth.[152]

Testament of Jacob

Together with the *Testament of Isaac, the Testament of Jacob* ultimately derives from an apocryphal book probably written in Greek during the first century C.E. by a Jewish author in Egypt, which deals with the death of Abraham. The three texts are collected under the title *Testaments of the Three Patriarchs*. In their present form, they all show obvious signs of Christianization. It is, however, certain that the original *Testament of Abraham* was a Jewish work, and its Jewish character is still apparent. There are more Christian elements in the *Testament of Isaac* and *Testament of Jacob* but it may nevertheless be worthwhile to take a look at the latter.[153]

Ladder of Jacob

The Pseudepigraphon the *Ladder of Jacob* (*Lad. Jac.*) is, in accordance with its name, an elaboration of Jacob's dream at Bethel. James H. Charlesworth calls the book an "… aggadic exegetical expansion of Jacob's vision (Gen 28:11-22) with apocalyptic elements."[154] It is only known from the *Slavonic Tolkovaya Paleya, or Explanatory Paleya*. The text in its present form is a compilation of many sources, and as such it is a

---

152 For more information, see Harrington's introduction to the book in *OTP*, vol. 2, 1985, 297-303. I use his English translation of *Liber Antiquitatum Biblicarum* in *OTP*, vol. 2, 1985, 304-377.

153 See Sanders' introduction in *OTP* vol. 1, 1983, 869-880. I use the English translation of the *Testament of Jacob* by Stinespring found in *OTP*, vol. 1, 1983, 914-918. The borderline between Christianity and Judaism was probably quite vague for a longer time in the region of the Eastern Churches than in the West.

154 Charlesworth 1992, 609.

complex work, containing both Jewish and Christian elements. Behind the present Slavonic version there is most certainly a Jewish narrative written in Greek.[155]

According to James Kugel, there are reasons to believe that this Greek text may in turn be a translation of a Hebrew or Aramaic original that possibly derives from the Second Temple era. He sees no reason to date the original source later than the first century C.E.[156] The underlying Jewish character of chapters 1-6 is apparent, while chapter 7 is generally considered to be a Christian addition, as it concerns the birth and crucifixion of Christ.[157] Accordingly, in the following discussion I will focus on the Jewish part of the book.

Prayer of Joseph

The major theme of this text is the idea that the patriarch Jacob was the earthly incarnation of the angel Israel, an interpretation based on Genesis 32.[158] Only three fragments of the Pseudepigraphon have survived. The title is enigmatic, since Joseph is not mentioned in the extant verses, but originally the text was most certainly an extended version of Jacob's blessing of Joseph's sons in Gen 48:15-16.

Fragment A is preserved in Origen's *Commentary on John* and described by him as "an apocrypha presently in use among the Hebrews."[159] Fragments B and C are quoted in the *Philocalia*, Gregory's and Basil's compilation of Origen.[160] Fragment C quotes fragment B and paraphrases fragment A. Due to Origen's knowledge of the *Prayer of Joseph*, the source must be dated before 231 C.E. According to Jonathan Z. Smith, a dating in the first century C.E. is probable because of the

---

155 I use Lunt's translation of the *Ladder of Jacob* in *OTP*, vol. 2, 1985, 407-411, see his introduction on pp. 401-406.

156 Kugel 1995, 209-227. Kugel's reasons are based both on the content of *Ladder of Jacob* and the many Hebrew words that survive in the transcription of the text. Kugel points out that there are many connections between this source and Rabbinic exegetical traditions. See also Kugel 1990, 117-119.

157 Lunt introduction in *OTP*, vol. 2, 1985, 402-405, see also Kugel, 1990, 117-119, and Charlesworth 1992, 609.

158 However, as will be shown below, the issue of whether Jacob is to be understood literally as the *incarnation* of the angel in this text is a moot point.

159 See Smith's introduction to the *Prayer of Joseph* in *OTP*, vol. 2, 1985, 699.

160 Additionally, fragment B is also quoted in Eusebius, *The Preparation of the Gospel*, and Procopius' Latin commentary on Genesis, see Smith's introduction in *OTP*, vol. 2, 1985, 699.

many parallels between the text and early Hellenistic and Aramaic material.[161]

Because of the few remains of the *Prayer of Joseph*, its original language is veiled in obscurity. Scholars who regard it as an original Jewish work assume that it was written in Aramaic, while those who claim Christian authorship advocate a Greek original. The opinions likewise differ concerning its provenance; either Alexandria or Palestine. According to Smith, a Jewish original context and authorship is the most probable, because the work contains many close parallels in technical terms, narrative traditions and theology to both Hellenistic and Palestinian Judaism. Thus Origen was probably correct when he defined the *Prayer of Joseph* as a Jewish composition.[162]

Joseph and Aseneth

Joseph and Aseneth is a romance written by an anonymous author. It is a Jewish composition, although it may contain some Christian interpolations.[163] The novel's origin can most probably be traced to the Jewish Diaspora of Egypt. All scholars agree that it is a fairly early work, possibly from the Second Temple era, and no one has dated the novel long after 200 C.E.[164] The original language is generally considered to be Greek.[165]

The main characters in the novel are the patriarch Joseph and his wife Aseneth, the Egyptian girl whom, according to Gen 41:45, Joseph married when he entered the service of Pharaoh. The story builds and elaborates on the biblical Joseph's and Aseneth's relationship and tries to answer the intriguing question of why the pious and God-fearing Joseph actually married the daughter of a pagan Egyptian priest.[166]

---

161 Smith's introduction in *OTP*, vol. 2, 1985, 700.
162 See Smith's introduction in *OTP* vol. 2, 1985, 699-712. I use his translation of the Pseudepigraphon in *OTP*, vol. 2, 1985, 713-714. See also Hayward 2005, 211-213.
163 Burchard, introduction to *Joseph and Aseneth* in *OTP*, vol. 2, 1985, 177, 186-187. I use Burchard's translation of the Pseudepigraphon in *OTP*, vol. 2, 1985, 202-247.
164 Burchard, introduction, *OTP* vol. 2, 1985, 187-188.
165 Burchard, introduction, *OTP* vol. 2, 1985, 181.
166 Burchard, introduction, *OTP* vol. 2, 1985, 177.

Demetrius the Chronographer

Six fragments are generally considered to be the preserved remnants of a work by Demetrius, a Jewish author who most probably lived in Alexandria during the reign of Ptolemy IV in the third century B.C.E. Demetrius is the first known Jewish author writing in Greek, and the first witness to the use of the LXX version of the Pentateuch. The two fragments of relevance here are numbers one and two. Fragment 1 contains a brief synopsis of the Aqedah while the second fragment provides a résumé of the patriarchal chronology, mainly focusing on the lives of Jacob and Joseph.[167]

4.2.2 Hagar and the Angel

Jubilees

Jubilees has no version of Gen 16:7-14, only an account based on Gen 21:9-21.[168] Perhaps the author viewed the two pericopes as two versions of the same story, the destiny of Hagar and her encounter with the angel of the Lord. Contextually it corresponds to the narrative in Genesis 21 and is placed just before the story of the binding of Isaac, Gen 22:1-19.

As in the Bible, it is said that Abraham drove away Hagar and his son Ishmael very unwillingly. God had to command him to obey Sarah's wish in this matter, *Jub.* 17.4-7. God promised Abraham that he would take care of Ishmael: "But regarding the son of this girl, I will make him into a great people because he is from your seed," *Jub.*17.7. The expulsion of Hagar and her son is described in *Jub.*17.17c-18a as one of the many trials of Abraham. We find the counterpart to Gen 21:17-21 in *Jub.*17.11-14:

> And *an* angel of the Lord, *one of the holy ones,* said to her, "What are you weeping for, Hagar? Having arisen, pick up the child and take him in your arms because *the LORD has heard your voice and he has seen the child.*" And *she opened* her eyes and she saw a well of water. And she went and filled the water skin. And she gave the child a drink and arose and went toward

---

167 Hanson, introduction *OTP* vol. 2, 1985, 843-844. I use his translation of the Pseudepigraphon in *OTP*, vol. 2, 1985, 848-854.

168 However, in *Jub.* 24.1 there is a reference to 'the Well of the Vision', i.e., the well where, according to Gen16:13-14, the angel of the Lord appeared to Hagar.

the desert of Paran. And the child grew and was a hunter. And *the LORD* was with him. And his mother took a wife for him from the maids of Egypt. And she [the wife] bore a son for him [Ishmael] and he called him Nebaioth because, she [Hagar?] said, *"the LORD was near to me when I called to him."* [my italics].

Jubilees' version is very similar to the biblical account, but there are also differences. The angel of God is here called *"an angel of the Lord, one of the holy ones."* *Jubilees* does not tell us from where the angel spoke to Hagar. In contrast to the Bible, the heavenly emissary is depicted in *Jubilees* as an unspecified angel, *one among many* in the heavenly court. The divine name used is the Lord/YHWH. The angel is not labeled as belonging to the angels of the Presence. As we will see, this is the case in *Jubilees'* account of the binding of Isaac. The angel of the Lord is there identified as the narrator himself.[169]

As in the Bible, the angel in *Jub*.17.12 speaks about God in the third person singular, as someone distinct from himself; "... because the Lord has heard your voice and he has seen the child ..." In Gen 21:17b we read; "... Do not be afraid; for God has heard the voice of the boy where he is." According to the biblical account, however, the angel of God thereafter switches to the first person singular and says to Hagar that "... *I will* make a great nation of him," Gen 21:18b. In *Jubilees*, the angel is not said to have made such a statement to Hagar, but the promise is mentioned as God's words to Abraham in *Jub*.17.7.[170]

Some differences of lesser significance are that in the Bible it is the voice of *the lad* that God heard, while in *Jub*. 17.12 it is the voice of *Hagar* and He is said to *have seen the child*, the latter being an addition to the biblical version.[171] Moreover, in the Bible, it is *God who opens* the eyes of Hagar in order for her to see the well, but *Jub*. 17.12b simply states that "... *she* [Hagar] *opened* her eyes and she saw a well of water ..." Maybe the wording "...God opened her eyes ..." appeared too anthropomorphic for the author of *Jubilees*.

Towards the end of the version in *Jubilees* we find some interesting information, not recorded in this context in the Bible: "And she [the wife of Ishmael] bore a son for him and he [Ishmael] called him Ne-

---

169 See also VanderKam 2001, 52, and Ashton 1994, 83-84.

170 See previous page.

171 This is probably an attempt by the author of *Jubilees* to harmonize the biblical story, wherein there is a contradiction concerning this matter: "... And as she [Hagar] sat opposite him [Ishmael], she lifted up her voice and wept. And God heard the voice of the boy; and the angel of God called to Hagar from heaven..." The Swedish Bible 2000 follows the LXX and states that it was the boy, not Hagar, who wept.

baioth because, she [Hagar?] said, 'The LORD was near to me when I called to him,'" *Jub*.17.14b-c. [172]

My interpretation, based on the context, is that the woman who inspires Ishmael to call his son Nebaioth must be identified as Hagar. The name refers back to the rescue of Ishmael's mother and himself by the angel of God in the desert: God heard Hagar weeping and in His mercy sent her an angel. This parallels the naming of her own son in Gen 16:11: "… Now you have conceived and shall bear a son; you shall call him Ishmael, for the LORD has given heed to your affliction."

Concluding Remarks

None of the Pseudepigrapha has a counterpart to Gen 16:7-14. The only source that has a version of Hagar's meeting with the angel of God is *Jubilees* in its rewritten version of Gen 21:17-21. The exclusion of a rendering of the parallel text Gen 16:7-14 may be explained by the fact that the author of *Jubilees* viewed the two pericopes as two versions of the same story. Another possible reason is that the author chose to avoid the theologically more complicated version of Hagar's encounter with the angel in Gen 16:7-14.

In *Jubilees*, the angel who addresses Hagar is an unspecified, anonymous angel, 'one of the holy ones'. He is an "ordinary" angel, one among many in the heavenly court. Nothing is said of his rank but it seems that he does not belong to the highest kinds of angels, namely the angels of the Presence or the angels of sanctification. The angel is clearly distinct from both God and the alleged narrator of *Jubilees*, the angel of the Presence, who refers to him in the third person. In contrast to the biblical account, the angel never speaks in the first person singular. There is no ambivalence in *Jubilees*' version of the story regarding the relationship between God and this unnamed angel.

---

172 In the Bible, Nebaioth is mentioned in Gen 28:9: "So Esau went to Ishmael and took Mahalath the daughter of Ishmael, Abraham's son, *the sister of Nebajoth*, to be his wife in addition to the wives he had." See also Gen 25:13.

4.2.3 The Aqedah

Jubilees

We find *Jubilees'* version of the Aqedah in chapters 17.15-18.19. At the beginning of the story we are informed that "... words came in heaven [maybe a discussion among the angels?] concerning Abraham that he was faithful in everything which was told him and he loved the LORD and was faithful in all affliction" (v. 15).[173] According to *Jubilees*, The reason for the trial was that prince Mastema[174] questioned Abraham's faithfulness and accused him before God.

Prince Mastema insinuates that Abraham's love of Isaac is greater than his love of and devotion to God. He proposes therefore that God should test Abraham by commanding him to sacrifice his son Isaac:

> [*Jub.* 17.16] And Prince Mastema came and he said before God, "Behold, Abraham loves Isaac, his son. And he is more pleased with him than everything. Tell him to offer him (as) a burnt offering upon the altar. And you will see whether he will do this thing. And you will know whether he is faithful in everything in which you test him."

God accepts this challenge.[175] *Jubilees'* version of the Aqedah thus includes an additional actor, prince Mastema, the Satanic character in *Jubilees*. He is a demonic angel, the chief of the evil spirits, see *Jub.* 10.1, 7-11; 11.11-24; 48.1-4; 9-19, and 49.2.[176] In *Jub.* 10.11, prince Mastema is explicitly identified with Satan. In the Qumran literature, Mastema is often equated with Belial.[177]

The introductory scene to Abraham's trial in *Jubilees* is probably inspired by the book of Job, wherein Satan plays a similar role.[178] The

---

173 According to *Jub.* 17.17-18, God had already tested Abraham in many ways and had found him faithful. The commandment to offer Isaac is depicted as Abraham's final and hardest trial.

174 Regarding 'prince Mastema', see also VanderKam 2001, 128-129.

175 *Jub.* 17.17-18; 18.1.

176 The name of this evil angel is probably derived from Hos 9:7-8, where the noun משטמה occurs, meaning 'enmity/hostility/animosity'. Verbal forms of this root are to be found in Gen 27:41; 49:23; 50:15, and in the book of Job (16:9; 30:21), where it is used to describe God's assaults on Job. See also Olyan 1993, 66-67, and chapter 2.2.2 above.

177 Cf., *Jub.* 1.20. See, e.g., Guiley 2004, 236, van Henten 1995c, 1033-1035, and Flusser 1971, 1119-1120.

178 See Job 1-2 and VanderKam 2001, 52-53.

'accusing angel' motif may even be labeled as a type-scene shared by the two books.[179]

Jubilees' answer to the question why God tested Abraham is thus that the whole idea was prince Mastema's suggestion, and God agreed to it. In *Jub.* 18.16 it is stated that "… And I [God] *have made known to all* that you [Abraham] are faithful to me in everything which I say to you." The purpose of the trial is thus to demonstrate the faithfulness of Abraham in front of prince Mastema and everyone else. Abraham is worthy of God's choice.[180]

The angel of the Lord who prevents Abraham from sacrificing his son is identified in *Jub.* 18.9-11 as the alleged narrator himself, *the angel of the Presence:*

> [*Jub.* 18.9] And *I* stood before him [Abraham] and before Prince Mastema. *And the LORD said, "Speak to him.* Do not let his hand descend upon the child. And do not let him do anything to him because I know that he is one who fears the LORD." [10] *And I called out to him from heaven and I said to him,* "Abraham, Abraham." And he was terrified and said, "Here I am." [11] And *I* said to him, "Do not put forth your hand against the child and do not do anything to him because now *I know that you are one who fears the Lord* and you did not deny your firstborn son to *me."* [12] And *Prince Mastema was shamed* […] [13] And Abraham called that place *"The Lord has seen,"* so that it is said *"in the mountain the Lord has seen."* It is Mount Zion.[181] [my italics].

James VanderKam points out that the only two contexts where the angel of the Presence and prince Mastema are explicitly mentioned together in *Jubilees* are the Aqedah and the events leading up to the Exodus from Egypt. In *Jub.* 48.2 prince Mastema is charged with the attempt to kill Moses but the latter was saved by the angel of the Presence.[182] According to *Jub.* 48.13, the angel of the Presence stood between the Egyptians and the Israelites, in the same way as he describes him-

---

179 See also Olyan 1993, 25, Bernstein 2000, 266-268, VanderKam 1997, 248-249, and Kister 1994, 10. van Ruiten (2002, 84-85), however, questions the dependence of *Jubilees* upon the book of Job by pointing out several differences between the narrative of the Aqedah in *Jubilees* and Job's trial. For example, in *Jubilees* it is God Himself who remains in charge. As in Genesis 22, it is God who tests Abraham. But in the book of Job, God puts Job into the hands of Satan.

180 *Jub* 18.16. The purpose of the trial was thus not to prove something to God, who is omni-scient, see also VanderKam 2001, 52.

181 Note that the angel of the Presence first talks about God in the *third person*, but in the end says; "… and you did not deny your firstborn son to *me."* Cf., the biblical text.

182 In the Bible the attacker is identified as God Himself: "And it came to pass on the way, at the encampment, that the LORD met him [Moses] and sought to kill him," Exod 4:24.

self as standing before (VanderKam reads "between") Abraham and prince Mastema in *Jub.* 18.9. These are also the only two occasions in *Jubilees* where prince Mastema is said to have been put to shame. In both contexts, the angel of the Presence appears as the Savior from mortal danger in a crucial event in the history of Israel, when the very existence of the people was threatened.[183]

By ascribing the initiation of the Aqedah to prince Mastema, the author of *Jubilees* follows, according to VanderKam, in the footsteps of the Chronicler, who similarly transferred king David's census on God's command (2 Sam 24:1) to the initiative of Satan (1 Chr 21:1), thus solving a theological difficulty. Both the Chronicler and the author of *Jubilees* seem to have been driven by a wish to justify God.[184]

However, according to *Jubilees*, the one who calls to Abraham a *second time* is not the angel of the Lord, nor the angel of the Presence, but *God Himself*:

> [*Jub.* 18.14] And the LORD called Abraham by his name again from heaven just as he caused us [the angels] to appear so that we might speak to him in the name of the LORD. [15a] And he said, "I swear by myself, says the LORD ..."

The angel of the Lord in Gen 22:11-12 is thus identified with the angel of the Presence in *Jubilees*, while the second calling to Abraham in Gen 22:15-18 is ascribed to God Himself. It is, however, puzzling that *Jub.*18.14 states that the Lord called Abraham by his name *again*, since according to *Jub.* 18.10-11 it was the angel of the Presence who called him by name the first time. When comparing the different manuscripts, VanderKam proposes that according to the original text it is still the angel who speaks to Abraham in *Jub.* 18.14, but we cannot be certain about the original wording of the verse.[185] There is a certain inconsistency in *Jub.* 18.9-15. In *Jub.* 18.9-13, the angel of the Presence speaks in the first person singular as the one and only angel in the Aqedah, while in the quotation above he seems to include other angels who were also active in the first calling to Abraham.

Concluding Remarks

In *Jubilees'* version of the binding of Isaac (Gen 22:1-19) it is the demonic prince Mastema who is the initiator of the action. In *Jub.* 17.15 we read

---

183 See VanderKam 1997, 248.
184 VanderKam 1997, 249.
185 VanderKam 2000a, 389.

that "…words came in heaven concerning Abraham that he was faithful in everything …" This refers most assuredly to an alleged discussion among the angels. Prince Mastema is said to have questioned the
truth of this statement. Because of his accusations concerning Abraham,
God decides to put the latter on trial. The scenario preceding the Aqedah probably partly originated as an interpretation of Gen 22:1; "After
these things God tested Abraham …" but foremost due to a wish to
justify God. The transferring of the initiative from God to prince Mastema explains the reason for the trial and solves a theological problem.

The angel of the Presence narrates the story in the first person singular and identifies himself as the one who called out to Abraham on
the first occasion in order to prevent him from completing the sacrifice.
The angel of the Lord in Gen 22:11-12 is in *Jubilees* thus said to be the
angel of the Presence. Like the angel of the Lord in the Bible, the angel
of the Presence first speaks about God in the third person singular but
in the end he refers to himself; "… I know that you are one *who fears the
Lord* and you did not deny your firstborn son to *me*" (*Jub.* 18.11b). Although the angel of the Presence in *Jub.* 18.9-11 appears to be distinct
from God, the biblical ambiguity still remains.

However, the angel of the Lord's second call to Abraham recorded
in Gen 22:15-18 is ascribed to God Himself in *Jub.* 18.14-15. *Jubilees* is
thus not entirely consistent in its identification of the angel of the Lord
in Gen 22:1-19. But if we are to believe VanderKam, it may have been
the angel of the Presence who once more spoke to Abraham in the original version of *Jub.* 18.14. Another puzzling issue in *Jub.* 18.14 is that the
narrator refers to other angels involved in the Aqedah.

4Q225

The only pericope of relevance to our study that has a counterpart in
this document is Gen 22:1-19; the text usually designated as the Aqedah
(even though the actual binding of Isaac is not mentioned in 4Q225).

The source has been labeled '*Pseudo-Jubilees*', and there are indeed
many similarities between the renderings of the Aqedah in the two
texts. Prince Mastema has the same function in 4Q225 as in *Jubilees*; he
accuses Abraham before God of loving Isaac more than God, and in
this way initiates the trial.

We also encounter some new information here. According to Geza
Vermes, 4Q225 bears witness to the tradition that Abraham saw a '*fire*'

marking the divine presence on the sacrificial site.[186] This tradition is moreover to be found in *Targum Pseudo-Jonathan*, *Genesis Rabbah*, and *Pirqê de Rabbi Eliezer*. The synagogue mosaic of Sepphoris also seems to testify to this interpretation of the Aqedah.[187] Florentino García Martinez, however, doubts this reading of 4Q225.[188]

A clearer difference between this source and *Jubilees* is the mention in 4Q225 of *the holy angels standing above* (the altar?) *weeping* for Isaac's sake, while *the angels of Mastema/the angels of animosity* are said *to rejoice* when they see that Abraham is about to kill Isaac. According to García Martinez, the purpose of Mastema's plan in testing Abraham was to abort the promise of posterity through Isaac.[189] The weeping of the holy angels is mentioned in other sources[190] but the presence of several demonic angels in the Aqedah is something unique to 4Q225. The angel's first call in order to prevent Abraham from sacrificing his son is not mentioned, but the one who finally stops him from sacrificing Isaac seems here to be identified as God Himself.

The ending of the Aqedah[191] in 4Q225 differs from both the biblical version and *Jubilees'* account. It is there stated that God blessed Isaac all the days of his life. The name of God is rendered אל יהוה 'God YHWH.'[192]

Concluding Remarks

As in *Jubilees*, prince Mastema is described as the initiator of Abraham's trial, but there are also differences between the two sources. If we are to

---

186 See the English translation of 4Q225 (4Q226) by Vermes, 1997, 509, and Vermes 1996, 140-146. See also the textual notes on 4Q225 in DJD XIII, *Qumran Cave 4. Parabiblical Texts*, part 1, 1994, 151.

187 See below. Cf., also Exodus 3.

188 García Martinez 2002, 51-52.

189 García Martinez 2002, 55.

190 See chapter 4.5. See also the textual notes on 4Q225 in DJD XIII, *Qumran Cave 4. Parabiblical Texts*, part 1, 1994, 152.

191 García Martinez (2002, 47) hesitates to use the designation 'Aqedah' concerning the rendering of Gen 22:1-19 in 4Q225, because the actual binding of Isaac is one of the elements of the story omitted in the document.

192 According to García Martinez, this detail contradicts a Qumran origin of the composition. He also claims that 4Q225 should be differentiated from *Jubilees*. He writes: "It belongs thus neither to *Jubilees* nor to the Qumran tradition. This characteristic makes it even more interesting, in so far as it witnesses to the development and growth of the traditions around the Aqedah, though not in a particular sectarian context of the Judaism of the time," see García Martinez 2002, 56-57.

believe Vermes, one is that 4Q225 bears witness to the tradition that Abraham saw a 'fire' marking the sacrificial site as holy. This reading of the manuscript is, however, very uncertain and doubted by among others, García Martinez.

Another and in this case obvious difference between *Jubilees* and 4Q225 is the appearance of several holy angels weeping for Isaac as well as the reference to a multitude of angels of animosity, who are said to rejoice when they think that Abraham is about to kill his son. These angels, both the good and the bad ones, have no counterparts in the Bible. The one who prevents Abraham from slaughtering Isaac in 4Q225 seems to be identified as God Himself, clearly distinguished from the weeping/rejoicing angels.

Liber Antiquitatum Biblicarum and Demetrius the Chronographer

In *Liber Antiquitatum Biblicarum* there are a few allusions to the Aqedah in the retelling of the revelation of God to Balaam, the victory chant of Deborah and Barak, and the story about the daughter of Jephthah,[193] cf., Numbers 22; Judges 5 and 11:30-40). It is only the first two references that are of interest for our quest. In *L.A.B.* 18.5 God says to Baalam:

> ... And I demanded his [Abraham's] son as a holocaust. And he brought him to be placed on the altar, but *I gave him back to his father* and, because he did not refuse, his offering was acceptable before me, and on account of his blood I chose them. And *then I said to the angels who work secretly,*[194] 'Did I not say regarding this, *I will reveal everything I am doing to Abraham ...*' [my italics].

In this version of the Aqedah, there is no mention of a specific 'angel of the Lord' who interferes and stops Abraham from sacrificing Isaac; the only heavenly actor is God Himself. The angels who God refers to are mere spectators in the drama, not active participants.

In the rendering of the victory chant of Deborah and Barak we encounter some angels indirectly involved in the Aqedah. Here we read that it was their jealousy that motivated God to test Abraham:

> [*L.A.B.* 32.1b] And he [God] gave him [Abraham] a son at the end of his old age and took him out of a sterile womb. And *all the angels* were jealous of him, and *the worshipping host* envied him. [2] And since they were jealous of

---

193 *L.A.B.* 18.5; 32.1-4, and 40.1-9. In the last mentioned reference, Jephthah's daughter compares herself with Isaac, whom she considers as a role model.

194 Or: "... the angels of the service..." [Eng. trans. Jacobson, 1996, 118]. See also his commentary on p. 584.

him, God said to him [Abraham], 'Kill the fruit of your body for me, and offer for me as a sacrifice what has been given to you by me.'[195] [my italics].

The angels thus play a similar role as prince Mastema in *Jubilees*. According to *L.A.B.* 32.4, Isaac is saved at the last moment by *God Himself*:

> And when he [Abraham] had offered his son upon the altar and had bound his feet so as to kill him, the *Most Powerful hastened and sent forth his voice from on high* saying, 'You shall not slay your son, nor shall you destroy the fruit of your body. For now I have appeared so as to reveal you to those who do not know you *and have shut the mouths of those who are always speaking evil against you ...*'[my italics].

The purpose of the trial was thus to prove the fidelity of Abraham to the angels and the rest of the world.[196] As in *L.A.B.* 18.5, no specific angel of the Lord is mentioned.

In contrast to *Liber Antiquitatum Biblicarum*, the rendering of the Aqedah in *Demetrius the Chronographer* is quite similar to the biblical account; there is only one angel mentioned, and as in the Bible it is he who prevents Abraham from completing the sacrifice. However, in contrast to the biblical story, there is no ambivalence between the angel and God. The one who saves Isaac is clearly an angel distinct from God:

> But no long after God commanded Abraham to offer his son Isaac […]. But when he was about to sacrifice him, he was prevented by an angel, who provided him with the ram for the burnt offering ...[197]

Concluding Remarks

Similar to 4Q225, *Liber Antiquitatum Biblicarum* refers to a multitude of angels involved in the Aqedah but they are not said to have either wept or rejoiced. Their role is instead described as similar to that of prince Mastema in both *Jubilees* and 4Q225, because according to *L.A.B.* 32.1b-2, it was the jealous angels who provoked God into subjecting Abraham to a trial. In both *L.A.B.* 18.5 and 32.1b-2, the angels are depicted as 'walkers-on' in the drama; they are spectators 'behind the scenes.' It is God Himself who calls out to Abraham at the last moment and saves Isaac from being sacrificed. There is no specific angel of the Lord who interferes.

However, in the short reference to the Aqedah in *Demetrius the Chronographer*, the saving of Isaac is ascribed to an angel, acting on

---

195 Cf., *Gen. Rab.* 60.4, see chapter 4.5 below.
196 See also Bernstein 2000, 271-272.
197 Fragment 1.

God's behalf, but distinguished from him. As in the Bible, there are no other angels mentioned in the story.

4.2.4 Jacob and the Angel

Jubilees

Jacob's dream at Bethel

The context of the narrative (Gen 28:10-22) is the same as in the Bible. Jacob is forced to leave his home because of the conflict with his brother. In contrast to the biblical version, however, Rebekah is said to have been informed in a dream of Esau's plans for revenge and thus advises her son to flee to her brother Laban in Haran. Isaac also agrees to Jacob's journey and with the blessing of his father Jacob thus departs from home.[198] When he has left, Rebekah grieves for her son; she is worried about him and weeps; *Jub.* 27.13. Isaac comforts her and says:

> [*Jub.* 27.14] "My sister, do not weep on account of Jacob, my son, because in peace he will journey and in peace he will return. [15] God Most High will protect him from all evil and he will be with him because he will not forsake him all of his days, [16] for I know that he will make his ways prosper everywhere he goes until he returns to us in peace and we see him in peace…"

Isaac is confident that God will protect Jacob on his journey and that he will return home safely. The theme of divine protection when traveling is something we recognize from both Genesis 24 and the book of Tobit. Although *Jub.* 27.13-18 is based on Gen 28:1-5,[199] many scholars have noted a remarkable similarity between Tob 5:18-22 and this passage.[200] In the same way as Isaac, Tobit comforts his wife when their son Tobias leaves home in order to go to Media: "A good angel will accompany him; his journey will be successful, and he will come back" [Tob 5:22]. In *Jubilees*, however, it is God in person who is said to directly exercise His protection, not an angel.[201]

---

198 See *Jub.* 26.35; 27.1-12.

199 Cf., the prayer of Isaac for his son Jacob in Gen 28:3-4.

200 See, e.g., Moore, 1996, 193-194.

201 Dupont-Sommer (1968, 411-426) claims that the "author" of Tobit was inspired by *Jubilees*. Because Tobit's angelology is more developed in this passage, he concludes that *Jubilees* is earlier than the book of Tobit. As shown in the quotation, Isaac refers to God's personal protection, but in Tobit the protection is exercised by the angel Raphael. However, most scholars consider the case to be the other way around; the "author" of *Jubilees* used Tobit as a model and source of inspiration. The book of *Ju-*

Jacob thus leaves the land of his birth in order to escape the revenge of his brother Esau and, as in the Bible, God encounters him on the way. We can read about Jacob's dream at Bethel in *Jub.* 27.19-27. *Jubilees'* version of the revelation is very similar, in fact almost identical, to the biblical account. Jacob sees in his dream a heavenly ladder with angels ascending and descending on it.[202] God stands above the staircase and speaks to him; *Jub.* 27.21-22.[203] In verse 24 we read that God says to Jacob:

> [*Jub.* 27.24] "… And behold, I shall be with you and I shall protect you everywhere you go. And I shall bring you back into this land in peace because I shall not forsake you until I do everything which I have said to you."

This verse is virtually identical to Gen 28:15 and it is also an echo of the words of Isaac in *Jub.* 27.15-16, as quoted above.

As in the Bible, the God who addresses Jacob is clearly distinguished from the angels who go up and down on the ladder. Jacob's reaction to the heavenly vision in *Jub.* 27.25-27 is the same as in Gen 28:16-18.

Jacob eventually arrives at his destination, works there for his uncle Laban and marries the latter's two daughters Leah and Rachel; *Jubilees* 28, compare Genesis 29-30.

Jacob's second dream

We find the shortened counterpart of Gen 31:2-21 in *Jub.* 29.1-4. Laban and his sons have become jealous of Jacob, who decides to flee. We read in verse 3:

---

bilees is generally considered to be later than Tobit. See, e.g., Moore, 1996, 194. As shown previously, angels play a more predominant role in other parts of *Jubilees*, and it seems evident that *Jubilees* generally has quite an advanced angelology. See also *Jub.* 35.16-17, a passage in which Isaac once again ensures his wife of Jacob's divine protection: "And you [Rebekah] should not fear on account of Jacob because the protector of Jacob is greater and mightier than the protector of Esau." In the light of *Jub.* 27.13-18, the most probable interpretation of Isaac's assurance in *Jub.* 35.16-17 is that "the protector of Jacob" is God Himself. However, if we are to believe Charles (1902, 209, note 17), the latter passage is the earliest reference to Jewish belief in guardian angels. The issue is in turn discussed by Hannah (2007, 423-424) who also interprets the passage in this way, with the reservation that he maintains that the angel Raphael's role in the book of Tobit must be counted as the earliest witness to the belief in guardian angels.

202 *Jubilees* does not offer any explanation of the meaning of the stairway/ladder or the presence of the angels in Jacob's dream.

203 Wintermute has here chosen the translation 'stairway,' not 'ladder;' God/the LORD is depicted as standing above it. However, Charles' English translation has the word 'ladder' which God is said to be standing upon; see *Jub.* 27.21-22 in *AOT*, 1984, 87.

> [*Jub.* 29.3] For he [Jacob] told them [his wives] everything, as he had seen it
> in the dream, and everything which *he* [God] told him, that he would re-
> turn to the house of his father.

In the context of *Jubilees* it is unclear whether the dream that Jacob refers to here alludes to the previously mentioned revelation in Bethel or
another, distinct vision. The most probable interpretation seems to be
that the "author" of *Jubilees* has in mind the second dream vision of
Jacob mentioned in Genesis 31. *Jub.* 29.3 is thus a summary of Gen
31:10-13. As shown in the quotation, the designation 'the angel of God'
is not used in *Jub.* 29.3, and in this way it differs from the biblical account of this event. According to O. S. Wintermute, 'he' who has told
Jacob to return home is God Himself, an interpretation that is very obvious in this context.[204] The angel of God in Gen 31:11 seems thus in
Jubilees to be identified as God in person, cf., Gen 31:13: "*I am the God of
Bethel ...*"

Jacob's pilgrimage to Bethel

Jub. 31.1-2 corresponds to Gen 35:2-4:

> [*Jub.* 31.1] And on the first day of the month, Jacob spoke to all of the men
> of his house, saying, "Purify and change your clothes, and having arisen,
> let us go up to Bethel, where on the day when I fled from the face of Esau,
> my brother, I made a vow to him who has been with me and has returned
> me unto this land in peace. [2] Remove the strange gods that are among
> you ..."

Unlike in the biblical narrative, Jacob is said in *Jub.* 31.3 to have invited
his father and mother to come to Bethel in order to participate in the
sacrificial service. Jacob visits his parents and his son Levi is or-
dained/blessed as a priest by Isaac: "May he [God] draw you [Levi] and
your seed near to him from all flesh to serve in his sanctuary as *the
angels of the Presence and the holy ones ...*" (*Jub.* 31.14). The angels of the
Presence are thus considered to perform a priestly role in heaven.[205]

Jacob tells his father that God has shown him mercy and protected
him from all evil, and now the time has come for the fulfillment of the
vow he once made to God in Bethel, *Jub.* 31.24-26.[206] Because of the
weakness of old age, Isaac does not follow Jacob to Bethel to participate

---

204 Wintermute *OTP*, vol. 2, 1985, 111. Wintermute is probably correct in his assumption. We must, however, consider the possibility that the wording in *Jub.* 29.3 may be
deliberately ambiguous, leaving it to the reader to interpret the pronoun as referring
either to God or to an angel. See also Hayward 2005, 114-116.

205 See also the *Testament of Levi*.

206 Cf., *Jub.* 27.13-18 and Gen 48:16.

in the service but Rebekah accompanies him, *Jub.* 31.26-30. The whole of chapter 31 is dedicated to Jacob's preparation for the sacrifice on the altar he has built at Bethel and hence the accomplishment of his vow.

Jubilees 32 describes Jacob's sacrifice and tithe at Bethel, while his son Levi functions as a priest during the service.[207] In the second night at Bethel, God appears once more to Jacob, blesses him and gives him his name Israel. *Jub.* 32.17-19 is thus a counterpart of Gen 35:9-13.[208]

In *Jub.* 32.16 we read that Jacob wants to build a sanctuary at Bethel, but he is later prevented by an angel from accomplishing this plan:

> [*Jub.* 32.21] And he [Jacob] saw in a *vision of the night* [a dream? Cf., I Sam 3:5; Isa 29:7],[209] and behold *an angel* was descending from heaven, and there were seven tablets in his hands. And he gave (them) to Jacob, and he read them, and he knew everything which was written in them, which would happen to him and his sons during all the ages [...] [23] And he [the angel] said to him, "Do not build this place, and do not make an eternal sanctuary, and do not dwell here because this is not the place ..."

This is thus an addition to the original biblical story of Jacob's pilgrimage to Bethel in Genesis 35. The angel who advises Jacob against building a sanctuary at Bethel is clearly distinguished from God, because according to the preceding verse, *Jub.* 32.20; when God had finished speaking to Jacob, he departed from him: "... And Jacob watch-

---

207 One night in Bethel, God confirms to Levi in a dream that he and his sons have been ordained as priests of God forever, *Jub* 32.1. See also *T. Levi* 2.4-12, where Levi is said to have been taken up to heaven by an angel and ordained a priest, cf., also chapters 8 and 9 in the Pseudepigraphon. According to Kugel (2006, 115-168), the tradition that an angel was involved in Levi's covenant with God is based on an ancient interpretation of Mal 2:4-7. Although the name of the holiday is not explicitly mentioned in *Jubilees* 32, Jacob's celebration in Bethel seems to be connected to Sukkoth, and *Jub.* 32.27-29 most certainly refers to the institution of *Shemini Atseret*:

And he [Jacob] observed there yet one (more) day and he sacrificed in it according to everything which he had been sacrificing on the previous days. And he called it "Addition" because that day was added, but the previous (days) he called "the feast." [...] Therefore it was revealed to him so that he might observe it and add it to the seven days of the feast. And it was called "Addition" because it is written (on high) in the attestation of feast days according to the number of days of the year.

Cf., Lev 23:36; Num 29:35-38; 2 Chr 7:9, and *Targum Pseudo-Jonathan* to Genesis 35. See also Hayward 2005, 139-153, and chapter 4.6.

208 *Jubilees* does not mention Jacob's struggle and his renaming at the ford of Jabbok but simply states; "And he [Jacob] crossed over the Jabbok in the ninth month on the eleventh day of the month. And on that day Esau, his brother, came to him and was reconciled to him ..." [*Jub.* 29.13]. See further Hayward 2005, 118-119, 132-139, 144.

209 See also Guiley 2004, 105.

ed until he [God] went up into heaven."[210] The angel on the other hand, appears to Jacob in an additional, separate vision and is said to be "*descending from heaven …*" According to the author of *Jubilees*, the 'right place' for the Temple is Jerusalem. The angel with the seven tablets in his hands is here anonymous, but he calls to mind the alleged narrator of *Jubilees*, the angel of the Presence:[211]

> [*Jub.* 1.29] And the angel of the presence, who went before the camp of Israel, took *the tablets of the division* of the years from the time of the creation of the law and testimony according to their weeks [of years] according to the Jubilees., year by year throughout the full number of Jubilees, from [the day of creation until] the day of the new creation when the heaven and earth an all of their creatures shall be renewed […] until the sanctuary of the LORD is created in Jerusalem upon Mount Zion …

Because of the obvious resemblance of the angel in *Jub.* 32.21-23 to the angel mentioned in the quotation, it seems probable that it is one and the same angel in both cases.

Jacob and Joseph

There is no counterpart to Gen 48:15-16 in *Jubilees*. However, when Jacob is reunited with his son Joseph and comes to live in Egypt he says to him:

> [*Jub.* 45.3] "Let me die now after I have seen you. And now let the LORD, the God of Israel, be blessed, the God of Abraham and the God of Isaac, who did not withhold his mercy and his kindness from his servant Jacob. [4] It is enough for me that I have seen your face while I was alive, *for the vision which I saw in Bethel was certainly true.* May the LORD my God be blessed forever and ever and blessed (be) his name."

In his happiness over the reunion with Joseph, Jacob looks back at his life and recalls the vision at Bethel. Jacob exclaims that God has indeed kept the promise he once made to him there; "And behold, I [God] shall be with you and I shall protect you …"

Concluding Remarks

In *Jubilees'* rendering of the Jacob narratives, God Himself stands out as the one who appears to the patriarch during his travels and hard-

---

210 Cf., Gen 35:13.
211 Cf., *Jubilees'* version of the Aqedah. As shown above, there are several angels of the Presence mentioned in *Jubilees*, but the alleged narrator of the book seems nevertheless to have a specific status.

ships.[212] The only exception is the angelophany in *Jub.* 32.21-23, which lacks a counterpart in the Bible. The angel who gives Jacob the seven tablets concerning the future of his descendants is anonymous but for contextual reasons we may assume that he is to be identified as the angel of the Presence, compare *Jub.* 1.29. The theme of divine protection of travelers is significant in *Jubilees* and recalls the book of Tobit as well as Genesis 24.

4Q158

A fragmentary paraphrase of Genesis 32 is preserved in the Qumran manuscript 4Q158. This version is quite similar to the biblical account with the noteworthy exception that, when blessing him after the fight, Jacob's contender refers to God in the *third* person:

> "… May the Lo[rd] make you fruitful […]. May he grant you kn]owledge and understanding and may he save you from all violence …"

Thus here, Jacob's opponent is obviously not identified as God in person.[213]

The Ladder of Jacob

In accordance with its title, this Pseudepigraphon is mainly an elaboration on Jacob's dream at Bethel and his vision of the heavenly stairway/ladder (Gen 28:10-22). There is also a short allusion to Jacob's encounter with 'the unknown man' in Gen 32:22-30. *Lad. Jac.* 1.3-8 reads as follows:

> [3] He [Jacob] had a dream. And behold, a ladder was fixed on the earth, whose top reached to heaven. [4] And the top of the ladder was the face of a man, carved out of fire. [5] There were twelve steps leading to the top of the ladder, and on each step to the top there were two human faces, on the right and on the left, twenty-four faces (or busts) including their chests. [6] And the face in the middle was higher than all I saw,[214] the one of fire, including the shoulders and arms, exceedingly terrifying, more than those

---

212 As shown, *Jubilees* has no version of Jacob's struggle at the ford of Jabbok, nor a direct counterpart of Gen 48:15-16, but all the other relevant Jacob narratives are rendered therein.

213 See also Hayward 2005, 28-37.

214 According to Lunt (note 1a in *OTP* vol. 2, 1985, 407), it is probable that the *Ladder of Jacob* originally began with Jacob's own account of the events that brought him to Bethel, considering the first-person narrative from v. 6 onwards.

> twenty-four faces. [7] And while I was still looking at it, behold, angels of God ascended and descended on it. [8] And God was standing above its highest face, and he called to me from there, saying, "Jacob, Jacob!" And I said, "Here I am LORD!"

As shown in the quotation, the revelation of the heavenly ladder is much more elaborate here than in the Bible, the appearance of the ladder being described in detail. On the top of the ladder there is a fiery face of a man, and God stands above it. The ladder and God are thus closely connected to each other.

H. G. Lunt writes that even though he has retained the traditional translation 'ladder,' the "author" certainly had a solid staircase in mind, lined with statues, as a ziggurat.[215] As in the Bible, angels of God are said to ascend and descend on it, in that order. According to Lunt, this angelic motion is characteristic of the traditions related to Jacob; elsewhere the emphasis is upon angels descending and then ascending.[216] From *Lad. Jac.* 1.6 and onwards, the alleged narrator of the revelation is Jacob himself.

God then talks to Jacob and promises to bless him and his offspring; *Lad. Jac.* 1.9-12 thus corresponds to Gen 28:13-14 but God's words to Jacob concerning his present situation (Gen 28:15) are here omitted.

As in the Bible, the revelation scares Jacob: "And when I heard (this) from on high, awe and trembling fell upon me" (*Lad. Jac.* 2.1). Jacob asks God to explain the meaning of his dream, *Lad. Jac.* 2.21-22. The "author" of the book thus presumes that the vision of the heavenly ladder has some deeper symbolic significance. The ladder conceals a divine message.

While Jacob is still praying, God answers him and sends out the archangel Sariel:

> [*Lad. Jac.* 3.1] … behold, a voice came before my [Jacob's] face saying, [2] "Sariel, leader of the beguiled, you who are in charge of dreams, go and make Jacob understand the meaning of the dream he has had and explain to him everything he saw; but first bless him."[3] And Sariel the archangel came to me and I saw (him), and his appearance was very beautiful and awesome. [4] But I was not astonished by his appearance, for the vision which I had seen in my dream was more terrible than he. [5] And I did not fear the vision of the angel.

---

215 Lunt, note b in *OTP* vol. 2, 1985, 407.
216 Lunt, introduction in *OTP* vol. 2, 1985, 405.

Lunt writes that here "… 'the voice' has ceased to be something heard [as in *Lad. Jac.* 2.1] and has become a hypostatic creature."[217] Jacob does not fear the appearance of the archangel; the vision in the dream was more terrifying.

This angelophany obviously constitutes a major difference between the *Ladder of Jacob* and the biblical account in Genesis 28. In the same way as the anonymous angel with the seven tablets in his hand (*Jub.* 32.21), the archangel Sariel is depicted as distinct from God. He is a heavenly messenger, the angel who is in charge of dreams who comes in order to unveil Jacob's mysterious vision. God is personified by 'the voice.' God commands Sariel to bless Jacob before he starts to explain the dream, and the archangel accordingly changes Jacob's name to Israel. *Lad. Jac.* 4.1-5 is thus an echo of Gen 32:24-30:

> [*Lad. Jac.* 4.1-5] And the angel said to me [Jacob], "What is your name?" And I said, "Jacob." (He announced), "Your name shall no longer be called Jacob, but your name shall be similar to my name, Israel." And when I was going from Phandana of Syria to meet Esau my brother, he came to me and blessed me and called me Israel. And he would not tell me his name until I adjured him.

According to the version of Gen 32:24-30 in *Targum Neofiti 1*, it was the angel Sariel who was Jacob's contender at the ford of Jabbok. The other Palestinian Targums also claim that Jacob wrestled with an angel, not God in person, but the angel is identified as Sariel only in *Targum Neofiti 1*.[218]

The appearance of an archangel by the name of Sariel is significant, because many consider him to have been the original fourth archangel, later replaced by Uriel/Phanuel.[219] He appears, for example, as one of the four archangels in *The books of Enoch, Aramaic Fragments of Qumran Cave 4*.[220]

---

217 Lunt, introduction in *OTP*, vol. 2, 1985, 406. See also Charlesworth 1992, 609.

218 See chapter 4.5 below and Vermes 1975, 159-166. Vermes interprets Jacob's words in *Targum Neofiti 1* Gen 32:31 "… I have seen angels from before the Lord face to face and my life has been saved" as an allusion to the angels on the ladder in Jacob's dream in Bethel. I find this interpretation doubtful. Jacob's words here may just as well allude to the angels who met him as described in Gen 32:1-3.

219 van Henten 1995b, 152. Variants of the name of this angel are Saraqel and Suriel, among others. There are also traditions concerning a fallen angel by the name of Sariel (and similar names). See Guiley 2004, 318.

220 Ed. Milik and Black 1976. See pages 170-174. Sariel is also mentioned in the *Qumran War Scroll*, 1QM 9.12-15. See also Vermes, 1975, 159-166.

According to Lunt, the archangel Sariel is hence linked to Jewish traditions that clearly predate the fall of the Second Temple in 70 C.E.[221] Sariel functions in the *Ladder of Jacob* as a so-called *angelus interpres*. His role is thus similar to that of the archangel Gabriel in the book of Daniel, cf., Dan 8:15-16:[222]

> [Dan 8:15] Then it happened, when I, Daniel, had seen the vision and was seeking the meaning, that suddenly there stood before me one having the appearance of a man. [16] And I heard a *man's voice* between the banks of Ulai, who called, and said, "*Gabriel, make this man understand the vision.* [my italics].

According to Kugel, Jacob's fearful reaction to the dream (Gen 28:17) was something that puzzled the early Jewish interpreters. What was it that scared Jacob so much?[223] As we have seen, according to *Lad. Jac.* 3.4-5, Jacob deemed the vision of his dream to be more frightening than the angelic visitation. The answer provided by the *Ladder of Jacob* is that the ladder in itself is a symbolic message concerning the future:

> [*Lad. Jac.* 5.1] Thus he said to me: "You have seen a ladder with twelve steps, each step having two human faces which kept changing their appearance. [2] The ladder is this age, [3] and the twelve steps are the periods of this age. [4] But the twenty-four faces are the kings of the ungodly nations of this age. [5] Under these kings the children of your children and the generations of your sons will be interrogated.[224] [6] These will rise up against the iniquity of your grandsons [...] [16] Know, Jacob, that your descendants shall be exiles in a strange land, and they will afflict them with slavery [...] [17] But the LORD will judge the people for whom they slave.[225]

The ladder represents thus the coming ages of history and the twenty-four faces symbolize the two "pagan" rulers of each period who will subdue Jacob's offspring. As the embodiment or representative of the people of Israel (cf., *Lad. Jac.* 4.1-5), Jacob is allowed to see the future of

---

221 Lunt in *OTP* vol. 2, 1985, 405. See also *1 Enoch* 20.

222 See also, e.g., Dan 9:20-27. As mentioned, Sariel appears to be another name for the angel Uriel (Phanuel) who figures in the *Prayer of Joseph* and frequently functions as an *angelus interpres* in *1 Enoch* (e.g., 72.1; 74.2; 78.10), and in *4 Ezra* (e.g., 4.1; 5.20; 10.28). Ashton (1994, 83-85) demonstrated that the same ambivalence that exists between the 'angel of the Lord' and God also applies to the relationship of Uriel and God in *4 Ezra*. See also Orlov 2004, 71-73.

223 Kugel 1995, 211-212.

224 According to Kugel (1995, 210), in place of Lunt's translation 'interrogated', we should probably here read 'tested'.

225 *Lad. Jac.* 5.16-17 is probably inspired by God's revelation to Abraham in Gen 15:12-17. The reference is clearly to the slavery of the Israelites in Egypt and their subsequent Exodus. See also the *Ladder of Jacob* 6.

the Jewish people. As the Master of world history, God is standing above the ladder and speaks to Jacob. God will bless Jacob and his descendants in all their tribulations, *Lad. Jac.* 1.8-12, cf., Gen 28:13-15.[226]

The notion that the Jewish people throughout history will suffer subjection under different foreign empires is something that we recognize from the book of Daniel; e.g., 7:3-27; 9:20-26. The function of Sariel in the *Ladder of Jacob* is similar to both Gabriel's role in the book of Daniel and that of the unnamed angel in *Jub.* 32.21-26: "... And he [the angel] gave (them) [the seven tablets] to Jacob, and he read them, and he knew everything which was written in them, *which would happen to him and to his sons during all the ages..."* (v. 21b).[227]

In my quotation of *Lad. Jac.* chapter 5 above, I omitted vv. 7-15. This was deliberate, and I will soon explain why, but let us first take a look at this passage:

> [*Lad. Jac.* 5.7] And this place[228] will be made desolate by *the four ascents* [...] through the sins of your grandsons. [8] And around the property of your forefathers a palace will be built, a temple in the name of your God and of (the God) of your fathers, [9] and in the provocations of your children it will become deserted by *the four ascents of this age.* [10] For you saw the first four busts which were striking against the steps [...] [11] *angels ascending and descending,* and the busts amid the steps. [12] The Most High will raise up kings from the grandsons of your brother Esau, and they will receive all the nobles of the tribes of the earth who will have maltreated your seed. [13] And they will be delivered into his hands and he will be vexed by them. [14] And he will hold them by force and rule over them, and they will not be able to oppose him until the day when his thought will go out against them to serve idols and (to offer) sacrifices to the dead. [15] (He will) do violence to all those in his kingdom who will be revealed in such guilt ...

In *Lad. Jac.* 5.1-6, the archangel Sariel explained the ladder as a symbol of the twelve future eras of world history, each period reigned over by two kings, in total 24 kings of ungodly nations. In the passage cited above, the emphasis is instead on the so-called *four ascents* of this age and the angels ascending and descending on the ladder.

Kugel connects 'the four ascents of this age' to the four beasts in the book of Daniel. The angels who are said to go up and down symbolize the rise and downfall of heathen empires. The angels in Jacob's dream

---

226 Cf., Westermann 1985, 460, where he states that God's presence in history and the importance of cultic worship are the two main messages of the text.

227 Cf., also *Prayer of Joseph,* Fragment B, see below. According to the *Prayer of Joseph,* Jacob is in reality an angel himself, by the name of Israel. See also the *Prayer of Jacob.*

228 According to Kugel (1995, 216), 'this place' refers to Jerusalem, not Bethel/Luz.

are thus interpreted as *the angelic princes of the pagan nations* (cf., Dan 10:13, 20)[229] and that is why they are depicted as first going up before descending, and not the other way around, which had been the case with God's ministering angels.[230] In the words of Kugel: "... the four beasts are transformed into (four) 'angels of God' said to go up and down Jacob's ladder."[231]

It is noteworthy that even though the angels are present in the initial description of the dream in chapter 1, there is no mention of the four ascents. The *Ladder of Jacob* in its present form seems to be a fusion of two originally distinct and slightly conflicting explanations of Jacob's vision. In the interpretation that Kugel considers the original one, the angels play no particular role in the dream, except perhaps to assure Jacob of angelic protection for his descendants. It is *the ladder in itself* that constitutes the message, as *'the staircase of history.'*[232] Kugel accordingly claims that the passage cited above is a later interpolation,[233] a conclusion that I find convincing. This is hence the reason for omitting *Lad. Jac.* 5.7-15 in my first quotation of the chapter.

The angels in the dream are either understood as God's angels who represent the heavenly protection of Jacob and his descendants throughout history or as the guardian angelic princes of the heathen nations. However, the two interpretations of the dream have in common the depiction of God as standing above the ladder/staircase. God is the One who controls world history, and he will eventually redeem Jacob's offspring. The archangel Sariel functions as the *angelus interpres*, in the same way as the archangel Gabriel in the book of Daniel. This biblical book is an important key to understanding the message of the *Ladder of Jacob*.[234]

The two human faces on each step of the ladder/staircase (*Lad. Jac.* 1.5) are said to represent future pagan kings who will subdue Jacob's descendants (*Lad. Jac.* 5.1-5). However, the fiery face of a man at the top of the ladder mentioned in *Lad. Jac.* 1.4, 6, is not identified by Sariel. The wording of *Lad. Jac.* 1.4 is peculiar: "*And the top of the ladder was the face as of a man, carved out of fire.*" The ladder is thus described as having a

---

229 See also Deut 32:8-9 in the LXX.
230 Kugel 1995, 211-216.
231 Kugel 1995, 215. Here Esau and his sons represent the Roman Empire, see also Kugel 1995, 214-216, 222. This interpretation is also found in *Gen. Rab.* 68.14 and *Pesiqta de Rab Kahana* 23, see chapter 4.5. See also Hannah 2007, 418-421.
232 Kugel 1995, 216-221.
233 Kugel 1995, 209-227, esp. pp. 221-227. To be exact, Kugel considers *Lad. Jac.* 5.7-16a as a later interpolation.
234 See also Kugel 1995, 211-221.

man's head at its very top. Who does this head represent? As we have seen, God is said to be standing "… *above its* [the ladder's] *highest face…*" see *Lad. Jac.* 1.8. Thus, God appears to be distinguished from the face at the ladder's top.

However, Andrei Orlov interprets the fiery face in *Lad. Jac.* 1.6 as the face of God.[235] In support, he refers to Jacob's prayer in response to the vision,[236] especially his words in *Lad. Jac.* 2.15: "… Before the face of your [God's] glory the six-winged seraphim are afraid […] and they sing unceasingly a hymn …" According to Orlov, the depiction of Jacob's vision gives the impression that God's voice is emanating from the fiery face of the ladder, which he sees as a distinct divine manifestation. God is speaking to Jacob from behind the 'face'.[237]

Moreover, Orlov refers to *2 Enoch* 22, which also contains a similar depiction of the face of the Lord as 'fiery and terrifying', and he further remarks that, in some biblical and intertestamental texts, 'face' is used as an equivalent to God's Glory, His *Kavod*.[238]

According to Kugel, the description of the ladder with the fiery head at its top is based on the fact that the Hebrew word ראש can mean both 'top' and 'head,' cf., Gen 28:12a.[239] As mentioned in the analysis of Gen 28:10-22 in chapter 3, it is linguistically possible to interpret v. 12b as meaning that the angels are going up and down "on"/for the sake of Jacob.[240] The Hebrew word בו may refer either to Jacob or to the ladder. The Hebrew wording of Gen 28:12 is as follows:

ויהלום והנה סלם מצב ארצה וראשו מגיע השמימה והנה מלאכי אלהים עלים וירדים בו

Kugel connects the head constituting the top of the ladder in *Lad. Jac.* 1.4 with the Rabbinic tradition that Jacob's portrait is said to be kept in heaven.[241] He points out that it is possible to interpret the suffix at-

---

235 Orlov 2004, 61-66.

236 *Lad. Jac.* 2.7-19.

237 Orlov 2004, 62.

238 See Orlov 2004, 63-64, and e.g., Exod 33:18-23, where Moses asks to see God's Glory, but receives the answer that no man can see God's face. See also Ezekiel 1. God's face, פנים denotes God's presence, see chapter 3 and, e.g., Exod 33:14-16; Deut 4:37, cf., the rendering of Isa 63:9 in the MT and the LXX. See also Seow 1995, 607-613, and the rendering of Gen 28:13 in the *Targum Onqelos*, see chapter 4.5.

239 Kugel 1990, 118.

240 Kugel 1990, 112-116. This interpretation is also found in, e.g., *Targum Neofiti 1* and *Genesis Rabbah*.

241 Kugel 1990, 112-124, 250, cf., also the Palestinian Targums to Gen 28:12 and *Gen. Rab.* 68.12, see chapter 4.5 below.

tached to the Hebrew word ראש/ 'head/top' as alluding to Jacob. According to Kugel, the verse could thus be translated as; "... *and his* [Jacob's] *head reached to heaven; and behold, the angels of God were ascending and descending upon him.*"[242] The reason for the shuttling of the angels back and forth between heaven and earth is thus their wish to behold Jacob; on the one hand his heavenly portrait at the top of the ladder, and on the other the "real" Jacob lying on the ground.[243] However, this interpretation is not expressly given in the Pseudepigraphon.

Orlov also takes this line of interpretation and discusses the scholarly suggestion that the fiery face at the top of the ladder may represent Jacob's heavenly counterpart; Jacob's portrait/image engraved in/seated on God's throne.[244] This heavenly double of Jacob has in turn been defined as his guardian "angel" and identified as the embodiment of the divine Glory. The idea of Jacob's heavenly counterpart also seems to be present in the *Prayer of Joseph*.[245]

Concluding Remarks

As the title implies, this Pseudepigraphon is based mainly on Jacob's vision of the heavenly ladder in his dream at Bethel (Gen 28:10-22). In a similar way to *Jubilees*, this source also contains an additional angelophany, not mentioned in the Bible.

God, who is depicted as standing at the top of the ladder, sends out the archangel Sariel in order to make Jacob understand the meaning of the dream vision. This angel is entitled the one 'in charge of dreams'. He is portrayed as distinct from God, who is personified by 'the voice'. The role of Sariel in the *Ladder of Jacob* is reminiscent of the archangel Gabriel's function in the book of Daniel; like him, Sariel is an *angelus interpres*. Sariel appears to be of a higher rank than the angels going up and down on the ladder. He is clearly depicted as separate from both them and God. Similar to the unnamed angel in *Jub.* 32.21-26, Sariel reveals to Jacob the future destiny of his descendants.

---

242 Kugel 1990, 117-119.
243 Kugel 1990, 112-119.
244 Orlov 2004, 66-71. See also Fishbane 2003, 247-249, the renderings of Genesis 28 in the Palestinian Targums, and chapters 4.5 and 4.6 below.
245 See further chapter 4.6 and Orlov 2004, 66-71, Rowland 1984, 500-507, and Fossum 1995, 135-151. However, Orlov (2004, 76) admits that there is a certain ambiguity inherent in the the *Ladder of Jacob*; "... the fiery face can be taken either as God's *Kavod* or an enthroned vice-regent associated with the Face (i.e. the enthroned Jacob-Israel)."

The angels ascending and descending on the ladder are either interpreted as Jacob's guardian angels or as the angelic princes of the heathen nations. A third variant suggested by Kugel to be hinted at in the Pseudepigraphon is the tradition of Jacob's head portrayed at the top of the ladder: The angels are thus shuttling back and forth between heaven and earth in order to compare the "real" Jacob on the ground with his heavenly image. According to Orlov, the head/'the fiery face' on top of the ladder may be interpreted as a manifestation of God's Glory. Be that as it may, the angels on the ladder are distinguished from God, who is depicted as the one in charge of world history.

In addition to Gen 28:10-22, there is also an allusion to Gen 32:26-29 in the *Ladder of Jacob*. Sariel is said to have blessed Jacob and given him his new name Israel, an interpretation that most certainly is connected to the tradition in *Targum Neofiti 1*, where Jacob's contender at the ford of Jabbok is said to be the archangel Sariel. With regard to the fact that Sariel is often replaced by the archangels Uriel or Phanuel, there appears to be a traditional link between the *Ladder of Jacob* and the *Prayer of Joseph*, wherein Jacob's opponent is the angel Uriel, see below.

Testament of Jacob

In this narrative, the background setting of the plot is an angelic visitation; when the end of Jacob's earthly life draws near, God sends him Michael, here designated as the chief of the angels. Michael's commission is to prepare Jacob for his approaching death. This angelic visitation is depicted as one of many in the life of Jacob, who is used to talking with angels; *T. Jac.* 1.4-10.

Some time later, Jacob is visited by yet another angel, an angelophany that initially scares him, because the angel resembles his father Isaac. This anonymous angel[246] says to Jacob:

---

246 In his introduction to *Prayer of Joseph* (*OTP* vol. 2, 1985, 711) Smith interprets this angel in *Testament of Jacob* as Michael, appearing to Jacob in the form of Isaac. According to Jewish tradition, the archangel Michael is the guardian angel of the people of Israel, see, e.g., Dan 12:1. In *T. Dan* 6.5, we read about an unnamed 'angel of peace' who is declared to be Israel's guardian, a tradition that also seems to be extant in 4Q369 and *T. Levi* 5.6, where the angel who speaks to Levi identifies himself as the angel who intercedes for the people of Israel. However, Jewish tradition is ambivalent on this point, since there are also texts which deny the idea of an angelic patron of Israel and proclaim God to be the people's sole protector, e.g., Deut 32:8-9; Sir 17:17 and *Jub.* 15.30-32. See also Kugel 2006, 186-206, and Hannah 2007, 422-423.

> [*T. Jac.* 2.5] … "Do not fear, O Jacob; I am the angel who has been walking with you and guarding you from your infancy. [6] I announced that you would receive the blessing of your father and of Rebecca, your mother. [7] I am the one who is with you, O Israel, in all your acts and in everything which you have witnessed. [8] I saved you from Laban when he was endangering you and pursuing you. [9] At the time I gave you all his possessions and blessed you, your wives, your children and your flocks. [10] I am the one who saved you from the hand of Esau […] [14] Blessed are you also, Jacob, for you have seen God face to face. [15] You saw the angel of God–may he be exalted!–and you saw the ladder standing firm on the ground with its top in the heavens. [16] Then you beheld the Lord sitting at its top with a power which no one could describe …"

This angel is thus Jacob's guardian, who has watched over him his entire life. In *T. Jac.* 2.8-9, we see that the angel identifies himself as the one who saved Jacob from Laban and blessed his family and flocks, a clear allusion to Gen 31:10-13, where 'the angel of God' is mentioned.

On the other hand, the angel who addresses Jacob in the passage cited above distinguishes himself from 'the angel of God' referred to in *T. Jac.* 2.15 and speaks reverently about him in the third person. Verses 14-15 are parallel and may accordingly be interpreted as referring to the same person; "… you have *seen* God face to face (v. 14). You saw *the angel of God*–may he be exalted!" (v. 15a), an allusion to Gen 32:30. In the same way as in Gen 48:15-16, the angel and God seems to be equated with each other. There appears thus to be a slight contradiction between *T. Jac.* 2.8-9 and 2.15.

In the reference to Jacob's dream vision at Bethel, God is said to have been sitting at the top of the ladder, possessing an indescribable power. The angels in the dream are not mentioned, nor the significance of the ladder, v. 15b-16. [247]

T. Jac. 4.15 corresponds to Gen 48:15-16; Jacob blesses his grandsons Ephraim and Manasseh and says:

> [*T. Jac.* 4.15] "May *the God* under whose authority my fathers, Abraham and Isaac, served in reverence, *the God* who has strengthened me from my youth up to the present time when *the angel* has saved me from all my afflictions, may he bless these lads, Manasseh and Ephraim."

In contrast to the biblical pericope, Jacob distinguishes between the angel who has saved him from all his afflictions (possibly a reference to the angel in *T. Jac.* 2.5-9) and God himself, who Jacob invokes in the prayer and asks to bless his grandsons. The angel is referred to as

---

247 In *T. Jac.* 3.5-6, Jacob tells his household that God Himself once appeared to him in Upper Mesopotamia and promised to bless him and his descendants, cf., Gen 28:13-15.

God's *emissary*, a being sent by God. Through His angel, God has protected Jacob but the angel here is not equated with God.

Demetrius the Chronographer

In Fragment 2 there is a preserved rendering of Jacob's confrontation with the 'unknown man' on his way home to Canaan:

> And while he was going to Canaan, an angel of the Lord wrestled with him, and touched the hollow of Jacob's thigh [...]. And the angel said to him that from that time on he would no longer be called Jacob, but Israel.

Thus, Demetrius understood the "man" whom Jacob struggles with in Genesis 32 as an angel. Unlike the biblical account, there is no indication in his version of the event that Jacob might actually have met God in person. However, in accordance with the Bible, Demetrius accredits the second bestowal of the name Israel in Genesis 35 to God Himself.

Concluding Remarks

According to the *Testament of Jacob*, the patriarch is visited at the end of his life by the archangel Michael in order to prepare him for his approaching death. Some time later, another angel appears, who resembles his father Isaac. This last mentioned anonymous angel introduces himself as Jacob's guardian and identifies himself as the 'the angel of God' who saved Jacob from Laban and increased his flocks (Gen 31:10-13).

In the same way as the angel of the Presence in *Jubilees'* version of the Aqedah, Jacob's guardian angel addresses him in the first person singular. On the other hand, it seems as if the author of the Pseudepigraphon interprets the 'unknown man' who encountered Jacob in Genesis 32 as God in person, because he makes the angel exclaim; "… you [Jacob] have seen God face to face. You saw the angel of God–may he be exalted!" (*T. Jac.* 2.14b-15, cf., Gen 32:30). 'The angel of God' referred to in *T. Jac.* 2.15 is apparently someone other than the speaker, and in the light of the preceding verse he seems to be identified as God Himself. It is also stated that it was God who addressed Jacob in his dream at Bethel.

The angel referred to by Jacob in Gen 48:15-16 is interpreted in *T. Jac.* 4.15 as a guardian angel sent by God. This angel is probably the same as the angelic speaker above.

Regarding the rendering of Jacob's struggle by Demetrius, the 'unknown man' is identified as an angel and, unlike the angelic contender in the *Testament of Jacob* who appears to be equated with God, there is no hint in Demetrius' text that Jacob's opponent is anything but an "ordinary" angel, distinct from God.

Prayer of Joseph, Joseph and Aseneth and Liber Antiquitatum Biblicarum

According to the *Prayer of Joseph*, Jacob is an angel himself by the name of Israel. Smith argues that this idea goes back to the Targumic and Midrashic traditions of the conferring of the name Israel on Jacob in Genesis 32 which will be discussed later.

Another motif behind Jacob's angelic identity in the Pseudepigraphon may be the collective use of Israel in the Bible, e.g., Exod 4:22b: "… Thus says the LORD: 'Israel is my firstborn son …' " a passage that has sometimes been interpreted as alluding to a heavenly or pre-existent being.[248] The name Israel is interpreted in the *Prayer of Joseph*, fragment A as 'a man seeing God', an understanding of the name that also appears frequently in the works of Philo.[249] As an angel, Israel constantly sees God in heaven. Smith classifies the Pseudepigraphon as "a myth of the mystery of Israel."[250]

The main exegetical point of departure is Jacob's combat with the "man" in Genesis 32. According to Smith, the *Prayer of Joseph* belongs to a circle in first century Judaism "… which sought a model for salvation in the ascent of the patriarchs to the full reality of their heavenly, angel-

---

248 See Smith, introduction to the *Prayer of Joseph* in *OTP* vol. 2, 1985, 701, and 1968, 253-271. A similar tradition is also extant in Philo's writings about the 'Logos', which he sometimes called Israel, see below. Cf., also Kugel 1998, 394-397. In Exodus the title clearly refers to the nation, as in 4 *Ezra* 6.58; Sir 36:12; *Jub.* 2.20, and *Pss. Sol.* 18.4, but sometimes Exod 4:22 is interpreted as referring to the patriarch in person, e.g., *Jub.* 19.29; *Exod. Rab.* 19.7. See also Smith *OTP*, vol. 2, 1985, 713, note d.

249 However, to be precise, Philo does not explain the name Israel as meaning 'a *man* seeing God' but always gives the shorter etymology 'the one who sees (God)', thus omitting the word 'man'. See further chapter 4.3 below.

250 Smith introduction in *OTP*, vol. 2, 1985, 704, and, 1968, 281-282. When discussing the incarnation of the angel Israel, Smith (1968, 281-283) refers to the 'descent myth' and compares the *Prayer of Joseph* with the descent of 'Lady Wisdom' into the midst of Israel in Sir 24:8. See also Hannah 1999, 89-90.

ic nature."[251] An obvious parallel to this concept of angelic incarnation is to be found in the Enoch literature, particularly in 2 *Enoch*.[252]

According to Smith and others, the tradition of an angel by the name of Israel is also connected to the idea of his heavenly portrait.[253] Even if Jacob himself is not an angel, he may have a heavenly counterpart, an angel with the same name.[254] In the *Prayer of Joseph* however, Jacob appears to identify himself as the angel:

> [Fragment A] "I, Jacob, who is speaking to you, am also Israel, an angel of God and a ruling spirit. Abraham and Isaac *were created before any work*. But, I, Jacob, who men call Jacob but whose name is Israel am he who *God called Israel* which means, a man seeing God, because I am the *firstborn of every living thing to whom God gives life*.[255]
>
> And when I was *coming up from Syrian Mesopotamia*, Uriel, the angel of God, came forth and said that 'I [Jacob-Israel] had *descended to earth* and I had tabernacled among men[256] and that I had been called by the name of Jacob. He envied me and *fought with me and wrestled with me* saying that his name and *the name that is before every angel* was to be above mine[257]. I told him his name and what rank he held among the sons of God. 'Are you not Uriel, the eighth after me? and I, Israel, *the archangel of the power of the Lord* and the *chief captain* among the sons of God? Am I not Israel, the *first minister before the face of God*?' And I called upon my God by the inextinguishable name."[258] [my italics].

Scholars are divided in their interpretation of Jacob's statement above; does Jacob claim to be the earthly *incarnation* of the angel Israel, Jacob being his earthly name, Israel the angelic name,[259] or is it Jacob's angelic

---

251 Smith, *OTP* vol. 2, 1985, introduction, 705. See also the *Prayer of Jacob* v. 19.

252 Smith *OTP* vol. 2, 1985, introduction, 705. See 2 *Enoch* chapter 1; 22.9; 33.11; 67.18. See also VanderKam 2000b, 428-432, and Fletcher-Louis 1997, 146-164.

253 See Smith *OTP*, vol. 2, 1985, introduction, 710, and 1968, 284-292, Kugel 1998, 397, and Orlov 2004, 66-71.

254 See Gieschen 1998, 137-142, and Fossum 1995, 142-149. Cf., *Pirqê de Rabbi Eliezer* 37. The title 'Israel' is sometimes given to the 'Logos' by Philo, see, e.g., *On the Confusion of Tongues* 146. See also chapters 4.3 and 4.6.

255 Cf., Col 1:15-17. See also Smith 1968, 268, and Gieschen 1998, 140.

256 Cf., John 1:14.

257 According to Smith, another possible translation of this passage is: "… his name (Uriel) should have precedence over my name (Israel) and of the angel that is before all."

258 The italics in the quotations of the *Prayer of Joseph* are the translator's. According to Gieschen (1998, 139-140) the reference to 'the inextinguishable name' implies a connection to the 'divine name-angel' of the Exodus tradition.

259 See Smith 1968, 281-292, Sullivan 2004, 98-101, Hurtado 1998, 64-65, and Kugel 1998, 398-399. Smith emphasizes the idea of incarnation and 'the descent-myth' in the *Prayer of Joseph*.

counterpart who is speaking?[260] In any case, it is clearly an angel-ic/divine being who speaks in the *Prayer of Joseph*. The interpretation of the etymology of the name Israel as 'a man seeing God' emphasizes his celestial status. According to Smith, the underlying idea is that the heavenly name is known only to other angels.[261] The tradition that the patriarchs were formed before the creation is also to be found in other Jewish works.[262]

In this context, we may mention *Jos. Asen.* 22.7-8 where Jacob is also described in angelic terms:

> [7] And Aseneth saw him [Jacob] and was amazed by his beauty [...] and his old age was like the youth of a handsome (young) man, and his head was all white as snow [...] and his eyes (were) flashing and darting (flashes of) lighting, and his sinews and his shoulders and his arms were like (those) *of an angel,* and his thighs and his calves and his feet like (those) of a giant. [8] *And Jacob was like a man who had wrestled with God.* And Aseneth saw him and was amazed and she prostrated herself before him face down on the ground ...

Jacob's features in this text are commonly ascribed to divine beings, see, for example, Ezekiel 1 and Daniel 7. Aseneth's prostration is a very typical response to angelophanies in the Bible, e.g., Dan 8:15-17. It is also noteworthy that the author of *Joseph and Aseneth* seems to have understood the patriarch's contender in Genesis 32 to be God. Possibly, the author regarded Jacob's angelic appearance as a result of that divine encounter.[263]

According to the *Prayer of Joseph*; when Jacob/Israel comes up from Syrian Mesopotamia[264] he is confronted by the angel Uriel. The geographical setting is the same as in Gen 35:9-10.[265] In the same way as Hosea 12, the *Prayer of Joseph* appears to combine the biblical traditions

---

260 See Fossum 1995, 148. These two interpretations of Jacob's claim need not exclude each other, the incarnated angel may very well be identical with Jacob's celestial counterpart, thus Smith, Kugel et al. However, Fossum explicitly denies the idea that the angel Israel in the *Prayer of Joseph* is actually portrayed as *incarnated* in Jacob. He instead speaks of a '*mystical identity*' between *two* beings, one earthly and one heavenly. See also the discussion regarding the interpretation of 'the fiery head' on top of the ladder in Jacob's dream at Bethel in the section on the *Ladder of Jacob* above and chapters 4.5 and 4.6.

261 Smith *OTP* vol. 2, 1985, 713, note e.

262 See, e.g., *Tanhuma* (ed. Buber) *Numbers,* Naso 19 and Smith *OTP* vol. 2, 1985, introduction, 704.

263 See also Sullivan 2004, 102-103, and Orlov 2004, 75-76.

264 Syrian Mesopotamia is the standard Septuagint translation of Paddan-Aram. See LXX Gen 31:18 and 33:18.

265 Cf., LXX to Gen 35:9.

regarding the bestowing of the name Israel on Jacob.[266] According to the Pseudepigraphon, Jacob initially seems to have been unaware of his heavenly identity, because Uriel is said to have enlightened him concerning this matter. The ignorance of Jacob may have been inspired by the portrayal of him in Gen 28:16 as an ignorant man sleeping on the ground.[267] See also Fragment C:

> [Origen writes] Jacob was greater than man, he who supplanted his brother and who declared in the same book from which we quoted "I read in the tablets of heaven" that *he was a chief captain of the power of the Lord and had, from of old, the name Israel; something which he recognizes while doing service in the body, being reminded of it by the archangel Uriel.*

Jacob's opponent, the 'unknown man' of Genesis 32 is thus identified as Uriel, usually designated as one of the archangels.[268] That Uriel has to remind Jacob of his heavenly identity and origin may be inspired by the biblical statement that it was his opponent who gave Jacob the name Israel, see Gen 32:28.

The *Prayer of Joseph* supplies a motive for the attack on Jacob that differs from the one contained in the Bible story. Uriel is said to have envied him. The conflict is described as rivalry between two angels regarding their heavenly status and rank.[269] The Palestinian Targums identify Jacob's combatant as the angelic leader of the celestial worship, a tradition that is also extant in *L.A.B.* 18.5b-6

> [5]... And then I [God] said to the angels who work secretly, 'Did I not say regarding this, "I will reveal everything I am doing to Abraham [6] and to Jacob his son, the third one whom I called firstborn, who, when he was wrestling in the dust with the *angel who was in charge of hymns*, would not let him go until he blessed him."'

---

266 See also Smith introduction in *OTP* vol. 2, 1985, 709-710.

267 See also Smith 1968, 284-286.

268 See, e.g., *1 En.* 9.10; 10.1, 4, 9, 11; 20.2 and Guiley 2004, 360-361. On page 361 Guiley writes: "In the Prayer of Joseph, Uriel states, 'I have come down to earth to make my dwelling among men, and I am called Jacob by name.' The exact meaning of this statement is not clear, but it suggests that Uriel might have become Jacob, thus making him the first angel of record to become a mortal." This interpretation is apparently based on a totally different translation/understanding of the wording of the *Prayer of Joseph.*

269 See also Smith 1968, 278-281. The name 'Uriel' means 'fire/light of God'. Cf., *Gen. Rab.* 77.2, wherein Jacob in his strife with the angel at Jabbok claims to be made complete by fire, like an angel. See also *Exod. Rab.* 15.6: "The angels are called 'fire', for it is written: *The flaming fire Thy ministers* (Ps. CIV, 4), and Israel is also so called, as it is written: *and the house of Jacob shall be a fire* (Obad. 1,18) ..." [Eng. trans. Lehrmann 1939].

This tradition concerning Jacob's/Israel's rival may be connected in the *Prayer of Joseph* to the early Jewish personification of the worshiping community as an angelic figure named Israel leading the heavenly choir before God's throne.[270] The theme of angelic rivalry is also to be found in, for example, *Apoc. Ab.*10.9 and chapter 18.[271]

The rivalry between Jacob/Israel and Uriel may also be seen as a reflection of the biblical conflict between Esau and Jacob. Esau's jealousy of his brother in the Bible is paralleled by Uriel's envy in the Pseudepigraphon as the motive for the attack. In later haggadic lore, the fraternal conflict is extended to include Jacob's and Esau's descendants and their respective guardian angels.[272]

As previously mentioned, Uriel is normally counted among the archangels together with Michael, Gabriel and Raphael, but in some sources he is replaced by the angels Sariel[273] or Phanuel.[274] Thus *Targum Neofiti 1* refers to Sariel as the angelic adversary of Jacob in Genesis 32 and, in the *Ladder of Jacob*, Sariel is the *angelus interpres*.[275] The name Phanuel may be derived from the place name Peniel 'face of God' in Gen 32:30[276]. Compare Jacob's identification of himself in the *Prayer of Joseph*; "… Am I not Israel, the *first minister before the face of God?*" The name Uriel was often conflated with Sariel to produce the name Suriel/Suru'el and variants.[277] This angel is often ascribed negative attributes and sometimes said to have been the one who attacked Mos-

---

270 See also Smith 1968, 262-265, and *b. Hullin* 91b.

271 See also Smith *OTP* vol 2, 1985, introduction, 702-703. In *Tanhuma*, Bereshit 1.10 there is a comment on Job 25:2: "Dominion and fear are with God; he makes peace in his high heaven." In *Tanhuma* 'dominion' is interpreted as Michael, 'fear' as Gabriel. According to the Midrash, God is the one who makes peace between these angels.

272 See e.g., *Gen. Rab.* 77.3, Smith *OTP* vol. 2, 1985, introduction, 706, and 1968, 274-276. Smith (1985, 706) interprets Jacob's encounter with the band of angels in Gen 32:1-2 as a military confrontation. See also chapter 4.5 below.

273 E.g., *The books of Enoch, Aramaic Fragments of Qumran cave 4*, ed. Black and Milik 1976, see pp. 170-174 and 1QM 9:12-15. In 4QHen 9:1 Sariel replaces Uriel in the Greek manuscripts. The classification of Sariel as an archangel appears to be unique to Qumran. See also Smith *OTP* vol. 2, 1985, introduction, 708, and Vermes 1975, 159-166. Smith mentions a third angelic name 'Istrahel (Israel)' which substitutes for Uriel in the Gizeh fragment of 1 *En.* 10.1.

274 In *1 En.* 40.9; 54.6; and 71.8, 9, 13 Phanuel replaces Uriel as one of the four archangels.

275 See also Orlov 2004, 71-73.

276 Smith *OTP*, vol. 2, 1985 introduction, 709. See also Olyan 1993, 108-109.

277 See, e.g., *1 En.* 9.1 and 20.1 and Smith *OTP* vol. 2, 1985, introduction 709. See also note 273 above.

es in Exod 4:22-26. However, according to Hugo Odeberg in *3 Enoch*, Suriel is none other than the angelic prince of the Presence.[278]

In contrast to the biblical story, Jacob/Israel identifies his opponent in the *Prayer of Joseph*; "… Are you not Uriel, the eighth after me?"[279] Jacob's knowledge of his adversary's name demonstrates his power over him.[280] The designation of Uriel as "… the eighth after me [Jacob/Israel]…" may imply that he is excluded from the group of the archangels, usually said to be four or seven in number.[281] Jacob however, claims to be no less than "… the archangel of the power of the Lord and the chief captain among the sons of God…" Smith suggests that the implicit idea in the Pseudepigraphon is an angelic hierarchy with seven archangels with Israel as the eighth highest angel, ruling the seven below him, a counterpart to the role of the *Ogdoad* in Gnostic traditions and the *Dynamis* of the eighth and highest heaven in Jewish Merkabah traditions.[282]

Jacob's designation of himself as "… the archangel of the power of the Lord and the chief captain among the sons of God …"[283] parallels the titles commonly given to Michael, the guardian angel of the people of Israel.[284]

Fragment B is presumably an elaboration of Gen 48:15-16. Jacob addresses Joseph and his sons: "For I [Jacob] have read in the *tablets of heaven all that shall befall you and your sons*." This passage of the *Prayer of Joseph* relates the Pseudepigraphon to the so-called 'testament-genre', and is clearly connected to *Jub*. 32.21:

> And he [Jacob] saw in a vision of the night, and behold a n angel was descending from heaven, and there were seven tablets in his hands. And he gave (them) to Jacob, and he read them, and he knew everything which

---

278 Smith *OTP* vol. 2, 1985 introduction, 709, and Odeberg 1928, 99.

279 Cf., Gen 32:29: "Then Jacob asked him, 'Please tell me your name.' But he said, 'Why is it that you ask my name?' And he blessed him." The "man's" blessing of Jacob demonstrates that, according to the biblical version, it is he who is Jacob's superior, not the other way around as in the *Prayer of Joseph*.

280 See also Smith *OTP* vol. 2, 1985, 713, note m.

281 See also Smith *OTP* vol. 2, 1985, 713, note n.

282 Smith, introduction in *OTP* vol. 2, 1985, 704.

283 As stated above, the designation 'sons of God' is commonly used regarding angels in the Bible, e.g., Gen 6:1-4 and Job 1:6.

284 Cf., Dan 12:1. The Greek word used here for 'chief captain' (ἀρχιχιλίαρχος) is unique to the *Prayer of Joseph* but appears to be synonymous with the designation of the archangel Michael in Hellenistic Jewish literature (ἀρχιστράτηγος), e.g., LXX, Dan 8:11 and *T. Ab*. 1.4 and *Jos. Asen*. 14.7-8. See also Gieschen 1998, 140-142, and Smith *OTP* vol. 2, 1985, introduction, 704.

was written in them, which would happen to him and to his sons during all the ages.[285]

Smith also suggests a link to the *Testament of Isaac* and the *Testament of Jacob*, in which the angel Michael appears to the patriarch in question in the form of his father (Abraham or Isaac). He writes: "… in the Prayer of Joseph, perhaps, [the angel] Israel appears to Joseph in the form of Jacob."[286]

Finally, we have seen that the 'unknown man' who comes from nowhere and wrestles with Jacob in Genesis 32 is identified as the angel Uriel in the *Prayer of Joseph*. The battle at the ford of Jabbok is depicted as a confrontation between two competing angels. In the light of early Jewish traditions, the interpretation that the competition concerns the leadership of the celestial worship is close at hand. According to *L.A.B.* 18.6, the combatant is the angel in charge of hymns.[287] In both Pseudepigrapha it is obvious that Jacob's opponent is an angel distinct from God.

However, the angelic depiction of Jacob/Israel in the *Prayer of Joseph* is more complex. Jacob's identification as the angel Israel may imply that it is Jacob's celestial counterpart who speaks[288] and/or Jacob is understood to be this angel's earthly incarnation.[289] Moreover, Charles Gieschen and Jarl Fossum, for example, consider the angel Israel to be more than an "ordinary" angel; he is the manifestation of the very Glory of God.[290] Orlov is open both to the interpretation that Jacob's celestial "twin" is an angelic servant of God/'the Face' and to the idea that he is identical with God's Face, i.e., God Himself.[291]

---

285 Cf., also *Prayer of Joseph*, Fragment C and *Lad. Jac.* 4.1-5, see above.

286 Smith *OTP*, vol. 2, 1985, introduction, 711.

287 Cf., the Palestinian Targums to Genesis 32, see chapter 4.5 below.

288 See, e.g., Fossum 1995, 142-149

289 See, e.g, Smith 1968, 284-292, and Sullivan 2004, 98-101.

290 Fossum 1995, 142-149, and Gieschen 1998, 137-142. As support for their interpretation, both of these scholars refer to Philo's writings, where the 'Logos' is also sometimes labeled 'the angel Israel', and the 'Logos' of Philo is indeed no "ordinary" angel. See further chapters 4.3 and 4.6 below.

291 Orlov 2004, 76, cf., also Jacob/Israel's claim in the *Prayer of Joseph*: "Am I not Israel, the first minister before the face of God?"

Concluding Remarks

The Prayer of Joseph

In the *Prayer of Joseph's* elaboration of Genesis 32, Jacob is depicted as the (incarnated) angel Israel who is challenged by the angel Uriel. The name Israel is interpreted as 'a man seeing God'. The competition concerns the status of the two angels in heaven. According to Smith, in the light of early Jewish traditions it is probable that their rivalry concerns the leadership of the celestial worship. The angel who confronts Jacob is elsewhere often depicted as the heavenly worship leader, e.g., *L.A.B.* 18.6.

Contrary to the Bible, Jacob identifies his opponent and designates him as "...Uriel, the eighth after me..." According to Smith, the statement may attest to an angelic hierarchy with Israel as the counterpart to the *Ogdoad* in Gnostic traditions and the *Dynamis* of the eighth highest heaven. Israel rules the seven archangels below him, Uriel being the lowest. Regardless of how we interpret Jacob's designation of his opponent in the *Prayer of Joseph*, it is beyond doubt that he is an angel and not God in person.

However, Jacob's own identity in this Pseudepigraphon is more ambiguous; is he the incarnation of a very high ranking angel, or is the angel Israel somehow to be understood as an embodiment of God Himself?

Joseph and Aseneth

As in the *Prayer of Joseph*, Jacob is described in angelic/divine terms but the focus is not so much on his heavenly status as on his external features. The narrator explains Jacob's extraordinary appearance by the fact that he has struggled with God. Thus, it seems implied that the mysterious "man" at Jabbok was God in person.

Liber Antiquitatum Biblicarum

The only Jacob narrative of interest for our study alluded to in this book is the patriarch's struggle with the 'unknown man' at the ford of Jabbok. Jacob's opponent is in *L.A.B.* 18.6 stated to be the angel in charge of hymns. He is the leader of the celestial worship and thus clearly a being distinct from God.

4.2.5 Summary and Conclusions

Our texts do not offer any homogeneous interpretation of the identity of the angel of the Lord, but there is a tendency to identify him as an angel, presumably of high rank but distinct from God. There is moreover no source that contains renderings of all the pericopes in question.

In *Jubilees* the angel of the Lord is identified in various ways. The angel who meets Hagar is depicted as an 'ordinary' angel clearly distinct from God; he is anonymous and appears to be of a lower status than the narrator, the angel of the Presence.

On the other hand, in the rendering of the Aqedah, the biblical ambiguity between God and His angel is to a certain degree still present in *Jubilees*. In 4Q225 and *Liber Antiquitatum Biblicarum*, the one who calls out to Abraham in order to stop him from sacrificing Isaac is identified as God Himself. The initiator of the Aqedah is, according to *Jubilees* and 4Q225, the demonic prince Mastema, and in *L.A.B.* 32.1b-2 it is the jealous angels who provoke God to test Abraham. These interpretations are most certainly based on the wish of the authors to justify God.

The reference to a multitude of angels involved in the Aqedah in 4Q225 and *L.A.B.* 32.1b-2 has no counterpart in the biblical story. Maybe the calling of the angel of the Lord to Abraham in Gen 22:11, 15-18, was understood as an implicit indication that all the angels had been watching the scenario at Mount Moriah. The presence and interest of the angels may also be an expression of the importance of the event in Jewish tradition. Besides prince Mastema, 4Q225 also mentions several angels of animosity. We thus encounter to some extent a dualistic worldview in the interpretations of Gen 22:1-19.

There are plenty of renderings/allusions to the Jacob narratives in the sources. In *Jubilees* the angel of God who calls to Jacob in Gen 31:11 seems to be identified as God in person. This interpretation may depend on the fact that the angel of God in Gen 31:13 identifies himself as the God who spoke to Jacob in his dream at Bethel (Gen 28:10-22). In addition to the great variety of the biblical texts, the variation of the interpretations in *Jubilees* may also be explained in the light of the importance of the stories in the Jewish tradition, an explanation that may also apply to other sources. The Aqedah is a highly crucial event in the history of the people of Israel, and Jacob is a very important person, being the ancestor of the nation.

According to the *Testament of Jacob*, the one who appeared to him in Gen 31:11 is his guardian angel, who refers to God in the third person, thus distinguishing between himself and God. In the rendering of Gen 48:15-16, Jacob accordingly refers to the angel as his guardian, a being sent by God in order to protect him. The Pseudepigraphon's interpretation of the 'unknown man' in Genesis 32 is, however, exceptional. The author makes his angelic speaker equate God with 'the angel of God' when alluding to Gen 32:30. There is hence a certain inconsistency regarding the interpretations of the Jacob pericopes in the source. *Jubilees*, the *Testament of Jacob*, and the *Ladder of Jacob* contain angelophanies without counterparts in the Bible.

The identification of the "man" in Genesis 32 as God can only be found in the *Testament of Jacob*, but this interpretation seems also to be implied in *Joseph and Aseneth*.

According to *Demetrius the Chronographer*, the *Ladder of Jacob*, the *Prayer of Joseph*, and *Liber Antiquitatum Biblicarum*, he is an angel. In Demetrius' rendering it is an unspecified angel whom Jacob meets, while in the other sources he is defined as the archangel Sariel or Uriel or the 'angel in charge of hymns.' This angelic identity of the contender may also be implied in 4Q158, since he refers there to God in the third person. The alternation and changing of the angelic names Uriel, Sariel and Phanuel and the connection of all these angels to Genesis 32 in ancient Jewish interpretation, not to mention the combining of the two first names into the variant Suriel etc., may imply that we are dealing with one and the same angel, but under different names.

Both in *Joseph and Aseneth* and the *Prayer of Joseph*, Jacob is also portrayed in angelic/divine terms, and some scholars even identify 'the angel Israel' in the *Prayer of Joseph* as the embodiment of God.

4.3 Philo of Alexandria

4.3.1 Introduction

The early Jewish philosopher Philo of Alexandria[292] was a very produc-
tive author who comments on more or less all of the texts discussed in
the present thesis.[293] Due to the vastness and complexity of the subject,
a detailed discussion of Philo's authorship and teaching is impossible
within the frame of this thesis, thus I will restrict myself to a brief overview regarding his person, theology and exegesis.

Philo's Teaching and Exegesis – Jewish and Greek

Philo Alexandrinus and Judaeus

Philo is known by two names, Philo Alexandrinus, in modern scholarship usually in the form of Philo of Alexandria, and Philo Judaeus, a
name given him by the Church Fathers.[294]

These names express significant information about Philo as a person. He was truly an 'Alexandrian', not only by birth and citizenship,
Alexandria being the metropolis where he spent his entire life,[295] but
above all by his extensive knowledge of and great devotion to Greek
culture and philosophy. He had a broad Greek education and was well
acquainted with many Greek philosophers and authors.[296] Philo shared
this positive attitude toward Greek culture with the majority of the
Jewish community in Alexandria. The Jews of Alexandria appear to

---

292 Philo lived approx. 30/10 B.C.E–50 C.E. See Williamson 1989, 1, Borgen 1984, 233,
     Runia 1990, I, 3, and Winston 2005, 7105.
293 Unless otherwise stated, I use the texts by Philo found in the Loeb series and thus
     the English translations by Colson, Whitaker, and Marcus.
294 Winston 2005, 7105.
295 Philo came from a wealthy, aristocratic, and influential Jewish family in Alexandria
     (according to Jerome, of priestly descent). Philo's brother, Alexander, was probably
     the chief inspector of customs on the Eastern border of Egypt and was rich enough
     to provide silver and gold plates for nine gates of the Temple of Jerusalem and to
     lend money to King Agrippa I. One of Alexander's sons (i.e., Philo's nephew) mar-
     ried the King's daughter Berenice See Josephus, *Jewish War* 5.205 and *Ant.* 19.276-
     277. See also Runia 1990, I, 2-5, Winston 2005, 7105, and Borgen 1997, 14-15.
296 Runia 1990, I, 4-5, and Borgen 1997, 16-17.

have been the most thoroughly Hellenized in the Diaspora[297] and Philo was certainly an exceptionally learned man.[298] The influence of Stoicism, Pythagorean, and Platonic traditions upon his authorship is generally acknowledged. Thus, for example, the impact of the Platonic distinction between the world of 'forms' or 'ideas' and the visible world is evident in his works, and Philo's method of interpretation, so typical of his exegesis, was had its origin in Greek (originally Stoic) allegorical tradition.[299]

However, although Philo was greatly influenced by Greek thought and literature, he identified himself first and foremost as a practicing Jew and biblical exegete, not as a Greek philosopher.[300] He was a devout Jew who regarded the Torah as the ultimate source of wisdom. [301] For Philo, Moses was the supreme teacher and he wished to demonstrate the truth of Judaism by means of the tools of Greek philosophy, both to his fellow Jews living on the brink of assimilation in an environment dominated by Hellenism and to a pagan audience. Thus, he had a somewhat apologetic aim in writing his treatises.[302] Philo had a basically universalistic outlook, although he believed in Israel's special role as the priestly nation in the world.[303] His works may be described as an attempt to read Greek philosophy into the Torah of Moses, thus reconciling Greek ideas with his Jewish heritage. Accordingly, the name Philo Judaeus is also appropriate.[304]

Philo and the Jewish society of his time

Philo's authorship represents the culmination of Alexandrian Jewish literature, and Demetrius the chronographer, Pseudo-Aristeas, and Artapanus can be mentioned among his predecessors. Philo was by no means the first Jewish writer to make use of allegorical and philosophi-

---

297 During Philo's time Alexandria had the largest and most influential Jewish community of the Diaspora. According to Philo (*Against Flaccus* 43), the Jews numbered over a million people, but that may be an overestimation. See also Williamson 1989, 5-6.

298 See Runia 1990, I, 4, Borgen 1997, 16-17, and Josephus' note in *Ant.* 18.259.

299 See Borgen 1984, 254-256, Winston 2005, 7106, and Amir 1971, 411-414.

300 See Runia 1990, I, 4-5, II, 189-190, and Williamson 1989, 2-5. However, the issue of the essential Jewish or Hellenistic character of Philo's writings has been the subject of much scholarly discussion. See e.g., Borgen 1997, 1-13,

301 Philo often mentions the synagogues of Alexandria, and he appears to have been a regular visitor. His writings express a high reverence for the Jewish Shabbat. See, e.g., *On the Embassy to Gaius* 132-134, and *On Dreams* 2.123. See also Borgen 1997, 17-18, 1984, 257, Williamson 1989, 2-5, and Runia 1990, I, 5, 7-8.

302 See Runia, 1990, I, 5, and II, 189-190.

303 See Williamson 1989, 3, Runia 1990, I, 12, and Borgen 1984, 269-272.

304 See Runia 1990, I, 5, 14, and Winston 2005, 7105-7106.

cal exegesis as testified by, for example, the earlier works of Aristobulus, and there are many connections between the Wisdom of Solomon and Philo's works.[305]

The place of Philo's thought within the religious context of his day has been the subject of much scholarly discussion; was he essentially a Middle Platonic philosopher, mystic, or Jewish exegete?[306] The answer is probably that all three of these designations encompass true aspects of this multifaceted personality and author. He was certainly a mystic in the sense that he regarded the ultimate purpose of life to be the vision of God. In *Questions and Answers on Exodus* 2.51 he writes: "For the beginning and end of happiness is to be able to see God." Thus, Philo's interpretation of the name Israel as 'he who sees (God)' expresses the heart and goal of his piety.[307]

As mentioned above, Philo was an Alexandrian Jew, and the question arises as to what extent his version of Judaism was representative of the Jewish community in which he lived. Erwin R. Goodenough advocated the view that Philo is a witness to a Hellenistic mystical branch of Judaism flourishing in the Greek-speaking world and particularly in Alexandria during his time, a Judaic-Hellenistic branch different to Palestinian Jewish faith.[308] Samuel Sandmel also argues that 'Philonic religiosity' differed from the emerging Palestinian Rabbinic Judaism:

> Philo's religiosity was quite unique and different from that presented and advocated in Rabbinic Literature. To labor the point, his religion was not distinctly different from that of the Rabbis, but his religiosity was [...] In Rabbinic Judaism the Laws are an end in themselves, in Philo they are a means to what he conceives as a greater end. There is no echo I know of in Rabbinic literature of the central goal in Philo's Judaism, that of mystic communion with the Godhead.[309]

---

305 See Borgen 1984, 279-280, 1997, 38-45, and Runia 1990, I, 15, Williamson 1989, 147, and Winston 2005, 7105-7106.

306 See Borgen 1997, 1-13.

307 Williamson 1989, 28-29, 71-72, and Winston 1996, 74-82. See also Borgen 1997, 3, and Tobin 1992, 351. In his works, Philo sometimes refers to personal mystical experiences, see, e.g., *On Special Laws* 3.1-6; *On the Cherubim* 27-29 and the *Migration of Abraham* 34-35.

308 See Borgen's (1997, 1-13) survey of the history of research in Philonic studies.

309 Sandmel 1979, 83. Commenting on this passage, Williamson (1989, 71) states that although it is indeed true that Philo's goal was "mystic communion with the Godhead" it need not *per se* exclude the importance of the Mosaic commandments in Philo's piety, in the same way as the Rabbinic emphasis on obedience to the law need not exclude the goal of communion with God, and I tend to agree with him.

As shown in the quotation, in contrast to Goodenough, Sandmel classifies Philo's religiosity as "quite unique", i.e., he does not consider him a representative of a large movement within the Hellenistic Diaspora-Judaism of the time but as reflecting a marginal viewpoint.[310] However, although Sandmel regards Philo as thoroughly Hellenized, he does not deny his loyalty to Judaism. The Torah was the centre of Philo's exegetical endeavors, not the writings of the Greek philosophers.[311] In the same way as Josephus, Philo considered Moses the greatest legislator and teacher of all time.[312] According to Philo, the highest philosophical truth is to be found in Judaism.[313]

The fact that Philo was a recognized leader in the Jewish community of Alexandria and was even chosen to head the delegation sent in 39/40 C.E. to Emperor Gaius Caligula in Rome in order to defend Jewish customs and rights indicates that he was not regarded as an outsider or a heretic by his fellow Alexandrian Jews.[314] In this light, Sandmel's classification of Philo as representing a marginal viewpoint seems rather unlikely.

An opposite view to those of Goodenough and Sandmel was proposed by Harry A. Wolfson, who argued that Philo only represented a Hellenization in respect of terminology, on a "superficial level" so to speak, and not in terms of religion. According to Wolfson, Philo's thoughts are to be seen as a Hellenistic philosophical adaptation of basically Pharisaic/Palestinian Judaism.[315]

Scholars today are generally agreed that it is impossible to draw a sharp dividing line between so-called Hellenistic and Palestinian Judaism.[316] The Judaic world of Philo's time was one of mutual influence and communication between various Jewish groups in Galilee, Judea, and the Diaspora.[317] Thus, scholars today tend to favor Wolfson's understanding of Philo, although he has been criticized for presenting

---

310 Sandmel 1979, 147.

311 Sandmel 1979, 134.

312 See e.g., *On the Creation* 1-3 and *Ant*.1.18-23. See also Borgen 1997, 78, and Runia 1990, I, 4-12.

313 Runia 1990, I, 7-8, 15, and Winston 2005, 7106.

314 See Williamson 1989, 2-3. In this context, it may be added that the Jewish community of Alexandria did not live in an entirely friendly environment, as demonstrated by the pogrom during the time that Caligula was Roman emperor and Flaccus governor of Egypt, an event that caused Philo to write his treaties *On the Embassy to Gaius* and *Against Flaccus*.

315 Wolfson 1947, vol. 1, 3-86. See also Borgen 1997, 4.

316 See Hengel 1974, Kugel (ed.) 2002, and Mason 1991, 336.

317 See Borgen 1984, 258-259, and 1997, 20-21.

Philo as a much more systematic philosopher/theologian than he was in reality.[318] However, the influence of Greek philosophy on Philo's authorship may be greater than Wolfson admitted.

As Josephus, Philo points out that Jerusalem was the center of a network linking the Diaspora and Palestinian Jews. It is evident that he regarded the Jews as *one* nation, regardless of whether they lived in Judea, Alexandria, Athens or Rome. Philo mentions Jewish pilgrimages to Jerusalem, and he himself visited the Temple at least once. His writings breathe great respect for the Temple-cult.[319]

Apart from the Bible, Philo indicates that he used other Jewish sources in his work and in the *Life of Moses* 1.4 he refers to information obtained from "some of the elders of the nation".[320] It has been discussed to what extent Philo's writings may share exegetical traditions with Palestinian Judaism, and according to, for example, Peder Borgen and Naomi G. Cohen, the answer is most certainly affirmative.[321] However, because no sharp distinction can be drawn between Palestinian and Alexandrian Jewish traditions, the whole question is subordinate. In the words of Borgen: "The main question is then to uncover traditions current in Judaism at that time and examine the various usages, emphases and applications within this common context."[322]

However, there were naturally differences between the Jews living in Alexandria and Palestine, an obvious one being the language. The question of Philo's knowledge of Hebrew has been much debated, and no consensus has been reached.[323] Wolfson maintained that Philo indeed knew Hebrew[324] but the predominant view today is that Philo probably did not master the language.[325] However, his lack of knowledge of Hebrew need not automatically exclude an acquaintance with, and use of, Palestinian traditions, as demonstrated by Cohen[326] but in contrast to their Palestinian brethren, the Bible which Philo and Alexandrian Jews in general knew and read was the LXX.

---

318 See Borgen 1997, 5.
319 Cf., Acts 2. See Borgen 1997, 18-21, and Williamson 1989, 2-5. See also *On Providence* 64.
320 See also Borgen 1984, 258.
321 Borgen 1984, 259-259, and Cohen 1995, 1-20. See also Segal 1977, 178-181.
322 Borgen 1984a, 124.
323 Borgen 1984, 257.
324 Wolfson, 1947 vol. 1, 88.
325 See e.g., Runia 1990, I, 13, and Winston 2005, 7106.
326 Cohen 1995, 14-20.

Philo's works and exegetical approach – some remarks

Although Philo's biblical interpretation has been briefly discussed above, e.g., his employment of the allegorical method and the impact of Greek philosophy on his authorship, I find it appropriate to make a few additional remarks.

As mentioned above, Philo's Bible was the LXX, which he considered divinely inspired, and he shows no awareness of the Hebrew underlying the Greek translation.[327] He regarded Moses as the supreme philosopher and spokesman of God and the author of the entire Pentateuch, on which his exegesis is mainly based.[328] Philo rarely refers to other biblical books but, as previously stated, he sometimes mentions extra-biblical traditions. Borgen suggests that the *Sitz im Leben* of Philo's exegetical work may have been the Alexandrian synagogues.[329]

Although he was a genuine advocate of allegorical exegesis, i.e., the symbolic exploration of Scripture, Philo also maintained that it should not be used in order to abolish the literal meaning, which may be illustrated by his statement in the *Migration of Abraham* 89-93:

> There are those who, regarding laws in their literal sense in the light of symbols of matters belonging to the intellect, are overpunctilious about the latter, while treating the former with easy going neglect. Such men I for my part should blame for handling the matter in too easy and off-hand manner: they ought to have given careful attention to both aims, to a more full and exact investigation of what is not seen and in what is seen to be stewards without reproach. As it is, as though they were living alone by themselves in a wilderness, or as though they had become disembodied souls [...] It is quite true that the Seventh Day is meant to teach the power of the Unoriginate and the non-action of created beings. But let us not for this reason abrogate the laws laid down for its observance, and light fires or till the ground or carry loads [...] It is true also that the Feast is a symbol of gladness of soul and of thankfulness to God, but we should not for this reason turn our backs on the general gatherings of the years seasons. It is true that the receiving circumcision does indeed portray the excision of pleasure and all passions, and the putting away of the impious conceit [...] but let us not on this account repeal the law laid sown for circumcising. Why, we shall be ignoring the Sanctity of the Temple and a thousand other things, if we are going to pay heed to nothing except what is shewn us by the inner meaning of things. Nay, we should look on all these outward observances as resembling the body, and their inner meanings as resembling the soul. It follows that, exactly as we have to take thought for the body, because it is the abode of the soul, so we must pay heed to the letter of the

---

327 Borgen 1984, 257-258, Williamson 1989, 168-169, and Winston 2005, 7106.
328 Borgen 1984, 258, Runia 1990, II, 189, and Winston 2005, 144.
329 Borgen 1997, 17-18.

laws. If we keep and observe these, we shall not incur the censure of the many and the charges they are sure to bring against us.

In this passage, Philo summarizes his exegetical standpoint. In spite of his philosophical outlook, he maintained the validity of the rite of circumcision[330], the celebration of the Shabbat and other Jewish holidays, and the temple-cult.[331] Although he gave preference to the allegorical interpretation of Scripture, he did not neglect the value of its literal meaning and recognized both forms of exegesis as equally valid. This was most unusual in Philo's time, and his authorship constitutes the earliest extant example of an attempt to reconcile the two modes of interpretation, an attempt that brought him into conflict with other Jewish exegetes. Philo debated both with the so-called literalists, who rejected the allegorical method,[332] and those interpreters who only accepted the allegorical meaning of Scripture. [333]

However, there is no doubt that Philo considered the allegorical reading of the Bible as the way of disclosing the profoundest truths of the texts. According to him, the biblical texts encompass two levels; the apparent, literal meaning and the allegorical, deeper one, beneath the surface so to speak.[334]

The allegorical interpretation of Scripture enabled Philo to maintain his conviction that it constitutes the inspired, infallible word of God, in spite of the fact that it contains passages which, if taken literally, would depict God in an unworthy way.[335] For example, Philo emphasized the absolute transcendence of God and therefore strongly opposed anthropomorphism.[336] The use of the allegorical method also enabled him to apply his insights gained from Greek philosophy to the Bible, while remaining faithful to his Jewish heritage.[337] In Philo's view, not only the

---

330 See also On the Special Laws 1.1-11.

331 See, e.g., Williamson 1989, 3-5, Borgen 1984, 259-261, and Winston 2005, 7106.

332 Among the so-called literalists, two main groups can be distinguished; those who rejected the allegorical method because they considered that it endangered the "authentic" meaning of the Bible and introduced alien ideas into Judaism and apostate Jews (and pagans) who used the literal reading of the texts in order to ridicule the Biblical message. According to the apostates, no allegorical interpretation whatsoever could justify the validity of the Bible. See Williamson, 1989, 152-158, and Borgen 1984, 260-261.

333 See also On Dreams 1.120 and, e.g., Borgen 1984, 259-261, Williamson 1989, 152-158, and Winston 2005, 7106.

334 See Williamson 1989, 157-163.

335 See Williamson 1989, 157-158.

336 See Williamson 1989, 52-54, 74-85.

337 See Williamson 1989, 157-158, and Borgen 1984, 262-264.

Bible but also the work of the allegorical exegete is divinely inspired.[338] In *On Special Laws* 3.1-6 he expresses his view on his life and work:

> There was a time when I had leisure for philosophy and for the contemplation of the universe and its contents, when I made its spirit my own [...], when my constant companions were the divine themes and verities [...] I had no base or abject thoughts nor groveled in search of reputation or of wealth or bodily comforts, but seemed always to be borne aloft into the heights with a soul possessed by some God-sent inspiration [...] But as it proved, my steps were dogged by the deadliest of mischiefs [...] which [...] plunged me in the ocean of civil cares [...] Yet amid my groans I hold my own, for planted in my soul from my earliest days I keep the yearning for culture [...] To this I owe it that sometimes I raise my head and with the soul's eyes–dimly indeed because the mist of extraneous affairs has clouded their clear vision–I yet make a shift to look around me in my desire to inhale a breath of life pure and unmixed with evil. And if I unexpectedly obtain a spell of fine weather and a calm from civil turmoils, I get me wings and rides the wages [...] wafted by the breezes of knowledge [...] it is well for me to give thanks to God even for this, that though submerged I am not sucked down into the depths, but can also open the soul's eyes [...]. So behold me daring, not only to read the sacred messages of Moses, but also in my love of knowledge to peer into each of them and unfold and reveal what is not known to the multitude.

Philo's treatises can be divided into three main categories; the exegetical, the historical-apologetic, and the philosophical.[339] The first category comprises Philo's exposition of the Mosaic Scriptures and consists in turn of three large series, the first of which comprises paraphrases of the Pentateuch, e.g., *On the Creation, On Abraham, On Rewards and Punishments* and *On the Special Laws*.[340] These works bear clear resemblance to the genre of 'rewritten Bible' and Borgen classifies them as such.[341]

The second series of the exegetical writings consists of purely allegorical commentaries on Genesis, e.g., *On the Cherubim, On Flight and Finding, On the Confusion of Tongues, On the Change of Names, On Sobriety, Allegorical Interpretation, On Drunkenness, On the Migration of Abraham, Who is the Heir,* and *On Dreams*.[342]

The third and final series of treaties belonging to the exegetical category are *Questions and Answers on Genesis/Exodus.* As the titles indicate, in these works Philo employs questions put to the biblical texts as the

---

338 See Williamson 1989, 169-172.
339 Runia 1990, I, 5, Winston 2005, 7106, and Amir 1971, 410-411.
340 See Winston 2005, 7106, and Runia 1990, I, 5-7.
341 Borgen 1997, 63-79, and 1984, 233-234.
342 Runia 1990, I, 5-6, and Borgen 1984, 243-246.

starting point for his exposition. The exegetical treaties comprise by far the largest part of the Philonic corpus (39 books). [343]

Among the historical-apologetic writings, we find *Against Flaccus* and *On the Embassy to Gaius*. As an example of the works of the last main category, the philosophical treaties, *On Providence* can be mentioned. In total, 48 of Philo's writings are still extant.[344]

Since the concern of this chapter is Philo's interpretation of 'the angel of the Lord-texts' in Genesis, it is the first main category that is of interest, i.e., the exegetical writings. The main books by Philo analyzed below are *On Flight and Finding, On Abraham, Questions and Answers on Genesis,*[345] and *On Dreams*. In these works we find Philo's interpretations of Genesis 16; 22; 24; 28; 31, and 32. Concerning Jacob's struggle at the ford of Jabbok, Philo comments upon Genesis 32 and Jacob's new name Israel on various occasions, for example, also in *On the Change of Names, On Drukenness*, and *On Sobriety*. As will be shown, there are also some scattered remarks on these pericopes in some of Philo's other texts, for example, *On the Cherubim*. He also briefly discusses Jacob's blessing of Ephraim and Manasseh in Genesis 48 in several of his books, for example, in *Allegorical Interpretation*, book three.

The Philonic concept of God and angelology – some remarks

Although there is much to say about Philo's doctrine of God[346] and his angelology, this is not the place for a detailed treatment of the subject and I will confine myself to say just a few words on the matter, since it concerns the main issue of this chapter; Philo's perception of the angel of the Lord and his relationship to God. The 'Logos-doctrine' of Philo constitutes an essential part of his concept of God.[347] As will be shown

---

343　Runia 1990, I, 5-7, and Borgen 1984, 241-242.

344　See Runia 1990, I, 5-7, and Amir 1971, 410-411. It is thanks to the early Church that Philo's writings were saved from oblivion, as the emerging Rabbinic Judaism after the fall of the Temple in 70 C.E. showed little interest in Philo's philosophical interpretations of the Bible. Many Church Fathers were influenced by Philo's allegorical exegesis and ideas, e.g., Clement of Alexandria and Origen. Until the 16th century Philo remained almost forgotten in Jewish society. However, R. Oshaiah Rabbah's saying in *Gen. Rab.* 1.1 seems to have been influenced by Philo's *On the Creation* 16. See Runia 1990, I, 14-15, Borgen 1984, 279-280, Winston 2005, 7107, and Amir 1971, 415.

345　Unfortunately, the main part of *Questions and Answers on Genesis* is only extant in an Armenian translation, probably dating from the 5th century C.E., the Greek original being lost, apart from a tiny portion (less than 10 per cent) of the book. See Marcus (introduction) 1953, vii.

346　See also Williamson, 1989, 28.

347　See also Williamson 1989, 103.

in the following, the angel of the Lord appears to be identified as the 'Logos' in many of Philo's interpretations of our pericopes. In order to illuminate the role of 'Logos' it is necessary to also briefly discuss Philo's theology in general.

A main theme in Philo's writings is polemic against on the one hand atheism, and on the other, polytheism; the two worst kinds of wickedness.[348] According to Philo, the creation bears witness to the existence of the one true God, its Creator:

> [*Questions and Answers on Genesis* 2.34] ... And this (reason), seeing with a sharp eye both these (celestial phenomena) and through them the higher paradigmatic forms, and the cause of all things, immediately apprehends them and genesis and providence, for it reasons that visible nature did not come into being by itself, for it would be impossible for harmony and order [...] to come about by themselves. But it is necessary that there be some Creator and Father, a pilot and charioteer, who both begat and wholly preserves the things begotten.

A cornerstone of Philo's theology is thus that God is both the Creator and the Sustainer of the world and, through the testimony of the creation, His existence is made known to all humankind.[349]

As stated previously, Philo stresses the absolute transcendence of God; humankind can only gain knowledge of God's existence but not of His essence. God's nature is far beyond human grasp and comprehension, He is indescribable and outside both space and time.[350] God is "... transcending virtue, transcending knowledge, transcending the good itself and the beautiful itself ..."[351] From this it follows that God is essentially nameless since, according to Jewish thinking, a name expresses the innermost nature of a thing or person. The only epithet that is adequate to denote God is 'He who IS'/'the (truly) Existent', the "name" by which God revealed Himself to Moses at Mount Horeb in the LXX version of Exod 3:14: ἐγώ εἰμι ὁ ὤν/"I am the one who is." In designating God, 'the Pure Being' Philo uses both the biblical masculine form ὁ ὤν 'He who is/exists' and the philosophical abstract neuter τὸ ὄν 'that which exists'.[352] By his employment of the former epithet,

---

348 Williamson 1989, 29-31.
349 Cf., Rom 1:18-23. See also Williamson 1989, 34-38, and the conclusion of *On the Creation* 170-172, where Philo presents a summary of his faith in five principles, which has been called 'the first creed in history'. See also Mendelson, 1988, 29-49.
350 See e.g., *On the Special Laws* 1.32. See also Williamson 1989, 38-43, and Runia 1990, I, 9.
351 *On the Creation*, 8.
352 See Williamson 1989, 39-42, and Runia I, 1990, 9, Sandmel 1979, 91-94, and Dodd 1953, 60-62.

Philo distinguishes himself from the Greek philosophers and reveals his Jewish heritage; in spite of His utter transcendence, the God of Philo is a personal being with whom we as human beings can enter into a mutual relationship.[353] Other Jewish characteristics of his theology are, for example, his belief that God hears and answers prayers, and the conviction that God is active in history.[354]

However, the utter transcendence of God leads to the question as to how it is possible for humankind to know anything at all about Him. Philo considered the Mosaic writings to contain the supreme divine revelation, but how was it communicated? How does God relate to His created beings? Philo's goal was the vision of God, but how is it possible for human beings to relate to a transcendent God? Philo's answer was that although the human mind cannot comprehend the essence of God, His activities or δυνάμεις/ 'powers' can be known. God makes Himself known by His actions. It is by means of these 'powers' or 'potencies' that God relates to His creation. The two main 'powers' are expressed in God's creative activity and in His governing and sustaining of the world. These 'powers' are in turn connected to the two main divine designations in the LXX; *Theos* 'God' represents God as the Creator and *Kyrios* 'Lord' represents God's sovereignty.[355] Moreover, in contrast to the Rabbis, Philo relates the former term to God's goodness and mercy, while *Kyrios* stands for God's retributive power.[356] In his depiction of the divine 'powers', Philo also applies the Platonic concept of the world of the ideas.[357] As stated previously, he believed in divine inspiration; by God's grace and initiative the human soul can receive a glimpse of the divine reality:

> [*Allegorical Interpretation* 1.36, 38] Breathed into, we note, is equivalent to "inspired" […]. For how could the soul have conceived of God, had He not breathed into it and mightily laid hold of it? For the mind of man would never have ventured to soar so high as to grasp the nature of God, had not God Himself drawn it up to Himself, so far as it was possible that the mind of man should be drawn up, and stamped it with the impress of the powers that are within the scope of its understanding.

By His Spirit, God makes Himself known to the mind of man. However, the human soul is unable to grasp God's nature in its fullness and

---

353 Runia 1990, I, 11.
354 See Williamson 1989, 31-34, and e.g., *On the Decalogue* 47. However, according to Runia (I, 1990, 12), Philo's version of Judaism was essentially a-historic.
355 See Runia 1990, I, 9, Williamson 1989, 48-54, Sandmel 1979, 91-94, and Borgen 1984, 273.
356 See Wolfson 1947, vol. 1, 224-225, and Segal 1977, 173-178.
357 Wolfson 1947, vol. 1, 217-226.

can only perceive God as He is manifested in His 'powers'.[358] In Philo's interpretation of Abraham's encounter with the three "men" in *Questions and Answers on Genesis*, he presents yet another example of his conception of the relationship between God, His 'powers,' and humankind:

> [*Questions and Answers to Genesis* 4.2] What is the meaning of the words, "He [Abraham] saw, and behold, three men were standing over him"? Most natural things, to those who are able to see does (Scripture) present, (namely) that it is reasonable, for one to be three and for three to be one, for they were one by a higher principle. But when counted with the chief powers, the creative and the kingly, He makes the appearance of three to the human mind. For this [the mind] cannot be so keen of sight that it can see Him who is above the powers that belong to Him, (namely) God, distinct from anything else. For so soon as one sets eyes upon God, there also appear, together with His being, the ministering powers, so that in place of one He makes the appearance of a triad. For when the mind begins to have an apprehension of the Existent One, He is known to have arrived there, making (Himself) unique [...] But, as I said a little earlier, He cannot be seen in His oneness without [...] the chief powers that exist immediately with Him, (namely) the creative, which is called God, and the kingly, which is called Lord ... [8] and He in His oneness is likened to a triad because of the weakness of the beholders...[359]

Thus, Philo interprets the three "men" who visited Abraham in Genesis 18 as God and His two powers. However, in reality, all three visitors were a manifestation of the one true God, and Abraham's perception of them as three was an illusion, due to the limitations of the human mind.[360]

As stated above, Philo objected to anthropomorphic depictions of God, and in, for example, *On Abraham* 107, 118, he firmly states that the three men appeared to Abraham "in the form of men" and that "it is a marvel indeed that though they neither ate nor drank they gave the appearance of both eating and drinking", thus interpreting the narrative in a docetic way.[361]

When describing Philo's theology, it is impossible not to mention the 'Logos', a most central term in his teaching. As stated above, Philo identifies the angel of the Lord as the 'Logos' in many of his interpretations of our pericopes. This should not surprise us, because the 'Logos' may be described as the connecting link between the creation and God.

---

358 See also Williamson 1989, 50-51, 59-62.
359 See also *On Abraham* 119-123.
360 See also Williamson 1989, 50-51, and Thunberg 1966, 565-570.
361 See also Williamson 1989, 52-54.

According to Philo, the sun may be likened to God and the sunrays to His 'Logos'; we as humans cannot gaze directly into the sun without being blinded but we can perceive the light which emanates from it.[362]

The above mentioned tension between God's transcendence and immanence finds its prime solution in the concept of the 'Logos', which encompasses and unites the 'powers' of God, both the creative and the ruling aspect.[363] The 'Logos' may also be described as the expressed thought of God; it is God in His self-revelation to the world. God in His essence remains unfathomable but, through His 'Logos', 'He who IS' reaches down to and makes Himself known to humankind. The 'Logos' is God in His knowability.[364] Philo also depicts the 'Logos' as the instrument by which God both created and sustains the world. Moreover, the 'Logos' is the image of God, and human beings are in turn created in the image of the 'Logos'.[365]

Philo's depiction of the 'Logos' is very complex, and it has been much discussed whether it is to be understood in terms of an independent entity, a 'hypostasis' or a manifestation/an aspect of God, as the 'powers' mentioned above.[366] It is beyond the scope of this thesis to elaborate this issue in detail but it will briefly be touched upon below, since the 'Logos' constitutes a key-term in Philo's exegesis of the pericopes in focus.

The religious-historical background to Philo's 'Logos' is both Jewish and Greek. For example, the term itself was borrowed from the Stoics, although given a new meaning, and there are apparent connections to Jewish wisdom tradition and perceptions of the creative 'Word of God'. Philo sometimes identifies the divine 'Wisdom' with the 'Logos' but 'Wisdom' is also metaphorically depicted as the mother of the 'Logos' and God as its Father.[367]

In this context, Philo's teaching has often been compared with the 'Logos' of John's Prologue, and it is generally recognized that the Evangelist and Philo draw upon common traditions. There are cer-

---

362 See the discussion below of *On Dreams* 1.239-240 and *Questions and Answers on Genesis* 3. 34-35. See also Williamson 1989, 105-106.

363 See e.g., *On the Cherubim* 27-28. In *On Flight and Finding* 101 quoted below, the 'Logos' is even depicted as being the "charioteer of the Powers". See also Williamson 1989, 105-109, and Wolfson 1947, vol. 1, 234-238.

364 See Williamson 1989, 103-109, Sandmel 1979, 94-97, Dunn 1989, 220-230, 241, and Dodd 1953, 68-71.

365 Williamson 1989, 108-109, 112-115. See also Borgen 1984, 264-266, Wolfson 1947, vol. 1, 261-282, and Dodd 1953, 68-71.

366 See Runia 1990, I, 9-10, and Tobin 1992, 351.

367 Winston 1989, 103-109, Tobin 1992, 350-351, and Wolfson 1947, vol. 1, 253-261.

tainly parallels between Philo's 'Logos' and John's description of the pre-incarnate Christ. However, the idea of the 'Logos' as incarnated in a historical person of flesh and blood would most certainly have appeared absurd in Philo's eyes.[368]

Philo also had a conception of angels as intermediaries between God and humankind. These angels are sometimes termed 'logoi' but are not to be confused with the supreme, divine 'Logos', the totality of the 'powers'.[369] The angels may be described as a special kind of immanent powers in the world. They are 'unbodied souls', i.e., souls that have not been incarnated as humans. Philo equated the δαίμονες/"demons" of Greek cosmology with the biblical angels. According to Philo, it is through His angels that God exercises His providence over humankind.[370]

In the same way as the 'powers' the angels are divided into two main categories, the beneficial and the punitive. The 'beneficial angels' are God's instrument in granting 'secondary gifts', such as deliverance from evil. For example, Philo identifies the angel who saved the city of Zoar from destruction[371] as beneficial, while the angels who destroyed Sodom and Gomorrah were punitive angels. The 'principal blessings', however, are granted by God Himself.[372] When discussing Philo's interpretation of Jacob's blessing of Ephraim and Manasseh in Genesis 48, we will return to this aspect of his angelology.

Finally, it must be stated that Philo also seems to have believed in evil "angels", who not are to be confused with God's punitive angels, acting on His behalf.[373]

---

368 See also Williamson 1989, 52-54, 115-119, Dodd 1953, 71-73, and Dunn 1989, 240-245. Many scholars point out that the similarities between Philo's Logos concept and the pre-incarnate 'Logos' of John do not necessarily imply any direct influence of Philo's works on the Fourth Gospel, but are due to the Evangelist's and Philo's common religious heritage. See, e.g., Brown 1966, LVIII.

369 Wolfson 1947, vol. 1, 366-385. See also Williamson 1989, 110-111, 135, and Borgen 1984, 273.

370 Wolfson 1947, vol. 1, 366-385. See also Runia 1990, I, 10, and Hannah 2007, 424-425.

371 See Gen 19:15-23.

372 Wolfson 1947, vol. 1, 381-383.

373 Wolfson 1947, vol. 1, 383-385. However, Philo's belief in evil "angels" has been disputed by scholars, see, e.g., Dillon 1983, 203-205.

4.3.2 Hagar and the Angel

Philo has some comments on Hagar's encounter with the angel in his works *On the Cherubim, On Flight and Finding, On Dreams* and *Questions and Answers on Genesis*.

In *On the Cherubim* 1.3, Philo describes Hagar's first flight as voluntary (Genesis 16) while the second one (Genesis 21) was a banishment. The first time Hagar returned to her master's house when she met the angel, here called 'the divine reason' by Philo. On the second occasion Hagar did not return. Apart from this brief commentary on Genesis 21, Philo mainly focuses on Hagar's encounter with the angel as recorded in Genesis 16.

According to *On Flight and Finding* 1.5, Hagar's motive for her escape in Genesis 16 was that she was ashamed. Philo argues for his interpretation in the following words:

> [*On Flight and Finding* 1.5-6] … A sign of this is the fact that an angel, a Divine Word, meets her to advise her the right course, and to suggest return to the house of her mistress. This angel addresses her in the encouraging words, "The Lord hath hearkened to thy humiliation" (Gen. xvi. 11), a humiliation prompted neither by fear nor by hatred […] but by shame, the outward expression of inward modesty. Had she run away owing to fear, the angel would probably have moved her who had inspired to fear to a gentler frame of mind; for then, and not till then, would it have been safe for the fugitive to go back. But no angel first approached Sarai […] But it is Hagar who is taught by the angel monitor, whose goodwill to her makes him at once friend and counselor, not to feel any shame, but be of good courage as well; pointing out that shame apart of confidence is but a half virtue.

As seen in the quotation, Philo designates the angel of the Lord who encounters Hagar as a 'divine Word/a divine Logos', and this identification of the angel is also extant in *On Dreams* 1.240 and in *Questions and Answers on Genesis* 3.28: "Why does the angel say to her, 'Hagar, maidservant of Sarah, whence comest thou and whither goest thou'? […] But as for the deeper meaning, forcefulness (is meant), for the divine Logos is a disciplinarian and an excellent healer of the weakness of the soul."

The angel appears in order to encourage and advice Hagar to return to her mistress. Philo also denotes him as 'the angel monitor', Hagar's teacher. The translators Colson and Whitaker understand this as

Philo describing the angel as Hagar's personified inner conviction.[374] Their interpretation seems to be confirmed by Philo's own words:

> [*On Flight and Finding* 1.203-205] The inward monitor [ὁ ἔλεγχος], then, speaking within the soul says to it, "Whence comest thou, and whither art thou going? (*ibid*. 8). In thus addressing her he does not express doubt or inquiry [...] for we may not think that an angel is ignorant of anything affecting us. Here is a proof of it: even the secrets of the womb, which are hidden from created beings, the angel knows with certainty, as his words shew: "Lo, thou art with child, and shalt give birth to a boy, and shalt call his name Ishmael" (*ibid*. 11). For it is not in the power of man to know that the embryo is a male [...] So the words "Whence comest thou?" are spoken to rebuke the soul that is running away from better judgement.

According to the translators' interpretation, the angel is here called 'the inward monitor' by Philo.[375] But the angel seems nevertheless to be addressing Hagar from the outside. Why else does Philo find it necessary to explain that the angel's question is not caused by ignorance? The angel already knew the reason for Hagar's flight, and he is rebuking her. The angel knows all about Hagar, including that she is pregnant with a male child. Philo's words are peculiar in this context; in contrast to created beings, the angel knows "the secrets of the womb." Does this imply that he is not a created being himself? Or does the term "created beings" in this case refer to humans as distinct from angels?

The angel is said to be speaking to Hagar's soul, which may imply that Philo regarded Hagar's meeting with the angel as an 'inner experience'. We are perhaps to understand Philo as saying that the angel spoke to Hagar through her own conscience.

Philo understands Gen 16:13-14 to mean that Hagar perceived the angel/'the divine Logos' as God Himself. In reality she did meet not God in person, but His servant; see, for example, *On Flight and Finding* 1.211-212. This interpretation is also to be found in *On Dreams* 1.239-240[376] and *Questions and Answers on Genesis* 3.34-35. Here, Philo compares God to the sun itself and the 'Logos' is likened to the sun rays, by some people misinterpreted as being the source of light itself:

> [*Questions and Answers on Genesis* 3.34] (Gen xvi. 13) Why does (Scripture) say, "And she called the name of the Lord, who was speaking to her,

---

374 Colson/Whitaker, Analytical introduction to *Flight and Finding*, 1949, 3, and note a on p. 12. The revised translation of Philo's works by Yonge (1993) contains a slightly different rendering of *On Flight and Finding* 1.6: "... But this angel, who is reproof, at the same time friendly and full of advice, out of his goodness teaches her not to feel only shame, but also to entertain confidence..."

375 Yonge's translation has here "...its [the soul's] convictor."

376 For a quotation of this passage, see section 4.3.5.

"Thou art God who seest me, for she said, "For indeed I have seen before (me) him who appeared to me"? Observe the first point carefully, that he was the servant of God in the same way (that Hagar was) the maid-servant of wisdom. Hence the angel was called (God) in order that she might harmonize the reality to his appearance. For it was fitting and proper that God, the Most High One and Lord of all, should appear to wisdom, while he who was his Logos (and) minister (should appear) to the maidservant and attendant of wisdom. But it was not strange (for her) to believe that the angel was God. For those who are unable to see the first cause naturally suffer from an illusion, they believe that the second is the first. (They are like those) who have poor eyesight and are not able to see the corporeal form, which is in heaven, (namely) the sun, and believe that the rays which it sends to earth are this itself. And all those who do not see the Great King ascribe the dignity of the first in sovereignty to his satrap and the one under him.

As we have seen previously, Philo states in *On Flight and Finding* that the angel did not need to approach Sarai. In the quotation above, on the other hand, he writes that God in person appeared to her, in the text symbolized by wisdom, while the 'Logos/angel' encountered Hagar, the maidservant of wisdom.[377] Hagar and Sarai are thus depicted as being on different spiritual levels. The 'Logos/angel' appeared like God to Hagar.[378]

Concluding Remarks

To conclude, it seems clear that Philo interpreted Gen 16:7-14 as an encounter between Hagar and the divine 'Logos', God's servant. According to Philo, 'the angel of the Lord' in Genesis 16 is not to be confused with God Himself. However, it is peculiar that the 'Logos' is contrasted with created beings in *On Flight and Finding* 1.203-205.

4.3.3 The Aqedah

Philo's rewriting of Gen 22:1-19 in *On Abraham* is philosophical and quite extensive compared to his renderings of other pericopes. However, it is Abraham who is the main character in Philo's version, not God/the angel.

---

377 See Marcus' footnotes g and i (*Questions and Answers on Genesis*), 1953, 222.
378 See also *Questions and Answers on Genesis* 3.35.

Philo is more interested in Abraham's emotions and thoughts, his 'inner life', so to speak, than in describing the external course of events. He mentions, for example, neither the binding of Isaac on the altar nor the ram[379]. Philo provides an allegorical interpretation of the event. According to Philo, God is the real owner and source of all true joy and Abraham demonstrates this by his willingness to sacrifice his son, his happiness in life. Philo thus draws attention to the name of the son, Isaac, which in Hebrew means 'he laughs'. God gives Isaac back to Abraham and shows thereby that He is not grudging. The message is that God is the rightful owner of all happiness and joy, and He gives it willingly to all who are worthy of it.[380] No angel is mentioned in Philo's version of the Aqedah. It is God Himself who calls out to Abraham and saves Isaac from being sacrificed.

> [*On Abraham* 176-177] ... *God the Saviour* stopped the deed half-way *with a voice from the air*, in which He ordered him to stay and not touch the lad. And *twice He called* the father by name to turn him and draw him back from his purpose and thus prevent his carrying out the slaughter. So Isaac was saved. Since God returned the gift of him and used the offering which piety rendered to Him to repay the offerer ...

Philo does not mention the second divine interference in Gen 22:15-18 and the blessing of Abraham but simply states that "twice He [God] called the father by name", a reference to the angel's words in Gen 22:11 where Abraham's name is repeated twice,[381] with the difference that in Philo's version the angel is substituted by God.

Concluding Remarks

In his account of the Aqedah, Philo appears to identify 'the angel of the Lord' as God the Savior. However, his substitution of the angel for God may also be interpreted to mean that Philo considers the angel *per se* as unimportant and not necessarily implying that Philo deemed the angel in Genesis 22 to be a manifestation of God but that he read the text as God speaking through the angel. In any case, it was God who interfered. Philo's ascribing of the rescue of Isaac to God may also be seen in the light of the importance of the Aqedah in Jewish tradition.

---

379 However, in *On the Unchangeableness of God* 4, Philo mentions that Abraham bound Isaac, but also here, it is Abraham's 'inner world' that is in focus, and no angel is mentioned in the short allusion to the Aqedah.

380 *On Abraham* 200-207.

381 See also Feldman 2006, 276.

Philo describes the divine interference in terms of a 'voice from the air', which calls to mind the concept of the *bath qol* as a representation of God in Rabbinic texts.[382] The epithet 'the Savior' is also noteworthy. According to Feldman, Philo emphasizes that God called Abraham by name twice, since he regarded God as the giver of principal benefits and blessings, whereas it is his servants, the angels, who bestow the secondary gifts as well as execute punishments.[383]

4.3.4 The Wooing of Rebekah

Philo has given us a detailed verse-by-verse analysis of Genesis 24 in his treatise *Questions and Answers on Genesis* 4.84-146. However, the role of the angel is not his main concern; Philo makes only a few comments upon the subject. According to Philo, when Abraham assured his servant that he would be accompanied by an angel, he prophesied:

> [*Questions and Answers on Genesis* 4.90] (Gen xxiv. 7) Why does he [Abraham] say, "The Lord God of heaven and God of the earth will send his angel before thy face, and thou shalt take a wife for my son Isaac."? Thus do I see that he is a prophet and legislates oracularly things that are to come [...] For whence does he know that the servant will be able to complete his journey through the guidance of the angel if not from some divination and prophecy? But perhaps someone will say, "What need did the servant have of an angel to go along, since he bore with him the command to complete the marriage with a virgin of their family? To this it must be said, "Not ineffectual Sir, did He wish the human mind to be in nature, but to be active [...] For this reason the steersman will not abandon the rudder even though the ship may be enjoying a favourable wind [...] This is the literal meaning. But the passage also contains an allegory [...] For inasmuch the uttered word, which in comparison with the mind has been called "servant," at once was in doubt and gave an appearance of weakness and deceit, the Saviour joined and fitted to it another word, not deceived or defrauded, which he calls "angel," (as) the interpreter of divine oracles and commands. And when he comes along and teaches man, he compels him not to vacillate in his reasoning or move about and be confused.

By divine inspiration, Abraham knew that the servant would be able to accomplish his task by the help of angelic guidance. The role of the angel is thus essential for the success of the commission. Philo goes on to compare human life to a ship and states that God, the steersman, is

---

382 Cf., *L.A.B.* 32.4; *Lad. Jac.* 3.1; *Pirqê de Rabbi Eliezer* 31 and *Tg. Neof.* Gen 22:10. See also chapters 4.2 and 4.5.

383 Feldman 2006, 276-279. See also *On the Confusion of Tongues* 180-181 and *On Flight and Finding* 66-67.

always involved in human affairs, even when we (the rudders) think that we are able to cope with life on our own. Philo also interprets the verse allegorically. The 'uttered word' represents Abraham's servant,[384] God is called 'the Savior,'[385] and the angel is 'another word', the teacher of mankind.

The servant's doubts concerning the willingness of the woman to follow him back to Canaan and Abraham's answer (Gen 24:5-8) are interpreted allegorically by Philo in the following way:

> [*Questions and Answers on Genesis* 4.91] You need but say that if the angel of God is not there, it would seem that the woman might not wish to go along. Wherefore he [Abraham] says, by way of sealing and confirming the matter, "If she does not go with thee as if perhaps wishing to go with a companion, she may wish to go along with the divine Word." And even though she may not have faith in this youth, she (will have faith) in him who instructs and leads to the elected way and the completion of a great work. And the work is the divine, holy and consecrated marriage of the soul, the harmony of the self-taught reason.

Although the woman may not trust 'this youth', that is, Abraham's servant,[386] she will have faith in his angelic guide, designated by Philo as 'the divine Word', the 'Logos'.[387]

In the same way as Abraham's words in v. 7, the servant's prayer (Gen 24:12-14) is interpreted prophetically by Philo;

> [*Questions and Answers on Genesis* 4.95] … since the angel of God was his companion on the journey and was near by, he was perhaps enthused by him and began to be possessed.

The arrival of Rebekah at the well even before the servant had finished speaking (Gen 24:15) is interpreted by Philo as proof of "… the surpassing kindness of God, which seem to be swifter than anything in creation."[388]

Concluding Remarks

It may thus be concluded that prophetic inspiration as well as divine guidance are main themes in Philo's interpretation of the pericope. The theme of divine providence is dominant in Philo's analysis of the narra-

---

384 See also Marcus 1953, note a (*Questions and Answers on Genesis*), p. 374.
385 Cf., Philo's commentary upon Gen 22:1-19, see above.
386 See also Marcus 1953 (*Questions and Answers on Genesis*), note a, p. 374.
387 See also Marcus 1953 (*Questions and Answers on Genesis*), note b, p. 374.
388 *Questions and Answers on Genesis* 4.96.

tive. The angel is by Philo equated with the divine Word, the 'Logos' but distinguished from God Himself, designated by Philo as 'the Savior'.

4.3.5 Jacob and the Angel

Jacob's Dreams

Introduction

In *On Dreams* 1, Philo made a thoroughly allegorical interpretation of Jacob's two dreams in Genesis 28 and 31. This was Philo's second treatise on dreams, the first one has unfortunately been lost.[389] According to Philo, Jacob's dreams are examples of the kind of dreams that enable the mind to perceive the future by divine inspiration.[390]

Jacob's dream at Bethel

In Gen 28:11 we read:

> He came [ויפגע][391] to a certain *place* [במקום], and stayed there for the night, because the *sun* had set. Taking one of the *stones* of the place, he put it under his head, and lay down in that place.

As mentioned in chapter 3 above, the Hebrew word מקום/'place' has a double connotation; it can also designate a 'holy site'. Philo states that this word (in Greek τόπος) has a threefold meaning:

> [*On Dreams* 1.62-64] ... *firstly* that of a *space filled by a material form, secondly* that of the *Divine Word* [ὁ θεῖος λόγος], which God Himself has completely filled throughout with incorporeal potencies; for "they saw," says Moses, "the place where the God of Israel stood." (Ex. xxiv. 10) [...] There is a *third signification*, in keeping with which *God Himself is called a place*, by reason of His containing things, and being contained by nothing whatever, and being a place for all to flee into, and because He is Himself the space which holds Him; for He is that which He Himself has occupied, and naught encloses Him but Himself. I, mark you, am not a place, but in a place; and each thing likewise that exists; for that which is contained is different from

---

389 See the "Analytical introduction to book 1," *On Dreams*, by Colson/Whitaker 1958, 285, in *Philo*, vol. V, LCL.
390 *On Dreams* 1.1-2.
391 Literally "... he *met* a certain place ..."

that which contains it, and the Deity, being contained by nothing[392], is of necessity Itself Its own place ...[393]

According to Philo, apart from its ordinary "physical" meaning, the word 'place' may either indicate the divine Word/'Logos' which God fills and in which he stands, or God Himself.[394] The divine 'Logos' is God's place, an interpretation Philo bases on Exod 24:10 according to the LXX, which differs from the MT:

> And they [Moses, Aron, Nadab, Abiud and seventy of the elders of Israel] saw *the place* where the God of Israel *stood* ... / Καὶ εἶδον τὸν τόπον οὗ εἱστήκει ὁ Θεὸς τοῦ Ἰσραήλ...", [instead of]; "... and they saw the God of Israel ... / ... ‏ויראו את אלהי ישראל‎ ... [MT].[395]

See also *On the Confusion of Tongues* 96-97 where Philo identifies 'the place' in the LXX version of Exod 24:10 as the 'Logos':

> For then they shall behold the place which in fact is the Word, where stands God the never changing, never swerving, and also what lies under his feet like "the work of a brick of sapphire, like the form of the firmament of the heaven" (Ex. xxiv. 10), even the world of our senses, which he indicates in this mystery. For it well benefits those who have entered into comradeship with knowledge to desire to see the Existent if they may, but, if they cannot, to see at any rate his image, the most holy Word, and after the Word its most perfect work of all that our senses know, even this world ...

The use of the word 'place' as signifying either God's 'Logos' or God himself recalls the early Rabbinic epithet ‏מקום‎/*Māqôm* as a divine title designating God as 'the Omnipresent.'[396] In addition to Exod 24:10, Philo also uses Gen 22:3-4 to support his interpretation:

---

392 Yonge proposes another translation: "... but the Deity, being surrounded by nothing, is necessarily itself its own place..."

393 As seen in the quotation, Colson and Whitaker have chosen to translate Philo's concept 'Logos' according to its literal English meaning "Word." I will therefore use both terms as interchangeable equivalents.

394 According to Segal (1977, 162-165), Philo's divine 'Logos' is the hypostasized intelligence of God; by His 'Logos', God reveals Himself to humankind. The 'Logos' is God's 'image', the visible emanation of God. Kleinknecht (1969, 89) writes: "Thus the λόγος is a mediating figure which comes forth from God and establishes a link between the remotely transcendent God and the world of man, and yet which represents man to God as a high priest ..." See also Hannah 1999, 79-83.

395 See also Segal 1977, 168-169, and Barker 1992, 118-122.

396 See also Jastrow 1971, 830, Segal, 1977, 161-162, Urbach 1975, 66-79, A. Marmorstein 1927, 92-92, and 148-153. According to Koehler/Baumgartner (2001, 627), the word *Māqôm* already has this meaning in Esth 4:14: "For if you keep silence at such time as this, relief and deliverance will rise for the Jews from another quarter ..." [‏ממקום אחר‎ = from God]. See also chapter 4.5 below.

[*On Dreams* 1.64-66] "He [Abraham] came to the place [the LXX: ... ἦλθεν εἰς τὸν τόπον] of which God had told him: and lifting up his eyes he saw the place from afar." (Gen. xxii. 3f.). Tell me, pray, did he who had come to the place see it from afar? Nay, it would seem that one and the same word is used of two different things: one of these is a divine Word, the other God who was before the Word [...] But when he has his place in the divine Word he does not actually reach Him Who is in very essence God, but sees Him from afar ...

The repetition of the word 'place' implies that it denotes two different "entities" in Gen 22:3-4; God and God's 'Logos'/Word.

After his survey of the three different definitions of the word 'place', Philo concludes that the proper interpretation of Gen 28:11 is that 'the place' denotes the Word of God: "... Jacob, having come to Sense-perception, meets not now God but a word of God, even as did Abraham ... "[397] Furthermore, Philo highlights the fact that the text does not say that Jacob *came* intentionally, by choice so to speak, to the place but that he *met* with a place. Hence the divine 'Logos' met him, manifesting itself suddenly to an unprepared Jacob.[398]

Philo provides several allegorical interpretations of 'the sun' in Gen 28:11. The sun, according to Philo, first and foremost represents God; 'the Father and Ruler of the Universe', to use his designation.[399] God is Light, the very source of all light.[400] The sun may also symbolize the divine 'Logos', the divine pattern or model which contains the fullness of God,[401] and finally it may represent the human mind, enlightened by God directly or by the means of His 'Logos'.[402] According to Philo, the latter applies to Jacob in Gen 28:11.[403]

The stones mentioned in this verse are also interpreted allegorically; the stones represent incorporeal 'words'/λόγοι, that is, immortal souls. Jacob takes one of these stones, the supreme Logos, the divine 'Logos' itself, to serve as the pillow for his mind. Hence Jacob lays his whole life "in the hands of" the divine Word, the 'Logos'.[404]

After this prelude, Philo discusses the dream vision itself. He interprets the ladder/stairway as symbolizing three things. Firstly, the ladder is a figurative name for the air, the abode of the unbodied souls.

---

397 *On Dreams* 1.70.
398 *On Dreams* 1.71.
399 *On Dreams* 1.72-74, 87-91.
400 *On Dreams* 1.75-76, 87-91. Cf., John 1:4-9.
401 *On Dreams* 1.75-76, 85-86. Cf., Col 1:15-17.
402 *On Dreams* 1.77-84, 115-119.
403 *On Dreams* 1.115-119.
404 *On Dreams* 1.127-128.

The angels ascending and descending on the ladder represent the movement of the souls; some descend into human bodies while others ascend and remain in the upper realms forever.[405] Some of these souls are even higher spiritual beings, by Philo called angels:

> [*On Dreams* 1.140-142] ... viceroys of the Ruler of the universe, ears and eyes, so to speak, of the great king, beholding and hearing all things. These are called "demons" [δαίμονες[406]] by the other philosophers, but the sacred record is wont to call them "angels" or messengers, employing an apter title, for they both convey the biddings of the Father to His children and report the children's need to their Father. In accordance with this they are represented by the lawgiver as ascending and descending: not that God, who is already present in all directions, needs informants, but that it was boon to us in our sad case to avail ourselves of the services of "words" acting on our behalf as mediators ...[407]

Secondly, the ladder in itself can be said to represent the human soul, upon which the divine Words ascend and descend, hence the soul constitutes the human link connecting with the divine.[408]

Thirdly, the ladder may be a picture of the future life of Jacob, with all the ups and downs that awaited him:

> [*On Dreams* 1.150, 153-156] It may be that the Practiser [Jacob] has his own life presented to him in his vision as resembling a stairway [...] The affairs of men are naturally likened to a ladder owing to their uneven course. For one day, the poet says, brings one man down from on high, and lifts another up, and nothing relating to man is of nature to remain as it is, but all such things are liable to changes of every kind [...] Such is the road on which human affairs go up and down, a road liable to shifting and unstable happenings [...]

Kugel compares this interpretation by Philo with the one given in the Pseud-epigraphon *Ladder of Jacob*, where the ladder is said to represent 'this age' as well as the future destiny of Jacob's descendants.[409]

According to Philo, the dream showed God, 'the Ruler of the angels' standing firmly upon the ladder, meaning that God is the unques-

---

405 *On Dreams* 1.133-139.

406 In this context, the Greek word is not to be understood as denoting 'evil spirits'.

407 Philo thus identifies the biblical angels with the demons of the Greek philosophers. But unlike the demons of, for example, the Stoic philosopher Posidonius, Philo's angels are not the necessary link between the upper and the lower stages of being. In Philo's view, the angels are instruments of Divine Providence, and their services could on occasion be dispensed with when God preferred to contact men directly. See Altman 1971, vol. 2. 973-976, and Hannah 1999, 84-85.

408 *On Dreams* 1.146-149.

409 Kugel 1995, 212. See also chapter 5 in *"Ladder of Jacob*. A New translation and Introduction," Lunt in *OTP*, 1985, vol. 2, 401-411.

tionable Lord of all creation, standing high above all created beings and things. It is God alone who establishes and holds together the creation and prevents chaos:

> [*On Dreams* 1.157-158] The dream shewed the Ruler of the angels [τὸν ἀρχάγγελον, κύριον] set fast upon the stairway, even the Lord, for high up like a charioteer high over his chariot or a helmsman high over his ship must we conceive of Him that IS [τὸ ὄν] standing over bodies, over souls, over doings, over words, over angels […] over powers descried by our senses, over invisible beings, yea all things seen and unseen: for having made all the universe to depend on and cling to Himself […] Let nobody […] think that anything co-operates with God to help Him to stand firmly […] For it is because He stablishes and holds it together that the system of created beings remains strongly and mightily free from destruction …

The one who addresses Jacob in Gen 28:13-15 is thus interpreted as God Himself, a statement that slightly contradicts Philo's previous assertion that God contacted Jacob through His 'Logos', because he was unable to see God directly (*On Dreams* 1.115-119). However, the meaning of Philo's statement in *On Dreams* 1.157 is disputed. The Greek wording is τὸν ἀρχάγγελον, κύριον /'the archangel, the Lord'. Since elsewhere in Philo's works the 'Logos' is also termed 'archangel' (*Who is the Heir* 205-206 and *On the Confusion of Tongues* 146-147) some scholars interpret *On Dreams* 1.157 as a reference to the 'Logos'.[410] However, the following designation "Him that IS" as well as the context in general indicates that Philo in this case is speaking about God.[411] This interpretation probably also lies behind the translation of the expression τὸν ἀρχάγγελον as 'the Ruler of the angels' chosen by Colson and Whitaker.[412]

God introduces Himself as "the LORD [YHWH] the God [Elohim] of Abraham your father and the God [Elohim] of Isaac" (Gen 28:13). Philo interprets this to mean that God is both the God of the universe and the God of Jacob's family. This is hence an example of concurrent Jewish universalism and particularism.[413]

---

410 E.g., Wolfson 1947, vol. 1, 377-379, and Segal 1977, 170.

411 See also Hannah 1999, 86.

412 Yonge translates *On Dreams* 1.157 as follows: "But the dream also represented the archangel, namely the Lord himself, firmly planted on the ladder; for we must imagine that the living God stands above all things …" Thus, Yonge also interprets the designation τὸν ἀρχάγγελον 'the archangel' as referring to God in this context.

413 *On Dreams* 1.159. According to Philo, The fact that God addressed Jacob by name indicates that God counted Jacob as one of his friends, *On Dreams* 1.193-196.

Philo poses the question as to why God designates Himself as 'the LORD God' in relation to Abraham, while in connection to Isaac He is just 'God'. One part of the answer is that the divine designations denote two different aspects of God's personality. To Philo, YHWH/*Kyrios* denotes the divine principle of justice and sovereignty, and the designation God/*Theos* represents the divine mercy and creative potency.[414] It is noteworthy that a similar doctrine of the two main divine attributes also appears in Rabbinic Judaism. However, in the words of Segal;

> ... Philo's identification of mercy and justice with the names of God is exactly opposite to the standard rabbinic doctrine. YHWH is merciful for the rabbis; *kyrios*, judging for Philo. Conversely, *Elohim* is judging for the rabbis; *theos*, merciful for Philo.[415]

Another part of the explanation pertains to the different characters of the two patriarchs,[416] a matter I cannot elaborate on here. According to Philo, Jacob reacts with surprise and fear when he awakes because he realizes that in fact God is not in any particular place but is omnipresent. 'The gate of heaven' (Gen 28:17) represents the visible world of the senses, through which we can perceive the divine.[417]

Jacob's second dream

After these remarks, Philo goes on to analyze Jacob's second dream, recorded in Gen 31:10-13. As a starting point it is worthwhile to take a look once more at the wording of the two crucial verses in the text:

> [Gen 31:11] Then *the angel of God* [מלאך האלהים] said to me in the dream, 'Jacob,' and I said, 'Here I am!' [13] *'I am the God of Bethel, where you anointed a pillar and made a vow to me.* Now leave this land at once and return to the land of your birth.'/ [אנכי האל בת אל אשר משחת שם מצבה אשר נדרת לי שם נדר עתה קום צא מן הארץ הזאת ושוב אל ארץ מולדתך]

Since it is stated in v. 11 that it was the angel of God who addressed Jacob, Philo concludes that the Bible considers dreams as God-sent, even though they are not mediated directly by God Himself but through the agency of His "... interpreters and attendant messengers who have been held to receive from the Father to Whom they owe their being a divine and happy portion," to use Philo's own words.[418]

---

414 *On Dreams* 1.160-163.
415 Segal 1977, 175. According to Segal (1977, 170, note 27), Philo also often links the two designations of God, Elohim and YHWH (*Theos* and *Kyrios*), to the 'Existing One' and His 'Logos' respectively. See also Hannah 1999, 84.
416 See *On Dreams* 1.160-172.
417 *On Dreams* 1.182-188.
418 *On Dreams* 1.190.

Philo then calls attention to the peculiar wording of v. 13a, which he quotes from the Septuagint version:

> [Gen 31:13] ... ἐγώ εἰμι ὁ θεὸς ὁ ὀφθείς σοι ἐν τόπῳ θεοῦ... / I am the God that appeared to you in the place of God ...

As a comment on this verse, Philo writes:

> [*On Dreams* 1.228-231] ... And do not fail to mark the language used, but carefully inquire whether there are two Gods; for we read "I am the God that appeared to thee," not "in my place" but "in the place of God," as though it were another's. What, then, are we to say? He that is truly God is One, but those that are improperly so called are more than one. Accordingly, the holy word in the present instance has indicated Him Who is truly God by means of the articles saying "I am the God," while it omits the article when mentioning him who is improperly so called, saying "Who appeared to thee in the place" not "of the God," but simply "of God." Here it gives the title of "God" to His chief Word, not from any superstitious nicety in applying names, but with one aim before him, to use words to express facts. Thus in another place, when he had inquired whether He that IS has any name, he came to know full well that He has no proper name [...] for it is not the nature of Him that IS to be spoken of, but simply to be. Testimony to this is afforded also by the divine response made to Moses' question whether He has a name, even "I am He that IS" (Ex. iii. 14) ...[419]

'The God' in definite form denotes the true God in Himself, while the word 'God' without the definite article denotes the 'Logos'. God appeared to Jacob in Gen 28:10-22 through His 'Logos', God's chief Word. According to Segal: "Philo derives the idea that the *logos* is a separate, second divine hypostasis from the fact that 'God' is repeated in 'place of God' instead of using the pronoun (i.e., *My* place) as one would normally expect."[420] See also Gen 35:1 (MT) where God/Elohim refers in the third person to the God/El who previously revealed Himself to Jacob in Bethel: "... Arise, go up to Bethel, and settle there. Make an altar there to *the God* [not to *me*!] who appeared to you when you fled from your brother Esau." God reveals Himself to humankind in the form of His 'Logos':[421]

> [*On Dreams* 1.232] To the souls indeed which are incorporeal and are occupied in His worship it is likely that He should reveal Himself as He is, conversing with them as friend with friends [the angels?];[422] but to souls which

---

419 Cf., *On the Change of Names* 14-15 quoted below.

420 Segal 1977, 162.

421 See also Segal 1977, 159-165, and Williamson 1989, 121-125.

422 My own interpretation is that Philo here probably refers to angels. Segal (1977, 163), however, interprets Philo to mean that some humans are indeed capable of seeing God directly, if they can transcend what is material, while other humans who only know the 'Logos' mistake the copy for the original.

are still in a body [humans], giving Himself the likeness of angels, not altering His own nature, for He is unchangeable, but conveying to those
which receive the impression of His presence a semblance in a different
form, such that they take the image to be not a copy, but that original form
itself.

Philo then continues to discuss the many anthropomorphic descriptions of God in the Bible and says:

> [*On Dreams* 1.237-241] … Broadly speaking the lines taken throughout the
> Law are these two only, one that which keeps truth in view and so pro-
> vides the thought "God is not a man" (Num. xxiii. 19), the other that which
> keeps in view the ways of thinking of the duller folk, of whom it is said
> "the Lord God chasten thee, as if a man should chasten his son" (Deut. viii.
> 5). Why then, do we wonder any longer at *His assuming the likeness of angels*,
> seeing that the succour of those that are in need *He assumes that of men*? Ac-
> cordingly, when He says "I am the God who was seen of thee in the place
> of God" (Gen xxxi. 13), understand that *He occupied the place of an angel only
> so far as appeared, without changing, with a view to the profit of him who was not
> yet capable of seeing the true God*. For just as those who are unable to see the
> sun itself see the gleam of the parhelion and take it for the sun [...] so some
> regard *the image of God, His angel the Word*, as His very self. Do you not see
> how Hagar, who is the education of the schools, says to the angel "Thou art
> the God that didst look upon me"? (Gen. xvi. 13); for being Egyptian by
> descent she was not qualified to see the supreme Cause. But in the passage
> upon which we are occupied, the mind is beginning, as the result of im-
> provement, to form a mental image of the sovereign Ruler of all such Po-
> tencies. Hence it is that He Himself says "I am the God", whose *image* thou
> didst aforetime behold deeming it to be I Myself, and didst dedicate a pillar
> engraved with a most holy inscription (Gen xxxi. 13); and the purport of
> the inscription was that I alone am standing [...] and sustained the un-
> iverse to rest firm upon *the mighty Word, Who is my viceroy*.

In, for example, *On Husbandry* 51, the 'Logos' is likewise labeled God's
'viceroy' and additionally identified as the 'divine name-angel' of Exodus 23.[423] The 'Logos', the image of God, the angel of God and the divine viceroy are thus equated to each other in Philo's teaching.[424] It is,
however, noteworthy that 'the angel of God' in singular form is not
mentioned in Genesis 28 but only in Genesis 31, where he in v. 13 identifies Himself as *the God*, in definite form, a term understood by Philo to
denote God Himself, not a mediator. Philo's statement that it was the

---

423 See also e.g., *On Flight and Finding* 101, 111-112, *On the Migration of Abraham* 174, and
     Gieschen 1998, 107-112.
424 According to Gieschen (1998, 107-112), Philo's use of the term 'angel' to denote the
     'Logos' reveals his dependence upon the Jewish angelomorphic traditions in his ela-
     boration of the concept.

'Logos' who appeared to Jacob in Bethel is not entirely consistent with his previous analysis of Genesis 28.[425]

There is also a contradiction in Philo's interpretation of Gen 31:10-13, since he deems it necessary in *On Dreams* 1.190 to assure the reader that Jacob's dream is divinely inspired, despite being transmitted by 'a messenger', not God in person.[426]

Jacob's Struggle at the Ford of Jabbok

In *On Sobriety* 65 there is an allusion to Jacob's encounter with the angels of God in Gen 32:1. The meeting with the angels is interpreted as a struggle against inner passions, a moral preparation for his wrestling bout at Jabbok:

> ... from Isaac's seed again comes the virtues of the laborious life in which Jacob exercised himself to mastery, Jacob trained in the wrestling-bout with the passions, with the angels of reason to prepare him for the conflict...[427]

According to *On Drunkenness* 82-83, Jacob's struggle at Jabbok is interpreted allegorically as the patriarch's final exercise in his pursuit of virtue. Philo quotes the statement in the LXX Gen 32:28; "Thy name shall no longer be called Jacob, but Israel shall be your name, because you have been strong with God and mighty with men" and takes this to mean that Jacob had showed himself worthy both in front of God and humans. As a reward, Jacob is blessed with the name Israel, which according to Philo signifies perfection and the sight of God:[428]

> Now Jacob is a name for learning and progress, gifts which depend on the hearing; Israel for perfection, for the name expresses the vision of God. And what among all the blessings which the virtues give can be more perfect than the sight of the Absolutely Existent? He who has the sight of this blessing has his fair acknowledged in the eyes of both parents, for he has gained the strength which is in God and the power which avails among men.

---

425 See the discussion of Philo's interpretation of Jacob's dream at Bethel (Genesis 28) above. As mentioned in the introduction, because of the inherent ambiguity in Philo's discussions of the 'Logos', there are also divergent views among scholars regarding the interpretation of Philo's writings on this point. There are basically two "sides;" those who consider Philo's Logos as nothing more than a way to express God's action in the world, e.g., Hurtado (1998, 44-48), while others argue that Philo's 'Logos' should be regarded as a hypostasis, e.g., Wolfson (1947, vol. 1. 231-252). See also Hannah 1999, 77-83.

426 See *On Dreams* 1.190 quoted above.

427 See also Colson/Whitaker, 1930, *On Sobriety* 65, footnote a, p. 478.

428 See also Hayward 2005, 169-172.

Thus, Jacob/Israel is presented as a role model in virtue who has obtained the most precious spiritual gift, the ability of seeing God as a
reward.[429] Philo presents a similar interpretation of the LXX Gen 32:28
in *On the Change of Names* 44-45, 81-82:

> [44-45] And so those were fitting words which were said to the victorious
> wrestler when he was about to be crowned with the garlands of triumph
> [...] To win honour in both spheres, in our duty both towards the un-
> created and the created, requires no petty mind, but one who stands in
> very truth midway between the world and God [but as for one which (if
> one must speak the truth) lies as a boundary between the world and God
> (κόσμου καὶ θεοῦ μεθορίου)...].[430]

> [81-82] ... The task of him who sees God is not to leave the sacred are-
> na uncrowned, but carry of the prizes of victory. And what garland more
> fitting for its purpose or of richer flowers could be woven for the victorious
> soul than the power which will enable him to behold the Existent with
> clear vision? Surely that is a glorious guerdon to offer to the athlete soul,
> that it should be endowed with eyes to apprehend in bright light Him Who
> alone is worthy of our contemplation.

As shown above, Philo depicts Jacob/Israel after the victory at Jabbok
as a boundary figure, a mediator between God and the created world, a
function that Philo elsewhere ascribes to the 'Logos':

> [*Who is the Heir* 205-206] To His word, the chief messenger highest in age
> and honour [τῷ δὲ ἀρχαγγέλῳ καὶ πρεσβυτάτῳ λόγῳ: To His archangel
> and eldest Logos[431]], the Father of all has given the special prerogative, to
> stand at the border and separate the creature from the Creator. This same
> Word both pleads with the immortal as suppliant for the afflicted mortality
> and acts as ambassador of the ruler to the subject. He glories in this pre-
> rogative and proudly describes it in these words 'and I stood between the
> Lord and you' (Deut v.5), that is neither uncreated as God, nor created as
> you, but midway between the two extremes, a surety to both sides...[432]

In this text, Philo defines the 'Logos' as a suppliant and describes it in
priestly categories, a role that he also assigns to the people of Israel;
Israel is the priestly nation, representing God in the world.[433] However,
in contrast to Jacob/Israel, the 'Logos' is said to be "neither uncreated as
God, nor created as you [humans]..."[434] There appears to be a close

---

429 See also *On the Migration of Abraham* 200-201.
430 Eng. trans. Hayward 2005, 162.
431 Eng. trans. Hayward 2005, 163.
432 See also Philo's interpretation of Genesis 18 in *On the Migration of Abraham* 173-174,
     where the 'Logos' is identified with the 'divine name angel' of Exodus 23. Cf., *On
     Flight and Finding* 112.
433 See e.g., *On the Embassy to Gaius* 3-4. See also Williamson 1989, 119-121.
434 See also Williamson 1989, 119-121.

connection between the 'Logos' and the nation of Israel in Philo's writings.[435] Indeed, in *On the Confusion of Tongues*, 146, the 'Logos' itself carries the name of Israel, a name that Philo throughout his writings interprets as meaning 'one who sees (God)':[436]

> But if there be any as yet unfit to be called a Son of God, let him press to take his place under God's Firstborn, the Word, who holds the eldership among the angels, their ruler as it were [... τὸν ἀγγέλων πρεσβύτατον, ὡς ἂν ἀρχάγγελον: the eldest of His angels, as the great archangel[437]]. And many names are his, for he is called, "the Beginning," and the Name of God, and His Word, and the Man after His image, and "he that sees," that is Israel [... ὁ ὁρῶν, Ἰσραήλ].[438]

According to Philo, it was this 'angel', the 'Logos', who bestowed the name Israel on Jacob. Moreover, the reason that Jacob, even after his renaming as Israel, is on occasions still called by his old name[439] is due to the fact that the new name was given to him by an angel, and not by God Himself; in contrast to the case of Abraham:

> [*On the Change of Names* 87] ...Therefore did Abraham in token of the even tenor of his future life receive his new name from God, the unchangeable [...] But Jacob was re-named by an angel, God's minister, the Word, in acknowledgement that what is below the Existent cannot produce permanence unswerving and unwavering ...

Thus, the 'Logos'/angel is in this context distinguished from God. According to Hayward, in identifying Jacob's opponent in Genesis 32 as an angel, Philo was most certainly dependent on text witnesses of the LXX Gen 32:24, which specify that it was an angel who wrestled with the patriarch.[440]

As mentioned previously, according to Gen 28:11, the stone which Jacob used as a pillow during his nightly sojourn at Bethel is allegorically interpreted as representing the divine 'Logos' in *On Dreams* 1.128. In this context, Philo briefly refers to Jacob's wrestling bout at Jabbok and identifies this 'Logos' as Jacob's contender. As his teacher and trainer, the 'Logos' disciplines Jacob and rewards him by giving him the new name Israel–he who sees:

---

435 See also Wolfson 1947, vol. 1, 377-379, Gieschen 1998, 111-112, and Hannah 1999, 88-89.
436 For a full list of references, see the 'Index of names'; 'Israel' in *Philo*, vol. X, LCL, 1962, 334.
437 Yonge's translation.
438 Cf., Col 1:15-17 and Heb 1:1-3.
439 See, e.g., Gen 34:5; 35:1-15; 37:1, 34; 48:2-3.
440 Hayward 2005, 167.

[*On Dreams* 1.129] The divine word readily listens to and accepts the athlete [Jacob] to be first of all a pupil, then when he has been satisfied of his fitness of nature, he fastens on the gloves as a trainer does and summons him to the exercises, then closes with him and forces him to wrestle until he has developed in him an irresistible strength, and by the breath of divine inspiration he changes ears into eyes, and gives him when remodeled in a new form the name of Israel–He who sees.

Since the 'Logos' in *On the Confusion of Tongues* 146 is designated by the very same title, 'Israel', that is given to Jacob, Gieschen suggests that Philo may have understood the renaming of Jacob as the 'Logos', i.e., the angel Israel bestowed his own name upon the patriarch.[441] Because of the close connection between Jacob/the nation Israel and the 'Logos' in Philo's mindset, others, for example, Wolfson and Darrell D. Hannah, interpret the 'Logos' in this context as the guardian angel of Israel, the archangel Michael.[442]

Although Philo does not explicitly offer any such specific identification of Jacob's contender in *On Dreams* 1.129, it seems implied that the 'Logos' is to be understood as an angel, akin to those others λόγοι/'angels' mentioned in the context.[443] However, as discussed above, scholars differ in the interpretation of 'the archangel, the Lord' who, according to *On Dreams* 1.157, addresses Jacob from the top of the ladder in his dream at Bethel, some identify him as God in person, others as the 'Logos'.

In the same way as the biblical account, the name of the antagonist remains unknown in Philo's interpretation of Genesis 32, which may be illustrated by his discussion of the narrative in *On the Change of Names* 14-15:

> So impossible to name indeed is the Existent that not even the Potencies who serve Him tell us a proper name. Thus after the wrestling-bout in which the Man of Practice [Jacob] engaged in his quest of virtue, he says to the unseen [ἀοράτῳ] master,[444] "Announce to me Thy name," and he said "Why dost thou ask this my name?" (Gen xxxii. 29), and he refuses to tell his personal name [... τὸ ἴδιον καὶ κύριον]. "It is enough for thee," he means, "to profit through my benediction, but as for names, those symbols which indicate created beings, look not for them in the case of imperishable natures."[φύσεσιν ἀφθάρτοις] Think it not then a hard saying that the Highest of all things should be unnamable [... τὸ τῶν ὄντων πρεσβύτατον

---

441 Gieschen 1998, 112. Cf., *Pirqê de Rabbi Eliezer* 37.
442 Wolfson 1947, vol. 1, 376-379, Hannah 1999, 88-89.
443 See also Hayward 2005, 172-177.
444 Yonge has here: [14] "And indeed, the living God is so completely indescribable, that even those powers which minister unto him do not announce his proper name to us [...] he [Jacob] says to the invisible Master ..."

ἄρρητον ...] when His Word has no name of its own which we can speak [ὁπότε καὶ ὁ λόγος αὐτοῦ κυρίῳ ὀνόματι οὐ ῥητὸς ἡμῖν]. And indeed if He is unnamable He is also inconceivable and incomprehensible. [Yonge translates: ...But as for names which are the symbols of created things, do not seek to find them among immortal natures. Therefore do not doubt either whether that which is more ancient than any existing thing is indescribable, when his very word is not to be mentioned by us according to its proper name ...]

And so the words "The Lord was seen of Abraham" (Gen xvii. 1) must not be understood in the sense that the Cause of all shone upon him and appeared to him, for what human mind could contain the vastness of that vision? Rather we must think of it as the manifestation of one of the Potencies which attend him ...

As in the Bible, Jacob's opponent refuses to reveal his name. According to Philo, the reason for the refusal is that names are symbols indicated for created beings and those of imperishable beings are not to be asked for, i.e., both God and his ministers. Thus, the "man" who confronts Jacob at the ford of Jabbok is here clearly identified as of a supernatural, celestial nature and origin; it is the 'Logos' of God, but not God in person. Ronald Williamson interprets the passage to imply that Philo understood Genesis 32 to mean that since God is unnamable, Jacob's request is denied, but even if God in His essence is beyond human comprehension, man is able to receive His blessings.[445]

According to David Runia, Philo distinguishes here between the 'Logos' and God. The 'Logos' is said to have a personal and proper name (τὸ ἴδιον καὶ κύριον), although he refuses to reveal it, but God is unnameable. Moreover, there is a difference between God, who is depicted as 'indescribable'/ ἄρρητος, and the 'Logos', whose proper name is "not to be mentioned"/οὐ ῥητὸς.[446] In this context we may also consider Philo's statement in On the Confusion of Tongues 146 that the 'Logos' has many names, while God is essentially nameless. God is beyond human comprehension but the 'Logos' is God's "face" turned toward humankind, His means of communicating with the world.[447]

The 'Logos' is depicted as 'the unseen Master', i.e., he is invisible to Jacob, but this may be explained by the fact that the battle took place at night, thus the appearance of the opponent was concealed by darkness.[448]

---

445 Williamson 1989, 86-92.
446 Runia 1990, XI, 78.
447 See Williamson 1989, 105-109, 113-125, and Runia, 1990, I, 9.
448 See Gen 32:22-24, 26 and Colson/Whitaker, footnote a (On the Change of Names), 1934, 150-151.

After his paraphrase of Gen 32:29-30, Philo compares the two patriarchs Abraham and Jacob to each other and claims that, since it is impossible to truly see God, neither of them encountered God in person but that it was one of God's potencies who manifested themselves to them. However, it is noteworthy that in the case of Jacob's antagonist, he is portrayed as distinct from 'created beings', compare Philo's description of the 'Logos' in *Who is the Heir* 206 and *On Flight and Finding* 1.203-205.

Philo and the Prayer of Joseph

Many scholars have pointed out parallels between the *Prayer of Joseph* and the Philonic corpus. An obvious one is the etymology of the name Israel, which is explained in both cases to signify the seeing of God. However, while the *Prayer of Joseph* explains the name to mean '*a man* who sees God', Philo always omits the word 'man' and employs a shorter form of the etymology, i.e., 'he/the one who sees (God)'.

The reason for Philo's omission of the word 'man' may be that he wished to loosen the epithet from its original context, i.e., the "historical" patriarch's renaming at Jabbok, in order to open up for a more abstract employment of the name. As already shown, 'Israel' is also the title that Philo assigns to the 'Logos' in *On the Confusion of Tongues* 146.

In this light, it is noteworthy that although the *Prayer of Joseph* retains the word 'man' in its etymology of the name, the Jacob/Israel who speaks in the Pseudepigraphon has apparent similarities with Philo's 'Logos'. Indeed, the description of Jacob/Israel in the *Prayer of Joseph* parallels in many ways Philo's depiction of the 'Logos', which may be demonstrated by a comparison between the Pseudepigraphon and two Philonic passages:

Prayer of Joseph	Philo
[Fragment A] "I, Jacob, who is speaking to you, am also **Israel, an angel of God** and a **ruling spirit**. [...] But, I, Jacob, who men call Jacob but whose name is **Israel** am he who God called **Israel** which means, **a man seeing God**, because I am the **firstborn** of every living thing to whom God gives life.[449]	[*On the Confusion of Tongues* 146] But if there be any as yet unfit to be called a Son of God, let him press to take his place under **God's Firstborn**, the Word, who holds **the eldership among the angels**, their **ruler** as it were [... τὸν ἀγγέλων πρεσβύτατον, ὡς ἂν ἀρχάγγελον: the **eldest of his angels**, as the **great archangel**[450]]. And many names are his, for he is called, "the Beginning," and the Name of God, and His Word, and the Man after His image, and *"he that sees,"* that is **Israel** [... ὁ ὁρῶν, Ἰσραήλ].
And when I was coming up from Syrian Mesopotamia, Uriel, the angel of God, came forth and said that I had descended to earth [...] He envied me and fought with me [...]	
I [Jacob/Israel] told him [the opponent] his name and what rank he held among the sons of God. 'Are you not Uriel, the eighth after me? and I, **Israel, the archangel of the power of the Lord** and **the chief captain among the sons of God**? Am I not **Israel**, the **first minister** before the face of God? [...]"	[*On Flight and Finding* 101] The Divine Word, Who is **high above all these** [the powers] [...] He is Himself the image of God, **chiefest of all Beings** [...] placed nearest [...] to the Alone truly Existent One. For we read: "I will talk to you from above the Mercy-seat, between the two Cherubim" (Ex. xxv.21) words which shew while the **Word is the charioteer of the Powers**, He who talks [God] is seated in the chariot ...[451]

---

449 Cf., Col 1:15-17. See also Smith 1968, 268, and Gieschen 1998, 140.
450 Yonge's translation. See also *Who is the Heir* 205 and *On Dreams* 1.157 quoted above.
451 See also *On the Cherubim* 27-28, where the 'Logos' is depicted as standing between and uniting the two Cherubim, representing God's highest powers, His goodness, and His sovereignty. However, in *Who is the Heir* 166 God Himself occupies this position.

As shown, many of the epithets that Philo assigns to the 'Logos' correspond closely to/are identical to those given to Jacob/Israel in the *Prayer of Joseph*, for example, 'archangel', 'firstborn', 'Israel', i.e., 'the man who sees'/'he who sees', 'the archangel of the power of the Lord'/'the charioteer of the Powers'.[452] However, Philo also employs terms not found in the Pseudepigraphon, e.g., he labels the 'Logos' as 'the man after His [God's] image'.

An additional connection between Philo's 'Logos' and the angel Jacob/Israel in the *Prayer of Joseph* may be that Uriel in the latter work is depicted as *the eighth* in rank, while Jacob/Israel is 'the archangel of the power of the Lord'. Philo assigns a similar title to the 'Logos', which he declares to be 'the charioteer of the Powers'. When commenting on the LXX Exodus 25 in *Questions and Answers on Exodus* 2.68, Philo describes the 'Logos' as part of a sevenfold hierarchy in which God has the prime position and the 'Logos' the second highest. Possibly, the author of the *Prayer of Joseph* also had such a heavenly hierarchy in mind and placed Uriel outside "the inner-circle of seven" but this conclusion remains hypothetical; perhaps there is only a "superficial" similarity between the terminology of Philo and the author of the *Prayer of Joseph*.

However, it is evident that both of them agree in ascribing to Israel the status of the highest angel but they arrive at this conclusion by different routes;[453] Philo never depicts the *patriarch Jacob* as an (incarnated) angel. In his works, it is the 'Logos' that inhabits this position. The description of the conflict at Jabbok as a confrontation between two rival angels, Uriel and Israel, in the *Prayer of Joseph* has no counterpart in Philo's exegesis.[454]

The only similarities between the elaborations on Genesis 32 presented by Philo and the Pseudepigraphon are the fact that Jacob's opponent in both cases is identified as an angel, Uriel and the 'Logos' respectively, and the etymology of the name Israel. However, in Philo's works, the name 'Israel' is generally described as a reward, Jacob has to *become* Israel *in order* to see God, it is not a quality he possesses from the outset.[455]

Based on these parallels and differences, there is no clear answer regarding the relationship between Philo's authorship and the *Prayer of*

---

452 See also Smith 1968, 267, and Birnbaum 1996, 75-76.
453 See Hayward 2005, 206-211, 215-217, and Smith *OTP*, vol. 2, 1985, introduction, 704.
454 See also Hayward 2005, 200-207, 215-216. For a detailed discussion of the *Prayer of Joseph*, see chapter 4.2 above.
455 An exception to this "rule", however, is Philo's statement in the *Posterity and Exile of Cain* 63. See also Hayward 2005, 201-208, 216-217.

Joseph. The latter may be contemporary with Philo's works but that does not imply any inter-dependence between them. Philo both might, and might not, have known the composition. Most probably, both Philo and the author of the *Prayer of Joseph* built upon common Jewish traditions regarding the etymology of the name Israel and angelology; traditions pre-dating both of them. They had a common religious heritage but used it differently in their respective authorships.[456]

The Blessing of Ephraim and Manasseh

Regarding the interpretation of Jacob's blessing of his grandsons Ephraim and Manasseh, Philo has three references to Jacob's words in Gen 48:15-16 relevant to the present thesis. The first is found in *Allegorical Interpretation* 3.177-178:

> Now those of whom we have been speaking pray to be fed with the word of God. But Jacob, looking even higher than the word, says that he is fed by God Himself. He speaks on this wise: "The God to Whom my fathers Abraham and Isaac were well pleasing, the God Who feedeth me from my youth up unto this day, the Angel who delivered me out of all my ills, bless these boys" (Gen xlviii.15f.). How beautiful is his tone and temper! He looks on God as feeding him, not His Word; but the Angel, who is the Word, as healer of ills [...] He thinks it meet and right that He that IS should Himself in His own Person give the principal boons, while His Angels and Words give the secondary gifts; and secondary are such as involve riddance from ills [...] Now His [God's] mode of dealing is the same in the case of the soul. The good things, the food, He Himself bestows with His own hand, but by the agency of Angels and Words such as involve the riddance of ills.

In this allegorical interpretation of Gen 48:15-16, Philo distinguishes between the 'angel'/the 'Logos' and God. It is God who bestows the prime benefits upon the soul, while the 'angel' gives the secondary gifts, such as deliverance from ills. God and His angels have different roles in relation to the pious. Thus, Philo identifies the 'angel' in Genesis 48 with the 'Logos', who is here portrayed as subordinate to God and distinct from Him.

In both of the other two references, *On the Confusion of Tongues* 180-182 and in *On Flight and Finding* 66-67, we encounter similar interpretations of Jacob's words:

---

456 See Hayward 2005, 216-219, and Smith 1968, 259-260. See also Birnbaum 1996, 72-90.

[*On the Confusion of Tongues* 180-182] ...God is the cause of good things only and of nothing at all that is bad, since He Himself was the most ancient
of beings and the good in its most perfect form [...] but that the chastise-
ment of the wicked should be assured through His underlings. My thoughts are attested also by the words of him [Jacob] who was made perfect
through practice, "the God who nourished me from my youth, the angel
who savest me from all evils [...] For he, too, hereby confesses that the truly good gifts, which nourish virtue-loving souls, are referred to God alone
as their cause, but on the other hand the province of things evil has been
committed to angels [...]. Therefore he says, "Come and let us go down
and confound them."[457] The impious indeed deserve to have it as their punishment, that God's beneficent and merciful and bountiful powers should
be brought in association with works of vengeance. Yet, though knowing
that punishment was salutary for the human race, He decreed that it
should be exacted by others ...[458]

[*On Flight and Finding* 66-67] ... He [God] punishes not by His own
hands but by those of others who act as His ministers [...] The Practiser [Ja-
cob] testifies to what I say in the words, "God who nourishes me... [quota-
tion of Gen 48:15-16] He ascribes to God the more important good things,
by which the soul is nourished, and the less important, which come about
by escape from sins, to God's minister.

In the same way as in *Allegorical Interpretation* 3.177-178, Philo uses
Jacob's words when blessing his grandsons to support his claim that
God is the giver of goodness only and cannot do anything evil, not
even punish.[459] Instead, He has appointed this task to His ministers,
the angels. It is noteworthy, that Philo in *On the Confusion of Tongues*
181 interprets the scriptural plural of Gen 11:7 "Come, let *us* go
down..." as referring to God's powers/angels. In this context, Philo
supplies the same explanation of the use of the plural form in the account of the creation of humankind (Gen 1:26):

[*On the Confusion of Tongues* 178-179] Man is practically the only being who
having knowledge of good and evil often chooses the worst [...] Thus it
was meet and right that when man was formed, God should assign a share
in the work to His lieutenants, as He does with the words "let *us* make

---

457 The reference is to Gen 11:7.
458 The translators Colson and Whitaker (1932, 110, note a) have a comment on this
     passage:

     Philo here seems to assign the work of punishment to the lower division of the mi-
     nisters rather than to the Potencies, though elsewhere he treats it as belonging to the
     Kingly Potency indicated by the name of ὁ Κύριος, e.g., *De Abr*.144, 145. Here the
     "angels" have the whole province of evil assigned to them, whether to save them
     from it, as with Jacob, or to inflict it.

459 See also *On Husbandry* 128-129.

men," that so man's right actions might be attributable to God, but his sins
to others. For it seemed unfitting to God the All-ruler that the road to
wickedness within the reasonable soul should be of His making, and therefore He delegated the forming of this part to His inferiors ...[460]

Because God is the origin of good only and human nature encompasses
both good and evil, Philo declares that God was assisted by His servants in the creation of humankind, a statement that comes perilously
close to the 'two powers-heresy' combated by the early Rabbis, although the Rabbinic interpretation of the same passage explains the
plural by saying that God consulted the angels.[461]

Concluding Remarks

Gen 31:13 as recorded in the LXX is a key verse for Philo's theological
system:

> [Gen 31:13] ... ἐγώ εἰμι ὁ θεὸς ὁ ὀφθείς σοι ἐν τόπῳ θεοῦ... / I am the
> God that appeared to you in the place of God ...

According to Philo, the God (in the definite form) here refers to His
'Logos', i.e., 'god' in the indefinite form. Philo's comment on this verse
implies that God initially appeared to Jacob through the 'Logos'. The
'Logos' is identified by Philo as the angel of the Lord, the image of God
and the divine viceroy. However, his interpretation of the verse is not
entirely in agreement with his comment on Genesis 28 since, according
to Philo, Jacob's dream showed God standing above the ladder, indicating that he is the Lord of all creation.

The sun as well as the word 'place' is said by Philo to symbolize
both God Himself and the divine 'Logos'. It is noteworthy that the
word *Māqôm*/'place' denotes God as the Omnipresent in some Rabbinic

---

460 See also *On the Creation* 72-75. If we continue to read *On Flight and Finding* (68-70) we
find the same explanation of the use of the plural form in connection with the creation of humankind.

461 See e.g., *Gen. Rab.* 8.4; *b. Sanhedrin* 38b, and *Tg. Ps.-J.* Gen 1:26. However, the Rabbis
strongly opposed the notion that God *had help* in the creation. See also Segal 1977,
176-177, and Fossum 1985, 198-211. There are also passages in Philo's works that
seem to contradict his "doctrine" of God as the origin of goodness only, e.g., *Allegorical Interpretation* 3.104-106. See also Wolfson 1947, vol. 1, 282, 349, and 382. It
must also be pointed out that, although according to, e.g., *On the Confusion of
Tongues* 178-179, God assigns the creation of the evil aspect of man to his servants,
God is still in control and has the ultimate responsibility for the whole creation, thus
there is no place for dualism in Philo's thinking. See also Williamson, 1989, 44-48.

sources, an interpretation in line with Philo's understanding of the word. [462]

To conclude, Philo is ambivalent concerning who really addressed Jacob at Bethel; it was either God or His 'Logos'.

There is also a certain ambiguity in Philo's interpretations of Genesis 32. As shown above, in his commentary on the narrative in *On the Change of Names* 14-15, Philo denies that humans (including Jacob) can see God but in other passages Jacob's "prize" for winning the battle is said to be the sight of God,[463] and Philo consistently interprets the name Israel as signifying 'one who sees (God)'. In *On Dreams* 1.79, Philo uses the LXX rendering of the place-name Peniel in Genesis 32 and writes that Jacob "passed by the appearance of God [τὸ εἶδος τοῦ θεοῦ]," a reference that may imply that he interpreted the narrative to mean that Jacob had indeed seen God's face at Jabbok. Moreover, as shown above, there is an ambivalence between God and the 'Logos' in Philo's portrayal of the latter in his writings and, although the 'Logos' is sometimes depicted in angelic terms, it/he also appears to be something more than an "ordinary" angel.

Regarding the first ambiguity, Philo's words in *On Rewards and Punishments* 43-44 may throw some light on this issue:

> But those, if such were be, who have had the power to apprehend Him through Himself without the co-operation of any reasoning process to lead them to the sight, must be recorded as holy and genuine worshippers and friends of God in very truth. In their company is he who in Hebrew is called Israel but in our tongue the God-seer who sees not His real nature, for that, as I said is impossible–but that He IS [...is denominated Israel, but in the Greek "seeing God;" not meaning by this expression seeing what kind of being God is, for that is impossible, as I have said before, but seeing that he really does exists ...][464] And this knowledge he has gained not from any other source, not from things on earth or things in heaven, [...] but at the summons of Him alone who has willed to reveal His existence as a person to the suppliant [i.e., Jacob].[465]

Jacob has not been granted the ability to see God's true nature but God Himself has revealed His existence to him, a statement that most probably alludes to Jacob's experience at the ford of Jabbok. Thus, according to this passage, it seems that Philo interprets Genesis 32 in

---

462 See for example *Gen. Rab.* 68. 9 (quoted below in chapter 4.5).
463 E.g., *On Drukenness* 82-83 and *On the Change of Names* 82, see quotations above.
464 Yonge's translation.
465 Yonge has here: "... not having learnt this fact from anyone else [...] but being instructed in the fact by God himself, who is willing to reveal his own existence to his suppliant."

terms of a revelation of God, who had willed to "… reveal His existence as a person to the suppliant."[466]

Regarding the comparison between Philo's authorship and the *Prayer of Joseph*, it may be concluded that the descriptions of the 'Logos' by Philo have many parallels with the angelic portrayal of Jacob in the Pseudepigraphon, as both are entitled 'Israel', 'archangel', etc. However, the respective interpretations of Genesis 32 differ considerably.

Finally, Philo's references to Jacob's words in Gen 48:15-16 clearly indicate that he conceived the angel in v. 16 as being distinct from and subordinate to God. According to Philo, the superior blessings are granted by God, the rescue from evil by His servant, the angel.

4.3.6 Summary and Concluding Discussion

Basically, it seems as if the biblical ambivalence between God and His angel, who Philo also called the 'Logos', is maintained in Philo's theological system. Just as the identity of the angel and God is merged in our pericopes, so is that of God and His 'Logos' in Philo's teaching. However, Philo was not a systematic theologian by modern standards, and there are certain inconsistencies in his works, for example, the depiction of the 'Logos' varies.

Philo generally identifies the 'angel of the Lord' with the divine 'Logos', which applies to his analysis of Genesis 16; 24 and 28. The only exception is his interpretation of Genesis 22, where neither the angel nor the 'Logos' is mentioned; the only heavenly actor is God in person. The reason for this may be that the angel does not play such a distinctive role in the Aqedah, in contrast to Genesis 16. In Philo's interpretation of Genesis 16, the 'Logos' appears to be distinguished from God but at the same time a clear distinction is made between "him" and "created beings." Hagar believed that she had met God, but it was only His servant. Philo contrasts Sarah and Hagar with each other and, unlike in Hagar's case, God appeared in person to Sarah.

Philo's interpretations of the 'man' who confronts Jacob at Jabbok are ambiguous. The "man" is identified as the 'Logos', who is depicted in angelic terms but at the same time the 'Logos' appears to be something more than a "mere" angel. This is expressed by the new name of Jacob, 'he who sees (God)', a name that also belongs to the 'Logos'. In many ways, the description of the 'Logos' in Philo's works parallels the

---

466 See also Colson, footnote a (*On Rewards and Punishments*) 1939, 338.

depiction of the angel Israel in the *Prayer of Joseph*, although the patriarch Jacob himself is never understood as an angel by Philo. It is the 'Logos' who is the supreme archangel. However, in *On Dreams* 1.157 God Himself seems to be designated as 'the archangel', standing on the stairway in Jacob's dream at Bethel (Genesis 28). In Philo's treatment of Genesis 28 and 31, the relationship between God and His 'Logos' is far from clear. The word 'place' in Gen 28:11 is, for instance, said to refer both to God and to the 'Logos'. However, in the case of Philo's interpretation of Gen 48:15-16, 'the angel' is portrayed as distinct from God.

The connection between 'the angel of the Lord' and the 'Logos' in Philo's exegesis is obvious but, as mentioned above, Philo's 'Logos-doctrine' is very complex and still an issue for scholarly discussion.

Many scholars maintain that although Philo calls the 'Logos' 'a second God,'[467] the 'Logos'/'the angel of God' is essentially a manifestation of the One God as He has chosen to reveal Himself to the world. For example, in the words of Alan Segal:

> Philo allows for the existence of a second, principal divine creature, whom he calls a "second God," who nevertheless is only the visible emanation of the High, ever-existing God. In doing this, he has an entirely different emphasis than the rabbis. He is clearly following the Greek philosophers. Like them, he is reluctant to conceive of a pure, eternal God who participates directly in the affairs of the corruptible world. So he employs a system of mediation by which God is able to reach into the transient world, act in it, fill it, as well as transcend material existence, without implying a change in His essence [...] So the *logos*, defined as the thinking faculty of God, can easily be described also as an incorporeal being [...] The *logos* becomes the actual figure of God who appears "like a man" in order that men may know His presence.[468]

According to Hannah, Philo was a devout Jewish monotheist, and he maintains that in spite of his often very exalted language when speaking about the 'Logos', Philo always distinguished carefully between God and His 'Logos'. As an example, Hannah refers to Philo's interpretation of Gen 31:13 where the 'true God' is distinguished from the 'Logos' by means of the definite article.[469] The same view is stressed by Williamson, who concludes that the 'Logos' is *God's* 'Logos', it is the uttered or expressed *thought of God* and thus not to be understood as a separate, distinct being having its own divine ontological status. It is generally acknowledged that it was Philo's belief in the absolute transcendence of God that necessitated his doctrine of the 'Logos', i.e., the

---

467 *Questions and Answers on Genesis* 2.62.
468 Segal 1977, 164-165. See Segal's whole chapter concerning Philo on pp. 159-181.
469 Hannah 1999, 77-79.

expression of God's communication with humankind. Thus, Williamson argues that, although the 'Logos' is often personified in Philo's teaching, it should not be mistaken for an independent personality.[470]

Margaret Barker, however, claims that the Jewish philosopher in fact considered the 'Logos' literally as a kind of a second God, a God Philo identified with the divine Wisdom and the angel of YHWH.[471] Barker questions Segal's statement that Philo actually derived the idea of the 'Logos' from his exegesis of Gen 31:13 in the Septuagint. According to Barker, Philo could hardly have invented the idea of a second deity in the Hellenistic Judaism of his day. She claims that Philo probably used Gen 31:13 as a proof text for something that he already believed in as a religious truth.[472]

Barker also questions Segal's conclusion that Philo was following the Greek philosophers. Even though Philo's theology is different from that of the Rabbis, Barker argues that Philo was not primarily dependent on Greek philosophy in his writings but drew his ideas of a divine mediator from ancient Jewish beliefs, presenting his conclusions in a Greek "costume."[473]

I am not entirely convinced by Barker's line of argument, although I also find it doubtful that Philo derived his 'Logos-theology' solely from Gen 31:13 but I am not sure that this is what Segal really means. Philo was a Jewish leader in Alexandria, and I agree with Barker that it is probable that his ideas were not unique but derived from his Jewish context and heritage. Philo's great contribution was to express Jewish theology in Greek terminology. Although there is no doubt that Philo was influenced by Greek philosophy, his works are essentially Jewish. It therefore seems to be an over-interpretation to claim that Philo and his fellow Hellenistic Jews should have literally believed in a second God. I tend to agree with Segal, who states that Philo's 'Logos' is merely "the visible emanation of the High, ever-existing God."[474]

---

470 Williamson 1989, 103-109, 119-125.
471 Barker 1992, 114-133.
472 Barker 1992, 119.
473 Barker 1992, 114-118.
474 Segal 1977, 164. In his discussion of Philo's 'Logos', Gieschen (1998, 112) seems to have taken a position somewhere between that of Barker and Segal, though slightly closer to the latter's interpretation. He writes: "... although the Word is not completely *separate* from God, Philo does use language that indicates the Word is a divine hypostasis with a degree of *distinct* personhood ..." See also Hannah 1999, 77-79.

4.4 The *Judean Antiquities* by Flavius Josephus

4.4.1 Introduction

A vast amount of scholarly books and articles have been written concerning Flavius Josephus, the famous Jewish historian, politician, and general, active during the first century C.E.[475] Since the focus of this chapter is Josephus' understanding of the angel of the Lord in Genesis, I will restrict myself to an outline of Josephus as a Jewish "theologian" and interpreter of the Bible.[476]

Josephus as an Interpreter of the Bible

It was in Rome that Josephus wrote his four known works; The *Jewish War/Bellum Judaicum* (ca 75-79 C.E.), The *Judean Antiquities /Antiquitates Judaicae* (ca. 93-94 C.E.), and his autobiography *Life/Vita*, an appendix to the latter work (ca. 95 C.E.). Finally, he wrote the polemical work *Against Apion/Contra Apionem* (ca. 95-100 C.E.), generally regarded as written in defense of the Jewish people and Judaism.[477]

---

475 See, e.g., Feldman's bibliographies: *Josephus and Modern Scholarship (1937-80)*, 1984, and *Josephus: A supplementary Bibliography*, 1986. Feldman has himself written/edited several books and articles about Josephus, e.g. *Josephus, the Bible and History*, 1988. I would also like to mention Mason's introduction in *Flavius Josephus. Translation and Commentary*, vol. 3, *Judean Antiquities 1-4* (ed. Mason, trans. and commentary, Feldman), 2000a,, XIII-XXXVI and the article "New Currents in Josephus research," by Bond in *Currents in Research: Biblical Studies*, vol. 8, 2000, 162-190. See also Mason's survey "Josephus and Judaism," 2000b, 546-563.

476 Josephus was born as Joseph ben Mattityahu in the year 37/38 C.E. in Jerusalem, which was also the place of his upbringing. He was of priestly descent, and on his mother's side he belonged to the royal Hasmonean family. According to Eusebius (*HE* 3.9.2.), he died in Rome, probably around 100 C.E., see also Sterling 1992, 235. After Josephus' death the Romans deposited his works in the city library and erected a statue in his honor. For surveys of his life, see Bilde 1988, 13-22, 27-60, Feldman 1992, 981-998, and 2006, 313-333, Sterling 1992, 229-235, Schalit 1971, 251-264, Attridge 1984, 185-192, and Bond 2000, 162-178.

477 In *Ant.* 20.268, Josephus mentions that he intended to write yet another work: *On Customs and Causes*, wherein he would deal with such theological issues as the reasons for the commandments, the practice of circumcision, etc., see also, e.g., *Ant.* 1.25, 29, 3. 94, 230, 4.198. However, this work does not appear to have been completed, see Feldman 1998, 205; 2000, 10, note 34, and 2006, 333, Schürer, vol. 1 (trans., rev., and ed. Vermes and Millar) 1973, 55-56, and Attridge 1984, 212. Because of his deference to the Romans and subsequent affiliation with the imperial family, Josephus' reputation among his fellow Jews suffered, and his writings have survived

The source focused upon in this chapter is the *Judean Antiquities*,[478] wherein all Josephus' renderings of the relevant Genesis texts are to be found. I will therefore say a few words in general concerning this work.

The aim and intended readership of the Judean Antiquities

The *Judean Antiquities* comprises twenty books and deals with the history of the Jews from the creation to the time of the Roman-Jewish war.[479] Roughly the first half of the work parallels the Bible and is a rewriting of Jewish history during biblical times.[480] As its title implies, Josephus' aim in writing the *Judean Antiquities* was to prove the antiquity and nobility of Jewish people and religion. The virtues of the biblical heroes, Abraham, David, etc., are emphasized.[481]

As to the question of the intended readers of his work, it is generally assumed that Josephus wrote primarily for the Gentile, Greek-speaking world, with a somewhat "missionary" and apologetic aim.[482] In Josephus' own words:

---

mainly because of their preservation by the early Church. Josephus' writings present a unique and invaluable source of information regarding Jewish society and history at the time of the birth of Christianity, see Bilde 1988, 15-17, and Bond 2000, 177-179. See also Feldman 1992, 995-996.

478 Most scholars translate the title of this work as the *Jewish Antiquities*. However, along with, for example, Mason and Feldman, whose translation I use (Feldman 2000a, ed. Mason), I have chosen the title *Judean Antiquities*, thus using the designation 'Judean' as referring to the people of Judea. Compare other ethnic designations; 'Egyptian,' 'Babylonian', not to mention Josephus' model, the *Roman Antiquities*, see below.

479 Although Jewish history begins with Abraham, Josephus follows the Bible and accordingly starts his work with the creation. It is generally assumed that Josephus aspired to produce a Jewish counterpart to the *Roman Antiquities* by Dionysios of Halicarnassus, written about a century earlier and also encompassing twenty books, see Thackeray's introduction in *Josephus*, vol. IV, in the Loeb series, reprinted 1978, p. IX, and Altshuler 2005, 4957.

480 Mason 2000b, 556.

481 See, e.g., Bond 2000, 172-174, Bilde 1988, 93, 99-101, and Feldman 1992, 988.

482 There are divergent views among scholars as to whether *Judean Antiquities* was an attempt by Josephus to proselytize. Mason and Feldman argue that by writing the *Judean Antiquities*, Josephus wanted to point out the attractions of Judaism to potential converts, see Feldman 1998, 46-49, and Mason 2000b, 553-558. See also Bilde 1988, 99. Other scholars have doubted Josephus "missionary" intention, see the survey in Bond 2000, 172-174. A difference between Mason and Feldman is that the former has played down the apologetic nature of the work arguing that it is mainly directed to an already interested and sympathetic Gentile readership. According to Mason (2000b, 556), the *Judean Antiquities* may best be described as "... a comprehensive manual or primer in Judean history, law, and culture." According to G. E Sterling (1992, 302-306), Josephus' main purpose in writing the *Judean Antiquities* was to gain respect for the Jewish people within the Greco-Roman world and not to proselytize, as in *Against Apion*.

[*Ant.* 1.5-6] I have taken in hand this present task thinking that it will appear to all the Greeks deserving of studious attention,[483] for it is going to encompass our entire ancient history and constitution of the state, translated from the Hebrew writings [...] to reveal who the Judeans were from the beginning and what fortunes they experienced, under what sort of lawgiver they were trained as to piety and the exercise of the other virtues ...[484]

The political constitution that Josephus refers to above is, of course, the Mosaic Law, the Torah, which he affirms is the most superb constitution in existence.[485] According to Mason, Josephus' interpretation of the Bible/Jewish history has an evident priestly perspective; the ideal Jewish government is theocracy, executed by means of a priestly aristocracy.[486]

However, in Josephus' worldview, the Mosaic constitution also has a universal dimension; the God of Israel is also the God of all humankind and He rewards everyone who obeys His decrees and punishes all who transgress them:[487]

[*Ant.* 1.14] On the whole, one who would wish to read through it [the Bible] would especially learn from this history that those who comply with the will of God and do not venture to transgress laws that have been well enacted succeed in all things beyond belief and that happiness lies before them as a reward from God. But to the extent that they dissociate themselves from the scrupulous observance of these laws the practicable things become impracticable, and whatever seemingly good thing they pursue with zeal turns into irremediable misfortunes.[488]

This "deuteronomistic" theology penetrates Josephus' interpretation of history. A major theme in his writings is the belief in divine providence and justice exercised through the events of world history.[489] According

---

483 Josephus specifically dedicates his work to one of these interested Gentiles; "...there were certain persons curious about the history who urged me to pursue it, and above all Epaphroditus, a man devoted to every form of learning, but especially interested in the experiences of history..." [*Ant.* 1.8] See also Attridge 1984, 187. Cf. also the dedication to Theophilus in Luke 1:1-4 and Acts 1:1.

484 Unless otherwise stated, I use the English translation of the *Judean Antiquities* by Feldman 2000a.

485 *Ant.* 1.14-26; see also Mason 2000b, 554.

486 Mason 2000b, 554-555, 560.

487 Although Josephus does not deny that a special relationship between God and Israel exists, it is not stressed in the *Judean Antiquities* and he never explicitly mentions the covenant. See Attridge 1976, 78-83.

488 See also *Ant.* 1.20: "God as the universal Father and Lord who beholds all things, grants to such as follow Him a life of bliss, but involves in dire calamities those who step outside the path of virtue."

489 See, e.g., Attridge 1976, 71-107, Sterling 1992, 295-297, and Bilde 1988, 184-185. Mason (2000a, XXII-XXXIV) lists four major themes in the *Judean Antiquities*: the antiqui-

to Josephus, the Mosaic constitution is founded upon the laws of nature and piety and is therefore universal and superior to all others.[490]

As a precedent for his rendering into Greek of the biblical history in the *Judean Antiquities*, Josephus mentions the LXX and refers to the legend of its creation, a fact that also implies that his work was primarily directed towards non-Jewish readers.[491] However, apart from the intended Gentile audience, most scholars assume that Josephus also had a Jewish readership in mind. Josephus' secondary aim may have been to strengthen the Jewish identity among his fellow Jews in the Diaspora and to warn against assimilation.[492]

The sources and genre of the Judean Antiquities

Josephus' reference to the LXX as a model for his work leads us to the question of which sources he used when composing the biblical paraphrase of the *Judean Antiquities*.[493] Most scholars assume that Josephus had at his disposal biblical texts in both Hebrew and Greek, possibly also an Aramaic Targum, and that his use of them varied from book to book. The facts that a multitude of text variants existed in Josephus' time and that he did not translate the biblical texts literally, but usually paraphrased and rewrote the biblical stories in his own words, make the whole issue very complex. Most likely, Josephus made use of a Greek biblical text but there are indications that it was not the LXX as we know it today. The Hebrew text he had before him may have been a different version from the later standardized MT.[494]

---

ty of Jewish culture, the Mosaic Law as an alternative political constitution, Judaism as an alternative philosophy of life and the moralizing perspective on history. See also Schwartz, 1990, 176-200, Attridge 1984, 217-227, and Betz 1987, 213-218.

490   *Ant.* 1.21-24, see also Mason, 2000b, 554, and Bilde 1988, 185-187.

491   *Ant.* 1.9-13. See also Feldman 1998, 47; 1992, 986-987, and Mason 1998, 79-80. In *Ant.* 12.11-118, Josephus retells the story of the origin of the LXX as it is recorded in the *Letter of Aristeas*.

492   See the survey in Bond 2000, 172-173, and Feldman 1998, 49. In *Ant.* 4.197, Josephus in fact addresses potential Jewish readers who might encounter his text, and *Ant.* 1.88 also seems to be intended for an audience familiar with the biblical tradition. See also Sterling, 1992, 306-307.

493   I will here limit myself to mainly discussing the sources behind the biblical part of the work, since Josephus' account of later Jewish history is not of interest in the present investigation.

494   Feldman 1992, 986-987, and 1998, 23-36. According to Feldman, for his rendering of the Pentateuch, Josephus probably mainly used a Hebrew text and/or a (written?) Aramaic Targum. See also Attridge 1976, 29-38, and 1984, 211. According to the latter (Attridge 1984, 211), the evidence for Josephus' use of a Targum is very scant.

Josephus' mother tongue was Aramaic, and although the earliest extant Targum for the Pentateuch, *Onqelos*, dates from the second century C.E., the rendering of biblical texts into Aramaic in the synagogue service is much older. Some scholars argue that, in his rewriting of the Pentateuch, Josephus was probably influenced by the Aramaic "translations" which he may have heard every week in the synagogue.[495]

As already pointed out, the *Judean Antiquities* does not constitute a literal translation of the Bible but is a free paraphrasing of its content and includes a great deal of interpretative material. Therefore, the claim of Josephus in *Ant.* 1.17 has puzzled many of his readers:

> This narrative will, therefore, in due course, set forth the precise details of what is in the Scriptures according to its proper order. For I promised that I would do this throughout this treatise, neither adding nor omitting anything.

Since, in his retelling of biblical history, Josephus has apparently both omitted certain episodes and interwoven a large number of additions,[496] his statement above has given rise to much discussion. Many solutions have been proposed[497] and I will mention just a few of them.

Louis H. Feldman suggests that like the Rabbis, Josephus considered it permissible to elaborate on the narrative parts of the Pentateuch but not to alter the biblical commandments. Another proposed explanation is that Josephus included not only the written Torah in 'Scripture' but also the Jewish tradition in general, the so-called oral Torah.[498] There is also the fact that Josephus and his contemporaries most probably understood the word 'translation' as including interpretation. The modern concept of literal translation, *verbatim*, so to speak, was unknown in Josephus' days. The Greek words Josephus uses for 'to translate', seem to encompass interpretation, paraphrasing and amplifying. To Josephus, it was the *content* of the biblical texts that mat-

---

495 E.g., Feldman 1992, 986-987, and 1998, 17, 23-30, Schalit 1971, 258, and Instone Brewer 1992, 183-184. Regarding the scholarly discussion of the existence of synagogues during Josephus' time, see chapter 2.

496 See Feldman 1998, 37-38. According to *Ant.* 4.196-197, Josephus himself acknowledged the restructuring of the biblical material as his only true innovation. See also Niehoff 1996, 44-45.

497 See Feldman 1998, 39-46, Bilde 1988, 94-97, and Inowlocki 2005, 49-51.

498 Regarding the aggadic and halakhic traditions in the *Judean Antiquities*, some of the material can be found in other extant sources, but there are also examples of unique traditions, only preserved in Josephus' work. For more information, see Mason 1991, 330-333, Schalit 1971, 257-258, Feldman 1992, 992-994, and Schwartz 1990, 170-171.

tered, not their external form.[499] A comparison with the rendering of the Bible in the Targums is appropriate.[500] All these theories seem fairly reasonable and do not necessarily exclude one another.

According to Feldman, the *Judean Antiquities* shares many of the characteristics of Midrash, e.g., the explanation of difficult passages, the addition of details, etc.[501] In many ways the work may be classified as a kind of 'rewritten Bible', as it retells the biblical narratives in its own words. In terms of literary genre, the *Judean Antiquities* has many similarities with books such as *Jubilees* and *Liber Antiquitatum Biblicarum*.[502] Feldman argues that there are indications that Josephus and the presumably contemporary Pseudo-Philo (*L.A.B.*) made use of a common oral or written extra-biblical source in their elaboration on Scripture.[503] There are also extra-biblical parallels between the content of Josephus' work and *Jubilees* as well as other Apocrypha and Pseudepigrapha, such as *1* or *3 Esdras* and the Wisdom of Solomon.[504] Feldman also points out affinities between the *Judean Antiquities* and the Rabbinic Midrashim.[505]

The impact of Hellenistic literature, both Jewish and pagan, on Josephus' works cannot be excluded. Thus, the influence of Philo is apparent in Josephus' account of the creation of the world.[506] Henry St. J. Thackeray argued that Josephus had two assistants when he composed the latter part of the *Judean Antiquities*, each of them influenced by a

---

499 Feldman 1992, 985-986; 1998, 42-46, and 2006, 343-345. See also Inowlocki 2005, 48-65, Bilde 1988, 95-97, and Sterling 1992, 252-258.
500 Feldman (1998, 17) proposes that Josephus used the Targums as models for his interpretative biblical paraphrase in the *Judean Antiquities*.
501 Feldman 1998, 16.
502 As shown in chapter 2, the definition of Midrash is much debated among scholars. Porton does not classify the *Judean Antiquities* as a Midrashic work, because in contrast to *Jubilees* and *L.A.B.*, the former seems to be directed to non-Jews (Porton 1992b, 72). However, in the light of Porton's own definition of Midrash as "... a type of literature, oral or written, which has its starting point in a fixed, canonical text, considered to be the revealed word of God by the midrashist and his audience, and in which the original verse is explicitly cited or clearly alluded to" (Porton 1979, 112), it could be argued that neither of the three works fits in. See also Feldman 1998, 14-17.
503 Feldman 1992, 986, and 2006, 322-323.
504 Feldman 1998, 51, 62-64. See also Attridge 1984, 212.
505 Feldman 1998, 65-73, and 2006, 322-323. See also Schalit, 1971, 257-258. According to Feldman (1992, 986), there are also parallels between the *Judean Antiquities* and Midrashim among the Dead Sea Scrolls.
506 Feldman 1992, 985-989, and 1998, 51-56. See also Schalit 1971, 258, Sterling 1992, 252-297, and Attridge 1984, 211-216. Attridge (1976, 36, and 1984, 211) is skeptical about Josephus' alleged dependence on Philo.

different Greek author.[507] This theory has been refuted by, for example, Feldman, and Josephus himself does not mention any assistants being involved in the work.[508]

Finally, the personal imprint of the author on his work must be taken into account. Feldman attributes several elements in the *Judean Antiquities* to the creativeness of Josephus himself and, like all authors, he was influenced by the environment in which he lived as well as by contemporary events and personal experiences. For example, Josephus emphasized the virtues of biblical heroes and exhibited a rationalizing tendency, e.g., his downgrading of miracles, traits that according to Feldman may be related to the fact that he wrote primarily for a non-Jewish audience.[509] Josephus frequently employs the formula "concerning such matters [miracles] let each one judge as is pleasing to him,"[510] a comment also found in many other ancient historians' writings, for example, Dionysius of Halicarnassus.[511] However, the formula is not due to personal doubts, as Josephus himself most certainly believed in miracles, but an expression of courtesy toward his pagan readers.[512]

All in all, Josephus was clearly not a systematic writer or theologian, and his writings display a certain ambiguity toward miracles. He frequently plays down the supernatural elements of the biblical stories and sometimes omits them from his narrative altogether, but he also assures his readers on several occasions of the historicity and accuracy of the miraculous character of the biblical narratives. For example, Josephus testifies that he himself has seen the pillar of salt identified as Lot's wife, see *Ant.* 1.203.[513]

---

507 See Thackeray's introduction in *Josephus*, vol. IV, xiv-xvii, 1978, in the Loeb series.
508 Feldman 1992, 988, 994-995. See also Instone Brewer 1992, 184-185.
509 Feldman 1998, 54-62, and 2006, 322-323. Koskenniemi (2005, 279) argues against this interpretation of Josephus' writings and states: "A skeptical pagan audience, which Josephus was allegedly concerned about, is the fantasy of some scholars. He did not write for skeptics; otherwise he certainly would have omitted more stories, and certainly he had not added or exaggerated miracles, as he sometimes does." There are, however, many examples in Josephus' rendering of Genesis where his rationalizing tendency is evident, as will be shown/illustrated below, and it seems reasonable to assume that this is due to the cultural context in which he wrote.
510 E.g., *Ant.* 1.108, 3.81, 3.322, 4.158, 10.281, etc.
511 See also Feldman 1998, 209, and Betz 1987, 212.
512 See Feldman 1998, 210, and Betz, 1987, 212-213.
513 See also Betz 1987, 212-213, and Moehring 1973, 376-383.

Josephus – a Pharisee?

As a teenager, Josephus decided to acquaint himself with the three Jewish "sects"; the Pharisees, the Sadducees, and the Essenes. He also spent three years in the desert with a certain hermit named Bannus. According to a common understanding of *Life* 12, Josephus finally decided to join the Pharisees, and the predominant view is that he either was a Pharisee, or at least wished (for political reasons) to present himself as such.[514] However, his Pharisaic allegiance is a matter of discussion.[515]

Many scholars have pointed out ideological differences between the *Jewish War* and the *Judean Antiquities*, but it is debated whether the historian's attitude toward the Pharisees changed significantly in the latter work.[516]

In addition to Josephus' statement in *Life* 12, scholars have sometimes referred to other issues in order to "prove" his alleged Pharisaic affiliation, for example Josephus' above-mentioned exaltation of the Mosaic Law, the inclusion of extra-biblical material in his writings, his emphasis on divine providence, and his belief in the resurrection of the dead.[517]

These arguments have all been refuted by Steve Mason, who claims that Josephus' theological outlook may very well be seen as representing

---

514 See, e.g., Feldman, 1992, 982. Franxman (1979, 399) identifies Josephus as a Pharisee based on his statement in *Life* 12. See also the survey of the scholarly discussion in Bond 2000, 170, Bilde 1988, 175, 189, Attridge 1976, 11-13, and Mason 1991, 18-39, 324-343.

515 See, e.g., Schwartz (1990, 170-222) who comments on *Life* 12 stating that the fact that Josephus says that he conducts his life according to the rules of the Pharisees does not imply that he claims to be a member of that group. See also Mason 1991, 342-356, and 2000b, 546-562.

516 The fact that Josephus often expresses criticism of the Pharisees has given rise to questions about his relationship to the group. Mason, for example, maintains that Josephus' attitude to the Pharisees was largely negative, see the survey in Mason 1991, 18-39, and 181-195, 325- 356. See also Schwartz 1990, 170-216, and Bilde 1988, 173-191. My supervisor Tord Fornberg suggests that Josephus' attitude toward the Pharisees may be connected to his relationship to the different "schools" within the group. Further, that Josephus probably disliked the nationalistic "school" of Shammai, which had ties to the militant, rebellious groups in Jewish society. After the war, this fraction lost its influence over the people. The surviving school of Hillel, however, was more moderate and pacifistic. Josephus' more favorable portrayal of the Pharisees in his later works may thus be seen as his approval of the school of Hillel. See also Fornberg 1988, 13, and Attridge 1984, 186, 226-227.

517 See the survey in Mason 1991, 330-341, and Bilde 1988, 185-186. Bilde (1988, 189) writes that "… Josephus' 'Pharisaic' theology runs like a red thread throughout his works…"

the general Jewish view of his day. He also refers to studies showing that Josephus' aggadic elaborations of the Bible point to a priestly rather than a Pharisaic influence.[518] Moreover, because of our relatively scant knowledge of the Jewish traditions of Josephus' time, it is difficult to make an accurate evaluation of his writings on this point.[519]

As will be shown in the following, Josephus appears to have shared the Pharisees' belief in angels as independent personalities, distinct from God.[520] However, the belief in individual angels and demonic spirits was not restricted to this group but a more wide spread phenomenon in Second Temple Judaism.[521]

Differences between Josephus and Hellenistic Judaism represented by, for example, Philo have also been proposed as indications of his Pharisaic affiliation. One such difference is the lack of a teaching on intermediary "hypostases," equivalent to the Philonic 'Logos'.[522] But, as Mason writes, "… it is no longer possible either to distinguish rigidly between 'Palestinian' and 'Hellenistic' or to equate 'Palestinian' and 'Pharisaic'…"[523]

Seth Schwartz concludes his analysis of Josephus' relationship to the Pharisees by stating that in the *Judean Antiquities* he promotes the emerging Rabbinic Judaism and the early Rabbis as the post-war Jewish leaders, a group related to, but not identical with, the Pharisaic movement.[524]

Harold Attridge argues that there are no clear connections between the major interpretative themes of the *Judean Antiquities* and the Pharisaic tradition.[525] If we are to believe Attridge, Josephus' retelling of

---

518 Mason 1991, 330-335.
519 See also Mason 1991, 330-333, and Schwartz 1990, 170-171, footnote 1.
520 For a survey of the Pharisaic "doctrine" of angels, see Finkelstein, 1929, 235-240, in Neusner 1990, 217-222. The Sadducees did not believe in angels as independent individuals, see chapter 1.4 above. Finkelstein (1929, 239) writes: "When the writer of Acts [see 23:8] implies that the Sadducees denied the existence of angels, he does not mean angels in the sense in which they are mentioned in the Pentateuch, for the Sadducees accepted the Torah as fully as did the Pharisees; he refers rather to their refusal to accept the new angelology of Maccabaean days, with its insistence that the angels were not mere ministers of the divine will but had wills and characters of their own."
521 See Gutmann/editorial staff 1971, 962-966, and Newsom 1992, 251-253.
522 See Attridge 1976, 9, 17, and Mason 1991, 336.
523 Mason 1991, 336. See also Gerdmar 2001, 15-18, and 324-330.
524 Schwartz 1990, 170-216.
525 Attridge 1976, 15 and 178-179. However, in his chapter about Josephus in *Jewish Writings of the Second Temple Period* (1984, 186), Attridge appears to adhere to the conventional interpretation of *Life* 12: "The account […] serves to indicate that Jose-

Jewish history bears the imprint of a very personal theological outlook and he emphasizes that there is a dimension of Josephus' authorship that cannot be explained as merely an influence of socio-political circumstances or his need for self defense.[526]

The importance of Josephus' priestly identity has been pointed out by several scholars. As a priest, Josephus considered himself a prophet and an inspired interpreter of the Bible, capable of discerning and hence transmitting its true message to his readers.[527]

4.4.2 Hagar and the Angel

Genesis 16

In contrast to the biblical version, in his prelude to the story of Hagar's encounter with the angel, Josephus mentions Abraham's distress caused by his childlessness. Abraham prays to God for the birth of a son and God promises him offspring. In this context, Josephus declares that it was on God's command that Sarah brought Hagar to the bed of Abraham in order to make her pregnant. The birth of Ishmael is thus described by Josephus as an outcome of a divine initiative. This differs from the biblical account, where the idea is solely ascribed to Sarah with Abraham agreeing to accomplish it (Gen 16:1-3). In Josephus' account, Sarah is simply depicted as obedient to God.[528] The transferring

---

phus made an informed choice in opting for the Pharisees. The claim to close association with that sect, as well as the particularly favorable picture of it, is a characteristic of Josephus' later writing. In contrast, the earlier account of the sects in the *War* (2:119-66) paints a glowing picture of the Essenes, as the most attractive [...]. Perhaps that portrait in *War* represents the earlier predilections of the historian, who had spent such a lengthy period with the desert hermit, although it also serves well the apologetic tendency in the *War* to portray authentic Judaism as distinct from that of the revolutionaries." See also Attridge 1984, 226-227.

526 Attridge 1976, 15 and 181-184.
527 See, e.g., Mason 2000b, 549-562, Instone Brewer 1992, 185-187, Attridge 1976, 16, Sterling 1992, 235-238, Bilde 1988, 189-191, Feldman 1998, 56-62, and 2000, 3-4. On several occasions in his writings, Josephus identifies himself with the prophet Jeremiah, among other biblical characters. See, e.g., Feldman 1992, 986; 1998, 59, and Mason 2000b, 549-550.
528 *Ant.* 1.186-187. See also Bailey 1987, 159, Franxman 1979, 139, and Amaru 1988, 147. Cf., *Gen. Rab.* 45.2 where it is stated that God was speaking through Sarah on this occasion.

of the initiative from Sarah to God is noteworthy, since Josephus often tries to diminish divine activity in his retelling of the Bible.[529]

When Hagar becomes pregnant she begins to look down on her mistress. Sarah punishes her and Hagar flees, as in the Bible. According to Josephus, Hagar puts her case to God: "... she planned flight, being unable to endure her hardships, and she besought God to take pity on her."[530] During her escape, Hagar meets a divine messenger:

> [*Ant.* 1.189-190] ... But as she [Hagar] went forth through the wilderness, *an angel of God* [ἄγγελος θεῖος] *met her*, bidding her to return to her masters. For she would attain a better life through being self-controlled (for, indeed, she was in these troubles because she had been thoughtless and stubborn toward her mistress): he said if she disobeyed God and went further on her way she would perish whereas if she returned she would be the mother of a son who would be king of that land. She obeyed this and returning to her masters she obtained pardon. Not long afterwards she gave birth to Ismaelos; someone might render it "heard by God," because God had listened to her entreaty.

Strictly speaking, Josephus calls the one who meets Hagar in the desert "a *divine* angel/messenger/ἄγγελος θεῖος." He does not say "an angel of the Lord/ἄγγελος Κυρίου" as in the LXX. However, Josephus' choice of designation is most probably not to be understood as referring to the divine nature of the messenger. Josephus simply states that the messenger was sent by God, which may explain Feldman's free translation of ἄγγελος θεῖος as "an angel of God."[531] In agreement with the LXX, Josephus interprets the divine emissary as an unspecified angel and uses an indefinite form; "*an* angel of God." The divine messenger refers to God in the third person. Josephus seems to clearly distinguish God from His messenger.

---

529 Amaru 1988, 147, and Feldman 1998, 205-214. In his retelling of Genesis 16, Josephus may very well have been influenced by Gen 21:12 where it is explicitly stated that Sarah's wish received divine sanction. See Feldman 2006, 370, and Franxman 1979, 138-139.

530 *Ant.* 1.188.

531 Also Thackeray translates ἄγγελος θεῖος as "an angel of God." See the *Jewish Antiquities* 1.189 in *Josephus*, the Loeb Classical Library, vol. IV, reprinted 1978. According to the *Greek-English Lexicon* compiled by Liddell and Scott (1968, 788), in addition to 'divine', θεῖος may also mean; 'of or from the god(s), belonging or sacred to a god, more than human...', etc. In *A Greek-English Lexicon to the New Testament and other Early Christian Literature* (rev. and ed. F. W. Danker 2000, 446-447) three main meanings are listed: 1) "...that which belongs to the nature or status of deity, divine. 2) persons who stand in close relation to, or reflect characteristics of, a deity... 3) that which exceeds the bounds of human or earthly possibility, supernatural."

Like the author of *Jubilees*, Josephus lacks an equivalent to Gen 16:10, where the biblical messenger speaks in the first person; "*I will* so greatly multiply your offspring ...*" Instead, according to the *Judean Antiquities*, the angel of God promises Hagar that if she obeys God and returns home, her future son will be prominent, a ruler of the country. There is no mention of the destiny of Ishmael to become "a wild man," as in Gen 16:12a.

The angel appears to regard Hagar's past behavior and flight as rebellious, since he assures her that "... she would attain a better life through being self-controlled..." This parallels the words of the angel of the Lord in Gen 16:9: "Return to your mistress, and submit to her," but in contrast to the biblical version, Hagar's own responsibility for her situation is emphasized and the angel in Josephus' account threatens her with the dreadful consequences that will happen if she does not return. He gives her a reprimand, but at the same time encourages her and promises that God will take care of her and her son if she is obedient.[532] The text is a kind of moralizing parenesis.[533] Josephus' elaboration on the speech of the angel seems to be clearly influenced by his "deuteronomistic" perspective mentioned above.

Josephus has omitted the biblical dialogues between the angel and Hagar. He refers to the angel's message in the third person. It is constantly the voice of the narrator that "we hear" in the text.

In the end we read that Hagar did return, was forgiven and had a son, who was named Ishmael, meaning 'heard by God'. The name is interpreted by Josephus as referring to the conviction that God listened to Hagar's prayer for mercy. It is not stated that the angel of God told her to call her son by that name, a clear difference compared to the biblical version, see Gen 16:11; "...you shall call him Ishmael, for the LORD has given heed to your affliction."

Another striking difference between the two versions is that Josephus completely omits to render Gen 16:13-14. The two last verses of the pericope, where Hagar seems to identify the angel of the Lord as God, are thus left out without comment, probably because of the theo-

---

532 All in all, Josephus stresses the insolence of Hagar and thus puts Sarah in a more favorable light in comparison to the Bible. See also Franxman 1979, 138-139, Bailey 1987, 139, Amaru 1988, 147, and Feldman, 1998, 180, 244. The angel's exhortation that Hagar "would attain a better life through being self-controlled" may be related to Josephus' high esteem of the Stoic philosophy. See Feldman, 1998, 192-197, 238.
533 Cf. Philo's comment upon the pericope.

logically problematic character of the passage.[534] To Josephus, it was an impossible thought that the handmaid Hagar could have seen God and survived. In his view, the divine emissary must have been an "ordinary" angel.

We must also remember that Josephus mainly wrote for non-Jews, which may have influenced his interpretations. Perhaps he assumed that his "audience" would have difficulties with Gen 16:13-14, so he preferred not to comment upon these verses.[535]

Genesis 21

Josephus also has a counterpart to the other biblical story about Hagar and the angel in his *Judean Antiquities*. As in the Bible, Abraham at first does not want to listen to Sarah and hence sends Hagar and Ishmael away. It is God's approval of the expulsion that makes him change his mind.[536] The counterpart to Gen 21:17-19 is to be found in the *Ant.* 1.219:

> But *an angel of God* [θεῖος ἄγγελος] *met* her [Hagar] and *told* her of a spring nearby and bade her to look after the nurture of the child, for great blessings awaited her through the preservation of Ismaelos. And she took courage through these promises, and meeting shepherds, escaped her misfortunes because of their attention.

Again, Josephus literally refers to the angel as 'a divine messenger', and as in his rendering of Genesis 16 he uses the indefinite form. It is an anonymous, unspecified divine emissary that Hagar encounters. In Gen 21:17 we read that "... God heard the voice of the boy; and the angel of God called to Hagar *from heaven* ..." But in Josephus' version, the divine messenger *meets* Hagar, probably on earth, in the desert, compare Gen 16:7. Although according to the Bible, the angel calls to Hagar from heaven, it is a kind of "meeting". In the Bible, the angel's intervention is described as God's response to Ishmael's crying.[537] This is not men-

---

534 As stated above in the introduction, Josephus usually tries to omit theological problems in his rendering of the Bible. See Feldman, 1992, 987, and 1998, 164-171.

535 This may probably have been the case even for Jewish readers.

536 Josephus does not render God's conversation with Abraham in Gen 21:12-13, but simply writes that "... later, for God also approved of the things decreed by Sarra, having been persuaded, he handed over Ismaelos ..." [*Ant.* 1.217]. See also Feldman, 1998, 250.

537 According to Gen 21:16, in the MT Hagar is the one who cries, but in the LXX it is Ishmael, a rendering that seems to be more logical, because it is stated in verse 17 in both versions that it was the voice of *the boy* that God heard.

tioned in the *Judean Antiquities*, a fact that Feldman explains as an attempt by Josephus to protect Abraham from charges of pitilessness.[538]

There are stylistic differences between the two versions. Josephus has chosen to simply summarize the content of the message of the angel to Hagar. As in his rewriting of Gen 16:7-14, he has omitted the direct speech of the biblical story. The angel of God says to Hagar in Gen 21:18; "... for *I will* make a great nation of him [Ishmael]." Josephus simply states that "... great blessings awaited her through the preservation of Ismaelos."[539]

The ambivalence between the angel and God in the Bible is nowhere to be found in Josephus' rewriting of the narrative. As a matter of fact, Josephus does not explicitly mention God. According to him, it was *the angel* who *told* Hagar about the spring, but in the Bible we read "...Then *God opened her eyes* and she saw a well of water..." [Gen 21:19a]. In the *Judean Antiquities* it is the angel, as God's emissary, who tells Hagar about the spring of water. Maybe Josephus, in the same way as the author of *Jubilees*, considered a literal rendering of this verse too anthropomorphic.[540] The insertion of the angel keeps the distance between God and Hagar intact. According to Feldman, Josephus' transferring of the action from God to the angel may also be seen as an expression of his rationalizing tendency. The miracle is diminished by the fact that it is not God Himself who opens Hagar's eyes but an angel who tells her of the spring of water.[541] An additional reason for the substitution of the angel for God may be that it was the angel who addressed Hagar first;[542] since he wanted to eliminate the ambiguity of the blurred identity of God and the angel, Josephus preferred to have only one heavenly actor in his version of the story.

The shepherds are not mentioned in the Bible. Their presence can be seen as Josephus' explanation of how Hagar and Ishmael managed to survive in the desert, a question that the Bible leaves unanswered. Josephus wanted to tone down the supernatural elements of the story, and hence rationalizes it.[543]

---

538 Feldman 1998, 244-245.
539 According to Feldman (1998, 254), Josephus' omitting of the angel's promise to make Ishmael a great nation was probably politically motivated.
540 See also Feldman 1998, 169, and 1992, 987.
541 Feldman 1998, 251.
542 Cf., Gen 21:17 and *Ant*. 1. 219, see above.
543 This is but one of many examples of Josephus rationalizing tendency in his rewriting of the biblical accounts, see Feldman 1998, 205-214, 249-252, and Betz, 1987, 212-213. However, another explanation of the presence of the shepherds has been proposed

Concluding Remarks

It seems apparent that Josephus interpreted the divine messengers of both Genesis 16 and 21 as "ordinary" angels, of no specific significance. Josephus has chosen to omit everything in the biblical texts that implies that the angel might be identical with God, e.g., the angel's direct speech in the first person in Gen 16:10 and 21:18, and the problematic verses Gen 16:13-14. The messengers are clearly distinct from God Himself but talking on His behalf. Josephus most certainly considered the biblical ambivalence between God and the angel in these texts a theological problem, and he thus chose to erase this ambiguity in his rendering of the narratives.

4.4.3 Josephus' Aqedah and His Version of Genesis 24

The Aqedah

Josephus makes a quite extensive elaboration of the Aqedah[544] in *Ant.* 1.222-236. However, as stated in the text analysis in chapter 3, the main characters in early Jewish exegesis of the narrative are generally Abraham and Isaac, not the angel of the Lord, and this also applies to Josephus' version.

Since this thesis deals with concepts of God and angelology, I will focus my analysis on these parts of Josephus' rendering of Gen 22:1-19.

Josephus begins his version of the pericope by transforming God's short appeal to Abraham in Gen 22:1-2 into a real theophany; God appears to Abraham and reminds him of all the benefits He has given him, of which Isaac is the supreme gift:

> [*Ant.* 1.223-224] … He [Abraham] attained this [his son Isaac], to be sure, by the will of God, who, wishing to make trial of his piety toward Himself, appeared to him and after enumerating all the things that He had granted, how He had made him stronger than his enemies and how he had his present happiness and his son Isakos owing to His benevolence, asked him himself to offer this one as a sacrifice and victim to Himself, and He bade him to lead him up Mount Morion, build an altar, and offer him as a burnt-

---

by Franxman (1979, 155). According to him, it is possible to "find" Josephus' shepherds in an alternate reading of the Hebrew text in Gen 21:19.

544 I use the term 'Aqedah' or 'Aqedat Isaac', i.e. 'the binding of Isaac' because this expression has become the general designation of Gen 22:1-19 in Jewish exegesis of the text. However, nowhere does Josephus mention the actual binding of Isaac on the altar. See also Feldman 2000a, 90.

offering. For thus he would demonstrate his piety toward Himself if he valued what was pleasing to God above the preservation of his child.

Josephus' implied message is that because Abraham owed all his benefits to the divine benevolence, God, as the giver of the gifts, also has the right to withdraw them, hence justifying the test.[545]

Abraham's reaction to the divine commandment is that "… nothing would justify disobedience to God and that in everything he must submit to His will, since all that befell His favoured ones was ordained by His providence …",[546] an insertion that very well mirrors Josephus' own conviction.[547]

Abraham thus travels to Mount Moriah together with Isaac and two servants in order to obey God's bidding.[548]

When the altar has been prepared, Abraham directs a long speech to his son and tells him that he is the intended sacrificial victim. The consensus is that since Isaac's birth was a divine miracle, God has the right to reclaim his life. Isaac was born supernaturally, so his death will equally not be a natural one.[549] In contrast to the Rabbinic elaboration of the Aqedah, Josephus' Abraham does not make any appeal to God.[550] Isaac, being 25 years old, receives Abraham's words with joy. He considers it an honor to die such a death and rushes to the altar.[551] Isaac's willingness to be sacrificed is depicted by Josephus as an act of great virtue.[552] He is a prototype for Jewish martyrdom.[553]

According to Josephus, it was God Himself who prevented Abraham from completing the sacrifice of Isaac, no angel being mentioned:

[Ant. 1.233-234] And the deed would have been done if *God* had not stood in the way. [κἂν ἐπράχθη τὸ ἔργον μὴ στάντος ἐμποδὼν τοῦ θεοῦ] For He called upon Habramos by name, preventing him from the slaughter of the child. For He said that He had decreed the slaughter of his child not because He longed for human blood, nor had He made him his father wishing to deprive him of his son with such impiety, but being willing to test his attitude, to see whether, if commanded, he would obey such injunctions. But having learned the enthusiasm and the high degree of his piety,

---

545 See also Niehoff 1996, 36, Feldman 1998, 252, and 2000, 86.
546 *Ant.* 1.225, English translation Thackeray in *Josephus*, vol. IV, the LCL, reprinted 1978.
547 See Niehoff 1996, 36-37, and Feldman 2000a, 87.
548 *Ant.* 1.225-227.
549 *Ant.* 1.228-231.
550 Cf., *Gen. Rab.* 56.10 and the Palestinian Targums to Gen 22:14. See also Feldman 2000a, 90.
551 *Ant.* 1.232.
552 *Ant.* 1.230-232.
553 See Feldman 2000a, 88-92.

He said that he took pleasure in what he had offered him and that He deemed it proper that he and his race would not fall short of receiving every consideration, and that his son would be very long-lived and having lived happily would bequeath to his virtuous and legitimate children a great realm.

As shown above, Josephus often prefers to let God replace angels in his paraphrase of the Bible. The absence of the angel may thus be a result of his "demythologizing" effort.[554] In the Bible, the angelic interference is expressed by a heavenly voice, calling from above. The substitution of God for the angel thus has no anthropomorphic implications. Moreover, since it was God in the first place who commanded Abraham to offer his son, it is logical that it is God who interferes and saves Isaac.[555] Another explanation is that Josephus considered the Aqedah such an important event that it must have been God in person who prevented Abraham from offering Isaac.[556] It is also worth noting that in Josephus' version, the two heavenly interventions are combined into one.[557]

Moreover, Josephus emphasizes that the God of Israel does not find pleasure in human sacrifice; it was not a craving for human blood that made God command Abraham to offer his son; it was "just" a test. According to Feldman, Josephus' intention is to stress the difference between human sacrifice among the pagans and the Aqedah.[558] In contrast to many other early Jewish interpretations of the pericope, Josephus does not delve into the problem of God's omniscience in relationship to His testing of Abraham.[559]

In the same way as in the biblical account, Isaac is thus spared and a ram takes his place on the altar:

[*Ant.* 1.236] ... Having said these things, *God brought forth a ram from obscurity for them* [Abraham and Isaac] for the sacrifice ...

According to Feldman, it is implied in the Bible that it was the angel who supplied Abraham with the sacrificial substitute, since it is the angel who is speaking in Gen 22:11. In contrast to the Bible, however, Josephus explicitly states that it was God who showed Abraham and Isaac the ram; God brought it forth from obscurity. He also omits to say

---

554 See also Feldman 1998, 212-213, and Bultmann, e.g., *New Testament and Mythology and other Basic Writings*, 1984.
555 Cf., Gen 22:1 and *Ant.* 1.223-224 quoted above.
556 See also Feldman 2000a, 92.
557 Cf., Gen 22:11-12, 15-18, respectively *Ant.* 1. 234-235. In contrast to the Bible, the divine promises are thus made to Abraham before the appearance of the ram. See also Franxman 1979, 161-162.
558 Feldman 1998, 284-285, and 2000, 92-93.
559 Cf., *Ant.* 1. 233-234, quoted above and , e.g., *Jub.* 18.16; *Gen. Rab.* 56.5-8.

that it was caught in a thicket by its horns. Feldman argues that in this way Josephus wanted to imply that the animal had been there all the time but merely hidden from sight; the sudden appearance of the ram would otherwise have seemed too miraculous for his Hellenistic readers.[560]

There is no clear distinction in the Bible between God and the angel in this biblical context. The ram is given by God[561] but its arrival is not necessarily supernatural.[562] It is, however, clear that in Josephus' rendering of the Aqedah, the only heavenly actor is God Himself.

The Wooing of Rebekah

In *Ant.* 1.242-256 Josephus refers to the guidance of God and the importance of prayer in his retelling of the servant's match-making trip in Genesis 24, but he does not mention the angel. Another important difference between Josephus' account and the biblical story is that, according to Josephus, Rebekah was appointed from the outset by Abraham as the future wife of Isaac.[563] See, for example, *Ant.* 1.245:

> Therefore, he [the servant] prayed God that Rebekka, for wooing whom for his son Habramos had dispatched him, if this marriage was destined to be contracted in accordance with his intention, should be found among them [the maidens at the well] and should be recognized by her offering him a drink when he requested it, whereas the others refused. [Cf. Gen 24:12-14]

As in the Bible, Rebekah meets him at the well and personifies the answer to his prayer;

> [*Ant.* 1.249] … on hearing these words, he [the servant] both rejoiced at the things that had happened and at the words that had been said spoken, seeing that God was so clearly supporting his journey … [cf., Gen 24:26-28]

Josephus thus refrains from mentioning the angel but he emphasizes the theme of divine providence.

---

560 Feldman 1998, 252, and 2000, 94.
561 That is, either directly or indirectly. As is mentioned in chapter 3, Gen 22:14 may be translated in various ways. The NRSV renders the verse as follows: "So Abraham called that place 'The LORD will provide'; as it is said to this day, 'On the mount of the LORD it shall be provided.'" According to this translation, it is near at hand to interpret the verse as Abraham alluding to God's provision of the sacrificial substitute, i.e., the ram, in his name-giving of the place.
562 Cf., Gen 22:11-14.
563 See also Franxman, 1979, 165-168, and Feldman 2000a, 97-98.

Concluding Remarks

The absence of the angel in Josephus' version of Genesis 24 may be due
to the fact that his presence is not an important factor in the biblical
story, since it is only mentioned twice.[564] In contrast to the angels in
Genesis 16 and 21, the angel of Genesis 24 does not speak. The angel is
not a main character; the story stands without it. Because of his rationalizing tendencies Josephus prefers to delete it from his narrative, in the
same way as in his rendering of the binding of Isaac.[565]

As shown above, apart from his wish to "demythologize" the biblical stories, Josephus' decision to omit the angel in his version of the
Aqedah may be based on additional reasons. One example is the logical
sequence of the story; in the Bible, it was God in person who ordered
Abraham to sacrifice his son and therefore Josephus transfers the rescue of Isaac to Him. The story needs no more than one heavenly actor.
Josephus evidently prefers to have the same divine/heavenly actor
throughout his narratives, compare his renderings of Gen 16:7-14 and
21:17-21, where it is the angel who constantly addresses Hagar. The
biblical ambivalence between God and the angel has disappeared in
Josephus' versions of the pericopes.

4.4.4 Jacob and the Angel

Jacob's Dream at Bethel

Josephus interprets the messengers/angels of God [LXX: οἱ ἄγγελοι τοῦ
θεοῦ] whom Jacob saw in his dream ascending and descending on the
ladder as ὄψεις, whatever that may be:

> [*Ant.* 1.279-284] … but he [Jacob] took up his quarters in the open air, plac-
> ing his head on stones collected by him, and he saw the following vision
> which appeared to him in his sleep [καὶ τοιαύτην κατὰ τοὺς ὕπνους ὄψιν
> ὁρᾷ παραστᾶσαν αὐτῷ] It *seemed* to him [ἔδοξεν] that he saw a ladder
> reaching from earth to heaven, and down it he saw *visions that had a form
> descending more awesomely than is found among men* [καὶ δι᾽ αὐτῆς ὄψεις
> κατιούσας σεμνότερον ἢ κατὰ ἀνθρώπου φύσιν ἐχούσας]. And last of
> all, above it, *God, appearing clearly to him*, called him by name and spoke the
> following words: "Iakobos, you who are the offspring of a good father and
> grandfather who achieved glory for his great virtue, it was not fitting for

---

564 See Gen 24:7, 40.
565 See also Feldman, 1998, 249-251.

you to be discouraged at your present circumstances but to hope for better things. For, indeed, an abundant presence of great blessings in every respect will await you by virtue of my assistance. For I led Habramos hither from Mesopotamia when he was being driven out by his kinsmen, and made your father prosperous. I shall allot to you a destiny no less than theirs. And taking courage, therefore, proceed on your way availing yourself of me as your escort [...] and good children will be born to you, and their multitude will be beyond number [....] But do not be apprehensive of any danger nor fear the multitude of toils, since I am exerting my providence over the things that will be done by you both at present and, far more, in future matters." Now God predicted these things to Iakobos. And he, being highly pleased with the visions [ἑωραμένοις] and promises, brightened up the stones, since a prediction of so many blessings had been made upon them; and he made a vow to sacrifice upon them ...

Thackeray translates Josephus' description of Jacob's nightly vision differently:

> ... He [Jacob] *thought* that he saw a ladder [...] down which were descending *phantoms of nature more august than that of mortals,* and above it last of all plainly visible to him was God ... [566]

The Greek word ὄψεις may be translated as 'appearances', 'visions', 'phantoms' or 'apparitions'.[567] It is noteworthy that these phantoms are only said to descend but not ascend back to heaven. According to Feldman, the reason may be that in Josephus' mind angels cannot be said to ascend from earth to heaven prior to their descent from heaven.[568] Moreover, Josephus points out that it only *seemed* to Jacob that he saw the heavenly ladder. Feldman sees this as yet an additional example of Josephus' rationalization of the biblical stories, and he also explains Josephus' identification of the angels as 'phantoms of nature' as a result of this tendency.[569]

I agree that visions/apparitions/phantoms may be less concrete than angels, and Josephus' statement that Jacob only *thought* he saw them descending on the ladder emphasizes the imaginary character of the vision. But even in the biblical version, the revelation is depicted as a

---

566 See his translation in *Josephus,* vol. IV, LCL, reprinted in 1978, *Ant.* 1.279. Whiston (new updated edition, 1987, *Ant.* 1.279, p. 47) has yet another translation of Josephus' version of Jacob's revelation: "At which time he saw in his sleep such a vision standing by him:– heaven, and persons descending upon the ladder that seemed more excellent than human; and at last God himself stood above it, and was plainly visible to him ..."

567 Feldman 2000a, 109. See also Liddell and Scott 1968, 1282-1283.

568 Feldman 2000a, 109.

569 Feldman 2000a, 109, and 1998, 212. In his commentary to the *Judean Antiquities,* Feldman seems in this case to be influenced by Thackeray's translation.

dream and thus less concrete than a real event.[570] Is it really only Josephus' attempt to rationalize the biblical narrative that may explain his
alterations of Jacob's vision of the ladder and its angels at Bethel? This
question needs further consideration, even though it is not the main
issue in the present investigation.

Could it be that Josephus' interpretation of the angels as 'phantoms
of nature' is inspired by Greek mythology? There are many other examples where 'phantoms' or 'specters' replace angels in Josephus' rendering of the Bible. However, in these cases he uses the synonymous
designation φάντασμα,[571] rather than ὄψεις, e.g., his versions of the
appearance of the angel of the Lord to Gideon (*Ant.* 5.213-214, cf., Judg
6:11-24) and his rendering of the angelic visitation to Manoah's wife
(*Ant.* 5.277-285, cf., Judges 13). We may also mention Josephus' renderings of Gen 32:1-2 and vv. 22-32, see below.[572] To return to his account
of Gen 28:10-22, the visions/phantoms on the ladder do not play any
significant role in Jacob's dream vision. Josephus makes no subsequent
comment about their presence.

The importance of the dream lies in the message that Jacob receives
from God. In contrast to Philo, Josephus shows no hesitation in claiming that Jacob in his vision actually saw God Himself; God is described
as standing above the ladder, plainly visible to Jacob. God is depicted
as the Master of all creation, standing above 'the apparitions/the phantoms of nature'.

---

570 See also Gnuse (1996, 149) who writes: "The visual aspect of the dream it unders-
cored by the use of the term, 'he thought (ἔδοξεν) he saw,' the expression common
to visual symbolic dreams (*Ant.*1.279). But an auditory aspect is clearly present, for
God 'called' [...] and spoke a rather long message [...]. The content of the message is
characteristic of auditory message dreams with its emphasis on divine direction and
presence. The dream combines elements of the auditory message dream and the visual symbolic dream, but this results from the presence of both modes in the original
biblical text."

571 According to Liddell and Scott (1968, 1916), the word φάντασμα has the meanings
'apparition', 'phantom', 'vision', and 'dream', etc. In *A Greek-English Lexicon to the
New Testament and other Early Christian Literature* (rev. and ed. Danker 2000, 846,) we
find the translations 'apparition' and 'ghost' as well as references to (among others)
Matt 14:26; Mark 6:49, and Luke 24:37.

572 See also Feldman 1998, 212-213. In his rendering of the angel of the Lord visiting
Manoah's wife, Josephus in fact alternates between the designations
φάντασμα/apparition/ spectre and ἄγγελος/angel. At the end of the story, it actually appears that Josephus identifies the heavenly visitor as God Himself. See also the
commentary on *Ant.* 5.277-284 by Bregg 2005, 69-71; 2007, 528, 532, and note 25 on
the last mentioned page.

In contrast to the biblical version of the dream, Josephus omits God's introducing of Himself as "the God of Abraham your father and the God of Isaac" (Gen 28:13). Perhaps Josephus wanted to avoid his readers' possible assumption of potential polytheism among the patriarchs, since God's self-identification might suggest His need to distinguish Himself from other deities.[573] Another reason may be that he wished to omit such a "nationalistic" statement. As mentioned in the introduction, Josephus has a universalistic perspective in his retelling of the Bible; the God of Israel is also the God of all humankind.

The dream is interpreted as a prediction of the future destiny of Jacob and his descendants. But whatever happens, God promises Jacob to watch over and protect him.

Josephus then goes on to relate Jacob's reaction to the revelation. He is described as overjoyed at God's promises and makes a vow to return and sacrifice on the site of his dream.[574] In veneration of the place Jacob names it Bethel, which according to Josephus can be translated as θεία ἑστία, 'divine hearth.'[575]

The Commission to Return

In contrast to Philo, Josephus does not comment on the appearance of the angel of the Lord to Jacob in Gen 31:10-13. His reason may be that he found it difficult that in the Bible it is 'the angel of God' who talks to Jacob and identifies himself as 'the God of Bethel'. We have seen before that Josephus tends to avoid such theological problems.[576]

Josephus simply states in *Ant.* 1.309 that after 20 years in the service of Laban Jacob decided to leave him in secret. Nothing is said about whether or not Jacob's decision was based on God's command. God is not mentioned here by Josephus.

---

573 See Gnuse, 1996, 149.

574 *Ant.* 1. 284. In contrast to the Bible, Josephus does not mention Jacob's fearful reaction to the dream, and he also omits Jacob's reference to God in the biblical text, cf. Gen 28:16-17.

575 *Ant.* 1.284. Thackeray (*Josephus*, vol. IV, LCL, reprinted 1978, 139) translates θεία ἑστία as 'God's heart stone.'

576 Gnuse (1996, 150), on the other hand, suggests that Josephus chose to omit Jacob's dream "… because it alludes to the sheep which were produced by 'magic' in the mating process. Josephus omits the account of Jacob's trickery in sheep production tactics, because it was an embarrassing story …" See also Feldman 2000a, 116.

On the other hand, Josephus has an expanded version of God's appearance to Laban in a dream, warning him not to act rashly toward his nephew and son-in-law.[577]

The Battle at the Ford of Jabbok

Whereas the Bible initially designates the opponent of Jacob as '*a man*'[578] who later in the story gives him the new name Israel, because he has striven *with God and with humans* and has prevailed,[579] Josephus at first calls Jacob's adversary '*an apparition*' whom he subsequently identifies as '*a divine angel/an angel of God*'. See *Ant.* 1.331-334:[580]

> ... And when they had crossed a certain torrent called Jabacchos, Iakobos, having been left behind, encountered *an apparition*,[581] [φαντάσματι συντύχων] and wrestled with it. When it began the battle, he overpowered the *apparition*[582] [φαντάσματος] And it, indeed, employed speech and words with him, urging him to rejoice in what had occurred and not to suppose that it was a small matter to prevail, but that he had defeated *a divine angel* [θεῖον ἄγγελον][583] and to consider this a symbol of great future blessings to come and an assurance that his race would never be extinguished and that his progeny would never disappear and that no man would be superior to him in strength. And he bade him to take the name of Israel. And this signifies, in the language of the Hebrews, *the opponent of an angel of God* [τὸν ἀντιστάτην ἀγγέλῳ θεοῦ]. Now he predicted these things at the request of Iakobos. For, perceiving that he was *a messenger of God* [ἄγγελον εἶναι θεοῦ], he [Iakobos] entreated him to signify what fate he would have. And *the apparition* [φάντασμα],[584] having said this, vanished. And Iakobos, pleased with this, called the place Phanouelos, which signifies "*the face of God.*" And because in the battle he had suffered pain in the broad tendon both he himself abstained from eating it and because of him neither is it permitted to us [the Jews] to eat it.

---

577 *Ant.* 1.312-313, cf., Gen 31:24. See also Gnuse 1996, 150-151.
578 Gen 32:24. The LXX has here ἄνθρωπος. MT (Gen 32:25) has איש.
579 See Gen 32:28. MT: Gen 32:29.
580 See also Franxman 1979, 204-205.
581 Thackeray (*Josephus*, vol. IV, LCL reprinted 1978, 159) has the translation 'phantom'.
582 Thackeray (*Josephus*, vol. IV, LCL, reprinted 1978, 159) has the translation "the struggle had been begun by the spectre, which now found a tongue..."
583 As shown above, the Greek text has here θεῖον ἄγγελον which Thackeray [*Josephus*, vol. IV, LCL, reprinted 1978, 159] translates as 'an angel of God', cf., Josephus' rendering of Gen 16:7-14; see above.
584 Thackeray (*Josephus*, vol. IV, LCL, reprinted 1978, 161) likewise here uses the designation 'the apparition'.

As in his description of the angelic visitors to Gideon and Manoah's wife in Judges chapters 6 and 13, Josephus employs the peculiar designation φάντασμα, 'phantom/apparition/spectre' for the opponent of Jacob. Likewise, according to the Bible, the angelic encounter which Jacob is said to have had on his way to Canaan (Gen 32:1-2) is described by Josephus in *Ant.* 1.325 as Jacob "... *had visions* [φαντάσματα συνετύγχανεν] which inspired him with good hopes for the future ..."[585] By the use of the same term, Josephus appears to connect the two passages.[586] Feldman translates the same passage slightly differently: "... *visions presented* themselves that suggested good hopes for the future ..." In both of these translations, the visions are unspecified and do not necessarily refer to angelic beings that Jacob met. They might just as well denote some other kind of (more abstract) revelation(s).

However, Robert Hayward understands the passage more concretely; on his way to Canaan Jacob *encountered* some *phantasms*, to use his expression. On the basis of the connection between the two stories and this more literal interpretation of *Ant.* 1.325, Hayward suggests that Josephus may have intended to imply that the phantom Jacob fought at the ford of Jabbok was one he had met previously. These phantoms had thus been with the patriarch for some time, and this may hence explain why Josephus refrains from mentioning that Jacob was alone at the ford of Jabbok.[587] This interpretation, however, seems far-fetched.

The designation φάντασμα 'phantom/apparition/spectre' is unusual in Jewish writings. The word is nowhere used in the LXX Pentateuch and it is only to be found in the Codex Alexandrinus in Job 20:8; Isa 28:7, and Wis 17:14/15, denoting visions of a negative character.[588] Hayward points out that by his use of this expression Josephus leaves

---

585 *Ant.*1. 325, Thackeray's translation in *Josephus*, vol. IV, LCL, reprinted 1978, 157. Cf., Josephus' depiction of the angels that Jacob (thought) he saw on the ladder in his dream at Bethel.

586 I.e., Gen 32:1-2 and vv. 22-32.

587 Hayward 2005, 230.

588 See *A Concordance to the Septuagint*, second edition (ed. Hatch and Redpath), 1998, 1424. See also Hayward 2005, 232. In Josephus' writings, the word φάντασμα occurs in: *Jewish War* 3.353, 5.381, *Ant.* 1.325, 1.331, 1.333, 2.82, 3.62, 5.213, 5.277, and 10.272. See *A Complete Concordance to Flavius Josephus*, vol. IV (ed. Rengstorf), 1983, 279. The negative connotation of the word in LXX may imply that it is a hostile, demonic angel whom Jacob encounters at Jabbok. However, we have seen that Josephus, for example, also employs this word in his rendering of the angelic visitation to Manoah and his wife, as well as in his version of Gen 32:1-2, which speaks against such an interpretation.

the Jewish discourse and steps into the world of Greek philosophy.
According to him:

> The word φάντασμα is common in learned treatises of the Greco-Roman
> period, and refers to an image presented by an object to the mind, a dream,
> or a vision. The sense of the word as dream or vision heightens the pro-
> phetic quality of the narrative ...[589]

Hayward points out that Josephus has transformed the biblical narrative into a prophetic vision, probably inspired by Gen 35:9-15,[590] where
Jacob's change of name to Israel is connected to a divine oracle.[591] Whereas in the Bible, Jacob's combatant blesses him in the end, Josephus
omits the blessing;[592] the phantom's function in the *Judean Antiquities* is
instead to foretell the future destiny of Jacob and his descendants. In
Josephus' version, the prediction of the indestructibility of Israel becomes the main message of the narrative.[593]

Besides the absence of the blessing of Jacob, there are also many
other items in the biblical story that Josephus has omitted in his rendering of it. For example, in the *Judean Antiquities*, the arrival of the dawn
is not connected to the departure of the phantom/angel.[594] The daybreak is nowhere mentioned by Josephus. In his version, the battle appears much shorter than in the Bible; Jacob certainly did not fight all
night long. Nor does Josephus directly mention that Jacob's adversary
during the fight hit him on the hip socket,[595] an omission that makes the
battle lose some of its concreteness. It is not until the end of the story
that he alludes to this detail.[596] Josephus has also removed all direct
speech in his account. In sum, compared to the biblical original, Josephus' narrative of Jacob's experience at the ford of Jabbok appears to be
more visionary in character, his use of the term φάντασμα being a

---

589 Hayward 2005, 232.
590 Hayward 2005, 221, 228-230, 234.
591 In the context where we expect to find it, this theophany is omitted by Josephus, see
   Ant. 1.341-342. In addition to the divine oracle in Gen 35:9-13, the prediction of the
   phantom in Josephus' account of Gen 32:22-32 also appears to be inspired by God's
   promises given to Jacob in his dream at Bethel, i.e., Gen 28:10-22. See also Hayward
   2005, 230, 234.
592 According to Hayward (2005, 238) the reason for the omission of the blessing was
   most certainly because Jacob had shown himself to be the angel's/phantom's superior, which made it illogical for his defeated combatant to bless him.
593 See also Hayward 2005, 226-235. However, it is of course possible to interpret the
   phantom/angel's prediction of Jacob's and his descendants' future success as a form
   of blessing.
594 Cf., Gen 32:24, 26, 31.
595 Cf., Gen 32:25.
596 *Ant.* 1.334, cf. Gen 32:32. See also Hayward 2005, 225-228.

main reason.[597] It is also because of Josephus' employment of this word that Robert K. Gnuse includes the story in his analysis of dreams and dream reports in the writings of Josephus:

> Most likely we are not reading a dream report in this text, at least not like the other dream reports recorded by Josephus. But its inclusion is warranted in our list because of this use of the word φάντασμα, which elsewhere can mean "dream." Also, we cannot be too sure just exactly what Josephus intends to describe here. One might be tempted to call this an εἴδωλον, a personage who gives a message, but otherwise this image acts in a most unusual fashion for typical Greek dream images when it wrestles with Jacob.[598]

But Josephus also refers to Jacob's opponent as a divine angel/an angel of God.[599] Whereas in the Bible, Jacob's combatant does not want to reveal his name, he openly discloses his identity in *Ant.* 1.332-333:

> And it [the phantom], indeed, employed speech and words with him [Jacob], urging him to rejoice in what had occurred and not suppose that it was a small matter to prevail, but that he had defeated a divine angel and to consider this a symbol of great future blessings and that his progeny would never disappear and that no man would be superior to him in strength. And he bade him to take the name of Israel. And this signifies, in the language of the Hebrews, the opponent of an angel of God...[600]

In the Bible, the opponent's identity remains a mystery but it is hinted at in the meaning of Jacob's new name Israel: "... for you have striven with God and with humans, and have prevailed"[601] as well as in the name Jacob gives the site of the battle, see below. In Josephus' interpretation of the narrative, the name Israel signifies the opponent of *an angel of God*, not an opponent of God in person.[602] Josephus emphasizes that the patriarch has not only striven with no less than an angel but has

---

597 Josephus' description of the departure of the φάντασμα also underscores the imaginary character of the event: "...And the apparition, having said this, vanished." [*Ant.* 1.333]. See also Begg 2007, 534.

598 Gnuse 1996, 152.

599 Cf., Josephus' account of the angel of the Lord's visit to Manoah's wife in *Ant.* 5.277-285. The word ἄγγελος is to be found in some extant manuscripts of the LXX, see Septuaginta, Vetus Testamentum Graecum, vol. 1, Genesis (ed. Wevers 1974), pp. 314-315.

600 Cf., Gen 32:29: "Then Jacob asked him, 'Please tell me your name. But he said, 'Why do you ask my name?' And there he blessed him."

601 Gen 32:28.

602 See *Ant.* 1.333 quoted above. The identification of Jacob's combatant as an angel is also well attested in other early Jewish sources, for example, in one reading in the LXX, the Targums, and the *Prayer of Joseph*. Josephus may have been influenced by the traditional Jewish interpretation. See also Hayward 2005, 231-236.

also shown himself to be his superior. The victory is a sign/symbol of great future blessings.[603]

According to Feldman, Josephus uses the designation ἄγγελος in order to retain the ambiguity of the biblical text, since the Greek word bears the meaning of both 'messenger' and 'angel'.[604] In the Bible, however, the opponent is never explicitly called "a messenger" or "angel"[605] but Jacob exclaims in the end: "… I have *seen God face to face*, and yet my life is preserved," hence the place-name Penuel.[606] Josephus renders the meaning of Penuel as 'the face of God' but he omits to explain the etymology of the name, presumably in order to avoid the anthropomorphism of seeing God face to face.[607] Josephus simply leaves it to the reader to figure out the connection between the place name and Jacob's encounter with the phantom/angel.[608]

The Return to Bethel

In contrast to Philo, Josephus provides an account of Jacob's return to Bethel:

> [*Ant.* 1.341-342] And God, approaching Iakobos, who had been stricken with consternation at the enormity of the deeds and was angry with his sons, [alluding to the episode concerning Dinah, Genesis 34], bade him have courage, and purifying his tents to offer the sacrifices that he had vowed when he first departed to Mesopotamia upon the vision of his dream. Therefore, while he was purifying those who were following, he came upon the gods of Labanos, for he did not know that they had been stolen by Rachela, and he hid them in Sikima […] and departing from there he sacrificed in Baitheloi [Bethel], where he beheld the dream while he was going previously to Mesopotamia.

The dream spoken about is, of course, Jacob's nightly vision at Bethel.[609] In the same way as in the Biblical version, Josephus states that God exhorted Jacob to fulfill the vow he once made in Bethel, compare Gen 28:20-22 and *Ant.*1.284. As usual, Josephus has simplified the narrative. In the Bible, God says to Jacob:

---

603 See also Hayward 2005, 231-236.
604 Feldman 1998, 328, and 2000, 121.
605 As stated previously, the designation 'man' in the Bible sometimes has the implied meaning of 'angel' and this may lie behind Josephus' interpretation of Gen 32:22-32.
606 Gen 32:30.
607 Feldman 1998, 328, and 2000, 121. See also Begg 2007, 530-531.
608 See also Hayward 2005, 239.
609 Gen 28:10-22, cf., *Ant.* 1.279-284, see above.

"Arise, go up to Bethel and settle there. Make an altar there to *the God* who appeared to you when you fled from your brother Esau." [Gen 35:1]

It is indeed very strange that God here seems to refer to Himself in the third person; Josephus accordingly omits this theological problem,[610] compare the absence of the angel of God in his version of Gen 31:10-13.[611] Josephus has deleted the second theophany at Bethel[612] but he has an abbreviated rendering of Jacob's fulfillment of his vow; "... and departing from there he sacrificed in Baitheloi ..." [*Ant.* 1.342, cf., Gen 35:6-7]

The Blessing of Ephraim and Manasseh

Josephus omits Jacob's blessing of his grandsons Ephraim and Manasseh in Gen 48:15-16. Jacob's "adoption" of them has been transformed in *Ant.* 1.195 into a request directed to his own sons to regard Ephraim and Manasseh as their equal brothers and to let them share the land of Canaan. Accordingly, Josephus eliminates Jacob's reference to the angel in this context. Maybe the equation of God and the angel in Jacob's prayer bothered him, so he decided to delete the passage.[613]

Concluding Remarks

It may be concluded that, according to Josephus, it was normally God Himself who spoke directly to Jacob, the sole exception being his rendering of Jacob's struggle with the 'phantom/angel of God' at the ford of Jabbok.

---

610 Another difference compared to the biblical version is that Josephus points out that Jacob did not know about the foreign gods stolen by Rachel. Whereas in Gen 35:2 it is Jacob who instructs his household to get rid of them, in Josephus' version it is God who reveals their presence to Jacob and orders him to purify his tents. According to Feldman, Josephus in this case inserts an appearance of God where the Bible does not mention Him. This statement seems peculiar, since in fact God is speaking in Gen 35:1, even though He does not expressly instruct Jacob to get rid of any strange gods. See Feldman 2000a, 124, note 963.

611 See *Ant.* 1.309 and above.

612 Cf., Gen 35:9-13. According to Feldman (2000, 124, note 968), the omission of the divine blessing of Jacob may be politically motivated.

613 There may also be other reasons why Josephus deleted the blessing of Ephraim and Manasseh, see Feldman 2000a, 185, note 549. See also Feldman, 1998, 328.

4.4.5 Summary and Conclusions

In our analysis of the *Judean Antiquities*, we have seen that the wish to avoid theological problems such as anthropomorphisms and ambiguities is characteristic of Josephus' rendering of the biblical pericopes.[614] One example of this tendency is his omission of Gen 16:13-14, wherein Hagar appears to identify the angel of the Lord as God. The ambivalence between God and the angel in both Genesis 16 and 21 is excluded from Josephus' interpretations of the texts. In his version of Gen 21:19 it is an angel who tells Hagar about the spring of water, but in the Bible it is God who opens her eyes, so that she may see it. God is nowhere mentioned in Josephus' rendering of Genesis 21. According to him, the divine messenger whom Hagar met was an "ordinary" angel, clearly distinct from God.

In Josephus' interpretation of the Bible, angels thus sometimes replace God, but there are also examples where the opposite is the case. For example, in his rendering of the Aqedah, Josephus does not mention the angel of the Lord; the one who calls to Abraham from heaven and prevents him from offering Isaac is God Himself.

Although there is a certain ambivalence concerning the identity of this angel in the biblical text, it is unlikely that Josephus understood the angel in Gen 22:11-12, 15-18 as a revelation of God in person. Most probably, he interpreted the biblical text as implying that God spoke to Abraham through the angel. The divine emissary is not important and therefore not mentioned. Josephus' omission of the intermediary may also be due to his general rationalizing tendency. Another possible explanation of the absence of the angel may be that Josephus considered the near sacrifice of Isaac such a crucial event that it must have been God in person who interfered. Moreover, because it was God who commanded Abraham to sacrifice Isaac (Gen 22:1, cf., *Ant.* 1.224), Josephus may have considered it logical to transfer the prevention of the sacrifice to God in person. In contrast, in Genesis 16 and 21 it is an angel who addresses Hagar in the first instance and Josephus hence saw no need to introduce God in his versions of the narratives.

As can be seen in the survey above, it appears that whenever possible Josephus prefers to avoid mentioning angels. Since the angel in Genesis 24 plays such an insignificant role in the story, Josephus neglects to mention him in his version of the wooing of Rebekah. In Gene-

---

614 However, Josephus is far from alone, since this tendency is common in Jewish exegesis in general.

sis 16, on the other hand, the angel who meets Hagar is a main character in the narrative and thus impossible to ignore. Josephus' omissions
of Jacob's dream in Gen 31:10-13 as well as the Patriarch's blessing of
Ephraim and Manasseh may be due to his wish to avoid theological
problems. In Josephus' version of the life of Jacob, it is generally God
who speaks to him, the only exception being Jacob's encounter with the
'phantom/angel' at the ford of Jabbok.

What then, is the difference between, for example, the narrative
about Jacob's struggle at the ford of Jabbok and the Aqedah? Why does
the angel replace God as the one who shows Hagar the spring of water
in Josephus rendering of Genesis 21, while he ascribes the prevention of
Abraham's sacrifice to God, contrary to the Bible? Why does Josephus
treat these stories differently? A possible answer may lie in the *nature of
the texts*. On the one hand, Josephus' "demythologizing" tendency
makes him eager to omit the activity of angels where possible but, on
the other, he also wants to avoid anthropomorphisms and other theological problems in his rendering of the Bible. The various natures of the
narratives should also be taken into account when considering Josephus' choice of terms in designating angels: ἄγγελος 'angel/messenger',
φάντασμα, and/or ὄψις 'vision/apparition/phantom'. For example, the
divine emissary who encounters Hagar is clearly a messenger, while the
angels on the ladder in Jacob's dream do not have this function. Moreover, Josephus' choice of the term φάντασμα in his version of Jacob's
struggle at the ford of Jabbok is most probably due to his wish to mi-
nimize the concreteness of the narrative and present it as a vision.

The divine intervention in the Aqedah (manifested by a heavenly
voice) conforms to Josephus' transcendent conception of God. However, concerning, for example, such an anthropomorphic tale as Jacob's
struggle at the ford of Jabbok, Josephus found it hard to believe that the
patriarch's opponent might actually have been God Himself. When
analyzing the *Judean Antiquities*, it is also important to bear in mind that
by modern standards Josephus was by no means a systematic author or
theologian.

In conclusion, it may be stated that it is apparent that Josephus
wanted to eliminate the biblical ambivalence between God and His
angel in the pericopes. The ambiguity of the biblical texts disappears in
Josephus' rendering of them. In his versions, the angel(s) is/are clearly
distinguishable from God, it is either God Himself or an angel(s) who
is/are depicted as active. Josephus seems to have a form of 'Phari-
saic/individualistic' view on angels, regarding them as distinct personalities, separate from God, although they all remain unnamed in his
treatment of these texts.

4.5 The Targums, Rabbinic Midrash and Talmud

4.5.1 Introduction

Targum Onqelos

Targum Onqelos (*Tg. Onq.*),[615] one of the two authoritative Targums of Rabbinic Judaism, is the most literal of the Targums to the Pentateuch. Nevertheless, it contains some interpretative material paraphrasing our pericopes.

As is the case with all of the Targums, the original composition and redaction of *Onqelos* is difficult to date, since it contains layers of material from different periods. We must distinguish between the dating of the traditions contained in the Targums and their final redaction. In the words of Anthony D. York:

> While the evidence indicates a great antiquity for written Targumim to many portions of the Bible, no effective method has as yet been devised to distinguish between the recension of a particular targumic text and the tradition that underlies that text.[616]

Many scholars agree that while the Targum (the so-called '*Proto-Onqelos*') originated in the land of Israel, the final revision and redaction of *Onqelos* took place in Babylonia, probably towards the end of the third century C.E.[617] The Targum may contain some pre-Christian elements.[618]

Most certainly, *Onqelos* was originally produced primarily for the benefit of the Aramaic-speaking masses and not for the scholars of the time. Both the aggadah and the halakhah of *Onqelos* disclose an apparent connection to the school of Rabbi Aqiba.[619] The Targum contains

---

615 Henceforth, I will use the shorter designation *Onqelos*, except when applying the abbreviation.

616 York 1974, 49.

617 There are, however, also scholars who advocate a Babylonian origin of *Onqelos*, e.g., P. Kahle. See Grossfeld 1988, 30-32.

618 Grossfeld 1988, 30-35.

619 Grossfeld 1988, 30-32. For more information, see his whole 'introduction', Grossfeld 1988, 1-35. See also Aberbach/Grossfeld 1982, 9-18, and Bowker 1969, 22-26. Alexander (1992, 321-322) writes that *Proto-Targum Onqelos* originated in Palestine/the land of Israel in the first or early second centuries C.E. According to him, the Babylonian redaction of the Targum was made in the fourth or fifth centuries C.E.

many parallel traditions with the Rabbinic Midrashim and the Talmuds, the Babylonian in particular.[620]

The Palestinian Targums to the Pentateuch

Similar to *Onqelos*, these Targums are very difficult to date. All of them most certainly contain material from different periods of Jewish history. As their designation indicates, they all originated in Palestine/the land of Israel. In contrast to *Onqelos*, the Palestinian Targums were never officially "canonized" by Rabbinic Judaism.[621]

Targum Neofiti 1

As mentioned in chapter 2.2.3, Alexander Díez Macho claims that *Targum Neofiti 1* (*Tg. Neof.*[622]) contains paraphrases that are pre-Christian, since they favor the Christian interpretation of Scripture.[623] According to Bowker, *Neofiti* in its present form can be assigned to the third century C.E., while M. McNamara suggests a dating of the Targum to the fourth century or maybe earlier.[624] *Neofiti* was (re-)discovered by Díez Macho in the Vatican Library in 1956.[625]

The Genizah manuscripts

The Genizah is located in the Ben Ezra Synagogue of Old Cairo. It contains Jewish manuscripts dating from approximately the 8th–9th centuries until the 14th century. The Cairo Genizah is the largest and, after Qumran, the most important source of ancient and medieval Jewish texts discovered in modern times. The Genizah fragments of Palestinian targumic manuscripts are counted among the earliest extant wit-

---

620 Grossfeld 1988, 15-18. If not otherwise stated, I use the English translation by Aberbach/Grossfeld, 1982.
621 McNamara (1992, 41), however, writes that "…The manuscripts of the *Palestinian Targums* of the Pentateuch have been transmitted to us by Rabbinic Judaism. This is evidence that even if not an official Targum, as *Onqelos* later was, the Palestinian Targum tradition was recognized by Rabbinic Judaism as its own." There are scholars (e.g., Klein) who see a connection between the Palestinian Targums and the halakah of the school of Rabbi Ishmael. McNamara 1992, 42.
622 Henceforth, I will use the shorter designation *Neofiti*, except when using the abbreviation.
623 Díez Macho 1960, 225-233.
624 Bowker 1969, 16-20, and McNamara 1992, 44-45.
625 McNamara 1992 (introduction), 7-9. I consult the English translations by McNamara/Maher 1968 and McNamara 1992. If not otherwise stated, I use the English translation by M. McNamara, 1992.

nesses of the ancient Aramaic translation of the Bible. Scholars have long acknowledged their significance in containing early midrashic traditions and non-normative halakha. The Genizah also contains targumic Tosefot, Fragment Targums, i.e., selections of verses, phrases and passages excerpted from the Palestinian Targum-tradition, festival-liturgical collections and introductory targumic poems, etc.[626]

The Fragment Targums

There are also Fragment Targums that have been preserved outside the Cairo Genizah. In contrast to most of the Genizah manuscripts, the incompleteness of the *Fragment-Targums* (*Frg. Tg.*) is probably delibe-rate and not due to accidents of transmission. A common theory is that the *Fragment Targums* constitute selective extracts put together by re-dactors from the now lost Palestinian Targums.[627] According to Philip S. Alexander, they represent a Palestinian exegetical tradition that typo-logically stands between *Neofiti* and *Targum Pseudo-Jonathan*.[628]

The origin of the *Fragment Targums* is veiled in obscurity. One view is that they originated as complements to *Onqelos*, in order to preserve the Palestinian targumic tradition when *Onqelos* became established as the "official" Targum of Rabbinic Judaism. Another view is that the *Fragment Targums* constitute variants of *Targum Pseudo-Jonathan*.[629] The liturgical nature of all the Pentateuch Targums is generally recognized, and the *Fragment Targums* may have been used in the synagogue as supplementary or alternate material to the main Targum being used.[630]

The *Fragment Targums* do not contain the very late elements found in *Pseudo-Jonathan*. On the other hand, they have passages that refer to the destruction of the Second Temple in 70 C.E.[631] Alexander writes: "It is not possible to put any kind of precise date on *Frg. Tg.*, but it proba-bly represents a recension or recensions of the PT [Palestinian Targum] earlier than *Ps.Jon* but later than *Neof.*"[632]

---

626 See Klein (introduction) 1986, vol. 1, xix-xxxviii. If not otherwise stated, I use the Aramaic texts of the Targum Genizah fragments collected by Klein along with his translations. For further information regarding the Genizah manuscripts, see Klein's introduction.

627 Klein 1980, 12, McNamara 1992, 4, and Alexander, 1992, 323-324.

628 Alexander 1992, 323.

629 Alexander, 1992, 324, McNamara 1992, 5, and Klein 1980, 13-19.

630 McNamara 1992, 6, and Klein 1980, 19.

631 Klein 1980, 23-26.

632 Alexander 1992, 324. If not otherwise stated, I use the English translation found in *The Fragment Targums to the Pentateuch. According to their Extant Sources*, vol. 1 (Ara-maic text) and vol. 2 (Eng. trans.). Ed. and trans. Klein, 1980.

Targum Pseudo-Jonathan

Targum Pseudo-Jonathan (Tg. Ps.-J.)[633] in its present form is considered to be of a later date, although it certainly contains ancient traditions. *Pseudo-Jonathan* probably received its final form after the emergence of Islam and the Arab conquest of the Middle East. This Targum is the only one that scholars generally consider to contain elements from the Islamic era and therefore it contains anti-Moslem polemic.[634]

Pseudo-Jonathan in its present form contains an amalgamation of material from different periods, perhaps to a higher degree than any other Targum to the Pentateuch. It reveals knowledge about Islam and refers to a wife and daughter of Mohammad (*Tg. Ps.-J.* Gen 21:21) as well as to 'Yohanan the High Priest' in *Tg. Ps.-J.* Deut 33:11 (John Hyrcanus, 134-104 B.C.E.).

As mentioned in chapter 2.2.3, this Targum contains interpretations that were censured in Rabbinic literature, sometimes as early as the Mishnah.[635] However, Michael Maher states that *Pseudo-Jonathan* "... in its *final form* cannot be dated before the seventh or eight century"[636] (my italics).

It has been proposed that the Targum constitutes an attempt to combine a Palestinian targumic tradition with material from the revised Babylonian *Onqelos*, with interwoven additions from various Midrashim, however, this has been disputed.[637] Many scholars agree that the redaction of the Palestinian Targums was probably completed in pre-Islamic times, with the exception of *Pseudo-Jonathan*.[638]

The Targum to Chronicles

Because of the relatively low canonical status of the book of Chronicles in Judaism, it is unlikely that it was read in the ancient Synagogue service. Thus, the Targum probably did not originate in the Synagogue

---

633 Henceforth, I will use the shorter designation *Pseudo-Jonathan*, when not applying the abbreviation.

634 Maher 1992, 11. Because of the language of *Pseudo-Jonathan*, some scholars do not consider it as belonging to the Palestinian targumic family, although it contains Palestinian material. Maher 1992, 9.

635 Alexander 1992, 322. See also Bowker 1969, 26-28.

636 Maher 1992, 12.

637 Alexander 1992, 322-323.

638 McNamara 1992, (introduction), 43-45, and Maher 1992, 11-12. For the Aramaic text of *Pseudo-Jonathan*, see Clarke 1984. If not otherwise stated, I use Maher's English translation (1992) of the Targum.

but in the religious school or/and private study. The *Targum to Chronicles* (*Tg. Chr.*) has an apparent Palestinian character and it was most certainly composed in that country, although it also displays affinities with the Babylonian Talmud. It also appears to have been influenced by *Pseudo-Jonathan*.

It is very difficult to date the *Targum to Chronicles*, as it probably constitutes the result of a long process of work by generations of interpreters at the Jewish academies. It may have originated in 4th century Palestine and was finally edited in the 8th century C.E. There are no Arabisms in the *Targum to Chronicles*. In many ways, it has a more developed angelology than the MT of Chronicles, e.g., in 1 Chr 29:11 angels are depicted as assisting in the giving of the Torah at Sinai.[639]

Genesis Rabbah

Genesis Rabbah (*Gen. Rab.*) is one of the oldest exegetical Midrashim. It is a Palestinian work edited during the late 4th/early 5th century C.E., although containing earlier material.[640]

The Midrash shares many traditions with the Jerusalem Talmud and *Onqelos*.[641] Ancient Jewish tradition ascribes the authorship of *Genesis Rabbah* to Rabbi Hoshaya, who belonged to the first generation of Amoraim in the land of Israel. However, such an early date for the final form of the Midrash is not tenable, since Palestinian Rabbis up to approximately 400 are cited therein.[642] It constitutes a running commentary on the book of Genesis.[643]

---

639 McIvor (introduction) 1994, 11-18. I use the English translation by McIvor, 1994.
640 Strack/Stemberger 1991, 300-305.
641 Grossfeld 1988, 16-18, and Bowker 1969, 78-79. See also Strack/Stemberger 1991, 303-304.
642 Strack/Stemberger 1991, 303-304, and Freedman 1939, xxviii-xxix. Freedman refers to Zunz, who claims that *Genesis Rabbah* was edited in the sixth century C.E.
643 Porton 1992a, 820, and 1979, 128. If not otherwise stated, I use the English translation by H. Freedman, 1939.

Pirqê de Rabbi Eliezer

In contrast to *Genesis Rabbah*, this is a narrative Midrash and as such similar to the 'rewritten Bible' genre. It was probably composed in Palestine/the land of Israel during the 8th or 9th century C.E.[644]

Pirqê de Rabbi Eliezer (*Pirqê R. El.*) is a composite work. While it contains many references to Islam and Arab rule, the redactor/author most certainly made use of earlier traditions.[645] The Midrash also appears to be closely related to the Pseudepigrapha, *Genesis Rabbah*, and *Pseudo-Jonathan.*[646]

Pesiqta de Rab Kahana

This is a homiletic Midrash containing sermons for the festivals and special Sabbaths. It is a Palestinian Midrash probably dating from around the 5th century C.E. *Pesiqta de Rab Kahana* (*Pesiq. Rab Kah.*) is considered by some scholars as the oldest known homiletic Midrash.[647]

Mekilta de Rabbi Ishmael

This is a halakhic commentary on the book of Exodus. The Midrash may probably be assigned to the school of Rabbi Ishmael. *Mekilta de Rabbi Ishmael* is a very old Midrash, probably originating during Tannaitic times, although its final redaction may be dated to the second half of the third century C.E.[648]

---

644 Strack/Stemberger 1991, 356-357. Although *Pirqê de Rabbi Eliezer* is generally considered to have been edited during the eighth or ninth century, much of the material in this Midrash is older. See, e.g., the introduction by Friedlander, 1916, pp. liii-lv and Strack/Stemberger 1991, 356-357.

645 Friedlander 1916, liii-lv, and Bowker 1969, 85. Strack/Stemberger, 1991, 356-357, classifies *Pirqê de Rabbi Eliezer* (in contrast to Friedlander) as the creative work of a personal author.

646 Friedlander 1916 xix- lv, Bowker 1969, 85, Maher 1992, 5-12, and Strack/Stemberger 1991, 357. I use the English translation by Friedlander, 1916.

647 See Strack/Stemberger 1991, 317-322, and Braude/Kapstein 2002, xi-ci. I use the English translation by Braude and Kapstein, 2002.

648 Strack/Stemberger 1991, 275-279. See also Lauterbach (introduction) vol. 1, 1961, xiii-lxiv. I use the English translation by Lauterbach, 1961.

The Talmuds

As is well known, the two Talmuds, in particular the Babylonian one, are the principal works of Rabbinic Judaism and further presentation is superfluous. For some general information, see chapter 2.[649]

4.5.2 Hagar and the Angel

Targum Onqelos

Genesis 16

Regarding Gen 16:7-10, *Onqelos* is very similar to the MT. Moses Aberbach and Bernard Grossfeld have chosen to translate מלאכא דיי in v. 7 in indefinite form: "Then *an* angel of the Lord found her by a spring of water in the wilderness ..." But we could equally understand the Targum as referring to a specific divine messenger, '*the* angel of the Lord', as in the Bible. To some degree, the biblical ambivalence between the angel and God remains in the Targum. As in the Bible, the angel refers to God in the third person (v. 11, see below) but he also talks with divine authority in the first person: "*I* will greatly multiply your descendants ..." (v. 10).

Onqelos interprets the coming of the angel as God's answer to the prayer of Hagar: "Behold, you are pregnant, and you shall give birth to a son; and you shall call his name Ishmael; for *the Lord has accepted your prayer*" (v. 11).

As mentioned in chapter 3, verses 13-14 are both linguistically and theologically problematic in the MT. As a consequence there are differences between the Targum and the Hebrew text in these verses. A comparison between the texts provides the following result:

---

649 I use the English translation of the Babylonian Talmud by Epstein, vols. 1-35, 1935-1948.

Gen 16:13-14: MT/NKJV   *Tg*. Onq. Aramaic and Eng. trans.

[13] וַתִּקְרָא שֵׁם יְהוָה הַדֹּבֵר אֵלֶיהָ אַתָּה אֵל רֳאִי כִּי אָמְרָה הֲגַם הֲלֹם רָאִיתִי אַחֲרֵי רֹאִי [14] עַל כֵּן קָרָא לַבְּאֵר בְּאֵר לַחַי רֹאִי הִנֵּה בֵין קָדֵשׁ וּבֵין בָּרֶד	[13] וְצַלִּיאַת בִּשְׁמָא דַּיָי דְּאִתְמַלַּל עִמַּהּ אָמְרַת אַתְּ הוּא אֱלָהָא חֲזִי כוֹלָּא אֲרֵי אָמְרַת אַף אֲנָא שָׁרִיתִי חָזְיָא בָּתַר דְּאִתְגְּלִי לִי [14] עַל כֵּין קְרָא לְבֵירָא בֵּירָא דְּמַלְאַךְ קַיָּמָא אִתַּחֲזִי עֲלַהּ הָא הִיא בֵּין רְקָם וּבֵין חַגְרָא
[13] Then *she called the name* of the LORD who spoke to her, *You-Are-the-God-Who-Sees*; for she said, *"Have I also here seen Him who sees me?"* [14] Therefore the well was called *Beer Lahai Roi*; [the well of the Living One who sees me] observe, it is between Kadesh and Bered.	[13] And *she prayed* in the name of the Lord who had spoken with her,[650] (and) she said, *"You are the God who sees everything,"* for she said, *"I, too, have begun to see* (visions) after He had been revealed to me." [14] Therefore the well was called the Well where the *living angel* appeared, behold it is between Rekem and Hagra [my italics].

The angel of the Lord who spoke to Hagar seems to be identified by her in *Onqelos* as God Himself in v.13, in accordance with the MT: "…You are the God who sees *everything*…" *Onqelos* interprets this verse as an allusion to the omniscience of God. God saw Hagar in her trouble. Grossfeld assumes that the targumic addition 'everything' is due to an attempt to diminish the anthropomorphism of the Hebrew אֵל רֳאִי, since it could be understood as Hagar calling the one who spoke to her "the God whom it is permitted to see."[651] This is theologically problematic, since no human can see God and live (cf., Exod 19:21 and 33:20). The LXX has "You are the God who sees me …" instead of "You-Are-the-God-Who-Sees." It all depends on how the word רֳאִי is vocalized.[652]

The idea that a maidservant should have given God a name was probably hard for the targumist to imagine, and he resolves the problem by translating וַתִּקְרָא שֵׁם יְהוָה /she called the name of the Lord" as בִּשְׁמָא דַּיָי וְצַלִּיאַת /"she *prayed in* the name of the Lord." Compare, for ex-

---

650 According to Aberbach/Grossfeld, it is significant that *Onqelos* translates the Hebrew phrase הַדֹּבֵר אֵלֶיהָ in v. 13 as דְּאִתְמַלַּל עִמַּהּ, using the Ithpael form of the verb מלל /'to speak'. *Onqelos* could just as well have used the translation דְּמַלִּיל עִמַּהּ. Aberbach and Grossfeld suggest that the reason was probably that the targumist wanted to make God's words to Hagar less direct. The use of this grammatical form renders the distance between God and Hagar greater: Aberbach/Grossfeld 1982, 99, note 10.
651 Grossfeld 1988, 73, note 12.
652 See also Chester 1986, 85-87.

ample, Gen 12:8: "...there he [Abram] built an altar to the LORD and *invoked* the name of the Lord [ויקרא בשם יהוה]." See also Gen 13:4; 21:33, and 26:25 both in *Onqelos* and the MT.[653] The reference to the prayer of Hagar in *Onqelos* may also be an influence from the synagogue-liturgy of the time.

The end of Gen 16:13 is also different in the Targum. According to *Onqelos*, Hagar is here saying: "... I, too, have begun to see (visions) after He had been revealed to me." The targumic addition in Hagar's exclamation; "I, too *have begun* .../...שריתי אנא..." might, according to Aberbach/Grossfeld, be connected to the midrashic view that several angels appeared to Hagar. The meeting with the angel of the Lord in the desert was thus only her first heavenly vision.[654]

Note that Hagar is saying "... *I, too*, have begun to see (visions) ..." This is possibly an allusion to the midrashic concept that divine revelations happened regularly in Abraham's household. Hagar is exclaiming that now she too, despite her low status as a servant, has had a heavenly visitation.[655]

Hagar meets the heavenly emissary in a revelation, a vision. It is thus not comparable to a 'face to face' encounter between two persons in the desert. Grossfeld writes that *Onqelos* in v. 13 presupposes an understanding of the Hebrew הלם; 'here/even' as חלם; 'dream (=vision).'[656] This reminds us of what God once said to Aaron and Miriam in Num 12:5-8:

> [5] Then the LORD came down in a pillar of cloud and stood at the entrance of the tent, and called Aaron and Miriam, and they both came forward. [6] And he said, "Hear my words: When there are prophets among you, I the LORD make myself known to them in visions; I speak to them in dreams. [7] Not so with my servant Moses; he is entrusted with all my

---

653 See also Grossfeld 1988, 73, note 9, Chester 1986, 89, and Aberbach/Grossfeld 1982, 99, note 10. This interpretation may be seen in the light of the fact that the Hebrew word קרא (especially in combination with the preposition ב) can also mean 'call upon/invoke/appeal to', hence 'pray'. Cf., also Rom 10:13 and the rendering of Gen 16:13 in the Palestinian Targums, see below and Maher 1992, 63, note 16.

654 Aberbach/Grossfeld 1982, 99-100, note 11. Aberbach/Grossfeld refers here to *Gen. Rab.* 45.7. I am doubtful about this reference, since *Genesis Rabbah* here comments upon Hagar's experience during her escape from Sarah in Genesis 16. It is true that the Midrash states that several angels appeared to Hagar, *but* on *one and the same occasion*.

655 Aberbach/Grossfeld 1982, 99-100, note 11. In addition to the Rabbinic tradition, Aberbach and Grossfeld base this on an assumption of the substitution of the word הלם in MT by אנא (I) in *Tg. Onq.* Gen 16:13. As shown above, Grossfeld also suggests another interpretation of *Onqelos* concerning the "translation" of the word הלם.

656 Grossfeld 1988, 73, note 13. See also Chester 1986, 87.

house. [8] With him I speak face to face–clearly, not in riddles; and he beholds the form of the LORD. Why then were you not afraid to speak against my servant Moses?"

The meeting between the angel of the Lord and Hagar is not described by *Onqelos* as a meeting 'en route'. It is not an 'ordinary' meeting between two persons in the desert, but depicted as a heavenly vision. This is a spiritualization of the biblical pericope. In this way *Onqelos* tries to diminish the anthropomorphism of the text, a typical targumic device.[657] The LXX also differs from the Targum on this point:

[Gen 16:13] καὶ ἐκάλεσεν Ἀγὰρ τὸ ὄνομα κυρίου τοῦ λαλοῦντος πρὸς αὐτήν, Σὺ ὁ θεὸς ὁ ἐπιδών με· ὅτι εἶπεν, Καὶ γὰρ ἐνώπιον εἶδον ὀφθέντα μοι/And Hagar called the name of the Lord who spoke to her, "You are the God who sees me/looks upon me;" for she said, "For I have openly [or: in person, see chapter 3] seen him that appeared to me." [14] ἕνεκεν τούτου ἐκάλεσεν τὸ φρέαρ Φρέαρ οὗ ἐνώπιον εἶδον... / ...The well of him whom I have openly seen ...

As is shown by the quotation, the LXX has no problem in stating that Hagar *openly saw* God. The LXX also distinguishes itself from *Onqelos* by the translation of v. 13a: "And she called the name of the Lord who spoke unto her..." According to the LXX, Hagar here names the God who appeared to her: "...You are the God who sees me..." In the LXX, there is no explicit reference to prayer in the name of the Lord in v. 13.

So far, it is possible to interpret the angel of the Lord in *Onqelos'* rendering of the pericope as identical to God. However, the last verse, Gen 16:14, changes everything. *Onqelos* has here inserted an angel; "... the Well where *the living angel* [קימא מלאך] appeared ..."[658] This interpretation has some support in the context, since it was an angel who is said to have found Hagar in v.7.[659] But this rendering of the verse nevertheless contradicts the wording of Gen 16:14 in the MT. In the words of Aberbach/Grossfeld:

---

657 See, e.g., Grossfeld 1988, 19-23, and 73, note 13.

658 Kasher (2007, 559) translates קימא מלאך in Gen 16:14 as 'the angel of the Covenant'. His explanations of *Onqelos'* insertion of the angel is that the Targum is adhering to the context of the verse (vv. 7-11) in which it is an angel who speaks to Hagar, or that the Targum wishes to sever the direct link between God and the alien maidservant.

659 This interpretation is also found in later Jewish commentaries. According to, for example, Rashi (see Rashi, *Commentary on the Torah*, vol. 1, *Bereishis/Genesis*, Eng. trans. Herczeg 1995, 181), the fact that the angel speaks in the first person singular and says to Hagar: "I will multiply your descendants exceedingly..." (Gen 16:10) does not imply that the angel himself has the ability to increase her offspring. The angel is speaking on behalf of God. But this does not explain why the angel in one and the same pericope first talks in the first person (v. 10) and then switches to the third person in v. 11. What is the reason for this ambivalence?

MT: באר לחי ראי (*the Well of Lahai-roi* or: *the Well of the Living One who sees me*). TO [Targum *Onqelos*], anxious to emphasize that it was an angel rather than God in person who appeared to Hagar, introduces "the living angel" to prevent any misconception. This was particularly necessary, since לחי ראי, whatever its precise connotation, undoubtedly refers to God described as אל ראי in the previous verse. [660]

The rendering of Gen 16:14 in *Onqelos* is in accordance with the Rabbinic tradition that God had addressed Hagar through (an) angel(s). According to, for instance *Genesis Rabbah*, God has never directly spoken to a woman, except to Sarah.[661]

In conclusion, when we look at the pericope Gen 16:7-14 as a whole in *Onqelos*, the biblical ambivalence between the angel and God is still present, despite the Targumist's attempt to smooth it out by inserting an angel in v. 14. 'The living angel' cannot be an ordinary one, since he is addressed by Hagar as "… You are the God who sees everything …" (Gen 16:13).

Genesis 21

Onqelos' version of Gen 21:17-20 is almost identical to the MT. The angel of the Lord calls to Hagar from heaven and speaks comfortingly to her, as in the Bible (v. 17).[662] The angel thereafter speaks to Hagar in the first person and says; "… for *I* will make of him [Ishmael] a great nation", v. 18. In the next verse we read that "…*God* [lit. the Lord/ יי] opened (lit. uncovered) her eyes, and she saw a well of water …" So far there are merely stylistic differences between the MT and *Onqelos*, i.e., the angel is labeled מלאכא דיי/ 'the angel of YHWH/the Lord', not 'the angel of Elohim/God'. However, the former designation of God is a usual characteristic of the targumic genre.[663]

---

660 Aberbach/Grossfeld 1982, 100-101, note 12.
661 Aberbach/Grossfeld 1982, 99-101, notes 10 and 12. See also *Gen. Rab.* 20.6; 45.10 and 63.7. The Midrash refers here to the annunciation to Sarah concerning the birth of Isaac: Gen 18:9-15. Here one of the three guests of Abraham is identified as God in person.
662 When I refer to 'the Bible' or the 'biblical/Hebrew text', I generally mean the Masoretic version.
663 Grossfeld (1988, 21): "In general, whenever Hebrew Elohim refers to God, it is rendered in the Targum by the Tetragrammaton, except when it is preceded in the Hebrew by the Tetragrammaton, in which case the entire phrase is left untranslated. E. T. Rasmussen ascribes TO's [*Onqelos*] preference for the Tetragrammaton in these cases to the fact that the more generic term Elohim could have been understood as a common noun referring to gods of other peoples, or as a proper noun referring to the God of the Hebrews, whereas the Tetragrammaton is more specific."

In contrast to v. 19, however, *Onqelos* in v. 20 uses the typical targumic circumscription for God: "And then *the Memra* of the Lord gave support to the lad ..."[664] The ambivalence between the angel and God remains in *Onqelos'* rendering of this pericope.

The Palestinian Targums

Genesis 16

Verses 7-12 of *Neofiti* and *Pseudo-Jonathan* are quite similar to each other and to the MT. The messenger who meets/finds Hagar in Gen 16:7 is מלאכא דיי.[665] The translators render this as '*the* angel of the Lord' (not in the indefinite form as Aberbach/Grossfeld, cf., above).[666]

As in the Bible, the angel of the Lord talks in the first person singular in v. 10 in both Targums: "... I will surely multiply your sons so they cannot be numbered for multitude" (*Tg. Neof.*). But in accordance with the MT, the angel in the following verse refers to God in the third person; "... you will call his name Ishmael, because your afflictions *have been heard before* the Lord"[667] (*Tg. Neof.*), "... because your affliction *has been revealed before* the Lord" (*Tg. Ps.-J.*). Thus in v. 11 the two Targums are closer than *Onqelos* to the MT, since there is no reference to the prayer of Hagar.

Unfortunately, we do not have any complete rendering of Gen 16:7-14 in the *Fragment Targums*. In v. 7, we have "on the road to Halusa," instead of "... on the way to Shur" (MT). Verse 13 is, however, available in its entirety in the *Fragment Targums*. Not surprisingly, they con-

---

664 The insertion of the Memra (Word) is a common targumic device used in reverence of God. The addition of the Memra obviates a direct relationship between man and God. According to Grossfeld (1988, 85, note 12): "...The use of the phrase 'the Memra of the Lord sustains' is an extremely common targumic phrase employed in translation for situations in Hebrew where God is depicted as assisting, protecting, defending and preserving man." Grossfeld also claims that "...It [the Memra] appears to be used euphemistically by God's personal manifestation." For more information on the Memra, see chapter 2.2.3.

665 *Neofiti* has וארע יתה/ "he (the angel) met her...", while *Pseudo-Jonathan* has ואשכחה / "he found her..."

666 *Neofiti* vol. 1, (Aramaic text) ed. Díez Macho 1968, Gen 16:7-14, p. 87. The words in italics are targumic deviations from the MT: McNamara 1992, ix.

667 A *Neofiti* marginal gloss has here "... he Memra/Word of the Lord has heard." McNamara 1992, 99.

tain a great deal of interpretative material. The same is the case in *Neofiti* and *Pseudo-Jonathan.*

Gen 16:13-14 read as follows in the Palestinian Targums and the MT, see next page.[668] Verse 14 is extant only in *Neofiti* and *Pseudo-Jonathan.*[669]

---

668 For comparison with *Onqelos*, see above.
669 Verses 13-14 of the Genizah Fragments are not extant.

MT/NKJV	Tg. Neof.	Tg. Ps.-J.	Frg. Tg. (P)[670]	Frg Tg.(V)[671]
[13] ותיקרא שם יהוה הדבר אליה	[13] וצליית בשם ממריה דייי דאתגל[י]ן עליה	[13]ואודיאת קדם ייי דמימריה מתמלל לה וכן אמרת	[13] ואודיאת הגר וצליאת בשם מימרא דיי' דאיתגלי עלה ועל שרי ריבונתהא	[13] ואודיית הגר וצליאת בשום מימרי דיי' דאיתגלי עלה ואמרת בריך את הוא אלהא קיים
אתה אל ראי	את הוא אלהא קיים כל אלמייא	אנת הוא חי וקיים דחמי ולא מתחמי	ואמרת בריך את הוא אלהא קיים לעלמיא וחמית	כל עלמייא די חמית בצערי ארום
כי אמרה הגם הלם ראיתי אחרי ראי	ארום אמרת הא אף כדון יתגלי עלי מן בתר דאתגלי על שרי רבונתי	ארום אמרת הא ברם הכא איתגליאת יקר שכינתא דייי חזוא בתר חזוא	בצערי ארום אמרת הלחוד עלי איתגליאת היך בתר דאיתגליאת על שרי ריבונתי	אמרת הא לחוד עלי איתגליתא היך בתר דאיתגליית על שרי ריבונתי
[14] על כן קרא לבאר	[14] בגין כדן קרא לבארה בא[ר]ה דאתגלי עלה קיים כל אלמייא הא היא בין רקם ובין חלוצה	[14] בגין כן קרא לבירא בירא דאיתגלי עלה חי וקיים והא היא יהיבא בין רקם ובין חלוצה		
באר לחי ראי הנה בן קדש ובן ברד				
[13] Then she called the name of the LORD who spoke to her, You-Are-the-God-Who-Sees; for she said, "Have I also here seen Him who sees me?"	[13] And *she prayed* in the name of the *Memra* [Word] *of the* Lord who *was revealed* to her: You are the God Who sustains *all* ages; [or: ex-ists for all ages][672] for	[13] *She gave thanks before* the Lord *whose Memra* had spoken to her, *and she spoke thus,* "You are *the Living and Enduring One, who sees but is not seen";* for she said, "Be-	[13] And Ha-gar gave thanks and prayed in the name of the *memra* of the Lord who was revealed to her and to Sarai her mi-stress, and she said: "Blessed art	[13] And Ha-gar gave thanks and she prayed in the name of the *memra* of the Lord Who was revealed unto her; and she said: "Blessed art Thou, God, Sustainer of

670 P= ms Paris – Bibliothèque nationale Hébr. 110, folios 1-16.
671 V=ms Vatican Ebr. 440, folios 198-227.
672 As stated, I use the translation by McNamara 1992, 100. His 1970 translation of *Neofi-ti 1* made together with Maher (p. 535) is very similar, but, as shown above, this verse differs slightly. According to McNamara 1992, 100, a *Neofiti* marginal gloss has "… sustainer, or living over all ages." The phrase קיים כל אלמייא can be translated in several ways; see the *Fragment Targums* (V) above: "…Sustainer of All Worlds…"

	she said: "Behold also now he has been revealed to me after he has been revealed to my mistress Sarai"	hold, here indeed the Glory of the Shekinah of the Lord was revealed, vision after vision."674	thou God. Who exists forever, Who has seen my distress; for she said: "Why even unto me You were revealed, just after You were revealed unto Sarai my mistress."	All Worlds, Who has seen my distress;" for she said: "Why even unto me You were revealed, just after You were revealed unto Sarai my mistress."
[14] Therefore the well was called Beer Lahai Roi; [the well of the Living One who sees me] observe, it is between Kadesh and Bered.	[14] Therefore the well was called: the well *beside which the One who sustains all ages*673 *was revealed*. Behold it is between *Rekem* and *Haluzah*.	[14] *Therefore the well was called* "The well *at which the Living and Enduring One was revealed*": *and* behold *it is situated* between *Reqem* and *Haluzah*.		

Grossfeld (2000, 149) translates it "… the preserver of all worlds." He suggests, however, that the original text in *Neofiti* was: קיים לכל עלמייא, / "who endures unto all eternity." Cf., Dan 6:27 and Targum *Jonathan* to Hab 1:12. The phrase קיים לעלמיא (*Frg. Tg.*/P) Klein (1980, 14) translates as "Who exists forever." See above.

673 Or: "… the well where he who exists for all ages was revealed." Eng. trans. McNamara/Maher 1968, 535. See above. A *Neofiti* marginal gloss has: "… above which was revealed the glory of the Shekinah of the Lord …" (McNamara, 1992, 100). Cf., *Pseudo-Jonathan.*

674 'Vision' is omitted in *Editio princeps* (*Ed. pr.*) of *Pseudo-Jonathan* (Venice 1598). Maher follows the reading of the British Library MS 27031 (Lond.) of *Tg. Ps.-J.*, since according to Rabbinic tradition Hagar was accustomed to divine revelations. Maher 1992, 63, note 18. Cf., the analysis of *Onqelos* above.

In the same way as *Onqelos*, the Palestinian Targums interpret ותיקרא שם/ יהוה "she called the name of the Lord" (MT) in Gen 16:13 as a reference to the *prayer/worship* of Hagar: "… Hagar/She gave thanks [or/and] prayed in the name of the *Memra* of the Lord who was *revealed* to her …" (*Tg. Ps.-J.*: "… before the Lord whose *Memra* had *spoken* to her …") [my translations].

The reason for this translation of the phrase is probably the same as in *Onqelos*.[675] However, in contrast to *Onqelos*, all the Palestinian Targums have inserted 'the *Memra*', to make the distance between God and Hagar greater than in the Bible.[676] In agreement with the MT and *Onqelos*, *Pseudo-Jonathan* alone of the Palestinian Targums states that God (through His *Memra*) had *spoken* to Hagar.

It seems apparent that Hagar identifies the angel of the Lord as God Himself, because according to Jewish belief one does not pray to, or worship, before anyone but God. Hagar gives the angel of the Lord divine epithets, for example: "You are the God who sustains *all ages* … [or: exists for all ages …]" (*Tg. Neof.*)/ "Blessed art Thou, God, Sustainer of all worlds…" (*Frg. Tg.*/V) Irrespective of the chosen translation of אלה קיים כל עלמייא it is undoubtedly a divine designation.

According to *Pseudo-Jonathan*, Hagar calls the angel of the Lord "You are the Living and Enduring One [חי וקיים], who sees but is not seen [דחמי ולא מתחמי]." Maher writes that *Pseudo-Jonathan*'s interpretation of אל ראי in the MT is influenced by v. 14, where the well is labeled באר לחי ראי/ "the well of the Living One who sees me" (my translation).[677] It is noteworthy that *Pseudo-Jonathan* apparently denies that Hagar had been able to see God and survive, since according to the Targum she calls God "… *who sees but is not seen* …"[678]

The divine title 'the Living and Enduring One' as well as the description of God as "He who sees but is not seen" occurs again in *Pseudo-Jonathan* in connection with Isaac; Gen 24:62 and 25:11.[679] *Pseudo-Jonathan* alone answers the question of what happened to Isaac after he was nearly sacrificed by his father: "*The angels on high took Isaac and brought him to the schoolhouse of Shem the Great, and he was there three*

---

675 See also Maher 1992, 63, note 16.

676 Concerning the use of Memra in the Targums, see chapter 2.2.3.

677 Maher 1992, 63, note 17.

678 See also Chester 1986, 87-88. See his entire discussion of Gen 16:13-14 in the Palestinian Targums, pp. 85-95.

679 See also *Tg. Ps.-J.*, Num 23:19. The designation of God as 'the One who sees but is not seen' is also found in the Koran and Rabbinic literature. See Maher 1992, 63, note 17.

years..." (Gen 22:19). After this, Isaac is missing until Gen 24:62: "Isaac was coming from the *schoolhouse of Shem the Great*, by the way that leads to the well *where the Living and Enduring One, who sees but is not seen, was revealed to him...*"[680] See also *Gen. Rab.* 60.14:

> AND ISAAC CAME FROM COMING, etc. (XXIV, 62): i.e. he came from a mission to fetch someone. And whither had he gone? TO BEER-LAHAI-ROI (*ib.*): he had gone to fetch Hagar, the one who sat by the well (*be'er*) and besought Him who is the life (*lahai*) of all worlds, saying, 'Look upon (*re'eh*) my misery.'

In all the Palestinian Targums except *Pseudo-Jonathan*, Hagar makes a comparison between herself and her mistress Sarai, e.g., "Behold also now he has been revealed to me after he has been revealed to my mistress Sarai" (Gen 16:13/*Tg. Neof.*). This may be a reference to the belief that divine revelations were usual in Abraham's household.[681] Compare *Onqelos*: "I, too, have begun to see (visions) after He had been revealed to me ..."

The words of Hagar in *Pseudo-Jonathan* v. 13: "... *vision after vision...*" may be an allusion to the midrashic interpretation that it was several angels who appeared to Hagar, cf., *Gen. Rab.* 45.7. It is apparent, though, that she is referring to a divine revelation in her speech: "...*here indeed the Glory of the Shekinah of the Lord was revealed ...*"[682] According to the *Fragment Targums*, Hagar in v. 13 also exclaims that God had seen her distress, which is reminiscent of Westermann's interpretation of the pericope.

As mentioned above, there is no preserved rendering of Gen 16:14 in the *Fragment Targums* as the verse is only extant in Targums *Neofiti* and *Pseudo-Jonathan*. Surprisingly enough, neither of these two Targums has inserted an angel in Gen 16:14, as *Onqelos* has done. This is noteworthy, since *Onqelos* is generally the most literal of the Targums. The explanation may be that this Targum is to a higher degree bound by Rabbinic traditions, *Onqelos* being the "official" Targum to the Pentateuch in Rabbinic Judaism.

---

680 Cf., also the *Frg. Tg.* (P) to Gen 24:62: "And Isaac was coming from the study-hall of the Great Shem to the well at which the Glory of the Shekinah of the Lord was revealed; and he was dwelling between Hagra and Haluzah" (My translation).

681 There may also be a contradiction in the Palestinian Targums to the Rabbinic opinion that God had never spoken directly to a woman, with the sole exception of Sarah, cf., *Frg. Tg.* Gen 16:13 (V and P): "...Why even unto me You were revealed, just after You were revealed unto Sarai my mistress."

682 Concerning the concept 'the Glory of the Shekinah of the Lord', see chapter 2.2.3.

Hagar's previous exclamation reveals that the name of the well in the two Palestinian Targums is "...the well *beside which the One who sustains* [or: exists for] *all ages was revealed...*" (*Tg. Neof.*), "...The well *at which the Living and Enduring One was revealed ...*" (*Tg. Ps.-J.*).

The Palestinian Targums seem to interpret the appearance of the angel of the Lord in Gen 16:7-14 as a theophany. The angel of the Lord is identical to God Himself and, although the holy angels are also carriers of the divine Glory, only God can be described as "*... the Living and Enduring One, who sees but is not seen*" (*Tg. Ps.-J.*, Gen 16:13). However, in the same way as in *Onqelos*, the "angel"/divine messenger reveals Himself to Hagar in a heavenly vision; it is not a meeting 'en route'.

Genesis 21

Concerning Gen 21:17-20 we are limited to the rendering of *Neofiti* and *Pseudo-Jonathan*, since the relevant verses are unfortunately not preserved in the *Fragment Targums* or the Cairo-Genizah.[683]

The rendering of *Neofiti* is quite close to the Hebrew original, despite the fact that one of the reasons for the expulsion of Ishmael is said to be that he practiced idolatry (Gen 21:9). The alleged idolatry of Ishmael may be explained as an attempt to justify Sarah's (and God's) behavior. Abraham unwillingly casts both him and Hagar out, on God's command to listen to Sarah's request. God, however, promises Abraham to make a great nation of the son of Hagar, his bondwoman, vv. 10-13.

As in the Bible, the heavenly messenger/ מלאכא דייי calls to Hagar from heaven in v. 17 and refers to God [ייי] in the third person; "... Fear not, because *the Lord* has heard the voice *of the prayer* of the boy..."[684] But in v. 18, the messenger switches to the first person singular; "... I will make him [Ishmael] a great nation ..." In v. 19 we read: "And the Lord[685] opened her eyes and she saw a well of water..." The only noteworthy difference from the MT is the use of the Tetragrammaton (albeit in shortened form) and the reference to the prayer of Ishmael in v. 17. The ambivalence between the messenger and God thus remains in *Neofiti*.

The interpretative material is more extensive in *Pseudo-Jonathan* but it mainly concerns Ishmael and not the identity of the heavenly emissary. According to Maher, there is an apparent anti-Moslem attitude in

---

683 In the *Fragment Targums* the only extant verses of Genesis 21 are vv. 9, 33 (P), and vv. 1, 7, 9, 15, and 33 (V).

684 A *Neofiti* marginal gloss has here "the Memra of the Lord (has heard) the voice." McNamara 1992, 114.

685 *Neofiti* marginal gloss: "the Memra of the Lord." McNamara 1992, 114.

the translation of the pericope. As previously mentioned, it is generally recognized that *Pseudo-Jonathan* received its final form after the emergence of Islam. Both Hagar and Ishmael are described as idolaters, vv. 11, 15-16. It is because of His relationship to Abraham that God listens to Ishmael (Gen 21:17-20):

> [17] The voice of the child was heard before the Lord because of the merit of Abraham. And *the angel of the Lord* called to Hagar from heaven and said to her, "… the voice of the child has *been heard before the Lord*, and he has not judged him according to the evil deeds he is destined to do. Because of the merit of Abraham he has shown mercy to him in the place where he is. [18] Arise, take the boy and hold him by the hand, for *I will make* a great nation of him." [19] *The Lord uncovered* her eyes, and a well of water was revealed to her… [20] The *Memra of the Lord* was at the assistance of the boy, and he grew up … [686] [my italics].

The biblical ambivalence concerning the identity of the angel of the Lord remains in *Pseudo-Jonathan*. But in contrast to the Bible, the deliverance of Hagar and her son is explicitly connected to the merit of Abraham. Because Ishmael is Abraham's son, God saves him and his mother in spite of his present and future sins, v. 17.[687] Why *Pseudo-Jonathan* finds it unproblematic to state that "the Lord uncovered her [Hagar's] eyes…" in v. 19 but inserts the *Memra* in v. 20 is a riddle.[688]

Genesis Rabbah

Genesis 16

The Rabbis behind *Genesis Rabbah* have the following to say about Hagar's encounter with the angel in Genesis 16:

> [*Gen. Rab.* 45.7] … the angel said: HAGAR, SARAI'S HANDMAID, etc. Hence, AND SHE SAID: I FLEE FROM THE FACE OF MY MISTRESS SARAI. AND AN ANGEL SAID UNTO HER: RETURN TO YOUR MISTRESS, etc […] AND AN ANGEL OF THE LORD SAID UNTO HER: I WILL GREATLY MULTIPLY THY SEED, etc (XVI, 9 f.). How many angels visited her? R. Hama b. R. Hanina said: Five, for each time 'speech' is mentioned it

---

686 Concerning the anti-Moslem mentality, see Maher 1992, 76, note 24.

687 We have some support for such an interpretation in the context of the MT. See the words of God to Abraham according to Gen 21:13: "Yet I will make a nation of the son of the bondwoman, because he is your seed."

688 A *Neofiti* marginal gloss states in v. 20: "the Memra of the Lord (was) at the aid of the child." McNamara 1992, 114. As mentioned previously, according to Grossfeld the use of the Memra is very common in targumic translations of verses in the Hebrew Bible where God is depicted as assisting people. Cf., the analysis above of *Jubilees*, the *Judean Antiquities*, and *Tg. Onq.* Gen 21:20.

refers to an angel. The rabbis said: Four, this being the number of times 'angel' occurs. R. Hiyya observed: Come and see how great is the difference between the earlier generations and the later ones! What did Manoah say to his wife? *We shall surely die, because we have seen God* (Judg. XIII, 22); yet Hagar, a bondmaid, sees five angels and is not afraid of them! R. Aha said: The finger-nail of the fathers rather than the stomach of the sons! R. Isaac quoted: *She seeth the ways of her household* (Prov. XXXI, 27): Abraham's household were seers, so she [Hagar] was accustomed to them.

According to the Rabbis, it was not only one angel who appeared to Hagar, but at least four. She had several heavenly visitations in the desert, compare the exclamation of Hagar in *Tg. Ps.-J.* Gen 16:13: "… *vision after vision …*" It was thus not God in person who met Hagar in the desert, but some of His angels. In contrast to Manoah, who was terrified when he realized that he had had an encounter with the angel of the Lord, Hagar was used to divine revelations. Heavenly visions were commonplace in Abraham's household; see all of the Targums to Gen 16:13 and *Gen. Rab.* 47.10:

> FOR SHE [Hagar] SAID: HAVE I EVEN HERE (HALOM) SEEN HIM THAT SEETH ME. She said: I have been granted not only speech [with the angel], but even with royalty too, as you read, *That Thou hast brought me thus far*–halom (II Sam VII, 18).[689] I was favoured [to see the angel] not only with my mistress [Sarah], but even now that I am alone.[690] R. Samuel said: This may be compared to a noble lady whom the king ordered to walk before him. She did so leaning on her maid and pressing her face against her. Thus her maid saw [the king], while she did not see him.[691]

As shown above, a similar interpretation of the end of Gen 16:13 הגם הלם ראיתי אחרי ראי/"Have I also here seen Him who sees me?" is also found in the Targums, explicitly in the Palestinian ones,[692] e.g., "*Behold also now he has been revealed to me after he has been revealed to my mistress Sarai*" (*Tg. Neof.*).

The epithet that Hagar gives God, אל ראי, is explained by R. Aibu to mean that she thereby proclaims that God sees the sufferings of the

---

689 According to Freedman/Simon 1939, 388, note 1, the biblical reference to David's royal rank and the word 'halom' expresses Hagar's gratitude that kings would spring from her. Cur. Edd. has here: "Not only was I favoured to see the angel together with my mistress, but even my mistress who was with me did not see him (while I did)." This might explain the comparison in the end.

690 Freedman/Simon 1939, 388, note 2: "Rendering: I have seen (the angels in the wilderness) after having seen them (at home); v. *supra*, 7."

691 The noble lady did not see the king because she was hiding her face in modesty: Freedman/Simon 1939, 388, note 3.

692 Except *Pseudo-Jonathan*, see above.

persecuted,[693] compare her exclamation in the *Fragment Targums* (P): "Blessed art thou God. Who exists forever, Who has seen my distress..."

The beginning of Gen 16:13 was problematic for the Rabbis of *Gen. Rab.*: "Then she called the name of the LORD who spoke to her ..."[694] Could it actually have been God in person who talked to Hagar? This is subject to discussion in the Midrash:

> R. Judah b. R. Simon and R. Johanan in the name of R. Eleazar b. R. Simeon said: The Holy One, blessed be He, never condescended to hold converse with a woman save with that righteous woman [viz. Sarah], and that too was through a particular cause. R. Abba b. Kahana said in R. Birya's name: And what a roundabout way He took in order to speak with her, as it is written, *And He said: Nay, but thou didst laugh (ib.* XVIII, 15)! But it is written, AND SHE [HAGAR] CALLED THE NAME OF THE LORD THAT SPOKE UNTO HER? R. Joshua b.R. Nehemiah answered in R. Idi's name: That was through an angel ...[695]

Sarah, as the supreme matriarch[696] of Israel, thus holds a unique position in the Rabbinic tradition; of all biblical women God has spoken directly only to her. This implies that the Rabbis interpreted one of the three visitors to Abraham and Sarah in Genesis 18 as God Himself.[697] However, the Rabbis are not in total agreement concerning Hagar's case. We do not have a univocal interpretation of Gen 16:13. There seems to be an apparent contradiction in the Midrash. On the one hand, Sarah and Hagar are contrasted to each other but, on the other, Hagar is said to have compared herself and her spiritual experience to that of Sarah: "I was favoured [to see the angel] not only with my mistress [Sarah], but even now that I am alone ..." (*Gen. Rab.* 45.10).

The connection in *Genesis Rabbah* between Genesis 16; 18; Judges 13, and 2 Samuel 7 is an apparent example of the intertextuality so characteristic of Midrash. As stated previously, the early Rabbis understood

---

693 Or: "You see the humiliation of those humiliated." *Gen. Rab.* 45.10, Eng. trans. Neusner, vol. 2, 1985, 155.

694 NKJV.

695 *Gen. Rab.* 45.10.

696 The Midrash continues to say that not even the matriarch Rebekah had a direct encounter with God.

697 Rashi (1040-1105), on the other hand, emphasizes that neither Sarah nor Hagar had a direct encounter with God in person. On both occasions (Gen 18:10-13 and Gen 16:7-14) it is an angel speaking on God's behalf. Rashi, Eng. trans. Herczeg, 1995, 181. This prominent medieval scholar, however, belongs to a later period than that covered in my thesis.

the Bible as a unity, in which everything belongs together. One biblical text can thus illuminate another.

Even though the Rabbis of *Genesis Rabbah* acknowledge that the title אל ראי in Gen 16:13 is given by Hagar to God, the majority nevertheless deny that He talked to her in person; God addressed Hagar through angels. The designation 'the angel of the Lord' in Gen 16:7-14 is interpreted as denoting several angels appearing to Hagar. This is why the phrase 'the angel of the Lord said to her' occurs more than once, each time it refers to the speech of a different angel. To the 'midrashic mind' there are no unnecessary repetitions in the Bible.[698] According to the Rabbis, one angel cannot have more than one task at a time.[699]

Genesis 21

Regarding Gen 21:17-20, *Genesis Rabbah* does not have any comment upon the identity of the angel of God who calls to Hagar but the Midrash mentions other angels, and he does not seem to be one of them:

> [*Gen. Rab.* 53.14] AND THE ANGEL OF GOD CALLED TO HAGAR (XXI, 17)–for Abraham's sake; while [GOD HATH HEARD THE VOICE OF THE LAD] WHERE HE IS connotes for his own sake, for a sick person's prayers on his own behalf are more efficacious than those of anyone else.
>
> WHERE HE IS.[700] R. Simon said: The ministering angels hastened to indict him exclaiming, 'Sovereign of the Universe! Wilt Thou bring up a well for one who will one day slay Thy children with thirst?[701] 'What is he [Ishmael] now? He [God] demanded. 'Righteous,' was the answer. 'I judge man only as he is at the moment,' said He. [Therefore Scripture continues] ARISE, LIFT UP THE LAD, etc. AND GOD OPENED HER EYES, etc. (XXI, 18 f.). R. Benjamin b. Levi and R. Jonathan b. Amram both said: All may be presumed to be blind, until the Holy one, blessed be He, enlightens their eyes...

The focus of the Midrash is not the identity of the heavenly messenger but the fact that God rescued Ishmael, in spite of the fact that he (his descendants) would become enemies of Israel. God saves Ishmael and Hagar, for Abraham's sake (cf., *Tg. Ps.-J.*) but also because of the prayer of Ishmael. At this moment, Ishmael is considered righteous by God,

---

698 See chapter 2.2.

699 See also Freedman/Simon 1939, 385, note 3. In *Gen. Rab.* 50.2 we read: "One angel does not perform two missions ..."

700 I.e., in his present state.

701 According to Freedman/Simon (1939, 473, note 6), this is a reference to Isa 21:13-15; "... which is interpreted as an unheeded appeal by the Israelites to the Arabs, regarded as descendants of Ishmael."

and He causes a well to spring up for him.[702] God opens the eyes of Hagar, interpreted as a statement that we all are (spiritually) blind, until God enlightens us. As is the case concerning *Neofiti*, it is worth noting that *Genesis Rabbah* dates from pre-Islamic times.

There is no mention of the promise of the angel of God to make Ishmael a great nation. The angel is, however, depicted as the spokesman of God, distinguished from the angels who question God's action.

Pirqê de Rabbi Eliezer

Genesis 21

As in *Jubilees*, the expulsion of Hagar and Ishmael is depicted in *Pirqê de Rabbi Eliezer* as one of the trials of Abraham. The two books also have in common that they contain a counterpart to the story of Hagar and the angel that can only be found in Genesis 21.

No angel is mentioned in *Pirqê de Rabbi Eliezer*'s rewriting of the pericope.[703] The only 'heavenly actor' is God Himself. Does this imply that the "angel" and God are assumed to be one and the same person? Or is the angel as God's messenger considered unimportant by the author? We cannot know for sure. As in, for example, *Pseudo-Jonathan*, Hagar is here depicted as an idolater. In contrast to the Palestinian Targums, nothing is said of Ishmael's idolatry, on the contrary, he entreatingly prayed to the God of his father Abraham to save him and his mother.

---

702 Cf., *Exod. Rab.* 3.2: "... the angels sought to bring charges against him [Ishmael] saying: 'Lord of the Universe, wilt Thou cause a well to come up for one who will one day try to slay Thy children with thirst'? [...] God retorted: 'But *now*, is he righteous or wicked?' They replied: 'He is righteous.' Whereupon God said: 'I judge a man only on what he is *now*'..." Eng. trans. Lehrman 1939, 60. According to a modern Jewish commentator, it is noteworthy that God in Gen 21:17-20 is named by His attribute of strict justice, Elohim: Rabbi M. Zlotowitz 1978, 764. See also *b. Rosh ha-Shana* 16b. According to *Gen. Rab.* 53.13, Hagar appealed to the justice of God: "... R. Berekiah said: The phrase connotes, as a woman who impugned God's justice, saying, 'Yesterday Thou didst promise me, I will greatly multiply thy seed, etc. (Gen. XVI, 10), and now he is dying of thirst!' "

703 Although *Pirqê de Rabbi Eliezer* does not make any reference to the angel of the Lord in the rendering of Genesis 21 (chapter 30), the angel is mentioned in a later chapter. Since according to Gen 16:11 the angel commands Hagar to name her son Ishmael, the Midrash states that he is one of six persons who were called by their names before their creation. The others are: Isaac, Moses, Solomon, Josiah, and King Messiah: *Pirqê de Rabbi Eliezer* 32. *Genesis Rabbah* also bears witness to this tradition, see 45.8.

The reason for their expulsion is said to be that Ishmael had tried to kill Isaac. [704]

Pirqê de Rabbi Eliezer states that God answered Ishmael's prayer and opened 'the well which was created at twilight' for him and his mother.[705] It is thus no ordinary well. According to Jewish tradition, it was created at twilight on the eve of the first Sabbath in the week of creation.[706] This interpretation may be derived from the name of the well in Gen 16:14: באר לחי ראי/"the well of the Living One who sees me." God showed Hagar the well and saved Ishmael. One may compare this with the Muslim legend of the holy Zam-Zam-well in Mecca, probably dating from pre-Islamic times.[707]

There is a parallel in Genesis 22; when Abraham is prevented by the angel of the Lord from killing Isaac, he discovers a ram to sacrifice instead of his son. According to *Pirqê de Rabbi Eliezer*, the ram was also created at 'the twilight'.[708] Compare the name of the well in Gen 16:14 with the name Abraham gives the sacrificial site: יהוה יראה אשר יאמר היום בהר יהוה יראה.../ " 'The LORD will provide'; as it is said to this day, 'On the Mount of the Lord it shall be provided'." The verse could also be rendered: "Abraham called the name of the place the Lord sees/chooses, as it is said today, on the mountain of the Lord it is seen/revealed" (Gen 22:14, my translation).

Concluding Remarks

There are many similarities between the interpretations of Gen 16:7-14 in *Genesis Rabbah* and the Targums. As we have seen, *Pirqê de Rabbi Eliezer* only comments upon Gen 21:17-20, possibly because the "author" of the Midrash considered the two texts as two versions of the same story. The narrative Midrash *Pirqê de Rabbi Eliezer* is close to the 'rewritten Bible' genre, and as such it is considerably freer in its relationship to the original texts than, for example, the exegetical Midrash *Genesis Rabbah* and of course the Targums.

---

704 *Pirqê de Rabbi Eliezer* 30.
705 *Pirqê de Rabbi Eliezer* 30.
706 See Friedlander 1916, 218, note 2. Cf., *m. Abot* 5.6 which refers to a well 'created at the twilight'. Neusner (ed. and Eng. trans. 1988, 686) connects it to the well mentioned in Num 21:16-18. I, however, think that it is doubtful that there should be *two* such wells in Rabbinic tradition.
707 According to Islam, it was the archangel Gabriel who opened the well.
708 *Pirqê Rabbi Eliezer* 31, cf., also *Gen. Rab.* 56. 9 and Rev 5:6-14.

The renderings of Gen 16:7-12 are quite similar in all the Targums and in the MT.[709] The messenger who meets/finds Hagar is referred to in definite form in Gen 16:7; מלאכא דייי/'the angel of the Lord'.[710] As in the biblical narrative, the angel of the Lord addresses Hagar in v. 10 in the first person singular, e.g., *Neofiti;* I will surely multiply your sons …" However, in the following verse, the messenger refers to God in the third person. The biblical ambivalence concerning the merged identity of God and His messenger thus remains in the Targums. In v. 11 *Onqelos* distinguishes itself from the others in stating that God had heard the prayer of Hagar. *Pseudo-Jonathan* reads for example "…your affliction has been revealed before the Lord," but this can be deemed merely a stylistic difference. Not surprisingly, we find the most expanded targumic paraphrases in Gen 16:13-14.

The idea that a slave-girl should have given God a name was probably hard to imagine for the targumists. Both *Onqelos* and the Palestinian Targums thus interpret ותיקרא שם יהוה /"she called the name of the Lord" (MT) in Gen 16:13 as a reference to the prayer/worship of Hagar. This translation may also have been influenced by the liturgy of the synagogue.

It is possible to understand the exclamation of Hagar in v. 13 in all the Targums as implying that she identifies the "angel" of the Lord as God Himself. For example: "You are the God who sustains all ages … [or: exists for all ages …]" (*Tg. Neof.*). Compare *Onqelos:* "… You are the God who sees everything …"

All of the Targums seem to allude to the Rabbinic tradition that divine revelations were common occurrences in Abraham's household. In *Neofiti* and the *Fragment Targums* (V and P) Hagar actually compares her experience in the desert to that of Sarah. This interpretation is also found in *Gen. Rab.* 45.7 and 10.

Regarding the relationship of the revelations of Sarah and Hagar, however, there is an inconsistency in *Genesis Rabbah*. On the one hand, Hagar is said to have compared herself to Sarah on an equal level: "I was favoured [to see the angel] not only with my mistress, but even now when I am alone …" (*Gen. Rab.* 45.10). On the other, the majority of the Rabbis of the Midrash emphasize that God has never directly

---

709 In the *Fragment Targums* we do not have any complete rendering of these verses. In v. 7 we merely have "… on the road to Halusa," instead of "… on the road to Shur" (MT).

710 *Neofiti* has וארע יתה/ "he (the angel) met her …", while *Pseudo-Jonathan* has ואשכחה / "he found her …"

spoken to a woman, except to Sarah, an interpretation that recalls Philo's distinction between the two women.

Only *Genesis Rabbah* explicitly refers to several heavenly messengers, and not merely one angel, who appeared to Hagar; God spoke to her via angels. According to the midrashic perspective, there are no unnecessary repetitions in the Bible. Therefore, each time the phrase 'the angel of the Lord said to her' occurs, it refers to the speech of a different angel. This interpretation may also be alluded to in the Targums, for example, *Pseudo-Jonathan*; "… here indeed the Shekinah of the Lord was revealed, vision after vision." Hagar experienced multiple revelations during her escape from Sarah.

According to *Pseudo-Jonathan*, Hagar calls the angel of the Lord "You are the Living and Enduring One [חי וקיים], who sees but is not seen [דחמי ולא מתחמי]." The Targum's interpretation of אל ראי in the MT may here be influenced by v. 14, where the well is labeled באר לחי ראי/ "the well of the Living One who sees me." It is noteworthy that *Pseudo-Jonathan* apparently denies that Hagar had been able to see God and survive, since according to the Targum she calls God "…who sees but is not seen…"

As a matter of fact, none of our sources interprets Gen 16:13 in accordance with Wellhausen's emendation: הגם אלהים ראיתי ואחי … … meaning: "Have I really seen God and remained alive/and I (still) live!" (my translation). According to both the Targums and *Genesis Rabbah*, the divine messenger(s) has revealed himself/themselves to Hagar in a vision. It is not a direct encounter 'en route', compare Philo's statement that the angel/'Logos' spoke to Hagar within her soul. In order to make the distance between God and Hagar greater and to circumvent anthropomorphism, there is a spiritualization of the event in all the Targums. The use of the Memra is a typical targumic device and not in any way exclusive to our two pericopes.

Alone of all the Targums *Onqelos* has in v. 14 inserted 'the living angel'/ מלאך קימא. This is most probably an attempt by the Targumist to avoid an understanding of the heavenly messenger as identical to God. As the "official" Targum, *Onqelos* is bound by Rabbinic tradition to a higher degree than the others. The Palestinian Targums paraphrase Gen 16:14 in accordance with the previous verse. "The well at which the Living and Enduring One was revealed …" (*Tg. Ps.-J.*). "… the well beside which the One who sustains all ages was revealed …" (*Tg. Neof.*). The *Fragment Targums* unfortunately do not have any preserved rendering of v. 14.

The renderings of Gen 21:17-20 in *Neofiti* and *Pseudo-Jonathan* are quite close to the MT, in *Onqelos* almost identical. In contrast to the

Bible, the heavenly messenger in the Targums is called 'the angel of YHWH/the Lord', instead of 'the angel of Elohim/God'. However, the use of the Tetragrammaton is a typical targumic trait.

The biblical ambiguity concerning the identity of the angel remains in the Targums. Ishmael is in focus, but in both Targums he is described as an idolater. Perhaps this is an attempt to justify Sarah's action, her wish to expel Hagar and her son? According to Maher, *Pseudo-Jonathan* contains an anti-Moslem polemic. However, in contrast to *Pseudo-Jonathan*, *Neofiti* is generally considered to have been completed before the advent of Islam.

Both Targums state that God hears the prayer/voice of Ishmael and rescues him. According to *Pseudo-Jonathan*, Ishmael's and Hagar's deliverance is solely due to the merit of Abraham. The Targum has no problem in stating that "the Lord uncovered her [Hagar's] eyes", v. 19. As we have seen, the relevant verses are not extant in the *Fragment Targums*.

The interpretation of Gen 21:17-20 in *Genesis Rabbah* seems to be in the same tradition as the Targums. The main character is Ishmael. He is saved for Abraham's sake and because of his own prayer. He (his descendants) is depicted as a future enemy of Israel, but for the moment, he is righteous. Again, we may ask ourselves about the reason for this dark depiction of Ishmael, since *Genesis Rabbah* dates from pre-Islamic times.[711]

The Midrash makes no comment on the identity of the angel of God, but mentions other angels who oppose God's rescue of Ishmael. God's response is that He judges man only as he is at the moment. The angel of God is clearly His spokesman, distinguished from the angels who question God's action.

As mentioned, our second Midrash, *Pirqê de Rabbi Eliezer*, only comments upon Gen 21:17-20. The angel is not mentioned at all, the only 'heavenly actor' is God Himself. This may indicate that the angel and God were understood as identical. Or is the explanation that, as God's agent, the angel was considered unimportant in himself? We cannot know for certain.

The well is here significant. God hears Ishmael's prayer and opens the well for him and his mother. According to the Midrash, it was created at twilight on the eve of the first Sabbath in the week of the creation. This may be derived from the name of the well in Gen 16:14:

---

711 A possible answer may be that the dark depiction of Ishmael is due to the fact that he and his descendants are outsiders, they do not belong to the commonwealth of Israel.

"The well of the Living One who sees me." *Pirqê de Rabbi Eliezer's* re-writing of Gen 21:17-20 may thus have been influenced by the parallel pericope Gen 16:7-14.

4.5.3 The Aqedah and the Angel

The Targums

Introduction

There are no significant theological differences between the MT and the Targums concerning the role of the angel of the Lord in Genesis 22. The land of Moriah seems to be identified with the future Temple Mount in all the Targums, which also contain an extended version of v. 14 and state that Abraham prayed/worshiped before the Lord on the mountain. All the Targums use the Tetragrammaton (albeit in shortened form) throughout the pericope.

Targum Onqelos

Except for the above mentioned derivations, there are merely stylistic differences between *Onqelos* and the MT, probably due to the targumic avoidance of anthropomorphisms, for example; "... by *My Memra* I swear, says the Lord ..." (v. 16, my italics).[712] *Onqelos* displays the same ambivalence concerning the angel of the Lord as in the original text. Not surprisingly, this is the Targum that contains the smallest amount of interpretation.

The Palestinian Targums

In the Palestinian Targums to the Pentateuch, we likewise find the same ambivalence between YHWH and the angel of the Lord. The wording of *Neofiti* in vv. 16 and 18 is a bit peculiar:

> [v. 16] And *he* [the angel of the Lord] said: "In the name of *his* Word *I have sworn* – says the Lord ..." [ואמר בשם ממריה קיימת אמר ייי]
>
> [v. 18, my italics].[713] "And because you [Abraham] heard *the voice of his Word*" [די שמעת בקל ממריה]

---

712 See the Eng. trans. and critical analysis of *Onqelos* by Aberbach/Grossfeld 1982, 128-133. As mentioned above, Alexander and Levine both claim that the concern in the Targums is *reverence of God* rather than an avoidance of anthropomorphisms. Alexander 1988, 226, and Levine 1988, 45-61.

713 *Targum Neofiti* 1, vol. 1, ed. Díez Macho 1968, 129. Eng. trans. McNamara/Maher 1968, 553.

Pseudo-Jonathan renders these verses as follows:

> [v. 16] ... and said, "By *my* Word have I sworn, saith the Lord... [ואמר במימרי
> קיימית אמר ייי]
>
> [v. 18, my italics] ... because thou hast obeyed *my voice*." [lit. *"my Me-mra/Word"* / דקבילתא במימרי][714]

All the Palestinian Targums mention angels in v. 10, e.g., the *Fragment Targums:*[715]

> ... Isaac's eyes were scanning *the angels of the heights*; Isaac saw them, Abraham did not see them; at that moment the *angels of the heights came forth* and said to one another: 'Come, see two unique righteous men who are in the world ...[716] [my italics]

Neofiti differs from the other Palestinian Targums and refers first to angels but says at the end of v. 10: "... In that hour *a voice* [*bat qol*/lit. *'daughter of a voice'*] *came forth* from the heavens and said ..."[717] (my italics). The angel of the Lord is distinguished from the angels mentioned in v. 10 and seems to have a higher status. He appears to be identified with God himself, yet he is distinct from Him, as in the original text.

Pseudo-Jonathan, together with a targumic Tosefta[718] among the Genizah fragments, refers to a cloud of glory in v. 4: "On the third day Abraham lifted up his eyes, and saw *the cloud of glory smoking* on the mountain ..." (*Ps.-J.*, my italics). It is only *Pseudo-Jonathan* that answers the question of what happened to Isaac after the Aqedah: "And *the angels on high* led Isaac and brought him to the school of Shem the great, and he was there three years...." (v. 19, my italics). According to *Pseudo-Jonathan* the reason for the death of Sarah in Gen 23:1-2 is that *Satan* came and told her that Abraham had really sacrificed Isaac. The trial, however, is not carried out on Satan's suggestion (cf., *Jubilees*) but because of the rivalry between Isaac and Ishmael (v. 1).[719]

According to all the Targums (including *Onqelos*), the angel of the Lord says in v.12 that Abraham now has proven that he fears God, e.g.,

---

714 *Targum Pseudo-Jonathan*, ed. Clarke 1984, 24. Eng. trans., Bowker 1969, 226.

715 See also a targumic tosefta to Isa 33:7 and Kasher 2007, 581-584.

716 This is the manuscript Vatican Ebr. 440. According to the ms Paris – Bibliothèque nationale Hébr. 110, it was a *voice* [lit. *berath qala* = 'daughter of a voice'] that emerged from heaven and said: "Come see two unique righteous men ..." Cf., *Neofiti*. Concerning the concept 'daughter of a voice', see chapter 2.2.

717 *Tg. Neof.* Gen 22:10. Ed. Díez Macho 1968, vol. 1, 127, Eng. trans. McNamara/Maher 1968, 551.

718 Cambridge University Library, ms T-S B 8.9, folio 2. See Klein (ed. and Eng. trans. vol. 1, 1986, 34-35.

719 *Tg. Ps.-J.* Gen 22:4, 19 and v. 1. Eng. trans. Bowker 1969, 224-226.

Neofiti "… because now I know that you fear before the Lord …" [720]
Thus, we here have no particular difference between the Targums and
the biblical account. But why did God have to compel Abraham to
prove his fidelity? The Targums give us no clear answer. However, in
Gen 22:14, the Palestinian Targums have put a long prayer in Abraham's mouth. Here Abraham declares that God knew all along that he
would pass the test, since He is omniscient.

All of the Palestinian Targums say at the end of this verse (after the
long prayer of Abraham) that the *Shekintah* (Aramaic: *Presence*) *of the
Lord was revealed* to him on the mountain. Does this refer to the revelation of the angel of the Lord?[721]

Genesis Rabbah, Pirqê de Rabbi Eliezer and Pesiqta de Rab Kahana

Genesis Rabbah presents several events that are said to have led up to
the Aqedah. One reason for the trial is said to be the angels' criticism of
Abraham (cf., *L.A.B.* 32.1-2):

> According to R. Leazar who maintained that the employment of wa-elohim
> where Elohim would suffice intimates, *He and His Court, it was the minister-
> ing angels* who spoke thus: 'This Abraham rejoiced and made all others re-
> joice, yet did not set aside for God a single bullock or ram.' Said the Holy
> One, blessed be He, to them: 'Even if we tell him to offer his own son, he
> will not refuse'[722] [my italics].

According to the Midrashim *Genesis Rabbah, Pirqê de Rabbi Eliezer* and
Pesiqta de Rab Kahana, both Abraham and Isaac saw the divine presence
manifested on the sacrificial site, either as a cloud (*Gen. Rab./Pesiq.Rab
Kah.* cf., *Tg. Ps.-J.* v. 4) or as "a pillar of fire standing from the earth to
the heavens" (*Pirqê R. El.*). The two servants of Abraham, however, did
not see this divine revelation on the mountain.[723] The Midrashim (and

---

720 *Tg. Neof.,* vol. 1, Gen 22:12. Ed. Díez Macho 1968, 127, Eng. trans. McNamara/Maher
   1968, 552.
721 *Onqelos* has a somewhat different rendering of this verse: "… On this mountain did
   Abraham worship before the Lord." According to Aberbach and Grossfeld (1982,
   131, note 10) *Onqelos* connects יראה from the root ראה with the root ירא – to fear, thus
   'to worship'. See also Chester 1986, 67-73.
722 *Gen. Rab* 55.4.
723 *Gen. Rab.* 56.1, *Pirqê de Rabbi Eliezer* 31, *Pesiq. Rab Kah.* 26.4. As we have seen above,
   the angel of the Lord is connected in Exod 14:19 to the pillar of cloud leading and
   protecting the Israelites during their exodus from Egypt, but in Exod 13:21-22 and
   14:24 it is stated that it was YHWH who manifested Himself in this pillar. In Exodus
   3 it is the angel of the Lord who is manifested in the burning bush but it is YHWH

Tg. Ps.-J.) explain in this way how Abraham knew which place God had chosen for the act, compare Gen 22:2b: "... go to the land of Moriah, and offer him [Isaac] there as a burnt offering on one of the mountains that I shall show you." The statement that the two servants did not see the divine manifestation explains why Abraham did not take them with him to the mountain.[724]

In *Gen. Rab.* 56.4, it is stated that *the demonic angel Samael* tried to make first Abraham, then Isaac, withdraw from accomplishing God's command in Gen 22: 2. Isaac was thus aware of what was about to happen (cf., *b. Sanhedrin* 89b, see below).

From the Amoraic period onward, Samael[725] is the main name of Satan in Rabbinic Judaism.[726] In the Pseudepigrapha he is referred to as a Satanic figure in, for example, *3 Bar.* 4.8, *3 En.* 14.2[727] and the *Martyrdom and Ascension of Isaiah*. In the latter source the name Samael is used synonymously with Satan and Belial (e.g., chapter 2). In *Pseudo-Jonathan* chapter 3, Samael is equated with the serpent called 'the angel of death' that caused the fall of Adam and Eve (v. 6). In *Pirqê de Rabbi Eliezer* chapters 13-14, he is the tempter of mankind and the leader of the rebellious angels.

According to *Gen. Rab.* 56.5, when Abraham bound Isaac on the altar, the princes (*the guardian angels*, cf., Daniel 8 and 10) of the heathens were also bound. When Isaac's descendants, the people of Israel fall into sin, these fetters are, however, broken.[728]

---

who talks to Moses. According to *Pirqê de Rabbi Eliezer* 31 and *Tg. Ps.-J.* Gen 22:3, the two servants are Ishmael and Eliezer. In *Pirqê de Rabbi Eliezer*, we read that they quarreled about who should inherit Abraham after the death of Isaac. God interferes and puts an end to the discussion: "*The Holy Spirit* answered them, saying to them: Neither this one nor that one shall inherit."

724 Cf., Gen 22:4-5. See also *Gen. Rab.* 56.2, Eng. trans and comment Neusner 1985, 279. Cf., also Vermes' interpretation of 4Q225, see above.

725 The name is derived from the word *sami* / סמי meaning blind. Many Gnostic works refer to Samael as 'the blind god'. See Scholem 1971, 719.

726 See Scholem 1971, 719-722.

727 This source distinguishes between Satan and Samael, the latter being identified as the guardian angel of Rome; see *3 En.* 6.26.

728 The meaning is that, when Isaac was bound on the altar, the guardian angels of the heathens became subservient to Israel, but when Israel sins the heathens and their angels gain dominion over them. Cf., *Gen. Rab.* 56.9: "At the end of [after] all generations Israel will fall into the clutches of sin and be the victims of persecution; yet eventually they will be redeemed by the ram's horn, as it says, '*And the Lord God will blow the horn*', [...] the Holy One, blessed be He, said to him [Abraham, my addition]: 'So will thy children be entangled in countries, changing from Babylon to Media, from Media to Greece [...] yet they will eventually be redeemed by the ram's horn, as it is written, *And the Lord God will blow the ram's horn* [...] *the Lord of hosts will de-*

According to *Genesis Rabbah,* Abraham was very eager to sacrifice Isaac, in accordance with God's initial command, and the angel of the Lord has to emphasize that He (i.e., God) does not want him to hurt his son:

> AND THE ANGEL OF THE LORD CALLED UNTO HIM OUT OF HEA-VEN, AND SAID ABRAHAM, ABRAHAM (XXII, 11)…..AND HE SAID: LAY NOT THY HAND UPON THE LAD, etc. (XXII, 12). Where was the knife? *Tears had fallen from the angels* upon it and dissolved it. 'Then I will strangle him,' said he [Abraham] to Him. 'LAY NOT THY HAND UPON THE LAD,' was the reply. 'Let us bring forth a drop of blood from him,' he pleaded. 'NEITHER DO THOU ANY THING TO HIM,' He answered – inflict no blemish upon him. FOR NOW I KNOW–I have made known to all– that thou lovest Me … [my italics][729]

Both *Genesis Rabbah* and *Pirqê de Rabbi Eliezer* say that *the angels wept* when they saw Abraham stretching forth his hand to slaughter his son (cf., 4Q225). According to *Pirqê de Rabbi Eliezer, the angels beseeched God* to have mercy upon Isaac.[730] As shown above, *Genesis Rabbah* states that the *tears of the angels* dissolved the knife. The angels are also said to have cried out that God had broken his covenant with Abraham. God's response was that He will not profane His covenant and that His intention was never that Abraham should slaughter Isaac, only 'to take him up'/העלהו:

> When the Patriarch Abraham stretched forth his hand to take the knife to slay his son, the *angels wept* … [my italics]
>
> … And who says that this verse refers to the angels?–Here it says, UPON (MI – MA'AL) THE WOOD, while in another passage it says, *Above (mi-ma'al) Him stood the seraphim* (Isa VI, 2).[731]
>
> … The angels assembled in groups above. What did they cry? *The highways lie waste, the wayfaring man ceaseth; He hath broken the covenant, He hath despised the cities* (Isa XXXIII, 8) –has He no pleasure in Jerusalem and the Temple, which He had intended giving as a possession to the descendants of Isaac? …
>
> R. Aha said: [Abraham wondered]: Surely Thou too indulgest in prevarication! Yesterday Thou saidest, *For in Isaac shall seed be called to thee* (Gen XXI,12); Thou didst then retract and say, *Take now thy son* (ib. XXII, 2);

---

fend them …" The quote is from Zech 9:14-15. See also Deut 32:8-9 according to the LXX.

729 *Gen. Rab.* 56.7. Niehoff (1995, 79) compares the role of the angel in the Aqedah with the role of the angel in the story about Balaam in Numbers 22. According to Num 22:20-21, Balaam is relying on God's command when he agrees to follow the Moabites, but he is prevented from cursing Israel by the angel of the Lord, Num 22:22-35.

730 *Pirqê de Rabbi Eliezer* 31.

731 *Gen. Rab.* 56.5.

while now Thou biddest me, LAY NOT THY HAND UPON THE LAD!
Said the Holy One, blessed be He, to him: 'O Abraham, *My covenant will I
not profane* (Ps LXXXIX, 35), *And I will establish My covenant with Isaac* (Gen
XVII, 21). When I bade thee, "*Take now thy son,*" etc., *I will not alter that
which is gone out of My lips* (Ps. loc. cit.). Did I tell thee, Slaughter him? No!
but, "*Take him up*". Thou hast taken him up. Now take him down.'[732]

Abraham is thus depicted as having misunderstood God. The reason
for the trial was to make known Abraham's love of God in the world.[733]
According to Maren Niehoff, the purpose of this interpretation is to
justify God.[734]

The angel of the Lord in Gen 22:11-12 who prevents Abraham from
completing the sacrifice is clearly distinguished from the weeping angels. *Genesis Rabbah* has no unequivocal comment upon the identity of
the "angel"/messenger of YHWH. In the above cited passage however,
Abraham appears to identify him as God: "...Thou didst then retract
and say, *Take now thy son* (ib. XXII, 2), while now Thou biddest me,
LAY NOT THY HAND UPON THE LAD!" It seems implied that the
"angel"/messenger is to be understood as God, who as a result of Abraham's faithfulness swears by Himself to bless him... (cf., Gen 22:15-
18).[735]

Likewise, in *Pirqê de Rabbi Eliezer*, it is said that Isaac's soul left his
body because of the tremor when the blade of the knife touched his
neck but that it returned when he heard *God's voice*

> ... *from between the two Cherubim*, saying (to Abraham), 'Lay not thy hand
> upon the lad' [...] And Isaac knew that in this manner the dead in the fu-

---

732 *Gen. Rab.* 56.8.

733 *Gen. Rab.* 56.5-8, *Pirqê de Rabbi Eliezer* 31. See also *Gen. Rab.* 60.2: " '*Shall have rule over
a son that putteth to shame*': this alludes to Isaac, who put all idolaters to shame when
he was bound upon the altar ..."

734 Niehoff 1995, 75.

735 *Gen. Rab.* 56.11. In the later *Midrash Wa-Yosha* 37-38, the angel of the Lord in Gen
22:11-12 is identified with the *archangel Michael*. Abraham, however, refuses to listen
to him and says: "God did command me to slaughter Isaac, and thou dost command
me not to slaughter him! The words of the Teacher and the words of the disciple–
unto whose words doth one hearken? Then Abraham heard it said: "By Myself have
I sworn, saith the Lord ..." In this Midrash we also find traces of the legend that the
angels were critical of the creation of humankind. God says to the angels: "Had I
hearkened unto you at the time of the creation of the world, when ye spake, What is
man, That Thou art mindful of him? And the son of man, that Thou visitest him? (Ps
8) who would there have been to make known the unity of My Name in this world?"
Eng. trans. Ginzberg, *The Legends of the Jews* vol. 1, 1942, 281-282.

ture will be quickened. He opened (his mouth) and said: 'Blessed art thou, O Lord, who quickeneth the dead.'[736]

The reason for Isaac's later bad eyesight (Gen 27:1) is said to be that he saw *the glory of the Shekinah* as he lay bound on the altar.[737]

In accordance with the biblical account, Isaac is not sacrificed in *Pirqê de Rabbi Eliezer*, and the ram takes his place on the altar.[738] However, it is said that the *demonic angel Samael* tried to distract the ram in order to annul Abraham's sacrifice. According to *Pirqê de Rabbi Eliezer*, it is Samael who was also responsible for the death of Sarah (Gen 23:1, cf., *Tg. Ps.-J.*).[739] In *Pesiqta de Rab Kahana*, on the other hand, it is Isaac himself who tells Sarah about the event and that he would have been sacrificed if *God/'the Holy One'* had not stopped Abraham. Sarah is so shocked that she dies.[740]

The Babylonian Talmud, the Targum to Chronicles and Mekilta de Rabbi Ishmael

Sanhedrin 89b

In the Babylonian Talmud tractate *Sanhedrin* 89b, Satan plays the same role in the Aqedah as Prince Mastema in *Jubilees*. In this interpretation

---

736 *Pirqê de Rabbi Eliezer* 31. The blessing of Isaac is taken from the second benediction of the *Shemoneh 'Esreh/* the Amida. The prayer originally included 18 benedictions (hence its name) but a 19th was added at a later stage, perhaps a polemic against Jewish Christians. It is thus one of the oldest prayers in the Jewish liturgy and constitutes to this day the central part of the Synagogue-service. Isaac's rescue is connected in Jewish thought to the resurrection of the dead. Cf., *Gen. Rab.* 56.1; Heb 11:17-18 and Rom 4:13-25.

737 *Pirqê de Rabbi Eliezer* 32. See also *Gen. Rab.* 65.10, where it is stated that the later bad eyesight of Isaac was caused by the tears of the angels falling into his eyes during the Aqedah. In *Tg. Ps.-J.* Gen 27:1, it is stated that Isaac's eye-problem was caused by the fact that he had looked upon the Throne of Glory while tied to the altar.

738 *Pirqê de Rabbi Eliezer* makes a connection between the pregnancy of Rebekah as an answer to prayer and the binding of Isaac at Moriah:

Rabbi Jehudah said: Rebecca was barren for twenty years. After twenty years (Isaac) took Rebecca and went (with her) to Mount Moriah, to the place where he had been bound, and he prayed on her behalf concerning the conception of the womb; and the Holy One, blessed be He, was entreated of him ... [*Pirqê de Rabbi Eliezer* 32. See also *Tg. Ps.-J.* to Gen 25:21].

739 *Pirqê de Rabbi Eliezer* 31 and 32.

740 *Pesiqta de Rab Kahana* 26.

of the Aqedah, it is also stated that Satan tried to get Abraham to waiver in his faith but failed, cf., *Gen. Rab.* 56.4, see above.

Berakot 62b

Another Talmudic tractate, *Berakot 62b*, records a Rabbinic discussion connected to the Aqedah. The text discussed in the tractate is 1 Chr 21:15:

> And God sent an angel to Jerusalem to destroy it. As he was destroying, the *Lord looked* [or saw: ראה] and relented of the disaster, and said to the *angel who was destroying* [מלאך המשחית] "It is enough, now restrain your hand." And *the angel of the Lord* stood by the threshing floor of Ornan the Jebusite.

What was it that the *Lord saw* that made him stop the destroying angel? One of the Talmudic Rabbis claims that it was *the ashes of Isaac that the Lord saw*.

The Targum to Chronicles

The above mentioned interpretation of the Aqedah is also found in the *Targum to Chronicles*:

> [1 Chr 21:15] Then *the Memra of the Lord* sent *the* angel *of the pestilence* to Jerusalem to destroy it. When he was destroying it, *he* observed *the ashes of the binding of Isaac which were at the base of the altar and he remembered his covenant with Abraham which he had set up with him on the mountain of worship; (he observed) the sanctuary-house which was above, where the souls of the righteous are, and the image of Jacob which was engraved on the throne of glory,* and he repented *in himself* of the evil *which he had planned to do*. So he said to the destroying angel: *"You* have had enough …"[741]

According to 2 Chr 3:1, the threshing floor of Ornan the Jebusite was the site of King Solomon's Temple. There is thus a Rabbinic connection between the Aqedah and 1 Chr 21:15 based on the verb ראה, 'see', which occurs in both pericopes.[742] It is clear that the angel of the Lord/the destroying angel in 1 Chr 21:15 is distinguished from God himself.

---

741 The words in italics are the targumic additions/interpretations of the Hebrew original.

742 See also Spiegel 1993, 38-44. Spiegel refers to a Rabbinic tradition claiming that the ram which was sacrificed in the place of Isaac bore his very name, i.e. the ram was called Isaac. According to Spiegel, the ashes of Isaac probably allude to the ashes of the ram. In *Pirqê de Rabbi Eliezer* 31, we read: "The ashes of the ram were the base which was upon the top of the inner altar." According to *Gen. Rab.* 56.10, the phrase 'Where the Lord is seen' in Gen 22:14 refers to the presence of the Lord in the rebuilt Temple during the Messianic era. Mount Moriah is the place of salvation. According to Rabbinic tradition, Abraham's ram was created at twilight on the first Sabbath eve of the week of creation. See, e.g., *Num. Rab.* 17.2, Eng. trans. Slotki 1939, 700.

Mekilta de Rabbi Ishmael

In *Mekilta de Rabbi Ishmael*, the Aqedah is connected to the Jewish Passover, Pesach. The blood of the paschal lamb sprinkled on the doors of the Israelites in Exodus 12 is said to remind God of the blood of Isaac:

> He seeth the blood of the sacrifice of Isaac, as it is said: *"And Abraham called the name of that place Adonai-jireh" (the Lord will see)*, etc. (Gen 22.14). And it is also written: "and as He was about to destroy, the *Lord beheld* and repented Him" (1 Chron. 21.15). What did He behold? He beheld the blood of the sacrifice of Isaac, as it is said: *"God will Himself see the lamb for a burnt-offering"* (Gen 22.8). [743]

In Jewish liturgy today, the Aqedah is connected to Rosh haShana. One important ritual during this festival is the blowing of the shofar, the ram's horn, to remind God of the binding of Isaac and the ram that was sacrificed in his place. The connection between Rosh haShana, the Aqedah and this ritual is very ancient, see *Gen. Rab.* 56.9.[744]

In Jewish belief, God rises from the throne of Judgment and moves to the throne of Mercy when He hears the sound of the shofar.[745] According to Niehoff, the crying angels in, for example, *Genesis Rabbah*, indicate the 'feminine,' emotional side of God, the divine mercy.[746]

This leads us to the Rabbinic interpretation of the different designations of God in Gen 22:1-19, YHWH, and Elohim. According to the Rabbis the name YHWH refers to the mercy of God, while Elohim refers to divine justice. It is thus no coincidence that it is *God/Elohim* who commands Abraham to sacrifice Isaac but the angel of the *Lord/YHWH* who prevents Abraham from slaughtering him. This may, however, be a somewhat later interpretation of our pericope although the interpretation of the divine "names" in the Bible is ancient.[747]

However, Robert Hayward points out that the targumic tradition does not seem to make any distinction between the designations YHWH and Elohim and, as has been demonstrated, the Targums usually employ the name YHWH, even where the MT has Elohim. Accord-

---

743 *Mekilta de Rabbi Ishmael,* vol. 1 Pisha 11.90-95. See also Pisha 7.78-82, p. 57. It is noteworthy that it is not clear in the MT Exod 12:22-28 whether it was God Himself who killed the firstborn sons of the Egyptians, because in v. 23b it seems as if God used *the Destroyer* to carry out this task. This issue is, however, not discussed here in *Mekilta de Rabbi Ishmael*. See also John 8:56: "Your ancestor Abraham rejoiced that he would see my day; he saw it and was glad."

744 See also *b. Rosh haShana* 16a, *m. Ta'an.* 2.4, Jacobs 1971, 481-482, Lewis 1971, 1443-1447, and Spiegel 1993, 51-59.

745 *Lev. Rab.* 29.4, 10, see also Jacobs 1971, 309.

746 Niehoff 1995, 75.

747 Spiegel 1993, 121-124.

ing to Hayward, it is the epithet 'the Memra' which signifies God's mercy in the Targums[748] and, as we have seen, it appears in the targumic renderings of "the angel's" promise to Abraham in v. 16, e.g., *Onqelos*: "… by My Memra I swear, says the Lord…"

Concluding Remarks

We may conclude that Abraham's final trial, the Aqedah, is depicted as a crucial event that highly engages the angelic world. According to the Babylonian Talmud, *Sanhedrin* 89b, Satan questions Abraham's piety and in this way provokes God to test him. The words in Gen 22:1; "After these things God tested Abraham …" in this Talmudic tractate thus refer to satanic activity, which forms the reason for the trial. According to Talmud, Satan later tries to make Abraham waiver in his faith, compare *Gen. Rab.* 56.4. The transfer of the initiative for a questionable act from God to Satan already appears in the Bible itself, see 1 Sam 24:1 and 1 Chr 21:1.[749]

According to *Pirqê de Rabbi Eliezer*, the demonic angel Samael is responsible for the death of Sarah (Gen 23:1) and in *Pseudo-Jonathan* Satan plays this role. Thus, we encounter to some extent a dualistic worldview in some of our sources. Although God is in control, he also has enemies in the heavenly realms.

However, the angels of God are also engaged in the Aqedah. According to *Gen. Rab.* 55.4, the angels were jealous of Abraham, which caused God to put him on trial in order to demonstrate Abraham's faithfulness.[750]

In many of our sources the angels of God play a more benevolent role. This applies to the Palestinian Targums (Gen 22:10) and the Midrashim *Pirqê de Rabbi Eliezer* and *Genesis Rabbah*. In the last two works, the holy angels are even said to have wept in compassion for Isaac. The angels pray that God will show him and Abraham mercy. The angels accuse God of having broken the covenant with Abraham, e.g., *Gen. Rab.* 56.8. Perhaps the angels were not aware that it was "only" a trial? Niehoff interprets the angels as representing God's merciful side.

---

748 Hayward 1981, 39-56.
749 Cf., also the LXX Exod 4:24, and *Jub.* 17.16, see chapters 3 and 4.2. It should be noted that, according to the *Targum of Chronicles* 21:15, God eventually stops the destroying angel because of the ashes of Isaac.
750 Cf., *L.A.B.* 32.1-2, see chapter 4.2.

Pseudo-Jonathan states that after the trial Isaac was brought by the angels to the school of Shem the Great, possibly because it is said in the biblical text that Abraham returned alone to his servants (Gen 22:19).

It may well be that the biblical angel of the Lord has inspired all these 'angel speculations' in the interpretations of the text. The angel's calling to Abraham in Gen 22:11 may have been understood as an indication that the angels had watched the scenario on Mount Moriah; how else could one of them interfere in the course of events?[751] Or is the presence and interest of the angels due to the importance of the Aqedah? Perhaps both answers encompass truth.

The angel of the Lord seems to have *a special status* in all of the sources, he is distinguished from the weeping angels/the angels of the heights in *Genesis Rabbah* and the Palestinian Targums. This is in many ways reminiscent of the difference between God who is standing above the ladder[752] and the angels ascending and descending on it in Gen 28:12-15 (cf., Gen 31:11-13, where God's angel seems to identify himself with God).

The portrayal of the angel of the Lord in all of the Targums is quite similar to the biblical version, most certainly because of the fact that the *meturgeman* was bound by the wording of the Hebrew original to a higher degree than, for example, the author/redactor of *Pirqê de Rabbi Eliezer*. The ambivalence of God and His angel remains in the targumic versions of the pericope. As usual, the Targums employ the epithet 'the Memra'.

The Aqedah is considered a decisive event in the history of salvation, being connected to Pesach (*Mekilta de Rabbi Ishmael*) and Rosh ha-Shana (*Gen. Rab.* 56.9). Abraham sees 'a cloud of glory'/ 'a pillar of fire' on the mountain (*Gen. Rab.*, *Tg. Ps.-J.*, Genizah fragment, *Pirqê R. El.*, *Pesiq. Rab Kah.*). God's presence, the Shekinah, is said to be manifested on the sacrificial site, which is identified as the future Temple Mount (e.g., the Palestinian Targums, *Genesis Rabbah* and *Pirqê de Rabbi Eliezer*). Because of the Aqedah, the Israelites were rescued from the last plague in Egypt and Jerusalem spared from destruction. Gen 22:14 is commented with the phrase 'God sees the blood/ashes of Isaac' (*Mekilta de Rabbi Ishmael*, *b. Berakot* 62b, the *Targum to Chronicles*, cf., *m. Ta'an.* 2.1, 4).

It was never God's intention that Abraham should sacrifice Isaac. The purpose of the trial was not to prove something to God, who is

---

751 Cf., the Palestinian Targums, where the angels are mentioned in the preceding verse; Gen 22:10.

752 Or: beside Jacob.

omniscient, but to demonstrate Abraham's faithfulness to God before the surrounding world, both in the heavenly and in the earthly realms, see, for example, *Genesis Rabbah*. This interpretation is probably based on an attempt to justify God. However, on this point the Targums are quite similar to the Bible (Gen 22:12), most certainly due to their character as "translations," although in his prayer in v. 14 Abraham declares God's omniscience.

Niehoff interprets the role of the angels in *Genesis Rabbah* in the light of the Rabbinic concept that the divine name YHWH represents the attribute of Mercy, while Elohim is connected to the divine Justice and Judgment.

As in the Bible, the identity of the angel of the Lord is ambiguous; is he "merely" a spokesman for YHWH, or is he in fact a manifestation of YHWH himself? The second alternative seems the most probable but I cannot find a clear answer in our sources. The focus is not on the identity of the angel but on the main characters, Abraham and Isaac.

4.5.4 The Wooing of Rebekah According to *Genesis Rabbah*

Of our Rabbinic sources, *Genesis Rabbah* is the only one that has a relatively elaborated interpretation of Genesis 24 including the role of the angel.[753] We read in *Gen. Rab.* 59.8 that it was Abraham who made God known in the world:

AND I WILL MAKE THEE[754] SWEAR BY THE LORD, THE GOD OF HEAVEN AND THE GOD OF THE EARTH (XXIV, 3).[755] R. Phineas said:

---

753 The targumic rendering of Genesis 24 is fairly literal. All the Targums state that Abraham says in v. 7 that God will send/appoint His angel to go with the servant, in order to ensure the success of the journey. In *Neofiti* the divine guide is called the 'the angel of mercy', v. 7. According to Guiley (2004, 39), angels of mercy stand at the right hand of God in the heavenly court of law in the seventh heaven. These angels are present at the judgment of humans. Most of the angels of mercy are not named. Among the angels whose names are known, we may mention e.g., Gabriel, Michael, Zadkiel and Uziel, who are subordinate to Metatron. *Pirqê de Rabbi Eliezer* 32 mentions that Isaac married his relative Rebekah, but the Midrash does not make any reference to the angel or the journey of the servant.

754 The servant of Abraham is identified as Eliezer in *Gen. Rab.* 59.9, cf., Gen 15:2.

755 According to *Gen. Rab.* 59.8, the commandment of Abraham to his servant to "...put your hand under my thigh..." in Gen 24:2 refers to the covenant of circumcision. Sarna remarks that the divine title 'the Lord, the God of heaven and the God of the earth' is unique in biblical literature. He writes: "In light of the fact that the mission involves travel to a distant land, it makes sense to invoke God's universal sovereignty. The epithet may be a monotheistic version of an ancient Near Eastern oath for-

[Abraham said]: 'Before I made Him known to His creatures He was the GOD OF HEAVEN; now that I have made Him known to His creatures, He is the GOD OF THE EARTH.

According to Rabbi Dosa, the angel who followed the servant is a particular one.[756] The Rabbi continues:

When our father Abraham said, HE WILL SEND HIS ANGEL BEFORE THEE, the Holy One, blessed be He, appointed two angels for him, one to bring out Rebekah,[757]and the other to accompany Eliezer.[758]

The single angel in Gen 24:7 has thus become *two* angels in the Midrash's understanding of the verse. As we have seen, according to the ancient Rabbis, one angel does not perform two missions. One angel was appointed to guide and protect the servant on his journey, while the other had the commission to arrange the meeting of Eliezer and Rebekah.[759]

The theme of divine guidance penetrates the commentary to the pericope in *Genesis Rabbah*. For example, according to one interpretation, the Midrash alludes to Isa 50:10 and identifies Eliezer as the servant of God who walks in darkness, only to have his path illuminated by God by means of meteors and lightning (*Gen. Rab.* 60.1).

The prayer of the servant in Gen 24:12 is interpreted as an invocation of the merits of the patriarchs, since he prays accordingly: "O LORD God of my *master Abraham*, please grant me success today, and show steadfast love to my master Abraham ..." According to Rabbi Haggai, this verse also teaches us that we all need God's kindness, even

---

mula in which the gods of heaven and earth were invoked as witnesses" (Sarna 1989, 162). For heaven and earth as witnesses, see Deut 4:26; 30:19; 31:29; 32:1, and Isa 1:2. The divine title 'God of heaven' is also found in, e.g., Jonah 1:9; Esra 1:2; 2 Chr 36:23; Dan 2:18 and Tob 5:17.

756 *Gen. Rab.* 59.10. According to a modern Jewish commentator, the midrashic view that a particular angel is meant is based on the fact that the angel in Gen 24:7 is called "*His* [God's] angel", rather than *an* [unspecified] angel. The angel in question is either Michael or the angel in charge of marriage. See Zlotowitz 1978, 901.

757 That is, bring her out to the well.

758 *Gen. Rab.* 59.10.

759 Jacob, Eliezer, and Hagar are compared in a comment on Gen 32:4 [v. 3 in the NRSV] in *Gen. Rab.* 75.4, where the Rabbis claim that the messengers whom Jacob sent before him were literally angels, because;

... If an angel escorted Eliezer, who was but a servant of the house, how much more to this one [Jacob], who was the beloved of the house! R. Hama b. Hanina observed: Hagar was but Sarah's handmaid, yet five angels appeared to her, how much more to this man [Jacob] who was the beloved of the house!

Abraham: "... who prophesied and said, He will send His angel before thee (ib.7), was yet in need of kindness ..." (*Gen. Rab.* 60.2).[760]

God was quick in answering the prayer: "Before he had finished speaking, there was Rebekah, who was born to Bethuel, son of Milcha, the wife of Nahor, Abraham's brother, coming out ..." (v. 15). Rabbi Simeon b. Yohai points out that Eliezer is one of the three persons in the Bible whose petitions were answered while their prayers were still on their lips, the other two being Moses and Solomon (*Gen. Rab.* 60.4).[761] The marriage of Isaac and Rebekah is thus understood by the Rabbis of *Genesis Rabbah* as a divine arrangement.

As in the Bible, the activity of the angel(s) is very much relegated to the background of the story. *Genesis Rabbah* does not even make any reference to the servant's repetition of Abraham's promise of angelic protection in v. 40. However, in contrast to the Bible, the Midrash refers to Isaac's guardian angel in its description of the first meeting of Isaac and Rebekah, *Gen. Rab.* 60.15:

> AND SHE [Rebekah] SAID UNTO THE SERVANTS: WHAT MAN IS THIS (HA-LAZEH) THAT WALKETH IN THE FIELD TO MEET US (XXIV, 65)? R. Berekiah said in the name of R. Hiyya his father: She saw that he [Isaac] was comely, [*ha-lazeh* having the same meaning] as in the verse, *Behold, this* (ha-lazeh) *dreamer cometh* (Gen. XXXVII, 19).[762] The Rabbis said: It refers to his guardian (angel), *halazeh* meaning, This one [the angel] is for his service.[763]

Concluding Remarks

Belief in divine providence is a key issue in *Genesis Rabbah*'s exposition of Genesis 24. God had already appointed Rebekah to be the wife of Isaac. This is evident in, for example, the interpretation of the words of Abraham in Gen 24:7 as prophetic.

The universality of YHWH is underlined in *Genesis Rabbah*. He is the God of both heaven and earth and not limited to the boundaries of Canaan, the Promised Land. Abraham is credited as the one who made God known to the world.

---

760 According to ibn Ezra, Abraham did not prophecy in v. 7 but he *prayed*: "May he send his angel before you ..." See Zlotowitz 1978, 901.

761 *Genesis Rabbah* refers here to Num 16:31 (Moses) and 2 Chr 7:1 (Solomon).

762 Isaac is here compared to Joseph.

763 Freedman/Simon (1939, 538) have in note 2 an explicative comment to the Midrash: "Reading *halazeh* as *elaw zeh*, he is for him." Curiously enough, Raphael is said to be the preceptor angel of Isaac. Lewis/Oliver 1996, 342.

The theme of divine guidance dominates the commentary of Genesis 24. The prayer of the servant, identified as Eliezer, plays a central role. It is stated that in his prayers Eliezer invoked the merits of the patriarch Abraham. The marriage of Isaac and Rebekah is understood as an answer to prayer, a divine arrangement.

As in the Bible, the angelic involvement is relegated to the background of the story in *Genesis Rabbah.*[764] However, there is a short comment on Abraham's reference to the angel in Gen 24:7. According to Rabbi Dosa, God appointed *two* angels to accomplish the task of finding a wife for Isaac. Since, according to the Rabbinic view, one angel does not perform two missions, one angel was appointed to accompany Eliezer on his journey and the other to arrange his meeting with Rebekah. The angels manifest God's guidance and help but are apparently depicted as distinct from God.

The angel(s) is (are) not mentioned any further in *Genesis Rabbah's* commentary on the narrative. The Midrash does not have any rendering of the servant's repetition of Abraham's promise of angelic guidance in v. 40. But in contrast to the Bible, *Genesis Rabbah* mentions Isaac's guardian angel in its description of the first meeting of Isaac and Rebekah. It is, however, unclear whether this angel has any connection to Eliezer's match-making journey.

4.5.5 Jacob and the Angel

Jacob's Dream at Bethel

The Glory of the Lord over Jacob
As usual, *Onqelos'* rendering of Genesis 28 is quite literal, but there are some minor differences between the MT and the Targum. In verse 13 we read: "And behold, *the Glory of the Lord* [יקרא דיי] was standing over [עילווהי] *him* [Jacob] and He said, 'I am the Lord, the God of your father Abraham...'"[765] Instead of referring to God directly, as in the Bible; "...

---

764 Cf., Philo's interpretation of the pericope.
765 According to the translators Aberbach/Grossfeld; "... since the subject of TO [*Tg. Onq.*] is not God Himself but 'the Glory of the Lord,' it could be depicted as standing above Jacob. The possibility that TO עילווהי refers to the ladder is less likely." Aberbach/Grossfeld 1982, note 6, p. 170. In *Tg. Onq.* Gen 28:12 the angels are said to be going up and down on the ladder (and not on Jacob, see the discussion below). This verse in *Onqelos* is almost identical to the MT-rendering. See Aberbach/Grossfeld 1982, p. 168 (Eng. trans.) and p. 169 (Aramaic text).

the Lord stood above it [the ladder]/him."[766] *Onqelos* uses the typical targumic concept 'the glory of the Lord' in order to avoid anthropomorphism.[767] However, in v. 15, the Targum has chosen another frequent circumscription for God: "And behold, my *Memra* [lit. 'Word'] will assist you, and I will watch over you wherever you go ..." In v. 16b, when Jacob awakes, according to the Targum he exclaims: "... In truth the Glory of the Lord dwells in this place[768], and I did not know it." However, in his subsequent vow, Jacob refers to the Memra of the Lord: "If the Memra of the Lord will assist me, and protect me on this journey [...] and I return in peace to my father's house–then the Memra of the Lord shall be my God" (vv. 20a, 21).[769] There is thus a correspondence between vv. 13 and 16 as well as between vv. 15, 20, and 21.

Unfortunately, the only preserved verses of Genesis 28 in the *Fragment Targums* are vv. 10, 12, 17 (P) and vv. 10 and 12 (V), and in the Cairo Genizah only vv. 17-22 are extant. The other Palestinian Targums contain a complete rendering of the chapter.

Neofiti has a literal rendering of Gen 28:13 and thus refers to God directly: "And the Lord stood beside him [Jacob] and said ..."[770] However, in a *Neofiti* Marginal gloss there is a noteworthy deviation from the MT; "an *angel of mercy* from before the Lord stood placed beside him ..."[771] Thus, according to this version, it was not God Himself who addressed Jacob in Bethel, but an angel! This interpretation is most probably influenced by Gen 31:11-13, where 'the angel of God' identifies himself as the God who appeared to Jacob in Bethel.

Pseudo-Jonathan refers to the divine revelation in v. 13 in the same manner as *Onqelos*: "And behold, *the Glory of* the Lord stood beside

---

766 Or: "... the Lord stood beside him/it ..." My translation.

767 See also Aberbach/Grossfeld 1982, note 5, p. 170.

768 According to Aberbach/Grossfeld, the Rabbis sought to associate the place of Jacob's dream with the Jerusalem Temple. See also Gen 28:17 in *Onqelos* and Aberbach/Grossfeld 1982, note 14, p. 171. This interpretation also seems to be implied in the Palestinian Targums to Gen 28:11, 17, see below. See also Maher 1992, 99-100, and McNamara 1992, 139-140.

769 According to Grossfeld (1988, note 12 to *Tg. Onq.* Gen 21:20), the targumic usage of the Memra is very common whenever God is depicted as assisting, protecting, defending or preserving man. See the chapter on Hagar and the angel above. See also McNamara 1992, 28.

770 Note that the Targum refers to Jacob, not the ladder. The Rabbis of *Genesis Rabbah* are of differing opinions concerning this matter. See *Gen. Rab.* 69.3.

771 Cf., *Neofiti*'s rendering of Gen 24:7, see note 753 above.

him ..." According to both *Neofiti* and *Pseudo-Jonathan* in Gen 28:16, Jacob refers to "... the *Glory of the Shekinah* of the Lord ..."[772]

Jacob's vow to God

The rendering of Jacob's vow differs slightly between *Neofiti* and *Pseudo-Jonathan*.[773]

Neofiti	*Pseudo-Jonathan*
[Gen 28:20] And <Jacob>[774] made a vow, saying: "If *the Lord* [ייי] *is at my aid,* and protects me	[Gen 28:20] And Jacob swore saying, "If the Memra of the Lord [מימרא דייי] comes to my assistance, and keeps me
	from shedding innocent blood, (from) idol worship, and (from) sexual immorality,
on the road on which I journey and gives me bread to eat and clothes to clothe myself,	on this journey on which I am going, and (if) he gives me bread to eat and clothing to wear,
[21] and (if) I return in peace to the house of my father, and (if) the Lord is for me a *redeeming* God, [ויהוי ייי לי לאלה פריק...][775]	[21] and (if) I return in peace to my father's house,
	the Lord shall be my God,
[22] (then) this stone which I set as a pillar will be *a sanctuary to the name of the Lord* ..."	[22] and this stone which I have placed as a pillar shall be *arranged as a sanctuary of the Lord, and the generations shall worship upon it to the Name of the Lord* ..."[776]

---

772 Cf., *Gen. Rab.* 69.7: "AND HE SAID: SURELY (AKEN) THE LORD IS IN THIS PLACE, AND KNEW IT NOT (ib.). Where (ekan) dwells the Shechinah? IN THIS PLACE, yet I did not know [...] R. Judah b. R. Simon said: This ladder stood on the Temple site...." In *Gen. Rab.* 68.12, the ladder is also said to represent the altar in the Temple and the angels its priests, see below.

773 The words in italics are the targumic deviations from the Hebrew text, see the editors' foreword to McNamara's English translation of *Neofiti*, 1992, viii.

774 "Jacob" is missing in the text.

775 *Neofiti* marginal gloss; "the Memra of the Lord is at my aid as a redeemer God." See McNamara, 1992, 141. Aramaic text, Díez Macho (ed.) 1968, 181.

776 The pillar is thus connected to the Temple in Jerusalem, see further below, cf., also the discussion of John 1:51 below.

In the same way as *Onqelos*, both of the Targums use the divine designation Lord/YHWH in Gen 28:20 and not God/Elohim as in the MT. As *Onqelos*, *Pseudo-Jonathan* refers to 'the Memra of the Lord'.[777] According to all the Targums, Jacob invokes the help of God in these verses, but *Pseudo-Jonathan* contains a unique moral aspect, not present in the others.[778] However, in contrast to *Neofiti*, the end of v. 21 in *Pseudo-Jonathan* is identical to that in the MT. In this verse the wording of the former recalls Gen 48:15-16, where Jacob invokes God in prayer and says: "...the God who has been my shepherd all my life to this day, the angel who has *redeemed me* from all harm, bless the boys; ..."

Miracles on the way to Haran

All of the Targums have an expanded version of v. 10 with a fairly similar content. According to the Targums, Jacob experienced no less than five miracles when he left his homeland to go to Laban in Haran. One of the miracles was that God made the sun set before its time because He desired to speak to Jacob. The Targums employ here yet another circumscription for God; 'the Dibbera'.[779] One of the other miracles is said to be that, in the morning, the stones that Jacob placed under his head had merged into one single stone.[780] Both of these miracles are discussed in *Genesis Rabbah*; concerning the first we read:

> [*Gen. Rab.* 68.10] The Rabbis said: This teaches us that the Holy One, blessed be He, caused the sun to set prematurely, in order to speak in privacy with our Father Jacob.[781]

Jacob's image in heaven

Neofiti and the *Fragment Targums* (mss P and V) have an almost identical rendering of Gen 28:12. However, there is one small but significant difference between them; while *Neofiti* says that Jacob's image is *engraved* in the throne of Glory, according to ms V, the version in the

---

777 But there is no reference to the Memra in v. 21, as in *Onqelos*, see above.

778 The same interpretation is to be found in *Gen. Rab.* 70.4.

779 Alternate forms are 'the Debbira/Dibbura'. This concept is a counterpart to 'the Memra'. In the words of McNamara (1992, 38): "In Hebrew, *dibberah* is the *nomen actionis* of the verb *dibber* ('to speak') and means 'divine discourse', 'revelation'. In the earlier Tannaitic period the form generally used in Jewish sources is *dibber*, while in the later Amoraic age it is *dibbûr*. *Dibbera, debira, dibbur(a)*, or however we write the words, signifies God as revealing his will to man."

780 This miracle is most certainly linked to the traditions of the holiness of the stone at Bethel. For a discussion of these traditions and their possible connection to John 1:51, see below.

781 Concerning the miracle of the stones, see *Gen. Rab.* 68.11 and *b. Hullin* 91a-b.

Fragment Targums states that Jacob's image is *on* the throne of Glory.[782]
As the differences between the two Targums are minor, I quote the
complete verse in *Neofiti* but only the last part of the verse in the *Fragment Targums* (ms V):

> [*Tg. Neof.* Gen 28:12] And he [Jacob] dreamed, and behold, a ladder was
> fixed on the earth and its head reached to the height of the heavens; and
> behold, the angels *that had accompanied him from the house of his father as-*
> *cended to bear good tidings to the angels on high, saying: "Come and see the pious*
> *man whose image is engraved in the throne of Glory, whom you desired to see."*
> And behold, the angels *from before the Lord* ascended and descended *and ob-*
> *served him.*
>
> [*Frg. Tg.* (V) Gen 28:12b] ... "Come and see Jacob, the pious man,
> whose image is on the throne of glory whom you have desired to see;" and
> behold the holy angels from before the Lord were ascending and descend-
> ing, gazing upon him.[783]

Both Targums state that Jacob had been accompanied by angels when
he left his home, and these angels now ascended back to heaven and
told their fellow angels that they now had an opportunity to get a
glimpse of the man "whose image is on/engraved in the throne of
Glory."

According to James Kugel, this midrashic paraphrase may be an attempt to answer the question as to why the Bible depicts the angels as
going up and down, in that order. The angels who had accompanied
Jacob went up and told others, who then went down in order to look at
Jacob. But the rendering of the verse in the Targums seems to suggest
that the angels kept going up and down looking at both Jacob's portrait
in heaven and the man himself asleep on the ground.[784]

As we have seen, this interpretation is presumably inspired by the
fact that it is linguistically possible to understand the Hebrew word בו

---

782 According to ms P, the *Fragment Targums* has here "... the pious man [Jacob], whose
     image is *fixed* to the throne of glory ..." See also Fossum 1995, 141-142, Rowland
     1984, 498-507, and the discussion of John 1:51 below.
783 This tradition is also attested in the baraitha in *b. Hullin* 91b:

> ... A Tanna taught: They [the angels] ascended to look at the image above and de-
> scended to look at the image below. They wished to hurt him, when Behold the Lord
> stood beside him [Jacob].

Here the angels are depicted as jealous of Jacob, but God protects him. Cf., the role
of the angels at the Aqedah in *L.A.B.* 32:1-2.
784 Kugel 1990, 114. See also Rowland 1984, 500-506.

in Gen 28:12b as referring to Jacob, and not the ladder, thus the rendering; "(up)on *him* [Jacob]/ because of him/for his sake."[785]

The idea that Jacob's portrait is engraved on God's throne is also attested in the *Targum to Chronicles*:

> [1 Chr 21:15] Then *the Memra of the Lord* sent *the* angel *of the pestilence* to Jerusalem to destroy it. When he was destroying it, *he* observed *the ashes of the binding of Isaac which were at the base of the altar, and he remembered his covenant with Abraham which he had set up with him on the mountain of worship, (he observed) the sanctuary-house which was above, where the souls of the righteous are, and the image of Jacob which was engraved on the throne of glory,* and he repented *in himself ...*

We also find the tradition referred to above in many Midrashim, see, for example, *Gen. Rab.* 68.12:[786]

> Shalmoni said in the name of Resh Lakish: He showed him [Jacob] a throne of three legs. R. Joshua of Sikin said in R. Levi's name: [God said to him]: 'Thou art the third leg.' That indeed is the view of R. Joshua in R. Levi's name, who said: *For the portion of the Lord is His people, Jacob the cord of His inheritance* (Deut. XXXII, 19): as a cord cannot be woven of less than three strands [so there were no less than three patriarchs]...
>
> R. Hiyya the elder and R. Jannai disagreed. One maintained: They were ASCENDING AND DESCENDING on the ladder; while the other said: they were ASCENDING AND DESCENDING on Jacob [...] Thus it says, *Israel in whom I will be glorified* (Isa. XLIX, 3); it is thou, [said the angels,] whose features are engraved on high, they ascended on high and saw his features and they descended below and found him sleeping ...[787]

---

785 See also Kugel 1990, 114-115. Cf., the *Ladder of Jacob* and John 1:51, see below. According to Kugel, another explanation of the origin of this interpretation may be that the Hebrew word for 'ladder/stairway' *sullam* (a hapax legomenon) is similar-sounding to the word *selem*, 'image'. Kugel 1990, 124. See also *Gen. Rab.* 68.13 and the discussion of John 1:51 below. In later Rabbinic texts, the human face of the Cherub in Ezekiel's vision (Ezek. 1:10, 26) is said to bear the features of Jacob. See Kugel 1990, 117, 250 and Guiley 2004, 194.

786 We may here also mention that this interpretation is attested in *Pirqe de Rabbi Eliezer* 35:

> And the ministering angels were ascending and descending thereon, and they beheld the face of Jacob and they said: This is the face like the face of the Chayyah, which is on the Throne of Glory..."

787 See also *Num. Rab.* 4.1. (Eng. trans. Slotki 1939, 95) where the motif of Jacob's heavenly portrait is based upon Isa 43:4:

> ...There is a scriptural text bearing on this: *Since thou art precious in My sight, and honourable, etc,* (Isa. XLIII, 4). The Holy One, blessed be He, said to Jacob: Jacob, thou art exceedingly precious in my sight. For I have, as it were, set thine image on my throne, and by thy name the angels praise Me and say: *Blessed be the Lord, the God of Israel, from everlasting and to everlasting* (Ps. XLI, 14).

The change of Jacob's angelic guard

In *Pseudo-Jonathan* we also encounter a similar interpretation of the activity of the angels in Gen 28:12 but, in contrast to the other Palestinian Targums, the angels who accompanied Jacob to Bethel are specifically said to be the two angels mentioned in Genesis 19:

> [*Tg. Ps.-J.* Gen 28:12] And behold, the *two* angels *who had gone to Sodom and who had been banished from their apartment because they had revealed the secrets of the Lord to the world*, went about when they were banished until the time that Jacob went forth from his father's house. Then, as an act of kindness, they accompanied him to Bethel, and on that day they ascended to the heavens on high, and said, "Come and see Jacob the pious, whose image is fixed in the Throne of Glory, and whom you have desired to see." Then the rest of the holy angels of the Lord came down *to look at him*.

There is a parallel to this tradition in *Genesis Rabbah*. After stating that the angels who escort a man in the land of Israel are not the same as those who escort him outside the country, thus it appears that a change in Jacob's 'angelic guard' took place at Bethel. [788] The Midrash goes on to say:

> [*Gen. Rab.* 68.12] … R. Levi said in the name of R. Samuel b. Nachman: Because the ministering angels revealed God's secrets, they were banished from their precincts a hundred and thirty-eight years [...] R. Hama b. Hanina said: [They were banished] because they boasted and said, *For we will destroy this place* [789] (Gen. XIX, 13). When did they return? On this occasion, ASCENDING first and then DESCENDING.

God as the Māqôm and Bethel as the Temple site

In Gen 28:11 we read: "He [Jacob] came [ויפגע/lit. 'met'] to a certain place [במקום] and stayed there for the night…" As we have seen previously, the Hebrew word *māqôm* has the connotation of 'holy site' and in Rab-

---

788 The angels who ascended were those connected to the land of Israel, who at Bethel returned to heaven, to be replaced by other angelic guards who descended from heaven, in order to accompany Jacob outside his native land. The belief that Jacob enjoyed angelic protection is also apparent in the interpretation of Gen 32:3 (v. 4 in the MT): "Then Jacob sent messengers before him…" The Midrash compares Jacob to Hagar and Abraham's servant Eliezer:

The rabbis said: It means literally angels. If an angel escorted Eliezer, who was but a servant of the house, how much the more this one [Jacob], who was the beloved of the house! R. Hama b. Hanina observed: Hagar was but Sarah's handmaid, yet five angels appeared to her; how much the more then to this man [Jacob], who was the beloved of the house! [*Gen. Rab.* 75.4.]

789 I.e., Sodom.

binic terminology *Māqôm* came to be employed as a divine epithet, meaning 'the Omnipresent.'[790] This understanding of the word is also implied in *Gen. Rab.* 68.9:

> ... R. Huna said in R. Ammi's name: Why do we give a changed name to the Holy One, blessed be He, and call him 'the Place'? Because He is the Place of the world. R. Jose b. Halafta said: We do not know whether God is the place of His world or whether His world is His place, but from the verse, *Behold, there is a place with Me* (Ex. XXXIII, 21) it follows that the Lord is the place of this world, but the world is not His place. R. Isaac said: It is written, *The eternal God is a dwelling place* (Deut. XXXIII, 27) ...

This discussion of the word 'place' calls to mind Philo's work *On Dreams*, where he writes that 'place' in addition to physical space may signify God or God's Word, the 'Logos'.[791]

In Rabbinic tradition, the holiness of Bethel is associated with the Jerusalem Temple. For example, instead of saying in Gen 28:11 "he came," to Bethel (*Onqelos*), all the Palestinian Targums state in this verse that Jacob *prayed* in that place. In verse 17b we read in *Neofiti*: "... *a place designated before the Lord, and this is the gate of prayer designated toward heaven*", and *Pseudo-Jonathan* has here "... *and this is (a place) suitable for prayer, corresponding to the gate of heaven, founded beneath the Throne of Glory*."[792] See also Rabbi Bar Kappara's comment in *Gen. Rab.* 68.12:

> No dream is without its interpretation. AND BEHOLD A LADDER symbolises the stairway;[793] SET UP ON THE EARTH–the altar, as it says, *An altar of earth thou shalt make unto Me* (Ex. XX, 21); AND THE TOP OF IT REACHED TO HEAVEN– the sacrifices, the odour of which ascended to heaven; AND BEHOLD THE ANGELS OF GOD–the High Priests; ASCENDING AND DESCENDING ON IT–ascending and descending the stairway. AND BEHOLD, THE LORD STOOD BESIDE HIM (XXVIII, 13)–*I saw the Lord standing beside the altar* (Amos IX, I)[794]

---

790 See also Jastrow 1971, 830. According to Koehler/Baumgartner (2001, 627), the word מקום already has this meaning in Esth 4:14: "For if you remain completely silent at this time, relief and deliverance will arise for the Jews from *another place*" [ממקום אחר = *from God*]. See also Marmorstein 1927, 92-93.

791 Philo, *On Dreams* 1.62-64.

792 A *Neofiti* marginal gloss has here: "this is not a profane place but rather the place of the sanctuary of the Lord and this temple corresponds to the gate of the sanctuary which is in heaven." See also v. 22 in *Neofiti* and *Pseudo-Jonathan* cited above and Clarke 1974/5, 367-377 and O'Neill 2003, 374-381.

793 Leading to the top of the altar in the Temple, see Freedman, 1939 note 2, p. 625. See also Grossfeld's commentary to *Neofiti*, 2000, pp. 200-205.

794 According to yet another interpretation of Gen 28:12 in *Gen. Rab.* 68.12, the ladder represents Sinai and the angels allude to Moses and Aaron. See also *Gen. Rab.* 68.9, where it is stated that Jacob was the patriarch who instituted evening prayer.

In *Pirqê de Rabbi Eliezer* chapter 35, Bethel is identified with Mount Moriah, the place where Isaac was bound, i.e., the Temple site, and there is also an explanation of the Rabbinic designation of God as *Maqôm*:

> … From Beer-Sheba as far as Mount Moriah is a journey of two days, and he [Jacob] arrived there at midday, and the Holy One, blessed be He, met him, as it is said, "And he *met* in the place, and tarried there all night, because the sun was set" (Gen xxviii. 11) Why is the name of the Holy One, blessed be He, called Makom? Because in every *place* where the righteous are He is found with them there as it is said, "In every place (Makom) where I record my name I will come unto thee and bless thee (Ex. xx. 24)." […] Jacob took twelve stones of the stones of the altar, whereon his father Isaac had been bound, and set them for his pillow in that place … [Cf., Philo, *On Dreams* I.71]

The ascending and descending empires

This interpretation is connected to the angels that Jacob saw ascending and descending.[795] There are many variants of this midrash; it is extant, for example, in *Gen. Rab.* 68.14 and *Pesiqta de Rab Kahana* 23.[796] Since the content of the midrash is roughly speaking the same in all its variants, it is sufficient to look at these two sources:

> [*Gen. Rab.* 68.14] … AND HE DREAMED foreshadowed Nebuchadnessar's dream. AND BEHOLD A LADDER–*And behold a great image, etc.* (Dan. II, 31). SET UP ON THE EARTH–*And whose brightness was surpassing, stood before thee* (ib.). AND THE TOP OF IT REACHED TO HEAVEN–*This image which was mighty* (ib.). AND BEHOLD THE ANGELS OF GOD ASCENDING–this intimates two; AND DESCENDING, another two: that alludes to the princes of the four empires whose power is complete through them. ASCENDING AND DESCENDING: it is not written, 'descending and ascending, but ASCENDING AND DESCENDING: they [the empires] do ascend [to power] and it is indeed an ascent for them, but each is nevertheless lower than the preceding. It is written, *As for that image, its head was of fine gold, its breast and its arms of silver*, etc. (ib.32). Babylon was the highest of all, as it is written, *Thou art the head of gold* (ib. 38); and it is written, *And after thee shall arise another kingdom inferior to thee* (ib. 39) […] AND BEHOLD, THE LORD STOOD BESIDE HIM: thus it is written, *And in the days of those kings shall the God of heaven set up a kingdom which shall never be destroyed* (ib. 44).

---

795 In *Gen. Rab.* 68.12 we also read that:

R. Berekiah said: He showed him the world and a third of the world, for ASCENDING cannot refer to less than two [angels] while AND DESCENDING likewise must refer to two, and each angel is a third of the world [in size].

796 See also, e.g., *Exod. Rab.* 32.7; *Lev. Rab.* 29.2, and *Pirqê de Rabbi Eliezer* 35.

As shown above, both the *Fragment Targums* and *Pseudo-Jonathan* define the angels in Gen 28:12 as 'holy angels' but this interpretation is not chosen in the Midrash above. Here the explanation of the direction of the angels' movement (first up and then down) is that they are not holy angels at all. Instead, they are identified as 'the princes of the four empires,' i.e., guardian angels of the heathen nations. As the heathen empires ascend and descend, so too do their 'angelic princes.'[797] The dream is thus interpreted as a vision of the future destiny of the world and Jacob's descendants. God is in control of history and, in the end, God Himself will establish a kingdom that will surpass all others. The meaning of this midrash is even clearer in *Pesiqta de Rab Kahana 23:*

> ... and angels of God (Gen 28:12). These angels, according to R. Samuel bar Nahman, were the princes of the nations on earth. Further, according to R. Samuel bar Nahman, this verse proves that the Holy One showed our father Jacob the prince of Babylon climbing up seventy rungs on the ladder, then climbing down, the prince of Media climbing up fifty-two rungs and no more; the prince of Greece, one hundred and eighty rungs and no more, and the prince of Edom[798] climbing... [and so on]

This midrashic interpretation of Jacob's dream-vision reminds us of the Pseudepigraphon the *Ladder of Jacob* 5.2-4, 7: "The ladder is this age, and the twelve steps are the periods of this age. But the twenty-four faces are the kings of the ungodly nations ... And this place [Jerusalem] will be made desolate by the *four ascents* ..."[799]

Jacob's Second Dream

The renderings of Gen 31:10-13 both in *Onqelos* and in the Palestinian Targums[800] are similar to the Septuagint-version. In the same way as the LXX, all of the Targums have inserted an explanatory gloss in v. 13. Compare, for example the MT, *Onqelos* and the LXX:

[Gen 31:13 MT:] ...אל בית האל אנכי.../... I am the God (of) Bethel... [LXX:] ...
ἐγώ εἰμι ὁ θεὸς ὁ ὀφθείς σοι ἐν τόπῳ θεοῦ... /I am *the God* that *appeared* to

---

797 See Freedman 1939, note 1, p. 629, and Dan 10:13, 20.

798 I.e., Rome, see below.

799 Eng. trans. Lunt in *OTP*, vol. 2, 1985, 409. See also chapter 4.2 above and Kugel 1995, 211-216.

800 That is, *Neofiti, Pseudo-Jonathan* and a Cairo Genizah-fragment (ms Antonin Ebr.III B III, folio 2v). Verses 11-13 are unfortunately not extant in ms P of the *Fragment Targums*. In ms V the only preserved fragment of Gen 31:11 is: "Jacob answered in the language of the Holy Temple, and he said: "Here I am." See also Chester 1986, 156-158.

you in the place of God … [*Onqelos:*] …אל בית עלך דאיתגליתי אלהא אנא … / I am
the God who *was revealed* to you at Beth-el …

Thus, in all of the versions of the verse, the angel who appears to Jacob
in his dream in Gen 31:11 identifies himself as the God who spoke to
him at Bethel. However, in contrast to both the MT and the LXX, all of
the Targums state that it was the angel of *the Lord/YHWH* who addressed Jacob in Gen 31:11 and not the angel of God/*Elohim/Theos*.

According to *Gen. Rab.* 74.3, the angel of God spoke on this occasion
both to Jacob and to future generations but the Midrash contains no
comment on the angel's identification of himself with the God of Bethel
(Gen 31:13). Nor does *Pirqê de Rabbi Eliezer* (chapter 36) make any reference to v. 13 but only to v. 3:

> … Because it is said, "And it was told Laban on the third day that Jacob
> was fled (Gen xxxi. 22). Why did he flee? Because the Holy One, blessed be
> He, said to him: Jacob! I cannot suffer My Shekinah to dwell with thee out-
> side the land, but return unto the land of thy fathers, and to thy kindred,
> and I will be with thee" (ibid. 3). Therefore he fled.

God's revelation to Laban in his dream, warning him from speaking
either good or bad to Jacob (Gen 31:24), is put into the mouth of an
intermediary, the archangel Michael:

> [*Pirqê de Rabbi Eliezer* 36]… And Laban took all the men of his city, mighty
> men, and he pursued after him [Jacob], seeking to slay him. The angel Mi-
> chael descended, and drew his sword behind him, seeking to slay him. He
> said to him: Do not speak to Jacob, either good or bad, as it is said: "And
> God came to Laban the Aramean in a dream of the night …"

This interpretation is probably inspired by the revelation of the angel of
the Lord to Balaam in Num 22:22-23. We have a similar rendering of
Gen 31:24 in *Pseudo-Jonathan*: "An angel came by the decree from before
the Lord and drew the sword against Laban…" However, the other
Targums all state that it was either the Lord Himself or the Memra of
the Lord who confronted Laban in his dream.

Concluding Remarks

It may be concluded that according to both the Targums and the Midrashim it was God Himself who met Jacob in his dream at Bethel. The
only exception is the Marginal gloss in *Tg. Neof.* Gen 28:13 which refers
to 'an angel of mercy'.

Moreover, as in the LXX, the angel of God who speaks to Jacob in
Gen 31:11-13 is identified in the Targums as the God who appeared to
him at Bethel. This interpretation also seems to be implied in the Mi-

drashim. There are at least no objections to such an assumption, since the connection between God in Genesis 28 and the angel in Gen 31:11-13 is not discussed; the "angel's" equation with God is neither openly denied nor affirmed. However, it is evident that God is depicted in our sources as speaking in person with Jacob. In contrast, God's revelation to Laban in Gen 31:24 is ascribed to an angel in *Pseudo-Jonathan* and *Pirqê de Rabbi Eliezer* 36, in the latter source identified as the archangel Michael.

The ascending and descending angels in Jacob's dream at Bethel are depicted either as holy angels or as the angelic princes of the heathen nations. In both cases they are clearly distinguished from God. In *Pseudo-Jonathan* there is a connection between Genesis 28 and 19; the angels who are described as Jacob's guards on his way to Bethel are identified in this Targum as the two angels who previously went down to Sodom.

Jacob's Battle at the Ford of Jabbok

The Targums

The Hebrew wording of Gen 32:25 ויותר יעקב לבדו ויאבק איש עמו עד עלו השחר / "Jacob was left alone; and a man wrestled with him until daybreak" [NRSV][801] is rendered in *Onqelos*: ואשתדל גברא עימיה עד דסליק ... צפרא / "... and a man *contended* with him until the morning dawned" (my italics).

Onqelos thus renders the Hebrew ויאבק 'wrestled' as ואשתדל, which Aberbach/Grossfeld translate as 'contended', since they understand the verb as indicating verbal strife rather than physical combat.[802] This interpretation seems to be supported by Jastrow.[803] According to Aberbach/Grossfeld, *Onqelos* chose this verb in an attempt to diminish the implicit anthropomorphism of the account; that Jacob *wrestled* with an angel[804] or indeed even with God Himself (cf., Gen 32:29, 31, MT).[805] The Targum's next major deviation from the MT is found in verse 29:

> Thereupon he said, "Your name shall no longer be called Jacob, but Israel; for you are great (or: a prince) before the Lord and among men, therefore you have prevailed." / ואמר לא יעקב יתאמר עוד שמך אילהין ישראל ארי רב את קדם יי ועם

---

801 Verse 24 in NRSV.

802 Aberbach/Grossfeld 1982, note 7, p. 197. See also Grossfeld 1988, note 13, 117.

803 Jastrow 1971, 1525.

804 As will be shown, this is the interpretation given in the Targum, see *Tg. Onq.* Gen 32:31.

805 Aberbach/Grossfeld 1982, note 7, p. 197.

גברייא ויכילתא [NRSV:] "… for you have striven with God [MT: כי שרית עם
אלהים] and with humans, and have prevailed."[806]

The simplest explanation for *Onqelos'* alteration of the verse is once
again the typical targumic dislike of anthropomorphic statements. The
Targum connects שרית 'you have striven', with שר 'prince/great one'
and exchanges the first עם for קדם in order to avoid the astounding implication of the Hebrew text; that Jacob had in fact striven with God.[807]

Onqelos' version also differs from the renderings of Gen 32:29 in the
Palestinian Targums,[808] which are very similar to each other.

> [*Tg. Neof*] "Your name shall no longer be Jacob but Israel, because you have
> claimed superiority *with angels*[809] *from before the Lord* and with men and you
> have prevailed against them."

> [*Tg. Ps.-J.*] "… because you have *gained superiority* over *the angels of the Lord*
> and over men …"

Like *Onqelos, Neofiti* and *Pseudo-Jonathan* also avoid the anthropomorphic idea that Jacob strove with God but their way of handling the Hebrew text is slightly different. The Palestinian Targums solve the "problem" by interpreting the Hebrew term אלהים in v. 29 as referring to 'divine beings', i.e., 'angels' and not God.[810] This identification of the unknown 'man' who confronts Jacob may also be seen in the light of
angels sometimes being designated as 'men' elsewhere in the Bible;
e.g., Gen 19:5; Ezek 40:3; Zech 1:8-12, and Dan 10:5-18.[811]

On the basis of this difference between *Onqelos* and the other Targums, Hayward proposes yet another reason for the former Targum's
particular rendering of the verse as well as an additional explanation
for its interpretation of the nature of the combat:

> TO [*Onqelos*] seeks to emphasize that Jacob-Israel is, and always has been, a
> 'prince', that is, a mighty angel, before the Lord, rather than a 'prince' with
> other angels. Here, perhaps, we perceive why TO was keen to play down
> the physical aspects of Jacob's struggle and injury: the reality was that he

---

806 Verse 28 in the NRSV.
807 See also Aberbach/Grossfeld 1982, note 9, p. 197.
808 I.e., *Neofiti* and *Pseudo-Jonathan*; the verse is unfortunately not extant in the *Fragment
     Targums*. The reading of the verse in the targumic fragments of the Cairo Genizah is
     as follows:

     … for you have contended with holy angels from before the Lord, in the form of
     men, and you prevailed against them. [Oxford Bodleian ms b 4, folio 18v].

809 *Neofiti* marginal gloss: "… in the form of men…"
810 Cf., Ps 29:1; 89:7-8 (89:6-7 in the NRSV); 82:1. In the first two Psalms, the designation
     בני אלים seems to signify angels, and in the latter one the term אלהים is used.
811 See also von Rad 1964, 40. Cf., also Judges 13 where the designations 'the angel of
     the Lord/God' and 'the man' are used interchangeably.

had always been an angelic prince before the Lord, and the episode at the Jabbok was principally designed to announce a fact which was already known.[812]

The Targums apparently do not interpret the name Israel in connection with שרה 'strife' but with שר 'prince/great one' or the related verb שרר 'rule/direct' and seem to understand it as a title signifying Jacob/Israel's superiority both in the heavenly and earthly realms.[813] Compare also the rendering in the LXX:

[Gen 32:28 (29)] ... ἀλλὰ Ἰσραὴλ ἔσται τὸ ὄνομά σου, ὅτι ἐνίσχυσας μετὰ θεοῦ, καὶ μετὰ ἀνθρώπων δυνατός.[814] / "... but Israel shall be your name; for you have prevailed/been strong/strengthen yourself with God and with men [you are] mighty/powerful."

All the Targums share the interpretation that the "man" whom Jacob encountered at Jabbok was *an angel* and not God in person; an identification of the opponent that most probably is mainly due to an avoidance of anthropomorphism. It is explicitly stated in Exod 33:20 that no man can see the face of God and live; consequently, it cannot have been God that Jacob saw 'face to face' at Jabbok.

However, there are some significant details distinguishing even the Palestinian Targums from each other. In order to illustrate this, I quote some selected targumic verses of the pericope:[815]

[Gen 32:25: *Tg. Neof.*] ...and *the angel Sariel* wrestled with him [Jacob] *in the appearance of* a man ... [*Tg. Ps.-J.*] ... And *an angel in the form of* a man wrestled with him.[816] *And he said, "Did you not promise to tithe all that would be yours? Now behold, you have twelve sons and one daughter and you have not tithed them."*[...] *And he began to count from Simeon, and Levi happened to be the tenth. Michael spoke up and said, "Master of the world, this one is your lot." It was on account of these things that he* [the angel Michael] *tarried beyond the stream until the column of* the dawn rose.

---

812 Hayward 2005, 303. Cf., the *Prayer of Joseph* treated above

813 See also Hayward 2005, 282–306. Sarna (1989, 405) points out that the verb ויישר in Hos 12:5 (which refers to this event) can only derive from שור, a by-form of שרר. As is evident in this verse, the prophet Hosea used the designation מלאך 'angel/messenger' to signify Jacob's contender at the ford of Jabbok. Thus, the targumic identification of the 'man' in Genesis 32 as an angel is most likely influenced by Hos 12:4-5 (vv. 3-4 in the NRSV).

814 Some mss add here ἔσῃ 'you shall be', see Wevers (ed.) 1974, text critical note to the LXX Gen 32:28.

815 The only extant verse of the pericope in the *Fragment Targums* of relevance for our quest is Gen 32:27.

816 The same rendering of Gen 32:25a is also extant in the Cairo Genizah ms Oxford Bodleian Heb. b 4, folio 18v. See Klein (ed. and trans.) 1986, 66.

[Gen 32:27: *Tg. Neof.*] ... And he [the angel Sariel] said: "Let me go because the rise of the dawn has arrived, *and because the time of the angels on high to praise has arrived, and I am the chief of those who praise.*" [817] [*Tg. Ps.-J.*] ... *and the hour has come when the angels on high praise the Lord of the world, and I am one of the angels who praise, but from the day that the world was created my time to praise did not come until this time.*" [*Frg. Tg.* ms P] And he [the angel] said: "Release me, [...] for the time has come for the angels of the heights [to give praise;][818] and I am head of those who give praise;"...[819] [ms V] "Release me [...] the hour has come for the angels to give praise;"...

[Gen 32:30: *Tg. Ps.-J.*] Jacob asked and said, "Tell me your name, I pray. And he said, "Why do you ask my name?" And *Jacob*[820] blessed him there.

[Gen 32:31: *Tg. Onq*] And Jacob called the name of the place Peniel; for (he said), "I have seen an angel of the Lord face to face, and yet my life has been preserved." [*Tg. Neof.*] ... called the place Peniel because: "I have seen *angels from before the Lord* face to face and my life has been spared."[821]

[Gen 32:33: *Tg. Ps.-J.*] ... because the *angel* touched *and held* the socket of Jacob's *right* hip ...

As shown above, both the *Fragment Targums* (ms P) and *Neofiti* identify Jacob's angelic opponent as the celestial worship-leader, and this is the reason for the angel's request to let him go when dawn comes. The same motif is also present in *Pseudo-Jonathan* and ms V of the *Fragment Targums*, although there the angel is not said to be the leader of the heavenly choir. The appearance of the angel is described by all the Targums to be man-like.

In contrast to *Onqelos*, the Palestinian Targums do not try to eliminate the physical character of the combat but otherwise *Onqelos'* rendering is closest to the Hebrew original and hence lacks many of the aggadic expansions found in the other Targums. For example, the liturgical aspect of the narrative[822] is not present in *Onqelos*. In the Palestinian Targums, the superiority of Jacob over the angels has liturgical connotations.[823]

Until Gen 32:31, Jacob's heavenly contender is called a 'man' in *Onqelos*, but when Jacob realizes his true identity, his angelic status is re-

---

817 *Neofiti* marginal gloss: "the time of the angels on high to be sent has arrived, and I am the chief of the ones who are sent."

818 "[to give praise]" is the translator's insertion and thus part of the quotation.

819 Almost the same rendering of the verse is found in the Cairo Genizah ms Oxford Bodleian Heb. b 4, folio 18v. See Klein (ed. and trans.) 1986, 66.

820 The addition of the name Jacob is unique to *Pseudo-Jonathan*.

821 Almost identical rendering (reference to angels in plural) in *Pseudo-Jonathan*. Cf., Gen 32:29 in the two Targums quoted above.

822 I.e., the reference to the heavenly service.

823 See also Hayward 2005, 308-309.

vealed. *Onqelos* is furthermore the only Targum that in this verse refers to an angel in the singular form;[824] Jacob's exclamation can thus only refer to the encounter with the 'man' at Jabbok.

In the Palestinian Targums, Jacob's earlier vision of the angels at Bethel may also be included in his statement.[825] Another reason for the reference to a multitude of angels in these Targums may be the same as the explanation suggested concerning Gen 32:29. Since no man can see God's face and survive, the *meturgeman* interpreted אלהים to mean 'divine beings', i.e., angels, as opposed to God.[826]

In *Onqelos* and the *Fragment Targums,* Jacob's angelic opponent is anonymous but in *Neofiti* and *Pseudo-Jonathan* he is identified by name. The reference to him as the angel Sariel is unique to *Neofiti* and not found in any other Rabbinic interpretation of the narrative.

This angelic name is on the whole very rare but is mentioned in a few sources, for example, the Qumran *War Scroll*, *1 En.* 9.1[827] and the *Ladder of Jacob.* Sariel seems to be an older name for the angel later labeled Uriel, who, as mentioned above, is depicted as Jacob's combatant at Jabbok in the *Prayer of Joseph.*[828] The appearance of the name in *Tg. Neof.* Gen 32:25 may also be connected to its phonological similarity to the name Israel,[829] cf., the *Ladder of Jacob*:

> [*Lad. Jac.* 3.3] And Sariel the archangel came to me [Jacob] and I saw (him), and his appearance was very beautiful and awesome… [*Lad. Jac.* 4.1-5] And the angel said to me, "What is your name?" And I said, "Jacob." (He announced), "Your name shall no longer be called Jacob, but your name shall be similar to my name, Israel." And when I was going from Phandana of Syria to meet Esau my brother, he came to me and blessed me and called me Israel. And he would not tell me his name until I adjured him

---

824 However, the Peshitta also refers to a single angel in this verse, in the same way as the Targum to Hosea:

> [12:4b] … And by his [Jacob's] might he contended with *the angel*. [5] Thus, he contended with the angel and prevailed, he wept and pleaded with him. In Bethel he *was revealed to* him and there he would speak with us. [6] *He is* the Lord, the God of hosts *who was revealed to Abraham, Isaac and Jacob.* [Eng. trans. K. J. Cathcart and R. P. Gordon 1989. The words in italics are the targumic derivations from the Hebrew text].

825 According to Hayward (2005, 293), the reference to a multiplicity of angels in the Palestinian Targums to this verse is due to the association of Genesis 32 in Jewish exegetical tradition with the vision of angels in Genesis 28. Another possible explanation is to read the statement in the light of Jacob's meeting with angels in Gen 32:2-3. See also Grossfeld's Commentary to *Neofiti* 2000, 227-228.

826 See also Chester 1986, 361, Kasher 2007, 562-563, and chapter 2.2.2 above.

827 I.e., in the Ethiopic mss. See also chapter 4.2.

828 See also Rebiger 2007, 638.

829 See Grossfeld's Commentary to *Neofiti*, 2000, 225-227, and Hayward 2005, 297-299.

In addition to the phonological similarities between the two names, Hayward also suggests an allusion in the Targum to the verb שׁיר 'to sing',[830] because Sariel is depicted as the choir-leader of the heavenly worship.[831]

However, a marginal gloss to *Tg. Neof.* Gen 32:27 refers to Sariel as the chief of the "ones who are sent", which gives quite a different dimension to the narrative, in the words of Hayward:

> … The notion of 'sending' arises directly out of the Scriptural verse, the angel presumably acknowledging that Jacob has power to 'send' him away so that he in turn may be sent on his duties to God […] it represents a Jacob-Israel whose angelic qualities consist not so much in liturgical service, as in the execution of divine commissions.[832]

In contrast to Sariel, Michael, the guardian angel of Israel[833] who appears in *Pseudo-Jonathan*'s version of Genesis 32, is well-known in Rabbinic sources. According to the Targum, the reason for the angel's appearance is to confront Jacob and remind him of his promise to give a tithe of all his possessions, including his children, to God, cf., Gen 28:22. In response, Jacob allots Levi to God.[834]

In contrast to Sariel in *Neofiti*, Michael is not depicted as the leader of the heavenly worship but just as "one of the angels who praise," and further on we read in *Tg. Ps.-J.* Gen 32:27: *"…but from the day that the world was created my time to praise did not come until this time."* This statement tells us that, according to the tradition extant in the Targum, angels have only one, single opportunity to praise God. Michael is thus depicted as being at the mercy of Jacob when he asks to be released in order to be able to return to heaven and praise God.[835]

Jacob's superiority over Michael is made explicit in *Pseudo-Jonathan* by its unique rendering of v. 30 that it was actually *Jacob* who blessed his opponent, and not the other way around, which is the natural interpretation of the Hebrew text, even though it is slightly ambiguous.[836]

---

830 Hayward 2005, 298.
831 Another possible interpretation of the name Sariel is to connect it to the Hebrew word שׂר 'prince', thus 'God is my prince'.
832 Hayward 2005, 300.
833 See e.g., Daniel 12.
834 Cf., the Jacob story in the version of *Jubilees* treated above.
835 See also Hayward 2005, 293.
836 See also Hayward 2005, 293. In the biblical text it is not explicitly stated who executed the blessing, although the context implies it to be the "man": "Then Jacob asked him, 'Please tell me your name.' But he said, 'Why is it that you ask my name?' And there he blessed him." [Gen 32:29 NRSV]. See also Miller (1984, 98-100) who also discusses the targumic renderings of Genesis 32.

The Rabbinic Midrashim and the Babylonian Talmud

In *Genesis Rabbah*, there is quite an extensive discussion of Jacob's nightly confrontation with the unknown "man" of Genesis 32.[837] However, all the Rabbis of the Midrash agree that Jacob's contender was an *angel* of some sort and not God Himself. There are various descriptions of this angel, for example, disguised as either a shepherd[838] or a brigand owning flocks and camels. Let us begin by looking at the second interpretation:

> [*Gen. Rab.* 77.2] AND THERE WRESTLED A MAN WITH HIM. The Rabbis said: He appeared to him in the guise of a brigand: each had flocks and each had camels, and he proposed to him: Do you take mine across and I will take yours. The angel then transported Jacob's in a twinkling of an eye, whereas Jacob took some across, returned, and found more, returned and found more [and so on]. You are a sorcerer he [Jacob] exclaimed […] Magicians do not succeed at night! R. Huna said: Eventually he [the angel] said to himself: Shall I not inform him with whom he is engaged? What did he do? He put his finger on the earth, whereupon the earth began spurting fire. Said Jacob to him: 'Would you terrify me with that? Why, I am altogether of that stuff! Thus it is written, *And the house of Jacob shall be a fire*, etc. (Obad. 1, 18).

This elaboration of Genesis 32 may appear very distant from the biblical account. In the Bible, the combat is apparently physical but in this interpretation of the event Jacob is said to be engaged in a kind of competition and verbal battle with the angel. As shown above, this interpretation of the pericope also seems to be implied in *Onqelos*. The concrete anthropomorphism of the biblical narrative has disappeared in *Genesis Rabbah*; the angel demonstrates his supernatural powers by transferring Jacob's flocks in the blink of an eye and by bringing forth fire from the earth. However, Jacob is not intimidated and says that he himself is made of fire. This claim may be an indication of Jacob's own angelic status.[839]

---

837 *Song of Songs Rabbah* to Song 3:6 has a similar exegesis of our text as *Genesis Rabbah*; Jacob's contender is identified as the angelic representative of Esau. Indeed, this Midrash reproduces much of the content of *Genesis Rabbah*. However, nowhere in this Midrash is the angel said to be involved in the heavenly worship. See also Hayward 2005, 279-282, and Miller 1984, 100-102.

838 *Gen. Rab.* 77.2. In *b. Hullin* 91a some other disguises are suggested: "R. Samuel b. Nahman said, He appeared to him as a heathen […] R. Samuel b. Aha said […] He appeared to him as one of the wise…"

839 Cf., *Exod. Rab.* 15.6: "The angels are called 'fire', for it is written: 'The flaming fire Thy ministers' (Ps. CIV, 4), and Israel is also so called, as it is written: 'and the house of Jacob shall be a fire' (Obad. 1,18)…'" [Eng. trans. Lehrmann 1939]. See also the *Prayer of Joseph* treated above and Smith 1968, 274-281.

Be that as is may, the quote from Obadiah, a prophet who thoroughly denounced Edom, implies in this context the angel's identity; he is the guardian angel of Esau/Edom, at the time of the Rabbis regarded as symbolizing the Roman Empire.[840] Further on in *Genesis Rabbah*, this identification becomes explicit:

> [*Gen. Rab.* 77.3] R. Hama b. R. Hanina said: It was the guardian Prince [angel] of Esau. To this Jacob alluded when he said to him [Esau]: *Forasmuch as I have seen thy face, as one seeth the face of Elohim,*[841] *and thou wast pleased with me* (Gen. XXXIII, 10) This may be compared to an athlete who was wrestling with a royal prince, lifting up his eyes and seeing the king standing near him, he threw himself down before him. (Thus it is written, AND HE SAW THAT HE PREVAILED NOT AGAINST HIM (XXXII, 26) which R. Levi interpreted: and he saw the *Shekinah*.)[842] R. Berekiah said: We do not know who was victorious, whether the angel or Jacob; since, however, it is written, WAYYE'ABEK A MAN WITH HIM (ib. 25), it follows: who was covered with dust (Abak)? The man who [strove] with him.[843]
>
> R. Hanina b. Isaac said: 'He [Jacob] comes against thee wearing five amulets,' [said God to the angel]: 'his own merit, and the merit of his father, of his mother [...] Measure thyself–canst thou stand against even his own merit?' [...] So, if the nations of the world come to join issue with Israel, the Holy One, blessed be He, will say to them: 'Your guardian angel could not prevail against Israel; how much less can you!'

In contrast to the widely spread practice during the time of the Rabbis, Jacob's amulets are not said to be inscribed with the names of angels, instead he is protected by his own and his parent's merits. Moreover, Jacob is depicted as the winner of the combat; in the end Israel will prevail against Rome. In the words of Hayward: "The victory over Rome is yet to come, but this is assured [...] That victory itself, indeed, was anticipated in Jacob's victory over Esau's angel ..."[844] Compare the interpretation of the ascending and descending angels in Jacob's dream at Bethel as the angelic princes of the heathen nations, see above.

---

840 See also Hayward 2005, 241, 255-256.

841 The Rabbis thus interpret 'Elohim' to mean angel. See Freedman 1939, 711, note 4.

842 The bracketed passage is inserted by Freedman from Cur.Edd. Because the angel saw the Shekinah, he allowed Jacob to win, see Freedman 1939, 712, note 2. The same interpretation is also found in *Song Rab.* 3.6.

843 As shown in the quoted passage, the Rabbis were aware of the ambiguity of the Hebrew text regarding who won the combat. However, based on a word play on similarly sounding Hebrew words for 'dust' and 'wrestle', they concluded that Jacob was the winner. According to the Rabbis, Jacob's combatant was covered in dust and had thus fallen in the wrestling match. See Feldman 1939, 712, note 4. In *b. Hullin* 91b there is also a discussion regarding the ambiguity of the text but it is finally concluded that Jacob was the one who prevailed.

844 Hayward 2005, 259. See also pp. 257-258.

In addition to the identification of the "man" of Genesis 32 as Esau's celestial patron,[845] *Genesis Rabbah* interprets the angel's request to leave when dawn comes similarly to, for example, *Neofiti*:

> [*Gen. Rab.* 78.2] AND HE SAID: LET ME GO, FOR THE DAY BREAKETH: For it is time to sing praises. 'Let your colleagues sing praises,' said he [Jacob] to him. I cannot [arrange it so], he replied…

As in *Neofiti*, the angel pleads with Jacob to release him, because the time for the heavenly worship has arrived. In contrast to *Neofiti*, however, the angel does not specify his position in the heavenly choir but only says that he wants to leave in order to partake in the angelic praise.[846]

The worshipping angels are described in *Genesis Rabbah* as transient in nature; God creates new angels every day and each company of angels praises God only once and then departs.[847] Only the celestial princes endure for ever. According to Rabbi Berekiah, Jacob's opponent belonged to the second group:

> [*Gen. Rab.* 78.1] … But it is written, AND HE SAID: LET ME GO, FOR THE DAY BREAKETH […] It was Michael or Gabriel, who are celestial princes; all others are exchanged, but they are not exchanged.[848]

In this statement, the Rabbi claims that the angel's request for release would be meaningless if he were to be exchanged after a day had passed. According to Freedman, Rabbi Berekiah's remark may be understood to mean that either he disagreed with the opinion that it was Esau's guardian whom Jacob met[849] or that it was no ordinary angel but one of superior status.[850] To me, the second alternative seems as the most probable, the Rabbi thus identified Jacob's opponent as one of the archangels; Michael or Gabriel.[851]

The blessing of Jacob and the bestowal of his new name Israel in Gen 32:28 [v. 29 in the MT] is interpreted in *Gen. Rab.* 78.2-3 as the angel's disclosure of the future:

---

845 As shown in chapter 3, Sarna likewise identifies the "man" in Genesis 32 in this way, his interpretation seems thus to have been inspired by this Rabbinic exegesis.

846 Cf., *Pseudo-Jonathan* and the *Fragment Targums*, ms V.

847 See also *Lamentations Rabbah* 3, Lam 3:22-24, which in commenting Genesis 32 is roughly identical to *Genesis Rabbah* and thus also testifies to the same angelology.

848 See also Rebiger 2007, 631.

849 It is worth noting that the Targums do not refer to the identification of the combatant as Esau's celestial counterpart, but the worship-motif is extant in some of them. Perhaps R. Berekiah himself adheres to this other tradition?

850 Freedman 1939, 714, note 5. See also Hayward 2005, 260-261.

851 See also the discussion in Miller, 1984, 103-104.

[*Gen. Rab.* 78.2] … he [Jacob] answered him. 'I WILL NOT LET YOU GO, EXCEPT THOU BLESS ME,' adding: the angels who visited Abraham did not depart without a blessing.[852] They had been sent for that purpose,' he pleaded, whereas I was not sent for that purpose.' 'Make an end, enough!' he retorted […] R. Huna said: Eventually he [the angel] decided, I will reveal [the future] to him […] Thereupon he told him: He [God] will reveal Himself to thee at Beth-el and change thy name, while I will be standing there. Hence it is written, At Beth-el He would find him, and there He would speak with us (Hosea XII, 5): it does not say, 'with him,' but 'with us'.

[*Gen. Rab.* 78.3] AND HE SAID UNTO HIM: WHAT IS THY NAME? AND HE SAID: JACOB. AND HE SAID: THY NAME SHALL BE CALLED NO MORE JACOB (XXXII, 28f.). […] *'That confirmeth the word of His servant'*[853] refers to the one angel who appeared to our patriarch Jacob and told him,: The Holy One, blessed be he, will reveal himself to thee atBeth-el and change thy name, and I too will be there […] God did appear to him to fulfil the degree of that angel, who had said to him, THY NAME SHALL BE CALLED NO MORE JACOB , and God too spoke thus to him, as it says, *And God said unto him: Thy name shall not be called any more Jacob* (Gen. XXXV, 10) …

According to *Genesis Rabbah*, it was not after the fight[854] at the ford of Jabbok that Jacob was given the new name Israel.[855] The angel did not really have the authority to rename Jacob, but revealed to him that God Himself would appear to the patriarch at Bethel and give him a new name. The angel gave Jacob a promise of a future blessing, a promise that God fulfilled when he returned to Bethel. Thus, the Rabbis of the Midrash interpret Gen 32:28 [29] in the light of Gen 35:9-10 and Hos 12:4 [v. 5, MT]. By interconnecting these three passages, they answer several questions that arise when reading them. For example; the reason for the renewed conferring of the name Israel on Jacob in Gen 35:10 is that on this occasion God confirmed the words of the angel, in his

---

852 Thus, the three "men" who visit Abraham and Sarah (Genesis 18) are here identified as angels.

853 The Midrash refers here to Isa 44:26.

854 As shown in the quotations, according to *Genesis Rabbah* the combat was apparently as much a verbal strife as a physical struggle, cf., *Onqelos* treated above.

855 The significance of the name 'Israel' in Gen 32:28 [29] is interpreted in *Gen. Rab.* 78.3 in two ways: Firstly, the name is understood to mean that Jacob/Israel had striven with celestial beings, i.e., the angel at Jabbok, hence the designation 'Elohim' in this verse is taken to refer to divine beings/angels and not God. Secondly, the name 'Israel' is interpreted as deriving from the Hebrew verb שרר 'to rule', 'to be a prince': Jacob/Israel is God's prince and his features are engraved in heaven, cf., *Onqelos'* rendering of the verse.

very presence. Accordingly, the curious 'with *us*' in Hos 12:4[5] is explained as referring to Jacob and this angel.[856]

By transforming the blessing of Gen 32:28[29] into a prediction of the future, the Rabbis also avoided the problem of having an angel possessing the authority to bless and rename Jacob,[857] especially an angel whom they explicitly state was defeated in combat and is inferior in spiritual status compared to the patriarch:

> [*Gen. Rab.* 78.1] R. Meir, R. Judah, and R. Simeon each made an observation. R. Meir said: Who is greater: The guardian or the guarded? Since it is written, *For He will give His angels charge over the in all thy ways* (Ps. XCI, 11), it follows that the guarded is greater than the guardian. R. Judah said: Who is greater, the bearer or the borne? [...] R. Simeon said: Who is greater: the sender or the sent? From the verse, AND HE SAID: LET ME GO [lit. 'send me away'], it follows that the sender is greater than the sent.[858]

Thus, the angels are understood to be the servants of the believers. Moreover, according to R. Simeon, Jacob's superiority over the angel at Jabbok is demonstrated by the fact that he has the power to send the angel away; [859]the angel is at the mercy of Jacob.[860]

As mentioned above, the Rabbis considered angels in general to be of transient nature, and this becomes evident once again in their discussion of Gen 32:29 [30]; the names of the angels change continually, so when Jacob asks for his opponent's name, he gets no proper answer, because the angel himself did not know his own name at that moment.[861]

In the Babylonian Talmud, tractate *Hullin* 91b, Jacob's contender is also identified as an angel. However, nothing is said of a connection to Esau/Edom. The reason for the angel's request to be released at dawn is here the same as in *Genesis Rabbah* and some of the Palestinian Targums; he wishes to join the heavenly worship:

---

856 See also Hayward 2005, 264-266, and Miller 1984, 104.

857 However, in the comment on Deut 33:1 in *Pesiqta de Rab Kahana* Supplement 1.10, Jacob is said to have received five blessings and, of these, the fourth blessing is accredited to the angel at Jabbok. See also Miller 1984, 105.

858 Freedman (1939, 715, note 4) remarks: "All three wish to prove that the righteous are greater than the angels."

859 Cf., the identification of the angel in a marginal gloss to *Neofiti* Gen 32:27: "the time of the angels on high to be sent has arrived, and I am the chief of the ones who are sent."

860 See also Hayward 2005, 264-266.

861 *Gen. Rab.* 78.4. In this context, the Rabbis compare Jacob's angelic opponent to the angel of the Lord who appeared to Manoah (Judg 13:18), who likewise did not reveal his name. See also Miller 1984, 105.

> And he said, *Let me go, for the day breaketh.* [Jacob] said to him, 'Are you a thief or a rogue that you are afraid of the morning?' He replied, 'I am an angel, and from the day that I was created my time to sing praises [to the Lord] has not come until now'…

The angel's statement is followed by a discussion concerning the liturgical function of angels and the people of Israel. The Rabbis finally conclude that Israel has preference in this respect: "… the ministering angels do not begin to sing praises in heaven until Israel has sung below on earth …" Thus, once more, the superiority of Israel over the angels is established.[862]

In *Pirqê de Rabbi Eliezer*'s version[863] of the biblical account, there appears to be an amalgam of different traditions. Jacob's contender is identified as an angel, and the reason for his request to be released is said to be that his time to sing praises to God has arrived, cf., the Palestinian Targums and *Genesis Rabbah*. As in *Pseudo-Jonathan*, the angel reminds Jacob of his promise to give a tithe of all his possessions, but in contrast to the Targum, this angel is not identified as Michael, although the archangel is also mentioned in this context:

> … Jacob whished to cross the ford of Jabbok, and was detained there. The angel said to him: Didst you not speak thus – "of all that thou shall give me I will surely give a tenth unto thee" […]. What did Jacob do? He put apart the four firstborn children of the four mothers and eight children remained. He began to count from Simeon, and finished with Benjamin, who was still in his mother's womb. Again he began (to count) from Simeon, and he included Benjamin, and Levi was reckoned as the tithe, holy to God […] Michael, the angel, descended and took Levi, and brought him up before the Throne of Glory …

The angel who encounters Jacob at the ford of Jabbok is thus distinguished from Michael, since we read that "… Michael, the angel, *descended* and took Levi …" (my italics). Michael had to descend from heaven in order to fetch Levi, whereas Jacob's opponent must already have been on earth. But the final proof that this angel was not Michael is *Pirqê de Rabbi Eliezer*'s version of the renaming of Jacob:

> Again the angel said to him: "Let me go" (Gen xxxii, 26). Jacob answered him: I will not let thee go until thou hast blessed me; and he blessed him […] Again he said to him: "Let me go" […] He answered him: I will not let thee go until thou tellest me what thy name is. And (the angel) called his name Israel, like his own name, for his own name was called Israel.

---

862 See also Hayward 2005, 273-279, and Miller 1984, 107-109.
863 *Pirqê de Rabbi Eliezer* 37.

Thus, unlike *Genesis Rabbah*, this Midrash seems to have no difficulty in stating that the angel actually blessed Jacob. The angel renames Jacob with his own name, Israel.[864] According to Gerald Friedlander, the idea of this aggadah seems to be that

> ... the angel is named according to the mission entrusted to him by God. Here it was to announce the ideal of Jacob to pursue, namely, that he was to live as Israel, the warrior of God, destined in his seed to do battle with everything which opposes the establishment on earth of the Kingdom of God. Therefore the angel is named Israel. Israel must neither fear man nor angel: he has prevailed over the powers above man, and need fear only God [...] It may also be that the angel was the guardian angel of Israel and therefore bore the name "Israel".[865]

Both of these meanings of the angel's name may be implied in the Midrash. Another striking difference between *Pirqê de Rabbi Eliezer* and the other sources is the fact that according to the Midrash the angel in question is sent to Jacob as an answer to his prayer for deliverance from the hand of Esau (cf., Gen 32:9-12). Consequently, far from being the celestial patron of Esau, this angel is instead depicted as a benevolent angel who comes to Jacob's support when he is faced with the impending confrontation with his brother.

Jacob's Pilgrimage to Bethel

Introduction
Pirqê de Rabbi Eliezer does not make any comment upon Gen 35:1-15, but there are some targumic paraphrases of the text that are noteworthy. In *Genesis Rabbah*, there are also some interpretations of the pericope of interest to our subject.

The Targums
As usual, when God addresses Jacob (vv. 1, 10 and 11) the Targums employ the Tetragrammaton 'YHWH/the Lord' instead of 'Elohim/God' as in the MT.[866] Otherwise, *Onqelos* and *Pseudo-Jonathan* have quite a literal translation of Gen 35:1, but *Neofiti* deviates slightly more from the MT:

---

864 Cf., the *Prayer of Joseph* treated above.
865 Friedlander 1916, 282, note 8 to *Pirqê de Rabbi Eliezer* 37.
866 Again, this applies only to *Onqelos*, *Neofiti*, and *Pseudo-Jonathan*, since the verses are not preserved in the *Fragment Targums* In these Targums the only preserved verses are vv. 9, 18 (ms P) and vv. 8-9, 16, 18, and 22 (ms V).

> And *the Lord* said to Jacob: "Arise, go up to Bethel and dwell there and
> build an altar there *to the name of the Memra of the Lord* who was revealed to
> you when you fled from before Esau your brother."

According to all the Targums the Lord/YHWH refers in Gen 35:1 to the
one who was revealed to Jacob at Bethel in the *third* person, as someone
distinct from Himself, in the same way as in the MT.[867]

In all the Targums, there is a correspondence between their renderings of Gen 35:3 and Gen 28:20; e.g., *Onqelos*:

> [Gen 28:20a] Then Jacob made a vow, saying, "If *the Memra* of the Lord *will
> assist me* and protect me on this journey that I am making... [Gen 35:3]
> Then let us arise and go to Bethel, and I will build (lit., make) an altar there
> to the God who accepted my prayer on the day of my distress and whose
> *Memra has been my support* on the journey ...

In agreement with Gen 35:1, *Neofiti* in v. 3 uses the same reference to
God: "... I will build an altar there to *the name of the Lord* who answered
me in the *hour* of my affliction and *was at my aid* on the journey ..."[868]
As in Genesis 24 and the book of Tobit, the theme of divine protection
of travelers is also expressed in the Targums. Jacob goes to Bethel in
order to fulfill his vow to the God who has supported him. As in Gen
28:16, *Neofiti* and *Pseudo-Jonathan* refer to 'the Glory of the Shekinah of
the Lord' in Gen 35:13,[869] while *Onqelos* uses the divine epithet 'the
Glory of the Lord': "Then the Glory of the Lord ascended from him
[Jacob] ..." The rest of the pericope in *Onqelos* is roughly similar to the
MT, but the Palestinian Targums show some striking deviations. In
Gen 35:7 we read in *Pseudo-Jonathan* and a Cairo Genizah–manuscript:

> [*Tg. Ps.-J.*] He [Jacob] built an altar there and called the place "El *who caused
> his Shekinah to dwell in* Bethel," because there *the angels of the Lord* had been
> revealed to him when he was fleeing from before *Esau* his brother./ ובנא תמן
> מדבחא וקרא לאתרא אל דאישרי שכינתיה בבית אל ארום תמן אתגליאו ליה מלאכייא דה במיערקיה
> מן קדם עשו אחוי[870]

---

867   Both *Onqelos* and *Pseudo-Jonathan* refer here to "... the God who revealed Himself ..."
868   The use of the divine epithet 'the name of the Lord' is relatively unusual in the
      Targums compared to such expressions as 'the Memra of the Lord'. The latter is es-
      pecially common when the meaning of the text is to express divine protection. The
      phrase "God/the Lord (or: I am) with you, is usually rendered as "the Memra of the
      Lord is (or: I, in my Memra am) at your aid." See McNamara 1992, 28.
869   See also Gen 35:13 in a targumic fragment of the Cairo Genizah; Leningrad,
      Saltykov-Schedrin ms Antonin Ebr. III B 542, folio 2v.
870   Aramaic text, see Ginsburger's edition 1971, 65.

[Cairo Genizah] And he built an altar, there; and he named the place El-Bethel; for there angels had been revealed unto him, when he was fleeing from before Esau his brother.[871]

[NRSV]: and there he built an altar and called the place El-bethel, because it was there that God had revealed himself to him …

In this quotation, we have an allusion to the appearance of the angels going up and down on the ladder that Jacob saw in his dream at Bethel, an interpretation most certainly based on the fact that the MT in Gen 35:7b has the verb גלה 'to appear/to reveal' in the *plural* form: … כי שם נגלו אליו האלהים … *Neofiti, Onqelos,* and the LXX, however, all render the verb in question in the third person *singular*, which according to Andrew Chester is most probably a response to the 'two-powers-heresy'. He further remarks that in this verse both *Pseudo-Jonathan* and the Cairo Genizah present an angelophany rather than a theophany.[872]

In both *Neofiti* and *Fragment Targums* (V and P) a long prayer is inserted in Gen 35:9: "Then God appeared to Jacob again [עוד], when he came from Paddan-Aram and blessed him."[873] I wish to point out a few things in the prayer. Let us look at the rendering of a part of verse 9 in the *Fragment Targums*:

ms P: … God of the World [אלהיה דעלמא],[874] may His name be praised […] And then You taught us to visit the sick, from our father Abraham, the righteous, unto whom you were revealed with Your good mercy, and You commanded him to circumcise his foreskin. And He sat at the opening of his tent, and You visited him; as it is written explicitly, and it says: "And the Lord appeared to him by the terebinths of Mamre."

ms V: […] as it is explicitly written […] "And the *memra* of the Lord was revealed to him in the Plain of the Vision …"[875]

ms P: And again you taught us to console the mourners from our father Jacob upon whom You were revealed when he arrived from Paddan-

---

871 Leningrad, Saltykov-Schedrin, ms Antonin Ebr. III B 542, folio 2r.

872 Chester 1986, 23-27, 156. See the Rabbinic discussion of this heresy and Gen 35:7 in *b. Sanhedrin* 38b. See also chapter 3 above and Segal 1977, 122. Other "dangerous passages" discussed by the Rabbis are, e.g., Gen 11:7; Deut 4:7; 2 Sam 7:23. Regarding *Onqelos*, it must be pointed out that there are other variants of Gen 35:7. According to Grossfeld (1988, 122), other readings are here "the angels of the Lord" (cf., *Pseudo-Jonathan* above) and "an angel of the Lord." As shown in chapter 3, Sarna interprets Gen 35:7b in a similar way to *Pseudo-Jonathan*.

873 This prayer is also extant in the Cairo Genizah; Leningrad, Saltykov-Schedrin, ms Antonin Ebr. III B 542, folio 2r and 2v.

874 This divine epithet could just as well be translated as 'God of Eternity'.

875 *Tg. Neof*: "….you were revealed to him in the Valley of the Vision while he was still suffering from circumcision …" Cairo Genizah: "… And the memra of the Lord was revealed upon him in the Plain of the Vision…"

Aram; and he had not rested from the pain of his hip-bone, he heard about the death of Rebekah his mother [...] and he sat down, screaming and wailing [...] and You in Your good mercy were revealed unto him to console him; You blessed him with the blessing of mourners; as it is explicitly written [...] "And the Lord appeared again to Jacob..."

ms V: [...] You were revealed unto him [...] when the way of the world occurred to Deborah [...] and Rachel died, to his sorrow [...] and You, Master of the Entire world [...] in the measure of Your good mercy were revealed unto him, and You consoled him, and You blessed him with the mourner's blessing on [the death of] his mother; it is therefore explicitly written [...] "And the *memra* of the Lord was revealed unto Jacob a second time when he arrived from Paddan-Aram, and he blessed him."[876]

This paraphrase of v. 9 is based both on the context of the verse and on the fact that the Bible says that God appeared *again* to Jacob and blessed him. God is praised in the Targums as the One who has taught His people to comfort the mourners. Why did God appear a second time to Jacob? The targumic answer is that God came in order to console Jacob in his grief because of the death of Deborah, his wife Rachel, and his mother.[877] The deaths of Deborah and Rachel are described in the biblical context, v. 8 and vv. 16-20 respectively. God appeared to Jacob at this dark hour and blessed him with the mourner's blessing.[878]

God is magnified in the prayer as the One who by His own example has taught His people to visit the sick, since He himself visited Abraham when he suffered because of his circumcision. One of the three men in Gen 18:2ff is thus identified as being a revelation of God Himself. God is here also depicted as reciting the mourner's benediction. The Jewish practices of blessing mourners and visiting the sick are hence derived from God Himself.[879]

In this context, ms V. of the *Fragment Targums* refers explicitly to one of God's main attributes: "... in the measure of Your good mercy..." In contrast to ms P, we see that ms V employs the targumic con-

---

876 *Tg. Ps.-J.* Gen 35:9b: "The Lord was revealed again to Jacob [...] and he blessed him *in the name of his Memra after his mother had died.*" Cf., Deut 34:6 according to *Pseudo-Jonathan.*

877 That Jacob was informed of the death of his mother during his stay in Bethel is presumably based on the fact that there is no mention in the Bible that Rebekah and Jacob ever met when he returned home. The reunion of Jacob and Isaac and the death of the latter, however, are mentioned in Gen 35:27-29.

878 This interpretation of God's appearance in v. 9 is also to be found in, for example, *Gen.Rab.* 81.5, and 82.3.

879 See also Maher 1992, note 13, p. 120, and McNamara 1992, note 12, 166.

ception 'the *memra* of the Lord'.[880] God is explicitly designated not only as the God of Israel, but as 'the Master of the Entire world'/ 'God of the World.'[881] The prayer inserted in Gen 35:9 tells us something important about how the Targumists perceived God's character.

This midrashic expansion of Gen 35:9 thus refers to God as the role model for certain works of mercy; being created in His image, humankind is to imitate God.[882]

As in the MT, it is YHWH who gives Jacob the name Israel in both *Onqelos* and the Palestinian Targums. With the exception of the Cairo Genizah rendering, where we read; "And the *memra* of the Lord said to him: Your name has been Jacob; you shall no longer be called Jacob, but rather Israel shall be your name ..."[883], all the Targums refer to God directly in Gen 35:10.

In Gen 35:11 we read that God designates Himself as "I am *El Shaddai*/ אני אל שדי*." As mentioned above, the exact meaning of the divine epithet *El Shaddai* is uncertain. The NRSV translates it as 'God Almighty'. This is also Freedman's translation of the epithet in the biblical quotation of Gen 35:11 in *Gen. Rab.* 82.4.

All the Targums employ the same epithet as the MT in the rendering of Gen 35:11,[884] with the exception of *Neofiti*, which has "I am God *of the heavens*."[885] This designation is the usual rendering in *Neofiti* of the biblical 'El Shaddai'. See, for example, Gen 17:1; 28:3; 43:14, and Exod 6:3.[886]

Genesis Rabbah

Gen. Rab. 82.2 records a Rabbinic interpretation of Gen 35:9:

> R. Isaac commenced: An altar of earth shalt thou make unto me ... in every place where I cause My name to be mentioned I will come unto thee and

---

880 As mentioned above, Hayward argues that 'the Memra' in the Targums represents God's mercy, a conclusion that seems to be supported by the use of the epithet in this context. See also Hayward 1981, 44.

881 As mentioned, the Aramaic epithet אלהיה דעלמא has a double connotation and may also be translated as "God of Eternity."

882 In this targumic prayer, the blessing of the bride and bridegroom is also said to be derived from God's blessing of Adam and Eve. A *Neofiti* marginal gloss to Gen 35:9 connects the obligation to bury the dead to God's burial of Moses. See McNamara (Eng. trans.) 1992, 166-167.

883 Leningrad, Saltykov-Schedrin, ms Antonin Ebr. III B 542, folio 2v.

884 The translators have left the epithet untranslated and render it as 'El Shaddai'. See Maher 1992, 120 (*Tg. Ps.-J.*) and Aberbach/Grossfeld 1982, 206 (*Onqelos*). Gen 35:11 is unfortunately not extant in the *Fragment Targums*.

885 LXX has here simply: "....Ἐγὼ ὁ θεός σου/I am your God..."

886 See also McNamara 1992, 35.

bless thee (Ex. XX, 24). If I bless him who builds an altar in My name, how much the more should I appear to Jacob, whose features are engraved on My Throne, and bless him. Thus it says, AND GOD APPEARED UNTO JACOB … AND BLESSED HIM.

R. Isaac thus connects God's blessing of Jacob in Gen 35:9 to the Rabbinic interpretation of Jacob's dream at Bethel (Genesis 28): Jacob's portrait is engraved on God's throne and the angels went up and down in order to look at, on the one hand, his heavenly portrait, and on the other the man himself sleeping on the ground.

The Rabbis of *Genesis Rabbah* also have a comment upon Gen 35:10 where we read that God changed Jacob's name and called him Israel:

> [*Gen. Rab.* 82.2] I am the Lord … that confirmeth the word of His servant, and performeth the counsel of His angels (Isa. XLIV, 24 ff.). Said R. Berekiah in R. Levi's name: Since He 'Confirmeth the word of His servant,' do we not know that He 'Performeth the counsel of His angels'? But [the explanation is this]: an angel had appeared to our father Jacob and said to him: "The Holy One, blessed be He, will reveal Himself to thee at Beth-el and change thy name, and I too will be present there. Thus it is written, At Beth-el He would find him, and there He would speak with us (Hosea XII, 5): it does not say, 'with thee,' but 'with us'. And so God appeared to him, in order to confirm the word of the angel [...] Thus, AND GOD APPEARED UNTO JACOB AGAIN…AND HE CALLED HIS NAME ISRAEL.[887]

The 'unknown man' who struggled with Jacob at the ford of Jabbok (Genesis 32) is identified by Rabbi Berekiah as an angel who foretold God's renaming of Jacob. The prediction of the angel, however, needed divine confirmation and this is the reason for God's second appearance to Jacob at Bethel. When Jacob returned to Bethel, God appeared to him once more and confirmed the new name in the presence of this angel. According to the Rabbi, that is why the prophet Hosea says; "… and there [in Bethel] He [God] would speak to *us* [Jacob and the angel] …"[888]

The Midrash contains additional interpretations of God's second appearance to Jacob when he returned to Bethel:

> [*Gen. Rab.* 82.3] R. Jose b. R. Hanina said: AGAIN implies, as on the first occasion. As on the first occasion [He spoke to him] through an angel, so on the second occasion it was through an angel. R. Abba b. Kahana said: [The word AGAIN implies]: I will not again unite My name with any human be-

---

887 See also *Pesiq. Rab Kah.* 7.3.
888 NKJV. See also the discussion of Genesis 32 above.

ing save one.[889] R. Judan said: [The word AGAIN intimates]: once again will I reveal myself unto thee.[890]

In the above passage, we have three different Rabbinic interpretations of the word עוֹד/'again' in Gen 35:9. According to the first, God spoke to Jacob through an angel "on the first occasion," which according to Freedman is a reference to Jacob's dream at Bethel (Gen 28:13-15)[891] and the same also applies to 'the second occasion'; the revelation described in Gen 35:9-12.[892] This understanding of the latter pericope thus contradicts the interpretation mentioned above, where God's personal appearance in Gen 35:9-10 is contrasted with Jacob's encounter with an angel in Genesis 32. Concerning the two other interpretations, see footnotes 889 and 890.

Jacob's Blessing of Ephraim and Manasseh

The Targums

According to *Neofiti*, Jacob says to Joseph in Gen 48:3: "The God *of the heavens* [MT: El Shaddai] was revealed to me at Luz [i.e., Bethel] in the land of Canaan and blessed me."[893] As in Gen 35:11, the other Targums use the same epithet as the MT; 'El Shaddai.'[894]

Both *Onqelos* and *Neofiti* render Gen 48:15-16 quite literally but, as usual, they refer to 'YHWH/the Lord' in v. 15, while the MT has

---

889 That is, Jacob. God has connected his name to the three Patriarchs, hence He is called; "the God of Abraham, Isaac and Jacob." See Freedman 1939, note 1, p. 754, and Hayward 2005, 270-273. In this context, it is also worth mentioning the interpretation of Gen 35:13 in *Genesis Rabbah*; "Then God went up from him [Jacob] in the place where he talked with him:"

[*Gen. Rab.* 82.6] AND GOD WENT UP FROM HIM, etc. (XXXV, 13). R. Simeon b. Lakish said: The Patriarchs are [God's] chariot, for it says, *And God went up from upon Abraham* (Gen XVII, 22); AND GOD WENT UP FROM UPON HIM; *And, behold, the Lord stood upon him* (ib. XXVIII, 13).

890 God will again reveal Himself to Jacob at Beer-Sheba, on his descent into Egypt (Gen 46: 1-4). See Freedman 1939, p. 754, note 2.

891 Freedman 1939, p. 753, note 4.

892 As shown above, Freedman interprets the "first occasion" mentioned in the Midrash in which God addressed Jacob as a reference to Gen 28:13-15. This is probably correct, but it must be pointed out that the reference is not clearly stated in the Midrash. Logically the "first occasion" could just as well allude to Gen 35:1 or Gen 31:10-13.

893 Cf., the targumic rendering of Genesis 35:11, see above.

894 The *Fragment Targums* have no preserved rendering of Gen 48:3. The only extant verses of this chapter are vv. 14, 22 (V) and v. 22 (P).

'God/Elohim.'[895] As in the Bible, the angel in v. 16 in these Targums seems to be equated with God, e.g., *Neofiti*:

> [Gen 48:15b] … *the Lord* who has *led* me from *my youth* until this day, [16] the angel who has redeemed me from all *tribulation*,[896] may he bless the boys …[897]

However, *Pseudo-Jonathan* has a unique rendering of Gen 48:15-16:

> [15] … *Lord*, before whom my fathers Abraham and Isaac worshipped, *Lord*, who *sustained* me since (the beginning of) my existence to this day, [16] *may it be pleasing before you that* the angel *whom you assigned to me to* redeem me from all evil, [יהי רעוא קדמך דמלאכא דומינת לי למיפרק יתי מכל בישא] bless the boys, and let my name be recalled in them, and the name of my fathers Abraham and Isaac.[898]

According to *Pseudo-Jonathan*, 'the angel' is thus not equated with God but is explicitly said to be *an emissary sent by God* to redeem Jacob from all evil. It is noteworthy that Jacob does not ask God himself to bless the boys, but prays that God will find it pleasing that *the angel* blesses Ephraim and Manasseh (cf., *T. Jac.* 4.15).

Genesis Rabbah

We have a similar interpretation of the pericope in *Gen. Rab.* 97.3 (Cur. Edd):

> R. Samuel b. Nahman said: It is even greater than redemption, for redemption comes through an angel,[899] whereas sustenance comes through the Holy One, blessed be He. Redemption comes through an angel: THE ANGEL WHO HATH REDEEMED ME. [Gen 48:16] Whereas sustenance comes through God: *Thou openest Thy hand, and satisfiest every living thing* (Ps. CXLV, 16).

The Midrash continues:

> [*Gen. Rab.* 97.3. Cur. Edd.] BLESS THE LADS. This alludes to Joshua and Gideon, as it is written, And it came to pass when Joshua was by Jericho,

---

895 According to Grossfeld (1988, 156), a variant reading of *Onqelos* has "God." *Neofiti*'s marginal glosses to Gen 48:15 refer to "the Memra of the Lord…" See McNamara 1992, 213.

896 *Neofiti* marginal gloss: "evil" = MT, *Onqelos* and *Pseudo-Jonathan*.

897 The rendering of these verses in the Cairo-Genizah fragment is roughly the same, with the exception that Jacob refers in v. 15 to the Memra: "The memra of the Lord, before whom my fathers […] worshipped loyally–the memra of the Lord who has led me […] [v. 16] The angel who redeemed and sa[ved] me from all evil, may he bless the youths…" [Cambridge University Library mss T-S AS 71.5v, 214r, 281r].

898 "Bless….and Isaac" is omitted in MS. Lond. See Maher 1992, note 16, p. 156. Clarke (1984, 61) has not included this part of v. 16 in his edition of *Pseudo-Jonathan*.

899 Neusner (1985, 338) translates "… for redemption takes place through the agency of a divine messenger …"

that he lifted up his eyes and looked, and, behold, there stood a man over against him … And he said: Nay, but I am captain of the host of the Lord; I am now come (Josh. V.13f.). R. Joshua said in the name of R. Hanina b. Isaac: He cried out from his very toe-nails, [900]'I am captain of the host of the Lord'; I am a prince of the celestial host, and wherever I appear the Holy One, blessed be He, appears.[901]

The angel who has redeemed Jacob from all evil, and whom he asks to bless his grandsons, seems thus to be identified with the unknown "man" with a drawn sword in his hand who appeared to Joshua according to Josh 5:13-15. It is striking that Joshua worshipped before this "man:"

> [Josh 5:13] Once when Joshua was by Jericho, he looked up and saw a man standing before him with a drawn sword in his hand. Joshua went to him and said to him, "Are you one of us, or one of our adversaries?" [14] He replied, "Neither, but as commander of the army of the LORD I have now come." And Joshua fell on his face to the earth and worshipped, and he said to him, "What do you command your servant, my lord?" [15] The commander of the army of the LORD said to Joshua, "Remove the sandals from your feet, for the place where you stand is holy." And Joshua did so.[902]

According to the midrashic passage quoted above, Jacob's angel also seems to be equated with the angel of the Lord who appeared to Gideon:

> [Judges 6:11b] … Gideon was beating out wheat in the wine press … [12] *The angel of the LORD* appeared to him and said to him, "The *LORD is with*

---

900 According to Freedman 1939, p. 939, note 3: "The expression 'from his toe-nails' means that he cried out with his whole body."

901 According to Freedman (1939, p. 939, note 1), this interpretation of Gen 48:16 is based on the facts that both Joshua and Gideon were descendants of Joseph, both are called young, and an angel appeared to both of them. Jacob thus prayed that Joshua and Gideon might be blessed. Concerning Joshua as a descendant of Ephraim, see, e.g., 1 Chr 7:20-27.

902 Cf., Exod 3:2-6:

> [2] There the angel of the LORD appeared to him [Moses] in a flame of fire out of a bush; he looked, and the bush was blazing, yet it was not consumed. [3] Then Moses said, "I must turn aside and look at this great sight, and see why the bush is not burned up." [4] When the LORD saw that he had turned aside to see, God called to him out of the bush, "Moses, Moses!" And he said, "Here I am." [5] Then he said, "Come no closer! Remove the sandals from your feet, for the place on which you are standing is holy ground." [6] He said further, "I am the God of your father, the God of Abraham, the God of Isaac, and the God of Jacob." And Moses hid his face, for he was afraid to look at God.

you, you mighty warrior." [13] Gideon answered him, "But sir, if the LORD
is with us, why then has all this happened to us? And where are all his
wonderful deeds … [14] Then *the LORD* turned to him and said, "Go in
this might of yours and deliver Israel from the hand of the Midian; I hereby
commission you. [15] He [Gideon] responded, "But sir, how can I deliver
Israel? My clan is the weakest *in Manasseh* … [16] *The LORD* said to him,
"But *I will be with you* …"

The identity of the angel of the Lord and the Lord Himself is merged in
the above passage. It is worth considering that in Judges 6 the angel of
the Lord and the Lord Himself seem to be one and the same person,
just as is the case with God and His angel in Gen 48:15-16.

Concluding Remarks

Considering the interpretation of Jacob's nightly struggle with the mysterious "man" of Genesis 32, we may conclude that the opponent is
consistently identified as an angel. Thus, all our sources deny that it
was God in person who Jacob met at Jabbok, most assuredly because
they wish to avoid the stunning implication that the patriarch in fact
strove with God in person. Moreover, since no man can see God and
live, it cannot have been God to whom Jacob refers in Gen 32:31, thus
'Elohim' is interpreted as meaning 'divine beings/angels' (e.g., *Tg. Neof,
Tg. Ps.-J.*) or 'an angel' (*Tg. Onq.*). In the two Palestinian Targums, Jacob's exclamation may be understood as referring to all his encounters
with angels, both at Bethel and at Jabbok, while in *Onqelos*, he only
seems to refer to the latter meeting.

The description of Jacob's angelic opponent differs between the various sources, sometimes even within one and the same text. In *Onqelos*
and the *Fragment Targums*, Jacob's angelic opponent is anonymous but
in *Neofiti* and *Pseudo-Jonathan*, he is identified by name, Sariel and Michael respectively. Both the *Fragment Targums* (ms P) and *Neofiti*[903] identify the angel as the celestial worship-leader, and this is the reason for
the angel's request to let him go when dawn comes. The same motif is
also present in *Pseudo-Jonathan*, ms V of the *Fragment Targums, Genesis
Rabbah*, the *Babylonian Talmud* and *Pirqê de Rabbi Eliezer* but in these
sources the angel is not said to be the leader of the heavenly choir. In
Genesis Rabbah, there is also an additional identification of Jacob's combatant as the guardian angel of Esau/Edom, who during the time of the

---

903 However, in a *Neofiti* marginal gloss, the angel is identified as 'the head of those who
are sent'.

Rabbis was seen as representing the Roman Empire. In this Midrash the transient nature of the angels is emphasized. However, Rabbi Berekiah argues that the angel who confronted Jacob was of higher rank and thus constant in nature. The Rabbi's statement can most probably be interpreted to mean that he regarded the opponent to be either the archangel Michael or Gabriel.

In *Pseudo-Jonathan*, the interpretation of the angel as Michael is evident. The alleged reason for his appearance is to remind Jacob of his promise to give a tenth of his possessions to God. In *Pirqê de Rabbi Eliezer*, this motif recurs, but here it is not Michael who reminds Jacob, although he also appears in this context. Instead, the angel who confronts Jacob at Jabbok is said to bear the name 'Israel' and, when the angel blesses Jacob, he gives him his own name, a motif that is not extant in any other of the discussed sources. Far from being the celestial representative of Esau, the appearance of the angel Israel is described in *Pirqê de Rabbi Eliezer* as an answer to Jacob's prayer for divine protection.

The idea of an angel blessing Jacob seems to have been a problematic issue in many of the sources, since the patriarch is considered to be his superior. Indeed, in *Pseudo-Jonathan*, Gen 32:30 is rendered; "... and *Jacob* blessed him [the angel] there ..." but in the other Targums it is the other way around, which is also the most natural interpretation of the Hebrew original.

However, in *Genesis Rabbah*, the blessing and renaming of Jacob in Genesis 32 is interpreted as the angel's disclosure of the future; when Jacob returns to Bethel, God will appear to him and give him the new name Israel. In this manner, the Rabbis interconnect Genesis 32; 35 and Hosea 12 to each other, an evident example of intertextual exegesis, so typical of Midrash. Thus, God's second appearance (Gen 35:9-12) is said to be in order to confirm Jacob's new name, Israel, in the presence of this very angel.

Accordingly, the dominant view in *Genesis Rabbah* seems to be that God in person spoke with Jacob at Bethel on both occasions (Genesis 28 and 35). There is nevertheless one passage in the Midrash according to which God spoke to him through an angel; both the first time (according to Freedman, an allusion to the dream in Genesis 28) and on the second occasion when Jacob returned to Bethel (Gen 35:9f: "Then God appeared again to Jacob ...", cf., *Gen. Rab.* 82.3). *Genesis Rabbah* thus has no consistent view on the matter. According to another interpretation, God appeared on the second occasion to comfort Jacob after the death of Deborah, among others. There is also an interpretation of Gen 35:9 in the Midrash which alludes to the tradition of Jacob's heavenly portrait.

God's (Elohim's) reference to the God (El) who appeared to Jacob in Gen 35:1 is preserved in the third person in our sources. The Hebrew verb גלה 'to appear/reveal' in Gen 35:7 is interpreted as referring to God in most of them. The Targums render the verb in the singular form, with the exceptions of *Pseudo-Jonathan* and a Cairo Genizah manuscript where the verb is interpreted as referring to the angels who Jacob saw going up and down on the ladder in his dream at Bethel (an interpretation we recognize from Sarna's commentary to Genesis). All the Targums, with the exception of a Cairo Genizah rendering, refer to God directly in Gen 35:10.

'The angel' of Gen 48:16 is understood in both *Onqelos* and *Neofiti* as an epithet referring to God. *Pseudo-Jonathan* differs from the other Targums in this case and distinguishes between God and the angel.

According to one interpretation in *Genesis Rabbah*, we are to understand Gen 48:16 as stating that redemption comes through an angel, while sustenance comes through God; the angel and God thus have different functions and are distinguished from each other. On the other hand, there is also a Rabbinic comment in this Midrash which connects the angel mentioned in Jacob's blessing of Ephraim and Manasseh with the revelations of Josh 5:13-15 and Judges 6 respectively. In the latter text, at least, it is again unclear whether it is an angel or God Himself who appears to Gideon.

4.5.6 Summary and Conclusions

The biblical ambiguity between God and the angel remains in the targumic renderings of Genesis 16 and 21. The most expanded paraphrases are to be found in the versions of Gen 16:13-14. Hagar gives the angel divine titles in the targumic renderings of Gen 16:13 but at the same time *Onqelos* inserts a reference to 'the living angel' in Gen 16:14, probably in an attempt to prevent the interpretation that it was God in person who appeared to Hagar. However, this rendering is unique for *Onqelos*. Regarding Gen 21:17-20, the Targums have a relatively literal rendering of the passage. There is a general tendency to avoid anthropomorphisms and to spiritualize the biblical accounts; Hagar did not meet the angel 'en route' but in a vision.

It is noteworthy that, according to *Neofiti*, the angel in Gen 24:7 is designated as 'the angel of mercy' and the same designation occurs in a *Neofiti* marginal gloss to Gen 28:13. This, however, is exceptional. In general, the translations of Genesis 24 in the Targums are relatively literal and the one who speaks to Jacob in his dream at Bethel in Genesis 28 is according to the Targums God Himself. Thus, it seems to be also implied that the angel who addresses Jacob in Gen 31:11-13 and identifies himself as 'the God who appeared in Bethel' in fact is God in person.

The sources clearly testify to a more developed angelology than the one found in the Bible, and there are references in many of them to additional angels who are not mentioned in the biblical accounts. They appear both in the various interpretations of the Aqedah and in the comments upon Genesis 16; 21; and 24 in *Genesis Rabbah*. According to the latter source, there were no less than four angels who appeared to Hagar. The Rabbis have no explicit comment on the identity of the angel of God in Genesis 21, but they have inserted other angels who oppose God's plan to rescue Ishmael. These angels are evidently distinguished from 'the angel of God' who acts as God's agent.

Since according to most Rabbis one angel does not perform two missions, one angel was appointed to accompany Eliezer on his journey and another to arrange his meeting with Rebekah.

In the interpretations of the Aqedah in *Genesis Rabbah* and Jacob's dream at Bethel, in this Midrash we encounter references to the angelic princes of the heathen nations, a motif that recurs in the identification of Jacob's angelic contender at Jabbok; the patriarch's opponent is said to be the guardian angel of Esau/Edom, i.e., Rome.

The dualistic perspective is evident in the interpretations of the Aqedah. For example, Satan is the alleged initiator of Abraham's trial in *b. Sanhedrin* 89b and, in *Pirqê de Rabbi Eliezer*, the demonic angel Samael is depicted as responsible for the death of Sarah.

In *Genesis Rabbah* the angels are said to have been jealous of Abraham. God therefore put him on trial in order to demonstrate Abraham's faithfulness. The presence of these angels can most probably be seen as an attempt to justify God and explain the reason for God's command to Abraham to sacrifice his son.

In addition to these accusing angels in the interpretations of the Aqedah, there are also those who are said to have cried and prayed on behalf of Abraham and Isaac. According to Niehoff, the crying angels represent God's merciful side. Whenever the 'angel of the Lord' figures in the interpretations, he is always clearly distinguished from these other, non-biblical angels. The difference between the descriptions of this angel and the weeping/watching angels in the Aqedah resembles the relationship between God who speaks to Jacob in his dream at Bethel and the ascending and descending angels.

Neofiti refers to a heavenly voice (*bat qol*/lit. 'daughter of a voice') addressing the angels in Gen 22:10 and, according to *Pirqê de Rabbi*

Eliezer, Abraham is prevented from sacrificing Isaac by God's voice calling to him. We saw in chapter 2.1.3 that the *bat qol* in Rabbinic sources is often used as an equivalent to the Holy Spirit. *Pirqê de Rabbi Eliezer* neglects mentioning the angel in its renderings of both the Aqedah and Genesis 21. It is God who speaks to Abraham and Hagar. In both *Pseudo-Jonathan* and, for example, *Pesqita de Rab Kahana*, the divine presence/Shekinah is said to have been manifested on Mount Moriah in the form of a cloud.

Another pattern of interpretation is the avoidance of theologically problematic issues. For example, the Rabbis of *Genesis Rabbah* omit to comment upon the angel's identification of himself with the God of Bethel in Gen 31:13, and this may also be the reason for omitting Hagar's encounter with the angel described in Genesis 16 in *Pirqê de Rabbi Eliezer*. For the early Jewish interpreters, it may have been very hard to imagine that a woman and servant like Hagar should have met God, and in addition to that astonishing fact, even given Him a "name", an epithet. Accordingly, the Rabbis of *Genesis Rabbah* emphasize that God never appeared in person to a woman, except to Sarah.

Moreover, all our sources claim that it was a distinct angel whom Jacob encountered at Jabbok, most certainly in order to avoid the stunning implication that Jacob strove with God. Since no man can see God and live, it cannot have been God who Jacob saw 'face to face'. Compare *Pseudo-Jonathan's* rendering of Hagar's statement in Gen 16:13: "You are the Living and Enduring One, who sees but is not seen."

The angel who struggles with Jacob is depicted in various ways in the sources; in the Palestinian Targums, *Pirqê de Rabbi Eliezer*, and *Genesis Rabbah*, he is depicted as a member of/the leader of the heavenly choir and in the latter source he is also described as the celestial patron of Esau. In *Neofiti, Pseudo-Jonathan,* and *Pirqê de Rabbi Eliezer*, he is called Sariel, Michael, and Israel respectively. Of all the Midrashim commenting on Genesis 32 discussed above, it is only in *Pirqê de Rabbi Eliezer* that the angel actually blesses and renames Jacob, presumably because the idea of an angel having the authority to bless the patriarch was a theologically sensitive issue.[904] *Genesis Rabbah* solves this problem by interconnecting Genesis 32; 35, and Hosea 12: The angel at Jabbok did not really bless Jacob; he only revealed God's plan to give him the name Israel when the patriarch returns to Bethel.

---

904 However, as stated in note 857 above, when commenting on Deut 33:1, *Pesiqta de Rab Kahana* also states that the angel blessed Jacob.

The general view in *Genesis Rabbah* is that God in person spoke to Jacob on both occasions at Bethel but there is one passage in the Midrash that claims that He spoke to him through an angel. It is typical of our sources that there is no consistent view on the matter. With the exception of the interpretations of Genesis 32, the tendency in our sources seems to be that Abraham and Jacob might have encountered God Himself while, in the case of Hagar, the situation is more ambivalent.

The identification of the angel whom Jacob refers to in Gen 48:16 is ambivalent in *Genesis Rabbah*; it is pointed out that redemption comes through an angel, but sustenance comes through God. On the other hand, this Midrash connects the verse with the revelation of the angel of the Lord to Gideon, a text where it is again unclear whether it is an angel or God Himself who appears.

Finally, we may conclude that there is no unambiguous or consistent interpretation of 'the angel of the Lord' and his identity in the sources. He is sometimes depicted as a divine emissary distinct from God,[905] while in other cases he appears to be seen as a manifestation of God Himself.[906] The ambivalence in the relationship between God and His angel remains in many of the interpretations of the texts.

In relationship to "ordinary" angels, 'the angel of the Lord' has a special, high status; he is always distinguished from other angels, whether they are already present in the Bible (Genesis 28, cf., Gen 31:11-13) or have been inserted into the biblical narratives by later interpreters (e.g., the Aqedah). A possible explanation for the many additional angelophanies may be that the biblical references to an angel inspired the imagination of the early Jewish interpreters of the texts.

Excursus 1. The Angel in Early Jewish Liturgical Poems

To the best of my knowledge, there are only two extant *piyutim*, i.e., liturgical poems,[907] of relevance to the present study that belong within the chosen time frame of this thesis. The poems are written in Aramaic

---

905 E.g., the interpretations of Genesis 32; 24 and Hagar's angels in *Genesis Rabbah*.

906 E.g., the renderings of Genesis 16 and 21 in the Targums (esp. the Palestinian ones) and the interpretations of Genesis 21; 22, and 31 in general.

907 The *piyutim* originated in the Palestinian Synagogues during the period of late Roman and Byzantine rule, i.e., the centuries before the Islamic conquest. The *paytanim*, liturgical poets, were generally cantors. For further information, see Carmi (introduction in *The Penguin Book of Hebrew Verse*) 1981, 14-50.

and Hebrew respectively and in both cases the authors remain un-known. Both *piyutim* concern the Aqedah. In the Aramaic *piyut* we read toward the end:

> The *angels stood up to appease their Lord,* we beg you to take pity on the boy, because of the love of his father we plead for the man in *whose house we have eaten salt.*

> The *Almighty* told him [Isaac]: be not afraid, boy, I am the Redeemer, and I shall redeem you, firm is God and strong are His deeds, there is no other like Him, none who resembles Him.[908]

In the same way as in, for example, the Palestinian Targums and 4Q225, this poem mentions angels involved in the Aqedah. However, it is *God/the Almighty* who saves Isaac, no specific angel of the Lord being mentioned. This is also the case in the Hebrew poem:[909]

> Then he [Abraham] went on to build the altar, stood up and placed his lamb [Isaac] upon it; he took the sword in his hand and took no pity at all.

> *The Almighty cried out to him* [Abraham]: 'Drop your hand at once! Instead of your son, I desire the ram caught by his horns in the thicket'.

> O God, heed these ashes, credit us with his covenant, favour us for his binding, reward our self-denial![910]

In the Aramaic poem, the angels plead for the life of Isaac and say: "*...we plead for the man in whose house we have eaten salt.*" This is proba-bly a reference to the visit of the three men to Abraham in Genesis 18, in Jewish sources often interpreted as angels. The angels pray that God will show mercy towards Abraham and Isaac (compare, e.g., *Genesis Rabbah* and *Pirqê de Rabbi Eliezer*, see chapter 4.5 above). God's response is to turn to Isaac and promise to redeem him. In contrast to the biblical account, God addresses Isaac, not Abraham,[911] but in the second He-brew poem it is Abraham who is the main character. The poems thus have different foci, Isaac and Abraham respectively, but have in com-mon that there is no reference to any specific 'angel of the Lord'.

In the two poems it is God Himself who saves Isaac, although angels pleading for his life are mentioned in the Aramaic one. The omission of a specific angelic savior recalls, for example, the account of the Aqedah

---

908 This poem is reconstructed from Genizah manuscripts and is to be found in the book *Jewish Palestinian Aramaic Poetry from Late Antiquity* (Sokoloff and Yahalom 1999, 124-131). See also van Bekkum 2002, 94-95.

909 This is the earliest known poem on the Aqedah. See Carmi (introduction in *The Penguin Book of Hebrew Verse*) 1981, 86.

910 See Carmi (Ed. and Eng. trans.), 1981, 201-202. See also van Bekkum 2002, 93.

911 Cf., 4Q225.

in *L.A.B.* 32.1-4 and the *Judean Antiquities*. The ascribing of the saving of Isaac to God in person in these sources may be due to the importance of the Aqedah in Jewish tradition and/or that the authors did not find it necessary to mention the angel, a mere messenger, speaking on God's behalf. In any case, it was God who intervened. However, the presence of the pleading angels in the Aramaic poem may be influenced by the appearance of 'the angel of the Lord' in Genesis 22.

Excursus 2. The Aqedah and the Angel in Early Jewish Art

Because of the Jewish prohibition against visual presentations of the 'holy', early Jewish artistic material connected to the 'angel of the Lord-texts' is scant, and the only depicted biblical scene of relevance to our study is the Aqedah.[912] The earliest known Jewish artistic presentation of this scene is the painting in the synagogue of Doura Europos (Syria)[913] from the middle of the third century C.E.[914] Next in terms of age are the floor mosaics in the Galilean synagogues in Beth Alpha[915] (ca. 525 C.E.) and Sepphoris (5th /6th century C.E.).[916]

In the synagogue of Doura Europos, the Aqedah is painted among the Torah shrine decorations. The Aqedah is portrayed on the right side of the shrine while other motives are the Temple (middle) and a huge Menorah to the left. The sacrificial site, the land of Moriah is thus identified with the Temple Mount.[917] The Aqedah is set in an obvious Temple context. The position of the painting tells us that it is an image of deep significance.

According to Eddy van den Brink, this constitutes a testimony to the Jewish conviction that the presence of God did not depart from Israel after the destruction of the Second Temple in 70 C.E. but was transferred to the synagogues, considered as holy places.[918] Isaac is painted as lying on the altar. The angel of the Lord who prevents Abraham from accomplishing the sacrifice is illustrated by *a hand* stretching

---

912 In the Doura Europos synagogue, there is a depiction probably showing the patriarch Jacob and a glimpse of the ladder, including two angels (see Goodenough 1988, illustration 52). However, the one who speaks to Jacob in his dream is not shown, thus the depiction is of little relevance for our subject.
913 See picture 1.
914 Thompson 1992, 241-243. See also van den Brink 2002, 142.
915 See picture 2.
916 See picture 3.
917 van den Brink 2002, 142.
918 van den Brink 2002, 144-145. Cf., chapter 2 above.

out from heaven above the altar. The hand is generally considered *to represent God.*[919]

The Temple context of the Aqedah is also apparent in the floor mosaic of the Beth Alpha synagogue.[920] In the upper center of the mosaic, the *hand of God* is pointing towards Abraham.[921] Above the hand, written in Hebrew are the words: אל תשלח "Lay not (your hand)." There are no angels portrayed in any of the pictures.

In both images of the Aqedah, the intervention of an angel of the Lord is thus represented by *a heavenly hand*. I conclude that it is *God Himself* who is depicted as preventing Isaac from being sacrificed. However, this does not necessarily imply that the artists identified the angel/messenger as God, the important fact is that God interfered and saved Isaac.

The imagery is biblical, God's activity as deliverer in the Bible is often symbolized by 'His right Hand'. One example is His deliverance of the Israelites from slavery in Egypt, see Exod 15:6, 12, an act that is also often ascribed to the angel of God, see, e.g., Exod 14:19 and 23:20-23.[922] It is noteworthy that this saving role has been taken over by the personified 'Lady Wisdom' in Wisdom 10, see, e.g., vv. 20-21, where the expressions 'your defending hand' and 'wisdom' seem to be equated with each other.[923] Moreover, a comparison of Wis 9:1-2 and 11:17 indicates that 'word' and 'hand" are alternate titles for 'wisdom':

Wis 9:1-2	Wis 11:17
[1] O God of my ancestors and Lord of mercy, who have made all things by your word, [2] And by your wisdom have formed humankind …	[17] For your all-powerful hand, which created the world out of formless matter …

These connections between 'God's Hand', 'the angel of the Lord', and 'Wisdom' may perhaps imply that the artists saw the angel of the Lord as God's "Hand;" a medium proclaiming God's will to Abraham, a "tool" in His hand?[924]

---

919 See, e.g., van den Brink 2002, 142.
920 van den Brink 2002, 144-145.
921 van den Brink 2002, 142-143.
922 See, e.g., Ps 118:15-16.
923 See also section 4.1.3 above
924 See Gieschen 1998, 101. Of course, the Jewish prohibition of portraying God may also have influenced the artists in question.

The mosaic in the Sepphoris synagogue is unfortunately not so well preserved, but two upturned shoes beneath a tree are still plainly visible in the right-hand panel. The implicit message is thus that Abraham and Isaac had removed their shoes out of respect for the holiness of the sacrificial site. Also discernible in the mosaic are the two servants, standing at the bottom of the mountain with the donkey. [925] In order to understand these details we must consider the midrashic tradition that Abraham and Isaac saw a manifestation of the divine presence at the site, marking it as the divinely chosen place for the act. The servants did not see this heavenly vision and were therefore left behind.[926] The depiction of the removal of the shoes due to the sacredness of the site recalls two other biblical texts; the angel of the Lord/God appearing to Moses from within the burning bush at Horeb (Exodus 3) and Joshua's encounter with the commander of the army of the Lord as recorded in Josh 5:13-15. [927]

1. Doura Europos synagogue, painting on the upper panel of Torah shrine (third century C.E.).

---

925 See also Weiss and Netzer 1998, 30-31.
926 Cf., *Gen. Rab.* 56.2.
927 See also Weiss and Netzer 1998, 30-31.

2. Beth Alpha synagogue, floor mosaic (ca. 525 C.E.).

3. Sepphoris synagogue, floor mosaic (fifth/sixth century C.E.). Courtesy of Prof. Zeev Weiss, The Sepphoris Expedition, The Hebrew University of Jerusalem. Drawing: Pnina Arad.

4.6 Scholarly Reflections on John 1:51

4.6.1 Introduction

The following chapter is a presentation of various scholarly interpretations of the Gospel of John, particularly John 1:51, in relation to Jewish traditions surrounding Jacob's divine encounters mainly as recorded in the Targums and Rabbinic Midrash, but also to some extent in the *Ladder of Jacob*, Philo's writings, and the *Prayer of Joseph*. Due to the difficulty in dating, for example, targumic material, the alleged connections between the Gospel and these Jewish interpretations remain largely hypothetical.

The Gospel of John

Since the Gospel of John is so well known, I find it sufficient to make just a few remarks regarding its general character.

The author appears to have been fully acquainted with Jerusalem's topography and Jewish theology, culture, and customs. Allusions to Old Testament themes and motifs are abundant. The affinities between the Qumran literature and the Fourth Gospel are well known.[928] Theories about the authorship of the Fourth Gospel are many and complex, but that is a topic for another thesis.[929]

While the gospel has a pronounced Jewish-Christian character,[930] a certain Hellenistic influence is also discernible, although the line between Hellenism and Judaism was blurred at the time of the Evangelist.[931] The gospel also contains anti-Gnostic polemic.[932]

---

928 See Lindars 1972, 36-38, Perkins 1989, 944-945, and Beasley-Murray 1987, lviii-lxiii.

929 According to tradition, the gospel was composed in Ephesus. Although its origins can be traced back to Judea, Ephesus may very well be the site of its final editing. The gospel may have wandered from Jerusalem to Antioch before acquiring its final form in Ephesus, see Beasley-Murray 1987, lxxv-lxxxi. The final form is often attributed to the Johannine School that is postulated to have emerged from the Johannine churches of Asia Minor, see Schnackenburg, 1980, vol. 1, 75-104, Brown 1966, lxxxviii-cii, and Perkins 1989, 946.

930 The language of the Gospel of John has obvious Semitic characteristics and Burney (1922) even suggested that it was originally written in Aramaic. See also Lindars 1972, 44-45. As is well known, the Gospel of John was composed at roughly the same time as the writings of Josephus.

931 From now on, I will simply use the term 'the Evangelist' when referring to the author(s) of the gospel.

The writings of Philo of Alexandria predate the gospel and have often been discussed in connection with it. Although both Philo and the Evangelist use the term 'Logos' in speaking about God's revelation, whether they are referring to the same phenomenon is a matter of debate.[933] Nevertheless, they evidently shared a similar Jewish-Hellenistic heritage[934] and both were influenced by Jewish Wisdom tradition.[935]

4.6.2 The Gospel of John and Jacob's Divine Encounters

John 1:51 and Jewish Traditions – Some Introductory Remarks

Although scholars agree that John 1:51 alludes to Jacob's vision of the heavenly ladder in Gen 28:10-22, there is no consensus regarding the precise interpretation of this allusion. It is generally acknowledged that the logion in John 1:51 does not only build upon the biblical text as such, but also upon a long tradition of Jewish exegesis of the pericope.[936] John 1:51 and its preceding context reads as follows:

> [John 1:47] When Jesus saw Nathanael coming toward him, he said of him, "Here is truly an Israelite in whom there is no deceit!" [48] Nathanael asked him, "Where did you get to know me?" Jesus answered, "I saw you under the fig tree before Philip called you." [49] Nathanael replied, "Rabbi, you are the Son of God! You are the King of Israel!" [50] Jesus answered, "Do you believe because I told you [σοι] that I saw you under the fig tree? You will see [ὄψῃ] greater things than these." [51] And he said to him, "Very truly, I tell you [ὑμῖν], you will see [ὄψεσθε] heaven opened, and *the angels of God ascending and descending upon the Son of Man*" [937] [my italics].

---

932 See Bultmann 1971, 7-9, Cullmann 1976, 30-38, Brown 1966, lxxv-lxxvii and Beasley-Murray 1987, liii-lxvi, lxxxix-xc.

933 See, e.g., Schnackenburg 1980, vol. 1, 125, 485-493, and Brown 1966, lvii-lviii.

934 See Beasley-Murray 1987, liv-lv, and Brown 1966, lviii and 520.

935 See, e.g., Brown 1966, lviii.

936 See, e.g., Rowland 1984, 500.

937 Some scholars (e.g., O'Neill 2003, 374, Neyrey 1982, 586-589, and Rowland 1984, 500) regard John 1:51 as an originally independent saying by Jesus. They refer to the sudden shift to the plural form in v. 51 as an indication that it is a later addition to the Nathanael story. Another way of explaining the shift to the plural is that Nathanael may be seen as a representative of all the followers of Jesus, compare the conversation with Nicodemos in John 3. Be that as it may, most scholars agree that in John 1:51 Jesus is not only addressing Nathanael but all his disciples. Most certainly, the reference is to disciples in a broader sense, i.e., including presumptive readers of the Gospel. See also, e.g., Ashton 1991, 348, and Fossum 1995, 151.

According to John C. O'Neill, the word 'see' constitutes a catchword linking the logion with its present context. Jesus' promise to Nathanael in v. 50 "... You will *see* greater things than these," reminded the Evangelist of the saying about *seeing* angels ascending and descending upon the Son of Man.[938] The designation of Nathanael as a true Israelite in v. 47 most probably also played a part in the insertion of the logion, since a common contemporary interpretation of the name 'Israel' was 'he who sees God'. [939]

Moreover, the allusion to the name of the third patriarch recalls the narrative of Jacob's dream-vision at Bethel in Genesis 28, which lies behind Jesus' statement in John 1:51.[940] As will be shown below, the logion also fits very well into the overall Christological context of John chapter 1 and indeed the Gospel as a whole.[941]

There is no mention of a ladder in John 1:51, the angels are instead depicted as going up and down on Jesus, 'the Son of Man', which in this context is not only a Messianic but also a divine title.[942] A common conclusion among scholars is that the Evangelist was influenced by the Jewish exegetical tradition which understands *bo* [בו] 'on it/him/for his sake' in Gen 28:12 as referring to a *person*, i.e., Jacob, and not the ladder.[943] The unusual order of the movement of the angels in both Gen 28:12 and John 1:51, i.e., first ascending and then descending, probably constitutes an additional link between the two texts.[944]

Up to this point, most scholars are prepared to accept a connection between the two texts, but there are manifold interpretations of the precise meaning of the allusion to Genesis 28 in John 1:51.

This is not the proper place for a detailed exegesis of the verse, thus I will restrict myself to presenting an outline of the various interpretations of concern for our quest. These interpretation models need not exclude one another; the logion most certainly contains many dimensions and there are no sharp distinctions between them. In the words of

---

938 O'Neill 2003, 374.

939 O'Neill 2003, 374. This interpretation of the name Israel is apparently shared by the Evangelist, see also Hayward 2005, 312-316.

940 See, e.g., O'Neill 2003, 374, and Neyrey 1982, 589.

941 See also Rowland 1984, 498-500, and Neyrey 1982, 586-605.

942 Cf., Dan 7:13-14 and Mark 14:61-62. See also Neyrey 1982, 587, 594-605, and Gieschen 1998, 280-283.

943 In making this connection, the Evangelist was dependent upon the ambiguous Hebrew text, and not the LXX, see the text analysis above and Burney 1922, 115-116. See also, for example, Odeberg 1929, 33-42, Brown 1966, 89-91, Clarke 1974/75, 374, Dodd, 1953, 245-246, Kugel 1990, 115, and Ashton 1991, 342-348

944 See also Rowland 1984, 500.

the Rabbis, the Scripture has many layers; see the famous saying in the *Mishnah Abot*: "Turn it over and over because everything is in it."[945]

Jesus as the Ladder

According to, for example, Charles Kingsley Barrett, Barnabas Lindars, and John Ashton, as 'the Son of Man' Jesus is the 'ladder,' that is, the connecting link between the divine and the human spheres.[946] In John 1:51, the angels are depicted ascending and descending upon ($\dot{\epsilon}\pi\acute{\iota}$) the Son of Man, thus Jesus takes the place of the ladder of Gen 28:12.[947] Such an interpretation of John 1:51 may also lie behind the *Ladder of Jacob* chapter 7, considered by many scholars to be of Christian origin:[948]

> [*Lad. Jac.* 7:1] "And as for the angels you saw descending and ascending the ladder, [2] in the last years there will be a man from the Most High, and he will desire to join the upper (things) with the lower. [3] And before his coming your sons and daughters will tell about him and your young men will have visions about him ..."

Jesus as the God who Appears in Genesis 28

Another way of interpreting John 1:51 is to see Jesus as corresponding to God[949] who stands above the ladder.[950] According to John 1:18, no one has ever seen God, thus all OT theophanies were in reality revelations of God the Son, not God the Father. Jerome H. Neyrey and Margaret Barker advocate this explanation and identify Jesus as the Deity

---

945 *m. Abot* 5.22. (Eng. trans. Neusner 1988, 689). See also chapter 2 above.

946 Barrett 1956, 186-187, Lindars 1972, 121-122, and Ashton 1991, 342-348, See also Beasley-Murray 1987, 28, Bultmann 1971, 105-106, Odeberg 1929, 33-42, and Perkins 1989, 953. In later Jewish Mystical literature, the angel Metatron is depicted as the ladder of Jacob's vision, see further Odeberg's introduction to *3 Enoch*, 1928, 123. Cf., Joh 14:6; Job 33:23-28, and 1 Tim 2:5-6: [5] "For there is one God and one Mediator between God and men, the Man Christ Jesus, [6] who gave Himself a ransom for all, to be testified in due time...

947 In Gen 28:12, the LXX uses the same preposition for 'upon', i.e., $\dot{\epsilon}\pi\acute{\iota}$.

948 See chapter 4.2.1 and Lunt in *OTP*, vol. 2, 1985, 402-405.

949 Neyrey 1982, 586-591. Cf., the reference to Christ inserted by Christians in vv. 19-20 of the second preserved prayer in the *Hellenistic Synagogal Prayers*: "And having placed our father Jacob in Mesopotamia, having shown (him) the Christ, through him you spoke, saying, *Look! I am with you* ..." [Eng. trans. Darnell in *OTP*, vol. 2, 1985, 678].

950 Or beside Jacob, see section 3.2.5.

appearing in the OT. It was actually the pre-incarnate Logos/Christ who appeared to Jacob and all the other saints during Israel's biblical history.[951] An identification of Jesus with the theophanic angel of the Lord seems thus to be implied in the Gospel.[952] In the words of Ashton:

> ... I believe that a reasonable case has already been made for the view that the מלאך יהוה tradition provides the most plausible and obvious explanation of John's presentation of Jesus as the emissary of God. The pages of the Bible are crowded with a host of intermediary figures–word, spirit, name, priests and prophets, not to mention dreams and visions–that represent God in his dealings with humanity; but nowhere else is there such an obvious analogue to the tantalizing equivocation that makes it impossible, when assessing the Christology of the Fourth Gospel, to settle definitely for either ditheism or subordinationism. Searching in the Jewish tradition for remnants of a possible bridge that could lead across to John's provocatively ambiguous portrayal of Jesus' relationship with the God who sent him (the Father–Son relationship is another story) where else should we look?[953]

On the other hand, when James Dunn discusses the angel of the Lord in the OT in relation to the Christology of the NT, he concludes that:

> ... no NT writer thought of Christ as an angel, whether as a pre-existent divine being who had appeared in Israel's history as the angel of the Lord, or as an angel or spirit become man [...] 'The angel of the Lord' in early Jewish texts is most obviously a way of speaking about Yahweh himself, and when 'the angel of the Lord' reappears in the writings of Luke and Matthew there is no real possibility of confusing him with Jesus. The idea of Jesus as an incarnation of an angel never seems to have entered the head of any NT author...[954]

At first sight, Dunn's statement differs from the interpretation of Jesus' identity in John 1:51 presented above. However, on closer examination the difference may not be that great. When Neyrey, Barker, and Ashton speak of Jesus as the theophanic angel of the Lord in the OT, they identify him as God. Obviously, they do not identify him as an independent angel in the terms of the later angelology of Second Temple Judaism,

---

951 Barker 1992, 227-228, Neyrey 1982, 589-594. See also John 8:56-58: "Your ancestor Abraham rejoiced that he would see my day. He saw it and was glad. Then the Jews said to him, 'You are not fifty years old, and you have seen Abraham'? Jesus said to them, 'Very truly, I tell you, before Abraham was, I am'." See also John 12:41 Cf., Isaiah 6: "Isaiah said this because he saw his [Jesus'] glory and spoke about him." See also Rowland 1984, 499-500, and Thunberg 1966, 563-570.

952 See Neyrey 1982, 590-594, Fossum 1995, 109-133, Borgen 1968, 137-148, and Gieschen 1998, 270-283. This interpretation is clearly stated in the writings of Justin Martyr, e.g., *Dialogue with Trypho* 56.4, 10; 58.3; 59.1; 61.1; 128.1. See also Daniélou, 1964, 132-134, and Talbert 1976, 430-431.

953 Ashton 1994, 82-83, see also the whole chapter, pp.71-89.

954 Dunn 1989, 158.

i.e., an angel such as Gabriel in the Gospel of Luke, see chapter 4.1. Most certainly, they would agree with Dunn that Jesus is not an incarnated angel in that sense of the word.[955]

As mentioned in chapter 1, the original meaning of the Hebrew word מלאך is 'messenger', 'one who is sent', and in the Gospel of John, Jesus clearly stands out as the messenger/agent of God the Father *par excellence*.[956]

In many ways, the ambiguous relationship between the angel of the Lord and God in the OT is mirrored in Jesus' intimate relationship with the Father. Jesus' teaching is not his own, but he speaks only as he is told by his Father.[957] Just as the identities of God and the angel of the Lord are blurred in the OT, so are the identities of Jesus and the Father in John's Gospel, see, for example, John 10:30, 38, where Jesus says: "The Father and I are one [...] the Father is in me and I am in the Father." See also John 5:30, 36-39; 7:16; 8:51-59; 12:49; 14:6-7, and 14:9b-10:

> [9b] "... Whoever has seen me [Jesus] has seen the Father. How can you [Philip] say, 'Show us [the disciples] the Father'? [10] Do you not believe that I am in the Father and the Father is in me? The words that I say to you I do not speak of my own; but the Father who dwells in me does his works."

As we know, Jacob was eventually named Israel by God, and as their ancestor he represents the people of Israel. It is therefore no coincidence that Jesus in this context addresses Nathanael as ἀληθῶς Ἰσραηλίτης, 'truly an Israelite' (v. 47). The name 'Israel' can be interpreted as meaning 'the one who sees God', compare John 1:50 where Jesus says to Nathanael; "... You will see greater things than these ..." [958] Jesus compares Nathanael to his ancestor Jacob/Israel and, like him, Nathanael will see the Glory of God [959] manifested in Jesus himself. In v. 51, not only Na-

---

955 Cf., also Jude 5, where according to some mss Jesus is credited as the one who delivered the Israelites out of Egypt, thus it seems implied that the author identified Jesus as the theophanic angel of the Exodus, see also chapters 3 and 4.1.

956 In the Gospel of John, Jesus often refers to the Father as the one who sent him. See, e.g., John 3:13-17; 5:30-38; 6:29, 35-40; 7:16-18, 28-29; 12:44-50; 13:20, and 20:21. See also Borgen 1968, 137-148, Evans 1993, 135-145, and Talbert 1976, 418-440.

957 See also North 2004, 155-166.

958 This etymology of the name Israel is to be found in, for example, Philo's writings, e.g., *On Dreams* 1.114. The fig tree under which Nathanael is depicted as having been sitting in v. 48 is also sometimes used as a symbol for the people of Israel, cf., Hos 9:10 and Jeremiah 24.

959 *Targum Onqelos* speaks about God's Glory, the *Yeqarah* standing over Jacob in Gen 28:13.

thanael but all of Jesus' disciples are cast in the role of Jacob. Like Jacob, they will see a theophany.[960]

As support for this interpretation, Neyrey mentions several other pericopes in the Gospel, e.g., John 5:37:[961]

> And the Father who sent me [Jesus] has himself testified on my behalf. You [the Jews] have never heard his voice or word or seen his form…

See also John 6:46:

> Not that anyone has seen the Father except the one who is from God [Jesus]; he has seen the Father. [Cf., John 1:18].

These sayings of Jesus seem to imply that not even Moses ever saw God the Father.[962] In this context, Neyrey refers to Philo who accepted the statement in Exod 33:20-23 that no one can see God and therefore interpreted the theophanies of the OT as revelations of God's 'Logos'/Word or a potency of God. According to Neyrey, although Philo understood the name 'Israel' as meaning 'the one who sees God', he nevertheless maintained that the patriarch did not see God in person, but the 'divine Logos'.[963]

However, in Philo's writings the name Israel is not only the name of the patriarch Jacob, but also a name that he gives the 'divine Word/Logos', which in turn is often identified with the angel of the Lord.[964] According to Philo, it is the heavenly Israel who truly is 'the one who sees God':

> But if there be any as yet unfit to be called a Son of God, let him press to take his place under God's Firstborn, the Word, who holds the eldership among the angels, their ruler as it were. And many names are his, for he is called, "the Beginning," and the Name of God, and His Word, and the Man after His image, and "he that sees," that is Israel [*On the Confusion of Tongues* 146].[965]

In his discussion of Philo's 'Logos' concept in connection with Johannine Christology, Craig Evans writes:

> This common identification of the *logos* with the 'angel of the Lord' [in Philo's writings] could make an important contribution to the bridge between

---

960 Neyrey 1982, 589-590. Cf., for example, John 1:14; 2:11 and 14:6-14.
961 Neyrey 1982, 589-594. He also refers to, e.g., John 1:18; 3:13; 8:56-58 and 12:41.
962 Neyrey 1982, 590.
963 E.g., *On Dreams* 1.157. See also Neyrey 1982, 592-594, Hayward 2005, 312-316, and Thompson 2007, 215-226.
964 See Evans 1993, 100-114, Borgen 1968, 144-148, Barker 1992, 114-133, and Gieschen 1998, 278-279. For references in Philo's works, see the quotation above and chapter 4.3.
965 Cf., Col 1:15. See also Dunn 1989, 165.

Wisdom and *logos* speculations and the Johannine confession that the 'Word became flesh'. If the *logos* could be identified as the angel that walked the earth and was seen by the patriarchs, then it would not be too difficult to equate the *logos* with Jesus who walked the earth and taught his disciples.

The Philonic identification of the Logos as the "angel" Israel recalls the *Prayer of Joseph* treated above in chapter 4.2.[966]

Jesus as Jacob's Heavenly Counterpart

As mentioned previously, many scholars connect the logion in John 1:51 with the Jewish tradition which interprets 'on it'/'on him' [בו] in Gen 28:12 as referring to Jacob. As we have seen above, this interpretation is for example attested in the Palestinian Targums, where the angels are said to ascend and descend between heaven and earth on/for the sake of Jacob. The reason for the shuttling up and down of the angels is said to be that they wish to gaze upon the man whose image is engraved on the throne of Glory. Although the Targums in their extant form postdate the Gospel, they contain early traditions.[967] Many scholars thus assume that the Evangelist was influenced by this targumic reading of Gen 28:12[968]

Christopher Rowland, for example, understands the targumic paraphrase of the verse to imply that Jacob's image on the heavenly throne is identical to 'the face of a man' mentioned among the 'living creatures' in Ezek 1:10. The angels wished to look upon Jacob because his features disclosed the mystery and Glory of God. According to Rowland, in the Evangelist's allusion to Gen 28:12, Jesus/the Son of Man substitutes for Jacob as the embodiment of the Glory of God and is thus the focal point of the angels' attention.[969]

A similar, but slightly different interpretation is offered by Jarl Fossum. Like Rowland, he takes his starting point in the Jewish tradition of

---

966 See also Smith 1968, 253-294, and *Pirqê de Rabbi Eliezer* 37, where Jacob's angelic combatant bears the name 'Israel', see further chapter 4.5. See also Fossum 1995, 142-151, and the discussion below regarding Jacob's guardian angel/heavenly counterpart. For a discussion of the *Prayer of Joseph* and Philo's exegesis, see chapters 4.2 and 4.3 respectively.

967 See, e.g., Rowland 1982, 502, and Hayward 2005, 318. As shown in chapter 4.2, the same tradition seems to be extant in the *Ladder of Jacob*. For further information, see also chapter 2.2.3 and 4.5.

968 See, e.g., Clarke 1974/75, 374-375, Rowland 1984, 501-503, and Hayward 2005, 318.

969 Rowland 1984, 500-507.

Jacob's heavenly counterpart and regards this idea as the key to the interpretation of John 1:51.[970] He firmly rejects the notion that Jesus is to be seen as the ladder in this logion:

> The message conveyed by the picture is not simply 'that there is no other *route* between heaven and earth than the Son of Man'. The view that John 1.51 represents the Son of Man as the revealer sidesteps the real issue, namely that of the *connection between* the figure of the Son of Man and the ascent and descent of the angels.[971]

As a basis for his refutation of the 'ladder-theory', Fossum declares that Jacob is never seen as a mediator in the Rabbinic exposition of Genesis 28.[972]

However, he doubts that the original targumic elaboration of Gen 28:12 suggested that the patriarch's image was *engraved* on the heavenly throne, and remarks that if this really is the case, it would be difficult to argue for a link to John 1:51; "... for the fourth Gospel does not teach that the Son of Man has an engraved image in heaven."[973] As support for this claim, Fossum refers to an alternate reading in two versions of the *Fragment Targum*, where the verb 'engraved' or 'fixed' is omitted in the rendering of Gen 28:12; Jacob's image [אקונין] is simply said to be *on* His [God's] throne of Glory.[974] Since this version is theologically controversial, Fossum argues that it represents the *lectio difficilior* and thus is the original targumic reading:[975]

> ... It is to be noted that the shorter reading of the Fragmentary Targum can easily explain the addition of the verb 'engraved', while it would remain difficult to explain why a scribe would leave out the verb and create a reading which appears to be rather provocative.[976]

In agreement with Rowland, he understands the heavenly image of Jacob as the manifestation of God's Glory[977] but goes one step further and identifies this 'image' as the patriarch's *guardian angel*. This angel bears his name, Israel, as well as his features.[978] As support for his

---

970 Fossum 1995, 135-139.

971 Fossum 1995, 136.

972 Fossum 1995, 136-137.

973 Fossum 1995, 140.

974 I.e., Editio princeps (Venice 1590/91), see the reprint in *The London Polyglot,* ed. Walton(us), 1655-57, and ms Vatican Ebr. 440. See Klein (ed. and trans.) 1980, vol. I, p. 144 (Aramaic text) and vol. II, p. 107 (Eng. trans.). See also section 4.5.5.

975 Fossum 1995, 141-142.

976 Fossum 1995, 141.

977 Fossum 1995, 138-142.

978 Fossum 1995, 142-149. In the Jewish tradition, both in the Bible itself and in extra-biblical sources, there is ambiguity concerning the heavenly guardianship of the

claim, Fossum refers, for example, to the *Prayer of Joseph*, which according to him implies that there exists a mystical identity between two beings; the patriarch Jacob and his heavenly counterpart.[979] However, Jacob's 'image' is no ordinary guardian angel but the angel Israel, the very Glory of God.[980]

Finally, Fossum concludes that the implications of John 1:51 in the light of these Jewish traditions is that "… Jesus, like Jacob-Israel, is both in heaven and on earth at the same time."[981] When he walked this earth, Jesus, the Son of Man, was simultaneously present in heaven with the Father.[982] The allusion to the angels ascending and descending between Jacob sleeping on the ground and his 'image' upon the throne of God constitutes a promise of a vision of the Glory of God manifested in the Son of Man on earth.[983]

Similarly, Gieschen sees in Jesus' words to Nathanael in John 1:50-51 an example of his self-identification with the enthroned Glory of God:

> Jesus is presented here as the angelomorphic Son of Man, namely, the Glory who has "the appearance like a man" (Ezek 1.26; Dan 7.13) and whom angels desire to see. Therefore, the "greater things" Jesus is promising that Nathanael, a true "Israelite" (cf. Philo's etymology of Israel = "he who sees God"), will see are those things associated with the visible manifestation of the Glory who is the Son of man, upon whom all the heavenly host wish to gaze.[984]

He further points out that, in the Gospel of John, Jesus refers to himself on many occasions as the only mediator of heavenly revelation by

---

people and nation of Israel. For example, in Deut 32:9 it is written that Israel is God's own portion (cf., *Jub.* 15.30-32) but in Dan 12:1, the archangel Michael is said to be the guardian of the people. Likewise, both in *T.Dan.* 6.5 and in 4Q369 there is a reference to an angel of peace as a guardian over Israel, see also Kugel 2006, 186-206, *Lad. Jac.* 4.1-5 and *Pirqê de Rabbi Eliezer* 37. For further discussion, see chapter 4.2.

979 Fossum 1995, 142-149. Fossum also refers to the Greco-Roman idea that every person has a guardian spirit who looks like him or her. This idea was incorporated into Judaism, see pp. 145-147 and *Deut. Rab.* 4.4. Cf., also Enoch's identification with the heavenly 'Son of Man' in *1 Enoch* 37-71 and VanderKam 2000, 425-429. See also Smith's introduction to the *Prayer of Joseph* in *OTP* vol. 2 1985, pp. 703-711, Smith 1968, 253-294, Borgen 1968, 144-148, and Ashton 1991, 342-348. For a detailed discussion of the *Prayer of Joseph* in this thesis, see chapter 4.2.

980 Fossum 1995, 142-149. Cf., also the 'face of a man, carved out of fire' in *Lad. Jac.* 1.4-6 and Jacob's subsequent prayer in *Lad. Jac.* 2.7-19. See also Orlov 2004, 59-76.

981 Fossum 1995, 149, see also pp. 150-151.

982 Fossum 1995, 149-150. See also John 1:18; 8:16, 23, 29; 10:30, and 16:32.

983 Fossum 1995, 149-151.

984 Gieschen 1998, 281.

means of the descent-ascent motif,[985] e.g., John 3:13,[986] where Jesus says to Nicodemus:

"No one has ascended to heaven but He who came down [i.e. descended] from heaven, that is, the Son of Man, *who is in heaven.*"[987]

Israel – the One Who Sees God: Genesis 32 and John's Gospel

In addition to Jacob's dream at Bethel, Robert Hayward reads John 1 in the light of Jacob's change of name to Israel after the struggle at the ford of Jabbok in Genesis 32.[988]

In agreement with other scholars, Hayward remarks that the Evangelist interpreted the name 'Israel' as meaning 'the one who sees God' and that this played an important role in his writing of the first chapter. Like O'Neill, Hayward points out that the matter of 'seeing' is a key issue in John 1, and he connects this to the traditions surrounding the bestowal of the name Israel upon Jacob in Genesis 32. For example, the assertion in verse 18 that no one has ever *seen* God appears to be a flat contradiction of Jacob's words in Gen 32:31"... For I have *seen* God face to face and yet my life is preserved."

The name Peniel/Penuel that Jacob/Israel gives to the place of the struggle in v. 30 is translated in the LXX as εἶδος θεοῦ 'form/face of God'. When speaking directly of God, the LXX only employs the word εἶδος in Gen 32:30-31. Hayward further reminds his readers of the single occurrence of the word in John's gospel, i.e., Jesus' statement in 5:37, where he says to his hearers, the Jewish people: "... You have never heard his [God the Father's][989] voice or word or seen his form [εἶδος] ..." The implication of this statement is thus that the patriarch Jacob never saw God or God's form, at least not directly.[990] As shown

---

985   Gieschen 1998, 280-283, esp. p. 282. See also Ashton 1991, 348-356, and Talbert 1976, 418-440.

986   See also e.g., John 6:42, 46; 6:62; 16:28, and 20:17.

987   Although the last clause in the verse "... who is in heaven" is missing in Codex Sinaiticus Codex Vaticanus (both of which are Alexandrian mss) and the Bodner papyri p⁶⁶ and p⁷⁵, it has considerable text-critical support. See also Fossum 1995, 149-150.

988   As a matter of fact, according to Hayward (2005, 312-320), the interpretation of the name Israel as 'one who sees God' and the analogy between Jacob/Israel and Jesus are central for the Christology of the entire Gospel.

989   See John 5:36.

990   Hayward 2005, 313.

above, this appears to be in accordance with Philo's interpretations of Jacob's theophanies.[991]

Moreover, John 1:47 contains the only reference in the Gospel to the title 'Israelite'; when seeing him, Jesus defines Nathanael as a true Israelite. During their conversation, Nathanael acknowledges Jesus as the Son of God and King of Israel. His real identity is thus beginning to be revealed to the people of Israel, here represented by Nathanael, cf., John 1:31.[992] Jesus' response to Nathanael's confession is that he will see even greater things; he will see heaven open and the angels ascending and descending upon the Son of Man.[993] According to Hayward, although Nathanael represents Israel, the Evangelist also portrayed Jesus as analogous to Jacob/Israel:

> On one level, Jesus may be compared with Jacob (John 1:51). The Hebrew Bible, read in one particular way, tells how angels ascended and descended on him at Bethel [...]
>
> Nathanael is a true 'Israelite' who will see what the Patriarch saw; he will see angels. But he will see more than that: he will also see Jesus *in persona Israel* with the angels going up and coming down upon him. This Jesus may be analogous to Jacob; but he is, for the Evangelist, greater than Jacob, inasmuch as he, as well as the angels, becomes the object of sight to whom the vision of the true Israelite Nathanael will be directed. Such status the Patriarch Jacob himself never quite enjoyed, since this Jesus is the Logos (John 1:1), that very reality with which, according to Philo, Jacob had wrestled in order to see God.[994]

Hayward interprets John 1:51 in light of the tradition of Jacob's heavenly image on the throne of Glory; similar to Jacob in Jewish tradition, Jesus' true home is in heaven, where the angels dwell.[995]

In order to demonstrate this analogy between Jacob and Jesus, Hayward also refers to Jesus' conversation with the Samaritan woman at the well of Jacob.[996] The woman asks Jesus: "… are you greater than our ancestor Jacob …?"[997] This question is obviously answered affirmatively in the gospel.[998]

Hayward further points out the importance of the feast of Sukkoth in the Fourth Gospel and connects this to the Jewish tradition which

---

991 See also Hayward 2005, 163-164, 208, 314-316, and above, chapter 4.3.
992 Hayward 2005, 313-314.
993 See also John 11:40; 14:9, and Hayward 2005, 320.
994 Hayward 2005, 317.
995 Hayward 2005, 317-318. See also e.g., John 3:13; 6:38, 41-42, 50, 51, 58; 8:23.
996 See John 4.
997 John 4:12.
998 Hayward 2005, 316-320.

associates the last day of Sukkoth, *Shemini 'Atseret,* with the confirmation of Jacob's gift of his new name Israel.[999] As we have seen in chapter 4.2, *Jubilees* narrates that Jacob wished to build a temple at Bethel but was dissuaded by an angel from doing so at this very feast. However, according to the Gospel of John, Jesus himself is the Temple of God, the contact point of heaven and earth.[1000] In the new covenant, there will be no need for an earthly temple, as the true believers will worship "in spirit and in truth;" John 4:21-26.[1001]

Jesus as the Holy Stone

Yet another line of interpretation is suggested by, for example, O'Neill who proposes that Jesus seems to identify himself in John 1:51 with the holy stone at Bethel; the stone that Jacob used as a pillow when God revealed himself to him in the dream and which he subsequently turned into an altar:

> The Son of Man is seen as the stone at Bethel upon which Jacob had his dream, and which he later set up and anointed with oil as an altar. The בו in Gen 28:12 is taken in its natural sense as referring to the ladder between earth and heaven, but the use of ἐπί with the accusative in John 1:51 shifts the emphasis away from the ladder to the symbolic object on the spot where the heavenly ladder rests, which can be nothing but the altar.[1002]

O'Neill then refers to *Gen. Rab.* 68.12, where the heavenly stairway/ladder which Jacob saw is compared to the stairway in the earthly temple leading to the top of the altar. The angels are in turn cast into the role of the high priests, bringing the sacrifices of the people to the altar and hence to God. This interpretation is thus linked to the Rabbinic identification of Bethel (meaning 'house of God') as the future temple site in Jerusalem.[1003]

---

999 E.g., *Jubilees* 32 and *Targum Pseudo-Jonatan* to Genesis 35. See above chapter 4.2 and John chapters 7 and 8. See also Hayward 2005, 139-150, and 315-316, 319.

1000 E.g., John 2:19-22, see also Hayward 2005, 315-320. In my view, at this point, Hayward's interpretation closely resembles the 'ladder-theory' mentioned above, but it could just as well be placed in the "Bethel-category", i.e., Jesus as the Temple of God, cf., O'Neill's interpretation below. See also Fossum 1995, 130-133, who interprets John chapters 7 and 10 as implying that Jesus is the new Temple-altar, the foundation stone of the world.

1001 See also Hayward 2005, 319-320.

1002 O'Neill 2003, esp. p. 376.

1003 O'Neill 2003, 377.

Furthermore, O'Neill points out that, according to Rabbinic tradition, the stone was made by God before the foundation of the world[1004] and it is identified as the sanctuary of the Lord in, for example, *Targum Pseudo-Jonathan* (Gen 28:22).[1005]

Consequently, if we read the Johannine allusion to Jacob's experience at Bethel in this way, Jesus thus claims to be the contact point between God and humankind; where Jesus is – there is the Glory of God. In John 1:51, the priestly service of the angels going up and down on the Son of Man therefore represents the communication between heaven and earth. The Evangelist may thus be alluding to the Jewish tradition of the angels as intercessors for Israel, bringing the prayers of the people up to God.[1006]

As shown above, there appear to be connections between Philo's Logos-speculations and the Christology in the Gospel of John and, it is interesting to note that Philo interprets the word 'place' in Gen 28:11 as referring to the 'divine Logos'.[1007]

The connection of a stone with a person appears in contemporary Jewish speculation, for example, the stone in Daniel 2 that crushes the statue representing the heathen empires is identified with the Messiah in *4 Ezra* 13.6.[1008]

In this context, O'Neill refers to 1 Cor 10:4 where Jesus is said to have been the rock which followed the Israelites in the desert.[1009] In the preceding verse this rock is linked with the manna, the heavenly food that nourished the people. Sometimes this manna is called the bread of angels, e.g., in Ps 78:24-25 and Wis 16:20.[1010] In light of these traditions, a connection between the imagery of angels ascending and descending upon the Son of Man and Jesus' self-identification as the bread of life is near at hand:

> [John 6:32] "Very truly, I [Jesus] tell you [the Jews], it was not Moses who gave you the bread from heaven, but it is my Father who gives you the true bread from heaven. [33] For the bread of God is that which comes down from heaven and gives life to the world." [34] They said to him, "Sir, give

---

1004 See, e.g., *Pirqê de Rabbi Eliezer* 35.

1005 See also *Tg. Ps.-J.* Gen 28:11, 17, and O'Neill 2003, 377.

1006 O'Neill 2003, 377-379. See also Tob 12:12, 15; *1 En.* 40.6-7; *Jub.* 30.20, and Rev 8:3-5.

1007 *On Dreams* 1.116, 118. See also O'Neill 2003, 378. In *On Dreams* 1.127-128, Philo even identifies the stone which Jacob used as a pillow for the night (Gen 28:11) as the 'Divine Logos'. For further details on Philo's interpretations, see chapter 4.3 above.

1008 See also Acts 4:11, and O'Neill 2003, 378-379.

1009 See also the discussion of the concept 'wisdom' and the reading of Jude 5 in chapter 4.1.3 above.

1010 O'Neill 2003, 379-381.

us this bread always." [35] Jesus said to them, "I am the bread of life. Whoever comes to me will never be hungry, and whoever believes in me will never be thirsty."

It is worth considering that in one of his writings, Philo links the manna with the divine Logos.[1011]

Ernest G. Clarke also advocates the interpretation of John 1:51 in light of Jewish traditions surrounding the stone at Bethel in Genesis 28. In the same way as O'Neill, Clarke refers to the Jewish connection of Bethel with the Temple and prayer.[1012] However, in contrast to O'Neill, he regards Jesus as corresponding to Jacob in the logion. In the same way as, for example, Rowland, Clarke interprets בו in Gen 28:12 as referring to Jacob, and in John 1:51, Jesus as the Son of Man has taken his place.[1013] In short, Clarke appears to have made a fusion of two lines of interpretation in his discussion of the logion; Jesus is seen as both the holy stone of Bethel, i.e., the Temple of God, and Jacob's counterpart.[1014] According to Clarke, this combination is also evident in Jesus' conversation with the Samaritan woman at Jacob's well in John 4.[1015]

4.6.3 Summary and Conclusions

Scholars generally agree that John 1:51 alludes to Jacob's dream at Bethel and his vision of the ascending and descending angels although there are divergent interpretations of the exact meaning of this allusion.

Some scholars regard Jesus in John 1:51 as corresponding to God who, according to Genesis 28, was standing above the ladder,[1016] while others argue that Jesus in the logion represents the ladder itself, i.e., the connecting link between God and humankind. Since the ladder is not mentioned in John 1:51, a common presumption is that the Evangelist was influenced by the Jewish exegetical tradition which understands *bo* [בו] 'on it/him/for his sake' in Gen 28:12 as referring to a *person*, i.e., Jacob, and not the ladder, and some scholars regard Jesus as analogous to Jacob in the Gospel of John.

1011 *That the Worse is Wont to Attack the Better* 118. See also O'Neill 2003, 380.
1012 Clarke 1974/5, 370-374.
1013 Clarke 1974/5, 374-375.
1014 Clarke 1974/5, 373-375. See also Hamerton-Kelly 1973, 225-230. As I understand it, he also fuses these two motives in his discussion of John 1:51.
1015 Clarke 1974/5, 373-375.
1016 Or beside Jacob, see chapter 3.2.5. Cf., Gen 31:11 where the angel of God identifies himself as 'the God of Bethel'.

Moreover, the matter of 'seeing' is pointed out as a key issue in the gospel, and it is argued that the Evangelist, like Philo, interpreted the name 'Israel' to mean 'the one who sees God'. Thus, Jesus' words to Nathanael in John 1:47b, 50b-51: "… here is truly an Israelite […] You will see greater things than these […] you will see heaven opened and the angels of God ascending and descending upon the Son of Man" are interpreted to mean that Nathanael and, by extension, all the disciples of Jesus represent Jacob/Israel. Like Jacob, they will see a theophany.

Finally, Jesus is seen as identifying himself as the holy stone/rock of Bethel and/or the Temple of God, i.e., Bethel, 'house of God'.

When considering all these interpretation models, my conclusion is that, in spite of their differences, the obvious, common denominator in all of them is that Jesus is seen as the focal point of God's Glory, in the words of Raymond Brown:

> … the theme that they [the interpretations] have in common is probably correct: whether it is as the ladder, the *shekinah*, the *merkabah*, Bethel, or the rock, the vision means that Jesus as Son of Man has become the locus of divine glory, the point of contact between heaven and earth. The disciples are promised figuratively that they will come to see this; and indeed, at Cana they do see his glory.[1017]

1017 Brown 1966, 91.

5. Comparative Analysis and Conclusions

5.1 Introductory Remarks

The purpose of this study has been to investigate the identity of 'the angel of the Lord' in early Jewish biblical interpretation and theology. Due to considerations of space, the focus has been restricted to the relevant texts in Genesis. How did the early Jewish interpreters solve the problem of the ambiguous relationship between God and His angel in these texts, and how is he related to God and to other divine emissaries? Is there a uniform answer, or is the appearance of 'the angel of the Lord' in the various biblical texts perceived differently? How is the angel of the Lord depicted in the discussed early Jewish sources? Was the "angel" understood as a manifestation/revelation of God Himself, or as an independent angelic being, distinct from God? A third alternative between those two extremes may be that he was regarded as a hypostasis of God, a personification/an extension of the divine will, possessing a certain degree of independent personhood, but not completely separate from God.

Related questions are in which ways the view of God is influenced by the angelology of early Judaism and/or vice versa, as well as how the relationship between man and the divine realm is constituted. Thus, the interpretations of the identity of 'the angel of the Lord' have been studied in the context of the development of angelology and concepts of God in the various forms of early Judaism. Is it possible to discern any patterns of interpretation in the discussed material?

As background information, I presented a survey of the characteristics of early Jewish exegesis in chapter 2. In section 2.2.2, it was noted that some scholars discern a connection between the increasing importance of exegesis and the development of angelology in early Judaism.

In chapter 3, I investigated the problem/phenomenon of the merged identity of God and His "angel" in all the relevant biblical texts, with particular focus on those in Genesis.

The main part of the dissertation is chapter 4, in which I have analyzed how the 'angel of the Lord-texts' in Genesis were interpreted in early Jewish sources.

The texts in question may be divided into two groups. I have chosen to focus primarily the first, namely those that explicitly mention 'the angel of the Lord': Gen 16:7-14; 21:17-20; 22:1-19; 24:7, 40; 31:10-13, and 48:15-16. Since the angel of God who appears to Jacob in Gen 31:10-13 identifies himself as the God of Bethel who spoke to him in Gen 28:10-22, the latter pericope has also been taken into consideration. The same applies to Gen 35:1-15, a text clearly connected to Jacob's dream at Bethel in Genesis 28 and thus also to Gen 31:10-13. Of these texts, only Genesis 24 contains a reference to an angel in the singular who seems to be distinct from God. Due to its exceptional character, the pericope has been included for reasons of comparison. Is it treated differently from the other pericopes by the interpreters?

The second group comprises pericopes that implicitly refer to 'the angel of the Lord'. Although we do not encounter the term 'the angel of the Lord', these texts describe divine revelations of a similar character and exhibit the same ambiguity between God and the divine emissary(-ies). The narratives concerning Abraham's three visitors in Genesis 18 and Jacob's struggle with an unknown "man" at the ford of Jabbok in Genesis 32 belong to this category. In spite of its implicit character the latter text has been included in my study for two reasons: Firstly, it constitutes an inseparable part of the Jacob saga and, secondly, the prophet Hosea explicitly identifies Jacob's contender as an angel, who in turn is equated with God; Hos 12:4-6 (NRSV vv. 3-5).[1] As pointed out in chapter 3, some scholars consider the word מלאך in Hosea 12 as a glossa and thus conclude that the prophet meant that Jacob had struggled with God.

A few texts in Genesis mention angels in the plural. These angels, who seem to be distinct from God, appear in the contexts of 'the angel of the Lord-texts'. In this thesis, I have thus taken a closer look at the angels Jacob saw in his dream at Bethel (Gen 28:12).

Jewish interpreters did not treat Genesis as an isolated book but read it in the light of the rest of the Bible. They understood the Bible as a unity, in which everything belongs together. This holistic view of the Bible is evident in, for example, the Rabbinic comparisons between Sarah in Genesis 18 and Hagar in Genesis 16.

I have used three kinds of interpretative material in my study. Firstly, sources that explicitly "translate," comment on, or rewrite the biblical narratives, e.g., the Targums, the works of Philo, the Rabbinic Midrashim, *Jubilees*, and the *Judean Antiquities* by Josephus.

---

1   Cf., Gen 48:15-16.

Secondly, sources that share the same motif(s), theme(s), and/or literary structure as the biblical texts. By the use of a biblical theme or
motif familiar to the presumptive reader, the "author" invites the audience to understand the story in the light of an already well-known
biblical text. This literary method has been classified as the use of type-
scenes and can be exemplified by the book of Tobit, where the role of
Raphael seems to have been modeled on that of the angel mentioned in
Genesis 24, although the latter does not play such an active part in the
narrative as Raphael. The depiction of Raphael is also reminiscent of
that of the angel of the Lord who appears to Manoah and his wife in
Judges 13. Another example is the annunciation to Mary, the literary
structure of which parallels the announcement of Ishmael's birth in
Genesis 16.

A third interpretative method can be described as explicit allusions
or references to biblical persons, events or circumstances. Wisdom
chapter 10, in which 'Lady Wisdom' assumes the role played by 'the
angel of the Lord' in many Genesis and Exodus texts, and the allusion
to Genesis 28 in John 1:51 constitute examples of this kind of biblical
interpretation.

As stated in chapter 1, I have focused on sources from roughly 200
B.C.E. to 650 C.E. and my ambition has been to investigate the material
chronologically. However, other issues such as genre and the kind of
interpretative method(s) employed in the sources have also been taken
into consideration.

In addition to the differences in genre and interpretative methods,
various Jewish contexts are also represented. For example, *Genesis Rabbah* and Philo's *Questions and Answers on Genesis* can both be classified
as Bible commentaries, although in many ways the works are worlds
apart. Some similarities between Philo's interpretations and the Rabbinic material can be discerned, but in general Philo's philosophical and
allegorical method of interpretation is unique in the studied material.
However, there are parallels between the *Prayer of Joseph* and Philo's
works as well as connections between Philo's 'Logos' and the depiction
of 'Lady Wisdom' in Wisdom, a book that most probably also originated in Alexandria.

Like Philo, Josephus wrote his work the *Judean Antiquities* for the
Greek speaking world, but otherwise it is very different in character to
both *Genesis Rabbah* and the Philonic corpus and in many ways constitutes a unique composition reflecting the personal outlook of the author. Both Philo and Josephus wrote in a Hellenistic context but yet
used different terms when referring to angels. Philo borrowed the
terms δαίμονες 'demons' and λόγοι 'logoi'/'words' from the Greek

philosophers, while Josephus called them ὄψεις/φαντάσματα, 'visions/apparitions' or ἄγγελοι 'angels/ messengers' in the same way as the LXX.

The Rabbinic material and many of the Pseudepigrapha, e.g., the Palestinian Targums, *Genesis Rabbah*, *Jubilees*, and the *Ladder of Jacob*, appear to share interpretative traditions, probably because most of these sources originated in a Semitic context. The different characteristics of the sources stand out as being of greater importance than chronological aspects when analyzing the interpretations of the relevant pericopes. Thus, it is important to bear in mind the miscellaneous character of the sources in the discussion of the results of the investigation.

Moreover, the (probably) earliest work analyzed in the thesis, the book of Tobit, contains a fairly well developed angelology, i.e., a conception of angels as individuals, bearing personal names and distinct from God. This perception of angels most certainly originated during the Second Temple era, the period in which our investigation takes its starting point. Thus, this is the kind of angelology encountered in the other post-biblical sources.

As stated previously, the Sadducean view on angels as impersonal extensions of God appears to have been rather archaic, while the Pharisees and other Jewish groups generally embraced the more "individualistic" conception. It should therefore come as no surprise that, for example, both the Rabbinic and Qumranic material testify to this later angelology. It is well known that the Sadducees gradually lost their influence after the fall of the Second Temple in 70 C.E. Thus, the chronological setting of the various post-biblical sources has proven to be of minor importance in the discernment of common denominators between them, i.e., patterns of interpretation. Instead, a more important factor turned out to be the *nature of the biblical texts*. There are clear similarities between, for example, the treatment of the Aqedah in many of our sources. Thus, the question whether the appearance of 'the angel of the Lord' in the various biblical texts is perceived differently can be answered in the affirmative.

However, there are obviously chronologically based differences when comparing the sources with the biblical texts. In contrast to the angel of the Lord in, e.g., Judges 13, the angel Raphael in the book of Tobit is apparently distinct from God. In this respect, the relationship between the book of Tobit and Judges 13 mirrors that of Genesis 16 and Luke 1. In the same way as Gabriel, Raphael introduces himself as an angel who stands in the presence of God (cf., Tob 12:15 and Luke 1:19). This is noteworthy, since according to *Jubilees* 'the angels of the Presence' and the angels of sanctification are the two highest orders of angels. As mentioned in section 2.2.2, this is the background of the concept of archangels. Both Gabriel and Raphael were later acknowledged as archangels.

Gen 24:7, 40 contain the only references in Genesis to an angel of the Lord in the singular who is clearly depicted as distinct from God. This angel is therefore more similar to Raphael in character than the angel of the Lord in Genesis 16 and Judges 13. But in contrast to Raphael, this angel is anonymous and does not play such a significant role in the story.

Unlike the angel of the Lord in Genesis, the divine messenger in Exodus is sometimes spoken of by God in the third person (e.g., Exodus 23) as someone distinct from Himself. However, by his possession of the divine name and the ability to forgive sins, the angel in Exodus 23 is depicted as sharing the divine nature.

Thus, the descriptions of the angels in Genesis 24 and Exodus seem to represent a stage in the evolution of the angelology in the religion of Israel that is midway between, on the one hand, Genesis 16 and Judges 13 and, on the other, Luke 1 and the book of Tobit.

5.2 Concluding Discussion

The ambiguity between God and the angel remains in the targumic "translations" of Gen 21:17-20 and in the targumic renderings of Gen 16:13, where Hagar gives the angel divine titles. But in Gen 16:14, *Onqelos* has inserted a reference to 'the living angel', probably in an attempt to prevent the "misconception" that it was God in person who appeared to Hagar. However, this is unique to *Onqelos*. The relative faithfulness of the Targums to the original biblical texts is most certainly due to their character as "translations."

On the whole, the tendency in the discussed sources seems to be that Hagar met (an) angel(s) distinct from God, while Abraham and Jacob encountered God in person. For example, the dominant view in *Genesis Rabbah* appears to be that it was God in person who spoke to Jacob in his dream at Bethel, although one passage in the Midrash claims that He spoke to him through an angel. This inconsistency is typical of most of the sources. The reference to the angel of God in Genesis 31 is often either ignored or the angel is (implicitly) equated with God. The *Testament of Jacob* constitutes an exception to this rule, as it identifies the angel as distinct from God.

It may have been very hard for the early Jewish interpreters to imagine that a woman and maidservant like Hagar should have met God

Himself. For example, the Rabbis of *Genesis Rabbah* emphasize that God never appeared in person to a woman, except to Sarah, and all the Targums interpret Gen 16:13 as a reference to the prayer/worship of Hagar, because it appeared impossible to the targumists that a woman and maidservant should have given God a name/an epithet. Similar to the Rabbis of *Genesis Rabbah*, Philo contrasts Sarah and Hagar with each other. God appeared in person to Sarah but not to Hagar. According to *Jubilees,* the angel who encountered Hagar in the desert was 'one of the holy ones', i.e., an "ordinary" angel, distinct from both God and the angelic narrator, the angel of the Presence.

However, in the Pseudepigraphon's account of the Aqedah, it was the angel of the Presence who called out to Abraham on the first occasion in order to prevent him from sacrificing his son, while the second call of the biblical 'angel of the Lord' in Gen 22:15-18 is ascribed to God Himself. *Jubilees* is the only source that identifies the angel of the Lord in Genesis 22 as a specific angel. Both Josephus and Philo mention the angel in their renderings of Genesis 16 but in their interpretations of Genesis 22 the angel is absent, the only heavenly actor being God.

In the same way as Philo and Josephus, the Midrash *Pirqê de Rabbi Eliezer* neglects mentioning the angel and states instead that Isaac was saved by a heavenly voice, i.e., God calling to Abraham from above. This recalls the 'hypostasised' voice addressing Jacob in the *Ladder of Jacob*.[2] We saw in section 2.1.3 that the *bath qol* in Rabbinic sources is often used as an equivalent to the Holy Spirit. This pattern recurs in the two discussed *Piyutim*, thus it is God Himself who saves Isaac. *Pirqê de Rabbi Eliezer* is the only source that omits the angel in its rendering of both Genesis 21 and 22. *Jubilees* and *Pirqê de Rabbi Eliezer* only comment on Gen 21:17-20, possibly because the "authors" considered the narratives about Hagar's meeting with the angel in Genesis 16 and 21 as two versions of the same story. *Jubilees* is the only Pseudepigraphon that contains a version of Hagar's encounter with the angel.

The omission of the angel in many of the discussed elaborations of the Aqedah may be explained by the fact that the interpreters understood the narrative to mean that God spoke through the angel, i.e., the messenger *per se* is not important and thus not mentioned. In contrast to the angel in the Hagar pericopes, the angel in the Aqedah is not a main character in the narrative, and the focus of the interpretations is on Abraham and Isaac. The transfer of the saving of Isaac need not necessarily imply that early Jewish interpreters identified the angel of

---

2   Cf., also *Tg. Neof.* Gen 22:10.

the Lord as God, although we cannot know for certain. An additional
reason for the angel's absence may be that they considered the Aqedah
such a crucial event that it must have been God in person who intervened. That the one who speaks to Jacob is generally depicted as God
in person is consistent with this idea, since being the ancestor of the
nation makes the patriarch a very important person.

An additional pattern of interpretation in the sources is the avoidance of theologically problematic issues such as anthropomorphism.
This is apparent in Josephus' renderings of the pericopes. He refrains,
for example, from commenting on the difficult verses Gen 16:13-14, and
there is an evident rationalizing tendency in his treatment of the pericopes. Of all the discussed sources, the *Judean Antiquities* contains the
most consistent interpretations of the 'angel of the Lord-texts'. In Josephus' rewriting of the pericopes, the ambivalence between God and the
angel has disappeared; it is either God or an angel who is the divine
agent in the narratives, not both. For example, since according to Gen
22:1 it was God who commanded Abraham to sacrifice Isaac, Josephus
may have considered it logical to transfer the prevention of the sacrifice
to God in person. In contrast, in Genesis 16 and 21 it is an angel who
addresses Hagar in the first instance, thus Josephus saw no need to
introduce God. Another example of Josephus' avoidance of theological
problems is his omission of Jacob's dream recorded in Gen 31:10-13, in
which the angel of God identifies himself as 'the God of Bethel'. In this
context it is worth mentioning that the Rabbis of *Genesis Rabbah* also
neglected to comment on these verses.

Thus, Josephus' elaborations of the pericopes are to be seen in the
light of the nature of the texts, and I consider this to have a decisive
influence on all the discussed interpretations, as shown by, for example, the renderings in the sources of Jacob's struggle with the unknown
"man" at the ford of Jabbok. Most certainly because of the grave anthropomorphic character of the narrative, Josephus identifies the opponent as a 'phantom'/an 'angel'. In the *Judean Antiquities*, this is the only
exception to the rule that it is God who speaks to Jacob. The *Judean
Antiquities* and other sources that discuss the text probably identify
Jacob's opponent as an angel for the same reason, i.e., the concrete
anthropomorphism in the pericope, compare Hamori's classification of
Genesis 32 as an 'îsh-theophany'. As shown in chapter 3, Jacob's opponent is depicted as an angel already in some late mss of the LXX. Due to
the fact that no one can see God and live, it cannot have been God
whom Jacob saw 'face to face' at Jabbok. The only clear exception is the
allusion to Gen 32:30 in *T. Jac.* 2.14-15. However, the identification of
Jacob's contender as God may be implied in *Joseph and Aseneth*, and

although Philo appears to identify Jacob's contender in terms of an angel, it must be admitted that his depiction of the 'Logos' in his interpretations of Genesis 32 is not entirely clear, see below.

The idea of an angel blessing and renaming Jacob seems to have been another problematic issue in many of the interpretations of Genesis 32. *Genesis Rabbah* solves this problem by interconnecting Genesis 32; 35, and Hosea 12. The angel did not really bless Jacob, he only revealed God's plan to give him the name of Israel when the patriarch returns to Bethel (cf., Gen 35:5-15). Of all the discussed Midrashim, it is only in *Pirqê de Rabbi Eliezer* that the angel actually blesses and renames Jacob.[3]

Liber Antiquitatum Biblicarum, the Palestinian Targums, *Pirqê de Rabbi Eliezer*, *Genesis Rabbah*, and the Babylonian Talmud present Jacob's angelic contender as a member of/the leader of the heavenly choir. In *Demetrius the chronographer's* rendering of Genesis 32, he is an anonymous, unspecified angel, and the same applies to *Onqelos*. *Neofiti* calls him Sariel, an angel whom we also encounter in the *Ladder of Jacob*, while in the *Prayer of Joseph*, Jacob's opponent is called Uriel, probably a somewhat later designation for the same angel. In the *Fragment Targums*, Jacob's angelic contender is unnamed, while in *Pseudo-Jonathan* he seems to be identified as the archangel Michael.

The appearance of the angel Sariel in the context of Jacob's dream at Bethel in the *Ladder of Jacob* constitutes an example of a third pattern of interpretation present in many sources, namely, the insertion of additional angelophanies not mentioned in the Bible. Apart from the Jacob narratives, this also occurs in the interpretations of the Aqedah and the comments in *Genesis Rabbah* on Genesis 16; 21, and 24. Since, according to the Rabbinic view, one angel does not perform two missions, at least *four* angels appeared to Hagar and God appointed *two* angels to accomplish the task of finding a wife for Isaac. One angel was appointed to accompany Eliezer on his journey and the other was charged with arranging his meeting with Rebekah. In their interpretation of Genesis 21, the Rabbis inserted angels who questioned God's rescue of Ishmael. The angel of God who addresses Hagar, however, is distinguished from them; he acts as God's spokesman.

The accounts of Jacob's life in the Pseudepigrapha *Jubilees*, *Ladder of Jacob*, and *Testament of Jacob* all contain extra-biblical angelophanies. The inserted angels are described as distinct from God. The interpreta-

---

3   In *Pirqê de Rabbi Eliezer* 37, the angel's name is Israel. He is thus said to give his own name to Jacob, see chapter 4.5.

tions of the Aqedah and Jacob's dream at Bethel in *Genesis Rabbah*[4] as well as, for example, in the *Ladder of Jacob*, include references to angelic princes of the pagan nations.[5] There is an apparent apocalyptic element in these interpretations and God is depicted as the Lord of the world and its history.

However, the dualistic perspective is more significant in the interpretations of the Aqedah, where prince Mastema/Satan is said to be the initiator of Abraham's trial in *Jubilees* and *b. Sanhedrin* 89b. 4Q225 even mentions several angels of animosity who are said to have rejoiced when they believed that Abraham would kill Isaac. Both *Liber Antiquitatum Biblicarum* and *Genesis Rabbah* refer to angels who are jealous of Abraham. Thus, in order to demonstrate Abraham's faithfulness, God subjected him to a trial, although the purpose of the test was not to prove something to God, as He is omniscient. Worth mentioning in this context is the appearance in *Genesis Rabbah* and *Pirqê de Rabbi Eliezer* of the demonic angel Samael who tries to make Abraham waver in his faith and causes the death of Sarah (see also *Pseudo-Jonathan*, where Satan causes Sarah's death). The insertion of these angels/Satan/prince Mastema/Samael into the narrative is most probably an attempt to justify God and explain the reason for God's command to Abraham to sacrifice his son.

In addition to the accusing angels, angels who are said to have watched the scenario on Mount Moriah and cried and/or prayed on behalf of Abraham and Isaac are also present in the interpretations of the Aqedah in the Palestinian Targums, 4Q225, *Genesis Rabbah*, *Pirqê de Rabbi Eliezer*, and the Aramaic *Piyut*. When the angel of the Lord is credited with the rescue of Isaac, he is distinguished from the other angels and appears to have a special status. The difference between the depictions of this angel and the weeping/watching angels in the Aqedah resembles the relationship between God who speaks to Jacob in his dream at Bethel and the angels ascending and descending on the ladder. A possible explanation of the many additional angelophanies may be that the biblical references to (an) angel(s) inspired the imagination of the early Jewish interpreters of the texts, in addition to their wish to justify God's testing of Abraham in Genesis 22.

A fourth discernable pattern of interpretation is the reference to the divine Presence/'Shekinah' manifested on Mount Moriah in the form of

---

4   See also *Pesiqta de Rab Kahana* 23.
5   Cf., one of the suggested interpretations of Genesis 32 in *Genesis Rabbah*, in which Jacob's opponent is identified as Esau's guardian angel, i.e., the angelic patron of Rome, see chapter 4.5.

a 'cloud of Glory'/'pillar of fire', e.g., *Pseudo-Jonathan*, a targumic Genizah fragment, and *Pesqita de Rab Kahana* (see also the excursus on the mosaic in the synagogue of Sepphoris).

The wooing of Rebekah in Genesis 24 did not attract the interest of the early Jewish interpreters to the same degree as the Aqedah and Jacob's life. However, the idea of angelic/divine protection of travelers is here a significant theme and the same also applies to the rendering of Jacob's escape to Laban in our sources. The angel's company guarantees the success of Eliezer's commission. Since the angel in Genesis 24 is distinct from God, the same applies to the sources that comment on his role in this text, i.e., Philo's *Questions and Answers on Genesis* and *Genesis Rabbah*.

However, it is noteworthy that, according to *Neofiti*, the angel in Gen 24:7 is designated as 'the angel of mercy' and that the same designation recurs in a *Neofiti* marginal gloss to Gen 28:13. This, however, is exceptional. In general, the translations of Genesis 24 are relatively literal in the Targums and the one who speaks to Jacob in his dream at Bethel is God Himself.

Philo usually identifies the angel of the Lord with the 'Logos'. The only exception is his interpretation of the Aqedah, where neither the angel nor the 'Logos' is mentioned, the only heavenly actor being God in person. A possible reason for this may be that the angel does not play such a distinctive role in the Aqedah, in contrast to Genesis 16. In the same way as the identity of the angel of the Lord and God Himself is merged in the biblical texts, the identity of God and His 'Logos' is merged in Philo's teaching.

However, his depiction of the 'Logos' varies from text to text, sometimes the 'Logos' seems to be a kind of divine 'hypostasis'/extension of God, while on other occasions it is described in terms of an angel, distinct from God. The latter case seems to apply to Philo's interpretation of Genesis 16; Hagar believed herself to have met God, but it was only His servant. However, there is a certain ambiguity in Philo's discussion of this pericope, because the 'Logos' is at the same time distinguished from 'created beings'. In Philo's comment on Genesis 24, the angelic guide, i.e., the 'Logos', appears to be equated with an "ordinary" angel. As stated in chapter 4.3, in addition to the term 'demons', Philo called the angels 'logoi' but these immanent powers are not to be confused with the supreme divine 'Logos', see for example Philo's rendering of Jacob's dream at Bethel, where the stones are allegorically interpreted as 'logoi'/'words'.

Philo's identification of Jacob's contender in Genesis 32 is ambiguous. On the one hand, he is explicitly identified as "an angel, God's minister, the Word [Logos]" and said to be "below the Existent" in *On the Change of Names* 87 but, on the other, he/the 'Logos' who confronts Jacob is portrayed by Philo as being something more than a "mere" angel. This is expressed by the new name of Jacob, i.e., Israel, 'he who sees (God)', a name that also belongs to the supreme 'Logos'.

In *Who is the Heir* 205-206 and the *Confusion of Tongues* 146-147, the divine 'Logos' is termed 'archangel', but in *On Dreams* 1.157, it seems to be God Himself who is designated by this title, although the interpretation of this passage is debated. In many ways, Philo's description of the divine 'Logos' parallels the depiction of the angel Israel in the *Prayer of Joseph*, although Jacob is never depicted as an (incarnated) angel by Philo, and in his writings it is the 'Logos' who is the supreme archangel.

In Philo's treatment of Jacob's dreams in Genesis 28 and 31, the relationship between God and His 'Logos' is far from clear. The word 'place' in Gen 28:11 is, for instance, said to refer both to God and to the 'Logos', which recalls the Rabbinic interpretation of the word in this text as representing God as 'the Omnipresent'.

The personified 'Wisdom' has many similarities with Philo's 'Logos' and his 'Logos-concept' is largely dependent on Jewish wisdom tradition. In Wisdom chapter 10, the 'divine Wisdom' is equated with the angel of the Lord who appeared to Abraham during the Aqedah, the angel of God who guided Jacob and increased his flocks (Gen 31:10-13) as well as the one who gave him the victory in "his arduous contest", probably an allusion to Jacob's combat as recorded in Genesis 32. According to *Jubilees*, it was the angel of the Presence who saved Isaac from being sacrificed. In *Jubilees'* account of the Aqedah, the angel presents himself as distinct from God, but in many other passages of the book the angel has taken over the function reserved for God Himself in the Bible.

Both 'Lady Wisdom' and the angel of the Presence are identified as the one who led the Israelites' exodus from Egypt, a deed that the Bible ascribes to either God Himself or the angel of the Lord. As we have seen, the concept 'the angel of the Presence' is probably derived from an interpretation of Isa 63:9 and, e.g., Exod 14:19; 23:20-23, cf., also Exod 33:14. The depictions in the synagogues of Doura Europos and Beth Alpha of a hand representing the divine intervention in the Aqedah have parallels in the biblical account of the exodus. In this context it is significant that the terms 'your defending hand' and 'wisdom' seem to be equated with each other in Wisdom 10.

Thus, in Philo's works and in Wisdom, the 'Logos' and 'Lady Wisdom' respectively have assumed the role of 'the angel of the Lord' in the Hebrew Bible. The relationship between God and His 'Logos'/'Wisdom' may be compared to the Sadducees' concept of angels as impersonal emanations of God. Based on these observations, a possible conclusion may be that although the angelology of Second Temple Judaism had developed in the direction of seeing angels as distinct personalities, Judaism still had room for the idea of divine hypostases.

Most certainly, this Jewish conception of divine hypostases constitutes a significant theological background for the development of early Christology, i.e., the belief in the divinity of Jesus. In the Gospel of John, the pre-incarnate Christ is called the 'Logos' and described in terms that are reminiscent of Philo's Logos-concept. We have seen in chapter 4.6 that some scholars interpret the gospel in the light of the 'angel of the Lord-traditions' and identify Jesus in John 1:51 as corresponding to God appearing to Jacob at Bethel. As James Dunn states, it is, however, true that no NT author perceived Christ as an angel, that is, assuming that we define 'angel' according to the angelology of Second Temple Judaism, i.e. angels such as Raphael in the book of Tobit and Gabriel in Luke 1. As shown, in many ways Luke presents Christ after his resurrection in angelic terms (chapter 24) but by depicting him eating in the presence of the disciples it is evident that Luke wished to counteract the assumption that the risen Christ is to be understood as an angel.

In this context, it is worth noting that many scholars point out that the Fourth Evangelist interpreted the name 'Israel' as meaning 'the one who sees God' and that this fact played a significant role in his writing of the gospel. Similar to Philo, the Evangelist states that no one has ever really seen God, except "the one who is from God", i.e., Jesus (John 6:46, cf., 1:18) and in Philo's teaching it is the 'Logos' who truly is "he that sees, that is Israel" (*On the Confusion of Tongues* 146). The same interpretation of the name recurs in the *Prayer of Joseph*, in which Jacob/Israel is depicted as a heavenly being, understood by some scholars as the patriarch Jacob's celestial counterpart and even as the very embodiment of the Glory of God. For example, Jarl Fossum advocates this interpretation and connects the "angel" Israel in the *Prayer of Joseph* with John 1:51 and the Jewish tradition concerning Jacob's heavenly portrait/counterpart, understanding 'on it'/ 'on him' in Gen 28:12 as referring to a person, not the ladder. According to Fossum, Jesus has taken the place of Jacob as the locus of the ascending and descending angels' attention in John 1:51.

The identification of the angel who Jacob refers to in Gen 48:16 is ambivalent in our sources. *Jubilees* seems to equate him with God but in *Genesis Rabbah* it is stated that the verse says that redemption comes through an angel but sustenance comes through God. On the other hand, the Midrash connects the verse with the revelations of the angel of the Lord to Joshua and Gideon;[6] in the latter case, at least, it is again unclear whether it is an angel or God Himself who appears. In both *Onqelos* and *Neofiti*, the angel in Gen 48:16 is understood as an epithet referring to God, while *Pseudo-Jonathan* distinguishes between God and His angel.

In commenting on Gen 48:15-16, Philo also makes a distinction between the roles of God and the angels in relation to humankind. In this context, Philo does not seem to discuss the 'divine Logos' but the role of "ordinary" angels, distinct from God, see, e.g., *Allegorical Interpretation* 3.177-178 and *On the Confusion of Tongues* 180-182.

In general, the angel of the Lord is connected to the redeeming agency of God in our sources. The Rabbis point out that it is God/Elohim who subjects Abraham to a trial, but it is the angel of the Lord/YHWH who rescues him. The divine name YHWH is connected to the divine attribute of mercy, while Elohim represents God's attribute of justice. Philo refers to the same two basic qualities of God's personality, but connects them with the opposite divine names. According to Maren Niehoff, the crying angels in the interpretations of the Aqedah represent God's merciful side.

Finally, the conclusion must be drawn that there is no unambiguous or homogeneous interpretation of 'the angel of the Lord' and his identity in our sources. He is sometimes depicted as a divine emissary separate from God, while in other cases he appears to be seen as a manifestation or a hypostasis of God Himself. The ambivalence in the relationship between God and His angel remains in many of the interpretations of the texts, and in relation to "ordinary" angels 'the angel of the Lord' is generally awarded a special, high status.

---

6   See Josh 5:13-15, Judges 6, and chapter 4.5.

Bibliography

(Abbreviations are from the list in *Anchor Bible Dictionary* (*ABD*), vol. 1, 1992. Not included abbreviation: *DDD* = *Dictionary of Demons and Deities in the Bible*.)

Primary Sources and Translations

Bible

Bibel 2000. Örebro, 1999
Biblia Hebraica Stuttgartensia: תורה נביאים וכתובים Eds. K. Elliger and W. Rudolph. Stuttgart, 1990
Bibeln eller Den Heliga Skrift. Gamla och Nya Testamentet, 1917 års översättning. Lund, 1967
Bibeln. Tillägg till Gamla testamentet. De apokryfa eller deuterokanoniska skrifterna. Bibelkommisionens utgåva. Stockholm, 1986
The Greek New Testament. Eds. K. Aland, M. Black, C. M. Martini, B. Metzger, A. Wikgren. Stuttgart, 4th edition 1983
Hebrew-English Bible: ספר הבריתות The Holy Scriptures, Hebrew and English: תורה נביאים כתובים וברית החדשה. עברית ואנגלית. The Bible Society in Israel, Jerusalem, 1997. The Holy Bible, New King James Version, copyright 1982 by Thomas Nelson, Inc. Modern Hebrew New Testament copyright, the Bible Society in Israel, 1995
The Holy Bible. King James Version. London (no year)
The Holy Bible. New International Version. Grand Rapids, 1988
The Holy Bible. New Revised Standard Version. With the Apocryphal / Deuterocanonical Books. New York, 1989
Septuaginta. Id est Vetus Testamentum graece iuxta LXX interpretes. (Ed. A. Rahlfs). Stuttgart, 1935:
– Vol. 1. Leges et historiae
– Vol. 2. Libri poetici et prophetici
Septuaginta. Vetus Testamentum Graecum. Auctoritate Academiae Scientiarum Gottingensis, Göttingen:
– Vol. 1, Genesis. Ed. J. W. Wevers, 1974
– Vol. 2, 1. Exodus. Ed. J. W. Wevers, 1991
– Vol. 3, 2. Deuteronomium. Ed. J. W. Wevers, 1977
– Vol. 8, 5. Tobit. Ed. R. Hanhart, 1983
– Vol. 12, 1. Sapientia Salomonis. Ed. J. Ziegler, 1980

– Vol. 13. Duodecim Prohetae. Ed. J. Ziegler, 1984
Septuaginta. Vetus Testamentum Graecum. Auctoritate Societatis Litterarum
    Gottingensis. Göttingen:
– Vol. 14. Isaias. Ed. J. Ziegler, 1939

Targums

The Aramaic Bible. The Targums. Project Director M. McNamara. Eds. K.
    Cathcart, M. Maher, M. McNamara. Editorial Consultants: D. J. Harrington,
    B. Grossfeld, A. Díez Macho:
– Vol. 1A. Targum Neofiti I: Genesis. Translated, with Apparatus and Notes by
    M. McNamara. Collegeville, 1992
– Vol. 1B. Targum Pseudo-Jonathan: Genesis. Translated, with Introduction and
    Notes by M. Maher. Collegeville, 1992
– Vol. 6. The Targum Onqelos to Genesis. Translated, with a Critical Introduction,
    Apparatus, and Notes, by B. Grossfeld. Wilmington, 1988
– Vol. 10. Targum Jonathan of the Former Prophets. Introduction, Translation and
    Notes, by D. J. Harrington and A. J. Saldarini. Wilmington, 1987
– Vol. 13. The Targum of Ezekiel. Translated, with a Critical Introduction,
    Apparatus, and Notes by S. H. Levey. Wilmington, 1987
– Vol. 14. The Targum of the Minor Prophets. Translated, with a Critical Introduc-
    tion, Apparatus and Notes by K. J. Cathcart and R. P. Gordon. Wilmington,
    1989.
– Vol. 16. The Targum of Psalms. Translated, with a Critical Introduction,
    Apparatus, and Notes by D. M. Stec. Collegeville, 2004
– Vol. 19. The Targum of Ruth. Translated, with Introduction, Apparatus, and
    Notes by D. R. G. Beattie and The Targum of Chronicles. Translated, with In-
    troduction, Apparatus, and Notes by J. S. McIvor. Collegeville, 1994
The Fragment-Targums of the Pentateuch. According to their Extant Sources. Vol. 1:
    Texts, Indices and Introductory Essays. Vol. 2: Translation. (Ed. and Eng. trans.
    M. L. Klein). Rome, 1980
Genizah Manuscripts of Palestinian Targum to the Pentateuch, 2 vols. (Ed. and Eng.
    trans. M. L. Klein). Cincinnati, 1986
Neophyti 1. Targum Palestinense Ms de la Biblioteca Vaticana, Vol. 1, Genesis. Eng.
    trans. M. McNamara and M. Maher (Ed. A. Díez Macho). Mad-
    rid/Barcelona, 1968
Pseudo-Jonathan. (Thargum Jonathan ben Usiel zum Pentateuch). Nach der Londoner
    Handschrift. (Ed. M. Ginsburger). Hildesheim/New York, 1971
Ps. Jonathan on Selected Chapters of Genesis. Eng. trans. J. Bowker. in: The
    Targums and Rabbinic Literature. An Introduction to Jewish Interpretations of
    Scripture. Cambridge, 1969
The Targum of Isaiah. Edited with a Translation by J. F. Stenning. Oxford, 1949
Targum Onkelos to Genesis. A Critical Analysis Together With An English Translati-
    on of the Text. (Based on A. Sperber's Edition). (Eds. and trans. M. Aberbach
    and B. Grossfeld). Denver, 1982

Targum Pseudo-Jonathan of the Pentateuch: Text and Concordance. (Ed. E. G. Clarke with collaboration by W. E. Aufrecht, J. C. Hurd, and F. Spitzer). Hoboken, 1984

Qumran Texts

The Books of Enoch. Aramaic Fragments from Qumran Cave 4. (Trans. and Eds. J. T. Milik with the collaboration of M. Black). Oxford, 1976
The Complete Dead Sea Scrolls in English. (Eng. trans. G. Vermes). London, New York, et al., 1997
Qumran Cave 4. VIII. Parabiblical Texts, Part 1. DJD XIII. (Eds. H. Attridge et al.). Oxford, 1994
Transcription and Eng. trans. of 4Q225 by F. García Martínez, 46-47, in: "The Sacrifice of Isaac in 4Q225", 44-57 in: *The Sacrifice of Isaac. The Aqedah (Genesis 22) and its Interpretations.* (Eds. E. Noort and E. Tigchelaar). Leiden et al., 2002

Pseudepigrapha

The Apocryphal Old Testament. (Including *Jubilees*: the translation of R. H. Charles revised by C. Rabin) Ed. H. F. D. Sparks. Oxford, 1984
The Book of Jubilees or The Little Genesis. Translated from the Editor's Ethiopic Text and edited with an Introduction, Notes and Indices by R. H. Charles. London, 1902
A Commentary on Pseudo-Philo's Liber Antiquitatum Biblicarum. With Latin Text and Translation by H. Jacobson, 2 vols. Leiden, 1996.
3 Enoch or The Hebrew Book of Enoch. Edited and Translated the First Time With Introduction, Commentary and Critical Notes by H. Odeberg. 1928. Reprinted 1973 in: LBS. (Ed. H. M. Orlinsky). New York
The Old Testament Pseudepigrapha (OTP). Vols. 1-2. (Ed. J. H. Charlesworth). New York, 1983/1985

Rabbinica

The Babylonian Talmud. Translated into English. Vols. 1-35. (Ed. I. Epstein). London, 1935-1948
The Crown Haggadah. Art Management and Production: R. Rausnitz. English text editing: Y. Fachler. (Facsimile edition). Jerusalem, 1995
Genesis Rabbah. The Judaic Commentary to the Book of Genesis. A New American Translation. Vol. 2. (Ed. and Eng. trans. J. Neusner). Atlanta, 1985
Jewish Palestinian Aramaic Poetry from Late Antiquity. (Eds. M. Sokoloff and J. Yahalom). Jerusalem, 1999

Lamentations Rabbah. An Analytical Translation by Jacob Neusner. BJS, 193. Atlanta. 1989

The Legends of the Jews. (Ed. L. Ginzberg), Vol. I. *Bible Times and Characters from the Creation to Jacob.* Philadelphia, 1942

Mekilta de-Rabbi Ishmael, vol. 1-2. (Ed. and Eng. trans. J. Z. Lauterbach). Philadelphia, 1961

Midrash Rabbah. (Eds. H. Freedman and M. Simon). London, 1939:
– Vol. 1. *Genesis.* Eng. trans. H. Freedman. London, 1939
– Vol. 2. *Genesis.* Eng. trans. H. Freedman. London, 1939
– Vol. 3. *Exodus.* Eng. trans. S. M. Lehrman. London, 1939
– Vol. 4. *Leviticus.* Eng. trans. chapter 1-19, J. Israelstam, trans. chapters 20-37, J. J. Slotki. London, 1939
– Vol. 5. *Numbers.* Eng. trans. J. J. Slotki. London, 1939
– Vol. 6. *Numbers.* Eng. trans. J. J. Slotki. London, 1939
– Vol. 7. *Deuteronomy and Lamentations.* Eng. trans. Deuteronomy, J. Rabbinowitz. Trans. Lamentations, A. Cohen. London, 1939

The Mishnah. A New Translation. (Ed. and Eng. trans. J. Neusner). New Haven and London, 1988

The Penguin Book of Hebrew Verse. (Ed., introduction and Eng. trans. T. Carmi). Harmondsworth, 1981

Pesikta Rabbati. Discourses for Feasts, Fasts and Special Sabbaths. (Ed. and Eng. trans. W. G. Braude), Vols. 1-2. Yale Judaic Series, vol. 18. New Haven and London, 1968

Pesikta de Rab Kahana. R. Kahana's Compilation of Discourses for Sabbaths and Festal days. (Eds. and Eng. trans. W. G. Braude and I. J. Kapstein). Philadelphia, 2002

Pirkê de Rabbi Eliezer. Translated and Annotated with Introduction and Indices by G. Friedlander. London, 1916

Rashi. *The Torah: with Rashi's Commentary, Translated, Annotated, and Elucidated: Genesis/*ספר בראשית (Eds. and trans. I. Z. Herczeg et al.). New York, 1995

Songs of Songs Rabbah. An Analytical Translation by J. Neusner. 2 vols. BJS, 197 and 198. Atlanta, 1989

Midrash Tanhuma: (S. Buber recension), translated into English with introduction, indices, and brief notes by J. T. Townsend. Hoboken, 1989

The Talmud of the Land of Israel. A Preliminary Translation and Explanation, vol. 16. *Rosh Hashana.* Eng. trans. E. A. Goldman. Chicago and London, 1988

Philo and Josephus

Josephus. 10 vols. With an English translation by H. ST. J. Thackeray et al. LCL, (Ed. G. P. Goold). Cambridge MA, London, 1926 – 1965

Flavius Josephus. Vol. 3. *Judean Antiquities 1-4.* Translation and Commentary by L. H. Feldman. (Ed. and introduction by S. Mason). Leiden et al., 2000a

Flavius Josephus. Vol. 4. *Judean Antiquities 5-7.* Translation and Commentary by C. Begg. (Ed. S. Mason). Leiden et al., 2005

The Works of Josephus. Complete and Unabridged in One Volume. New Updated Edition. Eng. trans. W. Whiston. Peabody, MA, 1987

Philo, 10 vols. With an English translation by F. H. Colson and G. H. Whitaker
LCL. Cambridge MA, London, 1927-1962
Philo, Supplement 1 and 2. *Questions and Answers on Genesis/Exodus*. Eng. trans.
R. Marcus. LCL. Cambridge MA, London, 1953
The Works of Philo. Complete and Unabridged in One Volume. New Updated Editi-
on. Eng. trans. C. D. Yonge, Peabody, MA, 1993

Church Fathers

Eusebius of Caesarea, *The Ecclesiastical History*: vol. 1. Eng. trans. K. Lake. LCL.
New York and London, 1926
St. Justin Martyr, *Dialogue with Trypho*: translated by T. B. Falls. Revised and
with a new introduction by T. P. Hallon. Selections from the Fathers of the
Church: vol. 3. (Ed. M. Slusser). Washington, 2003

Secondary Literature

Glossaries and Concordances

Danker, F. W. 2000. *A Greek-English Lexicon of the New Testament and other Early
Christian literature*. Third edition. Revised and edited by F. W. Danker ba-
sed on W. Bauer's Griechisch-deutches Wörterbuch zu den Schriften des
Neuen Testaments und der früchristlichen Literatur, sixth edition, ed. K.
Aland and B. Aland with V. Reichman and on previous English editions by
W. F. Arndt, F. W. Gingrich, and F. W. Danker. Chicago and London
Hatch, E. and Redpath, H. A. 1998. *A Concordance to the Septuagint. And the
Other Greek Versions of the Old Testament (Including the Apocryphal Books.)* Se-
cond edition. Grand Rapids
Jastrow, M. 1971. *Dictionary of the Targumim Talmud Babli, Yerushalmi and
Midrashic Literature*: ספר מלים. New York (reprint)
Koehler, L. and Baumgartner, W. 2001. *Lexicon in Veteris Testamenti Libros*. Stu-
dy Edition. Leiden et al.
Liddell, H. G. and Scott, R. 1968. *Greek-English Lexicon*. Revised and Augmented
Throughout by Sir H. S. Jones. With a Supplement. Oxford
Rengstorf, K. H. 1983. *A complete Concordance to Flavius Josephus*, vol. 4. Leiden

Dictionaries and Encyclopedias

Alexander, P. S. 1992. "Targum, Targumim", 320-331 in: *ABD* vol. 6. (Ed. D. N.
Freedman). New York, London, Toronto
Altman, A. 1971. "Angels and Angelology. In Jewish Philosophy", 973-976 in:
EncJud, vol. 2. (Eds. C. Roth, G. Wigoder, et al.). Jerusalem

Altschuler D. 2005. "Josephus Flavius", 4957-4958 in: *EncRel*, vol. 7. Second Edtion. (Ed. L. Jones). Detroit, New York et al.

Amir, Y. 1971. "Philo Judaeus", 409-415 in: *EncJud*. vol. 13, Jerusalem

Bamberger, B. J. 1971. "Angels and Angelology. Bible", 956-962 in: *EncJud* vol. 2. Jerusalem

Charlesworth, J. H. 1992. "Jacob, Ladder of", 609 in: *ABD* vol. 3. (Ed. D. N. Freedman). New York, London, Toronto

Collins, J. J. 1995. "Gabriel גבריאל", 640-642 in: *DDD* (Eds. K. van der Torn, B. Becking and P. W. van der Horst). Leiden et al.

Fabry, H.-J., Freedman, D. N. and Willoughby, B, R. 1997. "מלאך *mal'ak*", 308-325 in: *TDOT* vol. 8. (Eds. G. J. Botterweck, H. Ringgren, and H-J. Fabry). Grand Rapids

Feldman, L. H. 1992. "Josephus", 981-998 in: *ABD* vol. 3. (Ed. D. N. Freedman). New York, London, Toronto

Flusser, D. 1971. "Mastema", 1119-1120 in: *EncJud* vol. 11. (Eds. C. Roth, G. Wigoder, et al.). Jerusalem

Grossfeld, B. 1971. "Translations, Ancient Versions", 841-851 in: *Enc Jud*, vol. 4. (Eds. C. Roth, G. Wigoder, et al.). Jerusalem

Guiley, R. E. 2004. *The Encyclopedia of Angels*. Second Edition. New York

Gutmann, Y. /Editorial Staff. 1971 "Angels and Angelology", 956-966 in: *EncJud*, vol. 2 (Eds. C. Roth, G. Wigoder, et al.). Jerusalem

van Henten, J. W. 1995a. "Angel II ἄγγελος", 90-96 in: *DDD* (Eds. K. van der Torn, B. Becking and P. W. van der Horst). Leiden et al.

– 1995b. "Archangel ἀρχάγγελος", 150-153 in: *DDD* (Eds. K. van der Torn, B. Becking and P. W. van der Horst). Leiden et al.

– 1995c. "Mastemah משטמה", 1033-1035, in: *DDD* (Eds. K. van der Torn, B. Becking and P. W. van der Horst). Leiden et al.

Herr, M. D. 1971. "Midrash", 1507-1514 in: *EncJud*, vol. 11. (Eds. C. Roth, G. Wigoder, et al.). Jerusalem

Herrmann, W. 1995. "El אל", 522-533 in: *DDD* (Eds. K. van der Torn, B. Becking and P. W. van der Horst). Leiden et al.

Hutter, M. 1995. "Asmodeus Ἀσμοδαῖος", 197-200 in: *DDD* (Eds. K. van der Torn, B. Becking and P. W. van der Horst). Leiden et al.

Jacobs, L. 1971. "Akedah", 480-484 in: *EncJud*, vol. 1. (Eds. C. Roth, G. Wigoder, et al.). Jerusalem

Kittel, G. 1964. C. "The Doctrine of Angels in Judaism" and D. "ἄγγελος in the NT", 80-87 in: "ἄγγελος", *TDNT* vol. 1. Grand Rapids

Kleinknecht, H. 1969. B. 4. "The λόγοι of Philo of Alexandria", 88-90 in: λέγω, *TDNT*, vol. 4. Grand Rapids

Knauf, E. A. 1995. "Shadday שדי", 1416-1423 in: *DDD* (Eds. K. van der Torn, B. Becking and P. W. van der Horst). Leiden et al.

Lewis, A. L. 1971. "Shofar", 1442-1448 in: *EncJud*, vol. 14. (Eds. C. Roth, G. Wigoder, et al.). Jerusalem

Lewis, J. L. and Oliver, E. D. (Ed. Sisung, K. S), 1996. *Angels A to Z.* New York

Mach, M. 1995. "Raphael רפאל", 1299-1300 in: *DDD* (Eds. K. van der Torn, B. Becking and P. W. van der Horst). Leiden et al.

Marmorstein, A. /Editorial Staff 1971. "Fallen Angels"/"Angels in the Talmud and Midrash", 966-971 in: "Angels and Angelology", *EncJud* vol. 2. (Eds. C. Roth, G. Wigoder, et al.). Jerusalem

Mason, S. 2000b. "Josephus and Judaism" 546-563 in: *The Encyclopedia of Judaism*, vol. 2. (Eds. J. Neusner, A. Avery-Peck and W. Scott-Green). Leiden et al.

Meier, S. A. 1995a. "Angel I מלאך", 81-90 in: *DDD* (Eds. K. van der Torn, B. Becking and P. W. van der Horst). Leiden et al.

– 1995b. "Angel of Yahweh מלאך יהוה", 96-108 in: *DDD* (Eds. K. van der Torn, B. Becking and P. W. van der Horst). Leiden et al.

Metzger, B. M. 1962. "Versions, Ancient, 1. Aramaic Targums of the OT", 749-750 in: *The Interpreters Dictionary of the Bible. An Illustrated Encyclopedia*, vol. 4. New York, Nashville

Mullen, E. T. 1995. "Go'el גאל", 706-708 in: *DDD*. (Eds. K. van der Torn, B. Becking and P. W. van der Horst). Leiden et al.

Murphy, R. E. "Wisdom in the OT", 920-931 in: *ABD* vol. 6 (Ed. D. N. Freedman). New York, London, Toronto

Newsom, C. A. 1992. "Angels", 248-253 in: *ABD* vol. 1. (Ed. D. N. Freedman). New York, London, Toronto

Niehr, H. 1995. "God of Heaven אלהי השמים", 702-705 in: *DDD*. (Eds. K. van der Torn, B. Becking and P. W. van der Horst). Leiden et al.

Noll, S. F. 1997. # 4855 "מלאך" 941-943 in: *New International Dictionary of Old Testament Theology and Exegesis*, vol. 2. (Ed. W. A, VanGemeren). Carlisle

Porton, G. 1992a. "Midrash", 818-822 in: *ABD* vol. 4. (Ed. D. N. Freedman). New York, London, Toronto

von Rad, G. 1964. B. "מלאך in the OT", 76-80 in: "ἄγγελος", *TDNT* vol. 1. Grand Rapids

Schalit, A. 1971. "Josephus Flavius", 251-263 in: *EncJud*, vol. 10. (Eds. C. Roth, G. Wigoder, et al.), Jerusalem

Scholem, G. 1971. "Samael", 719-722 in: *EncJud* vol. 14. (Eds. C. Roth, G. Wigoder, et al.). Jerusalem

– 1971b. "Raphael", 1549-1550 in: *EncJud*, vol. 13. (Eds. C. Roth, G. Wigoder, et al.). Jerusalem

Seow, C. L. 1995. "Face פנים", 607-613 in: *DDD* (Eds. K. van der Torn, B. Becking and P. W. van der Horst). Leiden et al.

Thompson, H. O. 1992. "Dura Europos", 241-243 in: *ABD* vol. 1. (Ed. D. N. Freedman). New York, London et al.

Tobin, T. H. 1992. "Logos", 348-356 in: *ABD* vol. 4. (Ed. D. N. Freedman). New York, London et al.
van der Toorn, K. 1995. "Yahweh יהוה" 1711-1730 in: *DDD* (Eds. K. van der Torn, B. Becking and P. W. van der Horst). Leiden et al.

Walters, S. D. 1992. "Jacob Narrative", 599-608 in: *ABD* vol. 3. (Ed. D. N. Freedman). New York, London, Toronto
Winston, D. 1992. "Solomon, Wisdom of", 120-127 in: *ABD* vol. 6 (Ed. D. N. Freedman). New York, London, Toronto
– 2005. "Philo Judaeus", 7105-7108 in: *EncRel*. Second Edition. (Ed. L. Jones). Detroit, New York, et al.

General Literature

Abelson, J. 1912. *The Immanence of God in Rabbinical Literature*. London
Ackerman, H. C. 1921. "The Principle of Differentiation between 'the Word of the Lord' and 'The Angel of the Lord' ", 145-149 in: *The American Journal of Semitic Languages and Literatures*, vol. 37.
Adania, B. 2002. *Rum i Talmud*. Skellefteå
– 2004, *Midrash. Bibeln mellan raderna*. Skellefteå
Alexander, P. S. 1985. "The Targumim and the Rabbinic Rules for the Delivery of the Targum", 14-28 in: *Congress Volume Salamanca 1983: Eleventh Congress of the International Organization for the Study of the Old Testament*. Leiden
– 1988. "Jewish Aramaic Translations of the Hebrew Scriptures", 217-254 in: CRINT. *Section two, the Literature of the Jewish People in the Period of the Second Temple and Talmud, part one, Mikra. Text, translation, reading and Interpretation in Ancient Judaism and Early Christianity*. (Eds. M. J Mulder, and H. Sysling). Philadelphia
Alter, R. 1981. *The Art of Biblical Narrative*. New York
– 1996. *Genesis. Translation and Commentary*. New York, London
Amaru B. H. 1988. "Portraits of Biblical Women in Josephus' Antiquities", 143-170 in: *JJS* vol. 39
Andersen, F. I. and Freedman, D. N. 1980. *Hosea. A New Translation with Introduction and Commentary*. AB, vol. 24. New York
Anderson, A. A. 1972. *The Book of Psalms*, vol. 2; Psalms 73-150. NCB. London
Ashton, J. 1991. *Understanding the Fourth Gospel*. Oxford
– 1994. *Studying John. Approaches to the Fourth Gospel*. Oxford
Attridge, H. W. 1976. *The Interpretation of Biblical History in the Antiquitates Judaicae of Flavius Josephus*. HDR, vol. 7. Missoula
– 1984. Josephus and His Works, 185-232 in: CRINT. *Section two, the Literature of the Jewish People in the Period of the Second Temple and Talmud, part two, Jewish Writings of the Second Temple period. Apocrypha, Pseudepigrapha, Qumran Sectarian Writings, Philo, Josephus*. (Ed. M. Stone). Philadelphia
Ausloos, H. 2008. "The 'Angel of YHWH' in Exod. xxiii 20-23 and Judg. ii 1-5. A Clue to the 'Deuteronom(ist)ic' Puzzle?", 1-12 in: *VT*, vol. 58

Bailey, J. L. 1987. "Josephus' Portrayal of the Matriarchs", 154-179 in: *Josephus, Judaism and Christianity.* (Eds. L. H. Feldman and G. Hata). Leiden

Barker, M. 1992. *The Great Angel. A study of Israel's Second God.* London

– 2006. "The Archangel Raphael in the Book of Tobit", 118-128 in: *Studies in the Book of Tobit. A Multidisciplinary Approach.* (Ed. M. Bredin). Library of Second Temple Studies, 55. (Ed. L. Grabbe). London, New York

Barr J. 1960. "Theophany and Anthropomorphism in the Old Testament", 31-38 in: *Congress Volume. Oxford 1959.* VTSup, vol. 7. (Eds. G. W. Anderson et al.). Leiden

Barrett, C. K. 1978. *The Gospel According to St. John. An Introduction with Commentary and Notes on the Greek Text.* Second Edition. London

Bauckham R. 1999. "The Throne of God and the Worship of Jesus", 43-69 in: Newman, C., Davila, J. R and Lewis, G. S. (Eds.) 1999. *The Jewish Roots of Christological Monotheism. Papers from the St. Andrews Conference on the Historical origins of the Worship of Jesus.* Supplements to the Journal for the Study of Judaism, vol. 63. Leiden

Beasley-Murray, G. R. 1987. *John.* WBC, vol. 36. Waco

Begg, C. 2007. "Angels in the Work of Flavius Josephus", 525-536 in: *Deuterocanonical and Cognate Literature, Yearbook 2007. Angels. The Concept of Celestial Beings – Origins, Development and Reception.* (Eds. F. V. Reiterer et al.). Berlin and New York

van Bekkum, J. W. 2002. "The Aqedah and Its Interpretations in Midrash and Piyyut", 86-95 in: *The Sacrifice of Isaac. The Aqedah (Genesis 22) and its Interpretations.* (Eds. E. Noort and E. Tigchelaar). Leiden et al.

Bernstein, M. J. 2000. "Angels at the Aqedah: A Study in the Development of a Midrashic Motif", 263-291 in: *Dead Sea Discoveries. A Journal of Current Research on the Scrolls and Related Literature,* vol. 7. Leiden et al.

Betz, O. 1987. "Miracles in the Writings of Josephus", 212-235 in: *Josephus, Judaism and Christianity.* (Eds. L. H. Feldman and G. Hata). Leiden

Bilde, P. 1988. *Flavius Josephus between Jerusalem and Rome. His Life, his Works, and Their Importance.* JSPSup, 2. Sheffield

Birnbaum, E. 1996. *The Place of Judaism in Philo's Thought. Israel, Jews and Proselytes.* Studia Philonica Monographs, nr. 290. (Ed. M. Hay). Atlanta

Bond, H. K. 2000. "New Currents in Josephus Research", 162-190 in: *Currents in Research: Biblical Studies.* Vol. 8

Borgen, P. 1968. "God's Agent in the Fourth Gospel" in: *Religions in Antiquity. Essays in Memory of Erwin Ramsdell Goodenough.* (Ed. J. Neusner). Leiden

– 1984. "Philo of Alexandria", 233-282 in: CRINT. *Section two, the Literature of the Jewish People in the Period of the Second Temple and Talmud, part two, Jewish Writings of the Second Temple period. Apocrypha, Pseudepigrapha, Qumran Sectarian Writings, Philo, Josephus.* (Ed. M. Stone). Philadelphia

– 1984a. "Philo of Alexandria. A Critical and Synthetical Survey of Research Since World War II", 98-154 in: *ANRW* vol. II:21:1

– 1997. *Philo of Alexandria. An Exegete for His Time.* Leiden et al.

Bowker, J. 1969. *The Targums and Rabbinic Literature. An Introduction to Jewish Interpretations of Scripture.* Cambridge

Boyarin, D. 1990 *Intertextuality and the Reading of Midrash.* Bloomington

van den Brink, E. 2002. "Abraham's Sacrifice in Early Jewish and Early Chris-
    tian Art", 140-151 in: *The Sacrifice of Isaac. The Aqedah (Genesis 22) and its
    Interpretations*. (Eds. E. Noort and E. Tigchelaar). Leiden
Brown, R. E. 1966. *The Gospel According to John (i-xii)*. AB, vol. 29. New York
– 1999. *The Birth of the Messiah: a Commentary on the Infancy Narratives in Matthew
    and Luke*. Reprint of Second edition. New York
Bultmann, R. 1971. *The Gospel of John*. A Commentary. Oxford
– 1984. *New Testament and Mythology and other Basic Writings*. Philadelphia
Burney, C. F. 1922. *The Aramaic Origin of the Fourth Gospel*. Oxford

Chester, A. 1986. *Divine Revelation and Divine Titles in the Pentateuchal Targumim*.
    Texte und Studien zum antiken Judentum, 14. Tübingen
Clarke, E. G. 1973. *The Wisdom of Solomon*. Cambridge
– 1974/75. "Jacob's Dream at Bethel as Interpreted in the Targums and the New
    Testament", 367-377 in: *SR*. vol. 4
Claussen, C. 2003. "Meeting, Community, Synagogue–Different frameworks of
    Ancient Jewish Congregations in the Diaspora", 144-167 in: *The Ancient
    Synagogue From its Origins until 200 C.E.* (Eds. B. Olsson, and M.
    Zetterholm), ConBNT, vol. 39. Stockholm
Cohen, N. G. 1995. *Philo Judaeus. His Universe of Discourse*. Beiträge zur Erfor-
    schung des Alten Testaments und des Antiken Judentums. Band 24. Frank-
    furt am Main et al.
Cohen, S. J. D. 1992. "The Place of the Rabbi in Jewish Society of the Second
    Century", 157-173 in: *The Galilee in Late Antiquity*. (Ed. L. I. Levine). New
    York and Jerusalem
Coleridge, M. 1993. *The Birth of the Lukan Narrative. Narrative as Christology in
    Luke 1-2*. JSNTSup, 88. Sheffield
Conrad E. W. 1985. "Annunciation of Birth and the Birth of the Messiah", 656-
    663 in: *CBQ*, vol. 47
Cullmann, O. 1976. *The Johannine Circle. Its place in Judaism, among the disciples of
    Jesus and in early Christianity. A study in the origin of the Gospel of John*. Lon-
    don

Daniélou, J. 1964. *The Theology of Jewish Christianity. A History of Early Christian
    Doctrine before the Council of Nicaea*, vol. 1. London and Philadelphia
Davies J. A. 1984. *Wisdom and Spirit. An Investigation of 1 Corinthians 1.18-3.20
    Against the Background of Jewish Sapiential Traditions in the Greco-Roman
    Period*. Lanham, New York, London
Davies, P. R. and Chilton, B. D. 1978. "The Aqedah: A Revised Tradition
    History", 514-546 in: *CBQ* vol. 40
Le Déaut, R. 1989. "The Targumim", 563-590 in: *CHB*, vol. 2. *The Hellenistic Age*.
    (Eds. W. D. Davies, L. Finkelstein, J. Sturdy). Cambridge, London, New
    York et al.
Díez Macho, A. 1960. "The Recently Discovered Palestinian Targum: Its
    Antiquity and Relationship with other Targumim", 222-245 in: *Congress Vo-
    lume. Oxford 1959*. VTSup, vol. 7. (Eds. G. W. Anderson et al.). Leiden

Dillon, J. 1983. "Philo's Doctrine of Angels", 197-216 in: *Two Treaties of Philo of Alexandria. A Commentary on De Gigantibus and Quod Deus Sit Immutabilis.* By D. Winston and J. Dillon. BJS, 25. Chico

Dimant, D. 1988. "Use and Interpretation of Mikra in the Apocrypha and Pseudepigrapha", 379-419 in: CRINT. *Section two, the Literature of the Jewish People in the Period of the Second Temple and Talmud, part one, Mikra. Text, translation, reading and Interpretation in Ancient Judaism and Early Christianity.* (Eds. M. J Mulder and H. Sysling). Philadelphia

– 1991. "Literary Typologies and Biblical Interpretation in the Hellenistic-Roman Period", 73-80 in: *Jewish Civilization in the Hellenistic-Roman Period.* (Ed. S. Talmon). Sheffield

Dodd, C. H. 1953. *The Interpretation of the Fourth Gospel,* Cambridge

Dunn, J. 1989. *Christology in the Making. A New Testament Inquiry into the Origins of the Doctrine of the Incarnation.* Second Edition. Grand Rapids

Dupont-Sommer, A. 1968 "L'Essénisme à la lumière des manuscrits de la mer morte angélogie et démonologie, le livre de Tobie", 411-426 in: *Annuaire du Collège de France.* Paris

Ego, B. "The Figure of the Angel Raphael According to his Farewell Address in Tob 12:6-20", 239-253 in: *Deuterocanonical and Cognate Literature, Yearbook 2007. Angels. The Concept of Celestial Beings – Origins, Development and Reception.* (Eds. F. V. Reiterer et al.). Berlin and New York

Evans, C. A. 1993. *Word and Glory. On the Exegetical and Theological Background of John's Prologue.* Sheffield

van den Eynde S. 2005. "One Journey and One Journey Makes Three: The Impact of the Readers' Knowledge in the Book of Tobit", 273-280 in: *ZAW.* vol. 117

Eynikel, E. "The Angel in Samson's Birth Narrative – Judg 13", 109-123 in: *Deuterocanonical and Cognate Literature, Yearbook 2007. Angels. The Concept of Celestial Beings – Origins, Development and Reception.* (Eds. F. V. Reiterer et al.). Berlin and New York

Falk, D. K. 2003. "Qumran and the Synagogue Liturgy", 404-434 in: *The Ancient Synagogue From its Origins until 200 C.E.* (Eds. B. Olsson and M. Zetterholm). ConBNT vol. 39. Stockholm

Feldman, L. H. 1984. *Josephus and Modern Scholarship (1937-1980).* Berlin, New York

– 1986. Josephus. *A supplementary Bibliography.* New York

– 1987. *Josephus, Judaism and Christianity.* (Eds. L. H. Feldman and G. Hata). Leiden

– 1988. *Josephus, the Bible and History.* (Eds. L. H. Feldman and G. Hata). Detroit

– 1998. *Josephus's Interpretation of the Bible.* Berkeley, Los Angeles and London

– 2006. *Judaism and Hellenism Reconsidered.* Supplements to the Journal for the Study of Judaism. (Eds. J. Collins and F. G. Martínez). Leiden, Boston

Finkelstein, L. 1929. "The Pharisees: Their Origin and their Philosophy", 185-261 in: *HTR* vol. 22. Reprinted in *Origins of Judaism,* vol. 2, part 1, *The Pharisees and Other Sects.* (Ed. J. Neusner, 1990). New York and London

Fishbane, M. 2003. *Biblical Myth and Rabbinic Mythmaking.* Oxford

Fischer, A. 2007. "Moses and the Exodus-Angel", 79-93 in: *Deuterocanonical and Cognate Literature, Yearbook 2007. Angels. The Concept of Celestial Beings – Origins, Development and Reception.* (Eds. F. V. Reiterer et al.). Berlin and New York.

Flesher, P. V. M. 2003. "The Literary Legacy of the Priests? The Pentateuchal Targums of Israel in their Social and Linguistic Context", 467-508 in: *The Ancient Synagogue From its Origins until 200 C.E.* (Eds. B. Olsson, and M. Zetterholm), ConBNT, vol. 39. Stockholm

Fletcher-Louis, C. H. T. 1997. *Luke-Acts: Angels, Christology and Soteriology.* WUNT, Reihe 2, Vol. 94. Tübingen

Fitzmyer, J. A. 2003. *Tobit. Commentaries on Early Jewish Literature* (Eds. L. T Stuckenbruck et al.). Berlin, New York

Fornberg, T. 1988. *Jewish-Christian Dialogue and Biblical Exegesis.* Uppsala

Fossum, J. E. 1985. *The Name of God and the Angel of the Lord. Samaritan and Jewish Concepts of Intermediation and the Origin of Gnosticism.* WUNT, vol. 36. Tübingen

– 1995. *Image of the Invisible God. Essays on the Influence of Jewish Mysticism on Early Christology.* NTOA, vol. 30. Göttingen

Fraade, S. D. 1992. "Rabbinic Views on the Practice of the Targum, and Multilingualism in the Jewish Galilee of the Third-Sixth Centuries", 253-286 in: *The Galilee in Late Antiquity.* (Ed. L. I. Levine). New York and Jerusalem

Franxman, T. W. 1979. *Genesis and the "Jewish Antiquities" of Flavius Josephus.* BibOr, 35. Rome

García Martínez, F. 2002. "The Sacrifice of Isaac in 4Q225", 44-57 in: *The Sacrifice of Isaac. The Aqedah (Genesis 22) and its Interpretations.* (Eds. E. Noort, and E.Tigchelaar). Leiden et al.

Gerdmar, A. 2001. *Rethinking the Judaism-Hellenism Dichotomy. A Historiographical Case Study of Second Peter and Jude.* ConBNT, vol. 36. Stockholm

Gieschen, C. A. 1998. *Angelomorphic Christology. Antecedents and Early Evidence.* AGJU, vol. 42. Leiden et al.

Ginsberg, H. L. 1961. "Hosea's Ephraim, More Fool than Knave. A New Interpretation of Hosea 12:1-14", 339-347 in: *JBL*, vol. 80

Gnuse, R. K. 1996. *Dreams and Dream Reports in the Writings of Josephus. A Traditio-Historical Analysis.* AGJU, vol. 36. Leiden et al.

Goldenberg R. 1984. "Talmud", 129-175 in: *Back to the Sources. Reading the Classic Jewish Texts.* (Ed. B. W. Holtz). New York

Goldin, J. 1968. "Not by Means of an Angel and not by Means of a Messenger", 412-424 in: *Religions in Antiquity* (Ed. J. Neusner). Leiden

Goodenough, E. 1988. *Jewish Symbols in the Greco-Roman Period.* (Edited and abridged by J. Neusner). Princeton

Goodman, D. 1986. "Do Angels Eat?" 160-175 in: *JJS*, vol. 37

Grabbe, L. 1997. *Wisdom of Solomon. Guides to the Apocrypha and Pseudepigrapha.* London, New York

Greenstein E. L. 1984. "Medieval Bible Commentaries", 213-259 in: *Back to the Sources. Reading the Classic Jewish Texts.* (Ed. B. W. Holtz). New York

Grossfeld, B. 2000. *Targum Neofiti 1. An Exegetical Commentary to Genesis. Including Full Rabbinic Parallels.* Complete Text Edited by L. H. Shiffman. New York

Guggisberg, F. 1979. *Die Gestalt des Mal'ak Jahwe im Alten Testament.* Neuenburg

Hamerton-Kelly, R. G. 1973. *Pre-existence, Wisdom, and the Son of Man. A Study of the Idea of Pre-existence in the New Testament.* Cambridge

Hamori, E. J. 2004. *When Gods Were Men: Biblical Theophany and Anthropomorphic Realism.* Ann Arbor

Hannah, D. D. 1999. *Michael and Christ: Michael Traditions and Angel Christology in Early Christianity.* WUNT 2. Reihe. 109. Tübingen

– 2007. "Guardian Angels and Angelic National Patrons in Second Temple Judaism and Early Christianity" 413-435 in: *Deuterocanonical and Cognate Literature, Yearbook 2007. Angels. The Concept of Celestial Beings – Origins, Development and Reception.* (Eds. F. V. Reiterer et al.). Berlin and New York

Hayward, R. 1981. *Divine Name and Presence: The Memra.* Oxford Centre for Postgraduate Hebrew Studies. Totowa

– 2005. *Interpretations of the Name Israel in Ancient Judaism and Some Early Christian Writings. From Victorious Athlete to Heavenly Champion.* Oxford and New York

van der Heide, A. 1999. "Midrash and Exegesis – Distant Neighbours?", 7-18 in: *Nordisk Judaistik/Scandinavian Jewish Studies*, vol. 20

von Heijne, C. 1997. "Aqedat Isak. Judisk tolkning av Genesis 22:1-19", 57-86 in: *SEÅ*, vol. 67

Hengel, M. 1974. *Hellenism and Judaism.* 2 vols. Philadelphia

Hogeterp, A. 2007. "Angels, the Final Age and 1-2 Corinthians in the Light of the Dead Sea Scrolls", 377-392 in: *Deuterocanonical and Cognate Literature, Yearbook 2007. Angels. The Concept of Celestial Beings – Origins, Development and Reception.* (Eds. F. V. Reiterer et al.). Berlin and New York

Holtz, B. W. 1984a. "Introduction: On Reading Jewish Texts", 11-29 in: *Back to the Sources. Reading the Classic Jewish Texts.* (Ed. B. W. Holtz). New York

– 1984b. "Midrash", 177-211 in: *Back to the Sources. Reading the Classic Jewish Texts.* (Ed. B. W. Holtz). New York

Horbury, W. 1988. "Old Testament Interpretation in the Writings of the Church Fathers", 727-287 in: CRINT. *Section two, the Literature of the Jewish People in the Period of the Second Temple and Talmud, part one, Mikra. Text, translation, reading and Interpretation in Ancient Judaism and Early Christianity.* (Eds M. J. Mulder, and H. Sysling). Philadelphia

Hurtado, L. W. 1998. *One God, One Lord. Early Christian Devotion and Ancient Jewish Monotheism.* Edinburgh

Illman, K-J. and Harviainen, T. 1993. *Judisk historia.* Åbo

Inowlocki, S. 2005. "'Neither Adding nor Omitting Anything': Josephus' Promise not to Modify the Scriptures in Greek and Latin Context", 48-65 in: *JJS*, vol. 56

Instone-Brewer, D. 1992. *Techniques and Assumptions in Jewish Exegesis before 70 C.E.* Tübingen

Isaacs, R. H. 1998. *Ascending Jacob's Ladder. Jewish Views of Angels, Demons, and Evil Spirits.* Northvale, Jerusalem

Jaffee, M. S. 1997. *Early Judaism.* Upper Saddle River
Johnson, A. R. 1942. *The One and the Many in the Israelite Conception of God.* Cardiff

Kalimi, I. 2002. *Early Jewish Exegesis and Theological Controversy; Studies in Scriptures in the Shadow of Internal and External Controversies.* Jewish and Christian Heritage Series 2. Assen
Karris, R. J. 1989. "The Gospel According to Luke", 675-721 in: *NJBC.* (Eds. R. E. Brown, J. A. Fizmyer and R. E. Murphy). London, New York
Kasher, R. 2007. "The Conception of Angels in Jewish Biblical Translations", 555-584 in: *Deuterocanonical and Cognate Literature, Yearbook 2007. Angels. The Concept of Celestial Beings – Origins, Development and Reception.* (Eds. F. V. Reiterer et al.). Berlin and New York
Kister, M. 1994. "Observations on Aspects of Exegesis, Tradition and Theology in Midrash, Pseudepigrapha, and Other Jewish Writings", 1-34 in: *Tracing the Threads. Studies in the Vitality of Jewish Pseudepigrapha.* (Ed. J. C. Reeves). Atlanta
Klein, H. 2007. "The Angel Gabriel According to Luke 1", 313-323 in: *Deuterocanonical and Cognate Literature, Yearbook 2007. Angels. The Concept of Celestial Beings – Origins, Development and Reception.* (Eds. F. V. Reiterer et al.). Berlin and New York
Kolenkow, A. B. 1976. "The Angelology of the Testament of Abraham", 153-162 in: *Studies on the Testament of Abraham.* SBL: Septuagint and Cognate Studies, vol. 6. (Ed. G. W. E. Nickelsburg). Missoula
Koskenniemi, E. 2005. *The Old Testament Miracle-Workers in Early Judaism.* WUNT, Reihe 2, vol. 206. Tübingen
Kugel, J. 1986. Part one, chapters 1-4 in: *Early Biblical Interpretation* by J. Kugel and R. A. Greer. Library of Early Christianity, vol. 3. Philadelphia
– 1990. *In Potiphar's House. The Interpretative life of Biblical Texts.* New York
– 1995. "The Ladder of Jacob," 209-227 in: *HTR.* vol. 88
– 1998. *Traditions of the Bible. A Guide to the Bible As It Was at the Start of the Common Era.* Cambridge MA and London
– 2002. *Shem in the Tents of Japhet: Essays on the Encounter of Judaism and Hellenism.* Supplements to the Journal for the Study of Judaism, vol. 74. Leiden
– 2006. *The Ladder of Jacob. Ancient Interpretations of the Biblical Story of Jacob and His Children.* Princeton and Oxford
Köckert, M. 2007. "Divine Messengers and Mysterious Men in the Patriarchal Narratives of the Book of Genesis," 51-78 in: *Deuterocanonical and Cognate Literature, Yearbook 2007. Angels. The Concept of Celestial Beings – Origins, Development and Reception.* (Eds. F. V. Reiterer et al.). Berlin and New York

Larsson, G. 1993. *Uppbrottet. Bibelteologisk kommentar till Andra Moseboken.* Stockholm
Larsson, H. 2006. *Jews and Gentiles in Early Jewish Novels.* Uppsala

Di Lella, A. 2000. "The Book of Tobit and the Book of Judges: An Intertextual Analysis", 198-206 in: *Henoch*, vol. 22

Letellier, R. I. 1995. *Day in Mamre, Night in Sodom: Abraham and Lot in Genesis 18 and 19*. Biblical Interpretation Series, vol. 10. Leiden et al.

Levine, E. 1982 . "The Biography of the Aramaic Bible", 353-379 in: *ZAW*, Band 94, Heft 3. Berlin/New York

– 1988. *The Aramaic Version of the Bible. Content and Context*. Berlin, New York

Levine, L. I. 1992. "The Sages and the Synagogue in Late Antiquity: The Evidence of the Galilee", 201-222 in: *The Galilee in Late Antiquity*. (Ed. L. I. Levine). New York and Jerusalem

– 2003. "The First Century Synagogue in Historical Perspective", 1-24 in: *The Ancient Synagogue From its Origins until 200 C.E.* (Eds. B. Olsson and M. Zetterholm), ConBNT, vol. 39. Stockholm

Lindars, B. 1972. *The Gospel of John*. NCBC. London

Lipton, D. 1999. *Revisions of the Night. Politics and Promises in the Patriarchal Dreams of Genesis*. JSOTSup, 288. Sheffield

Maccoby, H. 1988. *Early Rabbinic Writings*. Cambridge et al.

Mach, M. 1992. *Entwicklungsstadien des jüdischen Engelglaubens in vorrabbinischer Zeit*. Tübingen

Marmorstein, A. 1927. *The Old Rabbinic Doctrine of God. I. The Names & Attributes of God*. London

Marshall, I. H. 1978. *The Gospel of Luke. A Commentary on the Greek Text*. NIGTC. Exeter

Mason, S. 1991. *Flavius Josephus on the Pharisees. A Composition-Critical Study*. SPB. (Ed. J. C. H. Lebram). Leiden et al.

– 2000a. "Introduction to the Judean Antiquities", xiii-xxxvi in: *Flavius Josephus. Vol. 3. Judean Antiquities 1-4*. Translation and Commentary by L. H. Feldman. (Ed. S. Mason). Leiden et al.

Mays, J. L. 1969. *Hosea. A Commentary*. OTL, London

McCarthy, D. J. and Murphy R. E. 1989. "Hosea", 217-228 in: *NJBC*. (Eds. R. E. Brown, J. A. Fitzmyer, R. E. Murphy, et al.). London, New York

Mendelson, A. 1988. *Philo's Jewish Identity*. BJS, 161 (Eds. J. Neusner et al.). Atlanta

Miller, W. T. 1984. *Mysterious Encounters at Mamre and Jabbok*, BJS, 50. Chico

Moehring, H. R. 1973. "Rationalization of Miracles in the Writings of Josephus Flavius", 376-383 in: *SE*, vol. 6. (Ed. E. Livingstone). Berlin

Moore, C. A. 1996. *Tobit. A New Translation with Introduction and Commentary*. AB, vol. 40A. New York et al.

Moore, G. F. 1922. "Intermediaries in Jewish Theology. Memra, Shekinah, Metatron", 41-85 in: *HTR*, vol. 15

– 1927. *Judaism in the First Centuries of the Christian Era. The Age of the Tannaim*, vols. 1-3. Cambridge

Müller, C. D. G. 1959. *Die Engellehre der koptischen Kirche. Untersuchungen zur Geschichte der christlichen Frömmigkeit in Ägypten*. Wiesbaden

Murray, R. 1984. "The Origin of Aramaic 'ir', Angel", 303-317 in: *Or*, vol. 53. Rome

Murphy, R. E. 1989. "Genesis" (comment on Gen 1:1-25:18 by R. J. Clifford and comment on Gen 25:19-50:26 by R. E. Murphy), 28-43 in: *NJBC* (Eds. R. E. Brown, J. A. Fitzmyer and R. E. Murphy et al.). London, New York
– 1996. *The Tree of Life. An Exploration of Biblical Wisdom Literature.* Second Edition. Grand Rapids, Cambridge

Neusner, J. 1987. *What is Midrash?* Philadelphia
Newman, C., Davila, J. R. and Lewis, G. S. (Eds.) 1999. *The Jewish Roots of Christological Monotheism. Papers from the St. Andrews Conference on the Historical Origins of the Worship of Jesus.* Supplements to the Journal for the Study of Judaism, vol. 63. Leiden
Neyrey, H. J. 1982. "The Jacob Allusions in John 1:51", 586-605 in: *CBQ*, vol. 44
Nickelsburg, G. W. E. 1984. "The Bible Rewritten and Expanded", 89-156 in: CRINT. *Section two, the Literature of the Jewish People in the Period of the Second Temple and Talmud, part two, Jewish Writings of the Second Temple Period. Apocrypha, Pseudepigrapha, Qumran Sectarian Writings, Philo, Josephus.* (Ed. M. Stone). Philadelphia
– 1996. "The Search for Tobit's Mixed Ancestry. A Historical and Hermeneutical Odyssey", 339-349 in: *RevQ*, vol. 17
Niehoff, M. 1995. "Return of Myth in Genesis Rabbah on the Akeda", 69-78 in: *JJS*, vol. 46. Oxford
– 1996. "Two Examples of Josephus' Narrative Technique in His 'Rewritten Bible'", 31-45 in: *JSJ*, vol. 27
Nolland J. 1989. *Luke 1-9:20.* WBC, vol. 35A. Dallas
North, W. E. S. 2004. "Monotheism and the Gospel of John: Jesus, Moses and the Law," 155-166 in: *Early Jewish and Christian Monotheism.* (Eds. L. Stuckenbruck and W. North). London, New York
Nowell, I. 1989. "Tobit", 568-571 in: *NJBC* (Eds. R. E. Brown, J. A. Fitzmyer and R. E. Murphy et al.). London, New York
– 2005. "The Book of Tobit: An Ancestral Story", 3-13 in: *Intertextual Studies in Ben Sira and Tobit. Essays in Honor of A. Di Lella, O. F. M.* (Eds. J. Corley and V. Skemp). CBQMS, vol. 38. Washington DC
– 2007. "The 'Work' of the Archangel Raphael", 227-238 in: *Deuterocanonical and Cognate Literature, Yearbook 2007. Angels. The Concept of Celestial Beings – Origins, Development and Reception.* (Eds. F. V. Reiterer et al.). Berlin and New York

Odeberg, H. 1929. *The Fourth Gospel. Interpreted in Its Relations to Contemporaneous Religious Currents in Palestine and the Hellenistic-Oriental World.* Uppsala and Stockholm
Olyan, S. M. 1993. *A Thousand Thousands Served Him. Exegesis and the Naming of Angels in Ancient Judaism.* Texte und Studien zum antiken Judentum, vol. 36. Tübingen
O'Neill, J. C. 2003. "Son of Man, Stone of Blood (John 1:51)", 374-381 in: *NovT*, vol. 45

Orlov, A. 2004. "The Face as the Heavenly Counterpart of the Visionary in the Slavonic Ladder of Jacob", 59-76 in: *Of Scribes and Sages. Early Jewish Interpretations and Transmission of Scripture*. Vol. 2. Later Versions and Traditions. (Ed. C. A. Evans). London, New York

Otzen, B. 2002. *Tobit and Judith. Guides to Apocrypha and Pseudepigrapha*. London, New York

Patte, D. 1975. *Early Jewish Hermeneutic in Palestine*. Missoula

Perdue, L. G. 1994. *Wisdom and Creation. The Theology of Wisdom Literature*. Nashville

Perkins, P. 1989 "The Gospel According to John", in: *NJBC* (Eds. R. E. Brown, J. A. Fitzmyer and R. E. Murphy et al.). London, New York

Perrot, C. 1988. "The reading of the Bible in the Ancient Synagogue", 137-159 in: CRINT. *Section two, the Literature of the Jewish People in the Period of the Second Temple and Talmud, part one, Mikra. Text, translation, reading and Interpretation in Ancient Judaism and Early Christianity*. (Eds. M. J. Mulder and H. Sysling). Philadelphia

Porton, G. 1979. "Midrash: Palestinian Jews and the Hebrew Bible in the Greco-Roman Period", 103-138 in: *ANRW*, vol. II:19.2. (Eds. H. Temporini and W. Haase). Berlin

– 1992b "Defining Midrash", 55-92 in: *The Study of Ancient Judaism*. Vol. 1. *Mishnah, Midrash, Siddur*. (Ed. J. Neusner). Atlanta

von Rad, G. 1962. *Old Testament Theology*. Vol. 1. *The Theology of Israel's Historical Traditions*. Edinburgh

– 1985. *Genesis. A Commentary*. London

Rebiger, B. 2007. "Angels in Rabbinic Literature", 629-644 in: *Deuterocanonical and Cognate Literature, Yearbook 2007. Angels. The Concept of Celestial Beings – Origins, Development and Reception*. (Eds. F. V. Reiterer et al.). Berlin and New York

Reiterer F. V. 2007. "An Archangel's Theology. Raphael's Speaking about God and the Concept of God in the Book of Tobit", 255-275 in: *Deuterocanonical and Cognate Literature, Yearbook 2007. Angels. The Concept of Celestial Beings – Origins, Development and Reception*. (Eds. F. V. Reiterer et al.). Berlin and New York

Ringgren, H. 1947. *Word and Wisdom. Studies in the Hypostatization of Divine Qualities and Functions in the Ancient Near East*. Lund

Rofé, A. 1979. *The Belief in Angels in the Bible and in Early Israel:* האמונה במלאכים במקרא. Jerusalem

Rowland, C. 1982. *The Open Heaven. A Study of Apocalyptic in Judaism and Early Christianity*. London

– 1984. "John 1:51. Jewish Apocalyptic and Targumic Tradition", 498-507 in: *NTS* vol. 30

van Ruiten, J. 2002. "Abraham, Job and the Book of Jubilees: The Intertextual Relationship of Genesis 22:1-19, Job 1-2:13 and Jubilees 17:15-18:19", 58-85 in: *The Sacrifice of Isaac. The Aqedah (Genesis 22) and its Interpretations*. Eds. E. Noort , and E. Tigchelaar. Leiden et al.

– 2007. "Angels and Demons in the Book of *Jubilees*", 585-609 in: *Deuterocanonical and Cognate Literature, Yearbook 2007. Angels. The Concept of Celestial Beings – Origins, Development and Reception.* (Eds. F. V. Reiterer et al.). Berlin and New York

Runesson, A. 2001. *The Origins of the Synagogue. A Socio-Historical Study.* ConBNT, vol. 37. Stockholm

– 2003. "Persian Imperial Politics, the Beginnings of the Public Torah Readings, and the Origins of the Synagogue", 63-89 in: *The Ancient Synagogue From its Origins until 200 C.E.* (Eds. B. Olsson and M. Zetterholm), ConBNT, vol. 39. Stockholm

Runia, D. T. 1990. *Exegesis and Philosophy. Studies on Philo of Alexandria.* Collected Studies Series, 332. Aldershot and Brookfield

Röttger, H. 1978. *Mal'ak Jahwe – Bote von Gott. Die Vorstellung von Gottes Boten im hebräischen Alten Testament.* Frankfurt am Main

Samely, A. 1992. *The Interpretation of Speech in the Pentateuch Targums. A Study of Method and Presentation in Targumic Exegesis.* Tübingen

Sanders, E. P. 1977. *Paul and Palestinian Judaism. A Comparison of Patterns of Religion.* Philadelphia

Sandmel, S. 1979. *Philo of Alexandria. An Introduction.* New York and Oxford

Sarna, N. 1989. *The JPS Torah Commentary. Genesis*: בראשית. Philadelphia

Schiffman, L. H. 1991. *From Text to Tradition. A History of the Second Temple and Rabbinic Judaism.* Hoboken

Schnackenburg, R. 1980. *The Gospel According to St. John*, vol. 1. HTKNT. London

Schwartz, S. 1990. *Josephus and Judean Politics.* Columbia Studies in the Classical Tradition, vol.18. (Ed. W. V. Harris). Leiden et al.

Schürer, E. 1979. *The History of the Jewish People in the Age of Jesus Christ (175 B.C. – A.D. 135).* A New English Version Revised and Edited by G. Vermes, F. Millar, and M. Black, vol. 2. Edinburgh

Schäfer, P. 1975. *Rivalität zwischen Engeln und Menschen. Untersuchungen zur rabbinischen Engelvorstellung.* Berlin, New York

Segal, A. F. 1977. *Two Powers in Heaven. Early Rabbinic Reports about Christianity and Gnosticism.* SJLA, vol. 25. Leiden

van Seters, J. 1975. *Abraham in History and Tradition.* New Haven and London

Shinan, A. 1983. "The Angelology of the Palestinian Targums on the Pentateuch", 181-198 in: *Sefarad*, vol. 43. Madrid

– 1992. "The Aramaic Targum as a Mirror of Galilean Jewry", 241-251 in: *The Galilee in Late Antiquity.* (Ed. L. I. Levine). New York and Jerusalem

Signer, M. A. 1994. "How the Bible Has Been Interpreted in Jewish Tradition", 65-82 in: *The New Interpreter's Bible*, vol. 1. Nashville

Skemp, V. 2005. "Avenues of Intertextuality between Tobit and the New Testament", 43-70 in: *Intertextual Studies in Ben Sira and Tobit. Essays in Honor of A. Di Lella, O. F. M.* (Eds. J. Corley and V. Skemp). CBQMS, 38. Washington DC

Smelik, W. F. 1995. *The Targum of Judges.* Leiden

Smith, J. Z. 1968. "The Prayer of Joseph", in: *Religions in Antiquity* (Ed. J. Neusner). Leiden

Speiser, E. A. 1964. *Genesis.* AB, vol. 1. New York

Spencer, R. A. 1999. "The Book of Tobit in Recent Research", 147-180 in: *Currents in Research*: Biblical Studies, vol. 7

Spiegel, S. 1993. *The Last Trial. On the Legends and Lore of the Command to Abraham to Offer Isaac as Sacrifice: The Akedah.* Translated with an Introduction by Judah Goldin. Woodstock

Steinsaltz, A. 1976. *The Essential Talmud.* New York

Sterling, G. E. 1992. *Historiography and Self-Definition. Josephos, Luke-Acts and Apologetic Historiography.* NovTSup, vol. 64. (Eds. C. K. Barrett, P. Borgen et al.). Leiden et al.

Stier, F. 1934. *Gott und sein Engel im Alten Testament.* Münster

Strack, H. L. and Stemberger, G. 1991. *Introduction to the Talmud and Midrash.* Edinburgh

Stuckenbruck, L. T. 1995. *Angel Veneration and Christology. A Study in Early Judaism and in the Christology of the Apocalypse of John.* WUNT, Reihe 2, Vol. 70. Tübingen

Suggs, M. J. 1970. *Wisdom, Christology, and Law in Matthew's Gospel.* Cambridge, MA

Sullivan, K. P. 2004. *Wrestling with Angels. A study of the Relationship between Angels and Humans in Ancient Jewish Literature and the New Testament.* AGJU, 55. Leiden and Boston

Syrén, R. 2000. "The Targum as a Bible Reread, or How does God Communicate with Humans?", 247-264 in: *Journal for the Aramaic Bible*, vol. 2. Sheffield

Talbert, C. H. 1976. "The Myth of a Descending–Ascending Redeemer in Mediterranean Antiquity", 418-440 in: *NTS*, vol. 22

Tate, M. 1990. *Psalms 51-100.* WBC, vol. 20. Dallas

Teugels, L. M. 2004. *Bible and Midrash. The Story of 'The Wooing of Rebekah' (Gen 24).* Leuven, Paris, Dudley MA

Thompson, M. M. 2007. "Jesus 'The One Who Sees God'", 215-226 in: *Israel's God and Rebecca's Children. Christology and Community in Early Judaism and Christianity. Essays in Honor of Larry W. Hurtado and Alan F. Segal.* (Eds. D. B. Capes et al.). Waco

Thunberg, L. 1966. "Early Christian Interpretations of the Three Angels in Gen. 18", 560-570 in: *Studia Patristica VII.* (Ed. F. L. Cross). Texte und Untersuchungen zur Geschichte der altchristlichen Literatur, Band 92. Berlin

Tov, E. 2003. "The Text of the Hebrew/Aramaic and Greek Bible used in the Synogogues", 237-259 in: *The Ancient Synagogue From its Origins until 200 C.E.* (Eds. B. Olsson, and M. Zetterholm), ConBNT, vol. 39. Stockholm

Trebolle Barrera, J. T. 1998. *The Jewish Bible and the Christian Bible. An Introduction to the history of the Bible.* Leiden et al.

Tuschling, R. M. M. 2007. *Angels and Orthodoxy. A Study in their Development in Syria and Palestine from the Qumran Texts to Ephrem the Syrian.* Studien und Texte der Antike und Christentum, vol. 40. Tûbingen

Urbach, E. E. 1975. *The Sages. Their Concepts and Beliefs.* 2 vols. Jerusalem

VanderKam, J. C. 1997. "The Aqedah, Jubilees, and PseudoJubilees", 241-261 in: *The Quest for Context and Meaning. Studies in Biblical Intertextuality in Honor of James A. Sanders.* (Eds. C. A. Evans and S. Talmon). Leiden et al.

– 2000a. "The Angel of the Presence in the Book of Jubilees", 378-393 in: *Dead Sea Discoveries. A Journal of Current Research on the Scrolls and Related Literature*, vol. 7. Leiden et al.

– 2000b. *From Revelation to Canon. Studies in the Hebrew Bible and Second Temple literature.* Supplements to the Journal for the Study of Judaism, vol. 62. (Eds. J. Collins and F. G. Martínez). Leiden et al.

– 2001. *The Book of Jubilees. Guides to the Apocrypha and Pseudepigrapha.* London, New York

Wassén, C. 2007. "Angels in the Dead Sea Scrolls", 499-523 in: *Deuterocanonical and Cognate Literature, Yearbook 2007. Angels. The Concept of Celestial Beings – Origins, Development and Reception.* (Eds. F. V. Reiterer et al.). Berlin and New York

Vawter, B. 1977. *On Genesis: A New Reading.* London

Weiss, Z. and Netzer, E. 1998. *Promise and Redemption. A Synagogue Mosaic from Sepphoris.* Jerusalem

Vermes, G. 1970. "Bible and Midrash: Early Old Testament Exegesis", in: *CHB* vol. I. From the Beginnings to Jerome. (Eds. P. R. Ackroyd, and C. F. Evans). Cambridge

– 1975. "The Archangel Sariel. A Targumic Parallel to the Dead Sea Scrolls", 159-166 in: *Christianity, Judaism and Other Greco-Roman Cults. Part Three, Judaism before 70.* SJLA. (Ed. J. Neusner,) Vol. 12. Leiden

– 1996. "New Light on the Sacrifice of Isaac from 4Q225", 140-146 in: *JJS*, vol. 47

Westermann, C. 1985. *Genesis 12-36. A Commentary.* Minneapolis

– 1988. *Genesis. A Practical Commentary.* Text and Interpretation. Grand Rapids

Wevers, J. W. 1993. *Notes on the Greek Text of Genesis.* SBLSCS, vol. 35. Atlanta

White, S. L. 1999. "Angel of the Lord: Messenger or Euphemism?" in: *TynBul*, vol. 50.

Whitt, W. 1991. "The Jacob Traditions in Hosea and Their Relation to Genesis", 18-43 in: *ZAW*, vol. 103

Williamson, R. 1989. *Jews in the Hellenistic World: Philo.* Cambridge Commentaries on Writings of the Jewish and Christian World 200 BC to AD 200. Cambridge, New York et al.

Winston, D. 1979. *The Wisdom of Solomon. A New Translation with Introduction and Commentary.* AB, vol. 43. New York

– 1996. "Philo's Mysticism", 74-82 in: *The Studia Philonica Annual. Studies in Hellenistic Judaism*, vol. 8. (Ed. D. T. Runia), BJS, 309. Atlanta

Wolff, H. W. 1974. *Hosea. A Commentary on the Book of Hosea.* Hermeneia. Philadelphia

Wolfson, H. A. 1947. *Philo. Foundations of Religious Philosophy in Judaism, Christianity and Islam*, vols. 1-2. Cambridge MA

van der Woude, A. S. 1963/64. "De Mal'ak Jahweh: Een Godsbode", 1-13 in: *NedTTs*, vol. 18

Wright, A. G. 1989. "Wisdom", 510-522 in: *NJBC* (Eds. R. E. Brown, J. A. Fitzmyer and R. E. Murphy et al.). London, New York

Wyler, B. 1996. "Mary's Call", 136-148 in: *A Feminist Companion to the Hebrew Bible in the New Testament*. The Feminist Companion to the Bible, vol. 10. (Ed. A. Brenner). Sheffield

York, A. D. 1974. "The Dating of Targumic Literature", 49-62 in: *JSJ*, vol. 5

Zetterholm, K. 2001. *Portrait of a Villain. Laban the Aramean in Rabbinic Literature*. Lund

Zimmerli, W. 1979. *Ezekiel, a Commentary on the Book of the Prophet Ezekiel*, vol. 1; Chapters 1-24. Hermeneia. Philadelphia

Zlotowitz, M. 1978. *Bereishis/Genesis. A New Translation with a Commentary Anthologized From Talmudic, Midrashic and Rabbinic Sources*. Vols. 1-3. Eds. N. Sherman and M. Zlotowitz. New York

Index of Modern Authors

Selective Source Index

The Apocrypha/ Deuterocanonical Books

Qumran Texts

Pseudepigrapha

Philo

Piyutim

Selective Index of Terms and Names

Other Terms and Divine Epithets